OF RULE AND OFFICE

Of Rule and Office

PLATO'S IDEAS OF THE POLITICAL

Melissa Lane

PRINCETON UNIVERSITY PRESS
PRINCETON & OXFORD

Published by Princeton University Press
41 William Street, Princeton, New Jersey 08540
99 Banbury Road, Oxford OX2 6JX

press.princeton.edu

All Rights Reserved
ISBN: 978-0-691-19215-4
ISBN (e-book): 978-0-691-23785-5

British Library Cataloging-in-Publication Data is available

Editorial: Rob Tempio and Chloe Coy
Production Editorial: Jenny Wolkowicki
Cover design: Drohan DiSanto
Production: Lauren Reese
Publicity: Alyssa Sanford and Charlotte Coyne
Copyeditor: Maia Vaswani

This book has been composed in Miller

10 9 8 7 6 5 4 3 2 1

For Andrew
whose loving care and inspiring creativity
have sustained me to this day

CONTENTS

Preface · ix
Abbreviations · xi

PART I	INTRODUCTION	1
CHAPTER 1	Overview: Why Rule and Office? Why Plato?	3
CHAPTER 2	Rule and Office: Figures, Vocabularies, Stances	42
PART II	RECONFIGURATIONS OF RULE AND OFFICE	85
CHAPTER 3	Rule and the Limits of Office (*Laws*)	87
CHAPTER 4	Rethinking the Role of Ruler and the Place of Office (*Statesman*)	115
CHAPTER 5	Defining the *Telos* of Rule (*Republic*, Book 1)	140
CHAPTER 6	Guarding as Serving: The Conundrum of Wages in a *Kallipolis* (*Republic*, Books 1–5)	172
CHAPTER 7	Philosophers Reigning: Rulers and Officeholders in a *Kallipolis* (*Republic*, Books 5–7)	213
PART III	DEGENERATIONS OF RULE AND OFFICE	247
CHAPTER 8	The Macro Narrative: Flawed Constitutions within Cities (*Republic*, Book 8)	249
CHAPTER 9	The Micro Narrative: Flawed Constitutions within Souls (*Republic*, Books 8–9)	318

PART IV   THEMATIZATIONS OF RULE
              AND OFFICE   351

CHAPTER 10   Against Tyranny: Plato on Freedom, Friendship,
              and the Place of Law   353

CHAPTER 11   Against Anarchy: The Horizon of Platonic Rule   381

              Acknowledgments · 411
              Glossary of Selected Greek Terms · 417
              Bibliography · 419
              Index · 439

PREFACE

THE IMAGES ON THE FRONT COVER are stylized abstractions of ancient Greek insignia of rule. The image at the top is inspired by a golden diadem signifying kingly rule from Mycenaean Greece, circa 1600–1100 BCE, of the kind that the Mycenaean king Agamemnon as depicted in Homer (and discussed in chapter 1) might have worn. The image at the bottom is inspired by an Athenian golden crown with which officeholders could be honored after having been held accountable for their actions in office, award of which to the orator Demosthenes is discussed in chapter 2 (as the subject of Aeschines's speech "Against Ctesiphon").

All abbreviations in the text and bibliography follow the *Oxford Classical Dictionary*, 4th edition, where applicable. A list of abbreviations used is also provided to aid the reader.

Transliterations of Greek quoted are set off by parentheses () when the Greek is quoted exactly as it appears in the text. Square brackets [] are used when quoted words have been modified morphologically so as to present them in a more readily recognizable grammatical form. The Oxford Classical Texts are the source of Greek quoted except where otherwise noted.

Translations are my own except where otherwise noted. While I have most closely consulted the translations contained in Cooper's *Complete Works* in making my own, and have sometimes (where noted) quoted them directly (doing so especially when helpful to achieve consistency with my own previously published work), I have also consulted a number of other translations into English and other European languages, as is evident in the footnotes.

An index locorum for this book will be made available upon its publication at the following web address, and will remain available there so long as no technical barriers arise in the future to its being so at: https://melissalane .princeton.edu/wp-content/uploads/sites829/2022/12/Lane-Of-Rule-and -Office-PUP-2023-index-locorum.pdf and at: https://press.princeton.edu /isbn/9780691237855.

In chapters dedicated to a single Platonic dialogue and identified as such in the chapter title, the name of that dialogue has generally been omitted from citations of line references, unless it is not clear in the context (for example, if a comparison is being drawn to another dialogue).

Many of my own previous publications are drawn on at points throughout this work; where I diverge from them, the present work represents my current view. The most significant and extensive correspondences of chapters (or, rather, parts of chapters) in this study with previous publications, incorporated with permission (and sometimes silently altered), are:

CHAPTER 2

"The Idea of Accountable Office in Ancient Greece and Beyond." *Philosophy* 95 (2020): 19–40.

"Persuasion et force dans la politique platonicienne." Translated by Fulcran Teisserenc. In *Aglaïa: Autour de Platon; Mélanges offerts à Monique Dixsaut*, edited by Aldo Brancacci, Dimitri El Murr, and Daniela P. Taormina, 165–98. Paris: Vrin, 2010.

CHAPTER 4

"Political Expertise and Political Office in Plato's *Statesman*: The Statesman's Rule (*Archein*) and the Subordinate Magistracies (*Archai*)." In *Plato's "Statesman": Proceedings of the Eighth Symposium Platonicum Pragense*, edited by Aleš Havlíček, Jakub Jirsa, and Karel Thein, 49–77. Prague: OIKOYMENH, 2013.

"Statecraft as a Ruling, Caring, and Weaving *Dunamis*: 303d4–305e7." In *Plato's "Statesman": A Philosophical Discussion*, edited by Panos Dimas, Melissa Lane, and Susan Sauvé Meyer, 195–216. Oxford: Oxford University Press, 2021.

CHAPTER 5

"*Technē* and *Archē* in *Republic* I." *Oxford Studies in Ancient Philosophy* 57 (2019): 1–24.

"Virtue as the Love of Knowledge in Plato's *Symposium* and *Republic*." In *Maieusis: Essays in Ancient Philosophy in Honour of Myles Burnyeat*, edited by Dominic Scott, 44–67. Oxford: Oxford University Press, 2007.

CHAPTER 8

"How to Turn History into Scenario: Plato's *Republic* Book 8 on the Role of Political Office in Constitutional Change." In *How to Do Things with History*, edited by Danielle Allen, Paul Christesen, and Paul Millett, 81–108. Oxford: Oxford University Press, 2018.

"Placing Plato in the History of Liberty." *History of European Ideas* 44 (2018): 702–18.

"*Antianarchia*: Interpreting Political Thought in Plato." *Plato Journal: Journal of the International Plato Society* 16 (2016): 59–74.

CHAPTER 10

"Placing Plato in the History of Liberty." *History of European Ideas* 44 (2018): 702–18.

ABBREVIATIONS

Aeschin. Aeschines

Arist. Aristotle

[*Ath. Pol.*] *Constitution of the Athenians* (Aristotle [Pseudo-Aristotle?])

Euthphr. *Euthyphro* (Plato)

Grg. *Gorgias* (Plato)

Hdt. Herodotus

Hec. *Hecuba* (Euripides)

Il. *Iliad* (Homer)

Isoc. Isocrates

Leg. *Laws* (Plato)

LSJ Liddell and Scott (rev. Jones), *Greek-English Lexicon* (9th ed.)

Lys. Lysias

Mem. *Memorabilia* (Xenophon)

Menex. *Menexenus* (Plato)

OCT Oxford Classical Texts (series of Greek and Latin Texts)

Od. *Odyssey* (Homer)

Pers. *Persians* (Aeschylus)

Plt. *Statesman* (Plato)

Pol. *Politics* (Aristotle)

Resp. *Republic* (Plato)

Thes. *Theseus* (Plutarch)

Thuc. Thucydides

Ti. *Timaeus* (Plato)

Xen. Xenophon

PART I

Introduction

CHAPTER ONE

Overview

WHY RULE AND OFFICE? WHY PLATO?

SIX CENTURIES AFTER PLATO, the polymathic Greek geographer Pausanias would recount a folk history of archaic Athens, contending that it was the stripping of the Athenian king of most of his unaccountable powers that had "transformed the kingship [*basileia*] into an accountable office [*archē hupeuthunos*]."[1] Spelling out kingship as unaccountable, office as accountable, Pausanias's folk-historical claim both connects and contrasts them.[2] The implication is that kingship is absolutely, or relatively, free of the kinds of procedural limits and controls that could enforce accountability. Office, by contrast, is accountable, underscored here by the adjective *hupeuthunos*, which is one signal that the noun *archē*—translatable as either "rule" or "office," depending on contextual clues—is being used by Pausanias in the sense of "office."[3]

1. Pausanius, 4.5.10, trans. Jones and Ormerod, modified; the same phrase is cited in Caillemer's "ARCHONTES" (383), where it is translated as "les Athéniens changèrent alors la royauté en une magistrature responsable" (the Athenians thus changed the kingship into a responsible magistracy [this being the French equivalent of "accountable office"]).

The reference is to the purported transformation of the archaic kingship into the figure of the so-called "king-archon" (*archon basileus*), also known as simply "the archon" in his unique function of giving his name to a calendar year. More broadly, Hall's "Rise of State Action" (12), dates "a shift towards authority based on ascribed status, where emphasis is given to the office itself rather than the person who holds it as with the Homeric king," back to the seventh century BCE. While Luraghi, in "Ruling Alone" (13, 15n17), calls this a "story-pattern" that lacks historical validity, he acknowledges that it "derives directly from Greek historiography."

2. Whereas Pausanias contrasts kingship with (accountable) office, other ancient Greek authors (like many medieval European ones) would treat it instead as a nonstandard kind of office itself, an issue discussed further in chapter 2.

3. Sometimes (as here by inclusion of the adjective *hupeuthunos*), ancient Greek uses of *archē* and *archein* clearly signal which idea is meant. For example, the noun in the plural almost always signifies "offices" (or, by extension, their holders), especially when used with

The accountability of political officeholders was conventionally understood as central to what it was for them to hold office at all, just as much in Pausanias's time as in Plato's, and indeed as at the time of this writing.

Introducing an overarching category of rule helps to capture the connecting transformation of kingship into office of which Pausanias speaks. A king is one kind of ruler, described by Pausanias as an unaccountable kind; an officeholder is another kind of ruler—broadly speaking, the accountable kind, in the sense of one subject to limits and control by another agent or agents.[4] To be sure, Pausanias does not use a separate word for rule as such a category. However, the noun *archē*, translated here as "office," is exactly the same word that in both his Greek and that of Plato would in other contexts be translated as "rule": namely, where it was not glossed or signaled to incorporate accountability (broadly conceived). The relationship between rule and office was understood by the Greeks not only in folk-historical terms but also in terms of a range of linguistic affordances of the noun *archē* and the cognate verb *archein*.[5] The nuances of these intertwining significations are what originally sparked this inquiry into the ideas of rule and office in Plato in the context of ancient Greek thought in dialogue with modern political theorizing.[6]

Why start an account of rule and office in Plato with Pausanias's much later dictum? To start, it has Platonic antecedents. Plato had included a more iconoclastic version of the same folk history in his *Menexenus* (containing a long speech about Athenian history attributed by Socrates, who tells it, to a female

---

certain verbs and prepositions. Other uses are more ambiguous, depending on context, which may not offer decisive signals either way. For example, the noun in the singular can signify either "rule" or "office"; the verb in participial forms such as *archontes* can signify either "rulers" or "officeholders." Further rules of thumb for interpreting the affordances of this vocabulary, which constituted common ground for Attic Greek authors who wrote mainly from the mid-fifth through the fourth centuries BCE (as well as some writing in other dialects of Greek and other time periods) are provided in chapter 2.

4. Office is on my analysis a kind of rule. When I speak of "rule and office," I use "rule" in that expression to indicate other kinds of rule (or sometimes rule in general, treated abstractly) as contrasted with the kind of rule that is embodied in office.

5. I cite an infinitive form of this verb as it provides a clearer visual contrast with the noun, and follow suit by citing most other Greek verbs in an infinitive form as well (but generally refer to entries for verbs in the Greek lexicon LSJ according to the first-person conjugations by which such entries are listed).

6. The vocabulary (by which I mean to refer also to its syntactical deployment) of rule and office was common ground, part of the language in a more literal sense than what the historian of ideas J.G.A. Pocock calls the "languages" that offer various "idioms, rhetorics, ways of talking about politics, distinguishable language games," each of which "may have its own vocabulary" (Pocock, "Concept of a Language," 21). By contrast, Plato's development of ideas of rule and office is well characterized as such a Pocockian "language"; it builds on the same vocabulary and linguistic affordances common to other authors at the time, but develops distinctive idioms (such as the strict evaluative, versus loose descriptive, uses of these and related terms, explained below).

associate of Pericles named Aspasia). Rather than contrasting kings then and accountable officeholders now, Plato puts the accent on continuity between the archaic Athenian kings and the office of the "king-archon" that featured in the constitution of his own time.[7] But more importantly, Pausanias's claim about how an unaccountable ruler might be transformed into an accountable one bears as much on politics today as it did on the Roman-dominated Greece of his day or the classical landscape of the *polis* in that of Plato. Both the value and the vulnerabilities of accountable offices as a way of organizing political rule have posed recurrent challenges for political theory and practice.

The value of making rule accountable in the form of political office (or, rather, offices, since the very nature of offices in being constituted by limited powers makes them typically plural) lies in the aspiration to ensure that rule is carried out for the benefit of those ruled. This aspiration is evident in the structure and exercise of accountable offices in ancient Greek polities, as in constitutional polities of later times. Accountability was not a vague term in ancient Greek thought or practice. Used most specifically (call this a narrow use), it referred to a widespread family of procedures (generally termed *euthunai*) by which those subject to an officeholder's powers were able to hold that office-holder to account. Those procedures consisted at a minimum in demanding the rendition of a set of accounts in the literal sense: a financial accounting of any public monies handled while in office. Sometimes (as in democratic Athens) they extended to demanding defense of a fuller account of one's conduct in office.

Beyond that narrow understanding of accountability as a matter of procedural audit, the aspiration to political accountability came more broadly in ancient Greek contexts, as today, also to stand for an overall ideal of limited constitutional government. Accountability broadly understood encompassed not only the *euthunai* but also a wider family of limits and procedures that conventionally regulated the offices more generally, usually through law. I refer to these as a family of conventional parameters of office—including term limits, selection methods, and the like—which contributed to making officeholders accountable in a broader sense than their subjection to the *euthunai* alone.

If one asks what the purpose of making officeholders accountable might be, the implicit but indisputable answer must be that of ensuring the good of those for whose sake officeholders' powers were meant to be exercised. Officeholders were expected not to exploit their powers for their own aggrandizement but rather to be accountable to fellow citizens (understood more widely in a democracy than in an oligarchy) for their proper use. That said,

---

7. Plato, *Menex.* 238d2–3: "We [Athenians] have always had kings; at one time they were hereditary, later elected" (trans. Ryan). All quotations of Plato are from the most recent edition of the relevant Oxford Classical Texts; all translations of Plato as well as other ancient and modern authors are my own, unless otherwise indicated.

conventional accountability procedures in ancient Greek constitutions (*polit-eiai*) were targeted at avoiding the most obvious bads (such as corruption) that would negate and undermine the good of the ruled.[8]

However, if the good of the ruled is the purpose (*telos*) of accountability measures broadly conceived, those measures—as part of an order (*taxis*) of accountable offices—were (and are) vulnerable to potential flaws. These put constitutional rule at risk. The most notorious expression of such vulnerability has long been associated with the name of the Roman poet Juvenal in the guise of the tag "Who shall guard the guardians?" The Juvenal conundrum, as I shall call it, one that Plato recognized in a particular context before him,[9] is in fact an ensemble of related vulnerabilities that threaten not only accountable officeholding but also any kind of political rule. Each of these vulnerabilities targets one aspect of a constitutional order: the design of its roles (including the roles of its various officeholders), the relationship between the role and the natural person who holds it, and the safeguarding of the first two aspects (to ensure that they are correctly maintained).

The first vulnerability lies in the procedures and norms associated with a given role. What are the optimal parameters for a given office, for example? The second asks about the availability and selection of persons capable of meeting the demands of each role. Are there procedures and norms to ensure that such persons emerge through the societal system of education, are selected to fill appropriate roles, and remain oriented to the purposes for which they will be held accountable? This vulnerability spans the motivation and competence of such persons as well as the orientation they display in their official actions. Rulers must care about playing their roles properly, meaning both that their roles require them to be oriented to the good of the ruled and that those who serve as rulers must be motivated to maintain that caring orientation.

The third vulnerability, for its part, reiterates the Juvenal conundrum with respect to the prior two. However the political roles of officeholders and other

---

8. I generally use "constitution" to translate *politeia* (singular), in line with many scholars, though others would translate it as "regime," and Arlene Saxonhouse has asked me in conversation to defend my choice in terms of its seeming to help itself to modern constitutional connotations. While I am aware of that risk, the articulation of *politeiai* (plural) in terms of offices and laws in much ancient Greek political thought from the sixth century through the fourth century BCE, as argued by Bordes (*Politeia*), offers support for my choice, and I discuss the similarities as well as differences from modern constitutions at points throughout this study. There were, however, also other significant ways of describing and categorizing constitutions, especially before the fourth century BCE. I return to the question of "constitutionalism" in ancient Greek politics in chapter 2.

9. Plato identifies this conundrum in the *Laws* (12.945b5–c2) with respect to the role envisaged there for the *euthunoi* (the officeholders who in that dialogue, as in some existing Greek constitutions at the time, carried out the *euthunai* procedures), as discussed further in chapter 3.

rulers are defined, however their incumbents are chosen, who can ensure that the defining limits of these roles are respected, that the accountability procedures are carried out properly, that the officeholders or other rulers act as they should? To what extent can any set of roles and procedures fully protect against a clever incumbent who is prepared to exploit them (or to make use of their loopholes) for their own benefit?

What do these concerns have to do with Plato? Beyond the folk history to which both he and later Pausanias refer, Plato's political thought in the high noon of his *Republic* is generally taken to be an effort to circumvent the theoretical force of the Juvenal conundrum. "Who shall guard the guardians?" is assumed to be a question that Plato's *Republic*—in prescribing that philosophers should rule—seeks not to answer but to reject as inapplicable, the assumption being that Plato's so-named "guardians" do not need any further oversight because they are wise.[10] So construed, his political thought is taken not to have participated in any kind of realist vein in the projects of constitutionally limited officeholding and institutional design that preoccupied democrats (and others) of his day, but rather to have stood aloof from all such projects on the ground that wise rulers would make them unnecessary. (Even though Plato's *Laws*—the third in the trio of major works that constitute the focus of this study—canvasses a political constitution that is articulated in terms of offices and laws in great detail, this is usually understood to be a late turn in his theorizing that takes his politics in a very different direction from the central thrust of the other two dialogues in question, the *Republic* and *Statesman*.)[11]

The thesis of this study is that Plato has much more to say about the Juvenal conundrum—including the nature of rule, the value and vulnerabilities of political office as a kind of rule, and the exploration of various ways in which both rule and office might be reconfigured so as to better address the conundrum—than has been previously recognized. The titles of his dialogues are clues to the different ways in which each tackles the conundrum in what I refer to broadly as their constitutional projects (meaning the constitutions that are laid out in detail in the *Republic* [composing much of books 2–7] and *Laws* [books 4–12], and the account of political rule that is laid out in detail in the *Statesman*).[12] The *Laws* does so in terms closest to ancient Greek

10. I consider Karl Popper's famous version of this line of interpretation later in this chapter.

11. In referring to these dialogues as constituting a trio, I speak of the way in which most studies of Platonic political thought treat them in tandem. They do not constitute a trio either in the dramatic framing of the dialogues or in ancient editorial groupings of them (the most influential of which is attributed to Thrasyllus).

12. The specific books of each dialogue mentioned above also contain much other material (general reflections on politics, and so on); conversely, all three dialogues have much to say about constitutions and rule outside the scope of their constructive constitutional projects—for example, in the narrative of flawed constitutions in *Republic* 8, discussed below

constitutional practices, doubling down on the aspiration to make all offices and positions of political power accountable (and so notably eschewing any political positions called "kingship" in the laws that it canvasses as a model for a newly founded city in a post-heroic human era), while infusing the content of the laws with the wisdom that good rule requires. By contrast, while both the *Statesman* and the *Republic* do, as I shall demonstrate, include offices in their main constitutional projects, both dialogues address the Juvenal conundrum by also positing rulers described as "kings" to reign over, and so safeguard, those who hold offices under them.

When I say that both the *Republic* and the *Statesman* (as well as the *Laws*) include offices and officeholders in their constitutional projects, I mean that Plato sometimes in the contexts of those projects (as well as in other passages of those dialogues) deploys the vocabulary of *archē* and *archein* in ways that his Greek contemporaries would conventionally have recognized as signaling the specific sense of "office" rather than the more general one of "rule." However, in neither the *Republic* nor the *Statesman* (in contrast to the *Laws*) does the institutional design of the offices so projected include mention of the *euthunai*, which were a conventional hallmark of accountable offices in his day. Whereas the *Statesman's* mention of office in its constitutional project is so brief that it is hard to infer anything from this silence, the *Republic* envisages offices that have been radically reconfigured in various ways that seem deliberately to exclude this conventional parameter of accountability to those ruled. In chapters 6 and 7, I take up the challenge of explaining in what sense these remain "offices" and how the function of accountability (or a functional equivalent to accountability) is in this dialogue, as in different ways in the *Statesman* and the *Laws*, to be secured.

It is because I take seriously the questions of how political rule might be organized to secure the good of the ruled, the extent to which some kind of constitutional order of offices is the best way of doing so, and the Juvenal conundrum of who shall guard the guardians (understood figuratively as the rulers) in any such order, that I take seriously Plato's varying explorations of these questions. It is because thinking about rule and office is so important that I seek in Plato a neglected guide in doing so, even though one might ultimately reject, as blueprints sufficient unto the modern day, any and all of the constitutional projects he explores. While Pausanias's later dictum would emphasize a historical contrast between unaccountable rule (which he describes as archaic kingship) and accountable office, Plato's dialogues suggest that one

---

in chapter 8; the discussion of constitutions and rule generally in *Laws* 1–2 and historically in *Laws* 3, considered in chapter 3; and the excursus on flawed constitutions and the role of law in the *Statesman*, considered in chapters 4 and 11. These references are not exhaustive; much can also be learned about the Platonic idea of rule from other aspects of each of these three dialogues (including their myths), as well as from other Platonic dialogues.

must think through the function that accountable office is meant to serve, reflect on the extent to which conventional accountability procedures succeed in achieving that function, and explore potential reconfigurations of both office and other kinds of rule as ways to do so. In so doing, it will turn out that although neither the *Republic* nor the *Statesman* makes use of *euthunai* procedures in characterizing the offices envisaged in their constitutional projects, they do explore other kinds of limits both for those offices and for other kinds of rule, in seeking to keep rulers (including officeholders) oriented toward the good of the ruled.

Notwithstanding these differences between Plato and Pausanias, another reason to take the latter's dictum as a useful starting point is that the language of kingship—the relationship between not just any kind of rule but specifically kingly rule and (accountable) officeholding—was itself central to Plato's political theorizing in certain dialogues.[13] Think not only of the philosopher-kings and philosopher-queens of the *Republic*, but of the figure variously described as the "kingly ruler" and the "statesman" in the *Statesman*. Plato's interest in kingship, and in an idea of rule mediated through that image, is situated within a broader Greek discourse going back to the Homeric image of the king as the "shepherd of the people."[14] That figure epitomizes the expectation that a king should serve the good of the ruled, while wider discussions of kingship treated kings as orderers of their domains, caring for the ruled by establishing forms of order. A Homeric king could be described as *kosmētōr laōn*, "orderer of the people,"[15] and while in context this described mainly the military role of ordering an army, the king's role in establishing a *kosmos* (a word for order) would have broader resonance also in later authors.

While Plato was interested in rule and the figure of the king, he was also, as this study contends, interested in officeholding as a distinctive kind of rule, one sharing overlapping vocabulary and developing a family of recognizable procedural limits in order to realize an aspiration of accountability broadly conceived. Office too had a long history in Greek thought and practices already by Plato's time, stretching back to seventh-century BCE Crete, from which survive the earliest known Greek laws regulating officeholders. Not only in the *Laws* but also in certain key passages of the *Republic* and *Statesman*, Plato discusses

---

13. I ascribe certain views to "Plato" despite the largely dialogical character of his writings. To introduce my approach to doing so, which is further developed in chapter 2: I identify "Plato" for the purposes of this study primarily with an overlapping set of repeated and broadly consistent positions, sometimes expressed through questions or converse denials, which certain protagonists—whom I characterize as "avatars" of Plato—adopt. Doing so is an interpretative choice that clearly comes at some costs, and has some limitations, as does any such choice.

14. Haubold, "'Shepherds of the People.'"

15. *Il.* 1.16, 1.375, 3.236; *Od.* 18.152. See Atack, *Discourse of Kingship.*

archē and *archein* in terms that sometimes unambiguously or arguably signal "offices" (usually found in the plural) by the conventions of the time, while at other times unambiguously or arguably signaling "rule" in a different or more abstract sense to be explored. In fact, Plato's discussion of office, and his sensitivity to office as a kind of rule, must be identified as a textual fact hiding in plain sight.[16]

Putting together kingship as a figure of rule oriented to the good of the ruled and office as a kind of rule, it emerges that Plato was (like Pausanias after him) grappling with the question of whether office can suffice to realize the purpose of rule, or whether office and rule need to be reconfigured in order to better enable them to do so, whether by reconfiguring the offices themselves, supplementing them in some way with a further kind of rule or with a special kind of law, or both. This, of course, is to speak only of rule and office in the political domain. While that is the primary concern of this study, it cannot be discussed without attention also to the question of rule within the soul (and, indeed, also that of divine rule within the *kosmos*). Political rule is described by Plato as necessary wherever, and for those for whom, psychic self-rule cannot be sufficiently achieved. This makes Plato an opponent of *anarchia* (anarchy) in the political domain in virtually all circumstances; his occasional rumination on whether psychic self-rule might be achieved without, and so not require, political rule, is considered in the final chapter of this study.

While Plato is an opponent of anarchy, however, the dialogues show him to be equally an opponent of tyranny. One way to appreciate the profundity of that opposition is to consider the often-overlooked valorization of office and law (law being the standard way in which offices are limited and controlled) in the *Republic*, as well as in the *Laws* (alongside the critique, but also the deployment, of office and law in the *Statesman* as well). The ultimate refutation of the putative happiness of the tyrant in *Republic* 9 is made by appeal to what I call the garden-variety constitutionalism of office and law; while rule need not always take this form, there are distinctive values of civic freedom and friendship that office and law are particularly well suited to foster. To understand Plato on (political) rule, one must understand what he has to say

16. To illustrate: *archai* is used twice in *Resp.* 5.460b6–8, denoting first the officeholders and then the offices assigned a task of supervising early childhood education. (Hansen [*Athenian Democracy*, 226] notes that the noun *archē* was "used with just about equal frequency of the person holding the magistracy," a point he made about Athens but which applies to other Greek constitutional polities as well.) As documented in chapters 2 and 7, translators of this passage into multiple languages correctly take the plural Greek noun to signal that "offices" and "officeholders" are meant, rather than abstract "rule," which would not here make sense in the plural. Yet scarcely any scholars have discussed the political or theoretical significance of these and other references to offices in books 5–7 of the *Republic*, as I do in chapter 7.

about the variety of ways in which rule can be ordered, which include but are not limited to office.

This project is insufficiently pursued in the discussions of "rule" in Plato offered by scholars such as Hannah Arendt and Jacques Rancière, each of whom is primarily interested instead in drawing a broad binary opposition between rule and democracy.[17] When, for example, Arendt glosses the Greek "concept of rule" as "the notion that men can lawfully and politically live together only when some are entitled to command and the others forced to obey,"[18] her insistence that rule entails its subjects being "forced to obey" fails to recognize the role played by office in Plato's writings as a kind of rule distinguished by its limited and accountable parameters and associated thereby with willing obedience. Indeed, for Plato in *Republic* 8, the democratic constitution features rulers who are officeholders within a constitutional framework of law, though their unwillingness (and that of those whom they rule) to act according to the constitutionally specified limits turns their roles into a kind of shadow play.

Arendt's effort to drive a wedge between democratic ideas and practices of politics (drawing especially on Athens) and Plato's idea of rule—followed by Rancière in accusing Plato of failing to grasp what is properly political at all— must be reconsidered once one recognizes Plato's subtle and varied grappling with office as well as rule, and with the relationship between them.[19] On my

---

17. Rule is a relatively neglected idea not only in Plato but in democratic theory more generally, as observed by Markell ("Rule of the People," 1), who writes: "In mainstream democratic theory, the term 'rule' has received relatively little attention, not because it has been thought to be unimportant, but because its meaning has seemed comparatively straightforward.... [T]he thought that politics is at bottom a matter of ruling, and that ruling consists in the exercise of authoritative control, remains part of the taken-for-granted background."

18. Arendt, *Human Condition*, 222. See also pages 8–9 and passim for her development of a connection between "beginning" and a notion of "natality" as part of the human condition and as arguably the "central category of political ... thought" (9); at 224, she mentions a passage in the *Laws* (without giving a precise citation) holding "that only the beginning (*archē*) is entitled to rule (*archein*)," perhaps thinking of 6.775e3, a passage she cites in both *On Revolution* and "What Is Authority?" I have argued in *Eco-Republic* for a related opposition between "initiative" and "inertia" as a neglected but fundamental axis of political life.

19. While influenced by Arendt, Sheldon Wolin's recognition of the importance of the language of rule for the Greeks and in Plato differed from her in valorizing its institutional realization in the form of constitutionalism. Wolin (*Fugitive Democracy*, 81) writes: "Ancient Greek theorists were the first to conceive the idea of codifying both the practices of ruling and the competing claims to rule while, at the same time, enclosing the dynamics of politics within a determinate structure and designated political space," one which he calls (as I do here) a project of "constitutionalism." Unlike Arendt, Wolin also recognizes and discusses, briefly but illuminatingly, what I call the characteristic limiting parameters of office, specifically in the context of Athens.

view, Plato's choices of language show him to have been keenly attuned to the variations of officeholding in existing Greek constitutions, democratic as well as oligarchic. His political theorizing involves working out the extent to which existing models of office could succeed in realizing their implicit purpose. And it involves reconfiguring those models in varied roles of office and (other kinds of) rule, designed to better grasp and realize that same purpose.

Having said that, Arendt's further diagnosis of Platonic politics as resting on mastery in the household, "where nothing would ever be done if the master did not know what to do and did not give orders to the slaves who executed them without knowing,"[20] raises an issue that must be confronted in Plato's willingness to use the language of slavery in describing rule—I take this up in chapter 10. The fact that virtually all ancient Greek accounts of rule, and of freedom, presupposed a society in which some were and would remain enslaved casts a profound shadow on them with which this work, like other studies of Plato, must contend. Setting aside Aristotle's theory of "natural slaves," virtually all such accounts likewise presupposed that actually existing Greek slavery was the domination and exploitation of those enslaved for the benefit of their enslavers. In using the language of slavery to describe certain relationships of rule among people not legally enslaved, Plato harnessed only the epitactic dimension that masters of slaves shared with political rulers;[21] he yoked this to an inversion of the *telos* of legal slavery, insisting that political rulers must qua rulers seek to serve the good of the ruled. This abstraction of a dimension of slavery to characterize rule keeps his theorizing within the ambit of the slave society within which it arose, but does not pretend that such legal enslavement was anything other than exploitation (a point which I find to be recognized in a passage of *Republic* 9, as argued below in chapter 10).

In following Arendt, Rancière, and others in speaking of "rule" in Plato, but understanding it as encompassing not only the register of *Herrschaft* (rule in the sense of mastery or domination) as it were, but also that of *Regierung* (rule in the sense of government or administration),[22] I owe the reader also a brief word as to why I have chosen the English word "office" as its complement in my title (and as one of the kinds of rule). The word "office" is derived from the Latin *officium*, glossed as "service, duty," and related to *opificium*, "the performance of constructive work";[23] *officium* connotes the "duty and

---

20. Arendt, *Human Condition*, 222–23.

21. This is complicated by the emphasis in Ismard's *Démocratie contre les experts* (74–79) on the fact that the actual powers of physical coercion were wielded in the Athenian democracy by enslaved people (such as the Scythian archers who served as a police force).

22. I draw this contrast from the observation in Markell's "Politics against Rule" that when Arendt writes of "rule" in German, she translates it with the vocabulary of *Herrschaft* rather than *Regierung*.

23. De Vaan, *Etymological Dictionary of Latin*, 431 (both quotations).

service attached to a role."[24] These Latin terms were not limited to politics—
Cicero's *De officiis* is an account of the virtues and duties attached to the role
of a good man, albeit that for him the good man would also be the citizen;[25]
likewise, the Greek *archē* was not limited to the sense of office or rule (it could
also mean more generally a "beginning," as Arendt emphasized, though in so
doing she neglected the sense of "office").[26] More challenging for my choice of
"office" to capture an ancient Greek (and Platonic) idea is the fact that even
when focusing on political offices, there have been significant historical shifts
in various epochs. For example, historians of English law trace a shift from
an eighteenth-century regime of offices understood as individually embody-
ing distinct assignments of public trust to "a model of salaried employment
and managerial control."[27] Nevertheless, contemporary administrative law in
common-law systems includes reference to "offices" often treated broadly as
positions of public powers delineated by legal limits and controls, which comport reasonably well with the "offices" that characterized the *archai* (and the
roles held by *archontes*) in Greek constitutions of Plato's day.

24. J. Allen, "Office of the Crown," 307. Schofield (*Cicero*, 185) observes, "*Officium* is in
fact a Roman moralizing transformation of the Greek *to kathēkon*, 'what it belongs to us
to do,' or 'what accords with our nature,'" noting further that "the transformation accordingly makes behaving virtuously also a matter of performing those actions that are *required*
of us . . . a matter of doing our duty (as a requirement conceived in that way)" (emphasis
original). Neither *officium* nor *to kathēkon* in its central role in Stoic thought was limited
to political offices alone.

25. For Cicero on magistrates (to use another Latinate term in its sense of "office"), see
De officiis 1.124 (on the magistrate bearing the *persona* [literally, a mask, in the sense of a
particular role or character] of the people); see also *De officiis* 1.97–115.

26. Arendt (*Human Condition*, 222–23) emphasizes the related verb *archein* in its
sense of "beginning" in discussing the *Statesman*:

> The problem, as Plato saw it, was to make sure that the beginner [the ruler]
> would remain the complete master of what he had begun, not needing the help
> of others to carry it through. In the realm of action, this isolated mastership
> can be achieved only if the others are no longer needed to join the enterprise
> of their own accord, with their own motives and aims, but are used to execute
> orders, and if, on the other hand, the beginner who took the initiative does not
> permit himself to get involved in the action itself.

There were also other senses of *archē*, including to designate empire or imperial domination, a sense related to that of "rule."

27. J. Allen, "Office of the Crown," 308. See also McLean's "Authority of the Administration" and Manners and Menand's "Three Permissions" for different aspects of the legal
history of office, as well as Condren's *Argument and Authority* for a broader historical and
conceptual account. In accounts of what is called a great shift "from office to contract,"
office is contrasted with a model in which bureaucrats are subsumed in a hierarchical chain
of command, with only those at the top typically being publicly accountable. But while this
restricted usage can be historically illuminating when so delineated, it does not negate the
survival of the broader and more flexible concept of office as I use it.

To focus in particular on ancient Greek officeholders: they were rulers who exercised epitactic and other powers, but whose roles in so doing were limited and constrained by a family (or a subset thereof) of conventional parameters. Each of these parameters (which have to be reconstructed from a variety of texts and material evidence) can contribute to controlling the officeholders and so making them accountable in the broad sense. As I noted earlier, accountability in a narrow sense revolved around the end-of-term audits (*euthunai*), which counted as limits on performance and could also be invoked as symbols of the whole of accountability (with Pausanias's adjective *hupeuthunos* already a key way of characterizing accountability in the classical period, being cognate to the word *euthunai*).[28] In the broader sense of accountability as meaning limited constitutional government, the parameters can be grouped into three further sets: limits on the powers of each office (often as a collegial member of a board), limits on the eligibility to serve (including term limits; specified selection procedures usually by means of lottery, election, or some combination thereof; and, mainly in Athens, scrutiny of those chosen before they were allowed to take up an office), and other potential parameters, sometimes including (of special interest in chapter 6) the payment of wages.

While procedural and institutional details differ, each of these parameters has parallels in many constitutions outside ancient Greece as well. Conversely, the parameters could in practice be filled out and combined in a wide variety of ways, and with some latitude, meaning that whether a role counts as a political office will ultimately be a matter of family resemblances requiring judgment and interpretation. Plato invites such interpretation by continuing to use the recognized vocabulary of office while pushing the bounds of these family resemblances to the extreme, exploring alternative ways in which offices might be limited and configured that diverge significantly, and some will think decisively, from those that could count as "offices" according to the standards of his time or ours.

Yet the laws and procedures of offices are not guaranteed to protect the good of the ruled. Accountability mechanisms sanction officeholders for corruption; term limits, rotation, collegiality, eligibility requirements, and so on, seek to prevent the abuse of power. Such procedures are likely to do better in warding off the worst abuses than in ensuring officeholders who fully grasp, reliably care for, and can effectively realize the good of the ruled. Moreover, the procedures themselves can break down or be abused by the persons who get into office, or by others able to manipulate them from the outside. These

---

28. The significance of being *hupeuthunos* or its opposite (*aneuthunos* or *anupeuthunos*) was drawn to my attention as relevant for this study by Kinch Hoekstra ("Athenian Democracy").

roles are not immune to the qualities and aspirations and habits—in short, the virtues—of the individuals who operate in and by them.[29]

How then might one address the Juvenal conundrum for constitutions predicated on offices? Fourth-century BCE Athenian appeals to an idealized "ancestral constitution" (*patrios politeia*) idealize the Areopagus Council, composed of selected former holders of offices, in playing a safeguarding role for current officeholders and for the constitution and city as a whole.[30] Indeed, an Athenian decree of 403 BCE, in the wake of the ousting of the Thirty, charged the Areopagus Council to "take caring charge of (*epimeleisthai*) the laws, so that the officeholders (*archai*) may employ the laws that have been passed."[31] Such a two-level model, in which officeholders are safeguarded by a higher body that does not itself hold or constitute an office, is comparable to the explorations that Plato would make in the *Republic* and the *Statesman* of ways in which superordinate rulers could safeguard the officeholders proper. Indeed, the language of ruling, caring, and safeguarding, which Plato develops, resonates more broadly with the *patrios politeia* debate and other interventions into ways of thinking about rule and office in his time and beyond, especially in the contributions of Isocrates.[32]

29. I adapt this sentence from my *Eco-Republic* (30).

30. In Plato's wake, for example, the late fourth-century *Constitution of the Athenians* (transmitted in Aristotle's corpus, though whether its authorship should be ascribed to Aristotle himself or others in his circle is a matter of scholarly debate) described the Draconian-era Areopagus Council as "guardian (*phulax*) of the laws," who "watched over the officeholders (*tas archas*) to see that they ruled (*archōsin*) in accordance with the laws" (4.4; see also 3.6 on the Areopagus's pre-Draconian *taxis* of "watching over (*diatērein*) the laws"); my translation, drawing on discussion in Wallace's *Areopagus Council* (esp. 39–47).

31. Wallace, "Councils in Greek Oligarchies," 200, so translating Teisamenos's decree as reported in Andocides, 1.83–84; [*Ath. Pol.*] 8.4. Wallace there also notes a presumably short-lived (if not entirely invented) institution, mentioned by Philochorus, who "reports that, probably after 462/461, the Athenians instituted a board of *nomophylakes* [*nomophulakes* in my preferred transliteration] to 'force the *archai* to abide by the laws,'" citing Jacoby (*Fragmente der griechischen Historiker* 328 F 64).

32. Isocrates in the *Areopagiticus*, in particular, stresses the epitactic role of the ancestral Areopagus Council (composed of selected and tested ex-officeholders) as a supervisor (*epistatousēs*; Isoc., 7.51), and conjoins this with the function of the *epimeleia* (care) which that Council exercised over adults and not only youths (Isoc., 7.37), in its overall role of caring for the good order of the city (*tēs eutaxias epimeleisthai*) (Isoc., 7.39). As has long been noticed in different currents of scholarship, Plato and Isocrates use mutually resonant language in this regard (setting aside the vexed debate over priority and influence, which goes back to Werner Jaeger and others). Socrates in the *Republic* describes the role of a philosopher-king or philosopher-queen as that of being a "supervisor" (*epistatēs*) whose role is necessary if the "constitution is to be safeguarded" (*ei mellei hē politeia sōizesthai*) (3.412b1), using language which recurs at crucial moments in the *Statesman* and the *Laws*; likewise, he refers to the need for philosophers to be compelled by chance to "care for" (*epimelēthēnai*) a city, using the same verb as Isocrates in 7.39, one which will play an

To be sure, in speaking of ancient Greek offices, it is significant that Greek polities did not distinguish between political offices (such as elected members of the legislative or executive) and administrative offices (appointed through a civil service) as many modern polities have variously come to do. Neither did a sharp distinction between executive, judicial, and legislative powers apply. In fourth-century BCE Athens, for example, every officeholder had the power to preside in certain kinds of court proceedings (a kinship of executive and judicial roles that Plato echoes in the *Laws*); as to legislative powers, these were transferred from the plenary Assembly to a judicial-like board of *nomothetai* who heard and judged motions to make any change to any of the codified laws. With these caveats, however, one may loosely treat ancient Greek *archai* as more or less comparable to modern executive offices, being more like political offices in their modes of accountability but administrative offices in their typical sets of duties.[33]

To compare ancient Greek offices to modern executive offices is to confront a new set of challenges, however, since, as Joseph Heath has remarked of modern states, "given that the state is constituted largely by the executive, it is surprising how undertheorized this branch of government is."[34] It has been

---

important role in all three Platonic dialogues considered in this study. Helmer (*Oikonomia*, 143) observes that *sōzein* and *phulattein/phulassein* (the verb corresponding to the role of "guardian (*phulax*)" in the *Republic*) are verbs widely used in Greek discussions of political economy, describing their relevant sense as "conserver, c'est ranger et calculer" (to preserve is to arrange and to calculate).

33. There was also an important group of administrators in ancient Greek cities who were so-called public slaves—enslaved persons owned by the city itself and deployed in civic tasks, many of them requiring considerable expertise—as has been emphasized by Ismard in *Démocratie contre les experts*. As he points out, this violates the very nexus between expertise and rule on which Plato would insist, and which modern societies have in some circumstances come to expect (though in fact that intuition is more fraught today than he admits). Notably, Ismard opens his second chapter (63–64) with a scene from Plato's *Statesman* in which "the group of slaves and servants" appear as rivals claiming the mantle (and title) of statecraft, a scene to which I shall return in chapter 4. However, his broader argument (30) that the role of public slaves challenges the sense in which the Greek state (say, the Athenian democracy) was in fact a state, to my mind goes too far in downplaying the role of the citizen officeholders (who could be designated by the term, *archai*, that could also designate their offices).

34. Heath, *Machinery of Government*, 19–20. One instructive exception, which appeared in the same year as Heath's study, is Cordelli's *Privatized State*, though the latter's discussion of "officeholders" (esp. 85–86, 102–13), focuses on administrative bureaucrats without theorizing the broader role of the executive per se. An earlier exception is Tuck's *Sleeping Sovereign*, although this is focused on the theoretical contrast between sovereignty and government (which includes constitutional officeholding) rather than on the nature of the latter. Several historians of early modern England have emphasized the role of office as a fundamental organizing political vision in that period, while noting its later retreat; here I have learned from Dauber's *State and Commonwealth*, Goldie's "Unacknowledged Republic," and Withington's *Politics of Commonwealth*, among others.

regarded by many political theorists and ancient historians alike as involving "mere administration," as it were, being overshadowed by interest in the powers of legislative and judicial bodies—in the case of scholars of democratic Athens, in the Assembly and the popular law courts. Officeholders have been of interest to many students of ancient Greece largely insofar as many of them were chosen by lottery, neglecting consideration of the significance of their powers once chosen (not to mention the fact that some were always, even in democratic Athens, chosen by election). Meanwhile, office has been regarded by some political historians and scientists to be a remnant of scholarly focus on the wrong kind of institutionalism, one that is too static and legalistic to illuminate political life in the ways that studies of ideologies and game-theoretic approaches can do.[35]

Thus office as a form of rule, and the idea of rule more broadly, is ripe for reconsideration from the perspective of the present work. Even those persuaded of the interest of office and rule as topics may be surprised to find Plato taken as a guide to development of what Heath calls "a philosophy of the executive,"[36] again using that modern vocabulary as a gloss on the roles of the officeholders and rulers who figure in classical Greek texts, and pointing to certain overlapping institutional formations then and now, such as the role of law in limiting and controlling officeholders so as to make them accountable. Yet Plato has a great deal to say about the proper role of rulers, the extent to which officeholders (who constitute one kind of ruler) can adequately fulfil the purpose of that role, and how both rule and office might be reconfigured so as to better realize that purpose. Or so it is the burden of this study to show.

To do so, I put some terms of art on the table, while noting that this overview makes many claims for which evidence can be given only in subsequent chapters. These terms of art are designed to capture Plato's ideas of rule and office, while also situating those ideas in a broader family of such ideas. Rule is a relationship between a ruler and one or more persons ruled, which can

35. See the discussion in Beck's introduction to the *Companion to Ancient Greek Government* (1–2), noting that recognition of the "anachronistic" presupposition of "a normative state law" in ancient Greek cities led scholars to turn away from what he calls "an overtly constitutionalist approach," and toward cultural and social scientific studies instead. The latter are well represented by the immense contribution made by the multifaceted works of Josiah Ober, including both his early work on the performative and ideological role of rhetoric in Athenian democracy and his more recent role in the turn to a game-theoretic "new institutionalism." I have learned much from these approaches as pursued by Ober and others, including his many students (among them Federica Carugati, Matthew Simonton, David Teegarden, and others). Yet the study of the constitutional structure of Greek offices, together with the practices associated with them, still has something important to teach us about the ideas and normative expectations implicit within them—not least because of the ways in which these came to animate (and be criticized and renovated) in the work of Greek philosophers, as I show in this study for the case of Plato.

36. Heath, *Machinery of Government*, 19.

be characterized in terms of two dimensions: a *telos* (purpose) and a *taxis* (order).[37] A *taxis* is an ordered set of roles and relationships (including institutions and procedures) through which a *telos* might be achieved.

A constraint on the *taxis* of any kind of rule is that the ruler have in principle the epitactic power of issuing orders (*epitaxis*, singular) to the ruled;[38] Aristotle would observe that "issuing orders is most characteristic of office."[39] What is essential to this epitactic power is, at least in principle, the form of a directive order: not the particular means of persuasion or coercion that a ruler may use to enforce it, nor the basis on which someone ruled may or may not be actually bound to obey the directive. Whether all those issued such an order are bound to obey, as well as whether they do or do not actually obey, does not affect the standing of a ruler as a ruler on this account. Plato is no Weberian in this respect. He does not treat coercion as fundamental to rule, a point discussed in chapter 11.

Within a significant tradition of thinking about ancient Greek rule, which can be traced from Homer to Plato, there is likewise a constraint on the *telos* of rule: that this should be the good of the ruled. Plato is no Weberian in this respect either, in not treating rule as an evaluatively neutral idea. That will undoubtedly seem tendentious. Why not take rule to describe a relationship in which a ruler may adopt any *telos* that they choose, including one that exploits

---

37. While Plato does not spell out these ideas in the way that I schematize them here, he uses both *telos* and *taxis* in the relevant senses of "purpose" and "order," though sometimes also using other words as well. Consider an illustration of each such use: on the one hand, his reference to "the *telos* (purpose) toward which . . . a man's appetites are directed" (*Resp.* 9.575e1, though this is not a reference to a political *telos*); on the other hand, his reference to "order [*taxis*] and law [*nomos*]" as virtues of a second-best form of rule that is contrasted with the case of someone engaged in "unaccountable and autocratic rule in a city (*anupeuthunos te kai autokratōr arxēi poleōs*)" (*Leg.* 9.875d4 and b3–4 respectively, parts of a difficult passage that is discussed further in chapter 3).

38. An order in the sense of a command is in Greek an *epitaxis*, which is part of an overall ordered arrangement (*taxis*), and thus contributes to realizing a state of *kosmos* (a fine arrangement); both *taxis* and *kosmos* can signify order in general. Rulers may also exercise other powers of ordering, through speech acts of persuasion, creation, and so on, as is noted by Landauer in "Drinking Parties Correctly Ordered," who criticizes my emphasis on ordering or commanding as essential to rule (expressed in an earlier publication of mine, "*Antianarchia*") by arguing that there are multiple "modalities of rule," such as negotiating and agenda setting. While this is true, my point remains that the capacity to issue orders remains central in principle to a relationship of rule. This is also the case with Raz's definition of practical authority, which hinges on the issuing of authoritative directives.

39. Arist., *Pol.* 4.1299a27–28, emphasizing this as most characteristic among a trio of powers of officeholders [*archai*], namely: "to deliberate and to judge and to issue orders." This passage is cited in Hansen (*Athenian Democracy*, 229), who also remarks of the fourth-century Athenian democracy in which Plato wrote: "the ephebic oath [taken by young men upon successfully attaining the status of adult citizen] included a promise to obey the magistrates [in my parlance, officeholders]," on pain of being fined.

the ruled rather than seeking to serve their good? Rule as inherently oriented to serving the good of the ruled might seem to be merely stipulative, not only to Weberians but also to Marxists, and indeed to many political scientists and some political theorists of various stripes. In fact, some of Plato's own contemporaries used the very vocabulary of rule that I have introduced (as well as other linguistic terms and idioms) to describe rulers who aimed at their own good instead. Plato too shows himself to be well aware of the existence of such cases, showcasing characters who describe or endorse self-serving rulers in several dialogues.

Nevertheless, Plato's adoption of this approach in context should not be taken as a novel philosophical intervention. Rather, he was working within a deeply ingrained evaluative nimbus of long-standing Greek approaches to the figuration of rulers, especially of kings. The Homeric trope of the king as shepherd, expected (if often failing) to care for the good of his flock, opened a source of imagery to which Plato would explicitly respond. Language of caring for the good of ruled, as would a caretaker put in charge of them, and of serving their good, as would a servant, can be found in idealizing depictions of the Athenian Areopagus in fourth-century BCE orators, and more generally in certain portrayals of politics in fifth-century BCE playwrights and tragedians (some of which will be quoted at later points in this study). Plato was in step with many of his predecessors and contemporaries in portraying rulers as expected to care for the good of the ruled, just as he was in emphasizing the epitactic dimension of rule (which clearly characterized, for example, portrayals of kingship).

Of course, some authors in ancient Greece (like many today) dissented from the assumption that kings and other rulers should serve the good of the ruled. Plato explicitly responds to such challenges as well, presenting them as voiced by the likes of Thrasymachus and Callicles in his dialogues. Moreover, many figures in power then (as now) dramatically flouted this expectation, yet their power was sometimes still described as "rule" (using *archē* or *archein*) in a looser use of language, showing that the evaluative nimbus of rule was a matter of clustered expectations rather than strict definition. My claim here is not that tyrants (say) were not sometimes described by Plato's contemporaries or predecessors as ruling in the vocabulary of *archein* and its cognates; indeed they were—for example, by Xenophon in presenting his version of Socrates.[40] "Rule" could sometimes be used to describe bad rule as well as good rule (though there was little effort made by Greek authors to develop an evaluatively neutral category). Notwithstanding all these caveats, Plato was far from isolated in taking the *telos* of rule to be the good of the ruled. He did

---

40. To illustrate: Xenophon (*Mem.* 4.6.12) ascribed the view to Socrates that "kingship and tyranny . . . were both kinds of rule (*archas*)" (an unusual instance in which a plural form of the noun *archē* should in context be translated as "rule" rather than "office").

so within a broadly shared social horizon of evaluative expectations, not as an isolated flourish or fetish of his own philosophical idealism.

The *telos* of rule as the good of the ruled, which for the Greeks was captured in the image of the king or ruler as shepherd, can also be picked up in modern philosophical vocabulary. Call this a service conception of rule, an expression that I adapt from the philosopher Joseph Raz's service conception of authority (focusing on his account of practical authority). A service conception is explicitly evaluative: it is oriented to the good of those persons whom it is the role of the party in question to direct (issue directives, for Raz, or orders, for Plato). Accordingly, both delineate a role—the role of ruler (Plato), the role of being a (practical) authority (Raz)—in terms of what it would be to perform the role rightly and well. It is consistent with this approach that any given natural person seeking to perform such a role might do so badly; that the persons whom they seek to direct should reject their direction, or that they should fail in some other way; and indeed that such a role might never be properly filled or recognized at all.[41] Both also independently take there to be objective grounds for those parties to accept directives or orders that are genuinely oriented to serving their good. Conversely, neither Plato nor Raz defines rule or authority in terms of its potential use of coercion.

With regard to the service conception and the *telos* of rule in particular, this was in context far less controversial (which is not to say not at all controversial) as a stance for Plato than it is for Raz. That politics should serve the good of the ruled appears to have been a view shared by a far greater number of Plato's predecessors than those relatively few iconoclasts who may have challenged it. That said, of course Plato would develop a profoundly original and counterintuitive account of the true nature of the good of the ruled, rooted in the Good as such—that is, the Form of the Good. A study of Platonic political thought without an account of his theory of goodness risks being *Hamlet* without the prince. Yet providing such an account, integrating the metaphysics, epistemology, ethics, and politics of even just the three dialogues on which I focus in this study, is beyond the scope of what this work can do. Fortunately, it

---

41. Plato does not discuss as explicitly as does Raz whether a measure of de facto power is needed for someone to count as a practical authority (which Raz says [*Morality of Freedom*, 56] there is "a strong case" for answering in the affirmative). The *Statesman* insists that someone with the requisite expertise is a statesman even if they are serving as an advisor to a ruler rather than ruling themselves, but invokes the closely related role of king to indicate someone with the same expertise who is actually engaged in ruling. As to the questions of feasibility and possibility: while Raz says little about these in *Morality of Freedom*, Plato addresses them explicitly in the *Republic* in books 5–7. I see Plato as similar to Raz in emphasizing the success conditions for a service conception, while separating this from the question of whether and how a constitution realizing such a conception could come into existence. In my "States of Nature," I discussed Raz's relative silence on the related question of the marks by which a genuine practical authority might be recognized.

is possible to draw on some basic presuppositions of Platonic ethics to explain the *telos* of rule, while also appreciating that the ways in which he presents the Good as operationalized in making political arguments do not always require a full account of the nature and content of that Good.

Among the basic presuppositions of Platonic ethics is that virtue is good for each individual, and that living virtuously is necessary for happiness (and probably also sufficient, though I leave that problem aside). Virtue consists in a proper ordering of the soul, and so of a person's life, toward that good. Thus rule within the soul is the ultimate aim of any kind of rule. Political rule aims at fostering rule within the souls of those who are unable to ensure such rule for and within themselves. Those who are sufficiently similar in having rule within their souls, whether achieved through self-rule or through political rule, are capable of participating in and so enjoying further relational goods: civic freedom and friendship. These are depicted in the dialogues especially as fostered by rule through office and law.

That said, the logics of self-rule and political rule are necessarily different. Self-rule aims to secure the good of the whole person; the only part that is capable of doing this—namely, the rational part of the soul—is part of that whole, and so seeks to realize its own good as part of the good of the whole. Political rule, however, requires someone to take up the role of ruler over another person. A natural person who plays the role of ruler has a different good from the good of the ruled in principle, in that each of them has their own virtue to pursue and realize, without which their individual life cannot be happy. A natural person who plays the role of ruler also has a different good from the good of the ruled in practice, in that their separateness as natural persons means that there is always a risk of the former using the powers of rule to pursue what they take to be their private good at the expense of the good of the latter.

On the one hand, this gap between the person(s) whose good constitutes the *telos* of political rule and the person(s) whose role is that of ruler is what makes a service conception of rule necessary. The role of the ruler is to serve the good of the ruled. On the other hand, this gap also makes it possible to discuss that service conception without invoking a full account of the content of the Good. For the Good can be operationalized in politics as "the good of the ruled," in the sense that the role of ruler be taken to be oriented to serving the good of the ruled as opposed to exploiting the ruled for the sake of the good of the ruler. This operationalization provides a helpful test, insofar as exploitation can often be assessed in mundane terms—personal financial enrichment, for example—without requiring a full grasp of the Form of the Good to determine.[42]

---

42. An even more literal test has long been applied by the town of High Wycombe in England, which annually weighs its officeholders to determine whether they have fattened

Of course, Plato also has in his repertoire the more fundamental ethical point that a ruler who seeks to exploit the ruled is making a mistake about their own good. Such a ruler is getting their own good wrong: the goods that exploitative political rulers take themselves to be pursuing will turn out not to be genuine goods at all (or, at least, not insofar as they are pursued by unjust means, and not insofar as they are to be used without knowledge of the true Good). But the account of rule offered in the *Republic*, as in the *Statesman* and *Laws*, does not hinge on that point. The point is that qua ruler, one must serve the good of the ruled, whatever that turns out to be (even though in fact its content will be Platonically determinate).

Considered as a natural person, one may derive some individual benefit from taking up the role of ruler. Those who rule so as to avoid being ruled by others less knowledgeable and virtuous than themselves do thereby derive a benefit.[43] But while that benefit may be their motivation as natural persons for taking up the role of ruler, it cannot constitute the *telos* that orients their actions in that role.[44] That *telos*, Plato argues explicitly in *Republic* 1 and in the *Statesman*, is the good of the ruled. In other words, the aim of one's actions as a ruler must be the good of the ruled, even if the aim for which one takes up the role of ruler may be different.[45] Qua ruler, one must pursue a service conception of rule all the way down.

To be concerned with a role that is directed toward a *telos*, one must be concerned with who will fill that role. Institutional design involves at least three interlocking issues (corresponding to the cluster of vulnerabilities associated with the Juvenal conundrum): design of the role; design of the selection procedure for identifying and assigning someone capable of meeting the demands of the role; and design of safeguards to ensure that, once installed in the role, the role holder will indeed pursue its proper purposes. Plato, on my view, is equally interested in each of these issues, not only in choosing the natural persons to serve as rulers, an issue that is too often taken to have exhausted his political thought. Each of the trio of Platonic dialogues considered in this study explores one or more of these issues (the *Republic* and *Laws* addressing each of them, the *Statesman* focusing especially on the first) and explores possible reconfigurations of the roles of rule and office to address them. Each such reconfiguration can be understood as exploring a way to keep the *taxis* of rule

---

themselves while in office (as an indication that further inquiry into private gain, in both senses, is needed): Freytas-Tamura, "British Town."

43. This distinction is drawn in a related context by Viehoff in "Authority and Expertise."

44. I seek to respond here to comments made by Josiah Ober on another part of this study in draft.

45. The point is analogous to a point often made about rule utilitarianism: one may have a utilitarian aim in designing an overall system of punishment, say, but insist that liability to punishment within the system be based on desert, even if that fails to maximize overall utility in any given case.

(which may include office) properly oriented toward its *telos*, in terms of both the shape of the roles and the orientation of the persons playing those roles. This is what I mean by "safeguarding": to arrange for the maintaining, so far as possible, of the orientation of those playing roles within a given political *taxis* toward the *telos* of the good of the ruled.

Republic 1 draws attention to a potential tension between the role of ruler, as there described, and any natural person who might take it up. Qua ruler, one must seek to serve the ruled. Yet the only natural person who can be trusted to take up that role is someone who does not want to rule but will take it up so as to avoid being ruled over by someone worse than themselves. The same underlying psychology that can make someone a suitable candidate to rule— subject to development by the right kind of education and experience—is what makes them naturally disposed to avoid becoming corrupted while doing so. This psychology marks out those who are philosophers by nature (as described in *Republic* 6), rooted in a hydraulic flow of their psychic energies away from physical appetites and toward the love of learning. The moral and intellectual virtues of these philosophers arise from this same root.[46] Nevertheless, Plato does not appeal to these natural virtues, as I call them, as a basis for untrammeled rule. To the contrary, these very candidate philosophers, and moreover the fully cultivated philosophers who are to rule as kings, are still to be subject to various kinds of legal and procedural safeguards (imposed by the reigning philosophers on others, and by their predecessors on themselves), some of them very drastic, as explained in chapters 6 and 7.

Putting together the role and its proper incumbent leads me to a final set of terms of art, building on ones used by Plato himself. For Plato sometimes speaks of true rulers, officeholders, constitutions, cities, and citizens as the only ones worthy of their respective names, speaking thus in a strict sense (*sensu stricto* is a useful Latin tag) that is inherently evaluative. A true ruler, citizen, and so on, is one who pursues the purpose proper to that role or entity.[47] This strict

---

46. Lane, "Virtue."

47. E.g., for constitutions, referring to the single *orthē politeia*, *Plt.* 293c5–6 (cf. 302b5–303c2), calling those in political power in all others "not statesmen, but experts in faction"; for constitutions and citizens, *Leg.* 4.715b5–6, arguing that certain kinds of putative constitutional regimes are not *politeiai* at all but rather *stasiōteiai* (factional regimes) (though here the contrasting reference to laws not being *orthous nomous* may mean only that these laws are not correct but not that they are not laws at all, as Jiseob Yoon has suggested to me), and *Leg.* 8.832c1–2, again renaming putative *politeiai* as *stasiōteiai* and claiming that none of them (*oudemia*) is a constitution at all; for a similar point about rulers and ruled, *Resp.* 8.552b9–11. These passages have been catalogued as making a discrete gesture of this kind by a number of scholars of Plato's works, as by Schöpsdau (*"Nomoi" (Gesetze) Buch IV-VII* and *Buch VIII-X*, respectively, ad loc. to the *Laws* passages cited in this note). But it has not been linked by these scholars, as I link it here, to Plato's following of existing patterns of usage distinguishing between rule and office; to his systematic analysis of office, rule, and the related idea of a constitution that could be articulated in terms of

sense contrasts with an alternative loose sense (*sensu lato*), which is merely descriptive. A ruler or citizen may be described as such in loose everyday terms even though they fail to be oriented to their proper *telos*. In the strict sense of "ruler," the everyday political figures with whom Plato or any of his contemporaries would have been familiar—imagine a statue gallery of kings, tyrants, officeholders, and so on, an image that is explored in chapter 2—reduces to just one genuine ruler, who may in fact have never yet existed, with the existing crew being largely or entirely imitations not worthy of the name.

While I am supplying "strict" and "loose," as well as "evaluative" and "descriptive," as terms of art for this distinction, I also follow Plato in making use of the vocabulary of "*alēthōs*" ("truly") or *ontōs* ("really") or *orthos* ("correct") or *dikaiōs* (in one of its senses, "really and truly")[48] to mark the strict evaluative side of the distinction. This vocabulary can be used when one wishes to deny that someone or something who may descriptively seem to count as an X is in reality an X at all, because they are not capable of fulfilling the proper evaluatively laden function of their role.[49] This kind of move is not made by Plato alone. On the contrary, modern linguists refer to the "dual character"[50] of certain concepts, which can be deployed either descriptively or evaluatively, with the latter use capable of invalidating the former in certain contexts. For example, one might describe someone with a PhD in biology working in a lab as a scientist, but also say (depending on whether they were flouting norms of research) that they are not a true scientist—that is, not truly a scientist at all. Similarly, just

---

archai (offices) and *nomoi* (laws); or to the inventive variations on roles of rule and office that feature in different configurations in the *Republic, Statesman*, and *Laws*.

48. LSJ, s.v.

49. For the Platonic concept of proper function, see the *ergon* discussion of *Republic* 1 (352d9–353e6). For all the scorn often heaped by modern political theorists on Platonic naturalism, many philosophers today make ready use of the concept of a goodness-fixing kind, one such that "merely by understanding what the kind is, we can order things of that kind from best to worst," and so are capable of "knowing a standard merely by knowing a kind." Examples of such kinds are typically drawn from the same sets as those of Plato—namely, artifacts on the one hand and biological kinds on the other. The notion of a goodness-fixing kind was introduced by Thomson in *Normativity* (21) and called to my attention by Michael Smith.

50. On such concepts, I follow Knobe, Prasada, and Newman's "Dual Character Concepts," an earlier version of which was drawn to my attention by Stout in "Religion since Cicero," with thanks to Emily Foster-Hanson for further advice. Leslie ("Hillary Clinton,"116) also invokes this formulation of dual-character concepts in discussing those social kinds that are also labeled "normative generics" in possessing a normative sense in which they are an "exemplifier of the ideals associated with being a [member of that kind]." In earlier versions of this study, I used the label "dual character concepts" more liberally in what follows, but I have been persuaded by Ian Walling that this could be misleading insofar as Plato is not making a point about concepts as distinct from reality, and have been further helped to think about these matters by Shapiro's "Essentialism" and by conversations with Gabriel Shapiro more generally.

as some of Plato's contemporaries could use "rule" to describe tyrants (even though Plato and others emphasized the positive evaluative nimbus of "rule"), so Plato could himself sometimes deploy the language of office and rule descriptively (referring to oligarchic officeholders, corrupt rulers, and so on).[51]

For Plato, however, the two alternative uses (strict and loose) are not on a par, nor is the character of a concept all that is at stake. He employs the strict sense when averring that only the evaluative use of certain ideas—such as ruler and constitution—correspond fully to the contours of reality. And while he sometimes in other contexts employs the loose sense, the implication of his work (so I argue) is that even seemingly everyday descriptive uses are ultimately illuminated by the underpinning evaluative expectations with which they cannot break altogether (as I show in part III, in chapters on *Republic* books 8 and 9).

Plato's drawing out, in this way, of the implicit evaluative presuppositions of existing models of rule and office,[52] and his philosophical renovations of them in the shape of reconfigured roles, are not radically distinct activities (contrary to what modern-day "practice positivists" would posit).[53] Instead, as I reconstruct his line of thought, Plato starts from the kind of investigation

51. Cf. Aristotle in *Pol.* 1276a2–3; I owe this reference to Josiah Ober.

52. While I use the word "implicit," I find Amanda Greene's approach to reconstructing the notion of the "implicit claim" made by an institution to be less helpful, remaining as it does ambiguous between the actual claim and the philosophically reasonable claim to be made. (Compare her account of a single [and implied normatively adequate] "implicit claim" made by the institution of a library ["When Are Markets Illegitimate?," 214–15] with Applbaum's reflections [*Ethics for Adversaries*, 57] on an old-fashioned librarian whose view of the institution rejects the transition from print to electronic collections.) Instead, I follow the political theorist Michael Rosen, who has observed (in "Liberalism" [2], while explicating the thought of Michael Sandel) that "philosophies carry within themselves assumptions that are expressions of particular forms of life while institutions are animated by practices within which political theory is already implicit," adverting to Sandel's *Democracy's Discontent* (4), which defines the "public philosophy implicit in our practices and institutions." In a similar spirit, I seek in this study to put text and context on a par: treating texts as contributions to a context, even as the vocabulary involved in articulating those practices serves also to structure a given text.

53. Defending "practice positivism," Arthur Applbaum (*Ethics for Adversaries*, 51 and 48–58 more generally), argues that "the rules of a practice are simply what they are, not what they ought to be or what we want them to be"; on which view, "we cannot criticize the schmocter [a doctor who views themselves as free of some of what a philosopher might consider the best case for the 'reasonable' moral duties associated with the role of doctor] on grounds that are internal to the concept of a professional practice or role." Applbaum insists that his own view does not reduce to the laxity of allowing that "a role is . . . simply whatever role occupants happen to do"—a position that he dubs "role realism"—because he takes it that a role can indeed be betrayed, traduced, and so on by a particular occupant (58). But he asserts that the evaluative criteria for determining whether an occupant is betraying or traducing their role are to be drawn from the social facts of how any such betrayal, and the role itself, are understood, not from the philosophical reconstruction (as

that another scholar has recommended in seeking to reconstruct the social norms, including the implicit evaluative criteria that they include, obtaining at any given time.[54] In particular, Plato identifies the *telos* of the good of the ruled as being implicit in the institutions and practices defining such offices, especially in the accountability mechanisms attached to them, which could potentially fail, however, to adequately protect the realization of that good. Accountability is a particularly sore spot, since this was part of the *taxis* of office meant to orient it toward a proper *telos*, but could fail in practice (as I take the dialogues to suggest) to do so with sufficient robustness. It is the recognition of such failures that leads Plato, in his sensu stricto moods, to claim that existing constitutions fail to count as genuine constitutions at all.

In each of the major dialogues that are the focus of this study—*Republic*, *Statesman*, and *Laws*—I show that Plato included variously reconfigured offices in constitutional and civic models of well-ruled cities. At the same time, he also reflected in various ways on their limits (pun intended) and vulnerabilities. Moreover, in so doing, he went a further step beyond existing models of how such Achilles' heels might be safeguarded against by considering how safeguarding might be achieved all the way down, or rather, up: not just how some further group of rulers might safeguard some subordinate officeholders, but also the further iterative question of how those superordinate rulers can be safeguarded themselves. The *Republic* in particular will contend that ruling at any level cannot be entirely unbounded or unlimited, entirely disordered, on pain of being unable to play its part in ordering others. The lack of any limits does not render rule pure; it negates rule altogether, yielding anarchy (literally, the privation of *archē*). At the same time, tyranny, which may seem to be an excrescence of epitactic power rather than its absence, turns out to count as a kind of anarchy as well. Tyrants undermine the order that is constitutive of any kind of rule.

So construed, Platonic political thought is exhausted neither by stating that the *telos* of rule must be the good of the ruled nor by identifying the knowers of that good or of the Good in itself. It is no simple epistocratic program of handing over absolute powers to such knowers.[55] On the contrary. The rule of knowledge in Plato is the *rule* of knowledge. Plato has as much to say about the nature of rule, including the value and limits of office, as he does about the nature of knowledge. And he is as interested in ways in which offices can be reconfigured as in the reconfiguration of other kinds of rule.

---

he terms it) of what the most "reasonable" boundaries of the role should be. In my view, Plato does exactly the opposite.

54. Rehfeld, "On Representing": a reference I owe to Darius Weil. The specific aim of Rehfeld's discussion is to formulate criteria for determining when someone is to be counted as "representing" someone else in a political sense.

55. I am grateful to Lisa Disch for suggesting the epistocratic framing in comments on a version of this chapter (Disch, "Comments on 'Rule'").

The trio of dialogues on which I focus each models such reconfiguration in different ways. Plato's *Laws* focuses on the limits (pun intended) of a *taxis* of offices; the *Statesman*, on the *taxis* of rule, with a subordinate role therein for offices—an inquiry matched by that of *Republic* 1 into the *telos* of rule as the good of the ruled; and the *Republic* as a whole, on constructing an elaborate mosaic in which two kinds of rule are reconfigured and related so that the philosophers reign as kings by safeguarding those in roles junior to them, including a cohort who are unambiguously linguistically signaled to be holding offices. To be sure, whether what are linguistically signaled to be "offices" in each of these reconfigurations should count as offices against the conventional standards of his time, or ours, is a matter for each reader of Plato to judge. Some will deny that they should count, taking their divergences from narrow mechanisms of accountability to be too profound for them to do so. My point is that Plato's deployment of the vocabulary of office and rule in all three dialogues implies that readers must at least ask themselves that question, and recognize it to be a genuinely Platonic one.

It may help to place the stakes of my reading of Plato in context by situating this between two poles, a Scylla in the shape of Karl Popper and a Charybdis in the shape of Adrian Vermeule. For his part, Popper famously proposed that political theorizing must "replace the question: *Who should rule?*"—a question that he ascribed to Plato—"by the new question: *How can we so organize political institutions that bad or incompetent rulers can be prevented from doing too much damage?*"[56] On my reading of the *Republic, Statesman*, and *Laws*, by contrast, Plato was far from limiting himself only to the question "*Who should rule?*" Neither did he rely upon what Popper ascribes to him as "the . . . general assumption that political power is practically unchecked, or . . . the demand that it ought to be so; together with the implication that the main question left is to get this power into the best hands."[57] Rather, he explored various models of offices and their relationship to other kinds of rule, so as to test how their *taxis* could prevent bad or incompetent rulers from coming into positions of rule at all. To illustrate with the *Republic*: the constitutional project thereof imposes limits of various kinds (including deprivation of any accumulation of wealth and dependence on wages, both limits that are said to be imposed by law) on the powers of the rulers, including those who are to hold various offices. Even the supreme philosopher-kings and philosopher-queens, who are described as reigning within the constitution (in a verb cognate with kingship), are shown to be subject to certain limits necessary to safeguard them in their very role of guarding others (the officeholders and others subordinate to them) and so of the city as a whole.

---

56. Popper, *Open Society*, 1:120–21.
57. Popper, 1:121.

Whereas Popper criticized Plato for (in effect) failing to attend to a project of liberal procedural limitation of power, the legal scholar Adrian Vermeule has recently advanced a theory of what he calls "common good constitutionalism," which puts a *telos* of the good of the ruled at the heart of a constitutional project. Vermeule's project may seem in keeping with that of Plato, in that it is fair to say that the latter shares the view that (as Vermeule puts it), "the end of the community is ultimately to promote the good of individuals."[58] As Vermeule attributes his own view to a broad classical tradition (drawing especially on Aristotle, Cicero, Roman law, and their later reception, while not in his book mentioning Plato), it is worth assessing the extent to which Plato's ideas of rule and office might be similar to or different from those of Vermeule, both for its own sake and as a way of clarifying the Platonic view.

Take first the content of the *telos* of the good. Vermeule argues that a "common good" must be "unitary and indivisible,"[59] and further, that "common goods are themselves the highest good for individuals."[60] On my reading in part IV of this study, Plato does identify certain common goods, such as the relational goods of civic freedom and friendship. These are fruits of certain kinds of *taxis* of rule, when those ruled obey the rulers willingly and more generally exhibit a cooperative disposition. And he speaks generally sometimes of the good of the city as a whole, as at the beginning of *Republic* 4, a passage discussed in chapter 6. But the primary *telos* of political rule is fostering the virtue (requiring ordered rule within the soul) of each of those who is ruled, virtue which for each of them is necessary to their individually enjoying a happy and flourishing life (a life of *eudaimonia*). Because the virtue of each embodied individual is, while not rivalrous, countably distinct from the virtue of another, the good as the *telos* of political rule must include the summation or aggregation of individual virtue.[61] Yet for Vermeule, any kind of aggregative approach counts as an antonym of the true "common good." Thus Plato's approach would fail Vermeule's test; conversely, Vermeule's approach fails to be in keeping with the Platonic source of any later classical tradition.

It is also worth noting that Vermeule's conservative approach to the content of common goods over time is very different from Plato's willingness to countenance breaking with long-standing social and political traditions where

---

58. Vermeule, *Common Good Constitutionalism*, 29.

59. Vermeule, 7. This is an introductory characterization, which is explained more fully as part of "the classical theory" as follows: "A genuinely *common* good is a good that is unitary ... and capable of being shared without being diminished. Thus it is inherently non-aggregative" (28).

60. Vermeule, 29.

61. Vermeule, 26. It must be noted, however, that while Platonic virtues can be both separated and summed up across individuals, they are not to be reduced to "the sum of separate private utilities," which is specifically what Vermeule decries under the heading of "aggregation."

philosophical insight can justify doing so. Consider, for example, the arguments in the *Republic* for qualified women to serve as rulers, and likewise Socrates's remark therein about a change in Greek male customs of exercising (from clothed to unclothed): "what reason had proved best lost its absurdity to the eye."[62] This is Plato summing up the process of bootstrapping changes in the political imagination, a process that Plato deploys in ways that were far more challenging to many practices of his own time than Vermeule's approach for its part generally countenances.

What of the *taxis* of the Platonic idea of rule, as compared with the *taxis* of Vermeule's common good constitutionalism? Again, there is an important shared starting point: both reject what Vermeule calls "ruling for private benefit."[63] But whereas Vermeule seeks to combat this by asserting a strong substantive account of the common good, I have argued that Plato does not simply fall back on his own metaphysics to make this point, but rather reconfigures the role of the ruler as being to serve the good of the ruled. For Plato, it is the role of ruling itself that puts constraints on the commonness of the good that ruling is to serve in its direct aims.

Moreover, Plato takes the risk of abuse of power far more seriously than Vermeule (and likewise more seriously than Popper allowed him to have done). Acknowledging that allegations of "abuse of power" are "a stock concern about political rule, under robust authority directed to the common good," Vermeule sketches two brief lines of response. He observes, first, that "the bad is privative and thus defined by the good"; second, that "the risks of abuse of power created by state organs" can overlook "the risks of abuse of power that public authorities prevent through vigorous government."[64] Neither of these responses, nor indeed Vermeule's downplaying of the concern altogether, is especially Platonic.

Plato's response to the risk of abuse of power explicitly attends to the nature, education, and selection of the persons who will hold constitutional roles of rule, simultaneously with applying safeguards of multiple kinds (including legal ones) to the ruling done by such persons.[65] To be sure, as Vermeule says of what he calls the classical tradition, the Platonic idea of rule too must finally rest "on the overarching principle of *bona fides* [good faith]," such that "where such good faith is systematically absent, the law may misfire."[66]

---

62. *Resp.* 5.452d5–7, trans. Lee, as quoted in my *Eco-Republic* (185), from which I adapt part of this paragraph.

63. Vermeule, *Common Good Constitutionalism*, 26, in context of 26–27.

64. Vermeule, 49 (first pair of quotations), 50 (second pair).

65. It is true that Plato does not concern himself with seeking to prevent risks of abuse of power by those who are not political rulers, even when those risks are obvious to modern eyes—as in the risks of abuse of power by slaveholders over their slaves. I confront this issue again in chapter 10.

66. Vermeule, 70.

Yet this is true of any form of rule, including liberal institutions as well. More-over, Plato is far more concerned to find ways in which good faith can be both cultivated and safeguarded in those filling the roles of different kinds of rulers than Vermeule shows himself to be. Systematic explorations of the relation-ship between those roles and the natural persons who serve them, and also among those roles as one can be deployed to safeguard another, shows Plato to have put prevention of corruption of the rulers and exploitation of the ruled at the very heart of his politics (as opposed to relegating it to a briefly rehearsed objection, as does Vermeule).

Pace Popper and Vermeule alike, a fundamental concern of Platonic politi-cal thought is how to prevent the abuse of power by political rulers, including explorations of various models of the kind of *taxis* of rule and office that could successfully prevent this: partly by precluding bad rulers from coming into those roles at all, but also by safeguarding the orientation to the good as the *telos* of those who hold them. At a deeper level, Plato recognizes that any pro-cedurally delineated political role risks being corrupted, if the person installed in that role (be it office or another kind of rule) is either by nature incapable or unwilling to carry it out for the good of the ruled, or is allowed owing to lack of limits and safeguards to exploit the ruled rather than serve them. This recognition has as much to say to radical critiques of legalism and procedural-ism (call it liberalism if you wish) as it does to conservative ones. Plato has no greater elective affinity with conservative than with radical politics; there are elements in his thought that can speak to both.[67]

Time to confront some objections. First, the tone and approach of this study will be rebarbative in several ways to a number of scholars whose rival approaches I very much respect. I unabashedly attribute views to "Plato" despite the fact that he is not writing assertorically in his own voice, but rather writ-ing different dialogues with different characters. I have adopted the method of treating some of these characters (in particular, in the three dialogues on which I focus, Socrates, the Eleatic Visitor, and the Athenian Visitor) as ava-tars of Plato, and in taking these three dialogues to be broadly complementary in the architecture of their treatment of the topics that interest me here (rule and office), even though they develop diverse models of how those roles might be organized (so taking up what one may call a complementarist position on the relationship among these dialogues, in between the traditional alternatives of unitarianism and developmentalism).[68] And I take the cities founded "in speech" in the *Republic* and the *Laws*, together with the city sketched briefly at the end of the *Statesman*, to be in their different ways propounded as models of

---

67. The reception history of Platonic political thought bears this out, as I argued in a selective survey in *Plato's Progeny*.

68. These interpretative stances involving avatars and complementarity are elaborated in chapter 2.

good cities (with the city of the *Laws* avowedly "second-best"), rather than as antitypes or critiques.[69] All these views will be controversial, and are undoubtedly in certain respects flat-footed. My defense is that it is impossible to do justice to the vast subtleties of these three Platonic dialogues (let alone all others) in a single study. By tracing the guiding thread of rule and office among them, I hope to derive insights that are relevant even to those starting from different assumptions, using different methods, or concerned with different questions.

Finally, committed democrats of many stripes will be normatively unsatisfied, indeed profoundly disturbed, by the picture of rule and office that emerges in Plato, and most intensively in the *Republic*, with its functional separation of roles between rulers and ruled that the rulers at any given time maintain by supervising the selection of their own successors. Democrats will object that it is impossible for a *taxis* of rule to achieve the postulated *telos* of the good of the ruled so long as that *taxis* does not include the participation of the ruled themselves. Such participation by the ruled is necessary, on this objection, both to determine the precise content of their own good and to contribute to constituting it in and through their own active engagement in politics. That might include potentially serving as rulers themselves, but in any case it must include being able to hold rulers accountable. For, on this line of objection, in dispensing with accountability mechanisms that are controlled by the ruled themselves, the very function of accountability is rendered moot.[70] The function of accountability simply cannot (they would contend) be achieved through any of the reconfigured institutional models that I take Plato to be exploring (at least, not through those of the *Republic* and *Statesman*; scholars are more divided on how to assess the democratic credentials of the *Laws*).[71]

In response, let me clarify that my aim in this study is not to endorse the value of the constitutional project outlined by Plato in the *Republic* or in any other dialogue, nor to defend its adequacy in seeking to address the challenge of how to keep a political order oriented toward the good of the ruled. It is, however, to insist that Plato recognized that challenge as one inhering in any kind of political constitution, including the proceduralist and institutionalist organization of rule through offices, which is broadly common to liberal democratic constitutions today. Those challenges are, for any kind of political constitution, ones to which Plato was not oblivious, any more than democrats today can afford to be. Consider the predicament of liberal democratic constitutions when those at the apex of the judicial order refuse to recuse themselves in

69. Here I am especially conscious of diverging from the erudite and challenging reading of the *Republic* offered by Frank in *Poetic Justice*.

70. This challenge has been pressed on me by a number of colleagues, among whom I am especially grateful to Jill Frank ("Comments on 'Rule'") for framing it in ways that I seek to capture here.

71. For a defense of the democratic nature of the constitutional project of the *Laws*, see Bobonich's *Plato's Utopia Recast*.

cases of conflict of interest, which Plato would consider a sign of rule oriented to the good of those in judicial office rather than the good of the ruled; when those at the apex of the executive branch refuse to uphold the fundamental constitutional duties of their office, including taking care that the laws be faithfully executed; when those at the apex of the legislative branch support the violation of the prescribed electoral procedures on which the constitution depends. It is far from clear that the existing remedies of accountability in liberal democratic constitutions today are capable of resolving that predicament.

Indeed, Plato recognizes the ways in which the procedures of office can be corrupted from within, if and when those seeking and holding them do so in a spirit of zero-sum rivalry rather than being animated for the good of those whom they rule. As I have asserted much about Plato in this overview while leaving its substantiation to subsequent chapters, let me introduce here a remarkable passage in book 4 of the *Laws* in order to give the flavor of the Platonic concern with such institutional corruption caused by the breakdown of the orientation of officeholders toward the *telos* of the good of the ruled. In that passage, the Athenian Visitor demonstrates that offices cannot fulfill the constitutional purpose that they are institutionally designed to achieve if their denizens themselves flout that very purpose. Moreover, he connects such potential abuse of office by its holders to their mistaken and dangerous views of the nature and role of law, and in so doing clarifies the interweaving of rule, office, and law in Plato's ideas of the political.

The Athenian Visitor makes his point by imagining a group (whom I shall call the "disputants") who object to the account of the purpose of office and the broader genus of rule that he has been laying out. In disputing the claim that one could aim at good laws simpliciter, as opposed to good laws relative to the interest of a certain party, these imagined figures bring a veiled confrontation with the position defended by Thrasymachus in the *Republic* into the heart of the *Laws*. This moment in the latter dialogue is accordingly important for the complementary reading of these two dialogues (together with the *Statesman*) that the present work undertakes.

The Athenian describes the position of the disputants by attributing to them use of several words that significantly mark Thrasymachus's position in the *Republic* as well.[72] The disputants (it is claimed) hold that laws are relative to a given kind of *politeia* (4.714b3–5). Accordingly, they reject any assumption that the purpose of law should be "attaining complete virtue" (the *telos* of legislation that had been proposed by the Athenian himself in book 1). Instead, the disputants insist that the laws should be entirely relativized to the advantage of the *politeia*, a view that in context turns out to be operationalized in terms

---

72. Compare Thrasymachus's language in *Republic* 1.338d9–e3 and passim in book 1 of that dialogue.

of the advantage of the group whose interests a given *politeia* is designed and operating to secure—as typically do the *oligoi* in an oligarchy, the *dēmos* in a democracy (4.714c1–4). And from this point about law, they, like Thrasymachus in the *Republic*, infer a point about justice, in this case described as "the best natural definition of justice"—namely, that justice is "whatever serves the advantage (*sumpheron*) of the stronger" (4.714c3–6).

To this point, the argument attributed to the disputants has been expressed quite abstractly: they are described as holding that both law and justice should be relativized to the interests of (those dominating within) a given constitution. However, as the Visitor continues to characterize the terms of the dispute, he suggests that the disputants' view has done real damage to political life in practice. That is, he describes a recurrent course of events ("the sort of thing that has happened thousands of times" in "some cities" [4.715a5–6]) in which this kind of cynical view of law and justice has been put into practice by those who seek to hold political office. As he describes in a remarkable and chilling passage that clearly refers to life within a constitution characterized by institutionally defined and limited offices:

> When officeholders are so made by fighting over their positions (*archōn perimachētōn genomenōn*), the winners take over civic affairs so completely that they totally deny the losers and the losers' descendants any share in office (*archēs . . . metadidonai*). Instead they live in close watch (*paraphulattontes*) on each other to prevent anyone from coming into office (*eis archēn*) who would, remembering the past wrongs, overturn the present arrangements. (*Leg.* 4.715a8–b2)[73]

An ominous feature of this passage is that the officeholders and would-be officeholders guard the good of their own faction only. *Paraphulattontes* is related to *phulax* ("guardian"), a term used in the title of the *nomophulakes* in the *Laws* as well as serving as the functional description of the guardians in the *Republic*. In this imagined dystopian city, rather than acting as proper guardians, the officeholders and would-be officeholders instead keep watch on one

---

73. While I have somewhat overtranslated the opening phrase of this speech (*archōn perimachētōn genomenōn*), the syntax overall strongly suggests that *archōn* here should be taken to be a plural participle being used as a noun, indicating the persons in a role rather than the abstract role itself. By contrast, the singular noun *archē* used with the verbs *metadidōmi* and *aphikneomai* (and in the latter case also with a preposition) suggests office rather than the more abstract rule (or the institutionally vague "power" and "position of influence" suggested by Schofield/Griffith). Finally, while the verb *epanistēmi*, which I have translated as "overturn the present arrangements," can mean to make a revolution (as both Saunders and Schofield/Griffith translate), in context here it suggests not so much seeking to overturn the entire system but rather only to put a different group on top within it via the elections. (The Saunders and Schofield/Griffith translations do capture well the way in which a different social group holding office is likely to bring with it a different set of laws and norms, which could amount to, or lead to, a change of constitutional regime.)

another for factional purposes, weaponizing the filling and wielding of this role in a partisan attempt to stymie their opponents.[74]

The Athenian Visitor's engagement with the disputants, and his survey of the real-world damage that such views have done to polities in the past, highlights an important point: that the establishment of the constitutional rule of law, including the establishment of offices, is not enough to secure the purpose at which such constitutional projects should aim. For even if procedures are followed to the letter, a rivalrous zero-sum attitude toward officeholding will undermine the very nature of a constitution. As the Visitor continues:

> What, then, we are now saying, is that those are not genuine constitutions (out' einai politeias), nor correct laws (out' orthous nomous), which are not established for the common sake of the whole polis. Rather, we call those groups for the sake of which they are established, not citizens (politas) but partisans (stasiōtas), and those who would say that such laws are just are speaking in vain. (4.715b2–6)[75]

This passage deploys the strict evaluative sense of politeia (constitution) and politēs (citizen) that was explained above. Plato here challenges those living in constitutional systems of rule through offices to recognize that offices too can be abused, and that the taxis of office is not guaranteed to secure the telos of the good of the ruled. Elsewhere in the Laws, as in the Republic and Statesman, Plato explores alternative parameters for offices and laws, as well as other procedural models for safeguarding the orientation of those officeholders and of other rulers within a given constitution toward the good of the ruled, in virtue of their education, selection, and the limits on their roles. His solutions may not suffice. Perhaps no solutions could fully suffice. But his questions, and his diagnoses of flaws in a range of failures to answer them adequately then (as also now), continue to repay attention for anyone concerned with whether and to what extent politics can indeed serve the good of the ruled.

74. In Republic 7, a similar dystopian city is briefly imagined with an almost identical phrase (perimachēton . . . to archein gignomenon). Socrates there contrasts the necessity of having rulers who do not wish to rule, because there is "a better way of life than ruling" for them, with the dystopian alternative: "if beggars hungering for private goods go into public life, believing that the good is there to be snatched up, then it is impossible [that a polis be well governed, supplying this from 7.521a2]. For in that case ruling comes to be something fought over, and such a war—being an internal civil war—will destroy these people themselves and the rest of the city also" (Resp. 7.520e4–521a8).

75. I borrow "partisans" from Schofield/Griffith's translation, though unlike their translation and Saunders's (and pace a misleading comma added to the Oxford Classical Text [OCT]), I take the hosoi clause of 4.715b4 to apply to the politeiai as well as to the laws in the previous part of the sentence: not only does the substantive point apply to both, but the reference to the groups of citizens in the next sentence picks up the analysis that had previously been made of the flawed politeiai, and the separated naming offered for such persons and laws also suggests a double but paired topic of the point being made in 4.715b2–4.

Overview of Chapters

The present chapter has sought to offer a bird's-eye view of the overall arguments and stakes of this long study. Those readers who are interested in its broad themes and implications for political theorizing, more than in the detailed reading of particular Platonic dialogues, should be largely equipped by it to turn to part IV. Those who are interested in particular dialogues should also be largely equipped to turn directly to the relevant chapters in parts II and III, as identified in the table of contents, should they so wish (while noting that the thematic chapters of part IV offer readings of some parts of the dialogues that are not included in the prior chapters devoted to each of those dialogues by name). While later individual chapters of the study may be the next destination of choice for readers with particularly focused concerns, those who are interested in the evidence for (and elaboration of) the historical, linguistic, and methodological points asserted in this overview, will find them developed in chapter 2, which completes the introductory work of part I. It considers the "figures" of king, tyrant, and officeholder as condensations of existing ideas of rule and office, which Plato both renovates (in filling in the precise content of these ideas) and reconfigures (in exploring various models of the roles and institutions that could best realize them); the "vocabularies" of rule and office both in ancient Greek (primarily Attic) and in a range of modern languages, including rules of thumb for their interpretation in context; and the interpretative "stances" adopted in the present work. Additional terms of art are introduced in that chapter, including "discursive legislation" (also described as legislation "in speech"), on which further chapters will rely.

Part II turns to these varied reconfigurations of rule and office in the chosen trio of dialogues. Rather than following the likely order of chronological composition of these three dialogues, which is also the order in which they are treated in almost all studies of Platonic political thought—namely, *Republic*, *Statesman*, *Laws*—I treat them in the reverse order. This is because it is most straightforward to identify the vocabulary of office in the *Laws*, and so to come to recognize Plato's familiarity with and alertness to it (even as he reconfigures the specific parameters of offices in the main constitutional project within that dialogue). That familiarity in turn is something that it is implausible to think was a fruit only of his relative old age, given that this vocabulary was endemic to Greek political practices and reflections by his time, as this chapter has asserted and the next will document. Recognizing Plato's deep and detailed engagement with the vocabulary and family of procedures and institutions of constitutional offices in the *Laws*, wherein it has long been acknowledged, prepares the way for recognizing the same engagement in the *Statesman* and *Republic*, wherein it has not.

That point allows chapter 3, on the *Laws*, to be selective, discussing only a subset of the offices outlined in the constitution legislated "in speech" in that dialogue, since these offices have all been treated in detail elsewhere (especially in work by Glenn Morrow).[76] Indeed, the key constituents of that constitution are offices on the one hand and laws on the other, exactly as fifth- and fourth-century BCE Greek constitutions (*politeiai*) were generally viewed as constituted (drawing on the work of Jacqueline Bordes).[77] The *Laws* tests the extent to which the *telos* of a constitution can be realized through a *taxis* of offices and laws alone, which depends in turn on the extent to which the offices and laws can themselves be safeguarded. While accountability procedures, which are heightened in the *Laws* and come to a paradoxical rest in the office of the "auditors (*euthunoi*)," are part of that safeguarding of the offices, the *Laws* also builds in several further steps that go beyond the existing constitutional orders of accountable office and law.

First, the laws themselves must be the results not of just any procedurally formulated decrees but rather of divine inspiration, so as to have the proper content to inform not just the exercise of accountability mechanisms for the officeholders by various groups of citizens but also the education and selection of properly oriented officeholders in the first place. That in turn enables the selection of virtuous auditors not through lottery but through election oriented to virtue. Whereas the bridling function of democratic accountability was in Athens carried out by groups of ordinary citizens chosen for various functions by lot (and each group of outgoing auditors was audited by the incoming ones), in the constitutional project of the *Laws* the Juvenal conundrum is instead solved by offering the auditors the most august civic-cum-religious rewards (and so punishments) to maintain their virtue.

Another feature of the *Laws* is that even the divinely inspired laws must be humanly safeguarded to ensure that their spirit, as it were, remains alive and well understood. This is carried out by a special role within the constitution usually described in English as that of a Nocturnal Council, which I reinterpret in terms of the various Greek expressions and descriptions used as a Daily Meeting. I argue that while this meeting is composed largely of current or former officeholders, participation in it does not itself constitute an office; nor is it a role of ruling understood centrally as giving epitactic orders. Rather, the Athenian Visitor at a late moment refers to the role of a ruler in the context of discussing the Daily Meeting, but this role has been entirely subsumed into the function of guarding the spirit of the laws. Thus the *Laws* remains in practice a constitutional *taxis* of office and law, with the question being the extent to which this can adequately safeguard and realize the true *telos* of rule.

By contrast, the *Statesman*, which is the subject of chapter 4, while describing a constitution under a true statesman as in practice including offices as well as laws (a point rarely recognized), does not allow the safeguarding of the

---

76. Morrow, *Plato's Cretan City*.
77. Bordes, *Politeia*.

telos of rule to depend on those offices and laws alone. Rather, the figure of the statesman is a superordinate ruler, also described as a king, who acts as what I call a safeguarding ruler. Paradoxically, although accountability procedures were meant to safeguard the *telos* of office (as a form of rule), the *Statesman* argues that a true statesman will be able to do so more perfectly, precisely so long as, and because, their role is itself free of conventional subjection to *euthunai* or other procedures of accountability. The *taxis* through which such a ruler acts is primarily epitactic ordering, directed to caring for whatever the *telos* of the good of the ruled turns out to be.

In the briefly sketched constitution involving offices at the end of the *Statesman*, however, the statesman as superordinate ruler plays the role of safeguarding a more familiar constitutional *taxis* of offices and laws. In this case, the safeguarding function is to be carried out by educative orientation of the officeholders and the citizens more widely, shaped through bonding beliefs and intermarriages. The *Statesman* emphasizes "caring" as a dimension of the role of ruler, which I take to be the proper orientation to the *telos* of rule. It is not enough that a ruler have inert knowledge of this *telos*; rather, to be a ruler is precisely to care about its realization. "Caring" in this sense is a structural feature of the role of ruler. The *Statesman* does not consider what kind of natural person would be capable of manifesting such a dispositional concern for the good of others, and so be capable of playing the rule of ruler— or of being willing to play that role. While the *Statesman* simply brackets off the question of how to fill the role so designed (that is, how a natural person capable of doing so could be educated and identified), this question is central to the *Republic*, which is the subject of the remaining three chapters of part II (as well as of the two chapters of part III).[78]

The first chapter on the *Republic*, chapter 5, complements the *Statesman*'s definition of the eponymous statesman as "the person who rules" by exploring the account of a ruler developed by Socrates in his refutation of Thrasymachus in book 1 of the *Republic*. The assertion by Socrates here that a true ruler must care for the good of the ruled has long left commentators cold, insofar as they take him to help himself to this normative idea of rule without justification. By appeal to the broader teleological nimbus of Greek ideas of rule and rulers (stretching back to Homeric kings) as set out in part I of this work, within which Plato's account should be situated, and by emphasizing the logic of rule itself as against those commentators who hinge the argument on the nature of a craft or profession (*technē*), I argue that the Socratic argument in this stretch of the dialogue should not be dismissed as abortive hand-waving but rather taken to be consonant with the fundamental Platonic idea of rule itself.

---

78. I am conscious that while this study treats aspects of *Republic* 1–9, it leaves out book 10.

Moreover, as chapter 5 also argues, *Republic* 1 advances that project in a way that the *Statesman* does not. Whereas the natural person who is capable of becoming a statesman remains in the *Statesman* a cipher, *Republic* 1 puts the question of the motivation of any natural person to take up this role squarely on the agenda, a question that is addressed by the account of the persons who are natural philosophers in *Republic* 6. The related problem of how to educate, test, and select those natural persons who are capable of undertaking such a role while caring for its *telos* of the good of the ruled is a problem to which various aspects of the dialogue further respond. I highlight two of these in the remaining chapters of part II.

Chapter 6 takes up one answer to the problem of the willingness of those suitable to rule to play that role, which is first mooted in *Republic* 1: namely, paying them some kind of wage for doing so. Whereas in book 1 of the dialogue such a wage is presented as necessary only to solve the motivational problem, once those who will become rulers are deprived of private land and wealth (already in the closing passages of book 3; reiterated in the "second wave" of book 5) a wage becomes necessary for an additional reason—namely, to provide them with subsistence. While this chapter digs into the details of precisely how and what kind of wage is in question in each context in which mention of it appears, and emphasizes that it is to be paid according to law, its broader contribution is to emphasize the theoretical contribution made by insistence on payment of a wage for ruling (and, more broadly, for all of those in the role of guardians in the constitutional project of the dialogue, including the auxiliaries who are being trained and tested to become rulers). Paradoxical as it may seem, a wage for rule—which in ancient Greek contexts was overwhelmingly associated with democratic offices, and not even with all of those in all time periods—turns out to be central to Plato's configuration of a service conception of rule in this dialogue.

Incorporating but going beyond payment of wages, chapter 7 tackles the larger agenda of how rule and office are related within the constitution of a *kallipolis* in the *Republic*—a topic that I argue is indeed central to that dialogue, though it has scarcely if ever been fully recognized as such. In books 5–7, it is the fully educated philosophers, aged fifty and above, who play the role of safeguarding rulers. Taking up Socrates's proposal in the "third wave" of book 5, calling for rulers who are described as "reigning" (a verb, *basileuein*, cognate with the role of a *basileus* or king), I interpret their role primarily as safeguarding the guardians who are junior to them (and who may one day be promoted to replace them), supervising their procreation and education, testing their suitability for promotion, and selecting those to fill the next ranks. The younger guardians include a cohort immediately junior to the safeguarding rulers, the cohort of those aged thirty-five to fifty, who are to play a role that is unambiguously described as holding various "offices" (unambiguously, that is, once one has been sensitized to the varying affordances of Greek vocabulary for rule and office). Junior to both groups are the auxiliaries, who are educated, tested, and selected for promotion to the middle-aged officeholding cohort, and then potentially the eldest cohort, in turn.

Thus Plato here (as in the *Statesman*) performs a separation between superordinate safeguarding rulers, on the one hand, and officeholders (who are also a kind of ruler, on the argument of this study as a whole), on the other. Yet in sharing the dialogical standpoint of discursive legislation with the *Laws*—that is, the standpoint of interlocutors who frame laws for a city "in speech" rather than "in deed"—the *Republic* also establishes a framework of laws within which its safeguarding rulers are envisaged as operating. Within that framework, they will be subjected to practices of collegial testing and dialectical exchange (which are described in terms that resonate linguistically with democratic scrutiny and accountability, respectively), through which the safeguarding rulers too are kept oriented toward the proper *telos* of rule. No cohort of safeguarding rulers is self-certifying. Each must be educated, tested, and selected by previous generations, so as to be properly formed, and informed, by an education making them capable of carrying out the ordering role required of them.

Part III continues to dwell on the *Republic*. Its primary subject is not, however, the dialogue's principal constitutional project, but rather Plato's depiction of what I call the degeneration of rule and office, in the flawed political constitutions of *Republic* 8, on the one hand, and in the flawed rule within the souls and lives of the corresponding kinds of persons narrated in *Republic* 8 and 9, on the other. (I call these corresponding types of individuals the "representative men," in a nod to Emerson;[79] they are gendered masculine, most being depicted as both a son to a certain father and a father to a certain son.) Both the narrative of political degeneration and the narrative of individual degeneration exhibit the ways in which the malfunctioning of office and rule results from distortions of both *telos* and *taxis*, and how they interact.

Recounted in chapter 8, what I call the macro narrative of the sequence of political constitutions demonstrates the ways in which constitutional orders of officeholding that lack safeguarding rulers can malfunction and then degenerate. Such malfunctioning is variously shown at work in the timocracy, oligarchy, and democracy depicted in *Republic* 8, with office and rule becoming a matter of mere shadow play in the democratic constitution. For its part, the tyranny depicted there turns out not to be a proper order of rule or office at all: it is, rather, a form of anarchy (*anarchia*), an absence of any kind of rule (including office as a species of rule), a term initially introduced in the context of the democracy that turns out to harbor the potential for transformation into a tyranny within itself.

---

79. Emerson, *Representative Men*—a series of seven lectures, the first of which is about Plato.

Recounted in chapter 9, the micro narrative of the sequence of representative men unpacks the ways in which rule in the soul can malfunction. Such malfunctioning is variously shown at work in the souls, or, more precisely, the embodied souls and the lives led, of the timocratic, oligarchic, and democratic men (all described in book 8). For his part, the tyrannical man described in book 9 turns out not to harbor any kind of ordered or (therefore) properly ruled soul at all: his soul is, rather, a manifestation of *anarchia*, an absence of rule or office, and so too is his life. This is an unusual kind of *anarchia*, however, as it results from an overreaching, an effort by the tyrant to exercise power without any of the bounds that make it count as ordered and so as rule, in an effort to realize the flawed *telos* that he takes to be his own good— namely, the exploitation of those whom he rules.

The same ambition means that no fruits of the relational orderedness of rule (most visible in the case of rule through office and law) can exist under a tyrant. That is argued in chapter 10, the first of the two thematic chapters of part IV, which together inquire into the interlocking *taxis* and *telos* of rule and its antithesis. Chapter 10 identifies the fruits of one potential *taxis* of rule— that of office and law—as being civic freedom and friendship, drawing on a neglected passage in the criticism of tyranny in *Republic* 9, as well as on *Laws* 3. I call this Plato's invocation of a garden-variety constitutionalism—albeit one for citizens only, which presupposes their ability to enslave others—of a kind that he is not generally considered to value outside the constitutional project that begins at the very end of *Laws* 3. The latter book, however, also depicts a case study, that of the postulated history of ancient Persia, in which it is rule that can secure civic freedom and friendship, without mention of office and law specifically. The key is that rule must be made compossible with civic freedom through willing obedience on the part of the ruled, a willingness that requires a disposition to cooperate, which likewise informs and makes possible the cultivation of civic friendship.

While highlighting these relatively neglected ways in which Plato values civic freedom and friendship, chapter 10 also explores some notorious moments in which both the *Republic* and the *Laws* use the language of slavery in order to describe rule. I argue that slavery in these contexts is being used to indicate the epitactic role that slave master and political ruler share as part of their *taxis*, but only for the latter is the *telos* the true good of the ruled, which is counterfactual for legal relations of slavery. Plato appeals to slavery counterfactually, only insofar as its epitactic dimension can be married to the *telos* of the good of the ruled, something that a passage in *Republic* 9 (mentioned above) implies was not actually the case for rule over legally enslaved persons.

Finally, chapter 11 explores the reason and extent to which Plato is committed to what I have elsewhere (in an article of that name) titled "*antianarchia*" and, conversely, to the value of rule, testing it against critiques of rule found in contemporary political theory and philosophy. I argue there that Plato's fundamental rejection of *anarchia* (anarchy) rests on a valorization of rule as a role of ordering (inherited from the nimbus of a longer Greek tradition, as shown in this introduction) but does not involve commitment to the use of coercive means to enforce that ordering. Political rule is understood as the orienting of a *taxis* of rule toward the *telos* of the good of the ruled; the means that rulers employ is not fundamental to the account. Ultimately, as noted earlier in the present chapter, political rule serves to shore up psychic rule as needed, in the service of cultivating the orderedness that produces virtue in the souls of the ruled. This means that Plato's commitment to *antianarchia* still allows him to entertain an idyll of philosophical anarchism in a purer form of what usually trades under that name (existing accounts of philosophical anarchism being better understood as being quietist forms of political anarchism instead).

For Plato, political rule is unnecessary only where psychic self-rule is already sufficient. But if that is the case, then while he may allow for an absence of political rule over such people, the underlying commitment is still to the orderedness of rule all the way down. Self-rulers must be capable of generating the cooperative disposition that will allow them to forge the civic freedom and friendship with others that must otherwise be the fruit of relationships of political rule, and are most recognizably depicted as the fruit of rule carried out through offices and laws (that is, through constitutional office as a kind of rule).

The *taxis* of rule, whether political or psychological, makes a difference to the goods that rule can realize. Conversely, and concomitantly, the *telos* of rule requires a certain kind of *taxis*, again either political or psychological, in order to be fulfilled. Far from the Platonic rule of knowledge being indifferent to the form of rule, Plato in his trio of key political dialogues is deeply concerned with the various configurations that form may take, in order to realize at least a nonexploitative, if not Platonically full-fledged, *telos* of the good of the ruled. Thinking institutionally for Plato, in a realist vein, always already requires one to think evaluatively as well, lest the institutional roles in question turn out to be hollow or perverse. Rule and office as Platonic ideas renovate a deep-rooted evaluative nimbus of rule as serving the good of the ruled, while exploring various reconfigurations of roles that might be adequate to that task, both in the distribution of their powers and in the ways in which natural persons might be capable of and identified for filling them. Plato's ideas of rule and office are ways of thinking through the challenges posed by the Juvenal conundrum, as opposed to pretexts for setting it aside.

CHAPTER TWO

Rule and Office

FIGURES, VOCABULARIES, STANCES

I OPEN THIS CHAPTER with two quotations from Plato's *Republic* (book 5) that feature respectively the Greek term *archē* (a noun that can be translated either as "rule" or "office") and the cognate verb *archein* (which has a similar range). I do so to illustrate a central claim of this study: that the relationship between rule and office (the latter being a kind of rule) is one to which Plato was as manifestly alert, and with which he was as deeply concerned, as were his contemporaries, though he would develop both ideas in his own distinctive way. The ideas of rule and office as expressed centrally (though not solely) in the varying deployment of *archē* and *archein* is an axis not just of this study but also of Plato's writings when read within the context of inherited political figures, vocabularies, and interpretative stances that this chapter lays out.

The first passage from *Republic* 5 is asserted by Socrates about the rulers of the city whom he and his main interlocutors for the bulk of the dialogue, Glaucon and Adeimantus, have been describing (the three of them constituting the plural "we" whom he invokes):

> It's likely our rulers [*archontes*] will have to make considerable use of falsehood and deception for the benefit of those they rule. (5.459c9–d2)[1]

The translation of the word I have quoted (changing it to the nominative case) as *archontes* here as "rulers" is likely to appear unsurprising, as most readers of the *Republic* assume that Plato is concerned with rulers who are far too

---

1. The Greek word that I have given in the nominative (*archontes*) is actually used in this passage in the accusative (*archontas*). I quote the translation by Grube/Reeve as I am making a point about standard translations into English (see note 4 in this chapter for other European languages); Bloom and Shorey both similarly translate "rulers" here. All quotations of Plato are from the most recent OCT, as are quotations of other Greek texts, unless otherwise indicated; all translations are my own unless otherwise indicated.

distinctive to be describable in the terms of conventional offices of the time. In fact, even if one brackets that assumption (which I go on to argue needs to be interrogated), "rulers" remains the most defensible translation here, since there are no clues in the immediate context that anything more specific is meant. (I elaborate on the kinds of clues that could potentially do so in the "Vocabularies" section below.)

But now consider another passage in *Republic* 5, which comes just a few lines after the one just quoted. In this next passage, Socrates proposes that the children born into the city being described should be taken in charge by a set of people who are designated by the noun *archē* in the plural. Specifically, he says that they should be taken in charge by:

> the officers (*archai*) established for this purpose—men or women, or both, for presumably the offices (*archai*) are common to women and men. (5.460b6–8)[2]

Here, Bloom (whose translation I have just quoted) translates the two incidences of *archai* as "officers" (a variant on my term "officeholders": nothing hangs on this distinction) and "offices" respectively. He does so justifiably, in tacit acknowledgment of the syntax of the sentence and its phraseology, since the use of the abstract noun, especially in the plural, is one of the idioms typically indicating the specific sense of "officeholders" rather than the more general one of "rulers" (again, these idioms will be elaborated more fully below).

Notice the result. Common and defensible translations of the initial book 5 passage have Socrates talking of the "rulers" of the constitution of the "beautiful city (*kallipolis*)" outlined in the dialogue.[3] Yet common and defensible translations of the latter one, just a few lines later, have him talking of its "officers" (or in my parlance its "officeholders") and "offices." This is true of translations not only into English but also into French, German, Italian, and Spanish.[4] In all these languages, translators of the dialogue generally recognize

2. Bloom's translation, again in order to make a point about standard translations of this passage. Similar choices of words for office here are made by Shorey and Grube/Reeve, but the latter get another aspect of the passage wrong (translating an intransitive verb as if it were transitive), so I quote Bloom instead.

3. The term *kallipolis* is discussed in more detail in chapter 6.

4. Many translations in other European languages recognize, in employing nonidentical terms, that there is some kind of distinction between the roles denoted in the two book 5 passages under discussion (with regard to the latter passage, addressing in this note only the first of its two uses of *archai*). In French, both Chambry and Leroux translate *tous archontas* as "dirigeants" (rulers, directors), with Chambry staying close to the same vocabulary for *archai*, while Leroux switches for *archai* to "ceux qui ont la responsabilité de veiller sur eux" (those who have the responsibility to watch over them). In German, Schleiermacher marks a sharp semantic distinction between "rulers" and "officeholders," with "Herrscher" (rulers or lords) for *tous archontas* and "Obrigkeiten" (authorities) for *archai*; likewise Rufener and Krapinger, who both contrast "Regenten" (rulers) with "Behörde"

that a semantic difference should be marked between *archontas* (as it actually appears in the initial passage, in the accusative case) and *archai* in the later one. But such recognition at the level of translation has attracted little explanation at the level of interpretation.

How are such "offices"—indicated with conventional vocabulary—to be understood? To what extent should they indeed be counted as offices, being described as such but configured very differently from typical expectations thereof? How might "rulers" and "officeholders" in these closely situated passages of the *Republic* be related? What does it mean that both figure in the presentation of the constitution depicted over the bulk of the *Republic*? These are issues about which other studies of Plato have had remarkably little to say (the same is true of similar passages and questions with regard to Plato's *Statesman*), despite the fact that, as I put it in chapter 1, reference to "offices" in the constitutional project of the *Republic* is hiding in plain sight.

This chapter supplies elaboration and support for the interpretation of Plato on rule and office offered in the study as a whole. This includes going over some of the same ground as the previous chapter in order to expand, clarify, and offer historical detail for the main points made there on which this study rests. Readers who are less concerned with such scholarly detail may wish to skim this chapter, but not to skip it altogether, since it introduces some further terms of art (as well as offering the promised rules of thumb for Greek vocabulary of *archē* and *archein*) on which further chapters will rely.

In the first section of this chapter I consider a range of "figures" in whom such ideas (or their antitheses) would have been assumed by Plato's generation and its forebears to be embodied. Building on the folk histories of the transition of kingship to officeholding in ancient Athens that were introduced in chapter 1, the first section introduces several inherited figures playing such roles—beginning with the antitype of the tyrant, and then focusing in particular on kings, officeholders (and alongside officeholders, constitutions)—in order to build up a schema of rule, including office as one specific kind of rule. The figures of both kings and officeholders suggest a schema that is already permeated by evaluative expectations: that a ruler exercises some kind of ordering (*taxis*) oriented to a purpose (*telos*) that includes the good of the ruled. The questions of just what that good requires and just what kind of ordering can adequately achieve it can be tested against each of these inherited figures.

(administrative authorities) in the respective loci. In Italian, Radice contrasts "regitori" (rulers) with "commissioni di magistrati" (boards of magistrates); Sartori, "governanti" (rulers) with "magistrati" (magistrates); Vegetti, "governanti" with "appositi uffici governativi" (appointed governing officers). In Spanish, Eggers Lan contrasts "gubernantes" (rulers) with "magistrados asignados" (appointed magistrates). I thank René de Nicolay for research assistance on these translations.

The second section of this chapter turns to what I call "vocabularies" (a term I stylize to refer to linguistic usages and idioms more generally). This section is essential to understanding the materials on which this study relies. It explains further the interrelated senses of both rule and office that could be indicated by the Greek noun *archē* and verb *archein*, as introduced in chapter 1; how their various affordances can guide interpreters as to their disambiguation and their remaining ambiguation in varying contexts; and how such patterned usages play a central role in the three Platonic dialogues under discussion. This is central to comprehending Plato's ideas of rule and office, making the relationship between those ideas in both Greek and English (or other modern languages) a puzzle inviting linguistic attentiveness as well as theoretical reflection.

Finally, the third section of this chapter turns to what I call "stances" in two senses: both the writerly positioning of the projects of particular Platonic dialogues, and the interpretative positioning adopted toward them by modern scholars (including me), in regard to how to read Plato as well as how to think about the political theory in which Platonic dialogues engage and its significance. Such stances are part of a broader question of scholarly approach that is interwoven throughout the chapter, focused on how Plato writes about the relationship of rule and office in the context of laws and constitutions as the latter were understood in contemporary Greek authors and practices.

Figures: Tyrants, Kings, Officeholders, Constitutions

Consider Plato writing in the course of the first half of the fourth century BCE,[5] setting almost all his writings in the last quarter of the fifth century, studding them with reference to prose and poetry composed both within and outside Athens (stretching back to Homer, whose epic poetry was alive in regular performances throughout the Greek world during his lifetime). In those writings, Plato sometimes has his characters test arguments by burnishing up imaginary statues for comparison and judgment.[6] In the same spirit, one can flesh out the ideas of rule and office that were sketched out in the previous chapter by imagining Plato surveying an imaginary statue gallery of figures of rule (and their antitypes), modeled on, but extending far beyond, the

---

5. Plato lived (on one good estimate: Nails, *People of Plato*, s.v. Plato) from 424/3 to 348/7 BCE, with most scholars believing that he did not begin to compose his dialogues until sometime after the death of Socrates in 399 BCE. All dates that follow are BCE unless stated otherwise.

6. Consider, for example, the unjustly unrewarded just man and the unjustly rewarded unjust man put forward by Glaucon in *Republic* 2, and the painting of a statue so as to make the whole statue beautiful advanced by Socrates in methodological riposte to Adeimantus in *Republic* 4.

Monument of the Eponymous Heroes, which he would have passed regularly in the Athenian *agora*. Moving from those roles as already figured to analyzing the functions they were intended to play, and how adequately from a Platonic perspective they could fulfill those functions, illuminates the handling of rule and office in the kaleidoscope of constitutional projects within his major political dialogues.

Such an imaginary statue gallery can be peopled by the varying figures celebrated or decried in the poetry, prose, and civic practices that Plato manifestly, as evidenced by his writings, knew well. Any Greek of Plato's day would have populated that gallery in part with images of kings; any Athenian from the late sixth century onward, also with the antitype of the tyrant (with which I begin); most would likewise have populated it also with figures of accountable officeholders, who were typically subject to institutionally organized and legally stipulated mechanisms of accountability. The reader may wish to populate a statue gallery of the cast of characters in political power in their own time or wider imagination, to test the extent to which Plato's ideas of rule and office can illuminate them as well.

TYRANTS

"Tyrant" is a translation of the Greek *turannos*, a figure that in late archaic and early classical descriptions was not necessarily viewed pejoratively: this was someone who came to similar power as a king but not through hereditary means.[7] In Athens in the late sixth century, two generations of the Peisistratid family held sway in the city, with their actions overall being ultimately subsumed by the memory of what was considered to be an outrage committed by a member of the family on another member of the elite, and whose ousting in consequence forged a cultural memory and practice of "tyrannicide" that anathematized such so-called tyrants. It was in the wake of that ousting that (especially in Athens) a *turannos* would become widely and pejoratively viewed as inverting, and so perverting, an expected *telos* of caring for the people.[8] When

7. Atack (*Discourse of Kingship*, 17) emphasizes that the ordering role of the king was specifically invoked in common contrasts with the tyrant, especially in Herodotus and in the tragic playwrights: "The *basileus* [king] takes responsibility for creating and maintaining order within his kingdom, whereas the *turannos* is more simply interested in maintaining personal, political and military control." (However, she notes the caveat that, as described by some authors, "tyrants can also establish good order," citing Herodotus on the Athenian tyrant Peisistratus (1.59.6), in which he used "tyrant" descriptively of a nonhereditary sole ruler (a term that I adapt from Ellis's "Sole Rule").) Atack returns to the same theme in discussing later authors, especially on page 106, in relation to Xenophon's relying on kingship as having "connotations of good cosmic order" in his effort "to separate it from ideas of tyranny."

8. Those home-grown tyrants of the Peisistratid dynasty were figures of the past, but there were recurrent fears in Plato's lifetime that an elite Athenian would seek to resurrect

so positioned, a tyrant was taken to seek not to care for the people but to exploit them.

Were kings and tyrants both viewed as kinds of rulers? As noted briefly in chapter 1, Xenophon—one of Plato's fellow Socratics[9]—claims that Socrates answered "yes" to this, while at the same time distinguishing them on evaluative grounds from each other:

> Kingship and tyranny, in his judgment, were both kinds of rule (*archas*), but he held that they differed. For the rule [*archē*] which is over willing humans and according to the laws of the city he judged kingly, while that which is over unwilling humans and not according to laws, but according to whatever the ruler should wish, is tyranny (*Mem.* 4.6.12)

Plato, in contrast, would ultimately in *Republic* 9 argue that tyranny at its core is a phenomenon of *anarchia*, within the soul of the tyrant and within his way of life, which thereby undermined all order in the interpersonal relations of the polity. So if kings and tyrants are both candidate rulers, at least at first glance, nevertheless, in penetrating their lives and souls, they will turn out (for Plato) not to share meaningful common features at all. But he also in the *Statesman* would at one moment draw a similar distinction between kingship and tyranny, stressing that kingship can be free from any external agential control even while conducted according to the ordered limits of law. Later in that dialogue, the theoretical implications of a statesman who should enjoy absolute freedom from external agential control, as implying an ability to override the laws themselves, is brought out—but even then only when still virtually ordered, as it were, and so regulated by the *telos* of benefiting the ruled.

KINGS

The eventual consolidation of the tyrant as an antitype relied upon a broader type of (good) ruler, which a Greek statue gallery would most readily exhibit in the figure of a king. This was true in general, and also in the Platonic dialogues in question, in that both the *Republic* and the *Statesman* employ "king" in describing their knowledgeable rulers. In the *Republic*, famously (and as discussed in chapter 7), Socrates asserts that for troubles in cities to cease, either philosophers must reign (*basileuein*: the verb that is cognate to the nouns for king and kingship), or, alternatively, kings (*basileus*, singular) and current power holders must philosophize (5.473c11–d6). In the *Statesman*, the true statesman—the person with expert political knowledge—is repeatedly also

---

such a role; there were also foreign tyrants in cities like Syracuse, where Plato is said to have traveled three times.

9. On the relationship between the Socratic projects of Plato and Xenophon, see Danzig's *Apologizing for Socrates*.

called a "king," using the same word (*basileus*). Evoked so explicitly in key dialogues, engaging with Homer and subsequent Greek thought, the figure of the king is a useful starting point for exploring how Plato thinks about rule.[10] I argue that Plato finds two aspects of kingship salient in this respect, both of which will feed directly into what I shall formulate as his schema of rule: kings as orderers, and kings as oriented to the good of the people (glossed most resonantly in the image of a king as shepherd of the people, though Plato will in the *Statesman* critically examine that image while developing an elaborate model of a human king as a political weaver).

Anyone, like Plato, raised on archaic and classical Greek poetry and prose would have been steeped in figures of royalty. To mention just a few: Zeus becoming king over gods and mortals in Hesiod's *Theogony*; the kings, queens, and royal families animating Homeric epic and Athenian tragedy; the kings of Persia, Media, and Macedon, who had threatened or allied with the various Greek *poleis* (including Sparta, with its own unique dual kingship): all of these figures, described with varying vocabularies, of which the most important for continuity with Plato is that of the *basileus*,[11] were in a range of works closely associated with roles of order and ordering, as noted in chapter 1.[12] For example, as Carol Atack has noted, Herodotus depicts the Median king Deioces as

10. Atack (*Discourse of Kingship*, 92–121) offers a helpful contextualization of kingship in what she terms "Socratic thought," treating Antisthenes, Xenophon, and Plato's *Gorgias*, *Euthydemus*, and *Republic*, but without highlighting the epitactic dimension that I emphasize specifically (or drawing the connection to the *Statesman*, of course not a primarily Socratic text in her sense). Studies of philosopher-kings as such in the *Republic* are legion, with the nature of their rule being framed mainly in terms of the kind of philosophical knowledge involved (whether or not expressed as a *technē* and what kind of activity ensues), a debate joined, e.g., by Irwin in *Plato's Moral Theory*, Schofield in "Disappearing Philosopher-King" and *Plato*, Steinberger in "Ruling," Duncan and Steinberger in "Plato's Paradox?," and Thakkar in *Plato as Critical Theorist*. None of these discussions identifies or analyzes the relationship of ruling and officeholding portrayed in *Republic* 5–7 as is pursued herein in chapter 7.

11. Translating *basileus* as "king," especially in Homer and Hesiod, is not uncontroversial. Raaflaub ("Homer to Solon," 79) remarks that in both Homer and Hesiod, "a strong *basileus* was no more than a *primus inter pares*" and their "leadership remained relatively weak and precarious," in both cases contrary to what the English word "king" might lead readers to assume; an even stronger claim that "kings" and "monarchs" never existed in archaic Greece is made by Luraghi in "Ruling Alone." Nevertheless, I follow many translators and interpreters in translating *basileus* as "king." Other Homeric terms for these figures, such as *anax*, retained less currency in later Ionic and Attic; as a contrast with hereditary kings, other terms such as *aisymnetēs* (for someone chosen for a similar role by election), would also emerge. The full relevant vocabularies of epic and of archaic and early classical poetry and prose are far more varied and complex than can be considered here; I trace only a few threads.

12. Brock, *Greek Political Imagery*, 1–24. Of course, both directions of the comparison were far from unique features of Greek thought, being features of a range of Near Eastern texts at the time as well, as Brock himself notes (1, 10–11).

"establish[ing] a kind of cosmic ordering in his kingdom of Media (1.97–8)" through a *kosmos* of court rituals within his palace; conversely, she observes that Aeschylus in the *Persians* articulates a similar aspiration for royal order to connect to cosmic order, while instead depicting the Persian king Xerxes in that play as "failing to order Persia properly, for example, leaving the forces as an 'uncountable' *plēthos* [multitude]."[13]

I refer to the ordering dimension of kingship, which would become paradigmatic for rulers in general, as that of establishing a *taxis* (a word for order). At the same time, ancient Greek political teleology was traditionally understood as pointing in one basic direction: toward the good of the people as its purpose, or *telos*. This teleological dimension of rule is illustrated in key moments in Homeric accounts of kingship—albeit that this figuration was not universally accepted, followed, or so interpreted. Consider Agamemnon's claim that his aim is to keep the people [*laos*] safe.[14] A similar expectation of a "blameless king" upholding justice and thereby ensuring the good of the people is articulated in the *Odyssey*.[15] To be sure, the same teleological expectation could be invoked to condemn its failure or perversion. Agamemnon himself is accused by Homer's Achilles of being a "people-devouring king,"[16] a description that resonates with the poet Hesiod's condemnation of the corrupted elite in his own *polis* as "gift-devouring kings."[17] Yet these very condemnations rely on an assumed if vague account of what the expected teleology should be.

An especially important image in this context, with an evaluative nimbus that Plato would evoke, is that of the king as shepherd of the people. There is more to the Homeric image of the king as shepherd than may immediately meet the modern reader's eye. On the one hand, the shepherd of Greek epic (associated with the names of Homer and others) is clearly understood as being charged with caring for the safety of the flock (of sheep) or herd (of cattle). On the other hand, "the shepherd of early Greek epic is not the owner of the animals he farms," but rather a young member of the family, a servant, or a hired hand working for payment, in any case of a lower social status than the owner.[18] The

13. Atack, *Discourse of Kingship*, 25 on Deioces (see also 17), citing Hdt., 1.99.1–2, and 43 on Xerxes, citing *Pers.* line 40, and noting also the use of *ochlos* (crowd) for his disordered subjects at *Pers.* lines 42, 53, cf. 936.

14. *Il.* 1.117; cf. 13.47–48 and 12.310.

15. *Od.* 19.109–14.

16. *Il.* 1.231: "*dēmoboros basileus.*"

17. *Works and Days* 38–39: "*basilēas dōrophagous.*"

18. Haubold, *Homer's People*, 18–19. For a brief alternative account, criticizing the methodology yielding Haubold's emphasis on the likelihood of Homeric shepherds failing, see Brock's *Greek Political Imagery* (43–52, esp. 43–44). In assessing their debate, one might conclude that, on the one hand, the formulaic application of the phrase "shepherd of the people" sometimes merely identifies someone as a king, but, on the other hand, that Haubold's use of the corpus of similes of failed (and sometimes successful) shepherds does at the very least suggest risks associated with the role as such.

paradox of the king (a superlatively high human social status, engaged in forms of lordly rule)[19] being figured as a shepherd (a role of low social status), and the associated problematic of a wage-earning caretaker who may not be sufficiently responsible either to his employer or to those for whom he is supposed to care,[20] would inform a general paradox of the figure of the ruler as serving the ruled, but not as their mere servant, which recurs throughout this study.

Even, or especially, in Homer, a metaphor is not an office. The image of the shepherd cannot make up for a lack of robust institutional offices and procedures. It confirms that the good of the people is paramount, but it also confirms the lack of institutional structures necessary to secure it. The underlying issue here is the absence of a worked-out institutional framework in Homeric society. While there are *themistes* (ordinances, often understood to be divinely established),[21] there is no system of law, *nomoi* as Greeks of the classical and archaic period understood it. In fact, the word *nomos*, in the meaning of "law," is not used in Homer. It is the lack of a robust institutional framework, along with associated problems of political education, accountability, and office, that means that Homeric rulers most often fail to work for the good of the people. The plots of the *Iliad* and (to a lesser extent) *Odyssey* are built precisely around the problems that arise as a result.

Homer, then, set his readers a puzzle: Given the issues he raises, what solutions might they suggest? Plato was one of many thinkers who (directly or indirectly) responded to this call, but he was not the first. The lyric poets envisaged the safety of the people (*laos*) in terms of the constitutional scaffolding that is missing in Homer—as for example in Pindar,[22] envisaging a people in a condition of *eunomia*, a condition of constitutional and broadly legal order aspired to by Solon and elsewhere in archaic poetry as well. These are prayers, and they express no more than a vague hope for the future. Still, they reference the kind of ordered constitutional framework that is missing in Homer. Others envisage founding a *eunomic* city as the decisive step toward ensuring the good of the people. Plutarch would later report that the legendary archaic king Theseus was believed to have "ordered a *politeia*" for Athens (*Thes.* 24.3), including the traditional Athenian imperative formula for gathering the people; this formula uses the word *leōs*, the Attic form of *laos*, as does Plato in raising a question of how the people for the envisaged pan-Cretan

19. Note, for example, the frequent use in the *Iliad* of the verb *koiraneō* (LSJ includes the sense "to be lord or master, rule, command")—e.g., 2.760.

20. The Homeric shepherd may fail in his duty owing to physical weakness, leading him to fearfully forsake it (as in the simile at *Il.* 5.136–39), or owing to "folly" and lack of valor, making him unable to meet its demands (as in the simile at *Il.* 16.352–57).

21. But note also *Il.* 16.387, describing Zeus punishing humans "because in violent assembly they pass decrees (*themistas*) that are crooked."

22. *Paean* F 52a.9–10, the relevant line reading, "Long may Paean wreathe the people's (*laōn*) offspring / with the flowers of wise order (*eunomias*)."

foundation of Magnesia in the *Laws* will be gathered (Plutarch, *Thes.* 25.1; Plato, *Leg.* 4.707e1–2). Both Plutarch explicitly and Plato allusively move from the heroic world of Homer, where kings rule haphazardly over a mixed and disordered people, to a properly constituted *politeia* with laws and offices, by which the people are prevented from becoming *ataktos*, or, literally, without *taxis* (Plutarch, *Thes.* 25.1).[23]

Both Xenophon and Plato would in presenting Socratic imagery draw deeply upon the Homeric figurative well of kings as shepherds.[24] Xenophon portrays Socrates as exploring in conversation the Homeric image of the king as "shepherd of the people": in speaking of kings as elected on the model of the generals whom Socrates has been discussing with Athenian compatriots, he remarks that "a king is chosen not to care well for himself, but so that those who have chosen him fare well," commenting on a line in Homer (*Il.* 3.179) in which a "good king" is one who makes his subjects happy.[25] Likewise, in the *Republic*, as in the *Statesman*, Plato connects rule to kingship, while recovering the underlying significance of rule itself as an idea.

Of course, by Plato's day, some voices, especially certain sophistic ones, had challenged the evaluative orientation of the traditional figure of rule. Plato himself presents powerful versions of these challenges within the dialogues. One gambit was to deny that any figures in the statue gallery actually pursue the purportedly traditional teleological purpose of rule: this is a strand in the debunking argument advanced by Thrasymachus in the first book of Plato's *Republic* that the purpose of the shepherd is simply to eat his sheep. Another was to invert the teleology, proclaiming rulers should direct their power toward their own good, not the good of the ruled: this is a strand in the argument advanced by Callicles in Plato's *Gorgias*. Grist to the latter mill was the pressing fact of empire, which could be described as an *archē*, as some called the Athenian Delian League of the mid-fifth century: this kind of imperial rule could be construed as the avowedly exploitative domination by one *polis* of others, as Thucydides portrays Cleon in the Mytilenian debate as having

23. The very proclamation cited by Plutarch (*deur' ite pantes leōi*: roughly, "come hither all of you") appears to have been used to introduce major festivals in classical Athens, a point that I owe to Johannes Haubold, as I do much of the discussion of Homer and Plato here more broadly. Haubold (*Homer's People*, 170–83) also argues that such occasions, especially the Panathenaea, reenacted the process of social ordering that Aristotle thinks Theseus performed in the heroic age, achieving something similar to the mythical Theseus in taking the *polis* back to a primeval situation of *ataxia* and then reaffirming existing social structures, as well as bringing the fundamental political issue of the safety and security of the community to the fore.

24. For a brief but valuable discussion, also considering other authors and the link between care and kingship, see Atack's "Shepherd King."

25. Xen., *Mem.* 3.2.3 and 3.2.2, respectively. "Fare well" (*eu prattein*) is also the expression used to conclude Plato's *Republic* (10.621d2–3).

described it (using the language of tyranny).[26] But while such dissenting voices rejected the evaluative account, they did so either by demonstratively inverting it or by claiming it to apply to a null set. No significant alternative teleology was ever consistently developed. Thus, to invoke kings was generally to take them to manifest the evaluative expectation (even if only in the breach) that the role of rulers be oriented to the good of the ruled.

So far, then, reflection on kingship furnishes what I call a schema of rule (as I take Plato to understand it):

> A ruler must act in and through some kind of *taxis* (order), which is oriented to some kind of *telos*.

The inherited and dominant version of this schema as deployed in Plato's time was already evaluative in both dimensions: *taxis* as order has a certain value, and the *telos* expected of a ruler has a certain value as including care for, rather than exploitation of, the ruled. In scrutinizing any kind of rule, then, including but not limited to kingship, one must ask how it fills in the variables of the schema with regard to both the *telos* and the *taxis*. The underlying challenge is not only to define the *telos* properly but also to deploy a *taxis* capable of maintaining the proper orientation of rulers (who may, specifically, be officeholders) toward it.

From a Platonic perspective, the questions to ask will be how correct and complete a given kind of rule's conception of the good of the ruled is, and how adequate the *taxis* is to realize it. Platonically, of course, the actual good of the ruled can be understood only in light of the true nature of the Good itself. This in turn can be fully grasped only by someone who is a true knower. So a schema of political rule in the figure of the king can be renovated into an idea of Platonic rule as ideally the rule of knowledge (and then configured in various ways within different kinds of constitutions, as I go on to show).[27]

But that is not the end of the story. For Plato also explores a spectrum of ways in which different kinds of rulers can engage in creating order (*taxis*). Essential to those powers, at least in principle, as the *Statesman* highlights, is the power of creating *taxis* by issuing an *epitaxis* (an order in the sense of command). Epitactic power can characterize the role of a king who is not

---

26. In Thuc., 3.37.1, Cleon employs the verb *archein* to describe Athenian imperial domination; in 3.37.2, he uses the noun *archē* in telling his fellow Athenians that "the empire (*archē*) that you possess is a tyranny."

27. In referring to Plato's ideas of rule and office, I do not mean that he conceived of either as an *eidos* in the sense of a Platonic Form (sometimes referred to as an upper-case "Idea"). Neither a ruler nor an officeholder (again, a kind of ruler, on my analysis) is the kind of thing that could correspond directly to a Platonic Form, any more than the just city could be (the latter point argued by Burnyeat in "Utopia and Fantasy" [298]), since both delineate particulars rather than universals. In my parlance, an "idea" may be identifiable as implicit within existing practices, from which an account can be drawn out. Making that account maximally coherent and adequate to reality may require a further renovation of its terms, as I take to be attempted in the Platonic fashioning of ideas of rule and office.

subject to any superordinate human commands (and, similarly, the role of the statesman-king as depicted in principle within that dialogue). But it can also characterize the role of another set of figures who were also familiar in the political life of Plato's day (and before): accountable officeholders.[28]

OFFICEHOLDERS AND CONSTITUTIONS

Just as the trio of Platonic dialogues central to this study make significant references to kings, so too they make multiple references to officeholders. Recognizable offices of this kind—while varying in their details from those of the Athenian, Spartan, and other existing offices that manifestly inform them—populate the constitution for Magnesia in Plato's *Laws*, as has long been recognized. As I illustrated in opening with a quotation from Plato's *Republic* (5.460b6–8), the vocabulary and idioms that conventionally in certain contexts indicated officeholding can be found at the heart of the constitutional project of that dialogue. Consider similarly a quotation from Plato's *Statesman* (311a1–2) that describes the statesman as entrusting the offices (*epitrepein tas archas*) to particular kinds of citizens, again speaking of the offices in the plural, which is one signal that "office" rather than "rule" is the right translation there.

To what are these (often unmistakable, sometimes ambiguous) references to offices referring? The paradigm for the vocabulary of "office" at the time was accountable office, meaning a position of power (typically one among others) subject to various kinds of limits, of which the conventional mechanisms of accountability were only one. Plato sometimes refers to these offices in their conventionally accountable form, as in *Republic* 8, and intensifies the mechanisms of accountability for offices in the constitutional project of the *Laws*. In the constitutional projects of the *Republic* and (much more briefly) the *Statesman*, however, the limits of offices are reconfigured in ways that diverge significantly, and some may think fundamentally, from the ways in which Greek offices were standardly configured, especially in replacing accountability to those ruled with what might be thought of as accountability to superordinate rulers. To recognize and to assess Plato's moves of this kind require a deeper acquaintance with the paradigm of accountable office with which he would have been familiar.

Accountable offices took shape gradually in the constitutions of most Greek polities, and became the predominant mode of organizing the use of epitactic powers within the *polis* by the mid-fifth century. Anyone observing not only the Athenian democratic *polis* but other polities in Plato's day would have recognized such officeholders as political figures whose tenure and powers are subject to specific kinds of control by agents other than the officeholders themselves, typically expressed in legal procedures and institutions, which

---

28. When I refer to officeholders in actual Greek constitutions, their broadly "accountable" nature should be taken to be implied, but it is sometimes useful to add the adjective (as did Pausanias [4.5.10] in the dictum with which I began chapter 1) to make this clear.

constituted the *taxis* of office.[29] Herein lies a paradox, which persists in regard to political offices today—though in making the comparison, it must be noted that the Greeks did not draw modern distinctions between political and administrative offices, or between executive and judicial powers, instead treating all office as of a single kind and typically mixing what one might call executive and judicial powers. The paradox is that officeholders are epitactic rulers while simultaneously being subject to controls by other agents, controls that are typically legally and procedurally defined and are implicitly intended to orient them to the good of the ruled.

Such controls typically involved legal mechanisms to impose a characteristic set of limits on the powers of officeholders, so as to make them accountable to some subset of those whom they ruled.[30] Already in the seventh century, the *kosmoi*, or officeholders, of Cretan Dreros (the very name for whose role draws on the same noun for order, *kosmos*, noted in chapter 1) were subjected to limits on their powers in the form of required rotation of office, as stated in an inscription:

> Thus has the polis decided: when someone has been *kosmos* the same person is not to be *kosmos* (again) for ten years. But if he should serve as *kosmos*, whenever he should give judgment, he is to owe double, and he is to be without rights as long as he lives, and whatever he should do as *kosmos* is to be void.[31]

This law demonstrates the importance of term limits and their enforcement, and so of limits and controls more broadly, to the emergence of offices and their constitutional roles.

29. I mean by "institutions" those relatively stable sets of practices serving to establish relatively explicit procedures by and through which, as March and Olsen (*Rediscovering Institutions*, 161) have put it, "rules are followed and roles are fulfilled," and specifically, in the political context, such institutions usually articulated by some kind of law. While adopting this perspective from these scholars' version of the "new institutionalism," I focus on the formal powers that such institutions created and the vocabulary and syntax by which they were characteristically described. My approach harks back to aspects of what one might call the "old institutionalism" that have receded in significance but still retain value, so aiming to complement the advances of "new institutionalism" scholars developing game-theoretical approaches to Greek constitutions.

30. Early Greek laws tend to take the offices as already established and then impose limiting powers or duties on them. The explicit use of law to establish the offices as well as to furnish rules for their activity may be a relatively late development; Plato highlights the peculiar status of "constitutional laws" (namely, laws setting up offices) in book 6 of the *Laws*, as discussed below in chapter 3.

31. Translation from Gagarin and Perlman's *Laws of Ancient Crete* (202). Raaflaub ("Archaic and Classical Greek Reflections," 78) notes that this law from Dreros (ca. 650), which is "the earliest extant [Greek] law," dating from the mid to late seventh century, shows that this constitution had already achieved "regulated rotation in the chief office by law." See also Gagarin, *Early Greek Law*, 51, and more generally 51–97 and 122–37, with Todd, "Writing the Law."

According to the evidence of classical Greek historians and orators, as well as epigraphical evidence, the limits defining offices characteristically included the following (in a list that I have collated for purposes of this study):

1. Performance audits: audits (known as *euthunai*)[32] upon vacating an office, with penalties if malfeasance of kinds specified in a given constitution was proven[33]

2. Limited powers of office (specified powers, often as a collegial member of a board)

3. Limits on eligibility to serve: term limits; specified selection procedures usually by lottery, election, or a combination of both; scrutiny of civic standing as a test (*dokimasia*) prior to installation in office (distinctive of classical Athens)

4. Other potential mechanisms of monitoring and sanctioning performance: these included: (a) accusations brought against officeholders during their term of office (distinctive of classical Athens);[34] (b) payment of wages, implying potential sanctioning for bad performance (mainly in Athens and other democracies, but only for certain offices at certain periods)

---

32. As Rhodes (*Commentary*, 155) explains the meaning of *euthunein* as involving straightening out: "The earliest meaning of εὐθύνειν is 'guide straight' or 'direct' (like the Homeric ἰθύνειν)," referring also to a fragment of Solon for the later related sense of "'making the crooked straight.'" *Euthunai*, which came to symbolize accountability of officeholders more generally, were widely required not only in Athens but also elsewhere, in both democratic and oligarchic regimes, though their character and details varied between those regime types and across individual regimes. Nevertheless, Athens boasted both the most offices (to our knowledge) and the most extensive system of limiting and controlling their powers. It is also the best attested case, especially in the fourth century, for which the textual corpus of orators, as well as the Aristotelian circle's *Constitution of the Athenians*, [*Ath. Pol.*], can be combined with epigraphic evidence.

33. In many constitutions, the focus of these procedures was on financial malfeasance only; the unique two-part structure of the *euthunai* in Athens (each stage carried out by a different board) allowed more general charges to be brought at the second stage. In terms of the sanctions that could be imposed at the end of an audit, Roberts (*Accountability*, 18) observes of democratic Athens that "only when his εὔθυναι [*euthunai*] were complete . . . was it legal for a man to set out on a journey, transfer his property to anyone else, be adopted into a different family, or even make a votive offering to a god. In other words, the state had a lien on the property and civic freedom of all officials until their accounts were settled." More generally, officeholders were in thrall to the political community until their accountability to it could be exhaustively resolved.

34. Fröhlich (*Cités grecques*, 323) notes that "Athens is the only city in which we know anything of procedures enabling sanctioning of a magistrate while in the course of his tenure." However, he observes elsewhere ("Governmental Checks and Balances," 263) that "Magistrates in many *poleis* were required to present their accounts for examination several times during their term of office."

While sometimes the term "accountability" is narrowly reserved for the *euthunai* alone, that very notion—with the aspiration of making of an officeholder *hupeuthunos*, or subject to audit—could be used in a more broadly metaphorical way. It is in that light that I gloss all of the mechanisms above as ones of accountability broadly speaking.

Each of these parameters (with the exception of the almost exclusively Athenian process of scrutiny, or *dokimasia*) could apply to offices in Athens as well as other democracies, and (with the further exception of the payment of wages to officeholders, which was characteristic of though not ubiquitous in democracies) to those in contemporary oligarchies as well. While I listed the *euthunai* first, given their symbolic importance in making offices accountable, I elaborate on the list by beginning with the basic contours of offices as delineated by their powers and terms. In contrast to rulers, who might have arrogated to themselves an unspecifed and unlimited set of powers, it was axiomatic that each office should have a limited set of powers. For example, in fourth-century Athens, officeholders held the following powers, each of which involved the power to issue orders to other citizens as needed: to preside over a court, to impose fines, to manage public funds, to supervise public works (note the characteristic combination of what today might be considered judicial and executive powers).[35]

Likewise, in contrast to lifelong kings or tyrants who clung to power until their deaths, it was axiomatic that officeholders would be selected for a fixed and limited length of term (typically in Athens of a single year). This led to rotation of office in the sense that upon the expiration of one term of office, a procedure had to be followed to install an officeholder afresh. A typical kindred requirement was a limit on the number of times anyone could serve in the same office, meaning that rotation also required a change of personnel (though this did not apply to the Athenian generals, for example, who could be reelected without limit).[36]

---

35. Put more technically, in Athens these powers included "the fundamental right of giving orders and of passing obligatory measures (ἐπιτάξαι [*epitaxai*]), which implied the right of punishing the delinquent (ἐπιβολὰς ἐπιβάλλειν [*epibolas epiballein*]": Glotz, *Greek City*, 204. There were also additional powers accorded to various officeholders, such as "power of initiative (*legein, graphein*), power to prepare business (*probouleuein, anakrinein*), power to decide (*kyrion einai*)": Hansen, *Athenian Democracy*, 228. While the tasks of the officeholders may have been restricted and the authority of the people in controlling them significant, their very role was to issue orders, at times taking executive (if not legislative) initiative: contra Bleicken, *Die athenische Demokratie*, 153 ("es konnte nicht einmal Initiative von ihnen ausgehen: Die Beamten waren reine Verwaltungsträger" [Not a single initiative could be taken by them [the officeholders]: the officials/civil servants were pure administrators]), and more generally 145–58 and passim.

36. In Thebes, for example, "any general who retained his office longer than the fixed period was called worthy of death," though this was not always put into effect in practice (Pritchett, *Greek State at War*, pt. 2, 17). A term limit in the sense of a limited period of office was compatible with an absence of term limits in the modern sense, meaning that the

Again, in contrast to hereditary kings or to tyrants who had come to power in some atypical way, selection procedures for officeholders typically consisted of lottery, election, or some combination of both (even in fourth-century democratic Athens, election was used for all military offices and some financial ones).[37] These procedures also set basic eligibility criteria, normally including a minimum age (thirty in most cases in fourth-century Athens), as well as characteristic differentiation for certain offices by age, in keeping with a general expectation that in certain respects elders should hold power over youths. Moreover, in classical democratic Athens and perhaps a few other *poleis* in the classical period,[38] anyone chosen by lot or election was subjected to a further test (*dokimasia*) before being allowed to take up any office. In Athens, this involved testing whether the prospective officeholder was a citizen in good standing (including being properly enrolled in their local deme, up to date with their taxes, and a participant in expected civic religious rituals). If not, they would be denied the opportunity to serve.

Most characteristic of offices was their subjection to audit or *euthunai*, as was argued by the Athenian orator Aeschines in 322 in the course of defining

---

single-year office of general or *stratēgos* could in Athens (for example; perhaps also that of *polemarch* in Chios) be held repeatedly through repeated election (Ehrenberg, *Greek State*, 72). Theoretically, while term limits serve to control the power of officeholders, they can also serve to protect their exercise of powers during their term, as argued in the context of English and early American common law by Manners and Menand in "Three Permissions."

37. The liminality of kingship with regard to these and the other parameters of office listed can be appreciated in this light. Consider, for example, the dyadic Spartan kingship, which continued to characterize the Spartan constitution in Plato's lifetime. There were no limits on the length of term of that role once assumed—but there was a threshold at which a youth "came of age" in assuming an inherited kingship. The selection procedures did not involve lottery or election or any combination thereof—but in sixth-century Sparta the succession to the dyarchic kingship followed "a fixed order of succession based on the principle of patrilineal male primogeniture," and this was institutionally determined by law (*nomos*) (Griffith-Williams, "Succession," quotation 43, remarks on *nomos* 45). In other words, while the procedural and institutional mechanisms for setting the limits of office familiar in other constitutions did not apply to the Spartan dyadic kingship, that institution was generally considered both within and outside Sparta to be subject to limits in some sense. Certainly to be a Spartan king was to serve in a role of rule that was delineated by some kind of limit and ordering, keeping it from descending into either anarchy or (a Platonic sense of) tyranny.

38. For Athens, Aeschin., 3.15. Feyel, in *Dokimasia*, studies *dokimasia* in Athens and gives some evidence that it was also used in the classical period in certain other *poleis* such as Rhodes, before spreading outward from Athens more widely in the Hellenistic period (see esp. 363–70). Athens also deployed *dokimasia* in different (but related) contexts of scrutiny, including that of scrutinizing eighteen-year-olds' qualifications to be entered on the citizen rolls in their respective demes. Farrar ("Taking Our Chances") emphasizes that the Athenians emphatically never assumed that anyone selected by lottery should automatically be deemed suitable to serve, noting that this should give pause to contemporary advocates of randomly selected citizens' juries and similar institutions.

just what counted as an office in the democratic constitution of his time.[39] While a number of knotty issues are raised in Aeschines's speech "Against Ctesiphon," the main issue for present purposes is the question of whether (as Aeschines contended) a role that had been taken up by the rival orator Demosthenes (on whom Ctesiphon had moved to bestow a civic honor) counted technically as an office.[40] For if it were an office, then Ctesiphon could rightly be prosecuted for having proposed a resolution to honor Demosthenes with a "crown" in violation of the existing laws with regard to when an officeholder could be so honored.[41]

To make his case, Aeschines surveyed the key requirements and application of the idea of office within the Athenian constitution at the time, citing existing laws in order to inform the jury (and in the process offering invaluable information about those laws to later historians). In particular, he invoked a law that prohibited the crowning of any officeholder until after the accountability procedures (*euthunai*) upon the conclusion of his term had been successfully completed (a condition not met by Demosthenes at the time that Ctesiphon's

39. Aeschin., 3.9–31. The date is admittedly late in the life of the fourth-century Athenian democracy (the democratic constitution established after the defeat of the Thirty in 403 BCE). Aeschines was writing about two decades after Plato's death, and in the decade after the Macedonian victory over Athens and other *poleis* at the battle of Chaeronea, which initiated a complex series of interactions between Athens and the forces of Macedon, which had become dominant in Greece. But for present purposes, Aeschines was referring to features of Athenian democratic offices that had remained broadly consistent from the mid-fifth century onward. Many authors follow Aeschines's account of an office as I do here, though some skepticism about the clarity of a definition of an *archē* in democratic Athens, as opposed to a broader category of different kinds of *timē* (civic role or honor), is expressed by Blok (*Citizenship*, 196–97 and passim).

40. Ctesiphon had proposed the resolution to recognize Demosthenes for having added his own money to a sum allotted to him in his office as a commissioner for the repair of the city's walls, and more broadly for his record of service to the city. The resolution was passed by the council and then challenged by Aeschines in the Assembly, which in turn passed the question to the popular jury courts to decide. The honor of a gold crown was legally required to be presented in an Assembly meeting, but Ctesiphon proposed that Demosthenes be crowned in the theatre of Dionysus at a coming civic festival. At the ensuing trial, Demosthenes (speaking on behalf of Ctesiphon and thereby defending his own record) carried the jury overwhelmingly, to the extent that Aeschines suffered the penalty for a frivolous prosecution that won too few votes. Yunis (*Demosthenes, Speeches 18 and 19*, 27) notes: "Aeschines had no political future in Athens, left the city, and ended up on Rhodes as a teacher of rhetoric."

41. Aeschines anticipates that his opponent will submit that Demosthenes's role had not been an office proper—an *archē*—but rather a kind of voluntary caretaking (an *epimeleia* or *diakonia*) (Aeschin., 3.13), though in the event Demosthenes did not avail himself of such a line of argument in his reply. The significance of *epimeleia* and of caring more broadly as part of ruling (and so officeholding) is developed in Plato's thought throughout this study.

resolution had been passed). The *euthunai* procedures, widespread among democratic and oligarchic constitutions alike, required officeholders to submit and defend an audit of their responsibility for any public funds; in late fifth- and fourth-century Athens, they involved a two-stage procedure, involving first any financial charges and then any broader charges that might be lodged against their performance in office.

The role played by the procedures of *euthunai* was especially important in limiting the powers of offices in Greek constitutions,[42] as Pierre Fröhlich has underscored: "The control of officeholders [by means of *euthunai*] is one of the characteristic features of Greek cities, in the classical and Hellenistic eras alike. . . . One must speak of Greek cities, and not only of democracies. For, even if the evidence is not very rich on this point, the control of officeholders is found equally in oligarchies."[43] Already in early fifth-century Gortyn, the officeholders known there (as in Dreros and other Cretan cities) as *kosmoi* were accountable for any violation of property law committed during their term, on pain of being fined by another body of officeholders, the *titai*.[44] Such a role for one group of officeholders (sometimes called *euthunoi*) in holding another group (individually) to account was typical of *euthunai* procedures and would be adopted by Plato in the discursive legislation of the *Laws*, as argued below in chapter 3.[45]

42. Accountability was not important only in democracy or only in Athens, a point on which the secondary literature is often misleading. Even Roberts's excellent book on Athens, *Accountability*, while it is entitled to take the limited scope that its title announces, occasionally falls prey to this temptation. While it is true that Athenian literature celebrated Athenian accountability and contrasted it paradigmatically with Persian unaccountability (as for example in Aeschylus's *Persians* [lines 212–14], as she remarks [5]), this should not be generalized or taken at face value to mean that the existence of accountability procedures was in fact unique or distinctive to democracies, albeit that, as I go on to observe here, certain ways in which they were configured and practiced in Athens were indeed unique so far as we know. By contrast, Landauer's focus in *Dangerous Counsel* on comparing the role of counsel in democracies and autocracies leads him to adopt an appropriately wider lens, highlighting that accountability procedures could be found across a wide range of regime types. See also the survey of Greek democracies in Robinson in *Democracy beyond Athens*.

43. Fröhlich, *Cités grecques*, 529—the French: "Le contrôle des magistrats est un des traits caractéristiques des cités grecques, à la époque classique et à l'époque hellénistique. . . . It faut parler des cités grecques, et non des seules démocraties. Car, même si la documentation n'est pas très riche sur ce point, le contrôle des magistrats se retrouve également dans les oligarchies." Note that the French word "magistrat," while sometimes translated "magistrate," means officeholders generally, rather than judges in particular as that English translation might mistakenly be taken to connote.

44. *Inscriptiones Creticae* 4:181–83, no. 79.

45. Aristotle would recognize its significance by ascribing to the sixth-century Athenian legislator Solon the granting to the people of "the minimum power necessary, that of electing officials and holding them to account (*euthunein*)" (since if they did not even

The requirement that officeholders be subject to *euthunai* was viewed widely as being of central importance. It became a metaphor for accountable rule more generally, as in its transposition by Aeschylus to the realm of the afterlife, with a chorus of Furies in the *Eumenides* describing the god Hades as the *euthunos* of mortals.[46] Indeed, Demosthenes would in his rejoinder to Aeschines expand the accountability of orators to the *dēmos* so as to make it a lifelong ethical expectation rather than a periodic procedural one: "Far from claiming that I was exempt from an audit (*ouk . . . hupeuthunos*), as [Aeschines] maliciously asserts, I submit that my whole life long I am subject to audit (*hupeuthunos*) by you for whatever public funds I have handled and for whatever public business I have undertaken" (18.111). Such proposing of a functional equivalent to a specific procedural requirement of office is a parallel for what Plato does in renovating and reconfiguring office and rule in the *kallipolis* of the *Republic* (chapter 7, below). Conversely, the formal unaccountability (being not subject to *euthunai*) of Athenian jurors and assemblymen was noted by many Athenian authors as a striking contrast to the role of officeholders. These jurors and assemblymen controlled the officeholders without being subject to the same kind of control themselves. But that control did not negate the epitactic powers that the officeholders possessed and wielded as an (accountable species of) rulers.[47]

While selection and scrutiny applied before an officeholder could embark upon a term of office, and *euthunai* marked the end of each such term, there were generally fewer controls on what officeholders could do during their term of office. Athens again was unusual in developing (especially in the fourth

have authority in these, the people would have been enslaved and hostile)"(*Pol.* 1274a15–18, trans. Reeve, modified; in particular, I have changed his "inspecting" to "holding them to account"): without these powers of accountability, the people would be in a state of enslavement, and hostility rather than civic friendship would characterize the *polis*. See Lane, "Popular Sovereignty."

46. Aeschylus, *Eumenides* l. 273. Sommerstein (*Aeschylus: Eumenides*, ad loc.) remarks that this "may allude to a procedure of Athenian law," and points out that in Aeschylus's *Persians* (l. 828), "Zeus as chastiser of the arrogant is called εὔθυνος βαρύς." Contrast the *Prometheus Bound* (l.324) where Zeus "rules alone, is harsh and undergoes no audit for his actions" (as translated and quoted by Roberts [*Accountability*, 5]). See also more generally the essays collected in Morgan's *Popular Tyranny*.

47. Consider how the assiduous elderly juror Philokleon in Aristophanes's *Wasps* plays on the fact that jury service was not in fact technically an office precisely because it was unaccountable: "And in doing all this [abusively exercising the powers of the jury] we are unaccountable (*anupeuthunoi*), something no other officeholder (*archē*) can claim" (Aristophanes, *Wasps* 587). The line is an evident paradox hinging on the fact that precisely in being *anupeuthunoi*, the jurors cannot claim to be holders of an *archē*, since accountability is central to what it is to be or hold an office. (The same line is cited in Landauer's "*Idiōtēs* and the Tyrant" [153], but his translation of the final phrase ["a power not given to anyone else"] misses the specificity and paradox of *archē* as office in the Greek text.)

century) a repertoire of opportunities for citizens to bring specified actions against officeholders for malfeasance of various kinds, which would then be heard by one or more public bodies for possible sanction. Athens also (like some other democracies) experimented with the payment of wages to office-holders for part of the fifth century. However, after the abolition of such wages for almost all offices (excepting the nine *archons* and a few others) by the short-lived oligarchic regime of the Four Hundred, they were not restored in the fourth century, even though wages were reintroduced for the council members, continued for jurors, and newly introduced for Assembly attend-ees.[48] The function of wages was never spelled out officially. It may have responded to a concern with making it possible for potential officeholders to serve (though those in the poorest group of citizens in Athens were never technically eligible, and wages were absent in the period in the fourth century when the poorest citizens are sometimes argued to have been allowed to serve nonetheless). But it may also indicate a potential form of control of the office-holders by those paying their wages. I argue in chapter 6 that Plato evinces special interest in the *Republic* in the question of wages for officeholders (whereas the *Laws* rejects such payment altogether). The question of wages in the *Republic* becomes a key to understanding in what ways these rulers and officeholders are to be understood as serving, and in what ways their roles are limited and ordered.

Depending on how these various parameters were fleshed out, one can see officeholders as fitting into a variety of Greek constitutions (*politeiai*, plu-ral). Such constitutions may be thought of on the model of a symphonic form, which is articulated by an expected set of movements, but which may vary both in the movements included and in the internal subforms they contain. This claim makes conceptual sense: a constitution centrally includes the formal assignment of powers to roles, which at once defines the roles and delimits their prerogatives. It makes political sense: a constitutional regime, unlike its uncon-stitutional counterparts (such as a lawless tyranny, considered as an ideal, or rather anti-ideal, type), is characterized by the limiting and controlling of the powers of offices that it maintains. And it makes historical sense: the earliest laws on record from ancient Greece, for various *poleis*, or city-states, in Crete, lay out particular powers of certain officeholders and the penalties to be assigned for their violation.

Those laws, as in the one from Dreros quoted above, already presupposed the existence of certain offices (*archai*). Together, offices and laws came to be viewed as the fundamental components of a constitution, a framework that Plato employs very clearly in the *Laws*, as argued in chapter 3 below. Indeed, a fundamental study of the meaning of *politeia* (constitution, in its primary

48. Hansen, *Athenian Democracy*, 150, 188–89, 240–42, 253–55, 315–16.

meaning in her account) in classical Greek texts by Jacqueline Bordes is organized in terms of the changing balance over time, from the archaic period
until Aristotle, between *nomoi* and *archē* (Bordes does not sharply distinguish
between its senses of rule and office) as its dominant constituents.[49]

Particularly in fifth-century texts, *politeia* could mean most broadly a
civic way of life and a citizen's participation in it, with *nomoi* concomitantly
referring to everyday customs and practices; it was not common there for the
role of *archē* to be relatively minimal.[50] For example, the fragments of Critias's various late fifth-century constitutional projects do not focus in detail
on offices (*archai*), and while offices are mentioned and briefly discussed
in pseudo-Xenophon's *Constitution of the Athenians*, also of the late fifth
century, the way of life of the Athenian *dēmos*, even in regard to democratic
political institutions, is of greater interest there.[51] However, Bordes argues that
in the fourth century, *archē* tended to become more prominent in articulating
the structure of a given constitution. The fourth-century Athenian orator Lycurgus, for example, in a speech titled *Against Leocrates*, enumerated the *archōn*—
using the term here as a label for a generic officeholder rather than a name for
one of the nine simply so-called Athenian archons—as holding one of the three
central roles of the *polis*.[52]

Broadly speaking, then, it was in and through a constitution, one typically from the late fifth century onward articulated in terms of written laws,
that the general power of ordering involved in any kind of rule is transmuted

49. Bordes's *Politeia* does not systematically explore the distinction between rule and
office as studied in the present monograph, though she generally assumes that *archē* is
defined in *politeiai* by certain kinds of institutional limits, comporting with the present
treatment of office herein, as also for example in emphasizing the role of *archē* as one
of "commandement" (238). Bordes typically translates *hoi archontes* as "les gouvernants"
(rulers) and *hoi archomenoi* as "les gouvernés" (the ruled) (129 and passim), and is more
interested in tracking shifts of emphasis from the "nombre" (number) of "gouvernants" (as
in the one/few/many distinction in its locus classicus in Herodotus 3.80–82), and their
individual "nature" (395 and passim).

50. Bordes, *Politeia*. See also Menn's "On Plato's ΠΟΛΙΤΕΙΑ," especially the survey on
politeiai in texts before Plato (3–13), though he says almost nothing about offices in that
section. While he draws a distinction that corresponds broadly to that drawn by Bordes
between *archē* and *nomoi*, he is (5n4) unduly dismissive of her substantial book in favor of
a brief survey by Treu in *Der neue Pauly* (*New Pauly*).

51. I am grateful to Malcolm Schofield for emphasizing these broad points to me in
conversation, and to Christopher Moore and Christopher Raymond for including me in
an illuminating conference on Critias held at the Pennsylvania State University in 2018.

52. Lycurgus, *Against Leocrates* 79. The other two are the juror and the individual in
his private capacity. Notice the absence of the assemblyman from this catalogue of the
central civic roles (the councilor being included in the category of officeholder), contrary to
the tendency among political theorists to inflate the significance of the Athenian Assembly
(often because of its seeming comparability to modern legislatures).

into the kind of rule that is carried out through offices. This was done by defining offices institutionally in terms of their ordering and limiting features: their legal capacities, their terms, their mode of selection, and the controls exercised over them. Just as an annual general meeting must establish offices, fill them, and hold their exercise accountable, so too did any ancient Greek constitutional order—in which epitactic subordination intersected with controlling mechanisms of accountability precisely in establishing office as a distinctive kind of rule.[53]

The implicit purpose of accountability in such constitutions of officeholders was as part of the *taxis* serving to orient the officeholders in relation to the good of the ruled. But the typical mechanisms of office were at best capable of orienting the officeholders away from egregious violation of that good. Accountable offices had the function of orienting officeholders as rulers in relation to the *telos* of the good of the ruled, but from a Platonic and indeed any kind of Socratic perspective would risk doing this inadequately. The risk stemmed both from the potentially inadequate nature of their understanding of that good (since the selection procedures of officeholders did not ensure their epistemic virtue) and from the inherently limited (in both senses of that term) nature of the mechanisms designed to orient them toward it.

Indeed, an accountable officeholder is a paradoxical kind of ruler. Like kings, officeholders are epitactic rulers who issue orders to others. Unlike kings (or at least to a much greater extent than most kings), officeholders are subject to controlling limits of their very powers of ruling. The function of those limits is, implicitly, to safeguard the officeholders' rule: to keep the

---

53. To speak of Greek constitutionalism is a somewhat controversial claim in the broader history of political thought. It is denied by Straumann in *Crisis and Constitutionalism*, though by largely equating "Greek" with "Aristotelian," while analyzing constitutionalism in terms of higher law rather than an order of offices and laws; Carugati, in *Creating a Constitution*, defends Greek constitutionalism, but defined only in terms of legislation rather than offices (8). I myself muddied the waters on the question of Greek constitutionalism in *Birth of Politics* (59), by writing that "no 'constitution,' even in the uncodified British sense, can be found in the political languages of classical Greece and republican Rome," a claim that I would now retract as having already been inconsistent with the overall context and argument of the relevant chapter of that study as a whole: the "topic" of that chapter is a few pages later summarized as "the connection between [the Greek word] *politeia* in the sense of citizenness, way of life, and *politeia* as a specific political structure" (61). As the present study argues, "constitution" is a useful and defensible way to translate *politeia* in the sense of a political organization of rule articulated in terms of offices and laws, understanding constitution as "an evolutionary process of political practice" even in "the absence of a constitutional document" (the latter approach drawing on the work on modern constitutionalism by Möllers, "Pouvoir Constituant" [191]). I am grateful to Linda Colley for pressing me to clarify this point.

taxis of their rule properly directed toward the *telos* of rule. Identifying that safeguarding function, however, enables one to ask to what extent the particular kinds of limits characteristic of accountable offices could succeed in fulfilling it. Athenian democratic accountability, in particular, made officeholders accountable to those whom they ruled (a kind of accountability "to below"): imposing periodic checks to protect against exploitation of the ruled, but not (from a Platonic perspective) systematically ensuring the formation or selection of officeholders who would be wise and virtuous in caring for their good. In other words, on my analysis, it is the very function of accountability—with its aim of orienting officeholders toward the true good of the ruled—that Plato would seek to conserve and to find ways to more robustly achieve. And this because the typical limits and parameters that defined Greek offices could not robustly succeed in orienting their holders toward what Plato would consider the true good of the ruled.

Accountability mechanisms broadly conceived can fall short for two reasons. On the one hand, that function, which is implicit in their workings, could be realized only imperfectly by the typical mechanisms controlling accountable offices: these could prevent gross corruption and exploitation of the ruled but were not structured so as to ensure the orientation of officeholders toward their true good. On the other hand, if the point of accountability is to ensure that orientation, there are other means and mechanisms than the typical limiting parameters of existing Greek offices that could more robustly do so.

These include, most importantly, broader attention to the formative education of persons who are capable of becoming officeholders (and of filling other ruling roles) of the desired kind, cultivating their knowledge and their virtue so far as possible. It is in their responsibility for education that the epistemically expert or wise character of the rulers (or the sublimated rule of reason in the shape of divinely inspired laws) shows itself to be most important. The rule of knowledge is as much expressed through shaping the education of the officeholders and those whom they rule as it is in giving direct epitactic orders—even though the capacity to do so remains a hallmark of rule. Thus, to consider the formation of officeholders is to consider office and rule not only as roles but in terms of the natural persons available to fill those roles, and the motivation that they might have to do so. This in itself becomes an important theme in certain Platonic works, especially in the *Republic* (as discussed below in chapters 5, 6, and 7), while being resolutely ignored in others, such as the *Statesman* (discussed in chapter 4), which shows no interest in the education of the statesman, who is treated instead as a kind of cipher. But it was not the only theme that interested Plato in addressing the vulnerabilities of officeholding; reconfigured offices, and their supplementation with superordinate rulers who might better safeguard an orientation to the good of the ruled, also attracted his attention, as this study contends.

Vocabularies: Archē *and* Archein
as *"Rule" and as "Office"*

The role of *archē* as a fulcrum between kingship and office, expressing a broader notion of "rule," had been already established from the sixth century. It has been described as signifying an "act of 'ruling'" that "amounts to a habit, status or position."[54] In fifth-century authors, the term was used concretely, to indicate rule considered as the possession of "an individual, a group, or a whole populace" (or to "signify a territory").[55] Significantly for present purposes, which are focused on its application to individuals, it was used in Herodotus and Thucydides to span the spectrum of figures highlighted so far in my imaginary statue gallery: including a king on the one hand and an officeholder on the other, with occasional applications to a tyrant as well.[56]

Indeed, it was in Herodotus and Thucydides especially that a political sense of *archē* was consolidated, complementing its older (and also continuing) sense of temporal beginning or originating cause: in this political sense, "unlike *kuriotēs* or *despoteia*, *archē* does not refer to an unrestricted lord or master," but instead to "power and authority."[57] A political theorist today might raise an eyebrow at that conjunction, since one common way to configure authority as a normative concept is to contrast it with power in the sense of de facto, or at best descriptively legitimate, domination. But, in general, the political use of *archē* in the fifth century suggested positions of respect, within the orbit of (while not always living up to what I earlier described as) the evaluative nimbus of the idea of rule attaching to most of the figures in the imaginary statue gallery.

Archē was not the only vocabulary that could span this spectrum.[58] Another familiar idiom used especially in fifth-century authors (and also found in some

54. Levin, "APXΩ and APXH," 120.

55. Spahn, *"archē,"* 60.

56. There are many other relevant terms that could be discussed in reference to office and officeholding, especially *timē* (plural *timai*), which described a broader set of civic institutional roles, including, for example, the priests and priestesses with civic roles in most constitutions. See Blok ("Citizenship," 168), positioning political *archai* and what she calls "military roles" (but which were also usually *archai*) as subcategories of *timai* ("cultic offices"), which were accorded more broadly than *archai* in that some could be accorded to women.

57. Spahn (*"archē,"* 59). He also notes there the Homeric use of the noun *ho archos* for "a military leader or naval commander," a noun that does not feature significantly in later Ionic or Attic dialects. In introducing the emergence of the political use of *"archē"* in the fifth century, Spahn (61, nn9–10) points out a metaphorical political use in Pindar (*Olympian Odes* 2.58) and a plural reference to *archas . . . polissonomous* in Aeschylus (*Libation Bearers* 865).

58. Again, there are many other relevant terms: *aisymnetēs* for an elected rather than hereditary ruler, a figure also sometimes described as a *turannos* in a neutral sense, for example.

inscriptions) to describe a similar spectrum was *hoi en telei*, those engaged holding political sway, exploiting a sense of *telos* that connects its finality and purpose to the role of the ruler. This idiom is especially common in fifth-century tragedians and historians, used by the former especially of Trojan War–era kings and heroes, by the latter of officeholders in Sparta as well as Athens, for example.[59]

Notably, however, Plato eschews the *hoi en telei* idiom. Perhaps this is because that idiom incorporates no semantic or syntactic clues as to where on the spectrum of different kinds of rule a given usage falls, insofar as *telos* was always used in the plural and the idiom came with no particular associated verbs.[60] In contrast, the linguistic usages of *archē*, as well as those of the verb *archein*, offered significant affordances for highlighting whether certain kinds of rule or office were specifically intended. While some ambiguities still remained (to be either glossed over or exploited, depending on context), the varied linguistic patterns that I now introduce are at work in Plato in passages that variously invoke, deepen, and problematize what kind of rule (potentially including office as a kind of rule) might in any given context be in question. The purpose of this section is ultimately to illustrate (as I began to do in chapter 1) a claim on which this study as a whole rests: that Plato clearly availed himself of the affordances of the vocabulary of *archē* and *archein*, even carving out further characteristic expressions involving them than are commonly found elsewhere and employing them to highlight cases of officeholding in particular.[61] What will be the significance of showing him to have done so? I give an overview of the implications before turning to the linguistic details.

On the one hand, Plato at times exploits and extends idiomatic uses of *archē* (especially in the plural), and *archein* (especially as a participle), to signal the sense of offices and officeholders. On the other, he sometimes uses the noun *archē* in the singular, and participles or other conjugations of the verb *archein*, to indicate a consideration of rule and ruler(s): sometimes in terms of their general nature, sometimes as instantiated in particular cases (whether genuine rulers or flawed ones). These linguistic formulations enable him to

59. For the tragedians, e.g., Sophocles, *Ajax* 1352, *Philoctetes* 385; for the historians' usage in the particular sense that I mention—e.g., Thuc., 3.36, and more generally of Ethiopian politics, Hdt., 3.18; Hdt., 9.106, refers to those in charge of the Spartan military forces at a certain juncture in the Peloponnesian War, meeting in council with their Athenian counterparts. I owe the point about the significance of this idiom, together with some other observations in this chapter, to Emily Greenwood.

60. Another speculation as to why Plato eschews the *hoi en telei* idiom is that it employs *telos* as if it were a description of the elevation of the rulers, rather than as directing their activity toward a *telos* of the good of the ruled, a suggestion that I owe to René de Nicolay.

61. My project here seeks to do for Plato, against the backdrop of broader Greek usages, what Condren (*Argument and Authority*, 2) has described in thinking about early modern England: conjecturing from "the evidence of language" to a "presupposition of office," while conversely placing officeholders on a broader spectrum of figures of rule.

collect what is broadly common to key figures of the imaginary statue gallery (as it were), to test and refine those commonalities, and ultimately to define (true) rule and the (true) ruler in his own way. He does so in holding his usages not just to the standard of existing linguistic conventions but to the adequacy of real essences, ultimately, of the Forms and in particular the Good.

In some passages involving the vocabulary of *archē* and *archein*, it should be taken to be unambiguous (based on the linguistic conventions reviewed below) that Plato (or any Attic author) has officeholders specifically in mind. In others it is unambiguous that Plato (more unusually) is instead inviting the reader to consider the abstract nature of rule and the role of a ruler as such. Nevertheless, it still remains in certain contexts ambiguous as to whether, especially in referring to *hoi archontes*, Plato (or any Attic author) means to refer to them as officeholders or as other kinds of rulers. In such cases the translator and interpreter can only judge how best to make sense of the ambiguity in context. These senses do not exhibit wholesale polysemy.[62] Rather, they are related and overlapping, both involving persons paradigmatically engaged in an epitactic role—that is, issuing commands to others—and doing so in a political context. Those to whom the sense of "officeholders" applies could also generally be described (and so sometimes the terms translated) as "rulers," but the converse is not true, in that some of the figures in the statue gallery who count as rulers clearly cannot count as officeholders.

Let me now offer evidence to flesh out the claims above. A first rule of thumb for this vocabulary is that while the noun *archē* can in the singular be translated either as "rule" or "office," in the plural (*archai*, citing the plural in the nominative) it virtually always signals "offices." This is because the noun in the plural typically "indicates the contrary of a monarchical government of the *polis* and implies a variety of administrative areas or functionaries."[63] Both in singular and plural, the noun could be used as the object(s) of verbs, sometimes in conjunction with certain prepositions, treating it or them as item(s) that could be given, shared, entrusted, and so on. Military commanders, who held epitactic roles, could be described as being "entrusted" with *archē* over their soldiers ("rule," though a kind of rule that in Athens was assigned on the basis of an office); so Xenophon describes himself in reference to his troops in the *Anabasis*.[64] Particular phrasing conventionally signaled that offices were in question, especially again when the noun was used in the plural.[65] This was because any officeholding polity—unlike, say, a kingship—would typically feature a multiplicity of such roles. Thus the plural noun features in the idiom "to hold the

62. For a discussion of polysemy, see Leslie's "Hillary Clinton."

63. Spahn, "*archē*," 61, with a note describing Sophocles's Creon as "ironically" using the plural noun of his own rule (*Antigone* 744) (n11).

64. Xen., *Anabasis* 6.1.31.6, using *archē* in the accusative as object of the verb *epitrepein*.

65. By contrast, a widespread use of the noun in the singular was to signify an empire, being a particular instance and kind of rule.

offices," combining the plural accusative *archas* with the verb *echein*, found in Thucydides in the fifth century and in Xenophon in the fourth.[66] Another verb and noun formed in a parallel way for similar purposes is the combination *didonai tas timas*, in which the broader term *tas timas* in context refers specifically to political offices that are given by the people of a city.[67]

A second rule of thumb applies to the cognate verb *archein*, which (already used in a political sense in Homer) came in Attic Greek to take on a distinctive configuration with regard to officeholding. This was especially true as regards its participles (such as *archōn*, nominative singular, and *archontes*, nominative plural). While these participles could sometimes be used to refer generally to those ruling, in fifth- and fourth-century Greek authors they could be used as a conventional way to characterize officeholders.[68] This means that participles of the verb should always be scrutinized as to whether (depending on the context) they should be interpreted as signaling the sense of officeholding, and so indicating officeholders in general (as "archons"), rather than simply a more general sense of ruling. Indeed, the participle had even been appropriated as the title designating certain particular offices (by the Greeks themselves and, following them, by later scholars writing in various languages). As an important case in point, the term *archon* used as a title to designate three particular officeholders in Athens (part of a group of nine who were also sometimes so titled) was simply the participle *(ho) archōn*.[69] Again, in his speech against Ctesiphon, the

66. Thuc., 6.95; Xen., *Cyropaedia* 8.3. Contrast Thuc., 2.36, using *echein* with *archē* in the singular, referring not to an office but to the Athenian empire, and Isoc., *Evagoras* 9.21, referring to descendants of a usurper who held the political domain.

67. Pseudo-Aristotle, *Rhetorica ad Alexandrum* 2.14.5, 11.6.4.

68. Cammack ("*Kratos*") asserts: "In fourth century Athens . . . it was no longer 'the one ruling' who performed an office," but instead (with the exception of "the nine historic archons") the "'*archô*-ing' agent was instead called by the name *archē*, 'office' (plural *archai*). Those whom the *dēmos* reconfirmed in office monthly were not *archontes*, after the old fashion, but *tas archas*." Even if confined solely to a claim about the titles of Athenian offices, her assertion (supported only by reference to Aristotle [Pseudo-Aristotle?], [*Ath. Pol.*], ch. 43) does not hold true of fourth-century usage more broadly. To take one significant example: in the speech ("Against Ctesiphon") discussed elsewhere in this chapter as key evidence for how offices were understood in fourth-century Athens, the orator Aeschines uses both participles and other conjugations of the verb *archein*, together with or instead of the noun *archē*, not (pace Cammack) just to describe the traditional nine *archontes* but also to describe other offices such as superintendent of the theoric funds (Aeschin., 3.24–26; cf. the usage in 3.9 cited in the main text above). (See also, as evidence for a broader use of the participle in the fourth century than Cammack allows, the quotation from Todd [*Shape of Athenian Law*] in note 69 below.) The same play with the affordances of *archein* and *archē*, both verb and noun, in regard to both ruling and officeholding, is shown in the present chapter and in this study as a whole to characterize Plato, himself a denizen of fourth-century Athens as well.

69. As Todd (*Shape of Athenian Law*, 363) explains for Athens (the term *archon* also being used similarly to name particular offices in Rhodes and elsewhere), this term was

fourth-century orator Aeschines illustrated this point in referring (speaking of earlier Athenian history) to the *"archontes* who manage the most important offices *(tas megistas archas)* and the public revenues" (Aeschin., 3.9). Here the *archontes* are clearly those in offices *(archas)* with key financial responsibilities, as opposed to the three (or more broadly nine) so-titled "archons" alone.

Moreover, just as the noun could occasionally take on an abstract sense to refer to rule in general, so too the verb and its participles could also be used in an abstract sense to refer to rulers in general, who were not necessarily officeholders.[70] Consider for example Herodotus's purported sixth-century Persian aristocrat Otanes's description of isonomic regimes (generally agreed by scholars to reflect the democratic vocabulary that had emerged by the mid-fifth century when Herodotus was writing). Otanes weaves together the noun *archē* and the verb *archein* into a complex portrait of two-level rule in such a constitution, in which the popular multitude are described as ruling in being able to hold the officeholders (also described as rulers) to account. Consider three clauses of his statement in turn (all drawn from, though not exhausting, a longer sentence in Hdt., 3.80.6):

1. "The ruling multitude *(plēthos . . . archon)*" is the subject of the clause, using a neuter participle of the verb.[71]
2. One way in which the multitude is described as ruling is that it "rules the officeholders by lot *(palōi . . . archas archei)*"—that is, selects them by lottery (though in actual Greek democracies, some officeholders were chosen by election, or a combination of lottery and election, instead).
3. A second way in which the multitude is described as ruling is that it "holds rule accountable *(hupeuthenon . . . archēn echei)*"—that is, holds the rule carried out by the officeholders to account, making implicit reference to the *euthunai* or audit procedures and perhaps to other ways of imposing accountability as well.[72]

Note the paradox in Otanes's presentation. On the one hand, the officeholders embody a kind of rule (they are described by the plural noun *archas,* which

---

"used in three senses: loosely, to refer to any Athenian public official; more strictly (usually a collective plural) to describe the 'nine arkhons'; specifically, as the title of the senior of the nine arkhonships, which were the titular chief magistrates of Athens." (Todd transliterates the Greek letter chi with "kh," as do some scholars, whereas I use "ch"; the "o" in *archon* signifies the Greek long vowel omega, rather than the short vowel omicron, but in the name of this office or officeholder it is typically transliterated without the long vowel marking.)

70. Hdt., 3.89.1: the Persian king Darius divides his *archas* (in the sense of his dominions) and appoints *archontas* over each one respectively.

71. Another of the Persian nobles depicted by Herodotus as contributing to the debate, Darius, uses a similar phrase, describing the ruling *(archontos* [another participial form of *archein*]) of the *dēmos* at Hdt., 3.82.4.

72. Otanes also lists a third way in which the multitude rules: by bringing resolutions about everything to the assembled community (meaning, roughly, for public decision).

could indicate both offices and their holders, and it is their rule [singular noun *archē*]) that is said to be held accountable by the multitude. On the other hand, the multitude themselves are described as ruling (*archon* as a participle of the verb), including in their role of selecting officeholders by lottery and holding them to account. This tension between the sense in which the office-holders exercise rule and count as rulers and the sense in which the people can be said to rule over their officeholding rulers (here in what Otanes describes as an "isonomic" [and, by fifth-century standards, democratic] constitution) would recur in a variety of fourth-century literary contexts as well.[73]

All this prepares the ground for Plato's own usages of *archē* and *archein*, which both invoke and build on those discussed above, enabling him sometimes to discuss ruling as an abstract matter, sometimes to signal that officeholding is the kind of rule in question in a given passage, and sometimes to play with the ambiguity between officeholding and other kinds of rule. Plato's writings evidence a plethora of these linguistic signals (indeed, more than the usual set) as to which sense was most likely in play in a given passage—but also evidence ambiguities that task the interpreter with making sense of what he is doing at crucial moments. Consider the following illustrative list of expressions in Plato, all making use of the plural noun with various different verbs (and in one case also a preposition) to signal that offices and officeholders are under discussion:

> *Echein tas archas* (to hold the offices)
>> Example in Plato's *Republic* (8.545d1–2):[74] *echontos tas archas*, using a participle of the verb *echein*
> *Didonai tas archas* (to give the offices)
>> Example in Plato's *Laws* (3.689d4):[75] *doteon tas archas*, using the verb *didonai* in an imperative form
> *Epitrepein tas archas* (to entrust, or leave, the offices)
>> Example in Plato's *Statesman* (311a1–2), using the exact phrase cited
> *Agein eis tas archas* (to vest [people] in the offices—i.e., to make eligible, select, and place certain individuals in the offices)
>> Example in Plato's *Ion* (541d3–4):[76] *eis tas allas archas agei*, done by the city, using the verb *agein* in a singular form

73. See my "Popular Sovereignty" for discussion of the trope of the multitude ruling by electing officeholders and holding them to account as a model for democratic theory; this trope is ascribed to the Solonian constitution in several fourth-century texts, including those of Aristotle, who also discussed this idea critically in his own terms (see, inter alia, *Pol.* 3.11, 1281b31–34).

74. At *Resp.* 8.553a1–2, however, the same verb is arguably used in a related sense, for those brought into office (see discussion in chapter 8).

75. See also *Menex.* 238d4.

76. See also *Ion* 541d3; *Leg.* 9.856b2, 856c3; *Resp.* 8.551a9, discussed below in chapter 8.

As this list shows, Plato makes use of an established verb-noun combination of *echein tas archas*. He also combines *didonai* as a verb with the plural *tas archas*, parallel to the phrase *didonai tas timas* that occurs (for example) in the anonymous *Rhetorica ad Alexandrum* (2.14). Likewise, he combines *epitrepein* as a verb with the plural *tas archas* (as opposed to the singular used for military command by Xenophon, as noted earlier in this section). Finally, he makes use of another verb with a preposition, which describes the vesting or instating of people in offices, *agein eis tas archas*. All of these expressions signal that the kind of ruling in question in these contexts is specifically office-holding, in the same way that other authors would signal this—though just what these references to offices designate in the constitutional projects of each dialogue (and in the deteriorating flawed constitutions featured in book 8 of the *Republic*) remains for further chapters to discuss.

Stances: Writerly Perspectives in Plato and in This Study

Consider the interrelationships among the Greek titles of the three Platonic dialogues to which I have been referring by the standard English titles of *Republic, Statesman,* and *Laws.* In the *Politeia* (which is perhaps most literally translated *Constitution,* in English typically now as *Republic*),[77] Plato articulates a *politeia* "in speech" in terms of its *archai,* or offices, and its *nomoi,* or laws, in keeping with the broad approach to a *politeia* outlined by Jacqueline Bordes, as discussed above. In the *Politikos* (*Statesman,* as in English), Plato draws out the dimension of political knowledge (*politikē*), which was already a topic of

77. The Latin translations of the dialogue titles played an important role historically in shaping their eventual English (and other European language) equivalents. For example, Cicero's decision to title his equivalent of Plato's *Republic* as *De re publica,* picking out a certain kind of constitution rather than constitutions as such, would ultimately bear on the prevalence of the title of that Platonic dialogue in English (and relatedly in other languages) as "*Republic.*" There is of course a much larger historical story to be told.

On the title of the dialogue being *Politeia,* as being also indicated by Plato at *Timaeus* 17c1–3 as *logoi peri politeias,* and on Aristotle's references to the same work under that title, see Menn's "On Plato's ΠΟΛΙΤΕΙΑ" (2), which I paraphrase. On the originality of the titles of the dialogues, Diogenes Laertius quotes Thrasyllus, the editor of Plato's dialogues into an order of tetralogies, as saying of Plato—in the translation quoted by Philip ("Platonic Corpus," 301): "He [Plato] uses a twofold title for each of his works, a name title and a theme title," with (as Philip further notes, 301–2), a further set of classificatory subtitles also being mentioned by Diogenes (3.49) but not ascribed to Plato. (To illustrate, the theme title of the *Politeia* is "on justice.") Despite the name titles and theme titles being treated by Thrasyllus (per Diogenes) as having a common origin, it is worth noting that the OCT editions do not generally print the theme titles either in their tetralogically organized tables of contents or on the title page of each dialogue (neither Burnet nor Slings doing so in the case of the *Politeia*).

discussion in Greek political thought, and (may have) invented a corresponding figure, the *politikos*, or expert statesman, defined in terms of possession of that expert knowledge,[78] who engages in rule in a manner that cannot be reduced to the occupation of an accountable office. And in the *Nomoi* (*Laws*, as in the English title, though the Greek *nomos* has a somewhat different semantic range), Plato again articulated a *politeia* in terms of its *archai* and *nomoi*, while delving more deeply into the relationship of both the rulers or officeholders and the citizens to the law, and into the nature of law itself.[79] The three titles of the dialogues and their respective projects all articulate relationships to constitutions as broadly defined above: constitution, rule, office, and law.

If the *Republic*, *Statesman*, and *Laws* all in different ways (and to different extents) develop projects of Platonic constitutionalism, questions arise about how their projects, and the dialogues more broadly, are related, and how they are to be interpreted. In none of these three dialogues could one reasonably take Plato to be endorsing injustice as a positive value, *anarchia* as a positive state of affairs, or tyranny as a positive kind of rule (in fact, the *Republic* will question whether it is a stable kind of rule at all, or whether it reduces to a kind of *anarchia* in the soul and so life of the tyrant, following on the shadow play of *nomos* in the depiction of a democracy).[80] Conversely, the idea of rule as having a fundamental evaluative purpose, that of serving the good of the ruled, likewise remains stable across the three dialogues. Channeling Tolstoy, one might say that for Plato, every good *politeia* will be alike in having a *taxis*

---

78. Called in the *Statesman* both an *epistēmē* and a *technē* (closely related terms for expertise, with somewhat different associations and usage patterns, on the relationship between which I have learned much from Hulme Kozey [now Hulme] ("*Philosophia and Philotechnia*")).

79. Menn ("On Plato's ΠΟΛΙΤΕΙΑ," 5–6) catalogues a handful of fifth-century references to works composed *peri politeias* or in some variation of that, as well as to works composed about the *politeia* of a particular people, though his discussion of the genre on 3–4 is framed by Aristotle's retrospective analysis. However, pace Menn ("On Plato's ΠΟΛΙΤΕΙΑ," 6), Schofield ("Plato, Xenophon," 451) suggests that the title of the Xenophontic work listed in the manuscript tradition as *Constitution of the Lacedaemonians* was more probably originally "Λυκούργου νόμοι [The laws of Lycurgus]" as that is the "explicit focus" of the treatise from 1.2 onward.

80. This kind of negative attribution to Plato mirrors the identification in Gerson (*Aristotle and Other Platonists*, 17) of "Platonism" as "the philosophical position arrived at by embracing the claims that contradict those claims explicitly rejected by Plato in the dialogues" (though, as I explain in the main text, I believe that we can also attribute certain positive claims and patterns of argument to Plato). Frank (*Poetic Justice*, 16–17) rejects Gerson's particular way of "reading Plato's dialogues negatively," while situating her own book in a "register of negation" that she takes to be one of "possibility"—though her own stimulating and provocative project rests firmly on rejecting one of the two models of reading that she finds in Plato, in favor of the other.

organizing its *archē* toward the *telos* of the good of the ruled, but every good *politeia* may do this in its own way.

It is because I have found all three of these dialogues to be centrally engaged in thinking "of rule and office" that I treat them as participants in the same broad inquiry, adopting the same schema of rule and drawing on similar patterns of vocabulary (in the stylized sense of "vocabulary" canvassed above, including syntax as well as semantics), even as their constitutional projects reconfigure the roles associated with realizing that account in diverse ways. It is this research finding (rather than a precommitment to any particular methodology) on the questions "of rule and office" in Plato that leads me to present this study as charting a course between two long-standing (and rather tired) rival interpretations of Plato's thought: the "unitarian" approach (on which all the dialogues say exactly the same thing) against the "developmentalist" one (on which a chronological order of composition is imputed to the dialogues and then used to infer changes of mind that are imputed to Plato across them). I would describe this study as yielding a "complementary" reading of Plato's political thought across my chosen trio of dialogues—without taking a stand on whether such a reading is appropriate to all topics or all dialogues.[81] This involves a broadly synchronic orientation both to Plato's works and to their context during his lifetime and in works that he can be presumed to have known, ranging across the fifth and fourth centuries as well as across various democratic and oligarchic constitutions, and also emphasizing the archaic and archaizing perspectives at work in the same period. I do so not to deny the significance of more specific differences and developments among such ideas and practices of office and rule for other inquiries, and indeed among the dialogues themselves on certain points, but in order to highlight broadly shared vocabulary, literary framing, and evaluative presuppositions, which bear on rule and office.[82]

81. I follow El Murr (*Savoir et gouverner*, 14), who argues for what he terms complementarity in regard to the main Platonic political dialogues. Compare Laks ("Legislation and Demiurgy"), who also identifies a dimension of complementarity among the three major Platonic political dialogues; he adds dimensions of completion and revision as well, which I would also acknowledge in respect of specific passages, while maintaining an overall position of complementarity in regard to the scaffolding of rule and office that underpins all three dialogues.

82. For an approach inspiring my own (in respect of synchrony), see Billings (*Philosophical Stage*, 11), proposing a focus on the "synchronic constellation of thinking" in classical Athenian drama and philosophical texts of broadly the same period, and going so far as a proposition of doing "intellectual history without chronology." My approach is also broadly consonant with that to Plato in particular articulated in Jordović's *Taming Politics*, which explores "the structure and development of some of Plato's concepts and their relationship to the historical context," in an effort "to fuse intellectual history, conceptual history and classical philosophy" (18).

In this perspective of complementarity, all three of the dialogues that are the focus of this study pursue the basic thought that knowledge alone can make action virtuous and so make people happy and their lives worth living. It follows that whoever possesses such knowledge—which Plato assumes throughout his work to be potentially and at most only a few people—must ensure that somehow or other it governs the actions of all. This view is compatible with the thought that in the chosen trio of dialogues, Plato explored what political philosophy could and should be from different angles and according to different understandings of philosophy itself.[83] Readers may feel that this remark illustrates a danger of complementarity as an interpretative perspective—namely, the risk of becoming vacuous: complementarity can cover both similarity and difference, after all. My response is that I have adopted complementarity as a result, rather than as a method or presupposition: it is meant to characterize the fruits of this study rather than to have determined them in advance, and to be addressed primarily to the topics of rule and office rather than any and every aspect of the dialogues.

A more action-guiding aspect of my approach is to take the protagonists (main questioners) in each of the three dialogues studied here as characters who can be considered, for present purposes, as avatars of Plato.[84] Socrates in the *Republic*, the Eleatic Visitor in the *Statesman*, and the Athenian Visitor in the *Laws* need not and should not be taken as rigidly designated "mouthpieces" for Plato.[85] Instead, it is illuminating to construe them as Plato's

---

83. In "Plato's Political Philosophy" (189), on this point I was already moving away from the more developmentalist perspective of my *Method and Politics*, though, again, the particular points of contrast drawn in that work between *Republic* and *Statesman* are themselves still consistent with a broader position of complementarity. A lovely metaphor was offered in a Florida State University class discussion of drafts of some chapters of this monograph by Svetla Slaveva-Griffin, who appealed to the way in which, from different angles, a given crystal may give off different colors of light.

84. I floated the idea of Platonic protagonists as avatars in *"Antianarchia"* (62), and develop it further here.

85. Examples of those attacking a "mouthpiece" reading include Gordon (*Turning toward Philosophy*, 8) and Wolfsdorf (*Trials of Reason*, 19). It is difficult to give examples of purported "mouthpiece" adherents; it is something of a straw man, since "mouthpiece" suggests a rigid transparency giving a simple one-to-one correlation of any utterance by a given character to the author's view, an approach that would founder in coping with the changing flow, and force, of dialectical argument in any dialogue. The scornful rejection incorporated into the very labeling of the "mouthpiece view" is itself rather ahistorical: there was an ancient debate over whether Plato "dogmatized," and at least some of the parties to the debate, such as Diogenes Laertius (3.52), had no difficulty in attributing views expressed by certain Platonic protagonists to their author. Later ancient authors, such as Aulus Gellius, had no qualms about attributing things written in the dialogues, including by Platonic characters, as being what Plato "says" himself: see Zadorojnyi's "Transcribing Plato's Voice" (470–71, citing Aulus Gellius [14.3.4 and 13.19.2] on Plato, and comparing these locutions in 1.1.1, 17.11.6, and elsewhere).

"representative in the virtual universe" of these three dialogues, serving to enact "a dynamic of agency by proxy," whereby diverse intellectual possibilities, such as invocations or reconfigurations of rule and office, can be explored by Plato without imposing an exclusive commitment to any one of them (he composed multiple dialogues, after all).[86] Adopting a variety of avatars is a way of exploring various configurations of ideas and models that may be viewed as complementary without being necessarily identical.

Identifying each of these dominant interlocutors as the dialogue's avatar enables us to see Plato as playing out the game of that dialogue primarily through the avatar's eyes, such that readers can best explore the world through Plato's eyes by looking through the avatar's eyes with him. Of course, nothing bars readers from sometimes adopting the perspective of other characters and benefiting from doing so: all the roles in the dialogue are available for exploration of this kind. Nevertheless, I propose that we find as readers that in each of these three dialogues it is in and through the avatars that Plato is most fully able to think through the questions to which he recurs in the context of variously revealing constraints.[87]

There is a significant caveat to be entered here. For Plato is not only the "user" of each of his avatars, creating different dialogues as varied games within which overlapping sets of questions can be explored in the context of different constraints, different additional characters, different settings, and so on. That is, he is not simply playing out an externally engineered game *through* his avatars, as video-game players play out a given game through theirs, exploring the virtual experiences made possible by the game designers. Rather, Plato is both maker and user, designing in the very experiences through which he is able to maneuver via his avatars, meaning that all of this exploration is done, as it were, in the past perfect tense. The dialogues constitute a painstakingly crafted literary universe of which it is reasonable to hold with M. M. McCabe, at least as a heuristic, that "Plato wrote nothing in vain."[88] They show us Plato

86. I am, of course, aware of significant rival approaches that emphasize irony or veiled renunciation in the claims made by various of the characters whom I treat as avatars: claims that the constitution sketched out in the main part of the *Republic* is intended as an antitype rather than a constructive proposal, for example, or that the Eleatic Visitor is an antitype of an interlocutor whose ideas are opposed to the more authentically Platonic ideas in other dialogues advanced by Socrates. There is no interpretative method by which such rival claims can be definitively settled; the proof of value can be only in the illumination offered by their application, and it is in this spirit, rather than one of methodological exclusivism, that I put my own approach and reading forward.

87. Dolgert ("Dungeon Master Socrates") offers an interesting account of what readers can learn by identifying with Glaucon and Adeimantus as youthful fantasists about tyranny who are made to play out the consequences of their fantasy within the dialogue.

88. McCabe, "Plato's Ways of Writing," 99. While McCabe is one of those who would generally be viewed as belonging to a "philosophical" camp of interpreters, against whom Blondell (*Play of Character*, 4) identifies her own preferred "literary" camp, the putative

depicting a set of philosophical adventures through the particular conversations engaged in by his avatars, rather than Plato actually experiencing such adventures in real time, as it were, in a world in principle beyond his full control.[89] Nevertheless, conceiving of Plato's dialogues as tracking the various experiences of his protagonists as avatars in working through a set of ideas in distinct conversational contexts, in ways that may diverge at the level of detail but can be attributed to him at the level of the overall identification of an author with their avatars, can still facilitate an escape from the overly restrictive terms of debate of putative "mouthpiece" theory and its deriders.

While the theorization of avatars may be applied to the dialogues more generally, my use of it here is limited to the particular dramatic setting of each of the three dialogues on which I focus, each affording a particular slant on recurrent questions and generating a range of claims made by the avatars (and other characters), which have to be assessed in context to determine whether, and with what kind of force, they should arguably be attributed to Plato. It allows a reader to appreciate the degrees of freedom that Plato afforded himself in writing such a range of dialogues with a more limited range of avatars, enabling him to depict how a set of recurrent claims and negations would play out in each particular context (each dialogue perhaps being akin to a single playing of a given game). Just as one would not expect a player deploying different avatars in different video games (or in repeated playing of the same game) to make exactly the same decisions and take exactly the same actions each time, so one may construe the freedoms of depicted exploration that Plato's various avatars afforded him.

---

contrast loses much of its utility when we consider that Blondell (4) takes her own camp to endorse "the fundamental literary-critical axiom that every detail of a text contributes to the meaning of the whole," a view very close to the sentiment quoted from McCabe in the main text.

89. In "*Antianarchia*" (61), I asked whether it might be a better interpretative stance "if one were to give up seeking a substantive noun to attribute (views, ideas) and instead associate a verb—as in David Sedley's lapidary characterization of the dialogues as 'Plato thinking aloud.'" Conversation with André Laks has since given me pause on this point, thanks to his reminder that the dialogues are carefully composed literary works rather than sallies of exploration (though the distinction between the order of discovery and the order of presentation is not sharply drawn in Plato's own depiction of the method of division, as I have argued previously in *Method and Politics*). Yet if the dialogues are clearly not jazz improvisations in the moment, they may still each count as a distinct foray into the forest of a topic, carving out distinct paths depending on their starting points, dramatic context, orienting questions, and so on, perhaps better represented as "Plato thinking through" the path that a given dialogue represents than as his purely exploratory and unanticipated "thinking aloud." Of course, one should not idealize a body of writing as fully within the author's control; even without deconstructing the figure of the author, there is commonsensical experience of the ways in which one's writing may elude one's full grasp.

I turn finally to a certain stance that I call "discursive legislation," or legislation "in speech,"[90] in which the constitutional projects of both the *Republic* and the *Laws* are carried out. The main interlocutors of the *Republic* on the one hand, the three interlocutors of the *Laws* on the other: each group constitutes itself as a group of discursive lawgivers, or legislators (I use the terms interchangeably), within the economy of the dialogue to which it is central. In each dialogue, the respective group of interlocutors undertakes to issue laws "in speech" as opposed to "in deed," albeit in designing a *politeia* envisaged as one that could eventually in some form come to exist in actuality.[91] In reviewing this stance in the two dialogues (and a related perspective within the *Statesman*), I shall argue that it is significant in at least two ways.

First, within the dramatic frame of the dialogues, the discursive legislative stance separates the role of lawgivers from the role of the rulers envisaged within the constitutions being articulated by the issuing of laws "in speech" (an idiom discussed further below). While both the *Republic* and the *Laws* do ultimately envisage that the constitutions if realized would require persons with an understanding of their purpose comparable to that of the original discursive legislators, those original legislators are not to become rulers themselves.[92] Second, at the level of the writerly project of the dialogues, the stance of discursive legislation means that the reconfigurations of rule and office in these dialogues are not being directly proposed as blueprints (as it were) for establishment by coercive force (even within the fictional frame of what is

90. I have already explored some of the details of this stance in the *Republic* in "Founding as Legislating," and in the *Laws* in "Persuasion et force."

91. While the modal force of "could" is complex, and must be interpreted in relation to the dramatic details of each of the two dialogues, the point I am making here is simply that there is a distinction between the legislation being laid down "in speech" and the actual legislation, as well as the roles of ruling and officeholding, which would obtain were the constitution "in speech" to be realized "in deed." On the related question of possibility in the *Republic*, see especially work by Laks, including most recently *Plato's Second Republic*; I have also learned from engaging with Beere's "Philosopher-Kings." There has been less discussion of the question of possibility in the *Laws*, though the point that the legislation set out in the course of the dialogue is proposed as a test of the ideas developed in its early books and with an eye to being useful to the Cretan legislative commission, which will eventually frame a constitution in actuality for the colony of Magnesia (in actuality within the fiction of the dialogue, of course), rather than as directly to be adopted by that colony, has been recently recognized (with Bartels, in *Plato's Pragmatic Project*, going too far in claiming that the constitution "in speech" has nothing to do with the envisaged new *polis* of Magnesia, whereas many of its details are explicitly framed with the setting of Magnesia in mind).

92. Even in the *Laws*, the proposal at the end of the dialogue by the other two interlocutors to draft the Athenian Visitor into a body that will actually issue laws for the founding of a new Cretan city (12. 969c4–d3) does not make the Visitor into an officeholder or ruler within that city itself. See the discussion of this issue in chapter 3.

presented as actual within the dialogues). Rather, they are explorations of the adequacy of these various roles to flesh out the schema of rule and to safeguard the playing of any role of rule. To explore the ideas of rule and office is not automatically to impose or defend the imposition of any version of them. The discursive stances taken within the dialogues underscore this point.

As discursive legislators, the dialogues' interlocutors are positioned as in a sense superior even to the legendary lawgivers of the various Greek cities (and perhaps, implicitly, to the board of *nomothetai* established in Athens after 403),[93] in their ability to frame a complete philosophically grounded *politeia* in terms of the appropriate level and type of *nomoi*. Yet they act as founders in leisure and in speech, rather than in necessity and in deeds or actuality; they act as legislators without actualizing coercion, lacking the need to threaten the actual coercion that characterizes real-world laws.[94] Moreover, the founder-legislators are not positioned as rulers within the cities in question. Rather, they frame laws in speech, which are models of the kinds of laws that any actual city would normally have to accompany with coercion (since a minimal form of law is that of a conditional coercive threat, as analysis in the *Laws* makes clear).[95] Those eventually imposed laws (not identical to the ones being issued discursively) would stand for the most part (barring later and minor changes) independently of the rulers and officeholders of those cities, whose actions they would constrain even as the rulers and officeholders are to act according to the laws.

The key to the parallel construction of the discursive legislative stance in the *Republic* and *Laws* is the use of the word *logos* in the dative, or in a dative construction. The word *logos* is notoriously slippery and ambiguously wide-ranging: among other possibilities, it can be used to mean account, either financial or narrative; proportion; explanation; reason or reasoning; word or speech. In the last-mentioned context, *logos* is frequently contrasted either implicitly or explicitly with *ergon*, another polysemous word, with such contrasts—typically involving both words in the dative—yielding a sense of "in word" versus "in deed," or "in speech" versus "in actuality." Many translations of both the *Republic* and the *Laws* render *logos* in the dative in such expressions with "in speech" or "in words," sometimes with "theoretically," adopting

93. Nails, "*Republic* in Its Athenian Context."

94. In both dialogues, the interlocutors also engage in intermittent exchanges that lack the illocutionary force of their discursive legislation. They discuss the nature of rule, office, law, and related topics, doing so with a view to their project of discursive legislation but not as part of its actual issuance ("in speech"). Both the content and the communicative force of these exchanges are variegated. The force of some parts is constative, with other parts being deployed to serve as hortatory advice to an imagined legislator (the very role that they themselves in other moments enact "in speech").

95. See chapters 10 and 11 on the theory of law in the *Laws*.

an implicit contrast with "in deed" or "actually." This contrast is instructive and concise, and, as already done above, I sometimes invoke it in my own translations and in referring to the stance of discursive legislation. However, I suggest that the sense of *logos* in these contexts should also be taken as generally involving not just any kind of speech or words but rather, more specifically, reasoning or argument carried out in words, and it is this that I mean in also calling it "discursive." It is helpful to bear in mind what in Plato's view all projects of legislation would share: a definition of law (*nomos*), offered in the *Laws* as *tēn tou nou dianomēn*, or the "distribution of reason."[96]

In the *Republic*, the stance of discursive legislation is linked to the broader project of discursive founding, which begins in book 2, when Socrates explains the significance of the fact that the city they have agreed to found is being founded only *logōi*.[97] This phrasing is often translated as "theoretical" or "in speech," as opposed to *ergōi* or "in deeds," in line with familiar ways of construing the endemic contrast in Attic Greek between *logos* and *ergon*. However, Socrates draws a less familiar contrast later, in book 8, remarking at a meta-level on the degree of realization of the timocratic constitution that he and his interlocutors have just been discussing (and generalizing his point to the whole project of outlining kinds of constitutions and individuals that was taken up at the start of book 8):

> "This, then," I said, "is the way such a *politeia* [the timocratic constitution] would come into being, and the kind of constitution it would be, the constitution having been outlined in argument rather than fully realized, since one can see the most just and the most unjust [this being the task set out in book 2 and reiterated at the start of book 8] sufficiently well from an outline, while it would be an impracticably lengthy task to explain all the constitutions and individual characters without leaving anything out."[98]

96. *Leg.* 4.714a1–2. I make this translation in line with arguments made by Yoon ("Role of Law"), among other scholars, pace the alternative interpretations of the Greek in the translations offered by Saunders in Cooper ("edicts of reason") and Schofield/Griffith ("provisions made by reason").

97. The stance is initially proposed by Socrates with the dative of *logos* (*logoi*, using an iota subscript) at *Resp.* 2.369a6 (in an invitation extended in 369a6–8, accepted by Adeimantus at 369a9); it is echoed again a few lines later by Socrates in an injunctive mood at 2.369c9–10, using a similar formulation of *logos* in the dative ("'Come then,' I said, 'let us, in speech, make a city from its origins.'") One could also translate these formulations as "in reasoning." Note that the contrasting stance of "in deeds" is not explicitly invoked in the book 2 context.

98. *Resp.* 8.548c10–d1. The *logos* clause uses the dative as in the book 2 invitation and injunction; the contrast clause uses a verb (*apergazesthai*) that had been thematized in *Republic* 5 as implicitly involving an *ergon*, as is discussed below in chapter 5, and also thematized (alongside the adverb *akribōs*) in the *Statesman*, as discussed below in chapter 4.

Here, the contrast between the constitution having been "outlined in argument" on the one hand rather than "fully realized" on the other is still a contrast within the horizon of speech, as Socrates makes clear by going on to flesh out the latter as a task of complete explanation. So it is not exactly the word versus deed contrast, but rather a contrast of sketched versus sufficient argumentative explanation. One might generalize the point to suggest that a *kallipolis* itself is only a sketch of a model of an ideal city, not the completed model itself; this suggestion should be brought to bear in reflecting on the relationship posited between a *kallipolis* as a model and the constitution elaborated with Magnesia in mind that is classified as second-best.[99]

There is a moment in the *Laws* when the project of discursive legislation comes into sharp focus. I excerpt it from a complicated context of discussion of the double theory of law as orders (in the sense of commands) prefaced by persuasive preludes, which is presented in terms of an analogy to doctoring in book 4 and then reprised in book 9. The reprise concludes with this remark by the Athenian Visitor (the full context of which I have treated elsewhere):[100]

> "Going through the laws in the way that we are now, is educating the citizens but not actually legislating." (*Leg.* 9.857e2–5)[101]

Note that the Athenian implies that he *agrees* with Cleinias's objection (though he adds "perhaps" at 9.857e2, echoed by Cleinias at 9.857e7): the Athenian expands on, rather than rejecting, the thought that what "we" are doing now is educating rather than, as it were, actually legislating. The question then becomes: What does he mean by "going through the laws in the way that we are now"? One view (defended by Christopher Bobonich) is that this must mean the work of any legislator engaged in issuing laws and preludes.[102] But the Athenian immediately goes on to distinguish the current position of himself and his companions from that of actual legislators. This shows that the "we" are the three interlocutors—himself, Cleinias, and Megillus—and the "now" is their sketching of model legislation for Magnesia, which is precisely free from force in that it is not "now" being imposed on anyone. "We," he says, are in the "fortunate position" of having "no necessity [*anankē*] to legislate." "We" are still engaged in inquiry (*skepsei*) and can choose between the examination of what Saunders translates as "ideal laws" and "the minimum standard we are prepared to put up with," or, more literally, "the best" versus "the most necessary" (9.858a1, a4–5).

Cleinias promptly chooses "the best" for their present project of freely contemplating legislation, so implying that actual legislators will have to pursue

---

99. This is a point made by Lisi in "¿Modelo, proyecto o utopía?"
100. Lane, "Persuasion et force."
101. This is my construal of the phrase *ou nomothetei* in context.
102. Bobonich, "Persuasion, Compulsion, and Freedom."

what is "most necessary" instead. He makes the same point in book 10 (887b4–5), insisting that the interlocutors have no need on the present occasion to choose "the briefest in preference to the best," which would be mean and ridiculous. Actual legislators, it is implied, will sometimes have to choose "the briefest in preference to the best." By contrast, the three discussants are not yet engaged in the task of actually legislating, but are rather at leisure, making it '"ridiculous" for them to act like legislators driven by "some overpowering necessity."[103]

What André Laks has called a "legislative utopia,"[104] in which force is reduced as much as possible, here reaches its zenith when one need not legislate at all: when persuasion, taken now to the level of an educative endeavor tantamount to philosophizing, is all that is required. It is consonant with Laks's emphasis on the impossibility of reducing force entirely that this highest idyll of pure philosophical persuasion is in book 9 located not *within* the city of Magnesia but outside it, in the leisurely discussion among the interlocutors of the *Laws* itself. It is not any actual legislator but the Athenian, Cleinias, and Megillus who are educating (one another, and those who will read their law code) rather than persuading and compelling (in the sense of forcing)— and this is precisely because they are acting only as discursive legislators, not legislating with constative force at all.[105]

While the strikingly parallel construction of this stance in the *Republic* and the *Laws* is not directly mirrored in the *Statesman*, the last-mentioned dialogue delineates the eponymous political expert, in certain moments described as a legislator as well as a king, as having the role of ruler in a city in which everyday offices will be held by particular groups of citizens. So one may take the statesman as having the capacity to engage in legislation in speech—for example, should they not occupy a ruling position—as well as in deed, and this in spite of the dialogue's critique of law in principle, since that critique comports with the expectation that laws will be used in any actual city in practice.[106] Were an ideal statesman as a "kind of legislator" to arise, their role would be to make (or at least superintend and when necessary revise or override) laws for an actual city, as it were from the outside (since no attention in the *Statesman* is given to their education or upbringing). But, again, no such coercive imposition (or lifting) of laws is directly proposed; that would be conditional on the emergence of a true statesman whom people in the city

103. All quotations in this paragraph, 9.857e8–858c3, if not otherwise cited.

104. Laks, "Utopie législative de Platon." In *Plato's Second Republic*, he echoes and elaborates this idea.

105. I draw on, but modify, Lane, "Persuasion et force."

106. I have argued the latter point in "Platonizing the Spartan *Politeia*." Schofield ("Disappearing Philosopher-King," 33–34) stresses a contrast between the legislative projects undertaken by the interlocutors of the *Republic* and *Laws* and the lack of such a project in the *Statesman*, but I think that one can draw them closer together on this point than he does.

would be willing to "stomach."[107] Thus the modality of discursive legislation is echoed, at least, in the *Statesman*, as well.

What then if one turns from discursive legislation as a stance of the characters within the dialogues to a project of illocutionary force as written by Plato himself? How can the writerly stance of discursive legislation be situated as a political-theoretical project? On the one hand, to adopt this stance requires immersion in the political vocabulary, conventions, and norms of Greek constitutional life, specifically those articulating a new constitution in terms of its offices and its laws. When Socrates in the *Republic* invites Glaucon and Adeimantus to join him in founding a city "in speech," he uses the word *tupos* first in issuing the patterns that poetic narratives should use in that city (2.379a2), and then (in one of those relatively rare moments in which a non-avatar's intervention is decisive) follows Adeimantus's lead in terming the ordaining of such patterns as a *nomos* (2.380c5, followed by Socrates at 2.380c8 conjoining *nomōn te kai tupōn*).[108]

Yet in other respects, to practice discursive legislation is precisely to open a gap between existing political and intellectual reality, and new possibilities to be conceived. It is to invite a critical reflection that, while framed and steeped in the immanent, can be in moments radically rejectionist. Plato himself compares the stakes of discursive legislation to the stakes of new political foundings (typically in the form of colonies sponsored either by a single *polis* or by several, a practice alluded to in the *Republic* with the verb *oikizein* (*Resp.* 2.369b9) and elaborated in the *Laws* with the related verb *katoikizein* (*Leg.* 3.702e2)). The leisure and lack of coercion or necessity that mark discursive legislation afford a freeing, and even in moments a ludic,[109] perspective that can be profoundly challenging to existing political constitutions and practices.

This perspective bears on another set of rival interpretative positions that address not Plato specifically but political theorizing more broadly. As framed by Michael Walzer, these positions contrast the "immanent social critic" who criticizes practices and conceptions of their society in the spirit of a participant seeking reform, with the "rejectionist social critic" who positions themselves outside a society and launches their criticism in the name of values that society may not share.[110] Instead of confining Plato to one box or the other, I envisage

107. In *Method and Politics* (161–62), I discuss passages in the *Statesman* that make this point.

108. This is discussed in my "Founding as Legislating," and in Annas's *Virtue and Law*, the original conference versions of which (in Annas's case, in regard to her treatment in that book of the *Republic*) were given independently of each other in 2010 and subsequently discovered by their authors to share much common ground.

109. Dolgert, in "Dungeon Master Socrates," emphasizes the ludic dimension of the *Republic* and other classic texts of political theory (not Platonic ones alone).

110. The contrast was developed in Walzer's *Company of Critics*; it has been influentially deployed in reading Plato, along with other classical Greek authors, by Ober in *Political Dissent*.

him as illustrating the value of complicating the two positions themselves. One may find in Plato *an intermittently rejectionist* stance that is fed by, and comports with, a series of *immanent critiques*.[111] Both dimensions of this stance make use of conventional vocabularies of rule and office while critically examining those ideas and arguing that in the strict sense they must be evaluatively characterized in light of what is truly good. Both dimensions combined enable Plato to propose and test the adequacy of different configurations of rule and office to that strict understanding, while also assessing the flaws in other configurations that can be only loosely described by that vocabulary.

The intermittent rejectionism relates to what was described in chapter 1 as the strict evaluative approach to certain ideas, according to which Plato sometimes (in each of the three dialogues that constitute our main concerns) declares only the ideal X to be an X at all. Sometimes, however, in other moods, he is entirely willing to use existing ideas (and vocabulary) as they are already circulating, or with only limited reconstruction in order to appropriate them for his own purposes. Nevertheless, in key moments, the internal critique of existing ideas leads to their renovation (having identified the evaluative purposes that the existing practices fail fully to realize, or even tend to betray).[112] It is in this sense that I characterize Plato as a realist in certain respects even as he insists that reality must be recognized to have an evaluative core: meaning that the political ideas of rule and office need to be renovated, and the corresponding roles reconfigured, so as to be adequate to that recognition.

111. I follow Schofield (*Plato*, 54) with respect to these immanent and rejectionist modes in his argument that "some of Plato's complexity comes from his writing now in one mode, now in the other, and sometimes in a style which simultaneously reflects *both* perspectives" (emphasis original; see also 81 and passim), and would add that these dynamics within the Platonic texts themselves help in part to explain the similar dynamics animating the extraordinarily wide and varied range of Platonic receptions, which I surveyed selectively in *Plato's Progeny*. However, I diverge in the present work fundamentally from another of Schofield's central claims: that Plato "shows comparatively little interest in constitutional theory or practice at any stage in his life" (*Plato*, 61).

112. I take heed of observations made by René de Nicolay and Emily Hulme in a panel that they proposed and cofacilitated at the Society of Classical Studies Annual Meeting in 2021 (in which I participated), pointing out that whereas Walzer's idea of "immanent critique" presupposes the calling of a society to account against standards that it already in some sense acknowledges, Plato's version of critique involved a renovation and reconfiguration of such standards in profound ways—as indeed the present work seeks further to show.

PART II

Reconfigurations of Rule and Office

CHAPTER THREE

Rule and the Limits
of Office (*Laws*)

Who of the officeholders will be sufficient to the task of being a straightener, should one of them, as someone might say, be crooked, being bent
out of shape in performing their office? That is to say, who would have
the power to make someone so lacking worthy of their office? For it is
far from easy to find an officeholder exceeding the other officeholders
(*tōn archontōn archonta*) in virtue, yet we must seek to identify such a
god-like straightener. (*Leg.* 12.945b5–c2)[1]

With these words, the Athenian Visitor in Plato's *Laws* introduces a political conundrum that would later became proverbial in a phrase from Juvenal's sixth satire: *Sed quis custodiet ipsos custodes*, commonly translated as
"But who shall guard the guardians?"[2] Plato's anonymous Athenian goes on

---

1. In Schofield's *Plato: The "Laws,"* the Schofield/Griffith translation of the words
tōn archontōn archonta is "a ruler of rulers," which is of course an option in line with the
understanding of rule proposed in the present work as including office as a kind of rule.
But the paradox of having to choose a group of officeholders by some variation on the procedures of lottery and election from a shortlist, which the Athenian has just mentioned for
choosing the officeholders so far created ("in speech") in the dialogue, counts in favor of my
more specific translation of "officeholders" instead (incorporating the limits and controls
that characterize this as a kind of rule, as argued in part I). All quotations from Plato in
this chapter are from the *Laws* (*Leges* in Latin, hence the standard abbreviation *Leg.* [or,
in some reference systems, *Lg.*]) according to the OCT, and in my own translation, unless
otherwise indicated.

2. Juvenal, 6.347–48. In the original domestic, patriarchal, and misogynistic context of
the poem, Braund (*Juvenal and Persius*, 266–67) translates the phrase as "But who's going
to chaperone the chaperones themselves?"

to propose that he and his fellow elderly legislators "in speech,"[3] the Spartan Megillus and the Cretan Cleinias,[4] who in this moment of the dialogue are engaged in a periodically resumed project of laying down laws "in speech" with a new pan-Cretan *polis* (to be named Magnesia) in mind,[5] address the Juvenal conundrum by establishing in the proposed constitution a collective office of auditors (*euthunoi*).[6]

The role of auditors to conduct the accountability procedures for other officeholders, procedures standardly known as *euthunai*, was one that, as shown in part I, was common to classical Greek constitutions (and not only to democratic ones), though not everywhere conducted by officeholders with such a neatly corresponding name as the Visitor adopts here.[7] Indeed, the Platonic legislators "in speech" in the *Laws* will adopt not only a version of the office of auditors but also a remarkably wide range of offices (some invented, some adapted from one or other actual Greek constitution) to populate the constitution that they outline. Each of these offices is marked by some version of all or almost all of the general characteristic features of office belonging to the family of parameters identified in part I: these included characteristic powers; age requirements and term limits; selection procedures involving lottery, election, or both, which are elaborated in the *Laws* in some cases in highly complex combinations; and specific audit mechanisms (standardly

---

3. The role of legislation "in speech," as contrasted with "in deed," in Plato, in both the *Laws* and *Republic*, was discussed in chapter 2.

4. I follow the standard practice of referring to the Athenian as "the Athenian Visitor" or simply "the Visitor" (when discussion of the *Laws* is the context, as opposed to the Eleatic Visitor of the *Statesman*), despite the fact that the other two characters are themselves (and are initially addressed by the Athenian as) also "visitors (*xenoi*)" to the particular locale of the dialogue's Cretan setting (1.624a1). Cleinias and Megillus are presumed to be characters invented by Plato; they are unattested outside this dialogue.

5. I explain further below the sense in which the constitution "in speech" both is and is not addressed to the proposed new colony of Magnesia; to indicate this, I sometimes speak of it as a constitution "for Magnesia" rather than "of Magnesia," though even "for Magnesia" is shorthand for the more complex dramatically envisaged status of the constitutional project of the dialogue.

6. Because Juvenal's words have become a standard way of articulating the political problem of who can guard the guardians, I use "the Juvenal conundrum" to label (anachronistically) that problem as tackled by Plato, as was explained in chapter 1.

The *euthunoi* are called by Stalley and Saunders, in their respective works on the dialogue, the "scrutineers," but in the terminology of the present book, that term risks confounding what I have called the "scrutiny" function of *dokimasia* with the "audit" function of *euthunai*.

7. Morrow (*Plato's Cretan City*, 219) notes that this was true in Athens, Sparta, Crete, and all Greek constitutions "except the most extreme oligarchies," though he also observes there that the members of the *gerousia*, or council of elders, in both Sparta and Crete were exempt from *euthunai*, and that "the kings at Sparta, as well as the holders of lifelong offices elsewhere, seem also to have been exempt."

called *euthunai*), to enforce accountability. The offices of Magnesia are notably also universally subject to the additional feature of *dokimasia* (the pre-
officeholding scrutiny), which was found almost exclusively in Athens at the
time of Plato's writing.[8]

The *Laws* envisages a variegated constitutional landscape of offices, and,
moreover, of offices that are explicitly established and defined by laws, in
contrast to the customary evolution of offices, which had attracted haphaz-
ard formal legal regulation in many Greek constitutions. It also makes distinctive use of further familiar, though not universal, features of existing
Greek offices. For example, oaths, invoking potential divine sanction, are to
be employed, though not in all the circumstances in which they were used
in existing constitutions.[9] Conversely, wages (an occasional but decidedly not
universal parameter of office at the time) are not to be paid to any officeholder
in the constitutional project of this dialogue—in stark contrast to the constitutional project of the *Republic*, as discussed below in chapter 6. The absence
of wages was more characteristic of oligarchic constitutions (which relied on
officeholders who were wealthy enough to have private means) than of democratic constitutions (which were divided, as was democratic Athens itself from
one time period to another, as to whether or not to pay wages for officeholding
and other civic roles).

In short, the constitutional framework of rule through officeholding, as
developed in the *Laws*, would have been relatively familiar to Plato's initial
readers. It consists in limits and controls that were broadly characteristic, in
varying respects, of existing Greek offices, though varied in terms consistent
with the family-resemblance approach taken in this book to the identification
of offices as such. And these limits and controls are set out by law, which is
analyzed according to the dialogue's "double theory" of law, noted briefly in
chapter 2, in which law in a narrow sense, consisting of an impersonally issued
conditional order (backed by coercive force), is prefaced by a persuasive
prelude. These officeholders are subject to accountability that is expanded
both horizontally and vertically (a metaphor unpacked below) by means of

8. Morrow (*Plato's Cretan City*, 217) observes that there are four procedures of *dokimasia* described in detail for various offices in the constitution for Magnesia, and infers
that every officeholder is to be subjected to *dokimasia* before being allowed to take up
their office. However, his additional suggestion there, that the Visitor evinces "an intention to use this procedure [sc. *dokimasia*] to establish also the special competence of the
individuals for the office concerned" is misleading, since what is being tested in most cases
is their general virtue rather than any "special" competence (albeit that, as he also notes,
the *dokimasia* of the officeholders charged with overseeing civic music involves testing the
extent to which the candidates are experienced [6.765b1]).

9. The Visitor proposes to ban the use of oaths in contexts in which people stand to
make private gains, so as not to tempt anyone to offer oaths without the intention of keeping them, or simply to break them, in either case incurring impiety.

institutions and procedures that build on (while reconfiguring) a range of existing models. These changes are all directed to the end of intensifying and expanding the controlled and limited exercise of rule through political office.

While the *taxis* of this constitution would have been broadly recognizable in its outline to Plato's contemporaries (albeit containing novel aspects), the dialogue's explicit statement of a *telos* for that constitution would not have been. To be sure, the content of that *telos*, the cultivation of virtue in the citizens,[10] was broadly traditional and shared at a pan-Hellenic level.[11] Yet the dialogue's explicit statement of virtue as the goal of the constitution contrasts with the aims of existing Greek constitutions having been at best implicitly stated, and when reconstructed from their offices and procedures (as done above in part I), primarily limited to avoiding corruption and incompetence rather than to achieving a full positive ideal of virtue.[12]

The implicit orientation of every constitution to some *telos* is brought out when Cleinias explains Cretan customs on the assumption that the historical Cretan lawgiver, Minos, had "looked toward (*pros touto blepōn*)" a specific purpose (in my parlance a *telos*, though no noun is supplied here) in framing them (1.625e1–2).[13] This means that those studying legislation, as the Athenian and his companions begin by doing, must start by inferring the putative purpose of a given lawgiver from the character of their laws. Moreover, in issuing laws, whether "in speech" or in actuality, a lawgiver or group of lawgivers must act so as to realize such a postulated purpose. Unlike existing Greek laws and constitutions, which seldom set out the overarching aim of their piecemeal procedural (and less often substantive) dicta, Plato in the *Laws* makes the purpose of legislation—specifically, the promotion of virtue in the citizens— central and explicit in his analysis of the figure of the lawgiver and the nature and role of both law and rule.

---

10. 1.630c1–4, 631a5–6; 12.963a1–10, a passage in which Cleinias summarizes the claim, adding that *nous* (reason) is the leading virtue of the standard four virtues; and passim.

11. The Athenian will argue, however, that the Spartan and Cretan constitutions cultivated too narrow a range of (primarily militaristic) virtues, while implicitly suggesting that full cultivation of virtue would require a more comprehensive set of both formal and informal means to realize it than did the Athenian constitution. As to the dramatic date of the *Laws*, the dialogue must be set sometime in the late fifth century, as it is not innocent of the Peloponnesian War, pace Zuckert (*Coherence*, 52–58); on the contrary, tactics used by the Athenians in this war are mentioned at 4.706b7–c7, as shown by Altman in "Tale" (261n154).

12. The Spartan and Cretan constitutions were exceptions in this regard, but their focus on virtue was as primarily achieved through education, rather than through the offices and procedures more generally; and Plato's Athenian Visitor argues that they too did not aim at the whole of virtue, only a martial subset thereof.

13. Minos was a legendary human king of Crete, believed to have been a son of the god Zeus; the Athenian obtains the agreement of his Cretan interlocutor, Cleinias, that Zeus had issued regular pronouncements that the king then laid down as laws: 1.624a7–b3.

A full conception of virtue for Plato always includes an epistemic dimension; wisdom is both one of the cardinal virtues and required to achieve any of the others. In the constitution of the *Laws*, that epistemic dimension of wise expertise will be embodied within the laws, which serve as a static content-repository of the *telos* of good rule, while virtuous agency will be embodied in the persons of the officeholders, who are selected for excelling in just that quality. Election (supplemented at strategic points by lottery) is used in a complex variety of ways to choose the best people to serve as officeholders. Their superior degree of virtue is presumed to be recognizable by their fellows, having been cultivated through education since childhood and practiced in various contexts of work, ritual, and play, involving not only cognitive but also motivational and physical attainments.[14] Yet these officeholders receive no special education for their offices, nor are they for the most part chosen or held to be epistemically especially suited. Instead, they are to rely on the general education shared by all citizens of Magnesia, itself shaped by and imparting the divine reason embodied in the laws, to guide and direct them.

At the same time, the dialogue demonstrates the limits of officeholding alone in seeking to achieve fully the purpose of rule. On the one hand, the dialogue cannot dispense with the task of safeguarding the virtue of the officeholders altogether. To begin with, the constitutional ball has to get rolling: some group needs to identify the initial holders of office, as will be detailed below in discussing the transitional arrangements for the vital office of the law guardians (*nomophulakes*). After that the regular processes of sortition and election among various subsections of the citizen body themselves will be relied upon to fulfill the identification of suitable officeholders going forward, even though these will not be guided by expert knowledge. On the other hand, in the absence of fully expert ideal rulers, the institutions and procedures of officeholding are able to achieve the *telos* of rule for the good of the citizens only insofar as, and because, they are governed by reason embodied in the laws.

The laws serve to safeguard the rule by officeholders in two respects. First, they incorporate the content of reason, so that the directives that they embody are oriented to a proper understanding of the *telos* of rule (the good of the ruled). And second, they structure the epitactic decisions that officeholders are empowered to take, by setting out a framework of orders involving conditional

---

14. At a later point in book 1, the Athenian highlights the insufficiency of expert knowledge alone, in the form of distinctive *epistēmai*, in making someone a good ruler. If a ship's ruler possesses the expertise of navigation but is prone to seasickness, or if a general possesses the *epistēmē* of war making but is cowardly in the face of danger, the Athenian avers, he will not be a good "ruler" (*archōn*, 1.639a9, b5; *archein*, b6). Seasickness is an interesting way to depict a constitutional unsuitability to rule, as it involves a lack of bodily stamina and resilience; both the *Laws* and the *Republic* argue that a certain kind of bodily constitution is necessary for the development of both moral and epistemic virtues, both of which are in turn required for virtue tout court.

coercive threats. The Visitor sums up the role of law that he recommends by proposing how both this city and its officeholders should be named. The city should be given "the name of the god who is in truth master of those who are reasonable" (4.713a3–4), a remark that has led to the glossing of this constitution as a "noocracy" (a constitution in which reason is in power).[15] And the Visitor remarks on the fact that, within it, those who are conventionally called the "rulers" or (to translate more specifically in context) "officeholders" (*tous . . . archontas*) should in the constitution for Magnesia be called "servants of the laws," and even be envisaged as "slaves" to the law, which is to be conceived as their "master" (4.715c6–d1, d4–5).[16] In the *Laws*, it is only when conceived (and so presumably conceiving of themselves) as subordinates of the law that those who rule can ensure (to the extent possible) that their rule is oriented to the good of the ruled.

The primary mode in which laws are issued within the dialogue is in the mode of what was described more fully in part I of this study as legislators acting "in speech." At the end of book 4, the Athenian and his interlocutors constitute themselves in this role, and so from time to time in the course of the rest of the work will issue laws for a constitution "in speech," with the proposed new daughter *polis* of Magnesia in view (when they adopt its geographical parameters to inform their exercise, for example), but without the coercive force of enacting actual legislation for that new *polis*. The illocutionary force that they exercise in so doing is both fictional and speculative, being leisured in a way that actual (even fictionally actual) legislators cannot be, and being free of any use of actual (that is, fictionally actual) coercive force.[17] (In contrast, the role of actual lawgiving is reserved for the fictional legislative commission being set up for the colony of Magnesia by the Cnossians, citizens of the *polis* charged by the rest of Crete with this responsibility, on which Cleinias discloses that he has been invited to serve.)[18] The interlocutors frame their

---

15. See also 12.957c5–7.

16. Compare the "terms of address" proposed for the rulers and subjects in *Republic* book 5, discussed below in chapter 6.

17. In "Persuasion et force" (189–90 and passim), I emphasized the leisure of the legislators "in speech" as contrasted with the pressure of the temporal and other necessities under which actual legislators "in deed" must labor, as in 9.857e10 (cf. 10.887b4–5). In that paper, I engaged with a number of works by André Laks on this question, including "Legislation and Demiurgy" and "Utopie législative de Platon"; in the chapters in part IV, below, I respond to his most recent engagement, in *Plato's Second Republic*, which has been shaped in turn by responding to my own prior and current work on this question.

18. While the interlocutors are not actually engaged in framing laws to be issued to this particular colony (a task that will rather be undertaken by the Cnossian-led legislative commission on which Cleinias has been asked to serve, and to which as the dialogue ends he proposes also to conscript the Athenian Visitor), the philosophical constitution that they delineate has that colony in view in terms of its site, population, and founding conditions. So, while the discursively framed constitution is not to be laid down in actuality, exactly as

own proposed laws in terms of a conditional epitactic structure: according to the dialogue's "double" theory of law, each law consists of a coercive threat, prefaced by a persuasive prelude (*prooimion*, a term alternatively translated as "preamble").[19] This applies even to the laws establishing the constitutional order of offices in book 6 (which must be organized and obeyed on pain of coercive enforcement), and it is this order of offices that is the focus of the remainder of this chapter.[20]

I do not provide a comprehensive account of the complex scheme of offices for Magnesia or its relationship to existing offices at the time in various Greek constitutions. That work has been done by others, above all Glenn Morrow, on whose shoulders this work stands.[21] Neither do I propose an overall interpretation of the dialogue, which would require reconsideration of further topics, including its psychology of human nature, its theology, the ideas of the mixed constitution and the middle or mean constitution, and other themes.[22] Instead, I focus primarily on three specific roles within the constitution of Magnesia as a means of discussing three aspects of the renovation, and reconfiguration, of office and rule within it.

These three roles are prefaced by presentation of some of the dialogue's analysis of rule and its relationship to office in the abstract. Having shared these points, I return to the Juvenal conundrum, fleshing it out in terms of the dialogue's broader discussion of accountable rule, before describing how the resultant aspiration to accountability all the way down (or up, as it were) is resolved through the extraordinary provisions made for the office of the auditors (*euthunoi*). Next, I describe the role of the *nomophulakes* and how

---

so framed, for the new colony, its framing does have Magnesia in view, pace Bartels's *Plato's Pragmatic Project* (126 and passim).

19. The "double" approach is contrasted with a "simple" approach, initially in describing two kinds of doctors (4.720b8–e6) and then applied to legislation from 4.720e6–7, with a reprise in book 9. I return to this topic in part IV.

20. The Visitor turns to the "establishment of office" in the city in book 6 (751a–2). He had anticipated this task in book 5's identification of "two kinds (*eidē*)" in the "order" (*kosmos*: like *taxis*, a word for an ordered system) of a constitution (*politeia*): "the one being the establishment of office (*to archōn*) [sc. by distributing it] to each [sc. officeholder]; the other being the giving of the laws to the officeholders" (5.735a5–6), in which I take *to archōn* to refer to the abstract idea of office, on the cusp of being converted from rule into individual offices, which are only then available for distribution to individuals who will hold them. In making these laws establishing the offices the first to be enacted (in the leisured, noncoercive mode of discursive legislation), Plato asserts a conceptual priority for offices in articulating a constitution that would become a standard understanding in the hands of Aristotle.

21. Morrow, *Plato's Cretan City*. See also the focused summary in Reid's "Offices of Magnesia," and the discussion interwoven in Schöpsdau's *"Nomoi" (Gesetze)*, especially in the volume on books 4–7 in commenting on book 6.

22. For a persuasive overall interpretation (itself, of course, selective in light of the great length of the dialogue), see Laks's *Plato's Second Republic*.

their selection is to be handled, especially during the initial establishment of the new *polis*, when the procedures of selection for the offices generally have not yet reached their steady-state reliability. The *nomophulakes* are also highlighted in my story for another reason: if one may think of the auditors as guarding the virtue of their fellow officeholders, the *nomophulakes* are to guard the role of the laws, modifying them in detail when necessary (though they receive no specialized education in order to do so).

Finally, I discuss a third role that will be set up by law within the constitution, but which (I argue) is not an office in the dialogue's own terms, nor in those typically expected of offices at the time. This is the role of the group often called in English the "Nocturnal Council,"[23] to which I instead refer for reasons explained below as the "Daily Meeting," and which I argue plays a distinct role of safeguarding the philosophical understanding of the constitution more broadly that the legislators would ideally have had. The chapter concludes by underscoring both the achievements and the limitations of a constitution that seeks to carry out the *telos* of rule primarily by means of laws and accountable offices (encompassing the orders that their holders are empowered to issue, within the ordered limits defining the offices themselves), without any figures comparable to the superordinate rulers who stand apart from subordinate officeholders in the *Statesman* and *Republic*. Rule in and through office and law, and the limits thereof, is the project of the *Laws*.

The Need for Office

In book 9, the Athenian explains that in continuing their program of legislation "in speech," he and his interlocutors should preface the laws to be issued on the subject of violent harm with general remarks about the purpose of law and its relationship to knowledge.[24] The reason (*aitia*) that laws must be laid down and that humans must live in accordance with them, if they are to distinguish themselves from wild beasts, is that "no human being grows up with a nature sufficient for them to grasp what benefits humans in living in a constitution, and, having grasped it, to be capable always of realizing the best and of being willing so to act" (9.875a1–4).

---

23. Though eventually he specifies that the group should begin meeting at dawn, the Athenian nevertheless twice uses the definite description "the group meeting at night," at 10.908a3–4 and 12.968a7, giving rise in relatively recent scholarship to the name "Nocturnal Council," though this is misleading in several respects, as explained further below.

24. While the language characterizing the preludes in the context of the "double theory of law" in book 4 (reiterated elsewhere in book 9) is not used here, the adjective *prorrhēteon* (9.874e7–8) alludes to it, as does an earlier use of the same term in the same book of the dialogue (9.854a3–5), which in featuring the technical term *prooimia* from the introduction of the theory in book 4, leaves no doubt as to which previous *logos* is being invoked.

The Visitor's proposed prelude to the laws of wounding goes on to identify two "difficulties," which together (he implies) explain why this *aitia* obtains. The first difficulty lies in:

> discerning (*gnōnai*) that with genuine political *technē*, one must care (*melein*) not for what is private but what is common (*ou to idion alla to koinon*). (9.875a5–6)[25]

And the second lies in the asserted fact that:

> even if someone were naturally to discern (*to gnōnai*) these things sufficiently by means of *technē*, and ruled (*arxēi*) in a city as someone unaccountable and autocratic (*anupeuthunos te kai autokratōr*), he would not ever be able to maintain his beliefs and use his power to nurture what is common to the city, but would rather pursue the private over the common, and his mortal nature would always drive him to act according to acquisitiveness (*pleonexia*) and self-servingness (*idiopragia*). (9.875b1–7)

The first of these two quotations establishes the purpose of political expertise as being inherently oriented toward caring for what is common or public (the role of caring for the public being closely reiterated as central to political expertise in the *Statesman*, as shown in chapter 4, below), using a verb that underscores that this is, however, difficult to discern in concrete cases. A form of the same verb is used in the second quotation, in which (in a complex and much-debated sentence) the Visitor asserts that even if someone were to succeed in discerning this *telos* of rule (as I would describe it), if they were to find themselves in the role of unaccountable ruler (*anupeuthunos*), that person would be driven by human nature to pursue a *telos* of private rather than public good.[26] The implication is that while human nature would drive pursuit of such an improper *telos* (for a ruler) even in someone fully possessed of political knowledge, what would allow them to actually carry out that wrongful purpose would be the absence of any accountability procedures or institutions.

---

25. In this and the following passage, I translate *gnōnai* and *to gnōnai* in the language of "discerning," a translation echoing my translation of *gnōstikē* in the *Statesman*, as offered in chapter 4. The underlying verb is *gignōskein*, which often has the sense of coming to know through grasping something perceptible, which "discerning" can in English connote.

26. Neither difficulty can be conceived as purely epistemic, as if that were separable from motivational force. Rather, both hinge on the complex interplay between coming to grasp something epistemically and coming to care about it appropriately, an interplay that hinges on the "irrational (*alogōs*)" promptings of pain and pleasure that (the Visitor goes on to assert) characterize human nature. In "Self-Knowledge," I have argued that full epistemic understanding for Plato (there focusing on the *Protagoras* and *Republic*) necessarily brings with it appropriate motivation and disposition to action; in "Value of Knowledge" I have argued similarly for the *Statesman*.

In other words, the prediction about the effects of mortal nature implies that the kind of rule suitable to the discursive constitution is that of office, which is (as argued throughout this work) precisely the constitutional form of rule that is typically subjected to some subset of a family of limiting parameters including audit, term limits, selection procedures, and others detailed earlier in this study. In the *Laws*, as in most Greek constitutions of the time, audit and accountability are the most prominent of these parameters (though in the constitutional project of the *Republic*, the configuration of parameters of what are called "offices" is very different, as argued in chapter 7). Because unaccountable (*anupeuthunos*) rule would pervert the *telos* of rule away from serving the public or common good toward private gain, establishing the characteristic limits of office—including (but not confined to) the audit procedures (*euthunai*)—can safeguard the *telos* of rule from such perversion. The *taxis* of constitutional ordering is meant to orient officeholders to the proper *telos* of rule, tested as the good of the ruled. Accountable officeholders, when coupled with laws incorporating a wise knowledge of that good and with additional figures who can safeguard the spirit of these laws, suffice in this dialogue to attain the *telos* of rule. Indeed, the law itself is described (figuratively) as a master, as noted above, and laws as rulers, in a passage to which I now turn.

A description of the laws as "rulers" is incorporated into a caveat that the Visitor immediately issues to his predictive claim, asserting that:

> If ever by divine fate a person were born with a nature sufficiently able to manage power, there would be no need for laws to be rulers (*tōn arxontōn*) over him. (9.875c3–6)

Can such an eventuality be expected ever to obtain? The Visitor comments enigmatically that "now (*nun*) no such person is to be found anywhere," adding the caveat "*all' ē kata brachu*" (9.875d2–3), the interpretation and translation of which are the subject of a heated debate, on which the larger issue of the political perspective of the dialogue hinges. Following Jacques Brunschwig, André Laks suggests translating this caveat as "except for a short time," meaning that while some such person might contingently arise, they would not be able to sustain an uncorrupted exercise of power.[27] For my purposes, the scope of that possibility, and the meaning of its exclusion from the "now" of the post-heroic human epoch, is less important than the subsequent specification of what is announced as the "second-best choice" (*to deuteron haireteon*) for

---

27. See Laks, *Plato's Second Republic*, 47–48, 48n44, adopting and discussing a translation suggested by Brunschwig ("Rule and Exception," 131n24); as Laks recounts, Brunschwig there further observes that the sense of the expression here is "temporal" rather than "quantitative," with the passage overall pointing to "inevitable corruption" due to "an incompatibility in principle, not between human nature and possession of the kingly science, but between human nature and durable possession of that science."

politics—namely, that of "order [*taxis*] and law [*nomos*]" (9.875d3–4).[28] This makes clear that the political constitution is to be understood in terms of its *taxis*—the order of offices, as well as the laws governing the role relationships among officeholders and citizens—that enables the overall *telos* of virtue of the citizens (constituting their true good) to be pursued.

In contrast to the hypothetical case of someone who might (not) be able to safely rule unaccountably (*anupeuthunos*) without the constraints of law, the constitutional project of the dialogue involves issuing laws to establish and be enforced by accountable officeholders. The achieving of accountability is not confined to the *euthunai* (audit procedures) that incorporate it by name, nor to the auditors (*euthunoi*) who carry them out. As argued below, the accountability of the *euthunoi* themselves is to be carried out through a vertical extension of accountability embedded partly in a broader form of life, rather than being restricted only to the procedures for *euthunai* applied to them and other officeholders in Magnesia (as in Athens and most other Greek constitutions at the time). It is also carried out through a horizontal extension of accountability, insofar as the imposition of *euthunai* is extended to all (or almost all) judges as well as all officeholders in the constitution.[29] This stands in evident contrast to Athenian democracy at the time, in which the *dēmos*—in their role as jurors and assemblymen—prided themselves on being unaccountable, in contrast to the officeholders who were held accountable by means of the *euthunai* and other procedures for their conduct of office.[30] Yet while some have read the *Laws* in this light as simply antidemocratic in the context of Athens at

28. In the Visitor's formulation in this sentence, *taxis* implies specifically a constitutional order of offices.

29. The two groups are interrelated in their functions, though not identified, at 6.761e5–6: "No judge or officeholder must judge or hold office (*archein*) unaccountably (*anupeuthunon*), except for those who issue final judgments, such as kings"; the last clause, while obscure, perhaps picks up the technical unaccountability of the Spartan kings, who were exempt from *euthunai*, a point that Morrow notes elsewhere (*Plato's Cretan City*, 219), but does not invoke in his reading of the sentence at 250–51 (though I agree with him that the force of the sentence is a general observation rather than a specific point about offices within the Magnesian constitution). Reid ("Changing the Laws," 415n3) suggests alternatively that "the one exception to the audit rule concerns the Guardians of the Law who act as judges for cases where somebody prosecutes a high court judge; this presumably prevents an infinite regress of appeals ([6.]767e3–9)." Note, however, the "almost all" in my text above: this signifies that while the Visitor's dictum applies at least to all judges at the highest level of a complex system of courts, jurors at the lower levels may be exempt from accountability (6.768a5 for wrongs against the public being decided by the general public, 6.768b4–c2 for wrongs against private individuals to be judged by jurors chosen by sortition in tribal courts).

30. The jurors who served in the Athenian *dikastēria* (the popular law courts) were exempt from *euthunai* (so too were the members of the Council of the Areopagus, a body composed of ex-officeholders, who were exempt from being called to account in their role of issuing judicial verdicts in cases of intentional killing and wounding).

the time, I suggest that the moral is more complex. Plato in the *Laws* is by implication testing all existing constitutions against the aspiration to accountable rule that they set themselves, and proposing that this very aspiration would require expanded vertical and horizontal application of accountability (through *euthunai* as well as other institutional means), together with knowledge of the true good embodied in the laws, if it is to be fulfilled. The family-resemblance approach to identifying office in Greek constitutions, adopted in this study, affords the latitude for Plato to be understood as reconfiguring various parameters of office in the constitution for Magnesia, while still remaining recognizably within its ambit.

Who Should Hold Office?

Almost as soon as he has mooted the constitutional laws establishing the offices, the Athenian turns to the crucial importance of the quality of the officeholders:

> When a *polis* has been well-prepared, to install unfit officeholders (*archas anepitēdeious*) in relation to laws that have been well-established, is not only to make what has been well-ordained superfluous—not failing to make the whole business into a mockery—but would make them [sc. the unfit officeholders][31] the causes of pretty much the greatest harms and mutilations that can be done to cities. (6.751b5–c2)

The damage that can be done by choosing unfit officeholders had already been graphically described in an important passage in book 4 (715a8–b2),[32] discussed above in chapter 1, which had traced out the consequences for the institutions of office of their being held by those animated by purposes at odds with the proper political *telos* of serving the good of the ruled. As that passage makes clear, officeholders must not be chosen on the basis of zero-sum partisan rivalry, lest they be rendered unfit and unwilling to care for the good of the ruled instead of exploiting the ruled for their own benefit. What, then, are the standards and processes that are proposed by the Visitor to seek to ensure that only those who are fit for office will hold it?

Earlier in the dialogue, a general principle for the quality of officeholders had been announced as their being "wise." But the Visitor had quickly

---

31. Unlike Saunders, I take *autōn* at the end of the sentence (c2) to refer back not to the laws but to the (unfit) officeholders of b7. (Schofield/Griffith takes it to refer generally to the city's appointment of such officeholders rather than to them as individuals, but I think my solution is neater in identifying a specific referent.)

32. Exceptions to this neglect include brief discussions in Meyer's "Two Questions" (tying it to the *Statesman* rather than to Thrasymachus or the *Republic*) and Long's "Political Analysis" (148–51).

explained that this is not a call for the rule of technical experts, but rather of those who avoid the "ignorance" of having their feelings of pleasure and pain diverge from their rational judgments (3.689a1–e2). So the qualification for office is "wisdom" as a virtue, signifying not epistemic excellence alone but also rationally appropriate motivation. However, this qualification must be modified to take account of the claims of wealth, not absolutely but to the calculated and measured extent necessary to avoid civic discord, a modification rooted in the reasons of human nature for allowing private property for all in the constitution in the first place.[33] Property classes accordingly play a role in some of the selection procedures and in some cases for the eligibility to hold particular offices (variously, for members of the council, temple treasurers, city wardens, market wardens, and officers of athletic competitions) and in assigning penalties for nonattendance at the assembly. These measures are designed to promote, though not to guarantee, the selection of officeholders who will be virtuous and wise in the appropriate sense.

While selection of officeholders is one dimension of an officeholding constitution, it must be complemented by the procedures to hold them accountable, and so seek to ensure that the virtue with which they (it is expected) begin is not corrupted during their time in office. And while all of the offices play their part in ensuring that rule in Magnesia would not be *anupeuthunos*, the central role in doing so is to be played by the *euthunoi*—who, in order to solve the Juvenal conundrum, must then be made accountable themselves. To that solution I now turn, in describing the role of the auditors, both with regard to their holding others accountable and with regard to how they are to be held accountable themselves.

Auditors (Euthunoi)

I suggested above that whereas in existing Greek constitutions audit procedures were standardly directed only at certain kinds of misuse of official powers— primarily, and outside Athens almost exclusively, financial corruption—the *Laws* seeks to connect such procedures and those (the auditors) responsible for carrying them out directly to the positive legislative goal of promoting virtue in the officeholders and the entire citizen body. That elevated role for audit makes the Juvenal conundrum an even deeper one for the *Laws* than it was for existing regimes of constitutional officeholding in Plato's time.

33. Compare 4.715b7–c2, justifying the existence of property classes in relation to officeholding and other political duties-cum-privileges, with the principle of proportionate (in)equality applied to both "honorific civic roles and offices (*tas timas te kai archas*)" at 5.744c2–4. A similar point is made in book 6 (757d5–e6) about the need to incorporate lot, and not only election, into selection procedures, as a matter of loosening the strict proportionate equity that might otherwise become intolerable to citizens.

In democratic Athens, the Juvenal conundrum of how to guard the guardians (that is, in the Athenian context, the officeholders), was addressed routinely and procedurally simply by having the outgoing auditors subjected to *euthunai* conducted by their incoming successors.[34] In the *Laws*, in contrast, this appears not to be nearly enough. Instead, Plato treats the Juvenal conundrum as requiring a solution going beyond the punishments that accountability procedures could typically impose. This is because, consistent with the *telos* of virtue toward which the constitution as a whole is directed, the auditors in keeping others accountable are not merely charged with ensuring the avoidance of malfeasance but rather with ensuring that each officeholder acts virtuously. And that in turn means that the auditors must themselves be superlatively, and securely, virtuous, if they are to be trusted in the role of holding others accountable for the virtuous exercise of office: "it is absolutely necessary that all of the auditors [*hoi euthunoi*] be remarkably and wholly virtuous" (12.945e2–3).[35] How is this remarkable degree of virtue to be ensured?

To incentivize not only avoidance of corruption and other misdeeds but also an extraordinary degree of virtue in those holding the office of auditor, the Visitor begins by instituting a special selection procedure, which, uniquely among all of the roles envisaged for the constitution of Magnesia (whether offices or other civic roles), involves the invention of a new civic cult. A joint cult of Apollo and Helios is to be established and associated with a sacred terrain on which the entire citizenry will meet every year following the summer solstice. In contrast to the selection procedures for many of the other offices, there is no special role in this case for those in the wealthier of the four classes into which the citizenry is to be divided (as the Athenian citizenry had been, it was believed, by Solon). Instead, every single citizen is to nominate three men (all over the age of fifty) to serve as auditors, twelve of whom will be initially elected to serve until they retire, subsequently complemented by three new ones chosen each year. The electoral procedure is complex. All

---

34. In Athens, which uniquely required two stages of accountability, this applied to those officeholders who conducted each of the two stages: the *logistai*, who in the fourth century, at least, carried out the first stage, which was focused solely on financial accounting, and the *euthunoi*, who could at the second stage hear accusations of any kind of malfeasance in office.

35. He says that the role of the *euthunoi* is a key element in whether a *politeia* will be "safeguarded (*sōizesthai*) or destroyed" (12.945c6–d1), because:

> If these officeholders (*archontas*) are better than those whom they straighten out (*exeuthunontes*), and are unblameworthy in their justice, then the whole place and *polis* will thrive and prosper. But if the audit procedures (*tas euthunas*) of those officeholders go otherwise, then the justice uniting the whole political class is destroyed, and by this means all of the rule is scattered into different places, and no longer aligned in the same direction, such that they make the *polis* from one into many, filling it with the *stasis* which will quickly destroy it." (12.945d1–e2)

citizens vote on the initial list of nominated candidates (a procedure that must assume substantial convergence in the nominations), half of whom (those who had received the fewest votes) are thereby eliminated; a second vote is held to choose and rank the top three from the remaining half of the original list.[36]

While there is no special education to prepare anyone to serve as an auditor, the common education of all of the citizens in virtue is to be carried out as prescribed by the laws, which embody a rational understanding of what is good. And while the resulting virtuous conduct should be widely shared, exceptional levels of virtue can be expected to be visible in exceptional conduct (the fear of secret misconduct being allayed by the underlying good education itself). This fosters the role of electoral procedures in seeking to select candidates of exceptional virtue, when supplemented by the cultic context, which would be expected to foster an exceptional spirit of civic dedication and solemnity in those participating in the election process. In contrast, the *nomophulakes*—the guardians of the laws, whose distinctive office and its role in the constitution will be discussed later in this chapter—will be chosen in a more complex procedure involving a period of public review of each person's nominations in advance of the next round of voting. But they too receive no specialized education to prepare for their roles.

For the auditors, as for all of the other officeholders in the constitution for Magnesia, the selection mechanism is only half of the equation for ensuring virtue.[37] The other half consists of accountability. In considering how this is

36. Reid ("Offices of Magnesia," 587) notes that in the first round of voting, "if the number [of total candidates divided by two] is an odd number, the one with the least number of votes is removed; if it's a tie, the younger of the candidates is removed," while in the second (and final) round, "if there is a tie, the ranking is determined by lottery." In a discussion focused on the similar procedure for the election of the *nomophulakes*, Landauer ("Drinking Parties Correctly Ordered") has advanced an illuminating analysis of its public and iterative nature, which (as he notes) applies to the election of the *euthunoi* as well. He argues that the public nature of the voting (signed ballots) in this nonsimultaneous, iterative procedure serves to "harness . . . coordinating effects," allowing the citizens to be influenced by the arguments of others ("influence . . . exercised by the exemplarity of the vote"), with time to be swayed by initially minority opinions when recognized (as encouraged by their carefully designed educational formation) to be those of the most virtuous among them. This public and iterative process is necessary for elections in which all citizens are to take part, as a way of coordinating and harnessing their varied degrees of virtue.

37. A different, more restricted process of election is used for the choice of the single "superintendent of education." (I prefer "superintendent" to "minister," as scholars including Landauer and Stalley translate, as the latter might imply a form of parliamentary cabinet governance that is belied by the relative independence [typical of Greek constitutions at the time] of the various officeholders in their assigned roles.) This officeholder "must be at least fifty years old, the father of legitimate children and a guardian of the laws," and is to be elected by all the other officeholders excluding the members of the council for a five-year term of office (Stalley, *Introduction to Plato's "Laws,"* 189). Of this case, Landauer ("Drinking Parties Correctly Ordered") argues that the use of a single secret ballot in this context,

to be achieved for the auditors, Plato's Athenian begins by seeming to treat it as a further occasion for the standard auditing procedure applicable to all other officeholders, asserting: "Now it is necessary to hear about the audits [*tas euthunas*] of these [sc. the *euthunoi*] themselves, what those will be and in what manner they will be done" (12.946e4–5). What follows on this assertion, however, is anything but a description of a standard audit.[38] Instead, the Athenian describes rewards, many of them unique to this office, to be given to these officeholders both in life and in death. Among these rewards are being granted front-row seats at all civic festivals; being crowned with laurel (to be given to no one else in the city); being made priests of Apollo and Helios in the new civic cult involved in their selection procedure, with the auditor who is ranked first of the three selected each year being made the chief priest and also given another honor, described below;[39] and being given unique funeral rites, including hymns, a prescribed special procession, a particular kind of tomb, and annual memorial games as a festival celebrating the departed auditors.

During their year in office, the auditor awarded the first prize is to serve not only as the chief priest of the Apollo and Helios cult, but also as the eponymous officeholder of the city: the eponymous officeholder being the one whose name is given to the year in which they serve so as to date it in an official civic calendar, as in most Greek constitutions. In Athens, the eponymous archon was the king-archon, believed to be the direct inheritor of some of the key powers of the legendary ancient kings of the city (albeit powers now bridled and controlled through the institutional limitations of office); the honor of giving his name to the calendar year in one of the city's calendars marked the high epitactic standing of such an office. In contrast, in the *Laws*, the Athenian Visitor proposes that it should be the top-ranked auditor who plays this

---

in contrast to the iterative public one for the boards of officeholders described above, is a function of the presumed exceptionally high level of virtue among the electors in this case—restricted as they are to the magistrates who have themselves emerged from complex processes of the kind stated above or other related procedures. As he observes: "When the pool of voters is restricted to the magistrates there is no need for multiple rounds and publicity. The Stranger instead privileges each voter's independent judgment, secured by the secret ballot. . . . The electors would consist entirely of *kaloi k'agathoi* [the good and virtuous men] who would not *need* to be led by one another's judgments."

38. While Reid ("Offices of Magnesia," 587) takes this sentence (cf. 12.947e6) to mean straightforwardly that "the auditors are also audited themselves," any prospect of punishment for an auditor is to arise not from any routine audit, but rather from the capacity of anyone in the city ("anyone who chooses") to launch a judicial prosecution of an auditor. Such prosecutions will be judged by a court composed of other officeholders, including their fellow auditors (11.947e8–948b2); Schofield (*Plato: The "Laws,"* 443n18) notes that "this is the same court—reinforced by the addition of the other auditors—as would hear charges against citizens accused of the capital offence of temple robbery: see 9.855c."

39. The auditor ranked first is the one receiving the highest number of votes or, in case of a tie, selected by lottery from those in contention.

role. As this unique elevation of the standing of the auditors suggests, Plato in the *Laws* explores the working of a constitution to which accountable officeholding remains central—the standard kind of constitution in ancient Greek *poleis* at the time—while at the same time deepening the meaning of such accountability by tying it not only to negative procedural avoidance of misdeeds but also to the positive achievement of the legislative goal of virtue.

Law Guardians (Nomophulakes)

While the auditors guard the virtue of the other officeholders, the *nomophulakes* play a wide range of roles, including one indicated by their very title of "law guardian," which resonates with those of offices elsewhere, such as the *thesmophulakes* of Elis (*thesmos* being an alternative term for law that was more common in archaic and early classical usage).[40] In an Athenian context, the title as a description of a role resonates with the combined executive and judicial functions that were believed to characterize the Council of the Areopagus, at least as the history and role of that body was construed in the fourth century. Glenn Morrow has observed that the board of thirty-seven *nomophulakes* outlined by the Visitor is to combine what we would today call executive, legislative, and judicial functions (a combination of functions characteristic of many Greek offices at the time, as I remarked in part I).

To outline these functions, following Morrow: the *nomophulakes* are to oversee the conduct of other officeholders, whom they are not unilaterally able to discipline or punish, but whom they can investigate and report to the *euthunoi* or indict in the courts.[41] They are to serve as "high officers on their own account and have special areas of administration," almost always performing these duties collectively.[42] They are to "have important judicial functions"—in particular, being among the members of the high court established as needed to try any auditor (*euthunos*) who may be indicted.[43] And, finally, they are "to act as a kind of legislative commission to revise and supplement the laws formulated by the legislator at the beginning,"[44] being referred to at one point as "*nomothetas te kai nomophulakas*" (lawgivers as well as law

40. Morrow, *Plato's Cretan City*, 210, noting Thuc., 5.47.9 on the *thesmophulakes* of Elis.

41. Paraphrasing Morrow, *Plato's Cretan City*, 198.

42. Morrow, 202. Schofield (*Plato: The "Laws*," 204n13) observes that "maintenance of the land register" is central to the initial presentation of their duties, as is the judicial role of "hearing as a court charges of improper financial gain or property acquisition."

43. Morrow, *Plato's Cretan City*, 203, referring to 12.948a[1–2].

44. Morrow, 200–201. Morrow observes that this is to be a permanent office in Magnesia, as opposed to the post-403 Athenian procedure of selecting boards of *nomothetai* as needed on an ad hoc basis, from the same annually empaneled body of six thousand who had taken the heliastic oath from which the juries for the popular law courts were also selected (Hansen, *Athenian Democracy*, 167–69).

guardians; 6.770a8), in the context of an analogy with painting that makes clear that their legislative role is supplemental only to the role of the original legislators in speech (and will also be time restricted).[45] While the functions combined here go beyond what would today be called executive roles, all of them involve the epitactic role of issuing orders that I have proposed as the speech act paradigmatic of officeholders as such: in this case, issuing indictments of other officeholders; issuing executive orders, as it were, on their own account; issuing judicial verdicts; and even issuing new laws when needed.

In the legislative dimension of their role, the law guardians would take over the role of legislator that would (in the fictional future actuality envisioned in the dialogue) have been carried out by the Cnossian-led legislative commission charged by the pan-Cretan founding group with enacting the laws that set up the constitution of the new *polis*. The laws to be enacted by the members of that commission may, the interlocutors of the *Laws* hope, be informed by the discursive legislation being reasoned out within the dialogue. How, then, are the *nomophulakes* to be educated, identified, and selected to fill this office?

On the one hand, the dialogue of the *Laws* itself is (the Athenian suggests) to form part of the educational curriculum of the new colony.[46] That means that all citizens, including those who will serve as *nomophulakes*, will study its discursive legislation as well as the supplemental conversation about rule, law, and office by which it is informed. On the other hand, no more than the *euthunoi* will the *nomophulakes* receive any specialized education to inform their specific role. Instead, as noted above, they will be chosen in an iterated public electoral procedure, which is arguably designed to harness the virtue present among the wider citizenry.[47]

That is, they would be so chosen within the constitution, if it were once to be up and running (though, again, this is all being presented as a constitution "in speech," not one designed or expected to be enacted exactly in this form).

---

45. 6.755a4–b1 has the relevant restrictions, which are age related: one must be fifty years old or older to become a *nomophulax*; no one can serve as a *nomophulax* for more than twenty years; no one can serve past the age of seventy. The significance of age fifty is marked in the *Republic* as well, where that is the age at which those guardians who have proved themselves worthy are brought to see the Form of the Good and then to undertake the highest role of ruling in the city (*Resp.* 7.540a4–c2; see chapter 7).

46. Nightingale, "Writing/Reading," 289, on 7.811b6–e1.

47. In this case (described at 6.753b1–d6), the voters are to be limited to those who have served in the cavalry or infantry, perhaps in the hope that their military experience will bolster their ability to guard well. They are to go to the most august temple in the state, where each elector puts down a tablet with the name, patronym, tribe, and deme of their preferred candidate, as well as their own. Then, for thirty days, anyone (presumably of those qualified as voters) can remove any tablet with a name to which they object and move it to the *agora*. The citizens then vote and the list is reduced to the top three hundred; a further selection (apparently by the same procedure) reduces these to one hundred; and then a final election to the requisite number of thirty-seven.

However, in this one case, the Athenian also considers the question of transition, as to how the very first officeholders in this role within Magnesia—thinking now of its purported (fictive) future establishment—could be selected. This is an instructive moment for my purposes, since it breaks the dramatic frame separating the founding sponsors of the *polis* (a federation of Cretan cities, among which Cnossos is the most important and has been charged with taking the lead) and its future citizens (albeit that both are still within the dramatic narrative of the founding of Magnesia, separated by a further dramatic frame from the legislators in speech themselves). It suggests, in other words, that a role external to that of any of the citizens within the city is essential in order to safeguard the orientation of the *taxis* of offices to the *telos* of the good of the ruled.[48]

The problem of transition is that the citizens, who will in the steady state of the new *polis* be its electors, brought up under laws and customs that elicit and sustain their virtue, are at the moment of the transition merely a newly assembled group of people from diverse backgrounds (all or most of them Cretan), who are "uneducated" and strangers to one another (6.751c5–d2).[49] As such, they cannot be trusted with choosing the first cohort of *nomophulakes* from among themselves. Instead, to solve this problem, the Visitor turns to "the Cnossians" (meaning, the citizens of Cnossos) to "choose" (*haireisthai*)[50] the thirty-seven members of the initial cohort of *nomophulakes* from two sources: nineteen of those who have already come forward to join the new city, plus eighteen of the Cnossians who are thereby to be drafted to join them as fellow citizens, including (the Athenian proposes), if they can persuade or otherwise forcibly make him do so, Cleinias himself (6.752e4–753a4).[51]

Beyond this explicit selection of the initial group of law guardians, the Cnossians are to identify a larger number from the same two sources—at least one hundred of the new colonists, "the oldest and most virtuous they can find" (so at least minimizing the bad-education problem), in addition to one hundred people (presumably similarly qualified) from among their own ranks—to

48. In fact, there are two such external roles: that of the founder-legislators "in speech," and then that of the founding sponsors of the new *polis* when it is actually founded—that is, actually within the fiction of the dialogue.

49. As noted in chapter 2, however, the colonists are said at 4.707e1–2 to constitute a *leōs*, an archaic ritual way of characterizing a people that might provide some resources to help solve the problem of transition.

50. This is the same verb conventionally used for political elections, as discussed in chapter 4.

51. Cleinias responds by asking why the Athenian and the Spartan Megillus should not also be included, as partners in their *politeia* in speech, but the Visitor demurs on the basis of their respective non-Cretan citizenship (Cleinias being the only Cretan among the three) (all 6.753a5–b1). At the very end of the dialogue, Megillus suggests to Cleinias's approbation that the Visitor must (whether by request or scheming) be made a partner in the founding of the city (the wording indicating now its founding in [fictive] actuality, as opposed to the discursive legislation of a constitution, which had been the project hitherto) (12.969c4–d3).

oversee the initial appointment of the officeholders according to the laws, and their proper scrutiny once selected.[52] In the case of this larger group, the Cnossians involved are not to be coopted permanently as citizens; rather they are to collaborate with their counterparts from the new city in the above task, before returning home.

A final point: the precise language is that the two groups chosen should "join in taking care (*sunepimelēthēnai*)" of the tasks just noted (that the office-holders be appointed according to the laws, and duly scrutinized once having been selected). The language of joint caretaking, or caring, picks up a broader description of the special responsibility of the people of Cnossos for the new city, who are charged with these responsibilities in virtue of their role in "taking care of the young city (*dia tēn epimeleian pros tēn nean polin*)" as if they were its parents (6.754b7–c1). In chapter 4, I shall show that *epimeleia*, or care, and related vocabulary denote in Plato's *Statesman* a key element in the complex of powers characteristic of statecraft and the statesman-cum-king who possesses this ruling expertise, and in chapter 7 that the guardians of the *Republic* are also similarly described as caretakers (using the same as well as other vocabulary). This suggests that the caring role of the people of Cnossos bears a family resemblance to the safeguarding role of the eponymous statesman in the other dialogue. Here, at least, it has been established that while the role of these one hundred Cnossians is related to the place of offices in the constitution, it is not that of holding such an office themselves. Instead, with their partners, who are among the most elderly and virtuous within the new city, they are responsible for overseeing the selection and suitability of those who are to hold the first cohort of offices.

A Role Distinct from Rule and Office:
The "Nocturnal Council" or, Rather, "Daily Meeting"

I turn now to a final role in the city, one that is also to be specified by law, but is not (as I shall argue) characterized as an office. This role is to "safeguard" the laws (translating as "safeguard" a word used as a noun in the Greek (*sōtēria*), and sometimes employing it in English as a corresponding verb). Those persons who collectively fill this role are not the "guardians" of the laws in the sense of having the paired powers to protect them as they are or when necessary to change them,

---

52. 6.754c7–d1 for the final clause of my sentence. The verb *kathistanai*, which is used twice in this context by the Athenian, can refer to the establishment of rule or office, but in the context, in which the appointment of officeholders (by which I mean generically whatever process of selection for each office is prescribed by the constitution) is paired with their subjection to a procedure of *dokimazein* (a cognate of *dokimasia*), the verb is best taken to mean the selection of the *officeholders*, as *office/officeholder* is a meaning that I have argued throughout this work the noun *hē archē* (used here in the plural form *hai archai* at c8) can be used to bear.

powers assigned to the *nomophulakes*, as noted above. Rather, I interpret this remaining role as that of "safeguarding" the constitution by maintaining a living philosophical understanding of it, continuous with that exercised by the legislators in framing it (and by extension with the discursive legislators whose work may have informed it). This living philosophical understanding ensures that the laws can sustainably play the educational role needed to safeguard the whole apparatus of office. While the body in question is often referred to in English as the "Nocturnal Council," I call it instead the "Daily Meeting."[53] Considering its role helps to clarify (by contrast) what the offices of the constitution involve, and how the offices function in conjunction with the laws.

The group that is to meet nightly—or, rather, as the Athenian later clarifies, to convene at dawn and meet into the morning[54]—is briefly introduced in book 10. It is then reintroduced in book 12, without the temporal markers brandished in book 10 (though these reappear later), but rather under the description of "the meeting (*ton sullogon*) that keeps watch (*epopteuontōn*) over the laws." It is to be composed of those who honorably hold or have held a set of other offices or played other roles in the city (along with younger individuals, each coopted by a senior member and approved by all of the latter). As Jeremy Reid summarizes, this group is to be composed of:

(a) the 10 oldest Guardians of the Law,
(b) all citizens who have won awards for excellence (as, e.g., some auditors receive),
(c) those who have been ambassadors to learn about other political systems,
(d) the current Officer [in my parlance, superintendent] of Education and all previous Officers of Education, and
(e) one person aged 30–40, selected by each of the people in (a)–(d) and approved by all of them ([12.]951d6–e5; [12.]961a2–b8).[55]

---

53. Due to similar dissatisfaction to my own with the label of "Nocturnal Council," Laks, in *Plato's Second Republic*, has plumped instead for the "Watch," as suggested to him by Luc Brisson, in order to preserve a singular group referent while also offering a gloss on the function of the body. I was tempted by the label "Vigil" (as suggested by Wintor Scott in a brainstorming session at Princeton in 2019), which prompted me to canvass "Invigilators," but explain below my reasons for adopting the "Daily Meeting" instead.

54. Despite the "nighttime" temporal references in the expressions at 10.908a4–5 and 10.909a3–4 (these being the first two mentions of this gathering) and at 12.968a7, elsewhere the Athenian suggests that in fact the body should meet after dawn (12.951d7–8, 12.961b6–8). The post-dawn timing of the meeting is noted by a number of scholars, including Lewis ("Nocturnal Council," 3n7), who also observes (15n47) that the "Nocturnal Council" kind of formulation is relatively recent and may derive from Victor Cousin's French translation of 1832.

55. The list is a quotation from Reid ("Offices of Magnesia," 589), into which I have introduced the spacing.

The evidence that membership in this group does not constitute holding an office is in my view manifold and decisive, especially when one takes seriously the constitutionally defined structure of officeholding both in Greek polities at the time and in the constitution in speech for Magnesia.[56] A first clue is the fact that, as V. Bradley Lewis has observed, *ho sullogos*, the term used repeatedly by Plato in this context and normally translated into English in this part of the *Laws* as "council," is not the same as the standard name for the regular council (*hē boulē*) used in Athens and in many other democratic and oligarchic *poleis* alike, nor for the council of Magnesia designated by the same term.[57] Instead, as Lewis documents, both in Plato and elsewhere, *sullogos* is most often used of informal gatherings (though sometimes also of a particular kind of meeting of an established body such as an assembly). As the name suggests, then, the daily dawn *sullogos* is not a rival to the Magnesian *boulē*; the word *sullogos* is best taken as putting emphasis on the activity of gathering, nightly or, rather, as I shall say from now on, daily. This is why I translate it for the most part (except when it would be awkward to do so) as "meeting," thinking of it as comparable to the way that the AA (Alcoholics Anonymous) holds a daily meeting, with the emphasis being on each particular convening.[58]

A second clue that membership in this group does not as such constitute holding an office is the contrast with the kind of selection procedure specified for most offices in the constitution for Magnesia, chosen for the most part through a mechanism involving (at least) an election by at least a significant subset of the citizenry. In contrast, the procedure for constituting the membership of this meeting alone allows the senior members to coopt junior ones, subject only to the other senior members' own approval. This cooptation mechanism is almost unparalleled in the selection procedure for offices in the constitution in involving no input for even a relevant subset of the general body of citizens in the selection. For their part, the senior members of the meeting are all (apart from one exceptional subgroup)[59] present or former

56. Reid (568 with n3) is doubtful as to whether they are, qua members of this body, officeholders, arguing subsequently in "Changing the Laws" (426–27) that they are not; Morrow (*Plato's Cretan City*, 500–514) is emphatic that they are not. I take the view that the members of this body do not hold office in the strict sense in serving on it, defended in the main text.

57. Lewis, "Nocturnal Council," 14–15.

58. Lewis (6) nicely picks up on the associated notion of a "practice (*epitēdeuma*)," which is used in the genitive plural at 12.962c6, in making a similar argument for a translation as "gathering" or "meeting," though he clings to the "nightly" temporal marking (14–15). I should note that in the case of the *Laws* the membership and so the attendance of this Daily Meeting is fixed, unlike in the case of AA meetings, which are open to all comers (as I understand it).

59. The exception is the ambassadors, who do not occupy an office within the dialogue (nor did they in democratic Athens). In the *Laws*, they are people with good military records who are chosen and approved by the *nomophulakes*, but whose role of studying

holders of certain offices, who have been subject each to a particular procedure of selection (sometimes involving having received a prize, such as for being the first-ranked auditor in each cohort).

Finally, the lack of any imposition of accountability procedures on the members of this meeting confirms the fact that such membership cannot plausibly be intended to count as an office, neither as offices are presented in the context of the *Laws* nor in terms of the family of parameters informing the understanding of office in Greek polities at the time (though in chapters 6 and 7, I shall suggest that the *Republic* pushes the reconfiguration of office still further in freeing it from such imposition). Every office in Magnesia is to be subjected to accountability—as argued above, even the office of auditor itself (in this case, through a unique mixture of rewards and punishment procedures, rather than a standard procedural audit). By contrast, no mention of accountability is made in the case of this meeting. Its role is rather, as Morrow has called it, an "informal" one, meant to embody a philosophical kind of knowledge and to bring it to bear in the content of the laws when needed.

I suggest that in the broad division of the constitution in book 6 between "offices" and "laws," the Daily Meeting is best understood not as belonging to the domain of the former, but rather as pertaining to the domain of the latter. Its role is related to the laws, without membership in it constituting the holding of an office. Instead, its members are human embodiments of the *nous* (reason) that is otherwise embodied in the laws, inheriting the role of the discursive legislators. But they do not exercise the epitactic role characteristic of officeholders, who issue orders to other persons. Even the task for which purpose the Daily Meeting is initially introduced in book 10, that of meeting regularly for five years with a certain group of avowed atheists who have been confined in a "moderatorium," involves no issuing of orders but, rather, only "consorting" and "admonishing."[60] In that context, their role is quite literally to *meet* with the atheists, in order to pursue the "safeguarding (*sōtēria*)" of their souls (10.909a4–5), an aim that is applied to the role of the Daily Meeting more broadly in book 12 through engaging in dialogue about the theology on the basis of which the constitution is founded.

In the reprise and extension of the role of the Daily Meeting in book 12, only one additional particular task is added to their plate—namely, that of meeting with each "observer of foreign legal usages (*nomima*)" who returns from abroad (12.952b5–7).[61] This task too is characterized in terms of meeting

---

foreign constitutions and meeting with virtuous people abroad involves a direct reporting back to the members of the Daily Meeting, and again involves no power to issue orders to citizens generally of the kind that would characterize office proper.

60. Lewis, "Nocturnal Council." I follow Lewis's translation of the words in quotation marks in this sentence.

61. Morrow, *Plato's Cretan City*, 502–3. One might think that the anonymous Athenian Visitor, who in the drama of the dialogue is visiting Crete and engaging in a conversation

for conversation, in this case for the meeting to learn about anything that the observer has learned from what people abroad have told him, or from what he has "figured out for himself," about "the laying down of laws or about education or upbringing" (12.952b7–9). No action items are attached to this agenda for the members of the meeting other than their judgment of the observer himself, as to whether he is to be congratulated for his energy, awarded honors for his improved virtue, or censured for having become corrupted. In this last case, he is to be isolated from any conversation with anyone else, but if he does not obey "those ruling" in this case and instead engages in conversation that amounts to "meddling in something regarding the educational system or the laws" (12.952c7–d2), he must be referred for trial in the *dikastēria* for a potential sentence of death—failing which referral, a penalty for "those ruling" themselves must be racked up when it comes to competitively assessing their excellence in regard to potential honors (12.952d2–4).[62]

A number of scholars (including Glenn Morrow and Jeremy Reid, whom I otherwise generally follow on the constitution of Magnesia) have suggested that the main point of the reception of the foreign ambassadors is that based on their learning, the Daily Meeting will be empowered to change the laws when necessary.[63] This is not, however, explicitly asserted; on the contrary, the role of supplemental changing of the laws is assigned instead to the *nomophulakes*, as noted above. Rather, the role of the Daily Meeting is to safeguard the laws, as well as other aspects of the city and constitution. This is made especially clear in book 12 with a discussion of the need within the constitution for "the safeguarding [*sōtēria*] of the laws" alongside "the rule of law [*eunomia*] in the souls of the citizens" and "the health and safeguarding [*sōtēria*] of their bodies" (12.960d2–3).[64] That leads the Athenian to compare the function assigned to the Daily Meeting to that of a steersman, general, or doctor,

---

about the benefits and flaws in traditional Cretan and Spartan education with interlocutors representing each of these locales, embodies the kind of ambassador whom the members of the Daily Meeting would send forth and from whose experience (perhaps even detailed in the course of a reported dramatized dialogue) they would learn.

62. The references in this context to "those ruling" (*archontōn*, 12.952d3; *tois archousin*, 12.952c7, 12.952d4) are not to the members of the Daily Meeting itself but, rather, to those officeholders whose job is to give orders of confinement, or to bring court cases against those who have returned corrupted from travels abroad.

63. See Reid's "Offices of Magnesia" (568 with n2) and "Changing the Laws," both of which in fact generally follow and depend upon my own previous work, including the 2018 Carlyle Lectures as written for delivery, in fundamental respects; I follow him here in turn on some matters of detail and analysis.

64. While the word *sōtēria* can be variously translated as "deliverance," "preservation," "security," or "safety," in this context translating it as "the safeguarding" has the advantage of linking it to the verbs used to characterize the nature and purpose of the meeting's activities, such as its role as "anchor" of the *polis* (being imagined as a ship) in "safeguarding (*sōzein*)" everything that the interlocutors could wish.

each of whom aims at "safeguarding" (12.961d1ff.), whether keeping ships and armies in a safe condition in the cases of the captain and general or restoring bodies to a healthy condition in the case of the doctor.[65]

In each of these cases, as in the role of the Daily Meeting in relation to the city as a whole, the aim requires having "understanding [*nous*]" of the entity in question (12.962a7). Whether that understanding is to be deployed so as to maintain the entity in a healthy state or to inform those whose role it is to reconfigure it so as to restore it to such a state is a secondary question. Thus the scholarly debate about whether and how the laws of Magnesia can be changed once the city has been established is orthogonal to Plato's own concerns. The question of the legal mechanism for making changes to the laws when necessary may well have mattered less to Plato than advancing a "spirit of the laws" approach to what such changes would mean and how they should be understood.[66] Similarly, the assertion by the Athenian near the very end of the dialogue, that "if this divine meeting (*ho theios . . . sullogos*) of ours can come into being, then the *polis* must be handed over (*paradoteon*) to it" (12.968b2–3), simply refers in my view to the general transition from the project of discursive legislation to some role within the *polis* once established, rather than specifying exactly what that latter role would entail.[67]

The safeguarding role played by the Daily Meeting, then, is not to solve Juvenal's conundrum by guarding the other officeholders directly, since that problem is solved, as argued above, by the special rewards and procedure for punishment attaching to the auditors. Rather, one might say that it is to serve as the guardians of the *spirit* of the laws in the sense of the constitution as a whole. And, indeed, the language of guardianship (both *phulakes* for guardians and *phulakē* for the abstract role of guarding) dominates the final pages of the dialogue,[68] linked to the language of safeguarding as their

---

65. References to *sōtēria* and cognate words in this passage include 12.961d1, d10, e2, e4; 962a1, b1; cf. the related function of the *phulaktērion* as what Saunders translates as an "organ of protection" (12.962c7).

66. My argument here is informed by and largely consonant with that of Reid in "Changing the Laws."

67. Pace Klosko, "Nocturnal Council." The term *paradoteon* is used in the dialogue also at 7.802e11, referring to how the discursive legislators should present the gendered nature of musical performance in both law and theory, and then, in the formulation *didaskalia kai paradosis* (7.803a1), to how they as legislators should teach and hand on these ideas to those who will live within the colony. At 4.715a1, the Athenian uses *paradotea* in asking to which side of a dispute the discursive legislators should "give" their *polis*; this is the dispute described in book 4 about whether offices should be filled in a rivalrous spirit that was discussed above.

68. *Phulax* appears in some form (singular or plural, sometimes in a compound or cognate) at 12.964b3 [*nomophulax*], b9, c7, c8 (a city that is "unguarded" (*aphulakton*), d3–4, d7 [*phulakē*], e2; 965b8, c10; 966a7, c6, d1 [*nomophulakes*]; 968a6 [*phulakē*], d1 [the nature of guarding, pace Saunders "the office of guardian"]; 969c2.

purpose.[69] While the members of the Daily Meeting are once described loosely as the "guardians of the others," meaning of their fellow citizens (12.964b9), in that same sentence they are also described as "the exegetes, the educators, and the lawgivers" (12.964b8–9). Here the reference to these members of the Daily Meeting as "lawgivers (tous nomothetas)" again has to be interpreted broadly: as I have emphasized, their role is not that of changing the laws (a role that was assigned to the distinct office of the nomophulakes earlier in the dialogue) but rather of sharing the full understanding of the laws that characterizes lawgivers.[70]

It is the specialized education they will receive that will allow the members of the Daily Meeting to guard the laws, by understanding them, and so by extension to serve as guardians of the whole community, safeguarding it in the sense of preserving its animating values. They are to have knowledge of virtue and of the "target" of the statesman, knowledge that is said to be both the basis for calling anyone a "ruler" and necessary for carrying out the role of safeguarding.[71] And this is to come from epistemic training, an education that will give them, just as it would "a really skilled craftsman or guardian in any field," the ability "not merely to see the many individual instances of a thing, but . . . to win through to a knowledge of the single central concept": in this case, a full understanding of the common definition and nature of the four virtues qua virtue (12.965c9–e5). This education requires knowledge of theology and cosmology, including both the nature of the soul and the nature of the kosmos itself as an order created by reason (to pan diakekosmēkōs) (12.966e4). They are to study arithmetic, the expertise of measurement, and astronomy (compare arithmetic and astronomy featuring in the curriculum of the Republic, and measurement being central especially to the Statesman and Philebus).

This range and level of knowledge is required for them to be "genuine guardians of the laws" (tous ontōs phulakas . . . tōn nomōn) and to "genuinely (ontōs) know the true nature of the laws" (12.966b5–6). As I have argued, their role is to serve as guardians of the laws in the sense of understanding and so safeguarding their true telos, in light of broader knowledge of the nature of the kosmos (its elements and its structure)—while being distinct from the nomophulakes, who occupy a distinct office. Likewise, "guardians" here is a

69. Sōtēria appears in some form (sometimes in a cognate) at 12.965a4 [sōzein]; 968a7; 969c3.

70. Note the similarly complicating terminological reference to the Daily Meeting as "genuine guardians of the laws" (12.966b5), discussed in the text below, and as nomophulakes again (in the genitive plural) at 12.966d1.

71. Indeed, the emphasis on their knowledge of the skopos of a statesman as consisting of virtue (the fourfold set of virtues, in fact) is dramatized by a brief dialogue that the Visitor imagines himself and his interlocutors carrying out as a kind of cross-examination of the nous of the statesman, as compared to that of the steersman, doctor, and general, each of whose nous is said to have its own particular target (12.963b4).

reference to a function rather than to a specific role of ruler characterized by epitactic powers, the latter being the role of the senior ranks of the "guardians (*phulakes*)" of the *Republic*.

It remains to explain two final twists at the very end of the dialogue. The first is that this same body is accorded the role of conducting "the guarding according to law for the sake of the safeguarding" (12.968a6–7). While this sounds pleonastic, it is actually informative. For it refers to the role of the Daily Meeting in carrying out the function of guarding as "guardians of the laws" (12.966b5, noted above), with it being it the laws that embody knowledge of the good, rather than individual rulers who do so as in the *Republic* and *Statesman*. Thus the "safeguarding" of the constitution as a whole happens at one remove, by safeguarding the laws that in turn both educate and control the officeholders so as to keep them properly oriented to the *telos* of the good of the ruled.

The second and final twist in these closing passages is a remark by the Visitor about the role of being a "ruler (*archōn*)" (12.968a7): "Someone who is not able to do these things [sc. achieve and share educational attainments relevant to customs and legal norms: my gloss on the preceding sentence] in going beyond the possession of popular virtues would hardly be able ever to become a sufficient ruler (*archōn*) of a whole city, but would have to be the servant of others who rule (*archousin*)" (12.968a1–4). This remark is made in the middle of an overall discussion of the education of the members of the Daily Meeting and their role as "guardians." Yet apart from this one very late and cryptic remark, the Visitor has never previously appeared to suggest that the role of members of the Daily Meeting might be to serve as "rulers."[72]

To be sure, the Visitor has occasionally made reference to the role of "rulers" and to the role of a "statesman" at various points in the dialogue, including in the extended context in book 12. There, he introduced such figures alongside steersmen, generals, and doctors—who I take to be models (rather than direct descriptions) of the role of the Daily Meeting.[73] Likewise in the cryptic

72. When the Athenian Visitor completes his reference in 12.967d–968b to what I have dubbed the Daily Meeting, he describes it as "the nocturnal meeting of the *archontōn*" (12.968a7). Its members are (I would contend) described as *archontōn* because most of them either hold or have held particular offices, rather than in virtue of their membership of the meeting itself, which does not as such (as I have argued) constitute an office. The relationship between the "nocturnal" temporal setting here, and the early morning temporal setting in other passages, is addressed earlier in this chapter.

73. Consider 12.962a9–b2 on a "ruler (*archōn*)" who should not be ignorant of the target pertaining to the "statesman [*politikos*]," and 12.963b2ff. on the "statesman [*politikos*]": while the flow of these passages is subtle, I take these comparisons and invocations to be identifying the *telos* of the laws (as a true statesman would frame them), which it is the task of the Daily Meeting to safeguard, rather than as assigning the role of ruler to the members of that meeting. Cf. 1.650b7–9, a somewhat surprising passage at the end of book 1, in which the Athenian Visitor describes [*hē*] *politikē* (the expertise of statecraft) as

remark quoted in the previous paragraph, the role of "ruler" and "statesman" can be read as a model for the intellectual attainment, whether glossed as wisdom or expertise, that is needed to grasp the *telos* that the laws are meant to embody and so enable the officeholders and all the citizens to pursue. In other words, Plato's emphasis here is on the knowledge of the *telos* that characterizes rulers, rather than on the epitactic role that would be associated with their *taxis*.

Indeed, as I have argued, there is no epitactic power associated with the safeguarding role of the Daily Meeting. Epitactic power is instead condensed into the conditional coercive threat contained within the laws themselves, as well as assigned by the laws to the various officeholders whose roles they delineate. The role of "ruler" is invoked at the end of the dialogue in order to emphasize the *telos* of the laws that the meeting is to safeguard, rather than to assign its members the kind of epitactic powers that rulers would characteristically enjoy.

Conclusion

The offices outlined in the discursive legislation for the constitutional project with Magnesia in view are intricately conceived and procedurally complex in ways designed to safeguard the *telos* of the good of the ruled so far as humanly possible through procedures alone. They comport with a general education designed to ensure that the officeholders are capable of the virtue required by their offices. The *Laws* pushes to the limit the possibilities for achieving good rule afforded by a constitution of limited and accountable offices.

Yet, ultimately, a reader of Plato would be led to conclude that the offices of the *Laws* share, if to a considerably lesser degree, the same limits (pun intended) as the offices of everyday existing Greek constitutions. They rely primarily on procedural safeguards, which must be construed as having an evaluative orientation toward the good of the ruled, but which are hamstrung by the flaw of any and all proceduralism. For procedures such as elections and accountability mechanisms are necessarily imperfect, allowing for mistakes and loopholes and, in particular, from a Platonic perspective, relying ultimately on the less virtuous to be able to identify the more virtuous and hold them to account. Potential ways in which office and rule might conceivably be reconfigured even more profoundly to escape these limitations are the subject of the chapters on the *Statesman* and *Republic* that follow in the remainder of part II.

---

that *technē* which "cares for (*therapeuein*)" souls—picking up a theme that is central to the *Statesman*, as the next chapter will show.

CHAPTER FOUR

Rethinking the Role of Ruler and the Place of Office (*Statesman*)

NEAR THE BEGINNING OF PLATO'S *STATESMAN*, the anonymous Visitor from Elea summarizes the object of the dialogue's inquiry into the eponymous statesman (*politikos*): "our pursuit is of the person who rules (*tou . . . archontos*), not their opposite" (*Plt.* 260e8–9).[1] That the statesman should be a ruler is axiomatically Platonic, expressing a commitment to the rule of knowledge, which the very formulation of the word *politikos* also bespeaks (the *-ikos* ending indicating a possessor of some kind of expertise). In Attic Greek parlance at the time, however, *politikos* was not a standard title or usual way of describing a ruler, a role that was still likely to be figured by a king, despite the archaizing or foreign connotations of kingship. While framing the inquiry of the dialogue as that of identifying the statesman,[2] the Visitor connects

---

1. All quotations in this chapter are from the *Statesman* (*Politicus* in Latin, hence the standard abbreviation *Plt.*), according to the OCT Duke/Robinson edition of the dialogue, and in my own translation, unless otherwise indicated. After various experiments in attempting to encompass both the masculine terms being used in the dialogue ("statesman" and "king," both masculine nouns in Greek) as well as the abstract nature of their expertise, and to do so consonant with the interplay between the words translated "statesman" and "statecraft" also in Greek, I adopt here the unsatisfactory but common expedient of gendering the statesman as male. I use plural pronouns ("they") when possible to point out that this dialogue makes no other comment on the gender of the person who might possess the relevant knowledge and so qualify for this name. Compare the *Republic* and *Laws*, in both of which it is made clear that women as well as men may serve as rulers in the various roles delineated in the constitutional projects thereof.

2. This is subsequent to the identification of the sophist in the eponymous dialogue that dramatically precedes it, in which Socrates had asked the same Visitor from Elea

the statesman also to the role of a king; for example, in asserting later in the dialogue that "kingly rule (*hē basilikē archē*) was one of the kinds of expert knowledge (*tōn epistēmōn*)" (292b6–7). "The person who rules," identified as such in the opening quotation above by a participle of the verb *archein*, furthermore, could in some contexts be a way of describing a person holding a constitutionally limited office, as this study has maintained. Thus the dialogue sets itself the challenge of clarifying the nature of rule, its connection to kingship and to constitutionally limited offices (kingship in this dialogue not being consistently positioned as such), and its basis in knowledge.

In so doing, the dialogue offers one important clarification of the *telos* of rule, highlighting that knowledge of the good must in political life be temporally indexed, involving knowledge of what action is opportune at a given moment (the *kairos*): a significant insight of the dialogue to which I have called attention in previous work.[3] However, notwithstanding that important contribution, the dialogue is otherwise remarkably vague and general in discussing the content of the *telos* of rule. The aspiration that an appropriately monarchical individual (I emphasize the identifications made between "statesman" and "king" below) who would be "willing and capable of ruling with virtue and expertise to distribute what is just and hallowed correctly to all" is about as detailed as it gets.[4]

To cast my point in the terms introduced in part I of this study: rather than specifying the *telos* (purpose) of rule in detail, the *Statesman* instead offers a class on the *taxis* (order) of rule (its epitactic expertise, its caring orientation, and its ultimate realization, or *ergon*). It does so in part through exploring the

---

who is the main protagonist of both dialogues (and who is in this chapter the "Visitor" so described, in contrast to the Athenian Visitor who features in the *Laws*, the dialogue under discussion in chapter 3) to explain whether, in his homeland, sophist, statesman, and philosopher are believed to be one, two, or three kinds, and named accordingly (*Sophist* 216d3–217b4). This question is picked up at the beginning of the *Statesman*, leading to a focusing of the inquiry on the eponymous figure at 258b2–3. The corpus leaves open the question of whether Plato ever intended to write a dialogue called *Philosopher*, or even to indicate dramatically in the *Sophist* and *Statesman* that he would do so; for one thoughtful answer in the negative, see Gill's *Philosophos*.

3. Lane, *Method and Politics*, 125–46, 171–202.

4. 301c10–d2. What I have excerpted is notable in several respects: the language of distribution (*dianemein*), which is connected etymologically to shepherding; the paired nouns for what is just and what is holy or hallowed by divine law, emphasizing that the monarchical kingly individual who has been sketched in the dialogue would act in accordance with divine law, even though sometimes overriding human laws when necessary; and the broader context of this statement, which is embedded in the Eleatic's observation that flawed constitutions have come about because people can't stomach the idea of such a monarchical individual being both capable and willing to rule correctly (Lane, *Method and Politics*, 161–62).

relationship between rule and office, the subtlety of which exploration suggests that it is a deliberate invocation, as well as reconfiguration, by Plato of
that very relationship. By the end of the inquiry, the reader will learn that
a true statesman does not hold an ordinary or even a reconfigured office in
the city, carrying out a role of rule that is epitactic and caring but not limited
by any of the parameters that would indicate the limits of office. But at its
inception, the Eleatic Visitor leaves open the possibility that he might: being
presented as allowing the participial use of *archein* to raise its conventionally
established resonance of institutional officeholding in the ears of his interlocutor and audience (and so Plato in the mind of his readers).[5]

In focusing more on the *taxis* than on the content of the *telos* of rule, the
Statesman also makes a suggestive and sometimes startling intervention into
the framing of a service conception of rule. At one point within the dialogue,
a group of rivals to the title of statesman is identified as "the remaining group
of slaves and all servants" (289c4). Despite that wording, the group is shown
to share not a common legal or social status but rather a common abstractly
described function: the group includes legally enslaved persons, but also
retailers, heralds, priests, and others. Some of them do not lay claim to the
names of "kingly expertise" or "statecraft" (the enslaved persons do not claim
the former; the merchants and retailers do not claim the latter: 289d11–e2,
290a4–6). But others do—namely, those who are "king-priests" in Egypt, or
"king-archons" chosen by lot in Athens, whose claims to kingliness in both
cases "make them see themselves as nonsubordinates; likewise, those who
turn out to be sophists, who see themselves as nonsubordinates and indeed as
entitled to the title of statesman" (290d5–291c7).

The statesman turns out to be the ultimate nonsubordinate, being the one
who can give orders based upon a special kind of knowledge to all the other
experts and forms of expertise to do with the city, who and which are therefore
to be counted as subordinates to him (as detailed for the final set of closely
related experts below). Yet, at the same time, the role of the statesman is to
care for the city and in that sense to serve it. The statesman is a nonsubordinate who plays a role associated with subordinates (compare the officeholders
of the *Laws*, who are envisaged as "servants" and even "slaves" of the law (*Leg.*
4.715c6–d5), noted in chapter 3). The statesman's rule is, I shall argue, a form
of serving.

5. The duality of rule and office is implicit in the very first use of the verb *archein* in
the dialogue, in the form of the participle *archōn* used as a noun at 259e10. This is the
very participle which in part I was shown to raise a systematic question of whether to
translate as "ruler" (generically or abstractly) or as "officeholder" (institutionally limited
and specified).

Kings and Shepherds in the Statesman

That the nature of rule is fundamental to the dialogue is flagged by the Homeric images of the ruler as king and as shepherd that are both employed and critically interrogated within it. While the topic of the inquiry is formally established as the identification of the statesman (*politikos*), early in the inquiry the Eleatic proposes that the statesman and king can be identified as possessing the same "single expertise" (258c1–2), leading him to posit statecraft, statesman, kingcraft (as it were), and king all "as one" (259d4–5).[6] The king continues to appear as a figuration for the statesman, or as a role conjoined with his, periodically throughout the dialogue. I take this to be an invocation of the commonly recognized epitactic role of the king—the king is in essence someone who is entitled to issue orders or commands—which would have been traditional and expected from archaic Greek literary sources and practices onward (as explored in part I of this study). By connecting, and sometimes identifying, statesman and king, Plato confers this epitactic role also on the statesman insofar as they are actually engaged in ruling. That is, while the Eleatic concedes that an advisor to a king, insofar as and in virtue of their possessing the expert knowledge of kingship, can also "be correctly addressed as king" (259b4–5), the very nature of ruling in exercising such knowledge (whether described as kingship or statecraft) involves issuing orders.

Thus, an advisor who is not exercising the role of king is not ruling, even if they possess expertise in how to do so, a point reiterated by the Visitor later as follows: "It is the person who actually possesses the expert knowledge of kingship [*hē basilikē . . . epistēmē*], whether they rule (*archēi*) or not, who must . . . be called expert in kingship [*basilikos*]" (292e9–293a1). On the one hand, as this passage indicates, Plato in the *Statesman* distinguishes between a pure epistemic competence or expertise and the exercise of that expertise in ruling. On the other hand, the very orientation of such expertise toward its potential exercise in ruling shapes the content and nature of that expertise in

6. This is the culmination of a discussion beginning at 258e8, which has seemed to some so problematically argued as to lead Robinson, in editing the dialogue in Duke et al.'s OCT, to transpose three later lines of text (259d4–6, the lines I translate in the latter part of my sentence above) so as to interpose them between 259b6 and b7, despite the lack of any manuscript support for so doing. For a recent discussion, arguing against such transposition but finding the flow of the argument in this part of the dialogue flawed, see Lawrence's "Trailhead." Note that at both junctures, the Eleatic further includes identification of the *technai* of the statesman and king with those of two other figures: the *oikonomos* (household manager) and the *despotēs*, a word typically interpreted here (as by Lawrence) in its sense of slave master, but which also had a sense of political despot, a possibility in interpreting the dialogue that could be explored further. I take the kind of *technē* in which all share to be the epitactic one of giving orders, the purpose of which has not yet at this stage of the dialogue been identified.

itself. Political expertise must be "command-apt," since a distinctive power of those with political expertise is their capacity to rule (a capacity not limited to those with expertise in the political domain, as the discussion of the master builder in the dialogue will show).[7] Political experts, whether we name them statesmen or kings, must be oriented to the ordering (and, as argued below, caring) that is characteristic of rule. The rule of knowledge is the *rule* of knowledge, not knowledge merely; conversely, such knowledge must be appropriately oriented in order to count as the kind of knowledge that can rule.

If the king is the embodiment of the epitactic dimension of rule, the shepherd is the embodiment of its caring orientation.[8] As argued in part I of this study, the figure of the shepherd intrinsically connects the production of order (*taxis*) with its purpose (*telos*). Herding more generally is a figure for a kind of knowledge that is both command-apt and oriented to caring for (rather than merely assertorically identifying) the good of the ruled. The early divisions of the *Statesman* identify the statesman as resembling a horse breeder or cowherd in being responsible for the care [*epimeleia*] of a whole herd at once (in contrast to the ox driver or groom, who might hand rear an individual animal) (261d4–10). But the Visitor soon pinpoints a distinction between herders and kings (267e1–2)—namely, that while no one contests the claims of the former to care for their respective herds, the latter are beset by rivals who claim that their own forms of expertise are also forms of "caring for human rearing" (268a1–4). Thus far in the dialogue, the language of *epimeleia* has not been restrictive enough to separate the king from these rivals.

In order to draw the requisite more fine-grained distinction, the Visitor invents a cosmic myth, weaving it out of an atypical reading of three traditional legends. In contrast to one recurrent kind of cosmic epoch (in which divine beings directly shepherd the human herd), in the present kind of cosmic epoch, human kingly rule should be understood to be an act of "care" (*epimeleia*, 276b8, d13, and passim) that is distinct from the other kinds of contributions to rearing that other kinds of expertise are able to make.[9] Part of the moral drawn by the Visitor from the myth is that a human king is not a shepherd of humans in the same way in which a shepherd of sheep is a shepherd: the latter is responsible for all the kinds of care that their sheep need, whereas the former offers a distinctive kind of care that is distinct from many other kinds of ministrations. The reader does not yet know exactly what kind of care is involved in human rule over humans, but the distinction having been

7. I introduced the language of "command-apt" in this context in my "Value of Knowledge."

8. I was struck while writing this chapter by the observation that "the presidency, as Biden says, 'is a duty to care,'" made in Egan's "Kamala Harris."

9. Lane, *Method and Politics*, 57, 118, where I note that *epimeleia* and its cognates are not the only terms used in the dialogue to signify care; *therapeia* and its cognates are used in similar contexts.

drawn, Plato allows the shepherd image to be reappropriated for the statesman when later described as a legislator,[10] while subordinating it to the
model of weaving in the final account of statecraft (a shift already understood
in Plato's day as marking an important shift in the anthropology of human
culture from a pastoral economy to an artisanal one, with important gendered
associations as well).[11] The Homeric image of the king as shepherd retains
some insight but is inadequate to provide a complete model for the Platonic
idea of rule.

Office and Rule

That the role of office is equally fundamental to the dialogue is far less evident.
But consider the following quotations from near the end of the dialogue, in
which the Visitor is painting a broad-brush portrait of a city ruled by a true
statesman. He describes the task or work (*ergon*, a term unpacked further
below) of "kingly interweaving" (using Rowe's translation of that phrase) to
include the production of a smooth, finely interwoven fabric out of two groups
of citizens who would otherwise be temperamentally hostile to each other. That
being done, the personified expertise of "kingly interweaving"—personified as
an agent in its own right, but elsewhere in the dialogue made definitionally
interchangeable with the statesman who possesses that expertise—would then
"always entrust the offices (*epitrepein tas archas*) in the city to them in common" (311a1–2). In this passage, the semantic signals identified in part I of
this work as indicating the sense of accountable office, rather than any other
kind of rule, are strong: the plural form of the noun *archē* being one, and that
plural noun as the direct object of a verb being another. The verb *epitrepein*
employed in the above passage was used in Athens to denote the submission
of a legal dispute to a private arbitrator (as opposed to a court trial).[12] Here,

---

10. At 294e9–295a1, the "legislator [*ho nomothetēs*]" is described as the person who
"orders" (in the sense of issuing commands to) his "herds"; at 295e5–7, the same kind of
person is again described as having acted "for all those herds of human beings that graze,
city by city, according to the laws of those who wrote them down in each case" (trans.
Rowe). I learned from the discussion of these points in coursework at Princeton by Ophelia
Vedder.

11. On the gendering of weaving in Plato's day, see my *Method and Politics* (164–69);
on the cultural shift and the characteristic associations of shepherding versus weaving, see
Blondell's "Fleece to Fabric." The discussion of shepherding in Foucault's "Omnes et singulatim" and elsewhere is misleading both in discussion of shepherding in the Near East and
in interpretation of the *Statesman*.

12. Harris, "Trials," 213–14, with references in n2, describing a process to which both
parties had to agree. The same article notes further (218–19) that the procedure of arbitration was expected both domestically and in inter-*polis* relations to result in the restoration of friendship between the parties. The verb *epitrepein* can also be translated as "to
leave" in the sense of leaving a task to someone else. This affordance should moderate the

by extension, it suggests a legal and institutional procedure within a constitutional framework of officeholding.[13]

Consider next how the use of the plural noun indicating office (*tas archas*) in the phrase just quoted comports with the use of the verb *archein* in the very next lines uttered by the Visitor, explaining what he meant in prescribing the entrusting of the offices in common:

> choosing [*haireisthai*] the person who has both qualities whenever there should be a need for a single officeholder (*henos archontos*) to put in charge, but mixing together a part of each of these groups where there is a need for several. (311a4–6)

Note that whereas at 260e8–9, the Visitor had used *tou . . . archontos* for a general description, which I translated as "the person who rules," here the participle follows immediately after a plural noun that signals "offices," providing grounds to translate *archontos* as "officeholder."[14]

The verb "choosing" (*haireisthai*) was the standard way of referring to election to office in the institutional context of democratic Athens.[15] Because the implied subject of this part of the Visitor's speech is not the statesman as a human being but rather "the task of kingly interweaving,"[16] it is at least possible that the choosing in question is to be done by means of establishing an institutional order for such election, or other form of selection, to be routinized. In this case, *haireisthai* could conceivably still bear its usual constitutional sense of "elect," opening the door to the possibility that the officeholders for these offices are to be elected by their fellow citizens (just as in the constitutional project of the *Laws*)—a question to which I return below.

Comparing these passages suggests that, while rarely thematized as such, the relationship between rule and office is central to the political theory of the

---

assumption that the statesman is necessarily choosing the holders of these offices individually; so far as the verb *epitrepein* goes, it may equally describe his leaving the selection of the holders of these offices up to the citizens.

13. The Visitor does not give any examples of offices here; I return to the question of which ones he might have in mind below.

14. It is notable, however, that in translating the participle of the verb *archein* in this passage at *Plt.* 311a4, many translators into various European languages do not pick up a specific sense of "officeholder"—in contrast to their doing so in translating the plural noun *archai* used twice in *Resp.* 5.460b6–8, for example, as documented in chapter 2. Translations of the participle *archōn* (as *archontos*, a genitive form) at *Plt.* 311a4 include: "chef [head or leader]" (Chambry, Brisson/Pradeau); "Herrscher [ruler or lord]" (Schleiermacher); "Führer [leader]" (Rufener); "governante [ruler]" (Migliori, Giorgini).

15. The LSJ entry for this verb (*haireō*) includes this sense: "*choose by vote, elect* to an office," citing inter alia its use by Plato, at *Menex.* 90b2 and (specifically in the context of electing generals) *Apology* 28e2.

16. In the speech quoted, *touto . . . esti . . . ergon* picks up this as the subject, named back at 310e7–8.

Statesman.[17] From the point of view of office, the quotations discussed so far should have already made clear that the dialogue is not politically "impoverished" to the extent of lacking reference to a constitutional order of offices in the idealized city ruled by a true statesman.[18] Instead, the city under a true statesman is to include a constitutional order of offices, some of which are exercised singly and individually, others of which are exercised by collective boards. This is of course an institutional design recognizable from the present work so far, which has emphasized the largely collective structure of offices in many classical Greek cities, as well as in the detailed constitution outlined in Plato's *Laws* (in which context the superintendent of education occupied a singular office).

To be sure, the place of office is not fetishized in the dialogue's exploration of what a Greek city would require in order to function. Offices are situated in the context of a wide range of recognized civic roles (*timai*).[19] Far from being an abstract analysis of political expertise only, the *Statesman* details how the constitutional offices of a city must be situated in the broader operations of a very wide range of kinds of expertise, from agriculture and artisanry to wholesale and retail commerce and on to the administrative infrastructure underlying the ordering roles of the officeholders.

Yet the complexity of that picture only intensifies the questions as to what, if anything, distinguishes the nature of political expertise (statecraft); where it is to be located in the city, in relation to accountable office; what its distinctive role is to be; and how that role comports with the personified statesman, who is in the dialogue defined entirely in terms of its possession. These questions revolve around the specification of the core elements in rule that have been identified earlier in the present work: its purpose (*telos*), and its activity of ordering in contributing to an ordered political framework more broadly (*taxis*). In the next section of this chapter, I summarize the account that the

17. An exception to its general neglect include my "Political Expertise," an article on which Sørensen builds in "Political Office" and "Second Best City."

18. As I discussed in "Political Expertise" (51–52), Schofield (*Plato*, 175) writes that "the *Statesman*'s thinking about politics—for all its brilliant intensity—is from other points of view more impoverished than what we are offered in *Republic* and *Laws*," in relation to their discussions of constitution (*politeia*), the statesman (*politikos*), and the nature of political expertise (*politikē*). While I do not disagree with the ranking made by Schofield's "relatively," I argue that the *Statesman* is in fact less impoverished with respect to the organization of the *politeia* and the function of the *politikos* than it is usually believed to be. I also challenge Schofield's further contentions that the *Statesman* as a whole considers that "the right *politeia* simply *consists* in one person ruling with expertise" (175, emphasis original), and that "for government to be scientific it is immaterial how society is organized" (176).

19. On *timai* as including but extending beyond *archai* in democratic Athens, see Blok (*Citizenship*, 188–98); for a rich discussion of a relevant portion of the *Statesman*, see Carpenter's "Civic Function."

dialogue gives of both of these elements, before unpacking the dimensions of the *taxis* of rule further in the remainder of the chapter.

Telos *and* Taxis *of Rule*

The idea of rule is in the *Statesman*, as I have argued in this study that it is generally for Plato (and for a significant strand of Greek tradition before him), an evaluatively laden one: it is a service conception of rule, seeking to serve the *telos* of the good of the ruled, as underscored by the Visitor's invocation and critical examination of the Homeric image of the ruler as shepherd. In Plato's hands, here as elsewhere, however, that evaluative *telos* of rule (shared with much, though not all, earlier Greek thought) turns out to come with a peculiarly strong epistemic demand: to serve the good of the ruled requires a distinctive form of expertise. Yet whereas in other dialogues that expertise may seem to be purely intellectualist, with ruling as a separate activity to which it may or may not be applied, here, the expertise in question turns out to be political expertise or statecraft interpreted as (as I shall sometimes call it) ruling expertise.

In other words, the very specification of the content of that expertise turns out to incorporate its epitactic role. In the special case of political expertise, which must be ruling expertise, *telos* and *taxis* are essentially intertwined. But that is not all. Serving the good of the ruled turns out, in the Visitor's hands, to require not only the activity of ordering but also an orientation of caring (itself an insight that Plato may have derived from contemporary political practice, as is discussed further below). And finally, as is made clear through the deployment of an elaborate model of weaving, the *taxis* of rule turns out to involve not only ordering and caring but also the praxis of weaving, meaning that its complex power *(dunamis)* yields a characteristic product or result: the very civic fabric that makes it possible for offices to be entrusted to appropriate types of citizens.

Above I have canvassed the ways in which the *Statesman* is the Platonic dialogue most directly (sometimes explicitly, sometimes implicitly) engaged in thematizing the nature and relationship of rule and office. Yet, as noted in part I, it does so at an angle that is athwart to the two other dialogues with which the present work is concerned. For while the *Republic* and the *Laws* mount parallel internal projects in setting out constitutions "in speech," the interlocutors of the *Statesman* never constitute themselves in this kind of fictive, leisured legislative role. Instead, the latter dialogue pursues a single inquiry, originating from the framing conversation of the *Sophist*,[20] in order to isolate and identify

---

20. The *Sophist* itself follows on, in dramatic temporal sequence, from the *Theaetetus*, with indications in the setting of the *Euthyphro* that its conversation intervened between them (the *Euthyphro* being set near the porch of the king-archon, the destination toward

the statesman (following on from the identification of the sophist performed in the preceding dialogue), a person who is posited to possess a distinctive kind of expert knowledge and indeed who appears as a cipher, identified only through their possession of that knowledge.

Rather than the interlocutors of the *Statesman* constituting themselves as discursive legislators of a particular constitutional project, it is the statesman they delineate who is to possess a legislative capacity. Yet this capacity is not definitional of, but rather supplementary to, the statesman's role as a ruler. That role involves issuing orders for the *telos* of the good of the ruled, whether done individually or collectively. The role of legislator is treated in the dialogue as one that a ruler may choose to adopt but that is not definitional of their expertise: issuing laws is one inflection of the more general power of issuing orders, which is paradigmatic (though not exhaustive) of the *taxis* of ruling expertise, enabling it to realize its *telos* of serving the good of the ruled. Precisely in lacking the dramatic play of interlocutors constituting themselves discursive legislators, the dialogue underscores the fundamental epitactic power of issuing interpersonal orders as central to ruling.

Elsewhere I have traced in detail the emergence of a distinction between *archein*, or the conception of rule that belongs to the statesman, and the *archai* to be occupied and exercised by select citizens (offices, presumed as such to be accountable, which count as a species of rule but are distinct from the kind of rule characteristic of the statesman).[21] The principled analytical distinction between these two closely related ideas emerges gradually, as the Visitor builds up an account of statecraft that is distinct in kind and level from the ordinary offices. As in many Platonic dialogues, it only gradually becomes evident to a nonphilosophical interlocutor, and even to a relatively sophisticated Platonic reader, that what is at stake is a radically new conception of ideas of rule and office, ideas that readers (then or now) may have thought that they already, on the basis of ordinary practice as lived or studied, understood.[22] Rather than here following the full sequential narrative of the dialogue, I turn next to the ultimate definition offered of political expertise, unpacking its three component participles in turn. This is followed by a discussion of offices in various parts of the work, and, finally, by a similar discussion of law, and the relationship of legislative expertise to political expertise or statecraft. While the dialogue offers an indispensable primer on the Platonic idea of rule, this chapter does not complete the explication of that idea; later chapters will expand it further by drawing on other dialogues as well.

---

which Socrates explains that he is heading to respond to the judicial indictment brought against him by Meletus, an errand mentioned at the very end of the *Theaetetus*).

21. Lane, "Political Expertise."

22. Compare "friends possess everything in common," initially slipped into *Republic* 4 (423e), yet which is then in book 5 elaborated by Socrates as requiring the guardians' deprivation of private families and possession of land or wealth.

Ruling, Caring, and Weaving:
The Ultimate Definition of Statecraft

Consider how the Visitor defines the nature of the expertise that he claims is most justly named statecraft (*politikē*):[23]

> The form of expertise that rules over all of these [sc. other closely related forms of expertise], and cares for the laws and all that is to do with the city (*sumpantōn tōn kata polin*), and weaves everything together in the most correct way—this we would most justly, it seems, call statecraft (*politikē*), encompassing its power with the name of the public domain [*to koinon*]. (305e2-6)[24]

Ruling, caring, and weaving: these are the three participles that collectively define the power or capacity (*dunamis*) of statecraft,[25] in line with a more general Platonic framework in which forms of expertise are each defined by their distinctive *dunamis*.[26] Each one of these participles has emerged from a strand of the dialogue to this point, in some cases from multiple strands, as I shall highlight. Together, they characterize statecraft as a form of expertise that is inherently apt to rule. One might be tempted to infer that statecraft is not only theoretical, but also practical—were it not that such a statement

---

23. This section of the present chapter draws extensively (sometimes verbatim), with permission, on my "Political Expertise," "Statecraft," "Politics as Architectonic Expertise?," and "Value of Knowledge." Any significant divergences herein from the claims made in those articles are noted below. On the role of naming in the dialogue, see also my *Method and Politics* (25-33).

24. I translate the genitive of *to koinon* "of the public domain" in order to pick up in the overall translation something of the resonance emphasized in the Greek between *politikē* and *kata polin*. While the usual pairing in Greek that is translated as public versus private is *to dēmosion* versus *to idion*, it is also possible for *to koinon* to play the role of "public." See my "Statecraft" for defense (and debts) of my overall construal of this passage. In brief, against Rowe, who takes the words "the laws" to fall within the scope of the participle *archousan* (dividing up the *te . . . kai . . . kai*), I take them rather to fall within the scope of the participle *epimeloumenēn*, in this respect following Brisson/Pradeau, Dixsaut et al., and Giorgini; I construe the phrase *sumpantōn tōn kata polin* as do Rowe and others, as a neuter plural, as opposed to construing it as do Dixsaut et al. as a masculine plural (which would make its referent not "all that is to do with the city" but rather "the citizens").

25. The *dunamis* of statecraft is described as such at 304d8-9, 305e5, 308c7, e6, and 309d2. It is matched by mention of the *dunamis* of each of the closest forms of expertise considered by the Visitor in reaching the definition of statecraft (by distinguishing it from each of those others), at 304c7-8 (rhetoric), 304e3 (generalship), and judgeship (305b2, picked up at 305c4-5). A complementary element to such a definition—namely, the *ergon* (the task, product, or result) that the *dunamis* is capable of producing—will be discussed further below.

26. In "Statecraft" (201-2), I argue that the *Statesman* builds on but moves beyond the *Republic* 5 account of *dunamis*.

would belie the fact that the very cognitive content of the expertise is itself oriented toward realizing the good of the ruled.[27] The lesson to be drawn is that the *taxis* of rule must be oriented toward, but therefore also by, the nature of its *telos*.

Ruling—and Serving

That fact about the nature of rule is rooted in a key moment in the early divisions of the dialogue, in which successive distinctions are drawn among different kinds of expertise (each of them subsuming various examples of the same kind, among which further distinctions may be drawn in turn). At the moment in question, the Eleatic Visitor identifies a kind of expertise that he names *epitaktikē*. This is epitactic expertise, with the characteristic power of issuing orders—the very kind of expertise that I have argued earlier in the present work rule must be (and here, rule is the role to be characteristically carried out by the statesman).[28] It is illustrated by the case of the master builder (*ho architektōn*) in a pivotal assertion by the Visitor:

> And every master builder (*architektōn*) too does not act as a worker themselves, but as a ruler (*archōn*) over workers. (259e9–10)[29]

Here the master builder has an epitactic role described as being a "ruler" over workers, rule being essentially the epitactic activity of ordering as defined in the present work in part I. But while translation in terms of "ruler" works best here, office is already also at the semantic table, in a way that any contemporary reader of Plato would have immediately recognized. For the *architektōn* (another participle being used as a noun) was not just any builder (commonly

---

27. Lane, "Value of Knowledge."

28. On the other side of the division is a kind of expertise named *kritikē*, defined by a characteristic power of judging without that judgment necessarily issuing in an order; here, I follow the translation of "judgment" that I employed in "Value of Knowledge" (57), though one might also venture "assessment." The illustration given of a person possessing this type of expertise is the accountant (*ho logistēs*, 260a5), using the same term that the Athenians used for the civic auditor belonging to the group charged with carrying out the first (financial) stage of the two-stage *euthunai* procedure. I do not here discuss the translation of *gnōstikē* as opposed to *praktikē*, terms that I would still insist must not be understood as "theoretical" versus "practical"; while I have continued to use "discernment" for *gnōstikē* to capture the orientation to ordering activity in the particular context of these dialogues, there is also merit in broader translations such as "thought-involving" (or, for shorthand, "cognitive," modeled on the Italian translation of the *Statesman* by Giorgini) versus, say, "action-involving," as well as of the objection put to me by Terence Irwin in conversation that "discernment" would be better reserved in an etymological perspective for *kritikē*.

29. Reading *kai mēn* with Duke et al.'s OCT. Contrast Rowe's translation, "but manage workers," translating *archōn* simply as a participle, whereas I take it to be one that is functioning here as a noun.

called an *oikodomos*). On the contrary: the relatively rare appellation of *architektōn* always derived from a fixed-term civic appointment, earning a civic stipend and being employed to oversee public building works on behalf of a particular polis.[30] Hence, a master builder described by the term *architektōn* gained the authority to rule over workers in virtue of having been appointed to a civic office. And the same was true in Athens of the contrasting type whom the Visitor described as *logistēs* in illustrating the contrasting kind of expertise, that which is not epitactic but merely that of an assessor (260a5).[31]

Against this backdrop, the fact that *ho archōn* was in Attic Greek standardly used both as a term for office in general and as a name for particular offices such as the board of ten *archontes* in classical Athens (as argued in part I), together with the variations in use of that very participle in the passages under discussion, testifies to Plato's artfulness. At this early stage of the dialogue, he proceeds in such a way as to allow his readers to assume that they know what is going on—that reference is being made to political roles in a conventional constitutional arrangement of offices—while also opening the door to a radically different role of ruler in the person of the ideal or true statesman.

The Visitor immediately adds a crucial additional dimension to his portrait of the master builder:

> It belongs to him [the master builder], I think, once he has given his professional judgment, not to be finished (*mē telos echein*) or to take his leave, in the way that the accountant took his, but to assign (*prostattein*) whichever is the appropriate task to each group of workers until they complete (*apergasōntai*) what has been assigned to them. (260a4–7, trans. Rowe, modified)

The epitactic role is not limited to just the issuing of orders. Instead it requires that the purpose of the ordering be realized. Notice that this orientation to realization is not portrayed as being a product of the application of a kind of expertise. It is intrinsic, rather, to the type of expertise by which the master builder is characterized. What distinguishes that figure from someone like the accountant is that the latter issues their judgment and then is done, leaving it

---

30. Lane, "Politics as Architectonic Expertise?," 453. Frank ("Comments on 'Rule'") challenges my reading of this figure, arguing that the practice of Greek architecture involved collective and interdependent agency; combined with her similar reassessment of weaving (Frank and Greenberg, "Weaving Politics"), this points toward a major alternative interpretation of the *Statesman*.

31. At an earlier stage of the divisions in the *Statesman*, the Visitor had appealed to a contrast between a doctor practicing privately or independently (*idiōteuōn*), on the one hand, and another doctor to whom the former might serve as an advisor: the latter is (in contrast) engaged in the affairs of the civic body (*tis tōn dēmosieuontōn iatrōn*) (259a1–4), and so constitutes another case of the divisions invoking a public *polis*-designated role, even if it did not strictly speaking constitute an office.

up to others (in the Athenian case, to a court) to decide how to act on the basis of the judgment and then to do so. The master builder, by contrast, is inherently oriented to the realization of their own judgment, and does so by issuing orders to other persons—in this case, construction workers—who carry out their own tasks so that the overall task of the master builder may be realized. The epitactic role as presented here is inherently hierarchical.

In fact, the dialogue has manifested a seemingly paradoxical play between what one might call the notions of mastering and serving as they pertain to rule.[32] For the statesman is defined as a king on the one hand, who is beholden to no human master, and yet also as someone who, while not subordinate to anyone else in the city, is engaged in serving in the sense of being oriented to the good of those whom he rules. Yet, at this same time, the statesman-cum-king's epitactic mastery is directed solely to caring for—or one might fairly say serving—the good of those over whom he rules, just as I argued in part I is true more globally for Plato's analysis of rulers as serving the good of the ruled. The repeated pattern by which the last set of other forms of expertise (three of them, which are called precious and related to statecraft) were successively separated off from statecraft involves the claim that each of them is subordinate to statecraft, which rules over them.[33] To say that the subordinate forms of expertise do not rule (over) themselves is to say that they do not rule—epitactically command—their own actions, but are rather subordinate, in each case described as a servant (*hupēretēs*), to the statecraft that has the role of doing so. This is a strong claim, though meant to be consistent with the thought that each of these forms of expertise is indeed master of its own domain in a way (as one might say, for generalship, being master of discerning and commanding how to make war).

Who or what are the subordinates to whom, or to which, the statesman is to issue orders? The dialogue sometimes analyzes this question in abstract terms, asking it about political expertise (statecraft), while at other times asking a similar question about the statesman as a human being (who is defined, as noted at the start of this chapter, by possession of the corresponding expertise). The ultimate account of statecraft and the statesman is formulated by contrast to three particular "precious and kindred" forms of expertise: rhetoric, generalship, and judgeship. The Visitor distinguishes statecraft from each of these in turn, using a common pattern: the very same pattern of ruling

---

32. I speak here of the dialogue as a whole, and of mastery both as epitactic superiority and as professional expertise. However, reference to mastery in Plato as in other ancient Greek authors cannot escape the shadow of the slave master (who can be termed a *despotēs*, as at 258e9).

33. These three are statecraft's closest kin, which need to be separated out not by the method of division but by means of a new process analogized by the Visitor to the smelting of metals in order to purify out gold. See Lane, "Statecraft," 194–200.

and subordination that was embodied in the case of the master builder and their workers. In the case of the three latter expertises (if the awkward plural can be forgiven), the key decision to be taken by political expertise in ruling the others is as to when they must or must not be either learned or practiced—a decision to be made on the basis of statecraft's unique mastery of the *kairos*, the time-sensitive objective standard for what action serves the good (in this case, of the ruled) in a given moment.[34] This discussion is summed up in the following statement by the Visitor:

> If then one looks at all the sorts of expert knowledge that have been discussed, it must be observed that none of them has been disclosed as statecraft.[35] For the genuine kingly expertise (*tēn . . . ontōs ousan basilikēn*) must not itself take action (*prattein*), but rule those with the power to take action (*archein tēn dunamenōn prattein*), because it knows when it is the right time and when it is the wrong time (*enkairias te peri kai akairias*) to begin and set in motion the most important things in cities; and the others must do what has been prescribed for them. (305c10–d5, trans. Rowe, modified)

Because they are not masters of a domain at the second-order level, none of these three other forms of expertise, relevant though they all are to aspects of the *telos* of statecraft, can be strictly said to be a ruler. They are instead subordinates or servants (*hupēretai*, plural, from the singular *hupēretēs*,[36] a word repeated in the same pattern of argument by which each of the final three forms of expertise is separated away from statecraft) serving under the one true or genuine "ruler" in the *polis* as a whole—that is, statecraft as exercised by the statesman. And this subordination is not merely among abstractions. If generalship (like the other two kinds of expertise separated off at this stage) is subordinate to statecraft, the general must be subordinate to the statesman. The relationship of rule is a relationship of command or order, at least in principle, over both other forms of expertise and the citizens. Its epitactic superiority holds even when exercised through speech acts that are not direct commands, and through creating mediating institutions such as subordinate offices (discussed further below).

---

34. Lane, *Method and Politics*, 132–55, 171–202.

35. I translate *anaphainō* here as "disclosed as" in place of Rowe's "declared to be"; the idea recalls the dialectical goal of *dēlōsis*, a manifestation or showing, at 287a3–4, a point I owe to Susan Sauvé Meyer.

36. See Rhodes (*Commentary*, 439) for its political sense: "The word ὑπηρέτης [*hupēretēs*] was sometimes used of public slaves," though he defends the view that it could be used of privately or individually owned slaves as well; it could also be used of servants who were not legally enslaved, and of subordinates in other contexts more generally. See also Ismard's *Démocratie contre les experts*, itself a work drawing extensively on the *Statesman* on this topic.

The relationship of the statesman to those subordinate forms of expertise, and, crucially, to their practitioners, had already become a vexed and subtle point earlier in the dialogue. Having divided off seven kinds of possessions and the relevant knowledge relating to each of them on the model of weaving, and making reference to having even earlier divided off the art of herd rearing of tame living creatures other than humans, the Visitor had announced that "what remains is the class of slaves and all those people who are subordinate to others, among whom, I strongly suspect, those who dispute with the king about the 'woven fabric' itself [of the city, on the model of weaving], will come into view" (289c4–6, trans. Rowe). And having then set aside legally enslaved persons, together with retailers, heralds, and others (some of whom are public slaves employed in political administration), the Visitor then again said that the remaining rivals to the statesman will appear in the larger group just described, even though "it would seem very odd indeed to look for these in some portion of the subordinate forms of expertise" (290b9–c1, trans. Rowe). This is odd precisely because any rivals to the statesman would logically be expected to appear in the domain of a similarly superordinate art, not a subordinate one. But, in fact, a proper understanding shows that all such rivals must ultimately be subordinate to the statesman or king. Thus the true statesman will be classed as a ruler rather than a servant, in keeping with their original identification with a king. Yet it is their purpose to serve the good of the ruled. As ruler, the statesman seeks to serve.

This understanding of the *dunamis* of statecraft furnishes a reply to a remark by Thomas Hobbes, who asked in the preface to *De cive*, "How many men have been killed by the erroneous doctrine that sovereign Kings are not masters but servants of society?"[37] In contrast to Hobbes, the *Statesman* suggests that the role of the king or statesman as ruler and as servant need not be understood as antithetical, developing and deepening the Platonic perspective on the ruler as serving that was introduced above in part I. For this dialogue treats kings, and rulers more generally, as both epitactically ruling and, in so doing, also serving (the good of) those they rule. The Platonic ruler in the *Statesman* rules by discerning and ordering what is for the good of the ruled. Their power is fundamentally the power (*dunamis*) of ruling, a power that they exercise with an orientation of caring and in the service of accomplishing the work (*ergon*) of political weaving—thus uniting the three participles central to the passage in which the *dunamis* of statecraft is finally identified and its name properly explained.

The *dunamis* of statecraft that has emerged so far in the dialogue involves not only the epitactic dimension that was established in the treatment of

37. Hobbes, "Preface to the Readers," 8: a passage called to my attention by Richard Tuck.

"ruling" in the early divisions. The role of statecraft was also specified as "caring" in the original shepherd divisions and especially in their reformulation in the wake of the myth (to ensure that "caring" was used instead of a too-narrow herd-rearing term). And, finally, statecraft was articulated in terms of the *paradeigma* of weaving, which was also itself termed as a form of "caring" for clothes. Having reviewed the role of "ruling," I now discuss "caring" and "weaving" more briefly in turn.

Caring

As noted above, in the criticism of the myth or story, the Visitor had specified that the statesman does not "rear" his herd but rather engages along with other herdsmen in a broader set of roles, for which he initially ventures several possible appellations (275e6–8)—it has to be "called some kind of expertise in 'herd-keeping' or 'looking after' (*therapeutikēn*) or 'caring for' (*epimelētikēn*)" (275e6–7)—before, in the case of "kingly rule," ultimately settling for the name of "care (*epimeleia*) of the whole human community together" (276b8–c2, trans. Rowe). Caring names the proper orientation of the role of a ruler, as specified by a given *taxis* of rule, toward the *telos* of rule—namely, the good of the ruled. A ruler is charged with caring for the good of the ruled in the sense that a doctor is charged with caring for the good of a patient. The point is not to guarantee that any actual ruler or doctor will be so motivated but, rather, to characterize the caring orientation built into the role itself.

Indeed, this was suggested throughout the Visitor's earlier comparison of the statesman to the expert trainers and doctors, whose concern after a period of absence must be with what is "better (*beltionōn*)" for their charges (295c9), as always with what is "precisely appropriate (*akribōs . . . to prosēkon*)" for each of them (295a2–3). In other words, like the herdsmen, trainers, and doctors, the statesman practices a *therapeia*, a form of expertise that is inherently and necessarily oriented to the good of its subjects.[38] The sole defining mark of a statesman and generally of "wise rulers" (*tois emphrosin archousin*) (297a6) is concluded to be doing "what is to the benefit" (*sumphora*) of the citizens (296d6–e4), so as "to safeguard them and so far as possible make them become better (*ameinous*) from having previously been worse" (297b2–3). All this, I suggest, is the content of the caring that orients the aim of political ruling and constitutes a distinctive dimension of its *dunamis*; it will occupy us again in chapter 11.

---

38. See chapter 5 on therapeutic *technai* in *Republic* 1 and elsewhere in Plato. The *Statesman* also uses *epimeleia* and *tina therapeia* to refer to the kinds of expertise that care for and look after clothes (281b4; cf. *pasan tēn . . . therapeutikēn*, also in the context of clothes, 282a2).

Weaving

While "caring" brings to bear the particular purpose and orientation with which the epitactic *dunamis* of statecraft (or of weaving) is to be exercised, "weaving" is the precise task that the statesman is to deploy his epitactic capacity oriented to caring to realize (and weaving itself was described as a form of "care" for clothes earlier in the dialogue). Moreover, all three are exercised by the statesman in a way that pertains to the city as a whole (*kata polin* is echoed at 305e10). For its part, the mention of weaving serves as a fulcrum, looking backward to the *paradeigma* of weaving earlier in the dialogue, but also forward, as the Visitor immediately goes on to suggest: "At this point we'll want, won't we, to pursue it [sc. the expertise of statecraft just defined] further by reference to the model (*paradeigma*) of the expertise of weaving, now that all the classes of things in the city have become clear to us?" (305e8–10, trans. Rowe, modified). And then he continues in his next speech: "Then it seems that we should discuss the intertwining that belongs to kingship—of what kind it is, and in what way it intertwines to render us what sort of fabric" (306a1–3, trans. Rowe). Picking up "intertwining" (*sumplokē*) as one of the great kinds of expertise from the division of weaving itself, the Visitor here points out that statecraft, like weaving, involves an activity of intertwining that produces a fabric—or to put it in the combined terms of the *Republic* and *Statesman*, it is an expertise with a *dunamis* that serves to realize (*apergazetai*) an *ergon*.[39]

Are ruling, caring, and weaving three entirely distinct activities? The answer is no.[40] The statesman is to rule over the other forms of expertise, giving epitactic orders to the three precious and kindred practitioners, and also (in the closing pages of the dialogue) to all of those practitioners who do the preliminary culling and preparing of citizens capable of receiving education (308d6–7), and more generally in the role of statecraft as commanding and ordering "those who prepare the other things it needs for its own work" (308d7–9, trans. Rowe).[41] So the epitactic role of the statesman in giving orders to the educators is part of what is involved in his caring for everything in the city, a task that includes caring for the citizens by overseeing their education and also by weaving their dispositions together as part of a fabric of civic

---

39. For the *Republic*'s introduction of the relationship among these terms, see my "Statecraft" (201–2), with references therein.

40. See the discussion of this question in El Murr's "Kingly Intertwinement," treating the end section of the dialogue, on which I comment only briefly here. Consider also the passage at *Leg.* 1.650b7–9, noted at the end of the preceding chapter of this study, describing *politikē* (political expertise) as the *technē* that "cares for (*therapeuein*)" souls.

41. The Visitor uses the same pair of verbs first as participles (*prostattousa kai epistatousa*, 308d6), and then as finite verbs (*prostattei kai epistattei*, 308d9).

unity.[42] This will enable those properly prepared to issue *kairos*-respecting orders themselves when they are entrusted by the statesman with the offices. Once again, the *taxis* of statecraft is inherently oriented toward its *telos*.

The inquiry as a whole, with its divisions followed by a new method of separative identification compared to smelting metals,[43] has elucidated not only all the forms of expertise relevant to politics but also all the kinds of objects relevant to the city, as in the initial divisions modeled on the *paradeigma* (model) of weaving earlier.[44] But now weaving will return as model not for identification of civic kinds but for the identification of the task of kingly weaving as intertwining. The fabric that is the *ergon* produced by weaving will be a fabric of civic virtues possessed and actualized by the educated part of the citizenry, a group divided into two, those inclined toward courage and those inclined toward moderation. Kingly statecraft must not only rule over the subordinate forms of expertise but also effect an intertwining to realize its *ergon*. And in so doing, it will rule not only over the practitioners of the other expertises but also over the citizens, a shift that comes to fruition in the final section of the dialogue.

Rule and Office Redux

In commenting on the deployment, and eventual circumscribing, of the Homeric figure of the shepherd, I elaborated the sense in which the statesman must be oriented to the good of the ruled in the mode of caring. It is not enough to know what the good requires; one does not have a rule-apt expertise unless one is oriented to caring for its achievement. This, however, is definitional of the role of statesman or king (a role that defines the person with the requisite expertise to play it), rather than a claim about the motivation of any one person to take up that role or how they will actually perform it. Indeed, the question of motivation to take up the role of ruler will be thematized as problematic in *Republic* book 1, as the next chapter of this study discusses.

There is still more to be said about the element of statecraft that consists in weaving. For this is not only an activity but an activity with a product. Weaving

---

42. A detailed account of the Greek model of weaving and the implications for politics that the reader of Plato has reason to draw from it, which offers some powerful challenges to my interpretation (especially by highlighting the collective agency involved in weaving, as opposed to my focus on that of the weaver or statesman alone), is offered by Frank and Greenberg, in "Weaving Politics," a forthcoming article that I benefited from being able to read as a working paper while finalizing this manuscript.

43. For analysis of this method, see my "Statecraft," correcting the assumption in *Method and Politics* (198–200) that the method of division continued to apply here.

44. I was persuaded by Gill ("Models") that "model" is the best translation of *paradeigma* in these Platonic contexts, contra my use of "example" to translate it in *Method and Politics*. See more recently Bronstein's "Learning from Models."

makes the *telos* of statecraft concrete (or rather, and paradoxically, abstractly concrete): not simply the normative goal of the good of the ruled but the production of a "civic fabric" in which opposing groups of citizens are interwoven in their own activities. Moreover, those activities are said to include the holding of the "offices." This brings me back to the question: Which offices might the Visitor have in mind, in the underspecified terms of his reference to them near the end of the dialogue (311a4–6), which stipulates only that some are collective and some individual offices? I have argued elsewhere that these offices can be understood as corresponding to the three precious and kindred forms of expertise that had (just before the definition of statecraft was reached) been successively distinguished from statecraft.[45] Each of those forms of expertise was related to an office, or a quasi-office, typical of Greek polities at the time. The general was an officeholder in many constitutions, including democratic Athens; the orator could hold civic quasi-offices (as when Pericles famously occupied the role of funeral orator appointed by the Athenian *polis* to mourn the war dead of a given year), or at least be subject to judicial procedures to hold them broadly accountable in other ways; and the judge or juror would be described by Aristotle in book 3 of the *Politics* (1275a32–33) as holding an "indefinite office," and was acknowledged as in some sense an officeholder by Plato in the *Laws* (in a dense passage discussed above in chapter 3). Thus, in associating those offices or quasi-offices each with a characteristic form of expertise, and then in suggesting that the citizens should in the city of the true statesman occupy (unspecified) offices, Plato is here (through his avatar the Eleatic Visitor) reconfiguring the qualifications for holding at least these offices to include a relatively high epistemic qualification. Among the offices envisaged may also be the roles of the educators and childcare attendants mentioned next as carrying out a role entrusted to them (using the verb *epitrepein*) by kingly expertise.[46] These subordinate educators, whose work is done "according to law" (*kata nomon*, 308e5), must be prohibited from producing persons who would be dispositionally incapable of joining in the appropriate mixing of persons and roles that kingly expertise requires. The Visitor underscores here the overarching epitactic capacity [*dunamis*] of kingship (308e5–6), assigning it the (to modern eyes deeply illiberal) task of killing, exiling, or punishing anyone who fails to share in the virtuous dispositions requisite.

---

45. The remainder of this paragraph summarizes arguments made in my "Political Expertise."

46. I translate *tropheusin* (308e6) as "childcare attendants" rather than "tutors," as the sense of a role in rearing and upbringing more generally (also picking up on the discussion of herd rearing earlier in the dialogue) seems more apposite here as a separate role to be paired with "educators (*paideutais*)" than does Rowe's "tutors." Note that this final section of argument is phrased largely in terms of the activity or task of the expertise rather than the corresponding person, as in *hē basilikē* at 308e4 (glossed in terms of its *dunamis* being one that is *epitaktikē*, 308e5–6).

The Visitor goes on to describe the task of creating both divine and human bonds among these people, here assigning it to the personified role of the *"politikos* and the good legislator" (309d1–4), who not only has the power of the musical kingly expertise to employ but also cannot be called by the names (presumably, statesman and king) under investigation should they not possess that power (309d6–8). But at the very end of the dialogue, he returns to taking the expertise, not the person, as his subject: the *ergon* of "kingly interweaving" is to create a smooth and fine-woven fabric (*uphasma*), and it is this expertise that is to "entrust (*epitrepein*)" the offices in common to the two groups of citizens (310d7–311a2), a task that the Eleatic explains as being that of "choosing" the appropriate candidates for individual or group office, as quoted above.

This brings me back full circle, to the problem of understanding what "choosing" (*hairoumenon*) the citizens to fill the offices should be taken to mean (311a4–6). Does the Visitor's ascription of it to the expertise of kingly interweaving, rather than to the person who possesses that expertise, signal that this may be a second-order kind of role, one of creating the conditions for others to choose rather than of directly choosing itself? When the same verb (*epitrepein*) was used as between the kingly expertise and the educators and childcare attendants, it was paired with a verb (*parakeleusthai*) that means "exhort" or "recommend," rather than "order" (308e4–8). That suggests that the role of the kingly expertise is to set up background conditions for the activity of others, a role consonant with its forging of the divine and human bonds as well. And that in turn would support an interpretation of *epitrepein* at 311a2 as likewise one of entrusting a sphere of operation that has been set up with certain conditions and parameters in order to enable others to act. The "choosing" (*hairoumenon*) of appropriate officeholders could then be conceived as the role of the kingly interweaving being to have set up appropriate conditions so as to "leave" (another possible meaning of *epitrepein*)[47] it up to the other citizens to "elect" the officeholders in the usual institutional sense of the verb *haireisthai*.

This is a speculative interpretation, but it pays closer attention to the syntax and semantics of these passages than most debates about the statesman's active role at the end of the dialogue have done (including my own previous contributions on this point).[48] The choice of whether to read these functions of statecraft as enabling background conditions rather than active interventional choices remains, I think now, open. However one interprets this, the dialogue is at least emphasizing that supervising education and overseeing the selection of officeholders are both part of the role of ruling with kingly expertise, so as to safeguard the officeholders and the constitution and city more broadly. Ruling expertise involves a two-part role of educating persons capable of filling

---

47. See the LSJ entry for the verb *epitrepō*.
48. Lane, *Method and Politics* (177–78); "Political Expertise" (70–72).

the roles of officeholding as well as setting up a way of matching persons to appropriate offices. Indeed, these functions are very similar to those that Plato most emphasizes also for the guardian-rulers of the *Republic*: for them, also, supervising procreative couplings so as to produce persons capable of ruling, and selecting those capable at each educational stage of fulfilling the requisite political roles are the fundamental tasks of ruling. It is their failure in judging the right timing for procreative couplings that leads to the downfall of the ideal regime in *Republic* 8, as this error leads to a breakdown of the education required to form the kinds of natural persons who are capable of rule.[49]

The *Republic* and the *Statesman*, that is, agree that an ideal city must be governed by genuine knowledge with respect to education and marriage. To put it in the terms of the *Statesman* in particular, the statesman's rule (*archein*) over the officeholders who exercise the arts of rhetoric, generalship, and jurisprudence is superordinate in that it shapes the conditions and the characters of the very officeholders who will be able to exercise those subordinate forms of expertise. The statesman cannot rule without such officeholders. Indeed, the role of the kingly ruler in engaging in *archein* (in the sense of rule) serves to safeguard the exercise of the limited constitutional powers belonging to those who hold the *archai* (in the sense of offices).

Office and Rule in Flawed Constitutions

The reference to offices comes at the end of the dialogue, as part of the depiction of the *ergon* of statecraft or kingly expertise, realizing its composite *dunamis* of ruling, caring, and weaving. But before moving on to the *Republic* in the next chapter, it is helpful to return to an earlier stretch of the *Statesman* offering an analysis and ranking of variously flawed constitutions, in the course of which the nature of correct rule was significantly elaborated. Indeed, in this context, the noun *archē* must be understood in the sense of "rule" (rather than "office"), as the Visitor launches his own version of a medical analogy to underscore that the only defining mark of "correct rule" [*hē . . . orthē archē*, 293a3] is that those who are ruling (*archontas*) are doing so on the basis of expertise [*kata technē*], irrespective of whether the rulers rule over willing or unwilling subjects, according to written laws or without them, and whether they (the rulers) are rich or poor (293a6–9). The analogy to doctors draws the same moral, about "medicine and any other kind of rule [*archē*] of any sort," spelling out that the "defining mark" [*horos*] of its correctness is again its expertise,

---

49. In the *Laws*, by contrast, the functions of supervising education and marriage are assigned to specific civic offices to be carried out by elected citizens (and the supervision of marriage does not there involve dictating the timing of procreative couplings). I argued in chapter 3 that the role of safeguarding there is primarily expressed in the safeguarding of the reason embedded in the laws themselves, rather than assigned to an epitactic role for particular human rulers.

regardless of whether it is done to willing or unwilling patients, according to written instructions or without them, and whether the doctors are rich or poor (these conditions being excluded in notably parallel language) (293b1–c3); I return to this discussion in chapter 11. A similar analysis of rule (*archē*) as the ordering activity common to the therapeutic *technai* is advanced in *Republic* 1, as the next chapter will show.

The Eleatic underscores this account of the single defining mark of rule by pairing it with an account of the kind of constitution that is "correct" and "alone a constitution" (293c6, trans. Rowe): namely, once again adopting the strict evaluative approach to certain ideas (introduced in chapter 1) in describing such a constitution as "the one in which one would find the rulers to be genuinely expert and not only seeming to be so" (293c6–8, trans. Rowe, modified). And then, having advanced an analysis of correct *archē* (rule) as an abstract noun, as well as of the corresponding correct *politeia*, he is confronted with a significant objection from Young Socrates: "The rest of what you have said, Visitor, seems to have been said measuredly. But what has been said as to it being necessary to rule (*archein*) without laws is harder to hear" (293e7–9).[50] Throughout the discussion of this objection, which takes up a considerable portion of the dialogue, the Eleatic continues to make references to ruling in an abstract and ideal sense as characterizing the ideal statesman-cum-king (e.g., "our kingly rulers" (*tous basilikous archontas*), 297e9). Anders Dahl Sørensen has argued persuasively that Young Socrates's discomfort should not be interpreted as being merely about laws. Rather, it should be taken to express the Greek constitutionalist assumption (one that has been laid out also in the present study) that Greek officeholders should be subject to institutional limits on power, including term limits, rotation in office, and *euthunai*.[51] Sørensen argues that the dialogue overall is working to replace the role of law in constraining and limiting offices in this picture with an

50. While the Visitor initially framed the excluded criterion in terms of whether or not rule is in accordance with (*kata*) written laws (239a7), in his subsequent speech he reframes it in terms of whether or not rule is in accordance with (*kata*) laws simpliciter (293c8–9), and it is the latter formulation with which Young Socrates then expresses discomfort ("objection," the term used above, may in fact be a bit too formal to capture his tone). Note that while the Visitor had both times framed the question as one of whether rule is *according* to (*kata*) laws or not, the youth instead frames the issue as whether rule *must* (*dein*) be carried out *without* (*aneu*) laws—thus raising the stakes considerably, as well as obscuring the possibility that kingly rule may comport with the existence of laws even if they are not always followed in individual decisions, which is in fact the position that the Visitor will end up defending.

51. Sørensen, in "Political Office," cites my "Political Expertise," but does not note the specific anticipation of this argument made there in the description of the thought experiment as "laws governing all the forms of expertise, of officeholders who are chosen by lottery and who then rule strictly according to the written laws" (77), though I welcome his further elaboration of what the institutional rules governing such officeholders would

alternative idea of law as "an approximation to the ideal rule of knowledge,"[52] in which the offices governed by law are to be exercised on the basis of "the right kind of professional expertise."[53]

Broadly speaking, my own views are aligned with those of Sørensen on this topic, especially in emphasizing that law-governed rotation of office is presented by the Visitor as insufficient to secure a meaningful rule of law (a point that I take Plato to make more generally about the insufficiency of proce-dure to ensure the proper *telos* of office).[54] However, I believe that Sørensen goes too far in suggesting that, by the end of the dialogue, "the relation between political office and rule of law has been wholly dislodged from the traditional understanding, on which the laws in question were first and foremost those formal and procedural limitations on official power embodied in the institu-tion of *archē* itself." While by "wholly dislodged" he may mean only to stress the underlying basis for law being changed, his argument fails to identify the significant ways in which those formal and procedural institutional limita-tions seem to remain in force in the sketch of the role of offices at the end of the dialogue, which involve mention of collective collegial offices (in some cases), the word for election, and an implicit principle of rotation of office.[55] The reconfiguration of such offices at the end of the *Statesman*, as laid out above, conserves some of their recognizable features in conventional practice and usage, even while here (as in the *Republic* and *Laws*) Plato renovates the proper understanding of the ethical and epistemic expectations of those who should hold them.[56]

---

have been in Greek constitutional thought and practice at the time (as well as his further engagement with my paper on other points).

52. Sørensen, "Political Office," 406.

53. Sørensen, "Political Office," 417.

54. I would also question his claim that by making the behavior of officeholders central to the way in which the posited law-abiding democracy might go politically wrong, Plato is offering a "strained and artificial" account (404), a claim echoed in Sørensen's asking why Plato offers an "analysis that focuses so one-sidedly on the role of political officials in government, even at the price of seriously distorting (by his own standards) his por-trayal of lawless democracy" (406). While it is true that Plato does elsewhere sometimes emphasize the role of the mass rather than the officeholders in a lawless democracy, the emphasis on officeholders is consistent with the portrayal of the degenerating democracy of the *Republic* (see chapter 8 below, anticipated in my "How to Turn History") and also with wider accounts of political change as revolving in important ways around the role of officeholders. This account is neither "strained and artificial," nor, as Sørensen also alleges (405), "peculiar."

55. Sørensen, "Political Office," 417.

56. In concluding that it is the judge's "capacity and disposition for judging correctly and impartially, that ensures that the city is governed in strict accordance with laws—those substantive laws that the expert statesman has laid down in imitation of his own individual instructions," and that it is "in this specific sense . . . [that] the institution of office-holding remains central to rule of law even in Plato's ideal city in the *Statesman*," it may seem that

In delineating the role of ruling expertise and the corresponding statesman-cum-king, the *Statesman* does not prescind from conventional constitutional analysis in the Greek context but rather presupposes it. The elevation of the statesman (*politikos*) completes the city. But it does not exhaust its political functions. The exercise of *archein* by the *politikos* is complementary to, rather than being a replacement for, the holding of *tas archas* by select citizens.[57] The dialogue delineates not only the content of political expertise but the role of the politically expert statesman in ruling, a role that serves to safeguard the holding of the offices within the constitutional order of the city briefly sketched at the end of the dialogue. Nevertheless, the dialogue says nothing about the qualities or motivations of the natural persons capable of playing the role of ruling as a statesman—that is, as a safeguarding ruler, superordinate to the officeholders whom it also envisages within the city. Its interest is in defining the role, not in how it could be filled. In contrast, the *Republic* attends both to the various roles of ruling within the constitutional project that it envisages and to the qualities, education, and selection needed to choose the natural persons capable of filling it. It is to that interwoven account that I now turn.

Sørensen (417) is making the same point. But in fact his argument here is that it is solely in (what he takes to be) the wholly epistemic qualification of the judge that the institution of officeholding is conserved in the ideal city, whereas I am stressing the conservation of a number of its broader institutional parameters as well.

57. I have significantly modified this paragraph from my "Political Expertise" to be consonant with changes in my views as expressed in the current chapter.

CHAPTER FIVE

Defining the *Telos* of Rule
(*Republic*, Book 1)

IN DISCUSSING PLATO'S *STATESMAN*, I remarked on Thomas Hobbes's rhetorical question in the preface to *De cive*, asking: "How many men have been killed by the erroneous doctrine that sovereign Kings are not masters but servants of society?" As argued in the preceding chapter, Plato in the *Statesman* insists that genuine kings, who possess the same political expertise as genuine statesmen, are rulers (or masters, as Plato, like Hobbes, sometimes puts it), whose purpose is to serve. Making this case by appealing to (while also critiquing) long-standing Greek figurations of rulers as shepherds or stewards, Plato argues that political rulers are not servants *simpliciter*, since their role is characterized by the power to issue orders (as part of a broader function of ordering). Indeed, they serve as rulers, in both senses of that phrase.

Kingship is thematized by Plato in the *Republic* as well, within the "beautiful city" (*kallipolis*) for which the dialogue's interlocutors—Socrates as avatar, and Plato's real-life brothers, Glaucon and Adeimantus—constitute themselves as discursive legislators in the middle of book 2.[1] That thematization, including the nature of kingly rule and its relationship to office within the *kallipolis* envisaged "in speech," will be considered further in the remaining chapters of part II. The present chapter begins instead with the thematization of rule outside the frame of the discursive legislation, in the provocative intervention into the discussion made by Thrasymachus and his subsequent exchanges with Socrates in book 1. Whereas the *Statesman* focuses especially on the *taxis* of rule, the argument between Socrates and Thrasymachus in *Republic* 1 focuses especially on its *telos*, underscoring the archaic evaluative expectation that the ruler is to aim at the good of the ruled. Yet whereas Homeric and other

---

1. "Avatar" and "discursive legislator" were introduced as terms of art in the present study in part I.

influential images of rulers as kings set political rulers apart from anyone else (even in comparing them with shepherds, since that comparison was a trope in Homer used for political rulers alone), the argument of *Republic* 1 treats political rule as but one instance of a more general category of rule characterizing the activity of *technai* more generally (or, at least, to go by the examples invoked, those I shall call the therapeutic *technai* that aim at the good of their subjects).

In so treating rule as an activity of ordering that is not unique to political rule but rather characterizes it alongside its role within a set of other *technai*, Socrates's arguments in *Republic* 1 are not incompatible with those advanced by the Eleatic Visitor in the *Statesman*. On the contrary, both sets of arguments emphasize the role of the ruler as defined by an evaluative *telos* directed toward the good of the ruled; an epitactic *taxis* of ordering, including paradigmatically the issuing of orders; and an epistemic grasp, which enables the *taxis* of rule to be correctly oriented to the realization of its *telos*. Beyond that, the *Statesman* rests content with treating the statesman as a cipher, inquiring neither into the kind of nature or education that would be required to create a person capable of occupying such a role nor into the motivation that such a person would then have for assuming that role. By contrast, *Republic* 1 is a portal onto a much larger and more complex set of arguments in the *Republic* as a whole, including the discursive legislating of a *kallipolis* (a beautiful or fine city), in the course of which such inquiries into the nature, education, and motivation of the persons capable of occupying the role of ruler are made visible and salient (while the extent to which they are successfully answered remains highly contentious), and which I discuss further in the subsequent chapter.

Preliminaries

Plato's character Thrasymachus is named for a person whose existence is historically documented outside of Plato, as an orator and author engaged in civic affairs for his *polis* of Chalcedon; he is often classed by scholars as a sophist.[2] In terms of the dialogue's setting in Piraeus, the port of Athens, at the home of a family of settled foreigners with the status of metics, his presence is explained by his serving as an ambassador from Chalcedon to Athens. He bursts into the discussion in order to offer a controversial account of justice— focusing on the political justice embodied in the laws of any given society— as inevitably imposed by the rulers of a city and so as serving their interest.[3]

2. As by Laks and Most in *Early Greek Philosophy*, vol. 8, and Anderson in "Thrasymachus' Sophistic Account."

3. His motivation in doing so has been a matter of dispute, most reading it as a matter of amoral political ambition, while S. White, in "Thrasymachus the Diplomat," has persuasively argued that it is rather a kind of world-weary regret. Whatever his motivation, the dialogue clearly depicts his savvy theoretical abilities (a point pressed upon me in private

Most studies of his ensuing exchanges with Socrates focus on the role played by *technē*, which we may understand as craft, skill, art, or, as I shall say here, following Emily Hulme, profession.[4] In contrast, I argue that the debate actually hinges on the idea of *archē*,[5] used primarily by both Socrates and Thrasymachus in their exchanges in the abstract and general sense of "rule"—notwithstanding that both characters show themselves also aware of the alternative sense of *archē*, more common in political practice as well as political theorizing at the time, to denote a defined constitutional office. Socrates treats rule as a hierarchical relation of subordination between individuals or entities, in which the relationship is a question of "who whom"—as Plato might, like Lenin, have been willing to say.[6] Yet it is likewise a relationship of service, in which the ruler has the role of providing benefit to the ruled, and in which the perfection of the rule qua rule lies in the realization of the ability to provide that benefit fully and precisely.[7]

---

correspondence by Terence Irwin), comporting with the evidence that survives of his writings (generally classed as being those of a sophist). For a discussion of the ancient sources on Thrasymachus's actual engagement with rhetoric, see El Murr ("Platon," 345–46). For a discussion of the overall tensions in Thrasymachus's stance, making sense of them by construing him as a genealogist of morals, see Anderson's "Thrasymachus' Sophistic Account."

4. Hulme Kozey, "*Philosophia* and *Philotechnia*" and "Another *Peri Technes* Literature." While no translation is perfect, Hulme has persuaded me that so long as one sets aside the connotation of the elevated social status that professionals receive (or at least assert) from the nineteenth century onward, this one has more advantages than any other. Compare the conception of an "expert" as "a well-qualified specialist on whom others may safely rely," which is developed in Woodruff ("Plato's Early Theory," 100).

5. Pace scholars such as Lycos (*Plato on Justice and Power*) and Allen (introduction to his translation of the *Republic*), both of whom who focus on the nature of *technē* alone as the key to the refutation of Thrasymachus here. See also Thakkar (*Plato as Critical Theorist*), whose interest is especially in the role of moneymaking in the argument and its relationship to various *technai*. My emphasis on *archē* does not of course belie the importance of *technē* within book 1, the *Republic*, and Plato more broadly: this is emphasized by Wallach in *Platonic Political Art* (234–49 and passim) and is the subject of divergent interpretations by Irwin in *Plato's Moral Theory* (contrasting the early dialogues with the *Republic*), Schofield in *Plato* (contrasting the *Republic* with the *Statesman*), and others.

6. The formula "who whom" (*kto kogo* in Russian) is an abbreviated version of a question attributed to Lenin in a speech of October 17, 1921, reporting to the Second All-Russia Congress of Political Education Departments, though not all English translations render it this way (including that available at "V. I. Lenin: The New Economic Policy," Collected Works vol. 33, Marxists Internet Archive, https://www.marxists.org/archive/lenin/works/1921/oct/17.htm). Geuss (*Philosophy and Real Politics*, 23–30) discusses the formula's political significance, as I did more briefly in *Birth of Politics* (3).

7. In "*Technē* and *Archē*," I experimented in this sentence, and at certain other points, with the gender-neutral pronoun "hir," as it is grammatically inclusive but sounds when spoken indistinguishable from the female pronoun "her." The aim was to provide an anticipation, by way of an unexpected aural jolt, of Plato's insistence in *Republic* book 5 that those of any gender can have the natures suitable to become philosophers and rulers (cf. Derrida on the oral indistinguishability of *difference* and *différance*). However, the

The Meaning of "Rule" and Thrasymachus's
Initial Political Examples

When Thrasymachus first offers his definition of justice, as "nothing other than the advantage of the stronger" (*Resp.* 338c2–3),[8] he expounds it by invoking a version of traditional Greek classifications of political constitutions as common knowledge: "Don't you know that some cities are ruled by a tyranny, some by a democracy, and some by an aristocracy?" as Grube/Reeve translate, or, more literally: "Don't you know that in cities some are tyrannical rulers, some are democratic rulers, and some are aristocratic rulers?" (338d6–7).[9] The more literal translation reveals Thrasymachus's focus on the individuals, or bodies of individuals, who are doing the ruling—that is, on those one might call the agents of rule—which he then glosses and generalizes by an abstract noun in his next question: "And in each city this element dominates, the ruling body (*touto kratei en hekastēi polei, to archon*)?" (338d9). I translate *to archon* as "ruling body" to bring out its abstract hypostatization. Yet this hypostatization is not of rule as such (as if it were disembodied from the agents and subjects of rule) but, rather, precisely of *rulers*—that is, the agents of rule, whether tyrannical, democratic, or aristocratic rule, across whom *to archon* is introduced to generalize.[10] Indeed, Thrasymachus, like Socrates in response to him, here is sensitive to the way in which even the lexical sense of *archē* that is closest to the abstract meaning of "rule" ("*first place* or *power, sovereignty*," a sense that is distinguished in the lexicon entry from that of "*magistracy, office*")—has in context still the meaning of a sovereign body or entity rather than the purely abstract notion of rule in general.[11] In other words, he uses the

---

typographical awkwardness of that usage has here led me to revert to more standard, if unsatisfactory, gendered pronouns.

8. All quotations in this chapter are drawn from book 1 of the *Republic* (conventionally abbreviated from the Latin *Respublica* as *Resp.*), unless otherwise noted; for this reason, I generally omit the leading digit (such as "1.") that I use elsewhere to indicate a book within a Platonic dialogue. Quotations of the Greek are according to the OCT edited by Slings, and in my own translation, unless otherwise indicated.

9. Strikingly, however, Socrates uses only the pejorative vocabulary of tyranny to describe rule by one—*hai ... turannountai*, 338d6; *turannis*, 338e2; *turannikous*, 338e2–3—while using the notably positive vocabulary of aristocracy for rule by the few: *hai ... aristokratountai*, 338d7.

10. Compare Otanes's invocation of *plēthos archon* in Herodotus (3.80.6). This likewise is often translated as "the rule of the multitude," as if "rule" were the (abstract) subject and multitude a qualification. But such a construal would require "rule" to be a nominative and "of the multitude" to be a partitive genitive. In fact, in Herodotus's Greek, "the multitude" is the subject and "ruling" is a present active participle of the verb *archō*: the phrase means "the ruling multitude," not "the rule of the multitude."

11. LSJ, ad loc.

noun here very often as a kind of shorthand for "the ruling (i.e., those ruling) over the ruled" (bringing this use of the noun close to the substantive use of the participle of the verb *archein*, as discussed in part I).

Thrasymachus then introduces a further gloss or substitution, moving from the neuter *to archon* to the feminine *hē archē*. But, again, because each of these is introduced as a way to gloss the threefold cases of tyrannical, democratic, and aristocratic rulers, *hē archē* too should be interpreted as a hypostatization of the ruling agents, not as a bloodless notion of rule in general abstracted from the relation of subordination between rulers and ruled. He then generalizes his claim to cover all these ruling entities, again using the feminine noun as a hypostatization of the ruling individual or group: calling justice in all cities "the advantage of the established ruling body (*to tēs kathestēkuias archēs sumpheron*), however it holds sway (*kratei*)" (338e6–a2).[12] And in continuing to read the dialogue, even where the noun *hē archē* may in later contexts be idiomatically best translated as "rule" (notwithstanding that this word itself does not appear in the LSJ entry for the noun in the closest relevant sense), one must keep in mind that the closest relevant lexical sense of "first place" or "power, sovereignty" still bears with it the idea of a being or entity holding that place or exercising that power or sovereignty. Rule is for Plato always a relationship of subordination: one person or entity ruling and another being ruled, with such subordination being, in the standard political case, interpersonal.

"In the Precise Sense": From Thrasymachus on Rulers and Professionals to Socrates on Rulers as Professionals

As argued above, Thrasymachus initially sets the agenda for treating ruling, and its ruling bodies or agents, within a relatively familiar and conventional political framework of the rule by one, few, or many, though given a particular accent by his word choices. And Plato has Socrates, too, remain within that broad paradigm as he begins to challenge the Chalcedonian on the problematic case of rulers making mistakes: as late as 340c8–d2, Socrates uses *tous archontas* (340c8) in the implicit context of political rulers only. It is in responding to that challenge—Socrates's argument from error, as I shall call it—that Thrasymachus makes the first move of the dialogue to broaden the family of examples of rule and, notably, to include professionals within it: introducing the doctor (*ho iatros*), the accountant (*ho logistēs*), and the

---

12. Grube/Reeve translate *to tēs kathestēkuias archēs* as "the established rule," which is ambiguous as to whether what is meant is an entity composed of individuals (as I argue) or a wholly abstract idea. The phrase should be interpreted in light of the preceding claim about cities being ruled alternatively by tyrannical, democratic, or aristocratic rulers.

grammarian (*ho grammatistēs*), all invoked in a neat sequence at 340d6–8.[13] It is again he who first introduces the notion of defining the figure of the ruler (*ton archonta*, 340b5) in a strict or precise sense, reiterating this move several times in related formulations in the same speech (his second major speech, ridiculing and rejecting Socrates's argument from error)—summed up in the claim that "the most precise answer (*to . . . akribestaton*) is this. A ruler, insofar as he is a ruler, never makes errors and unerringly decrees what is best for himself, and this his subject must do" (340e8–341a3).[14] From this he infers the vindication of his original claim (now understood in the *akribestaton* sense): "Thus, as I said from the first, it is just to do what is to the advantage of the stronger" (1.341a3–4).

In fact, whereas Thrasymachus had advanced the "precise sense" stipulation in the context of observing a claim about rulers pursuing their own good, but doing so without error, Socrates will turn the "precise sense" definition of a ruler into one in which the teleological flow of a ruler's activity must flow toward the good of the ruled. Thus despite the jujitsu appropriation by Socrates of the Chalcedonian's terminology,[15] the teleological directionality toward the good of the ruled built into the Platonic idea of a ruler gives that terminology an evaluative dimension in Socrates's hands that it lacked when first formulated by the sophist. From a strictly (Socratically) precise standpoint, as opposed to a Thrasymachean one, a ruler who cares for his own good instead of the good of the ruled is simply no ruler at all.

13. The first two are actually introduced for the first time earlier in the same speech, at 340d3 and d4 respectively. The doctor and the accountant, of course, featured in important ways in the early divisions of the *Statesman*, as argued in the previous chapter.

14. The relevant expressions used by Thrasymachus to this end include *tōi akribestatōi* (341b8), *ton akribē logon* (340e1–2), *to . . . akribestaton* (340e8), all of which he connects with an appeal to the idea that a professional who errs "is no professional" (340e4), generalized to the claim that "no professional, expert, or ruler makes an error at the moment when he is ruling" (*archōn . . . archōn*) (340e4–5). To be sure, Thrasymachus acknowledges that in common parlance people do sometimes say that "a doctor is in error, or an accountant, or a grammarian" (340d6–8), reiterating this point toward the end of the speech ("everyone will say that a physician or a ruler makes errors," 340e6–7), and exculpating himself from earlier self-contradiction by claiming that what he said earlier must be understood in this way (340e7–8, presumably referring to the chain of inferences that Socrates had pressed upon him at 339b4–e8). But he insists that, strictly or precisely speaking, "no professional, expert, or ruler makes an error at the moment (*tote*) when he is ruling" (340e4–5; more literally, "whenever he is ruling").

15. Socrates uses the "precise sense" terminology at 341b3–7, 342b6, 346b3, 346d2. Socrates also introduces related vocabulary in the course of the discussion—*ho orthōs kubernētēs*, 341c10; *hōs alēthōs iatron*, 345c2, *hōs alēthōs poimena*, 345c3, *hōs alēthōs iatron*, 345e2; *tōi onti alēthinos archōn*, 347d4–5—in the speech summing up the debate about the definition of justice as the advantage of the stronger. It is interesting to compare these formulations with one that Plato uses elsewhere referring to what people generally say, the so-called (*hōs legomenon*) doctor and so forth; on this turn of phrase in Plato, I have benefited from the discussion of Geiger in "So genannten Könige."

This is connected to the fact that while Thrasymachus compares being a professional with being a ruler, it is Socrates who eventually identifies them, treating being a ruler as a case of having professional expertise. Thrasymachus relates the cases of selected professionals to the (political) ruler simply through comparison—still holding to the meaning of "ruler" as "political ruler" only (and specifically). So he uses the phrase quoted above ("no professional, expert, or ruler," 340e4–5), following this up with the comparative formulation "a physician or a ruler" (340e6),[16] and ending up with the claim that matters most to him, which the discussion of the professionals has evidently been designed to illustrate and support:[17] "A ruler, insofar as he is a ruler, never makes errors and unerringly decrees what is best for himself, and this his subject must do" (340e5–341a3).

Having gotten Thrasymachus to reaffirm that he means this precision in the case of the (political) ruler, Socrates immediately picks up on the example of the doctor that Thrasymachus had ventured. Invoking the doctor, and then pairing this figure with his own example of the steersman (while leaving aside Thrasymachus's remaining examples of accountant and grammarian), the crucial move comes in my view when Socrates asks, "What about a ship's steersman (*kubernētēs*)? Is a steersman in the precise sense a ruler of sailors or a sailor?" (341c10–11).[18] Notice that what distinguishes the steersman from the other sailors is his role of ruling over them, their subordination to his orders. It is the sailors who are here the subjects of the steersman's skill, in a double sense: they are at once the objects of the steersman's rule and those subjected to it, its subjects—a point to which we shall return. And while this understanding of the steersman may seem strange to modern ears, as one might today think that the purpose of the steersman's skill is to navigate to an externally chosen destination (an assumption made by Renford Bambrough in an influential article),[19]

16. I follow Grube/Reeve in translating the *kai* in this line as "or."

17. On the "empirical" dimension of Thrasymachus's case, see El Murr ("Platon," 355; see also 360–64).

18. I have modified the Grube/Reeve translation of *kubernētēs* (cognate with the Latin *gubernator*) from "captain" to "steersman" with the benefit of advice from Paul Cartledge. The background to Socrates's choice of examples may well be the *Gorgias*, where (in the conversation with Callicles), he gives a list with doctor and steersman on it (512b–d), and also discusses the caretaking *technai* that are identified at various moments as *therapeiai*; see also *Ion* 540b6–d3, where Socrates introduces similar examples of professionals—including, strikingly, the *kubernētēs*; the *iatros*, or doctor; and the *boukolos*, or cowherd (who will appear in *Republic* 1 in what I call "Thrasymachus's last stand" below); as well as the woman weaving and the general—precisely as illustrations of rulers (*archonti; Ion* 540b5, b6, c1). I owe these thoughts to Emily Hulme and Alex Long respectively, in private communications.

19. See Bambrough's "Plato's Political Analogies" on the "ship of state" passage at *Resp.* 6.488a–489a, a passage that discusses the *technē* of navigation or steersmanship and the role of the "true steersman (*tou . . . alēthinou kubernētou*)" (6.488d4–5).

it makes more sense in considering that the ship in question here could well be (since the civic context is at the forefront) a ship crewed on behalf of the *polis*—that is, a warship, fighting on behalf of the *dēmos* who are also (metonymically, in the sense that a subset of them are) the sailors who crew it.[20] The good of the ship's journey is the good of the sailors in that broader sense, and the steersman orders them to act as sailors accordingly.

In any case, Socrates follows up his question to emphasize his counterintuitive claim that the steersman in the precise sense should be defined not as sailing but as ruling over sailors:

> We shouldn't, I think, take into account the fact that he sails in a ship, and he shouldn't be called a sailor for that reason, for it isn't because of his sailing that he is called a ship's steersman, but because of his profession and his rule over sailors (*kata tēn technēn kai tēn tōn nautōn archēn*). (341d2–4)

Again, this is a claim to which Thrasymachus is for the moment content simply to agree. In this, and in the preceding question, rule (*archē*) is no longer merely being compared to *technē*. Rather, it is being incorporated into the very structure and meaning of (at least certain kinds of) *technē*. In other words, what is now doing the work is not the notion of *technē* as a specific idea but rather the notion of *archē* that structures this *technē* from within.[21] Moreover, in connecting *technē* to *archē*, Socrates—like Thrasymachus—puts the figure of a ruler (who is also a professional), and so the idea of rule, at the center of his argument.[22]

Socrates then restates the point more broadly, as a generalization about professions, though one that arguably applies only to those that are in fact structured as he describes (in terms of rule):

> Now, surely, Thrasymachus, the professions rule over (*archousi*) and are masters (*kratousin*)[23] of that of which they are the professions? (342c7–8)

20. This would be in keeping with the *Statesman*'s repeated appeal to experts and kinds of expertise in the guise of specific civic roles, as was argued in the previous chapter.

21. Compare also the way that the Eleatic Visitor, in the *Statesman*, uses the verb *archein* to articulate a parallel between the statesman and the doctor, comparing the criterion of knowledge for defining medicine with that "of any other sort of rule [*archē*] whatsoever" (*Plt.* 293c2–3). This sentence is adapted from my "Political Expertise" (76).

22. Kamtekar ("Politics of Plato's Socrates", 221–23) anticipated this point, as I had not previously noticed.

23. I translate *kratousin* as "master" in contrast to Grube/Reeve who translate it as "are stronger than." To be sure, while one sense of the verb *krateō* in LSJ is "*to be strong, powerful,*" it is also among "verbs signifying *to surpass, be inferior* [sic] *to*" when used with a genitive of comparison (Smyth, sec. 1402). However, while this use is akin to that of the genitive with verbs of "*ruling*" (Smyth, sec. 1370), that latter usage is more specific to "verbs

It is just here that Thrasymachus is (within the present stretch of dialectic, which began at 341b–c) first said to concede only "very reluctantly" (342c9).[24] What is the crux that Thrasymachus senses will prove so dangerous to his case? It is that Socrates has for the first time made a claim about the nature of ruling as such—a claim that applies to those *technai* that rule over, both commanding and caring for, their objects (or subjects), as well as to political rulers ruling over, and so both commanding and caring for, their subjects. Whether or not people are inclined or willing to see all political rulers as thieves, as Thrasymachus had insinuated them to be, has no bearing on the kind of general claim that Socrates has established. Thus, the force of the argument that Thrasymachus originally made, to the effect that all political rulers seek their own advantage (before qualifying it with the "precise sense" caveat), has now been nullified. The experience and observation of political life on which Thrasymachus had relied has had its relevance voided by Socrates's newly general claim about the nature of rule (or we might, more precisely, say "ruling knowledge") in those *technai* that it structures.[25]

Immediately after Thrasymachus's "very reluctant" concession noted above, Socrates spells out what looks like a general claim, though one that may include indication of a limitation to its scope, as I explain below:

> No [kind of] knowledge (*ouk ara epistēmē ge*) seeks or orders the advantage of the stronger, then, but the advantage of the weaker and that which is ruled (*archomenou*) by it. (342c10–d2)[26]

---

signifying *to rule, command, lead.*" Levin ("APXΩ and APXH," 62–63) comments that in fifth-century inscriptions and literary texts, using the verb *archein* with "the genitive . . . continues the old idea 'to be in command of,' or 'to have supreme power over, to control'". In regard to fourth-century usage, Levin ("APXΩ and APXH") notes that the same verb "with the genitive . . . implies absolute, unrestricted power" (98); can be used metaphorically for controlling things rather than people (99); and is extended (with the genitive) by philosophers such as Plato, Xenophon, and Aristotle "to cover any and all cases that have a certain analogy" to supreme power over people in various combinations (100–101). I would add that at this point of the dialectic in *Republic* 1, it is the notion of ruling (*archein*) that has been doing all the work, and so the political sense of *kratein* would arguably be the one to come to a reader's mind in seeing the verbs paired. However, the close connection between the two genitives will be important shortly.

24. To be sure, he has begun introducing distancing language into his agreements from 342b8 onward.

25. Compare the remark by Arendt (*Human Condition*, 224) that "the concept of rule" was "for Plato a much more general category," rather than, as in the twentieth century, "invariably connected with politics," though she is not discussing this particular part of Plato's corpus there.

26. The Grube/Reeve translation is unhelpfully nonliteral here: they translate "what is advantageous to itself," but the Greek says "the advantage of the stronger," and the stronger/weaker contrast is what is structuring Socrates's point.

For Socrates to venture this complete generalization about every *epistēmē* (used here seemingly interchangeably with *technē* in the surrounding argument, as is sometimes Plato's wont) seems incautious, since his illustrations—the doctor and the steersman so far, and the shepherd and cowherd to come, as well as political rulers themselves—have all been drawn from what a practiced Platonic reader would recognize as a certain subclass of *technai*:[27] what we may call the *therapeiai*, which are a subset of *technai* that are "by definition oriented towards some kind of benefit for the animal or human that the practice is caretaking of," as in the cases of medicine, physical training, and horse training.[28] And indeed it may be that, in the passage quoted immediately above, Plato uses a particle (*ge*) so as to limit the sense of the noun *epistēmē* that it follows, to indicate that the claim generalizes only to those forms of *epistēmē* that are in fact ordered in terms of rule, meaning (at least, or only) the therapeutic ones.

Even if understood to be focused implicitly on the therapeutic *technai*, however, Socrates's language of stronger and weaker can be startling. For English speakers today tend to describe those entities that *technai*, and forms of knowledge more generally, engage as their *objects*—one would say, in the "strict sense," their "proper objects." Yet Socrates here analogizes these objects to the kinds of persons who are ruled over by political superiors. Not only political rulers have subjects for whom they must care in giving their commands. *All* rulers—that is, I take it, the practitioners of the expertise involved in all forms of knowledge characterized by rule—have subjects of that kind.[29] And Socrates claims that it is the nature of this rule—the nature of rule as such—that it seeks the advantage of its weaker subject, not of itself, being stronger.

Of this claim that knowledge seeks the advantage of the weaker, not of (itself) the stronger: in one sense, one might think, so far so seemingly Thrasymachean. The stronger rules the weaker. And yet Socrates has here sublated the original meaning of this claim that Thrasymachus had intended. Whereas Thrasymachus had meant this as a generalized claim about the politically

27. I borrow the phrase "practiced Platonic reader" (converting it to American spelling) from Schofield in "Religion and Philosophy" (3).

28. I quote the felicitous phrasing of a private communication from Emily Hulme, on file with the author, offering the following illustrative list of references of such therapeutic *technai*: medicine: *Protagoras* 345a and 354a; *Grg.* 464b and 517e; *Euthphr.* 13; physical training: *Grg.* 464b and 517e; horse training: *Euthphr.* 13a–b. Hulme also remarks the categorization of certain *technai* (such as piety, horse training, and herdsmanship) as *therapeiai* in the *Euthyphro* (12e–13c) (cf. *Laches* 185c–d, *Grg.* 464b–465b), noting further that "the Eleatic Visitor refers to a *therapeia* of leatherworking at *Plt.* 280c7," but this is a "metaphorical use."

29. The grammatical parallel in the Greek between the genitive case used with verbs of ruling, commanding, and leading and the genitive case of comparison used with verbs of surpassing or being superior may help in explaining why these connections come readily to Socrates's hand and are accepted, albeit with marked reluctance, by Thrasymachus.

strong and the politically weak, the dominators and the dominated, Socrates has transformed it into an assertion of the nature of rule that results in the stronger, by their nature as rulers, exercising their rule and so benefiting their subjects. The advantage of those who rule in the precise sense lies solely in exercising their rule as completely and perfectly as possible.[30] Ironically, it was Thrasymachus's original choice to introduce the *technai* and their practitioners as comparators to political rulers that has now opened the door to a much more general claim by Socrates, one serving to devastate the Chalcedonian's original view. For if all rulers share in the general nature of ruling, including both political rulers and the professionals who share the political rulers' task of (in some fashion) caring for living beings, then the nature of political rulers will be dictated by that nature of rule as such rather than by the political experience that is usually taken to delineate it.

Hence Thrasymachus's original definition is indicted as being not just a mistake about political rulers as they happen to be but a definitional and even a metaphysical mistake, as it were, about the nature of rule as such.[31] Indeed, it is not only indicted; it is inverted. Thrasymachus had originally proposed that "justice is, the same in all cities, the advantage of the established ruling body" (338e6–339a2), and had then claimed that "since the established ruling body is surely stronger," then "anyone who reasons correctly will conclude that the just is the same everywhere, namely, the advantage of the stronger" (339a2–4). At this stage of his response, building on the leading question as to whether "there [is] any advantage for each of the professions themselves other than (*allo ē*) to be as complete or perfect as possible" (341d11–12, modifying the Grube/Reeve translation),[32] and the postulate that "there is no deficiency or error in any profession" (342b2–3), Socrates infers that there can be no advantage to the doctor qua doctor in enriching themselves by malpractice, or to the political ruler qua ruler in doing so by using their power for corrupt ends.[33]

---

30. Compare Alon Harel's inversion of the usual law and economics approach to privatization: in his view, "it is not that *who ought to do the task depends upon who can succeed in doing it*; rather, it is that *who can succeed in doing it depends upon who ought to do it*": see Harel, *Why Law Matters*, 105–6, emphasis original.

31. In "*Technē* and *Archē*," I used the word "conceptual" here, rather than "definitional"; I have made other changes in this chapter as compared with that article, though most lines of argument are broadly the same.

32. Taking up a suggestion from Terence Irwin in correspondence (which I had failed to recall in preparing "*Technē* and *Archē*"), I now discard the Grube/Reeve translation of *allo ē* as "except" and instead translate it as "other than."

33. Harte ("Knowing and Believing," 154) argues similarly, about a recurrence of this line of argument in a slightly later stretch of the dialogue: whereas, she writes, "Thrasymachus, presumably, wanted to argue that acquisition of benefits such as power and money and so forth is not merely a possible atypical result of ruling, but the task to which ruling is assigned and hence constitutive of its best understanding," Socrates is in contrast making

Once again his chosen examples are limited to *technai* that are *therapeiai*; while he does not say so, it makes most sense to construe his claims as being implicitly (or at a minimum, most plausibly) about this subclass, rather than as being generalizable to any and every one of the *technai* as such.[34]

In this way Socrates reaches the conclusion that the advantage of any established ruling body—not only the ruling body in cities but the ruling body that operates respectively within the various examples of *technē* and *epistēmē* that he has been discussing—is by its very nature the advantage of the profession, or rule, in perfecting itself, which entails serving the advantage of its subjects. And notice that this conclusion is reached before, and independently of, a controversial distinction that Socrates will offer between other *technai* and a postulated *technē* of wage earning. That move is not needed in order for Socrates to contend that what is the advantage of the ruler can only be the advantage to the ruler qua ruler. Ruler and rule, or profession, become completely identified. The human being wielding the power drops away, in favor of the role, or as Cicero and Hobbes will say the persona, of the ruler.

I will return to the metaphysical nature and indeed necessity of rule below. But first, notice that this claim, too, Thrasymachus is said to resist: "He conceded this finally, though he tried to resist it" (342d3–4). Socrates then drives the point home, with respect to the case of "the doctor in the precise sense" (*ho akribēs iatros*, repeated at 342d7) and "the ship's steersman in the precise sense" (*ho kubernētēs ho akribēs*) (342d10)—who was earlier glossed as "a ruler of sailors, not a sailor"' (342d10–e1). And he then asks:

> Doesn't it follow that such a person (*toioutos*) who is a steersman and (*te kai*) a ruler won't pursue and command what is to the advantage of the steersman, but that which is to the advantage of the [person who is a] sailor and (*te kai*) [a] subject?" (342e3–5)[35]

This question is meant to sum up what has preceded (*toioutos*, such a person, pointing backward in this case). The steersman qua steersman is a ruler. It is specifically qua ruler that he does not seek out his own advantage, but the advantage of the subject whom he rules.

---

the point that money may in fact be "a result that may be produced by ruling," but one "for whose production ruling is not in fact specifically tasked and which, in addition, would not benefit a ruler if it were so produced."

34. For pressing this point on me, I thank Emily Hulme, Jonny Thakkar, and Katja Maria Vogt in comments on previous versions of this chapter.

35. Grube/Reeve translate "a ship's steersman or ruler," which in choosing "or" for the first *te kai* in this sentence, obscures the flow of the Socratic argument that has defined a steersman precisely as a kind of ruler.

Thrasymachus is once again marked as agreeing only "reluctantly" (*mogis*, 342e6). And that brings us to Socrates's final conclusion of this stretch of dialogue:

> So, then, Thrasymachus, no one in any position of rule (*archē*), insofar as he is a ruler (*kath hoson archōn estin*), considers or orders what is advantageous to himself, but that which is advantageous to that which is ruled, that on which he practices his profession. It is to the ruled and what is advantageous and proper to it that he looks, and everything he says and does he says and does for its sake. (342e7–11, trans. Grube/ Reeve modified)

Once again it is the person in a position of rule (or ruling, as we might say) in whom Plato is interested, and once again he is also interested in the concomitant relationship of subordination between the ruler and the ruled. And in drawing this conclusion, Socrates has drawn a conclusion that is general to rule—so understood—as such. Socrates's argument has identified rule as the architecture of at least some kinds of knowledge; as noted above, while he has put forward a general claim, he has chosen to illustrate it (solely) with examples of the subclass of *technai* identified above as the *therapeiai* (therapeutic professions). In so doing he has laid out an account of rule and its intrinsic purpose that transcends politics while also encompassing it.

In Socrates's account, rule structures the knowledge that in turn defines its purpose. While *technē* may itself be an evaluatively neutral term (so that one could have a *technē* of piracy or perhaps even murder),[36] those *technai* that are structured in terms of *archē* are not evaluatively neutral, aiming as they must at the good of their subjects. Readings of *Republic* 1 that take it to be fixated on a neutral sense of *technē* overlook this crucial role played by *archē*, which, as treated here and elsewhere in Plato (as in Homer and others, as argued in chapter 1 of this study) bears a positive charge, even if honored only in the breach.[37]

Compare a remark made by the Eleatic Visitor in the *Statesman* (noted above in chapter 4) that the constitution that is correct and "alone a constitution" is "the one in which one would find the rulers to be genuinely expert and not only seeming to be so" (293c6–8).[38] It bears underscoring also that statecraft in that dialogue is ultimately defined as belonging to a larger kind

---

36. A case for the normative neutrality of *technē* in Plato is made by Hulme Kozey in "Good-Directedness of Τέχνη."

37. Both here and in some other chapters, I have for the most part changed the language of normativity, which I used in earlier work, to the language of evaluative status, in order to avoid seeming to imply that Plato would have subscribed to any kind of is/ought distinction. Since normativity need not however imply this distinction (albeit that it is often taken to do so), I do sometimes retain it as well.

38. This sentence is adapted from my "Political Expertise" (77), but with the Greek translated by me afresh.

of "commanding" knowledge (*epitaktikē*), which involves a form of discerning that is already such as to be command-apt, as it were.[39] But whatever one makes of that comparison, Socrates's argument here in *Republic* 1 is that ruling has an evaluative purpose not merely in an ethical sense but in a constitutive one. The only proper rule is rule that serves the interest of the ruled. Rulers are in epitactic command, but solely in order to serve those whom they rule. And so the fact that therapeutic professionals benefit the objects of their skill or craft is in virtue of the very nature of rule itself. No ruler in the precise sense—using the vocabulary that Socrates adopts from Thrasymachus, only to give it an evaluative cast so as to undermine the sophist's original claim—could do otherwise.

The point is that ruling is for Plato, as for at least key strands of Homer and more generally in much of the inherited (if contested) landscape of Greek thought before Plato, inherently oriented to an evaluative purpose. The directionality of political teleology that Plato adopts is not willfully blind to the nature of reality, nor is it perversely original; it is rather rooted in many of the figures and expectations that clustered together in exhibiting what most Greek onlookers, as it were of an imaginary statue gallery, would have taken to be rule. More precisely, Plato sometimes (when speaking precisely) employs rule in the strict evaluative sense introduced in chapter 1; as argued there, implicit in existing constitutional practices of office, and now explicit in Plato's clarified account of the idea of rule, is the thought that rule in the strict sense (as opposed to cases that may merely be loosely described as such) must be rule that serves the good of the ruled. And, crucially, in Plato's account of rule here, together with his reconfiguration of office in the *Laws* (chapter 3), the *Statesman* (chapter 4), and elsewhere in the *Republic* (chapters 6 and 7)—as opposed to the rough and ready institutional efforts of the actual practice of classical Greek constitutional officeholding—this can only be nonaccidentally achieved through the possession of expertise. Hence the fact that professionals benefit the objects of their skill or craft is inherent in the notion of rule as Plato reconfigures it.

To be sure, that kind of argument may seem to beg the question against the starting point from which Thrasymachus began. For Thrasymachus is presented as being more certain of his claim that all political rulers are exploitative than he could be of any argument that could be deployed against it. If Socrates's argument implies that Xerxes was no ruler (being no ruler in the precise sense), so much the worse, Thrasymachus might reply, for Socrates's argument. Now Socrates can be taken to agree with Thrasymachus that no political rulers known in history have been rulers in the precise sense: for Thrasymachus, because none have been error-free; for Socrates, further, because

39. On "command-apt" and this passage in the *Statesman*, see the preceding chapter, and notes there.

none have aimed solely at the good of their subjects. But Socrates holds by the possibility of rulers in the precise sense, both within the *technai* and within the political domain. Thrasymachus, by contrast, deliberately punctures whatever evaluative expectations or aspirations for existing or past rulers his audience might have inherited from elements of Homer and later poetry and prose.

He does this by reading the Homeric image of the shepherd in what he implies is a more literal vein than traditional audiences of that image have done. For if shepherds in the Greek world were taken literally, the sophist contends, one would see that they raise their animal charges in order for them to be eaten or otherwise exploited by humans (whether by the herder themselves or, more likely, the master who owned the herds and employed the herders). And that counterintuitive rereading of the Homeric image of the political king or ruler as a shepherd is matched by a counterintuitive reading of cases of actual political rulers—his original and continuing primary interest—whom he takes to be equally exploitative.[40] This brings me to what I call "Thrasymachus's last stand" (last, that is, in the particular stretch of dialogue that is my focus in this chapter).

Thrasymachus's Last Stand

In making his last stand, Thrasymachus drops the comparison between political rulers and professionals such as doctors, accountants, and grammarians that has gotten him into such trouble. Going back to illustrate his core interest of the case of the political ruler, he chooses a far more prosaic pair of examples, which he interprets with a cynical spin: that actual shepherds and cowherds aim to fatten their charges for the taste or profit of themselves or, rather, of their masters (Thrasymachus refers to them using familiar nouns for their roles: *tous poimenas, tous boukolous* [both, 343b1]). But then he swiftly leaves the shepherds and cowherds behind to return to his original and continuing prime interest: political rulers, whom he calls "rulers in cities—those who are true rulers, that is" (343b4–5).

In so doing, the Chalcedonian offers evidence for the claim that "a just man always gets less than an unjust one" (343d2), which he draws from a jaundiced view of everyday political life.[41] All of this evidence is confined to the domain of the political: first, that the just are always cheated by the unjust in contracts

---

40. I have significantly rethought the argument of this paragraph, and of some related points below, thanks to comments of Johannes Haubold on my "*Technē and Archē*." I now emphasize the ways in which Thrasymachus's treatment of his examples would have been counterintuitive for Plato's Homerically educated readers, rather than intuitive for them.

41. He condescends to Socrates as unable to appreciate what should be obvious common wisdom: calling him "my most simple Socrates" (343d2), and using similar expressions passim. Again, however, I would no longer describe Thrasymachus's presentation of these examples as "intuitive," as I did in "*Technē and Archē*" (11, 14, 18–21).

between them; second, that the just pay more in taxes and get less in refunds than the unjust (some refrains never change). The third piece of evidence is specifically to do with office, which is the contextually warranted translation of *archē* in this stretch of the dialogue, since Thrasymachus is now talking about everyday Greek political affairs, which were conducted in most constitutions around him by persons holding offices. The sophist contends that "when each of them [a just person and an unjust person] holds a ruling position in some public office (*archēn tina*)" (343e1–2), a just person suffers disadvantage in the form of possible penalties, forced neglect of his own private affairs, and resentment from friends and relations whom he refuses to help with unjust favors—whereas the unjust experience the opposite in each case and are able to profit from holding office (this being the specific framework of power in question here, as the noun *archē* indicates).

Socrates's response is to force Thrasymachus back onto the terrain of the *technai* and of the ruling that must animate them. Plato here may well be coining a term for shepherding as a *technē*, a form of expertise, referring to *hē poimenikē* at 345d1, for which there is no prior evidence in the *Thesaurus Linguae Graecae* corpus.[42] This is not the only moment of possible Platonic linguistic innovation in the vocabulary of the *technai*; in particular, Christopher Rowe has pointed out the *Statesman*'s possible coinage of *politikos*, while noting the expertise signaling of *-ikos* and *-ikē*.[43] Here, however, Plato may be practicing the same form of possible linguistic innovation on behalf of a kind of farming practice that was not normally considered a candidate for being a *technē*.[44]

While in the *Statesman*, such linguistic innovations serve the course of the Eleatic Visitor's own constructive arguments, I suggest that here in *Republic* 1 Plato may have Socrates coin "shepherding" as a dialectical move. Thrasymachus in his third outburst has made a concerted effort to shift his ground, away from the terrain of the *technai* (notwithstanding that he had been the one to move the dialectic onto that terrain in the first place) and back to his counterintuitive rereading of the culturally loaded examples of shepherd, cowherd, and, most importantly, the source of his original focus (stated as "what I say justice is, the same in all cities," 338e6–339a1)—namely, political rulers as they exist and have existed. But Socrates returns him to the terrain of the *technai*

---

42. The *Thesaurus Linguae Graecae* is a Special Research Program at the University of California, Irvine, with a searchable database of digitized Greek texts covering the period from Homer to the fall of Byzantium in 1453 CE. It can be found at http://stephanus.tlg .uci.edu/index.php.

43. Rowe, introduction to *Plato: Statesman*, 1. See also Wallach, *Platonic Political Art*, 338n21.

44. Part of this paragraph is adapted from my "Political Expertise" (55); its adaptation is partly indebted to a comment by Emily Hulme. See also Hulme Kozey, "Is Farming a *Technē?*"

(345bff.), reinvoking the original meaning of the "precise sense" caveat, arguing that the original "precise sense" reading of the doctor has to be applied mutatis mutandis to the shepherd. Qua shepherd, on the Socratic account, the shepherd must care for the good of his flock: this is inherent in the nature of his rule.

Now, even though Thrasymachus is not allowed a further riposte here, many modern readers have caviled at this point on his behalf. For, they ask, what allows Socrates to help himself to the idea that a *technē*, just because it involves a structure of *archē*, and even if we fill that in terms of *archē* over living beings, must necessarily aim at the good of the ruled and solely at their good? Consider the gooseherd who cares for a gaggle of geese, feeding and fattening them, but doing so for the purpose of producing foie gras from their livers. (To simplify, suppose that the gooseherd does this not for a wage but simply to enjoy the resultant feast.) Is Socrates entitled simply to help himself by excluding this case from counting as gooseherding in the strict sense?[45]

My response on Socrates's behalf would operate in three steps.[46] First, by recognizing that in terms of the dialectic with Thrasymachus, since the Chalcedonian has already moved the discussion to a conceptual plane by formulating the idea of an X in the precise sense, it is he who is not then entitled to fall back on what he might take to be cases of empirical plausibility to defeat Socrates's rival conceptual proposal (though in calling it conceptual, I do not mean to lose sight of the fact that Plato's Socrates would take it to correspond to the nature of reality). Second, by pointing out that in the context of the Homeric framework that had made shepherds a preeminent image for rulers, as surveyed in chapter 1, the plausibility is in fact more on Socrates's side. The Homeric poems and other early Greek hexameter poems had taken it as axiomatic that shepherds should care for the good of their sheep and, indeed, that they would do so for a wage, being employed by someone else, so that their own exploitation of the sheep for a personal barbecue would have been off the imaginative table.

That said, the third step in my response is an acknowledgement that Plato is extending the limits of the cultural repertoire in regard to the exploitativeness of shepherds by having Thrasymachus ask this question. Just as in the criticism of the king as shepherd image in the *Statesman* by means of the elaborate myth, so here, too, Plato is at once acknowledging and calling attention to argumentative weaknesses in traditional approaches to political rule. Yet he

45. For formulation and discussion of this case, I am indebted to several participants in Jonathan Beere's seminar on the *Republic* in May 2018 at the Humboldt University, though my response may not satisfy all or any of them.

46. While the first step of the reply is the same as that given in my "*Technē* and *Archē*," the second and third steps are very different from the ones given there; I have changed my mind after further reflection on the significance of the Homeric background to the image of the shepherd, as presented by Haubold in *Homer's People* and "'Shepherds of the People.'"

does so ultimately in order to bolster the traditional case (here both Homeric and Socratic) that one may rightly expect a shepherd to care for the good of their sheep.

Overall, one must acknowledge the limits of *Republic* 1's focus in this stretch of the discussion only on the role of ruler qua ruler, which excludes any question of the motivation of a natural person to assume this role (or, conversely, to violate its norms for their own exploitative purposes). The next stretch of the dialogue with Thrasymachus will introduce the question of why natural persons might be (un)willing to rule, and in the larger arc of the dialogue as a whole, Socrates will argue that the only natural persons who will in fact be safely and reliably, because unwillingly, inclined to assume the role of political ruler are those whose nature is philosophical and whose education and development do not corrupt that nature. But while that analysis will be important in establishing the possibility of instantiating true rulers, it does not vitiate the value of considering the nature of such rulers qua rulers, as I have argued that Socrates in book 1 does (and, indeed, as Plato's *Statesman* in different but related terms does also).

Coda to the Argument So Far

Socrates completes the stretch of argument that has been the focus of this chapter by offering a retrospective summary of it, which at the same time includes a further powerful statement of precisely what it is that a *technē* does in relation to its subjects. Here, he asserts that "shepherding is concerned only to provide the best for that which is ordered (*tetaktai*) by it" (345d1–2, trans. Grube/Reeve, modified).[47] This claim extends the analysis of rule by telling us that what rule does is to order its subjects and to order them for their good ("provide the best"), in accordance with the schematization of the Platonic idea of rule in part I of this study. The *taxis* of rule must be such as to aim at its true *telos*.

Ordering for the good, of course, will be a fundamental element of the role of philosophy in enabling philosophers to serve as rulers, which is developed in the *Republic* more broadly. Socrates drives his point home here by contrasting the "provisions" that a *technē* gives to its subjects with its own lack of need for any such "provision": "it is itself adequately (*hikanōs*) provided with all it needs to be at its best when it doesn't fall short in any way of being the profession of shepherding" (345d3–5). And this in turn means that, qua exerciser

---

47. On *epi* plus the dative, plus the verb *tassō* (the very elements found in the present passage), see discussion of a parallel discussion in *Republic* 5 in Vogt (*Belief and Truth*, 63) and Harte ("Knowing and Believing") (though neither of them cites the earlier passage in book 1 that I discuss; Harte, who does briefly discuss book 1, picks up primarily from 345d1–3). I am grateful to Victor Caston for advice on translating this passage.

of that profession, the person who practices it and so rules over their proper subjects needs no provisions (including, but not limited, I think, to no money or wage—anticipating the focus on wage earning to come in the next stretch of the discussion) to be earned from doing so.

The service of the ruler to the ruled is an evaluative purpose inherent in the identification of the ruler with their therapeutic profession, not a separate and optional supplement to it. And so Socrates reiterates the conclusion that he and Thrasymachus had putatively agreed upon earlier:

> that every kind of rule, insofar as it is rule (*archē*), doesn't seek anything other than what is best for the thing subject to it and cared for by it, in the case of both public and private forms of rule. (345d6–e1, trans. Grube/Reeve, modified)[48]

As this once again confirms, it is rule (*archē*)—and not simply *technē*—that is at stake between Socrates and Thrasymachus in *Republic* 1. And it is a conception of *archē* that at once reveals Plato's oft-neglected, but actually frequent and astute, employment of technical Greek political and constitutional vocabulary, in this case emphasizing that rule is always in fact an interpersonal relationship between rulers (those ruling) and those ruled, while also that rule qua rule, rule in the strict evaluative sense, can and must serve the good of the ruled alone.

Will Rulers Rule Willingly?

That is the nature of rule, and not the nature only of a profession. But it will shortly be yoked by Socrates to a final puzzle, which he puts, quite abruptly at this juncture, to Thrasymachus: "Do you think that those who rule cities, the true rulers, rule willingly?" (345e1–3). Thrasymachus's response to that question is uniquely emphatic and unexpectedly positive. As Grube/Reeve nicely translate his response: "I don't [think it]; by god, I know it" (345e4).[49]

Before following out how Socrates explains and expands upon this puzzling question, I should like to underscore its peculiarity. It is a familiar problematic in political thought that subjects may not be willingly ruled, and an ideal of political theorizing in many different epochs and contexts that they should be (a topic to which I return in chapter 10). The willingness to rule on the part of the rulers, however, is seldom doubted. To survey the ancient Geek world only: from Homeric kings who have inherited their chieftaincies to "tyrants" (*turannoi*), who were called such as arrogators of nonhereditary

---

48. Socrates's reference to both "public and private forms of rule" reinforces the point that rule is a widespread phenomenon. In the *Ion*, Plato includes a woman weaving in the household as an example of someone ruling, which is a striking way of exemplifying "private rule" as compared with the male householder, whom Aristotle or Xenophon would celebrate.

49. Grube/Reeve translation with modified punctuation.

powers from roughly the sixth century onward, to aspiring Athenian generals and orators who jostled one another for public influence, the willingness of those who exercise public power to play such a role would seem to be virtually tautologous. In modern politics, too, it is relatively rare, at least until very recently, to find any political scientist or political theorist worrying about the reluctance of candidates to seek or exercise rule or office.[50]

Scholars of Plato's *Republic* have perhaps become desensitized to how strange and unexpected a question Plato poses at this juncture, because the paradox that the only good rulers are reluctant rulers—because only they can be trusted not to be ruling for the sake of their own advantage, and so to carry out the proper purpose of rule, which is the advantage of their subjects—is further thematized as the dialogue progresses. While commentators divide as to how, and how successfully, the project of the *kallipolis* can resolve that paradox, both sides have generally identified the problem, as well as the potential solution (if any), as lying in the nature of the human individuals who will rule within it—namely, those who are philosophers, with knowledge of the Forms and ultimately of the Form of the Good.

In contrast, in reading this puzzling question and what ensues, I wish to emphasize that the reluctance of rulers is presented as a problem intrinsic to the role of rule itself. While any solution must lie (as I agree and explore further below) in the human nature of the occupants of the role, who bring their own motivation to the table, the role itself is indifferent to that question of psychological motivation, and so the need for a natural person to have such motivation remains a separate question. That said, its presentation here in the sole terms of reward or sanction is too limited. A solution could in principle draw on the natural disposition of such natural persons and their formation through education (though care will still have to be taken to prevent such persons from succumbing to the temptations of corruption). Yet such a solution does not make the role of ruler redundant; it rather fills that role.

To see that the problem of reluctant rulers is inherent to the Platonic analysis of rule itself, rather than peculiar to the case of the philosophers, let me return to how Socrates goes on to explain his point. Immediately, he generalizes the question away from political rule to "other kinds of rule (*archas*)," which in the context of the discussion to this point means the rule inherent to the *technai* (and specifically, as I have argued, to the therapeutic *technai*). In that expanded context, he sets out his reasoning as follows:

> But, Thrasymachus, don't you realize that in other kinds of rule (*archas*) no one wants to rule willingly (*archein hekōn*), but demands

50. However, such reluctance as there has been has often been gendered or racialized owing to real vulnerabilities as well as real lack of concomitant support, and has become less rare more recently, as risks of being victimized through social media have escalated and done so disproportionately for different groups.

a wage [*misthos*], assuming that the advantage arising from their rule
will come not to themselves but to those whom they rule (*tois archomenois*)? (345e5–346a1)[51]

In explaining himself further, Socrates remains on the general terrain of the
technai, identifying each in terms of its particular *dunamis* (the same kind
of analysis of expertise that occurs in *Republic* 5 and in the *Statesman*, as
noted in chapter 4), each of which brings about a particular benefit. Without
reviewing the subsequent argument in detail,[52] he ultimately arrives at the
conclusion that those who rule properly (whether in the political domain or
in practicing other therapeutic professions) will demand a wage for doing so:

> No one willingly chooses to rule and to take other people's troubles
> in hand and straighten them out, but each asks for a wage [*misthos*];
> for anyone who intends to practice his profession well never does nor
> orders what is best for himself—at least not when he orders as his pro-
> fession prescribes—but what is best for his subject. (346e7–a3, trans.
> Grube/Reeve, modified)

He goes on to specify that by a wage (*misthos*), he means not solely money but
rather a range of possible instantiations: "money or honor or a penalty if he
refuses" (347a4).

Now the very idea of a wage for a ruler is an interesting one in the broader
Greek context. On the one hand, it would have been simply and widely
assumed that both hereditary and nonhereditary rulers enjoyed a myriad of
material benefits in virtue of their ruling position: high-status political power
was simply that kind of good, bringing with it most other earthly goods in turn.
On the other hand, the Homeric image of the ruler as a shepherd—a shepherd in everyday life being often a hired hand paid a wage (albeit sometimes
a household or family member who might have played this role unwaged)—
opened the door to thinking of rulers as a kind of servant, with which much
play would be made by Aristophanes and others in the context of democratic
Athens (as explored below in chapter 6).

The problem of wages and more generally material benefit from holding
a position of rule carried over in practice into the role of office as a kind of
rule. Wages were not intrinsic or necessary to the idea of office as it flour-
ished across existing Greek constitutions in the classical period. Rather, as noted
earlier in this work, whether or not wages were paid to officeholders varied

51. Grube/Reeve translate *hekōn* here as "for its own sake," which obscures the crucial
issue.

52. The argument involves the claim that each *technē* works to realize (*apergazetai*)
its own *ergon* and to benefit that which it is set over (*eph' hoi tetaktai*), using exactly the
same language that defines a *technē* as such in *Republic* 5; see Lane, "Statecraft," 201–2, for
references on this point.

with types of constitution, including within different cities across different historical periods, as well as with types of offices and other roles.[53] And in Plato's other dialogues, wages for office or rule are treated in a variety of ways. The *Laws* offers forms of civic honor, though no wages in a monetary sense, to induce officeholders to serve well (while drafting them rather than inviting them to come forward); the *Statesman* rests content with an analysis of the role of ruler, treating its occupant as a cipher defined by properties that all derive from the role itself, and mentioning no wage for rule (while remaining silent on whether the offices, which are only alluded to at the very end of the dialogue, will receive wages either).

What of the three disjunct types of wages—money, honor, and penalty— mentioned by Socrates in the quotation above from *Republic* 1 as types of wage that rulers might demand? In the course of the *Republic's* exploration of whether and why philosophers might be willing to rule, both honor and money are invoked (wages in the form of money, or at least subsistence wages, being prescribed in books 3–5, as I argue in the subsequent chapter). Both of these are familiar in light of existing Greek practices, though, as I shall argue, the question of a financial or in-kind wage is actually a subtly vexed one in the presentation of the *kallipolis*. By contrast, the third disjunct (a penalty) is inexplicable by appeal to existing Greek practices. This is underscored by the fact that Glaucon—who, together with his brother, embodies the kind of well-brought-up, wealthy youth whom Socrates will in the larger arc of the *Republic* be seeking to ensure is on the side of justice[54]—interrupts the exchanges with Thrasymachus to ask Socrates to explain himself, saying that while he is for his part familiar with the first two alternatives (money and honor), he doesn't understand what kind of penalty is meant "or how you can call it part of a wage" (347a8).

Socrates's reply marks another turn in the dialogue, in that he introduces in layperson's terms three distinct groups of people who will later in the dialogue be distinguished from another in terms of the technical tripartite

53. Morrow (*Plato's Cretan City*, 138 and 191) contrasts the lack of pay in the constitutional project for Magnesia, in Plato's *Laws*, with what he claims to be the principle of payment for offices in Athens "from at least the fifth century onward" (191). There is a scholarly debate as to whether such payment (for all but a few offices) was restored after its abolition by the Four Hundred, and if so, whether it was restored again after the similar overall (but not exceptionless) abolition by the Thirty: see p. 61, n. 48, and p. 184, n. 29 in this study.

54. Scott (*Listening to Reason*) argues that the aim of the *Republic* is to reinforce Glaucon and Adeimantus (and, by extension, Plato's readers) who are already well habituated in their moral commitments, rather than to convert moral skeptics or anyone who does not already share this basic outlook. While I agree with his emphasis on the overall significance of Glaucon and Adeimantus (as opposed to a hostile interlocutor) becoming the main interlocutors from book 2 onward, I think that a less credulous reading of their book 2 challenges, on which they may be protesting too much about their habituated commitment to the cause of justice, is also possible.

psychology of the soul. Here, by contrast, his terminology (in the next two speeches, in which he responds to Glaucon's question) is almost flagrantly loose, interchangeably invoking conventional epithets that would appeal to the wealthy and politically aspirational elite among whom his interlocutors (and Plato's family as a whole) belonged: "the best people," "the most decent people," "the good people," "the decent people."[55] Especially interesting is that, in part through a further choice of language, Socrates insinuates that this group of the self-approving elite (to which Glaucon would unquestionably take himself to belong) would not be motivated to rule by either money or honor. He initially replies to Glaucon's question thus:

> Then you don't understand the wage of the best people, for the sake of which the most decent types rule, when they are willing to rule at all. Or don't you know that the love of honor (*to philotimon*) and the love of money (*to philarguron*) are disgraceful, as they are said to be? (347a10–b3).

Glaucon immediately agrees to the latter question, which is striking in itself. For the ardent pursuit of honor (*philotimia*) is often celebrated as a key motivating force in both archaic and classical Greece. But in the elite circles of late fifth-century and early to mid-fourth-century Athens (the broad time frames in which the dialogue is dramatically set, on the one hand, and was probably composed, on the other),[56] *philotimia* had become in some contexts a problematic aspiration—especially in regard to the participation in ruling, taking as it did the form of officeholding in the democratic constitution (to leave aside the two short-lived oligarchical regimes of the late fifth century).[57]

While, up to this point, the dialogue with Thrasymachus has been steadfastly cast in terms of a broad extensionality of rule, as pertaining not only to politics but also other professions, Glaucon's ready endorsement of the suggestion that *to philotimon* is disgraceful implies that he hears Socrates's question as pertaining to ruling in the guise of democratic officeholding, the only kind that at this point in the dramatic date of the dialogue he would have known in his lifetime. This reading is supported by the way in which Socrates phrases the long speech on which he then embarks to explain the third type of wage (the penalty) in response to Glaucon's initial question. I translate the first part of the long speech interpreting the abstract noun *archē* now as office, as a way of marking the tacit shift from rule to the species of office made through

55. Respectively, *hōn beltistōn* (347a10); *hoi epieikestatoi* (347b1); *hoi agathoi* (347b6); *hoi epieikeis* (347c6). *Hoi agathoi* is a version of the famous *kaloi kagathoi* epithet for the Greek ideal of the elite, purportedly cultivated few.

56. On what may be deliberately created difficulty within the dialogue in assigning a firm dramatic date, see Nails's "Dramatic Date." On the likely dates of composition (which are necessarily inexact), see Wallach's *Platonic Political Art* (216–17).

57. As charted by Carter in *Quiet Athenian*.

Glaucon's response (that of a youth who has only ever lived, to this point in his life, in a democratic officeholding constitution):

> Therefore, because of these facts, the good people are not willing to rule either for the sake of money or for the sake of honor [*timē*]. For they don't want to be perceived publicly as engaging in office [*archē*] for the sake of a wage [*misthos*], being called mercenaries (*misthōtoi*); nor do they want to be such in secret, seizing a wage through thievery from their office (*ek tēs archēs*). Nor are they willing to rule [sc. from 347a5–6] for the sake of honor [*timē*]. For they are not honor-lovers (*philotimoi*). (347b5–10)[58]

The love of honor will, in the tripartite psychology, be located in those dominated by the *thumos*, and that group will eventually, in the constitution for a *kallipolis*, furnish the auxiliaries, whose love of honor leads them to engage in the military and logistical support for the rightful rulers (and, indeed, as I shall argue in a coming chapter, leads the auxiliaries to hold the offices that the constitution will involve). Here, however, Glaucon is being invited by Socrates to set that motivation and the desire for office, among other *timai*, which it would typically in that moment in Athens have evoked, aside. Instead, Socrates implicitly asks him to class himself among the decent, indeed self-perceived elite, people who are not willing to rule (in practice, through holding office) for the sake of either money or honor.

The alternative, as already intimated, is that such elites must be motivated instead by a penalty. Socrates continues by spelling out what that means:

> Therefore, they must submit to some necessity or penalty, if they are to be brought to be willing to rule (*ethelein archein*)—which is likely why it is thought to be shameful to approach ruling willingly (*to hekonta epi to archein*) rather than awaiting a necessity to do so—of which the greatest penalty is that of being ruled by someone worse [sc. than oneself], were one oneself to be unwilling to rule (*archein*). And it seems to me that it is fearing this that decent people rule (*archein*), when they do rule (*archōsin*), and that they then approach ruling (*epi to archein*) not as if going toward something good or as something which they will enjoy in itself, but rather from necessity, and being unwilling to entrust it to anyone else as being better or equal to themselves.[59] (347b9–d2)

In this part of the speech, Socrates consistently uses either the verb *archein* or an abstract substantive formed from it (*to archein*), in contrast to the

---

58. This category of *timē* encompasses political office, as noted in chapter 2.

59. I have added "as being" to make sense of the argument, though it is not explicit in the syntax.

preceding lines, in which, as shown above, the noun *archē* was doing the work. I vary translations of these terms because, as explained in part I, this verb (especially in an infinitive form as *archein*) is often conveniently translated as "ruling" in general (whereas, by contrast, the cognate noun is in certain contexts a signal of the more specific kind of rule that is "office"—that is, limited and broadly accountable rule). The kind of rule in question here is office.

In this argument, a penalty functions as does what could be a broader category of necessity: it imposes a requirement to act that is independent of one's estimation of what is positively and independently good. The final clause makes clear that, at least in some cases, the necessitation is that of a reasoned set of consequences—unless I rule, someone worse will rule over me—rather than an externally imposed force majeure.

Socrates goes on to link this conclusion back to his overall analysis of the idea of rule, which I have been analyzing throughout this chapter:

> In a city of good men, if such were to happen to come into being, there would be fighting (*perimachēton*) *not* to rule, just as there is nowadays *to* rule,[60] and it would become clear there that the person who is truly a ruler (*archōn*) does not by nature (*pephuke*) aim at his own advantage but at the advantage of the ruled. And therefore, in regard to all matters, everyone there [sc. in such a city] would be the kind of person who would seize the chance of being benefited by someone else, rather than benefiting another. (347d2–8)[61]

It is telling that this city is described by the very same participle as the one used in the *Laws* to describe the inverse kind of city, a kind of city said to have existed many times in history—namely, a city in which people battle to hold office and to keep their opponents out of office (4.715a8–b4), discussed in chapter 1 above, where I noted it as a passage that also resonates intertextually with the definition of justice issued earlier in the *Republic* by Thrasymachus. By contrast, the city imagined here is described in the optative, signifying "if it were to come into being." And the key specification of this city, its being a city "of good men (*andrōn agathōn*)," is not a vague or unspecified description. It is rather a definite description denoting a city populated by the very "decent" and "good" (indeed, "most decent" and "best") characters whom Glaucon has just agreed would not be motivated to hold office (or, a fortiori, to rule) for the sake of either money or honor. Only in such a city, one stripped of people with such extraneous and mistaken motivations, would the truth of the account of *archē* that Socrates has pressed on Thrasymachus become clear: that "the

60. I have added the emphases on *not* and *to* to bring out the contrastive force of the Greek phrases.

61. I have added some clarificatory words to the translation.

person who is truly a ruler does not by nature aim at his own advantage but at the advantage of the ruled."[62]

Roles and Natures

Because Socrates redirects the discussion after this point to the question posed by Thrasymachus in what above I called his "last stand," as to whether "the life of an unjust person is expected to trump that of the just person" (347e2–4), the discussion of ruling as a role, and the possible motivations of natural persons to pursue it, disappears from the remainder of book 1. In this final section of the present chapter, I survey how these topics raised in book 1 recur at later points of the dialogue (notwithstanding the fact that this will involve interpreting some difficult and much-debated passages without the space to engage with the relevant literature fully).

I begin by picking up on the rather surprising use of the word "by nature (*pephuke*)" in the passage inset most immediately above. I have been describing the claim about the *telos* of rule (treated as inherently evaluative) as a claim about the role of ruler, rather than about the human nature of any individual who might occupy that role. And yet, in restating the claim as above, Socrates adds the qualification "by nature." I read this as a play on words: the claim is that "by nature" a role occupant must be such and such, or, in other words, that the role is "by nature" such and such, perhaps underscoring the impossibility at the limit of an ordered role being entirely valueless (since order itself is for Plato inherently of value). By invoking the idea of nature, however, Socrates is also signaling the relevance of a different question, indeed one to which the burden of his thoughts in this passage has been tending: namely, what it is that might motivate a natural person to take up the role of ruler, and what specific kind of nature a person requires in order to become (at least in certain circumstances) willing to do so.

Now, what is counterintuitive about the way that the problem is formulated by Socrates in the exchange culminating at 347d8 is that one obvious way to solve a very similarly formulated problem might precisely seem to be through the assumption of an office or a professional role. Insofar as one is a statesman, one practices that profession—even though being a statesman deprives you of the leisure that would otherwise be yours as a philosopher,

---

62. Socrates goes on to link this point back to his broader objection to Thrasymachus's original definition of justice ("This is why I can in no way assent to what Thrasymachus said, that justice is the advantage of the stronger" [347d8–e1]): the genuine ruler, in aiming at the advantage of the ruled, is acting justly, whereas Thrasymachus had originally posited that rulers, being stronger (in the sense of being more conventionally powerful that he originally meant), aim at their own advantage.

as I have argued elsewhere.[63] Indeed, the earlier stretch of argument seemed to be pointing in this same direction. Insofar as one possesses a *technē*, one practices that *technē*, or, at least, it seemed earlier that one could not (qua professional) fail, in ruling, to aim at the benefit of one's subjects. That was simply the nature of rule: that the ruler, the person with the skill of ruling, benefits their subjects.

But Socrates has thrown a spanner in those works. For now it seems that even the possessors of the *technai*, and even—or, rather, especially—those with the skill and nature (as will be explained in book 6) to be political rulers need a special inducement or "wage" (but actually in the form of a negative penalty) to exercise their skill for the benefit of others. It is illuminating to contrast this predicament to the *Statesman*. There, the figure of the true statesman is a cipher, with no psychology or education specified, defined merely by their role as possessor of the corresponding expertise.[64] Here in the *Republic*, however, a potential chasm looms between the natural person and the (same person in) the role of ruler.

This potential chasm between natural persons and the role of ruler poses at least three challenges. One is to separate out the role of ruler from the natural person who might occupy that role, and to argue, as Socrates has done against Thrasymachus, that to count as a (genuine) ruler, one's aim must be the good of the ruled. Another is to consider why any natural person might be willing to take up the role of ruler, and, in particular, why philosophers— who are asserted in book 5 to be the only salvation of cities, whether philosophers who become kings or kings who become philosophers—might be willing to do so. Solutions as to how to span the chasm in this respect have been manifold.[65]

---

63. I discussed the statesman's characteristic lack of leisure in "'Emplois pour philosophes.'"

64. Lane, "Value of Knowledge," 61.

65. Scholars have offered solutions lying on a continuum from more negative to more positive. To illustrate: Sedley ("Philosophy") connects the book 1 discussion of this problem to the recurrent mention of "necessity" in later moments of the dialogue, such as the "necessity" (a translation of *anankē*, also translatable as "compulsion") imposed on the prisoner who is brought out of the Cave and then eventually pressed to return to it; the theme of compulsion is also emphasized by Brown in "Justice and Compulsion." Others, such as Cooper ("Psychology of Justice") and Kraut ("Return to the Cave"), have in different ways appealed to the more positive role played by the Form of the Good (or, relatedly, by the nature of justice: 7.540e) in orienting philosophers to its realization in the world through the activity of ruling. By contrast, others would deny that the dialogue adequately or consistently resolves this problem; see respectively Frank (*Poetic Justice*) and Weiss (*Philosophers*). My own view is that the negative approach—invoking a penalty for not ruling (in the shape of then having to be subjected to the rule of others worse than oneself) as the "wage" for reluctant rulers, canvassed above—is at least sufficient to resolve this challenge, even if more positive arguments could render it not necessary.

For present purposes, I am most interested in a third dimension of the chasm—namely, how to explain whether the role of ruler would be likely to be abused by a natural person who has taken it up, or, rather, to explain why it would not. This dimension of the issue is addressed within the architecture of the dialogue in book 6. That book, however, picks up on the two-part procedure outlined in book 5 to justify the claim that philosophers must rule:

> It seems to me necessary, if we are to escape from the people you mention [the people whom Glaucon had just imagined rushing to attack them on hearing the claim that philosophers should rule], [1] to define for them who are the philosophers whom we dare to say must rule (*archein*), so as, by clarifying how they are to come into being, to be able to ward off such a person, in showing that [2] to those people [the philosophers who must rule], it is fitting by nature (*prosēkei phusei*) both to engage in philosophy and to lead (*hēgemoneuein*) in a city, while to others it is fitting not to engage in philosophy but to follow (*akoulouthein*) the person who leads (*tōi hēgoumenōi*).[66] (5.474b3–c3).

Clause 1 of this passage is established by introducing the philosophers as full knowers at the end of book 5 and in the early part of book 6. In other words, the establishment of clause 1 focuses on the philosophers' developed knowledge. But clause 2—their fittedness by nature both to doing philosophy and to ruling—is explained in a further section of book 6 (6.485a4–487a8) by appealing to the motivations intrinsic to those who have philosophical natures, which produce these natural virtues.

As I have argued elsewhere, Socrates in *Republic* 6 positions a set of natural virtues as originating with a primitive version of temperance, which arises from a psychological, and even physiological, drive to learn. This drive is a form of love, one so powerful as to exert what I call (following an image in *Republic* 6) a hydraulic effect: psychic energy flows into this love, depriving other desires of the energy to oppose or distract one from the desire to learn:[67]

> Now, we surely know that, when someone's desires (*epithumiai*) incline strongly for one thing, they are thereby weakened for others, just like a stream that has been partly diverted into another channel. . . .

66. I have translated this afresh, so differing from the translation on which I relied in "Virtue." Socrates uses the same verb, *akoulouthein*, as used in the final clause of this quotation in subsequently inviting Glaucon to follow him in seeking to adequately set out the definition mentioned (5.474c5–6). Numbers [1] and [2] are my insertions.

67. I use "hydraulic" to refer to the protean motivational energy that in being directed toward one goal draws energy away from any other. For a step-by-step reconstruction of the argument, which I summarize as the claim that "the natural philosophers are naturally fitted for philosophy, and are therefore—through their initially hydraulically generated natural virtues—also morally fitted for ruling; they are also those who can become epistemically fitted for ruling, by gaining knowledge through philosophy," see my "Virtue" (56).

[T]hen, when someone's desires flow towards learning and everything of that sort, he'd be concerned, I suppose, with the pleasures of the soul itself by itself, and he'd abandon those pleasures that come through the body—that is, if he's a true philosopher. (6.485d6–8, d10–e1).

This passage and its extended book 6 context explain the nature of philosophers by comparing their desire to a flowing stream of water: a comparison that leads me to call this a hydraulic model of desire (6.485a10). Philosophers are lovers of learning (6.485b1), whose psychic energy flows so strongly into a loving pursuit of the truth (6.485d3) as to sap the flow of the same energy into bodily desires. This does not originate in a reasoned judgment that bodily desires and experiences are unimportant, nor in a deliberate policy of asceticism by which they are forcibly suppressed. It originates rather in a hydraulic redirection of psycho-physiological energy effected by the sheer power of the love of learning in the soul of the natural philosopher.

On the one hand, natural virtues are preconditions for the acquisition of knowledge-based virtues because only someone who is naturally abstemious as a result of their love for philosophy could go on to develop the panoply of full virtues. Without the right natural predisposition, they would sooner or later become distracted from the correct path by bodily desires that were not yet controlled by governing knowledge. On the other hand, natural virtues remain part of the psychological makeup of those who go on to develop full virtues. This claim plays a crucial role in the overall argument of the *Republic*, as the natural virtues of those with philosophical natures explain why the same people who are suited to do philosophy are also morally suited to rule. Nevertheless, the psychological structure of natural virtue differs from that of full virtue. The many virtues of the fully virtuous person pivot around their knowledge; those of the naturally virtuous person pivot around their temperance or discipline (*sōphrosunē*).[68]

Originating with a natural and dispositional form of temperance, the love of learning then develops in a complex interplay between disposition and evaluation. But from the standpoint of answering the question about why a ruler would not abuse their powers, appeal to the natural virtues alone (not yet perfected by knowledge) is already sufficient—or, rather, as sufficient as any appeal can be, given that there is no absolute guarantee that corruption

---

68. While translations of this term in English have been "traditionally 'temperance' or 'moderation,'" as observed by Moore and Raymond in their translation of Plato's *Charmides* (introduction, xxviii), they have advanced a strong case for "discipline" as the best translation of the term in that dialogue instead (xxxvi–xxxvii). I draw on their proposal in translating *sōphrosunē* and its cognates in some Platonic passages, while retaining the more familiar translations in others (especially where I have previously translated or quoted those passages in that way).

will not set in.[69] Indeed, Socrates goes on to explain how such corruption can be engendered, ironically especially in those with potent natural virtues, in corrupt societies, doing so in a response to an objection put by Adeimantus in book 6 (6.487c4–d5) that, of those who take up philosophy, most become either vicious or, at best, useless to the city. Nevertheless, Socrates suggests that within a *kallipolis*, philosophers who have received a good education in a noncorrupted civic culture and polity are at least likely to rule uncorrupted. The broader point is that, as it were, the virtuous cycle mentioned back in book 4 can be established between *psyche* and *politeia*, soul and city, at least for some period.[70] Hence, the challenge that I identified above—how to ensure that someone who takes up the role of ruler will not (or at least is maximally unlikely to) abuse the powers afforded by that role—is answered by appeal to a combination of the philosophical nature of someone taking up that role (since Socrates stipulates in the famous crux of book 5 that only persons who are philosophers should rule; see chapter 7) and the broader setting of a *kallipolis* as a *politeia* in which such persons will not become corrupted (at least until their natures begin to degenerate, as sketched at the beginning of book 8: see chapters 8 and 9).

The latter point is spelled out toward the end of Socrates's reply to the objection from Adeimantus noted above. Adeimantus has remarked that if a philosopher takes refuge from a city in which they have no prospect of allies in opposing injustice, that would be "not the least of the things that he could accomplish" before dying (6.497a1–2). Socrates responds with a caveat:

> But not the greatest either, since he didn't chance upon a constitution befitting him. Under one fitting him, his own growth would be much fuller (*mallon auxēsetai*), and also, in addition to his own affairs, he would safeguard the common ones. (6.497a3–5)[71]

In what sense would his own growth be fuller in a *kallipolis*, the kind of constitution befitting him because it corresponds to the kind of person he is, in the city-soul (or rather, city-person) analogy? The answer lies in the contention that only in such a constitution would he not risk becoming corrupted, as Socrates and Adeimantus have just been discussing is likely in other kinds of constitutions. Corruption would choke off philosophical development,

69. Here I enter an important caveat not noted in my "Virtue."

70. Socrates remarks in book 4 that a city with sound education "will go on as if growing in a circle" (4.424a5–6), a reference I owe to Rachel Barney, which encapsulates the argument that I made (without noting that reference) in my *Eco-Republic*. For the decline beginning in *Republic* 8, see chapters 8 and 9 below.

71. I am grateful to the B Caucus Reading Group of the Cambridge Faculty of Classics, in which context I first appreciated the Greek of the latter of these two sentences, which is perhaps my favorite line of Plato.

redirecting drives instead to honor or appetite, whereas in the absence of such corruption, psychic development allows the full development and perfection of wisdom along with the other virtues.

This brings me finally to consider whether Socrates's argument in book 1 in which, as this chapter has emphasized, he appealed to the role of ruler qua ruler retains its standing in the overall argument of the dialogue. Jill Frank has objected to me that it does not; in particular, that Socrates's book 1 account of the ruler qua ruler as aiming at the good of the ruled, in contrast to their own good, is inadequate and must be replaced with a definition of the ruler as aiming at both their own and their subjects' good.[72] Against this, I would draw a similar distinction to the one that I drew in chapter 3, in discussing the *Laws*' definition of the true legislator compared to the true doctor. What makes someone a doctor, legislator, or ruler is, indeed, on Platonic accounts throughout the three dialogues considered herein, the *telos* of aiming at the good of the ruled, as determined and enabled by the expertise that informs the activity of ordering (*taxis*) by which they do so. The acid test of the *taxis* of political rule, as deployed in *Republic* 1 and elsewhere, is a simple question about orientation toward its *telos*: whether any given ruler cares for the good of the ruled or instead seeks to exploit them.

Conclusion

Philosophically and politically, the ultimate challenge posed by *Republic* 1, which remains alive in the course of the dialogue, is that of the relationship between the natural person and the role of being a ruler. While this challenge remains central to the *Republic*, it is one that the *Statesman* leaves entirely aside, while the *Laws* addresses it in practical terms by setting up institutions that draft people to serve rather than asking them to choose to stand or run.[73] *Republic* 1 puts on the table a gulf between the motivation of ruler qua ruler, absorbed in their professional role, and of ruler qua natural person, considering at a distance, as it were, whether or not to accede to the demands of that role, that the later books of the dialogue cannot fully set aside. Plato dramatizes an unfamiliar set of dangers in this dialogue: not merely the usual dangers of corruption and ignorance but the special dangers that arise when a gap opens between the natural person and their role or office, in the sense of their being unwilling to comport themselves as their actual possession of skill demands that they should. Since on his view, those who actually have the skill cannot help but exercise it correctly, the gap lies instead in the

---

72. In conversation and comments on earlier versions of this work.

73. I owe this point to Reid, who in "Voting for the Guardians" insightfully observes: "Magnesians don't so much *run for office* as they do *find themselves in office*, having been nominated and elected by others" (emphasis original).

willingness of those with the skill to exercise it at all: to assume the office or role and fulfill the demands that it imposes, even at the cost of their own leisure and perfect happiness.

In comparing this problematic with that of Hobbes, say, there is a sense in which it may have been Plato who was the more truly realist. For Hobbes in *Leviathan* was notoriously less than deeply troubled about the danger that a sovereign might be inclined to abuse the powers and purposes of their office— that their subjects might, in Locke's penetrating criticism, avoid the dangers posed by polecats or foxes only to risk being devoured by a lion (or as Socrates in *Republic* 1 would put it, find themselves subject not to a guard dog but to a wolf).[74] Hobbes, for his part, falls back on the abstract and impersonal office of the sovereign to ward off such criticism, with debatable success. But for Plato, a still more fundamental issue lies below: not that the properly ruling person will abuse their power in exercising it but, rather, that they will not bother to exercise it at all.

Underidentification of a person with their professional role poses familiar political and ethical dangers—in the space of corruption. Overidentification too poses some familiar potential dangers—in the space of the pathologies of office, occupied by the unfeeling or by the overzealous bureaucrat. Yet Plato here adds a paradoxical combination of overidentification and underidentification as a danger that is far less commonly recognized—lying in the space of motivation, the danger that someone who overidentifies with the skills of a role may nevertheless underidentify with the motivation to undertake its practice. A supreme insight of Plato as a philosopher of politics is to bring out the full dimensions of these tensions between roles and natural persons, both in the political realm narrowly conceived, where those roles may take the form of inadequately safeguarded offices (as in *Republic* 8) or of ideal ruler, and in other forms of interaction in which persons play roles in relation to one another, as in the professions, or *technai*.

Thus Plato identified a gulf within classical Greek ideas of office and rule between person and role, whether the general role of ruler or the specific (and specifically limited) role of officeholder. While one can travel across that gulf by means of argument, such as the *Republic*'s arguments for why the philosopher should return to what Plato figures as the Cave, it remains an endemic challenge in political life. The gulf becomes a chasm in the flawed constitutions of *Republic* 8, which are incapable of educating the persons capable of properly playing the role of rulers, as I argue in chapter 8. Before that, I trace the question of the wages of rule in the constitutional project of the *Republic* as it unfolds beyond book 1 and use this to open up a broader discussion of the relationship between rule and office in that constitution.

---

74. Locke, *Second Treatise of Government*, in *Two Treatises*, 328.

CHAPTER SIX

Guarding as Serving

THE CONUNDRUM OF WAGES IN A
KALLIPOLIS (*REPUBLIC*, BOOKS 1–5)

IT WAS ARGUED in the preceding chapter of this study that book 1 of Plato's *Republic* raises, without resolving, the motivational question of why a natural person who is fit to rule would take up the role of ruler. Socrates there insists that any natural person would require a special kind of "wage" (*misthos*) in order to be willing to take up that role, given that such a role aims at the *telos* of benefiting others (the ruled) rather than the role holder themselves. In making that proposal, Socrates converts the nature of the "wage" in question away from the common meaning of monetary pay for hire or service, into a particular kind of penalty: the penalty suffered by someone in being ruled by someone else who is less virtuous than they are.

As the previous chapter observed, Socrates in book 1 explains the rejection of money as the content of such a wage as hinging on the revulsion of decent people against being considered money-grubbing mercenaries, should they engage in the everyday battle for political office (here, as he is commenting on existing attitudes and practices, the sense of *archē* as "office" is in view):

> Therefore, because of these facts, the good people are not willing to rule either for the sake of money. . . . For they don't want to be perceived publicly as engaging in office [*archē*] for the sake of a wage [*misthos*], being called mercenaries (*misthōtoi*); nor do they want to be such in secret, seizing a wage through thievery from their office [*archē*]. (1.347b5–10)[1]

---

1. Socrates also refers to positions of *timē* (honor), which in Athens included offices, as noted above in chapter 2. All quotations in this chapter are from Plato's *Republic* according to the Slings OCT, and in my own translation, unless otherwise indicated.

The reader should, therefore, experience some shock when, in book 4, Adeimantus raises the following objection to the nature of a *kallipolis* as so far described:[2] that the guardians (*phulakes*), whose way of life and role in the city has so far been described, seem to be settled in the city "like military mercenaries" (*hōsper epikouroi misthōtoi*) (4.419a1–420a2).[3] In contrast to Socrates's positioning in book 1 of the true rulers of a good city as the polar opposite of mercenaries, Adeimantus here positions its rulers precisely *as* such mercenaries. Indeed, as is established in recurrent (and subtly different) passages in books 3, 4, and 5, and is implied here in virtue of their name and role, the guardians of a *kallipolis* are indeed to receive a kind of wage.

Before tackling the implications of the guardians' status as mercenaries (a status on which Plato doubles down in using the label of *epikouroi* to describe some of them, as argued below), it is worth noting that Adeimantus's objection betrays his failure to appreciate the deeper significance of the book 1 argument (to which he and the other interlocutors were privy) about wages and rule at all. He presses the expectation that happiness will be enjoyed only by rulers who exploit their power for what they take to be their own benefit (land, houses, household religious rites, guests, and gold and silver are all mentioned by him; Socrates even bolsters the case for the sake of argument by adding mention of travel and other expenditures, including the keeping of women for sex, a perquisite of the powerful in the patriarchal society of the time). On this view, which resonates with aspirations expressed or endorsed by certain characters in other Platonic dialogues (think especially of Polus and Callicles in the *Gorgias*), those who seek power do so not to serve others but rather to exploit them in the service of enriching themselves.

This ominous intervention by Adeimantus reinforces the observation made earlier in this study that Plato was far from oblivious to the fact that a service conception of rule could well be rejected, and was rejected by many of his contemporaries. Reasons for such rejection had already been advanced

2. Reference to a *kallipolis* is made in the dative at 7.527c2, in the phrase "in your *kallipolis*" addressed by Socrates to Glaucon, meaning something like "in your fine city," as Grube and Reeve translate (*kalos* being a complex evaluative term that can be used to mean "beautiful," "fine," "noble," and related ideas). Barney ("Last Night in Suburbia") argues against the scholarly convention of using *Kallipolis* as a name, pointing out that the phrase in that book 7 passage functions more as a generic identification than as a name. In order to acknowledge this point, and to signal that the term refers to any city identified by a certain constitution rather than a unique civic entity, I use the term in the lowercase and modify it mainly by an indefinite article ("a" rather than "the" *kallipolis*).

3. I note below that *misthōtoi* can also be translated more generally as "hired hand" in nonmilitary contexts, especially for manual laborers. That sense could be apposite to the book 1 passage here, and will be shown below to be invoked at one point in book 2. However, the book 4 objection from Adeimantus, described in the main text immediately below, clearly has the military connotations, as it describes settlement as if in a military encampment.

within the frame of the *Republic* by Thrasymachus in book 1, as discussed in the previous chapter, in a caustic reframing of the shepherd as aiming to eat the sheep, striking at the heart of the Homeric evaluative nimbus of expectation that rule should serve the good of the ruled (even if it might often fail to do so in practice). While many readers find Socrates's response to Thrasymachus in book 1 to have been weak, insofar as it simply asserts the purpose of rule to be serving the ruled against the latter's denial of that claim, fewer have considered the endorsement by Adeimantus in book 4 of a position similar to that described by Thrasymachus, or the significance of the fact that the rulers and other guardians of the constitution outlined in the *Republic* are indeed to receive wages and to be limited by them in exactly the ways that Adeimantus accurately describes in decrying them.

In other words, Socrates accepts Adeimantus's objection and runs with it, accepting the positioning of these rulers as having no alternative (in virtue of the legal deprivations to which they are subject) but to serve the people, justifying this as their playing their part in ensuring that "the whole city is happy" (4.420b7–8).[4] To the underlying concern that the guardians themselves will not be happy, expressed in Adeimantus's objection, which presupposes a certain conventional image of such happiness (using wealth and power to buy material pleasure and social status), Socrates responds here enigmatically that their happiness will come from their "nature"—that is, as books 5–7 will show, from their nature as philosophers and the supreme pleasure of that way of life.[5] The rulers' happiness is irrelevant, however, to the question of their role in serving the good of the ruled as part of seeking the happiness of the whole city. And that role is to be enforced upon them by a set of legally imposed deprivations amounting to deprivation of any opportunity to exploit their power for the sake of material goods and opportunities, a deprivation that functions to make them dependent on wages instead.

Hiring someone for wages presumes that they are to serve the good of those who hire them. A waged servant is, precisely, a servant, serving the benefit of their employer. It also typically indicates that the person who hires them is able to control them—at least by ceasing to pay their wages so as to sanction or fire them. Military mercenaries could be hired by any kind of ruler or regime, as paid servants who could be hired and fired at will by starting or stopping their wages. In political contexts, in Greek constitutions of Plato's lifetime, the only kind of rulers who might sometimes have received wages were officeholders, and specifically some democratic officeholders; while not

---

4. This aim is reiterated at 4.420c1–3 and 4.420e6–7, contrasted with the aim of simply making certain individuals within the city happy. That latter aim would risk making each group of people happy in a way that would be incompatible with their function and so undermine the city's happiness overall (4.420c5–421c5).

5. The happiness of each such group must be left up to "nature" (4.421c4–5).

all democratic officeholders received wages (this varied from city to city and across time), officeholders in nondemocratic constitutions typically did not. (Certainly, no tyrants or despots or kings would have been expected to receive wages.) Aristotle would note that wages for political roles, including especially offices (*archai*), were characteristically democratic, explaining this (in the context of at least one kind of democracy) in terms of the necessity of purchasing sufficient leisure for the poor to participate in political roles.[6]

Thus, in establishing *misthoi* for guardians, some of whom are also to serve as rulers, the *Republic* trenches not just on a service conception of rule but on a feature especially (though not always) associated with democratic rule. The reason that wages are necessary in a *kallipolis* is superficially the opposite of the reason that they are necessary in a democracy (on Aristotle's account). In a democracy, wages are necessary to provide the poor with their (partial) livelihood, buying them, as it were, the leisure time to serve in politics. In a *kallipolis*, wages are necessary to provide the guardians with their (total) livelihood, as they are deprived of family and wealth, being conscripted into the service of the polity (I use the term "conscripted" in light of the necessity that is variously said, in books 1 and 7 in particular, to constrain them). Wages were necessary in a democracy like Athens to enable the poor to serve part-time in politics; in a *kallipolis*, to enable a class that is legally deprived of all opportunity to acquire wealth to serve as required.

What, then, is Plato doing, as a matter of political theorizing, in making the guardians of a *kallipolis* dependent on wages, depicting them (as, again, Adeimantus does accurately enough) as living like military mercenaries in encampments, while imposing a wage (described as a legal entitlement) for those of them who are to rule? I argue in this chapter that wages for the rulers and other guardians (those junior to the ones who rule) are, on the one hand, clearly intended to buttress the Platonic idea of rule as a service conception, which had been set out in *Republic* 1 and is also fundamental to the *Statesman* and *Laws*. The rulers of a *kallipolis* are to serve those whom they rule and are to view themselves as dependent on them. On the other hand, those ruled, while supplying the wages so that the rulers can benefit them, are to view the rulers as their "safeguarders"—as providing a service from above, as it were, without any adverting to the possibility that the wages could be stopped as a way of controlling those ruling from below. This complex geometry of objective dependence and different subjective attitudes toward wages on the part of the rulers and the ruled bespeaks Plato's most explicit grappling with the relational implications of a service conception of rule. I argue that the role of wages for the rulers in the *Republic*'s service conception of rule is deliberately paradoxical. The rulers are to see themselves as dependent on the wages (as they will genuinely be for their subsistence), yet the ruled are not to see

6. Arist., *Pol.* 6.1317b35–39, 4.1293a1–10.

themselves as political superiors of their rulers in virtue of paying their wages. Only in this paradoxical way can the epistemic superiority and epitactic subordination that ruling requires (on Plato's account) be preserved, even while the function of ruling as serving is safeguarded so as to avoid the corruption of those with power.[7]

The role of the rulers as safeguarders is spelled out succinctly at one point in book 3: Socrates there describes a ruler as someone who is "set over others [*epistatēs*]" in order to "safeguard the constitution (*hē politeia sōzesthai*)" (3.412b1).[8] But the question then becomes, if the rulers' role is to safeguard the constitution, how is their role in so doing to be safeguarded in turn? (As in chapter 3, my framing of this issue deliberately echoes the conundrum stated by Juvenal—"Who shall guard the guardians?"—and will recur again in the next chapter.) The answer developed in the *Republic* does not rely on simply the wisdom or benevolence of the rulers, even though they will eventually be identified as having to be philosophers if they are to rule well, with philosophical natures that tend toward bodily asceticism due to a passion for learning that makes possible the philosophical education that can ultimately perfect those natures. Rather, the rulers—along with the broader group of guardians from which they emerge as the best of the senior generation—must be subjected to laws depriving them of any incentive for, as well as power of, exploitation. Those laws in turn create the need for them to serve as wage earners in the sense of affirmatively receiving some kind of wage (and not just suffering a penalty).[9]

A wage is necessary for the guardians in such a constitution because its legislators "in speech" are to lay down as laws [*nomothetein*][10] a set of arrangements

7. Compare the paradoxical challenges involved in electing judges in modern democracies.

8. There is a striking resonance of this phrase with the role assigned in the *Laws* to the Daily Meeting (the term I proposed in chapter 3 in lieu of the nomenclature more familiar in modern English of "Nocturnal Council"). In the *Republic*, safeguarding is carried out by human rulers, those who are the eldest group of guardians. In the *Laws*, safeguarding is done by the content of the laws themselves, the spirit of which is preserved by the Daily Meeting; the latter body is not primarily described as ruling, though there are subtleties in the closing text of the dialogue that discuss its role in the context of the roles of statesmen and rulers, which I addressed in chapter 3.

9. On the structuring role of the issuing of "laws" in the founding of a city, and delineating of its constitution, in the *Republic*, see my "Founding as Legislating" and Annas's *Virtue and Law* (9–31). Not only the founders "in speech" but the philosophers themselves are described as having to engage in a project involving "writing laws" (*graphein nomous*), at 6.501a6.

10. *Nomothetēsōmen*, 3.417b8. See also 5.458c3–4, when Socrates insists that "the rulers themselves will be obeying our laws" whenever the discursive legislators have issued such laws, whereas in other cases the rulers (in this passage distinguished from the junior auxiliaries) will be imitating such laws where matters have been left up to them to endeavor to do so. These latter observations are made in the context of the "second wave," which

for the guardians' housing and property (as mooted at the end of book 3, and developed with further stipulations in book 5) that will deprive them of the private holdings of land and wealth, and (as per book 5) also of private kinship ties, through which the money to obtain, or direct access to, provisions necessary for subsistence would otherwise in existing cities be supplied.[11] Such laws are introduced in order to safeguard the city against the possibility of the guardians becoming corrupt—that is, of pursuing a *telos* of their own private good through indifference to or exploitation of the good of those whom they are to guard and, in some cases, rule. Laws that place limits on the role of the guardians—including the rulers—are part of the essential fabric of the constitution of a *kallipolis*;[12] their renewed discussion in book 5 confirms that they carry over into the fully fledged constitution ruled by philosophers as described in books 5–7.[13]

Yet, this only deepens the puzzle of wages in the *Republic*. By making wages necessary for the guardians for reasons that are simultaneously economic (deprivation of any alternative means of livelihood) and political (deprivation of any incentive to exploit those being guarded), Plato makes them necessary

---

emphasizes the lack of private kinship for the guardians as a whole but also reiterates that they are to "have common houses and public meals, none of them acquiring any such thing as a private individual" (5.458c8–9).

11. Even the Spartan *homoioi*, the "similars" who counted as full-fledged citizens, lost their civic standing if they lost the private wealth requisite to contribute to the city's needs.

12. On the significance of laws within a *kallipolis* in the *Republic*, I agree with Schofield ("Law and Absolutism"), who offers a persuasive rebuttal of the rival absolutist reading of the city of the *Republic* as eschewing laws in Barker's *Greek Political Theory*.

13. One may ask whether books 2–4 and 5–7 articulate the same constitution, being built up in stages, or whether only the constitution as described in 5–7 should be termed a *kallipolis* proper. Socrates opens book 5 with a clearly backward-looking summative remark: that "this therefore is the kind of city and constitution which I call correct, and so too is this kind of man" (5.449a1–2). However, the backward-looking summation with which Socrates opens book 8, while appearing to be a close narrative parallel to the backward-looking summation that had opened book 5, leads Glaucon to draw a distinction between the claims that had been advanced then and the claims that should be made at the stage that the argument has now (in dramatic terms) reached: "You were saying that you would set down as good both the city, and the man who is like it, which you had then described, but [sc. setting down] these, as so seeming to you, despite there still being a finer city and man to describe" (8.543c8–544a2). This retrospective gloss draws a distinction that was absent from Socrates's retrospective gloss at the beginning of book 5, driving a wedge between the city and man set down as good in the backward-looking summary at the start of book 5 and those described in the course of books 5–7, which are now set down as "a finer city and man." Nevertheless, because the changes introduced into the constitution of the city "in speech" in the course of books 5–7 originate in response to a demand for clarification of the city as it had previously been sketched, I take the constitution of a *kallipolis* to be under gradual construction from the introduction of the *phulakes* (guardians) in book 2 onward, and the continuity in that vocabulary to be itself indicative of that overall continuity of construction.

not only for guarding but for ruling. For while the role of mercenary soldier was clearly not one of rule or office within a constitutional polity, within the constitution of a *kallipolis* some of the "guardians" described with the language of mercenaries, and receiving a mercenary wage, are also to serve as "rulers."

In receiving a wage, the "guardians" (some of whom are also the "rulers" in a *kallipolis*) are therefore marked out by one of the parameters typically (though not essentially) characteristic of ruling in the sense of officeholding: involving powers, as argued in part I, that are inherently limited. This is significant from a theoretical standpoint. A wage is a relational entity. It is not inherited or received from the ether; it is paid by some human agent(s) to other(s), in its focal use as a recompense for services rendered—whether affirmatively provided, as was usually understood, or in the shape of a negative penalty, as per the argument of book 1. Wages were a signal (typically) of democratic power and control: the dependence of officeholders on wages was an indication of their subjection to external control by the *dēmos* through various legal mechanisms and procedures. Thus, wages for the guardians invoke one of the limiting parameters that could be characteristic of ruling as officeholding in Plato's time.

Rule, in the constitutional project of the *Republic*, as the task that the best of the guardians must fulfill, takes on the coloration of limited powers that is functionally similar (though not identical) to a limiting parameter of Greek offices as constituted in and before Plato's day. A similar analysis of the other parameters indicative of offices, and the extent to which functional analogues mark and limit the roles of the rulers in a *kallipolis*, is offered in the next chapter. There, a varying set of roles for the auxiliaries is divided according to age cohorts, and likewise a set of roles for the rulers, with the eldest guardians above age fifty "reigning" (described by a word for kingly reigning, *basileuein*) while the next most junior age cohort is described (I shall argue) as officeholders who rule over other citizens while gaining political and military experience between ages thirty-five and fifty. In this chapter, I focus on the question of wages for the guardians as a whole, taking note of the broad division between senior rulers and junior auxiliaries, but not otherwise of the subdivisions by age cohort that will be central to the discussion of ruling and officeholding in the next chapter. The question of wages applies to all the guardians considered as such, introduced with regard to their military function; the fact that some of them are rulers, and that some of those (as shown in the next chapter) rule as officeholders, brings these wages within the ambit of the democratic debate about wages for office as well.

The next section reviews the introduction of the "guardians" and how some of them come to be identified as "rulers." Subsequent sections step back to explain more fully why wages are necessary for the reasons canvassed above, and then just what sort of wages they will be, reconciling the subtle variations on this point expressed in passages in books 3, 4, and 5 respectively. Those sections establish the role and nature of wages in a *kallipolis* objectively, as it were. The final two sections of the chapter turn instead to their subjective role in shaping the attitudes of the rulers and ruled to each other. Textually, this subjective role hinges on a crucial passage in book 5, which discusses the terms of address to be used in a *kallipolis* among the rulers and the ruled. These proposed terms of address position the objective fact of wages as shaping the subjective dispositions and attitudes of the rulers to the ruled, but not of the ruled to the rulers. The final section of the chapter then considers the Platonic approach to the subjective significance of wages theoretically, in light of broader Greek figurations of servants and wages, arguing that these afforded Plato an approach to rule as a service conception that modern analyses of accountability (especially those focused on the control of an agent expected of their principal) fail to capture. The larger moral of the argument is that the function of ruling itself requires a recognizable *taxis* (order) of limits if it is to be able to realize the *telos* of the good of the ruled—a moral that in the next part of this study will be explored in the breach, in flawed constitutions in which *taxis* and *telos* degenerate in tandem.

Throughout this chapter, I use the term "guardians" to signify the entire group who are to receive such wages. In calling the group as a whole "guardians" in the context of focusing on that point (the topic of the present chapter), I build on the illuminating analysis by Alexander Long of the expertise of "guarding" (*phulakikē*) that they are ascribed.[14] The role of guarding, however, is not limited to knowledge of the proper *telos* of rule. Knowing the *telos* is indeed constitutive of rule. But so is the deployment of the proper *taxis* (order) in order to achieve that *telos*. A service conception of rule requires rulers whose *taxis* is so ordered as to enable them to properly serve those whom they rule through the pursuit of the *telos*. Receiving a wage for ruling is part of that *taxis* in the conditions of a *kallipolis*, and that fact illuminates what might be required, and entailed, in seeking rulers whose role as rulers is genuinely to serve.

"The Function of Guarding"

Despite the fact that the interlocutors of the dialogue at the outset often, as later, invoke en passant the vocabulary of *archein* and *archē* in expressions that sometimes signal specifically "offices," sometimes more generally "rule,"[15]

---

14. The term itself is introduced by Glaucon (as part of a set of answers to leading questions by Socrates) in book 4, identifying this expertise (4.428c11–d9) as "guardianship . . . being in those rulers (*tois archousin*) whom we just now named 'complete guardians'" (4.428d6–7); see Long, "Political Art," 28 and, more generally, 27–31. The distinction is drawn here on the basis of age, which was a common basis for the assignment of political and other roles in Greek constitutions; Aristotle makes age a basis for political turn taking in *Pol.* 7.9, 1329a13–17 and 7.14, 1332b26–27, for example, references recalled to me by Jeremy Reid.

15. For example: as Plato's brothers set out their reformulated versions of Thrasymachus's challenge to Socrates, Adeimantus refers in passing to "offices" (*archai*) among the

that vocabulary is strikingly absent from the initial founding "in speech" of the city in book 2, which in its earliest iteration has become known (owing to a disgruntled remark about it by Glaucon) as the "city of pigs." There is no mention of rule, office, or constitution (*politeia*) in this earliest phase of "making" a city "in argument," not even of *politeia* in the related but broader sense of a way of life.[16] Instead, Socrates in the *Republic* approaches the founding of a city not in the constitutional framework of laws and offices, nor even in a more general framework of rule, but rather in terms of the function of a wider set of professional forms of expertise, which had been debated throughout book 1 (as discussed in the previous chapter).

Beginning from the respective human needs to which each professional role responds, Socrates introduces the respective *ergon* (work, function, task, or product) of each of the latter (2.369e3). This populates the city initially with a farmer, a builder, a weaver, a cobbler, and a doctor; eventually, carpenters, metalworkers, cowherds, shepherds, other herders, more craftsmen of these and other kinds, merchants, retailers, and wage earners. Notice in particular the introduction of the last-named group. Having described retailers as engaged in "serving" [*diakonein*] in the marketplace (*agora*), alongside merchants who do so in importing and exporting with regard to other cities, Socrates uses a plural noun [*diakonoi*] in describing another group of "servants" needed in such a city—namely, those who "sell the use (*chreia*) of their physical strength, the reward of which we call a wage, they being called, as I think, wage-earners (*misthōtoi*)" (2.371e2–4). This is the first appearance of the role of *misthōtoi* in the context of the city being established "in speech"— signaling in this context not mercenary soldiers but wage-earning daily laborers.[17] Wage earners are thus already denizens of the healthy city, before the

---

kinds of goods that someone might gain through unjust conduct (2.363a3–4), harking back to Glaucon's earlier claim that such a person "rules (*archein*) his city" because he is believed to be just (2.362b2). Both brothers' easy allusions show how readily a use of the verb *archein* for rule could be convertible into the institutional species of office that such rule in Athens (the city in which Glaucon and Adeimantus were living, and in which the dialogue is set, hence plausibly their main frame of political reference), as in many other Greek cities at the time, presupposed. Again in book 10, officeholding as a good, even a reward to which a just person might aspire, is reinforced, in keeping with the chiastic structure of the dialogue: see the reference to what in context should be translated as "office" (*archē*) at 10.608b5–7, and to the intertwining of "rule" and "office" at 10.613d2–3.

16. Note that at 2.369c9–10, Socrates invites the brothers to join him in "making" (*poiōmen*) a city from the beginning. He does not introduce the language of "founding"— which in Greek practices at the time would have carried expectations of giving laws and of the establishment of a constitution—until 3.378e7–379a1, when he chides Adeimantus that "we are founders (*oikistai*) of a city."

17. The significance of daily laborers as central to the group of those earning wages (though not this textual locus in particular) was highlighted to me by Demetra Kasimis in an exchange on an earlier version of this chapter.

guardians whom Adeimantus will (correctly, though disapprovingly) describe as *misthōtoi* have yet been introduced.

Famously, Glaucon's disgust with this "healthy city" leads to its being made "luxurious" (2.372e2), a move that Socrates observes may be what enables them to see "when and in what way justice and injustice grow up in cities" (2.372e4–6),[18] conducing to the overall undertaking that he has given the brothers in book 2 of reinforcing their commitment to a just life being preferable and advantageous (as opposed to an unjust life, of which the extreme case is that of the tyrant).[19] Luxuries lead to a need for more land,[20] which (Socrates assumes) can be acquired only by being seized from neighbors, which will lead to war—offensive and, insofar as neighboring cities have followed the same path, defensive as well.[21] War will require an "army" (2.374a1); warfare is made according to a *technē* (it is *technikē*, 2.374b1–3); but by a general principle that had been articulated in the founding of the city, recalled here, it is impossible for one person to practice many *technai* well (2.374a4–6, recalling 2.370b5–c7).[22]

Socrates then infers, notoriously contrary to the practice of democratic Athens at the time, that one cannot expect it to be "easy" for "a farmer or a cobbler or any other person practicing another *technē*" to be able to practice war well (2.374c4–6). And this leads him to introduce "the function of guarding" (*to tōn phulakōn ergon*) (2.374e1). Carrying out the function of guarding well will, he cautions, require possession of the relevant "expertise" [*technē*] (2.374e2–3). But to the extent that this is the "greatest function," it will also require possession of the greatest "care" [*epimeleia*], and this in turn requires

18. The pairing of "justice and injustice" here leaves open the possibility that justice could already have been found in the healthy city, from which injustice was absent. The addition of "leisure" is underwritten by the argument in which this passage is embedded, that the guardians need to be free from the demands of other professions, as well as the broader (and related) one-person-one-job principle that structures the dialogue; the mention of "care" resonates powerfully with the centrality of that attribute and activity to the definition of statecraft in the *Statesman*.

19. For the focus on reinforcing moral views that the brothers already share, see Scott's *Listening to Reason.*

20. Not necessarily because of population size alone but because of the increased and varied demands of consumption, as Socrates explains his reasoning.

21. The justice of waging offensive war is conspicuously left undiscussed, a point the ramifications of which demand more discussion than can be given here.

22. A famous puzzle resulting from this principle is how to explain why it should not be violated by the "third wave" enjoining that philosophers must rule as kings, or kings philosophize (discussed in the next chapter). An answer in brief: to be a philosopher is to have the nature of a philosopher, the natural virtues and disposition as to how to live thereof, as argued in my "Virtue." Being a philosopher is a condition of a natural person, and so is not another job or task on top of being a ruler; rather, being a ruler is a job or task that philosophers will from time to time perform, as argued in my "'Emplois pour philosophes.'"

that the person carrying out this function have a "nature" [*phusis*] suited to this kind of pursuit, as well as the requisite leisure to fulfill it (2.374e1–5). Thus the book 1 question of the natural person who is suited to develop not only the epistemic expertise but also the appropriate orientation of care, in order to fulfill the work or role of guarding, returns here: Socrates emphasizes that their own corresponding *ergon* (that is, as founders of the city "in speech") is to identify precisely those natures that are suited to guarding in the city (2.374e7–9).[23]

Phulax is the term typically translated in English as "guardian," though it is important to note that it is initially introduced in a military context, and there is also merit in the choice made by Alexander Long of translating it consistently as "guard," insofar as this can highlight the functional cast with which the word is initially introduced. Used alone,[24] the term *phulakes* is more typically a reference to a military role, but not the name or title of any particular military office in any constitution (despite the fact that military commands were very often constitutional offices).[25] That said, the function of serving as guardians in order to safeguard the city could in fourth-century Athenian discourse be discussed in nonmilitary contexts as well. The speaker for whom Demosthenes's "Against Timocrates" was written, for example, addresses the jurors (in a case brought during Plato's lifetime) as "guardians [*phulakes*] of the law" (Demosthenes, 24.36).[26] So while Plato's introduction of specialized mercenaries as the sole military guardians of the city would have been

23. In Greek social practice and widely shared expectations, to possess a *technē* required a combination of nature, learning, and practice, as shown by Hulme Kozey's "Another *Peri Technes* Literature," "Good-Directedness of Τέχνη," and "Is Farming a *Technē*?," as well as her doctoral dissertation, "*Philosophia* and *Philotechnia*."

24. At 4.421a6–7, Socrates refers to the guardians of the city they are founding in speech as "guardians of the laws and of the city" (supplying the definite articles for convenience in English), emphasizing that these must be "guardians in truth" (4.421a9), a point that I owe to Long ("Political Art," 22n19). But that definite description is never converted into the title (such as *nomophulakes*) of any office more specific than the overall role of "guardians" simpliciter.

25. It was, however, an established constituent in the title of the role of *nomophulakes*, an office that existed in Athens in the fourth century, for example, and also in a number of cities much earlier, as I noted in chapter 3 in discussing its featuring as an office in the constitutional project of the *Laws*.

26. The same passage also ascribes a guarding function (*phulattomenos*) to the lawgiver who is imagined as having framed the law that prohibited the passing of any law contradicting the existing ones; cf. Demosthenes, 24.37, describing the *dēmos* as a whole, embodied in the jury, as such a guardian of the law. These passages are discussed in Wohl (*Law's Cosmos*, 297); they indicate that, as I have argued more broadly in this study, Plato was participating in a broader discourse about the need for safeguarding the functions of various political roles, and how such safeguarding could best be carried out, though he did not position the founder-legislators of his dialogues as rulers of the cities for which they legislate in speech.

anathema to democratic Athenians and their citizen army and navy, the language of guarding participates in a broader civic discourse about the need for guarding, and will be developed in the *Republic* in the context of political roles as well as military ones, and how all such roles may best be safeguarded.

As so far observed, the "guardians" are initially introduced as such in the military context of both offense and defense necessitated by the introduction of luxuries into what had been a "healthy city," without any initially identified role of rule. However, Socrates in book 3 begins to refer to the role of "rulers" in a city in the course of discussing the ethics and politics of lying (from 3.389b8),[27] and then later in that book introduces a discussion of which ones among the guardians "will rule and which ones will be ruled" (3.412c1). There, he divides the group of guardians into the older and the younger, specifying that it is "the best" of the older ones who must be the rulers: after a lifetime of testing, each of those qualified will "be established as a ruler of the city as well as a guard (*archonta . . . kai phulaka*)."[28] The distinction between rulers and ruled within the wider group of guardians will be scrutinized in the next chapter of this study. Here, I focus on a feature that they retain in common: their dependence on and receipt of wages.

Why Wages?

Why are these guardians to be paid wages? Or, more precisely, given that *Republic* 1 argued that some kind of wage would be necessary to induce natural persons to take up the role of ruler (an argument that I discussed in chapter 5), the question now to be asked is this: Why do these wages from book 3 onward turn out to be affirmative provisions of some kind, rather than simply the negative penalty that had been envisaged in book 1? The significance of the issue is underscored by the fact that the constitutional project of the *Laws* incorporates no such wages for the rulers (all officeholders) of its constitution envisaged "in speech." Wages were a possible feature of Greek offices,

27. And passim from that point: e.g., 3.389c1 in the context of the use of falsehoods; 3.389e1 and 3.390a2 in the context of moderation as part of the education of the city's youth.

28. 3.412b9–c12, 3.413e5–414a2, the latter passage leading into the "noble lie" that Socrates specifies he would try to persuade the "rulers" as well as the soldiers and then the rest of the city to believe (3.414d2–4). The initial question of who should rule and be ruled is raised about "these same people" (3.412c1), a back reference to the guardians whose education has been the major topic of the last book and a half. Recall from chapters 1 and 2 also the illustration of "rulers" in book 5, in which *hoi archontes* features in a syntactical context that I suggested is best translated as "the rulers"—"it looks as though our rulers [*hoi archontes*] will often have to make use of lying and deception for the advantage of those they rule" (5.459c9–d2)—and which in its dramatic context refers to the more senior rulers who are overseeing the procreative mating of the more junior auxiliaries (all of them serving the function of "guardians"). I return to this passage in chapter 7.

and, in particular, characteristic of some democratic constitutions.[29] In the constitutional project of the *Laws*, however, they are not necessary because the officeholders are drawn from the ranks of ordinary citizens, each of whom is to be distributed an allotment of private land (which should provide both the material provisioning and whatever level of cash income they require).[30] Indeed, Plato in the *Laws* points up the absence of *misthos* for officeholders by inverting the principle, suggesting instead imposing penalties or fines on officeholders who transgress their duties.[31]

This is not, of course, to say that, in lacking wages for officeholders, the *Laws* lacks a service conception of rule. Such a service conception could comport with the absence of wages for a given political role, as in Isocrates's idealizing invocation of Athenian officeholders having been expected, in the era of the broadly Solonian ancestral constitution, to "devote themselves to caring for what is common, like servants."[32] Rather, a service conception of rule is expressed by other means, including legal arrangements for election, audit, punishment for malfeasance, and so on. The difference between dialogues on this point does not invalidate the overall general approach to their

29. The practice of paying a wage to officeholders had been well established in fifth-century Athens, though possibly never restored after its general, though not exceptionless, abolition in at least the first of the upstart oligarchic regimes of the late fifth century (that is, the Four Hundred), or, if restored after the Four Hundred, possibly never restored after its similar overall (but again not exceptionless) abolition by the Thirty. In the debate on this question, I am persuaded by Hansen ("Magistrates in Classical Athens" and "Magistrates in Fourth-Century Athens?"), who argues against a fourth-century restoration of *misthos* proper for Athenian officeholders (with a separate consideration of councilors). The latter article by Hansen responds to criticisms and rival accounts by Gabrielsen (*Remuneration of State Officials*) and Pritchard ("Public Payment of Magistrates"); Pritchard reiterated his argument in a later book, *Public Spending*.

30. The sole use of *misthos* in the *Laws* in the sense of a wage is an exception that proves the rule (it is also used in a more unusual sense of a financial penalty at *Leg*.1.650a7). In book 11, the Athenian envisages generals in the law code being set out ("in speech") as receiving "honor," this being the "wages (*misthoi*) of fighters" (*Leg*. 11.921e1–2). In other words, the "wages" to be paid the military in Magnesia are not monies or in-kind provisions but solely honors.

31. Morrow, *Plato's Cretan City*, 191, making reference to the Athenian Visitor's proposals at *Leg*. 6.764a[3–7], which often use the verb *zēmioō* for the imposing of a monetary fine: "for example, instead of paying for attendance at the assembly, he [sc. the Athenian Visitor] imposes fines for nonattendance, except for members of the third and fourth property classes." In the context of the rigorous and all-pervasive civic education specified in this constitution, the idea that citizens would still need the threat of penalties to participate is surprising. It may indicate the fact that what André Laks calls the "legislative utopia" of the dialogue is always, as he contends, at the horizon of realization rather than actually being realized: see Laks, *Plato's Second Republic* and "Utopie législative de Platon."

32. Isoc., 7.26: *epimeleisthai tōn koinōn hōsper oiketas*. This passage is discussed by Brock (*Greek Political Imagery*, 26), though he observes (n9) that "Isocrates' commitment to the ideal is questionable."

complementarity on questions of rule and office that was sketched in chapter 2. Differences are compatible with being complementary. In this case, while both dialogues can be shown to be committed to a service conception of rule, the different ways in which such a conception is to be institutionally realized in their respective constitutional projects illuminate rather than invalidating that common commitment, by making clear the conditions, benefits, and costs of each possible arrangement.

Why, then, are wages necessary in the constitutional project of the *Republic*? The answer is that they are necessary because of the laws that will deprive the ruling group as a whole (junior auxiliaries and senior guardians alike) of private land and property (beyond minimal objects for daily use, it is implied). As noted earlier, these arrangements are specifically described as being laid down as laws at the end of book 3 (3.417b8, summing up from 416d4) and will be analyzed in detail later in this chapter. For present purposes, I highlight their overall function, and then return to their status of being issued as laws.

Socrates sums up the intention of these laws, which (inter alia) prohibit the guardians from possessing any but necessary private property and from touching or using any gold or silver objects, and specify their receipt of a "wage" [*misthos*] (3.416e2), as follows: "Whenever they come to acquire private land and houses and coined money, they will be household managers and farmers instead of guardians, becoming despots and enemies instead of allies of the other citizens" (3.417a6–b1). As this statement makes clear, the purpose of the deprivation of private land, wealth, and use of gold and silver is to protect the integrity of the role of guarding against corruption; that is, to keep the guardians, as rulers, focused on the good of the ruled as the *telos* of their rule, rather than either indifferently or exploitatively pursuing the good of themselves as private persons instead. Conversely, Socrates had put the function of these laws in positive terms a few lines earlier: the overall goal of the arrangements to be made with regard to their housing and property (later described as laws) is to be such as to "neither prevent them from being the best guardians nor induce them to wrong the other citizens" (3.416c5–d2).

Without drawing a connection to the need for wages, Alexander Long has usefully summarized key aspects of how and why these restrictions are introduced:

> In his discussion of private property Socrates' aim is to ensure that property will not prevent the guardians from guarding the city well . . . motivated by the thought that private property can cause the most serious dereliction of the guardians' duties, namely for the guardians to harm the citizens whom they are charged to protect.[33]

---

33. Long, "Political Art," 23, and see 23–24 more generally. I have elided a further part of his claim on that page, which I think gets matters just slightly wrong: namely, his claim that "in part [Socrates] wants to ensure that maintaining property will not distract the

Notice that neither the nature nor the education of the guardians is treated by Plato in the design of the dialogue as sufficient to ensure the persistence of their orientation to the proper *telos* of rule, namely (as argued in *Republic* 1, and discussed in the preceding chapter of this study as well as in its introduction), the good of the ruled. Rather, legal prohibitions are required within the constitution in order to ensure (so far as possible) their uncorrupted motivation to rule.

That the main constitutional project of the *Republic*, no less than that of the *Laws*, is framed as a project of the issuance of legislation "in speech" (as opposed to "in deed" or, as the Greek may also be translated, "in actuality") was emphasized in the opening chapters of this study. The language of laws and lawmaking is introduced in the course of the founding of the city "in argument" by Adeimantus, who refers to one of the proposals offered by Socrates as a *nomos* and endorses it as if he were voting for the establishment of such a law (2.380c5–6).[34] And as noted above, that language is explicitly used at the end of book 3 in establishing the legal prohibitions on property, wealth, and currency ownership for the guardians.

These legal prohibitions are significant because rather than simply auditing the potential (mis)use of powers after the fact, they cut off this possibility at the root: preventing even the very possibility of such malfeasance from the ground up. That is, they can be construed as functional analogues to the procedures of *euthunai*, the audits that were at the heart of Greek conceptions of accountable officeholding, as argued in part I. If a guard has no ability to accumulate wealth and, as book 5 will further stipulate, no private kin for whom to accumulate it, both the incentive and the feasibility of the kind of behavior that *euthunai* were designed later to catch have been eliminated ex ante. These legal prohibitions achieve a function similar to the one that audit and accountability more broadly were (implicit in their structure) designed to achieve—that of orienting those in power to use their powers for the good of those over whom they rule, and of ensuring that they do so. Arguably, in fact, the peculiar legal prohibitions on the guardians of a *kallipolis* achieve this function more robustly, by cutting off the very possibility that their powers could be misused.

That being so, the absence of provision for such audits in the constitutional project of the *Republic* is less surprising. Instead of such procedural audits, that constitution features a set of laws that are designed to serve a similar function, orienting the rulers to the good of the ruled, not simply

---

guardians from their duties," referring to the point about their becoming "household managers and farmers" rather than guardians, as if this were a mere matter of a sliding scale of attention, rather than, as I read it above, a point about the very nature of the role of guarding.

34. Lane, "Founding as Legislating," 105.

an aspiration that the rulers will be so oriented. The constitutional project of the *Laws* makes wages for officeholders (the specific roles of the rulers in its constitution) unnecessary, but audit necessary, as was described at length in chapter 3. The constitutional project of the *Republic* makes audit unnecessary by imposing this other set of laws, which for their part make wages necessary. (The question of whether laws can be expected to work well and be properly enforced without the tool of a procedural audit is addressed further in the next chapter.)

To be sure, the robustness of that solution depends on those in power abiding by the laws. To that extent, a democratic objection to this solution still holds weight:[35] whereas in democratic cities such as Athens, the people ruled had powers of audit and other accountability mechanisms to intervene when necessary to enforce the laws against the officeholders who ruled over them, in a *kallipolis*, no such powers are assigned to the people (barring any power to cease paying the rulers' wages, which is nowhere implied, as argued below). In other words, if there is a functional equivalent of audit and accountability in a *kallipolis*, it is not democratic accountability to those who are ruled, who are situated, as it were, below the rulers. Instead, the highest rulers have to be safeguarded against corruption by a combination of their philosophical nature, philosophical education, selection for service by a previous generation of wise rulers, laws including both legal deprivation of wealth and the reliance on wages, and ultimately, as a result of all of these factors, having the appropriate caring disposition toward the good of the ruled.

None of those safeguarding limits is fail-safe. A *kallipolis* remains vulnerable to an Achilles' heel of exploitation. But so too do democracies and other constitutional regimes, all of which share with a *kallipolis* at least the official commitment to a *telos* of power as being used to benefit rather than to exploit the ruled. In democracies, for example, audits and other accountability mechanisms will not suffice to deter or to detect abuse of power to exploit the ruled. Indeed, a structural weakness of democracies and other procedurally focused constitutions is that however well designed the procedures, they are vulnerable to abuse or failure if manipulated by bad actors. In paying attention to the nature of those who will serve as guardians (initially to their general virtues, ultimately to their philosophical nature), and not only (but, importantly, also) to installing legal safeguards on them, Plato shows himself to be more rather than less attentive to the fundamental causes of political corruption. A service conception of rule requires rulers who are oriented to the good of the ruled, and the nature of the persons who serve in the role of ruling is as important

---

35. Landauer (*Dangerous Counsel*) stresses that Athenian democratic accountability was accountability to the people. I am responding in this paragraph to challenges pressed on me by a number of colleagues and friends, especially Nannerl O. Keohane, to whom I am grateful.

as the legal limits on that role itself in safeguarding such an orientation to the maximal extent possible.

This reflection on the radical ways in which Plato in the *Republic* (as varyingly in the *Statesman* and *Laws*) reconfigures the roles through which a service conception of rule might be realized raises once again a methodological challenge confronted in earlier chapters of this study: namely, how to draw the line between reconfiguration, on the one hand, and a radical break on the other. In other words, the challenge is how to judge when a reconfiguration that clearly alludes to or is built upon aspects of an existing idea or practice is so radical as to constitute a break with that idea or practice altogether. Or, alternatively, whether such a radical reconfiguration might count as the truest, or even the only, instantiation of the point of the original flawed idea or practice at all.[36]

To illustrate: in arguing that the function of procedural audits (*euthunai*) was to safeguard the orientation of officeholders to the good of those whom they ruled, I am prescinding from the thought that in a democratic constitution, it is essential to that function that it be carried out by (some subset of) the ruled themselves. I raise the issue so that readers can recognize the choices that must underlie any argument about functions and the ways in which practices and institutions are configured, and might be reconfigured, to realize them. (Such arguments need not rely on a wholesale functionalist analysis of social evolution; the functions served in a developed constitution may have been introduced originally for quite different reasons or causes.) As in any "family resemblance" model, interpreters must make their own judgment about the threshold for reconfiguration, versus "abandonment," of a given idea or practice. I return now to the content of these wages in order to test how their role in a *kallipolis* fares in such an assessment.

The Content of Wages for Guarding

Deprived by law of the possibility of acquiring private land, wealth, coined money, or fine metals, the guardians will need their provisions to be furnished somehow. And in the same passage at the end of book 3, this provisioning is described as a kind of wage that the guardians will receive from the other citizens. This connection is explicitly spelled out by Socrates in this first of three significant passages about the nature of those wages, which must now be considered in detail (in books 3, 4, and 5 respectively), in order to see whether and how their prima facie differences may be reconciled.

Those differences revolve around the use of the term *misthos* and the extent to which it could in Attic Greek, and in specific contexts, encompass

---

36. I am grateful to Nikhil Menezes, Jeremy Reid, Emily Salamanca, and Darius Weil for helping me formulate this issue.

not only standard monetary wages but also two different ways of providing in-kind provision: monies paid only so as to enable such provision to be purchased (not intended for the recipient to be able to save up or put aside) and direct in-kind provision of foodstuffs and other necessities. Given that democratic Athens provides the most extensive evidence for the payment of *misthoi* to officeholders in the fifth century (before the temporary coup resulting in the power of the Four Hundred from 411 to 410, and then the temporary installation of the Thirty from 404 to 403) and debatably again in the fourth century, when such wages were definitely paid at least to the councilors, a brief review of debates over the content of those wages for officeholders is helpful in providing context for what Plato is doing in regard to the content of *misthoi* in the *Republic*.

In these debates over the content (and payment) of Athenian wages for officeholders (generally referred to in this mini-literature as "magistrates"), I generally follow Mogens Herman Hansen, who argues that in both the fifth and fourth centuries, *misthos* was paid daily but "only . . . to those . . . who, on that particular day, had participated in politics or administration" (and in the fourth century only, he contends, to the councilors, who then received five obols per day).[37] Hansen himself follows W. Kendrick Pritchett in arguing that a distinction emerged in the fourth century, with the advent of large mercenary armies, between *misthos* on the one hand, as "pay for service," which the soldiers could choose to "lay up" (so Pritchett, quoted by Hansen), and "money for rations," which they were expected immediately to expend: the latter could be described as "money paid out *eis sitēsin*," with both money for rations and food rations themselves being describable as *sitēsis*, the latter also as *trophē*. Hansen tracks this distinction in the description of the mid-to-late fourth-century Athenian democratic constitution in the *Constitution of the Athenians* (62.2), in which "the verb μισθοφορεῖν [*misthophorein*] is restricted to money paid out to the *ekklesia* [assembly], the *boule* [council] and the *dikasterion* [court], whereas the allowance paid out to the *prytaneis* [one group of officeholders presiding within the council], to the archons [another group of officeholders] and to various other officials" is described with the language of *sitesis* and was paid out every day.[38]

However, Hansen also cautions that "[a] warning must be issued . . . against making too sharp a distinction," citing Thucydides (8.29) for a fifth-century use of *trophē* as a case of *misthos*, or military pay, and conversely, some fourth-century uses of "a daily allowance referred to as a *misthos*," as

---

37. Hansen, "Magistrates in Classical Athens," 7, citing [*Ath. Pol.*] 62.2 for the amount of five obols, mentioned there as being paid to the councilors. He also surveys the question of whether wages for most *archai* were restored after the Four Hundred or after the Thirty, arguing in the negative.

38. Hansen, "Magistrates in Classical Athens," 7, drawing for the military case on Pritchett, *Greek State at War*, pt. 1, 3–29.

in Aeschines's reference (1.103) to a stipend paid to the disabled poor.[39] This caution must be borne in mind in assessing Plato's complex and varying references to the content of *misthoi* for the guardians in the *Republic*. On the one hand, as I have been arguing, he is emphatic in using the language of *misthos*. On the other hand, the exact content of that *misthos*, and whether it is to be paid as money for provisions in kind, or even simply provided in kind, remains to be determined in context. His language makes subtle play with the kinds of distinctions in both military and Athenian constitutional pay and provision that have just been noted.

BOOK 3: "A WAGE FOR GUARDING"

Expounding in book 3 how those who are to play the role of "guardians" are to live, Socrates makes five points in spelling out the detail of the arrangements that I have partially summarized above: namely, about "the houses and other property" that they are to have, in addition to the education that has been already described in books 2 and 3, such that these arrangements will "neither prevent them from being the best guardians nor induce them to wrong the other citizens" (3.416c5–d2). Here I collect and translate these five points (made at 3.416d4–417b8; the first four are explicitly enumerated as such by Socrates, who goes on to make a further point which I enumerate as the fifth):

1. "None of them should acquire any private property that is not wholly necessary."

2. "None of them should have a house or treasury [i.e., a storeroom for keeping valuables] into which anyone who wishes cannot enter."

3. "Whatever provisions (*ta . . . epitēdeia*) moderate and courageous warrior-athletes need, they will receive a wage for guarding (*misthon tēs phulakēs*) from the other citizens by agreement (*taxamenous*), such as to have neither shortfall nor surplus in a given year."[40]

4. "They'll regularly receive common meals (*phoitōntas . . . eis sussitia*) and live together like soldiers in a camp."[41]

39. Hansen, "Magistrates in Classical Athens," 20n21.

40. My translation makes the following choices: (1) rendering *ta . . . epitēdeia* with the sense of "provisions"; (2) rendering *taxamenous* as "by agreement" (LSJ, *tassō*, middle voice, where this very passage is cited for the sense of "Med., generally, *agree upon, settle*"); (3) construing the relative clause *tosouton hoson . . .* as modifying *misthon*, rather than assigning it as Grube/Reeve do to the first half of the sentence, an unwarranted shift. Shorey in his Loeb edition translated *taxamenous* in context here as "receive an agreed stipend," as pointed out to me by Malcolm Schofield.

41. Grube/Reeve translate the phrase that I have transliterated in this quotation as "they'll have common messes"; but LSJ suggests for the verb *phoitaō* the sense "of things, esp. of objects of commerce, *to come in constantly* or *regularly*," with examples including the regular receipt of corn, tribute, or taxes, which makes sense of a regular provision of

5. "For them alone in the city, it is unlawful (*ou themis*) to touch or handle gold or silver, meaning that they should not be under the same roof as it, wear it, or drink out of it."

Notice that the prohibitions on which I focused in the last section—as stated here, on private property and wealth (1) as well as use of gold and silver (5), enhanced by the prohibition on any part of a dwelling being reserved for private access (2)—are here complemented by a certain type of affirmative provision: the provision of common meals as part of a collective way of life, which is likened to that of soldiers in a military camp (4). Common meals (for which *sussitia* was one standard term) were a widespread feature of Greek civic practices, often including military organization.[42] The nutritional needs of the guardians are to be supplied through common meals of the sort that Greek soldiers would typically eat, while their housing is to be supplied akin to the way that soldiers were housed in military encampments.

Provision 5 puts pressure on the interpretation of the provision of primary interest here—namely, the provision of a wage for guarding (3)—for the usual monetary sense of *misthos* in provision 3 stands in prima facie tension with the prohibition on the guardians' handling of gold or silver that is imposed in provision 5. And this all the more so as during the period in which the dialogue appears to be dramatically set,[43] and for most if not all of Plato's lifetime, the only official Athenian coinage was silver.[44] Given the proximity of these two stipulations as part of the same overall set of provisions to be legislated, it is difficult to accord *misthos* in provision 3 its most common sense of a coined monetary wage payment. Moreover, in light of Pritchett's observation that *misthos* for soldiers was expected to be money that they could "lay up," the condition in 3 against either shortfall or surplus also points against a

---

sussitia as common meals. (Nothing hinges on my choice of translation of "meals" instead of "messes.")

42. They took different shapes in Sparta (where common messes were how adult men ate for the duration of their active military service) and in Athens (where they were provided for officeholders and for others whom the city wished to honor, such as its Olympic victors).

43. Nails ("Dramatic Date") canvasses explanations for the contradictory textual and contextual evidence, which, she contends, makes it impossible to settle the dramatic date of the *Republic* (most often argued to be set in either 421 or 411), in contrast, for example, to the exact dating indicated for the *Symposium* (set in the year 416).

44. Camp and Kroll, "Agora Mint," 144: "Whereas the earliest Athenian bronze coinage is now usually dated no earlier than the middle years of the 4th century B.C. owing to the Athenians' reluctance to attach their name and coin types to a coinage of base metal, the earliest regular bronze coinage with the AOE ethnic and Athena/owl types did not appear before the third quarter of the 4th century." The authors also note there (n15), however, that this earliest regular Athenian-marked bronze coinage was preceded by "an emergency issue of bronze-plated coinage in 406–5 B.C.," (subsequent to any of the possible dramatic dates for which evidence can be found in the *Republic*).

monetary pay for service sense of *misthos* here, even though that was the most common sense.

The solution that I propose is to read 3 as a gloss on 4. That is, the *misthos* is itself to consist of the foodstuffs to be provided in the form of common meals, provisioned out of the resources of the citizen body. This would fall within the scope of the caveat noted by Hansen above, that the distinction between *misthos* as pay for service and either money for rations or rations themselves being directly provided was not a hard and fast one. While such a solution is not perfect (it has difficulty accounting for the separation of the two stipulations 3 and 4, which seem redundant), nevertheless it will receive a paradoxical kind of support from the next passage in which the question of a wage for the guardians is taken up, in book 4. Support, because that book 4 passage emphasizes the provision of foodstuffs in kind. Paradoxical, because it does so by denying that the guardians will receive a wage (*misthos*) at all. After reviewing that conundrum, consideration of a final passage on the topic of wages, in book 5, will provide an overall resolution as to how to read the three passages together.

BOOK 4: "RECEIVE NO WAGE IN ADDITION TO THEIR RATIONS"

Book 4 begins with Adeimantus interrupting to take issue with the way of life of the guardians that Socrates had just closed book 3 by sketching. He does so by alleging that the city being described by Socrates "is not making these men very happy and . . . this is due to they themselves" (4.419a2–3). The allegation rests on a redescription of their way of life, governed by the stipulations 1–5 that Socrates has just outlined, from a different perspective—namely, that "the city in truth belongs to them, but they do not enjoy any good (*agathon*) from it" (4.419a3–5). This complaint highlights Adeimantus's inversion, at this stage of the dialogue, of the schema of rule that had been outlined by Socrates in book 1 (and which I sought to capture in the abstract in the second chapter of this study). According to that schema, the *telos* of rule inheres in the good of the ruled—whereas Adeimantus's inversion of that schema posits that one observes, and should also expect, rulers to use their rule to pursue their own good instead.

As Adeimantus explains his objection further:

> Others [sc. powerful people in existing cities] acquire land and build big and grand houses, acquire suitable furnishings for them, make their own private sacrifices to the gods, host guests, and also, of course, acquire what you were talking about just now, gold and silver and all the things that are thought to belong to people who are to be blessedly happy. But it would seem that they [sc. the rulers of the city they are

founding "in speech"] are simply settled in the city like military mercenaries (*hōsper epikouroi misthōtoi*) and . . . all they do is watch over it
(*phrarountes*). (4.419a1–420a2)[45]

In the *Republic*, the term *epikouroi* had been introduced by Socrates in book
3 as a term of art (usually translated as "auxiliaries") for the young people who
are to serve as "supporters" of the "convictions" of those who are "complete
guardians (*phulakas panteleis*)" and who serve as "rulers (*tōn archontōn*)"
(3.414b1–5),[46] drawing the differentiation within the group of guardians that
was mentioned earlier and to which the next chapter will return. It was a term
already well established in a particular context of Greek politics (and the politics of contemporary empires)—namely, in the hiring of missionaries. Indeed,
the specific phrase used by Adeimantus (*epikouroi misthōtoi*) has roots in
prior literary form, being conjoined by Herodotus, for example, in referring
to the "military mercenaries" (*epikouroi te misthōtoi*) employed in a battle
against a rebellious group of his own people by Polycrates, king of Samos.[47]

Moreover, *epikouroi* had figured as a loaded term in recent Athenian history, in a speech (either delivered, or at least written and circulated) by Lysias,
the real-life brother of *Republic* character Polemarchus, who would survive the
short-lived, violently antidemocratic regime of the Thirty in 404/3, fighting in
which Polemarchus perished. Attacking Eratosthenes, who had been a member
of the Thirty, for his actions during that period, Lysias adjured the Athenian citizens in the restored democracy before whom the proceedings were being held to
recall the misdeeds of the Thirty and their henchmen more generally: "Remember the mercenaries [*epikouroi*] that the defendants [sc. members of the Thirty]
stationed in the Acropolis as guardians [*phulakes*] of their power [*archē*][48] and

45. Cognates of the verb *phrarountes* were used to designate various Greek military
roles (the *phrourarchos* was the commander of a military garrison; the *phrouroi* were
members of such a garrison, the word also being used to designate the watchmen over the
Athenian naval yards). "Military mercenaries" is a loose translation to capture the sense of
the phrase in context.

46. Grube/Reeve obscure the reference to the role of rulers (*tōn archontōn*) by translating it as "guardians," as if this were instead another occurrence of the word *phulakes*.

47. Hdt., 3.45.3.

48. In "Idea of Accountable Office," I argue that the Thirty were not generally viewed
or described in classical sources as holders of offices, in the conventional sense outlined
above in chapters 1 and 2. Lysias himself earlier in the same speech uses the noun *archē*
several times in contexts describing the Thirty, which may look like (and are translated by
Todd as) references to conventional offices. I read these rather as either (as in 12.40) purely
descriptive uses similar to *archein* in 12.94 (to which cf. also 12.24, 44, 52) or as subtly indicating the nonconventional nature of the *archē* in question: e.g., in 12.5 and 12.36, in both
of which sections the phrase *eis tēn archēn* employs the noun in the singular, in contrast
to the more familiar plural form, which would, with that preposition, signal the context of
constitutional officeholding. Todd translates "power" in the same spirit.

your slavery" (Lys., 12.94).[49] The quoted translation by Stephen Todd glosses *epikouroi* not in the generically literal terms of "allies" or "helpers" but specifically in the sense of hired mercenary troops, as it had been used, for example, by Thucydides (2.33.1); this makes sense in the context of the hiring of these troops by the Thirty from their Spartan allies.[50] So precisely in the kind of military context in which they are introduced in the *Republic*, the so-called *epikouroi* would be most readily understood as hired mercenaries.

The language of Lysias's condemnation of the mercenaries hired by the Thirty reinforces the aggressive skepticism of the challenge directed by Adeimantus at the start of book 4 against a service conception of rule as the appropriate political aspiration for any city. Lysias puts together not only the role of mercenaries but their function of serving as "guardians" (*phulakes*), in the service of the *archē* of the Thirty, which is implicitly cast as a form of domination outside the scope of any service conception of rule. Without assuming that Plato was thinking of this particular speech, the constellation of the Thirty as a regime of domination enforced by guardians who were hired as mercenaries—using the very language of *epikouroi*, *phulakes*, and *archē* around which the *Republic* revolves—cannot be absent from the pointed appropriation of that language here. This shows, once again, that Plato is acutely aware of the existence of dissension from the very service conception of rule that he draws out of some past figurations of rule and seeks to defend and realize.

In the present context, Adeimantus is complaining to Socrates along the following lines: you may call these people "auxiliaries," but they are really just "mercenaries"—and not only they but the senior guardians as well are going to be made to live like soldiers for hire living in a military camp, not as if they were comfortably at home and well off in a city that belongs to them and that they can exploit entirely for their own benefit. Socrates initially responds to Adeimantus by piling on the same kind of charges in an a fortiori spirit, to make the charges as seemingly serious (at least to the youth himself) as possible:

> Yes, I said, and what's more, they [the *phulakes* whom Socrates had been describing] are people who work for rations alone (*episitioi*) and receive no wage (*misthon*) in addition to their rations (*tois sitiois*),

49. Lys., 12.94, trans. Todd, who silently accepts Markland's emendation of the manuscripts to *spheteras* in translating "their" rather than "your" (*humeteras*, as per the MSS). As Todd notes, it is likely though not certain that Lysias prepared this speech as part of the *euthunai* that were imposed after the restoration of a democratic constitution, in order to hold accountable the conduct of the Thirty and others during their time in power.

50. Xenophon also details the role of these mercenaries in his history of the period, though he uses the term *phrouroi* instead, in its sense of members of a garrison, and refers to the Thirty as undertaking to provide their food, without mention of wages (*Hellenica* 2.3.13). I discuss Xenophon's account in "'Thirty Tyrants.'"

as the others [those whom Adeimantus has just described as being comfortably at home and well off in any city] do. Hence, they won't be able to travel out of the city at will, or to give money to courtesans, or to spend money in whatever other ways they wish, as those who are considered happy do spend money. You've omitted these and a host of other similar points from your accusation. (4.420a3–8)

On the face of it, Socrates here directly contradicts what he had just proposed at the end of book 3. There, in provision 3, he had prescribed that the guardians "receive a wage for guarding (*misthon tēs phulakēs*) from the other citizens by agreement (*taxamenous*)" (3.416e1–2). In contrast, here—only a couple of paragraphs later[51]—he describes them as people who "work for rations alone (*episitioi*) and receive no wage [*misthos*] in addition to their rations" (4.420a3–4). The point in book 4 must be an absence of any monetary income, if one is to make sense of the references to being unable to support mistresses or enjoy foreign travel, both activities that could not be funded solely from the in-kind receipt of meals.

The appearance of contradiction can be resolved by reading provision 3 in book 3 according to the tentative solution proposed above. If the *misthos* stipulated there was in fact to be an in-kind provision of rations in the form of common meals, then there is no strict contradiction with the statement in book 4 that the guardians are to "receive no wage in addition to their rations"; indeed, this would adhere to the general (though not exceptionless) fourth-century distinction between *misthos* and either in-kind provision or money received for rations that Hansen and Pritchett identified. Nevertheless, a paradox remains. In book 3, Socrates had insisted that the guardians are to receive a wage, an insistence that at once makes common cause with wages as an incentive for ruling that he had advanced in book 1 and stands in some tension with the inverted content of wages as penalties in book 1, given the affirmative provision of something (whether foodstuffs or money) in book 3. Then, in book 4, he seems to cut this Gordian knot by denying that the guardians receive any wage beyond their rations, leaving an open question as to why he had started to use the language of *misthos* in the first place.

To summarize the paradoxical relationships among these passages: passages in books 1, 3, and 5 make it appear, at least prima facie, that the guardians both are and are not to receive a wage. This paradox points up a tension between these two dimensions of a wage: on the one hand, its association with being in the service of another agent or agents, and how receipt of a wage shapes the specific lineaments of a service conception of rule; on the other, the problematic incorporation into a monetary economy that it implies. This

---

51. Some Stephanus numbers are elided in the transition from book 3 to book 4.

tension finds a subtle resolution in the final main context in which wages for the rulers figure, in book 5.

BOOK 5: "RECEIVE THEIR UPKEEP . . . AS A WAGE"

Wages for the guardians—this time discussed solely with reference to the auxiliaries—are discussed one final time in book 5. This arises in the context of the "second wave" of book 5, in which Socrates explains that his previous reference in book 4 to a version of a Pythagorean proverb, asserting that "friends to the greatest extent get all things for themselves in common" (4.424a2–3) with reference to acquisition of wives, marriages, and childrearing by the guardians, will require that formation and knowledge of private kinship ties by birth and marriage be abolished among them. Because procreation applies to the younger group of auxiliaries among the guardians, the discussion of wages is here also focused on the auxiliaries only. In the context of the "second wave" of book 5, this is actually the primary textual locus in which the ban on privatization of kinship is in the "second wave" associated with a ban on privatization of property and wealth also. In it, as I shall argue, Socrates splits the difference between the emphases of books 3 and 4 on the question of whether wages are to be paid to the guardians and, if so, of precisely what kind. He does so by making a back reference (flagged as such) that weaves together, with some modifications, the language of the two passages (in books 3 and 4) considered above:

> And moreover, this [sc. the having of wives and children in common by the auxiliaries (*epikouroi*)] agrees with what we said before, for we said somewhere that, if they are genuinely to be guardians, they must not have private houses, land, or possessions, but must receive provisions [*trophē*] from the others [sc. the other citizens] as a wage for their guardianship (*misthon tēs phulakēs*) and enjoy it in common. (5.464b8–c3)[52]

The careful qualifications in the first and second stipulations of the book 3 passage have here been jettisoned. Socrates now recalls himself as having prescribed that "they mustn't have private houses, land, or possessions," whereas in fact in book 3, he had included qualifications to the effect that "none of them should acquire any private property that is not wholly necessary" (provision 1 from book 3), and "none of them should have a house or storeroom that isn't open for all to enter at will" (provision 2 from book 3). It is as if now, in this back reference, Socrates is reinterpreting the meaning of having

---

52. Note that Grube/Reeve translate *gēn* at 5.464b9 as "property," rather than the more specific "land."

private houses or possessions at all: as if the guardians will not truly have private houses if their houses are open for all to enter at will, and as if they will not really possess private property if their possessions are strictly limited to what is wholly necessary.

Nevertheless, while Socrates here reiterates his book 3 prescription of a *misthos* for the guardians, he does so using language that is also closely related to his book 4 prohibition of a *misthos* for them.[53] To be precise: he turns what had been a prohibition in book 4 (they are to "receive no wage in addition to their rations") into an injunction in book 5 (they are to "receive provisions . . . as a wage"). In this choice of language, calling *trophē* (which clearly refers to in-kind provision of food) a *misthos*, Plato breaks with the dominant way of contrasting these (albeit that, as noted above, there were at least some fifth- and fourth-century examples in which this dominant distinction was elided).

This audacious literary recombination of what had been (prima facie) a paradoxical prescription of a wage and then prohibition thereof is perhaps the best possible evidence that the reader is meant to focus on the paradox inherent in paying a wage for the guardians. A surface dimension of that paradox—the problem of paying a wage to guardians who are meant to eschew any use of gold and silver—can be resolved in the text as a whole, despite prima facie appearances, by taking their wages to be paid in kind through the provision of upkeep. The deeper dimension of the paradox, however, is theoretical. On the one hand, a wage is one fitting way to indicate a service conception of their role as guardians (a subset of whom are also to rule), orienting their rule toward the good of those who are guarded and ruled. On the other hand, a wage suggests some kind of relational dependence on the paymaster of the wage, both objective and subjective, limiting the powers and independence of the wage recipient.

In order to tackle these theoretical implications of wages, I turn next to another important passage in book 5. This is the "terms of address" passage, in which Glaucon, responding to a line of Socratic questioning, distinguishes between the terms used by rulers and ruled in existing cities to refer to themselves and each other, and those that would be so used in the context of a *kallipolis*. In fact, the "terms of address" passage is placed also in the overall account of the "second wave," indeed very shortly before the passage that I

---

53. Compare the book 4 "work for rations alone (*episitioi*) and receive no wage (*misthon*) in addition to their rations" to the book 5 "receive provisions [*trophē*] from the others." The book 5 passage does not use the book 4 plural noun *episitioi* (referring to the persons who work for rations alone), but instead uses the singular noun *trophē* to denote what I call the provisions (in the sense of nouriture) that such persons receive, while adding in a straight quotation of book 3 in the phrase "the wage for their guardianship" (*misthon tēs phulakēs*), which had appeared also in the provision I designated 3 in the book 3 passage.

have just been arguing will ultimately resolve the seeming paradoxes around the nature of the guardians' wage in a *kallipolis* by stating that they "must receive provisions . . . as a wage."

While that solution still makes the best overall sense of books 3 and 4 on the nature of the wage for guarding, Glaucon in the "terms of address" passage nevertheless emphasizes two distinct dimensions of the role of the future ruled as they are to be seen by their future rulers: their role as "paymasters," and their role as "provisioners" (*misthodotas te kai tropheas*) (5.463b2). Perhaps this is meant to reflect his own failure to follow the subtle distinctions and elisions between wage and in-kind provision that have taken place so far (which Socrates has not yet reconciled in what I called the audacious literary strategy of the passage discussed above, which is a Stephanus page still to come). Whatever Glaucon's grasp of the finer points of the issue, however, and even if in fact the wage to be paid is to be paid in kind through the furnishing of rations as provisions, Glaucon's highlighting of the two dimensions of acting as paymasters and provisioners draws an analytical separation that requires reflection.

Terms of Address in a Kallipolis: "Paymasters and Provisioners"

Socrates initiates the "terms of address" passage by contrasting "our own city" (a *kallipolis*) (5.462e4–5) with "those other cities" (5.463a1), meaning existing cities. He begins by asking (leaving the term *archontes* untranslated so as to discuss the rulers-or-officeholders question in what follows; though, for now, the reader can gloss *archontes* as "rulers"): "Are not there *archontes* and people (*dēmos*) in them [sc. those other cities], as well as in that one [sc. "our city" from 5.462e4–5]?" Glaucon replies "There are," and then offers the following replies to further questions from Socrates.

> In reply to a question about how those *archontes* are addressed by the people in other cities, how they address the people, and how they address one another, Glaucon avers (reordering his replies):
> (a) In many cities they are called "despots" (*despotas*), but "in those governed democratically they are called this name— *archontes*."[54]
> (b) In other cities, the *archontes* call the people "slaves" (*doulous*).
> (c) In other cities, the *archontes* call each other "co-*archontas*" (*sunarchontas*).

54. Reading *tounoma* with MSS A and D. In his questions to Glaucon eliciting the replies summarized in (a) and (b), Socrates adds the rider "besides fellow citizens," but as he applies this caveat to both "our own city" and the other cities, it is not a differentiating factor between them.

In reply to a subsequent series of questions from Socrates about what the *archontes* "call the people" in each of the contrasting kinds of city, Glaucon answers (I reorder his replies):

(a′) In our city, the people call the *archontes* "safeguarders and auxiliaries" (*sōtēras te kai epikourous*).[55]

(b′) In our city, the *archontes* call the people "paymasters and provisioners" (*misthodotas te kai tropheas*).

(c′) In our city, the *archontes* call each other "co-guardians" (*sumphulakas*) (5.463a1–b8).[56]

Notice that throughout this passage, Glaucon follows Socrates's lead in the overarching introductory question, by using *archontes* as a blanket or generic term to cover those figures who rule either in existing cities or in a *kallipolis*. In democracies and some other existing cities at the time, these *archontes* would all have been, specifically, officeholders, though Glaucon also refers to despotisms, in which the language of ruling more generally would (in a loose rather than strict sense) apply. In so readily grouping together despotisms and democracies in his description, Glaucon implies that it is only what he calls "our city" (a *kallipolis*) in which evaluatively correct terms of address apply, overriding the standard political distinctions among other kinds of constitutions that one might in fifth-century Greece have otherwise applied.

Beginning with what Glaucon avers of existing cities, (a) is a descriptive claim: in some cities, the people call their rulers "despots"; in others, which are democratic, they call them *archontes*, which was (as explained in chapter 1) not only a generic term for rulers, and sometimes specifically for officeholders, but also the title of nine of the particular officeholders in democratic Athens (and the title used for certain offices in some other cities as well). (c) is also a descriptive claim, one that seems fairly anodyne: in at least some existing cities, the *archontes* call one another "co-*archontas*."

(b), however, contains dynamite. It suggests that in at least some existing cities, without specifying whether these are the despotisms or the democracies that had just been mentioned as among those populating that range, the *archontes* (whether rulers in a despotism or officeholders in a democracy) call the people whom they rule "slaves." This was hardly an established term of address in any such city, so this cannot be a descriptive claim about avowed political practices. Rather, it is a diagnostic claim, perhaps purporting to

---

55. This is arguably a reference in the former term to the senior guardians, who are differentiated from the younger ones as the rulers following a reference to those needed to "safeguard (*sōzesthai*) the constitution" (3.412b1); see also *hoi sōtēras* ("the safeguarders") (6.502d1).

56. Socrates then goes on to a further elaboration of the ways in which the *archontes* of a *kallipolis* will address and consider one another using "kinship names" (*ta onomata . . . oikeia*) (5.463c7).

describe what goes on behind closed doors: the rulers of this range of existing cities, from despotisms to democracies, think of those whom they rule as
their "slaves." And why? Because, and insofar as, one must infer, they view
those they rule as subjects to be exploited, rather than as subjects whose good
it is the *telos* of their rule to pursue. Contrary to the more sanguine view of
Greek officeholding constitutions for which I argued in part I, which took
the implicit aim of their accountability mechanisms to be that of avoiding the
exploitation of the ruled by their rulers, Glaucon is here suggesting that the
actual motivation of rulers and officeholders in all constitutions other than a
kallipolis would remain fundamentally exploitative. The limits imposed on
accountable offices might constrain that exploitation in practice but not alter
the underlying motivation of the persons in those roles. Rulers might officially
refer to their subjects as fellow citizens, say, in public, but hidden beneath any
other terms would be their real attitude to their subjects as being tantamount
to their slaves.

In contrast, all three of the terms of address attributed by Glaucon to "our
city" are positively evaluative through and through (a', b', c'). In (b'), which
is the primary focus of the present discussion, *misthodotēs* (the nominative
singular of *misthodotas*) has the sense of "paymaster," illustrated by contexts
ranging from Xenophon on Cyrus as king of Persia ceasing to pay his soldiers
(*Anabasis* 1.3.9) to a somewhat more metaphorical use by Aeschines (3.218),
needling Demosthenes about on whom the latter is financially dependent
in being paid by them to write and deliver speeches in court.[57] Glaucon is in
(b') contending that as he understands the constitution of the city that they
have been founding "in speech," its rulers will not simply receive provisions
from the ruled for their upkeep, nor will they simply regard the ruled as the
source of such provisions. Rather, they will regard the ruled as their paymasters: a role common to the paymasters of mercenary soldiers for hire, as well
as to those who hire other kinds of people to serve them. While there was no
established linguistic expression using "paymasters" in regard to those holding political offices, the fact that such officeholders did in some constitutions
receive wages brings this reference within the ambit of office as well—and the
fact that these propositions all apply to *archontes* who must be rulers (not
simply guardians), whether or not they are specifically officeholders, certainly
brings it within the ambit of rule.

Notice that the terms of address proposed in (b') and (a') are not phrased
reciprocally. That is, the attribution of the terms "paymasters and provisioners" is to be confined (as per Glaucon) to the outlook of the rulers themselves.
These are not the terms of address that the ruled in the city are envisioned as
using of their rulers: there is no indication that the people will see themselves
as paymasters, even if, and as, the rulers see them in that light. The people,

---

57. LSJ, s.v. *misthodotēs*.

rather, in (a'), are to consider the functional services that the rulers perform for them, those of safeguarding them and of assisting in such safeguarding (here "rulers" must have the broad extension of covering the whole group of guardians, though elsewhere as noted earlier Socrates restricts it to the senior or "complete" guardians only). Nevertheless, while this lack of match is significant in distinguishing the different kinds of perceptions of the rulers by the ruled and the ruled by the rulers, the payment of a wage to the rulers is not a matter of such perceptions alone. As argued above, it is a structural feature of a *kallipolis*, indeed a structurally necessary one, and so whether or not the people address their rulers as waged servants, they will pay them wages and must know themselves, as least in descriptive terms, to be doing so.

How is *archontes* best to be translated in propositions (a'), (b'), and (c'), each referring to terms of address within a *kallipolis*? The question is rooted in the fundamental framework of this study, which is that *archein* and *archē* in different contexts, and with more or less degree of ambiguity, can have the sense either of ruling and rule or of officeholding and office (understood as a limited and institutional kind of rule). The argument of this chapter gives some support to translating it as "officeholders" in (b'), at least, given that officeholders were the type of rulers who might be paid a wage. But what about in (a')? The people are to view the *archontes* of a *kallipolis* in functional terms, in terms of their efficacy in serving as safeguarders; in this proposition, the extension of *archontes* in a *kallipolis* is unusually broad, covering both the senior reigning figures and the junior auxiliaries, a distinction that will come into clearer focus in the next chapter. Likewise, in (c'), the *archontes* of a *kallipolis* are to view one another in terms of their efficacy in carrying out their shared function of serving as guardians for the people, and doing so in a collegial relationship with one another. There are no special marks of "officeholding" in (a') or (c') that would point to this as a better translation in context than the more generic notion of "ruling." In (b'), however, the orientation to the ruled as paymasters could be taken to bespeak officeholding, given that the payment of wages by the ruled was especially characteristic of democratic officeholding. But the mercenary connotations of paymasters could alternatively defeat that implication and leave "rulers" the best translation here as well. In sum, the relationship between ruling and officeholding in the *Republic* cannot be settled on the basis of the "terms of address" passage alone. It is the topic of the next chapter.

One potential objection remains to be addressed. Note that Glaucon contrasts proposition (c), "In other cities, the *archontes* call each other "co-archontas (*sunarchontas*)," with proposition (c'), "In our city [the *kallipolis*], the *archontes* call each other "co-guardians (*sumphulakas*)." This contrast should lead one to infer (so the objection) that the term *archontes* itself is to be abandoned in a *kallipolis*, and that the conceptual framework of ruling and officeholding revolving around *archein* (and the associated noun *archē*) is to be abandoned with it.[58]

I reject this objection for two reasons. First, note that *archontes* plays two distinct roles in (c) and reprises one of those in (c′). In both (c) and (c′) it is relied upon as the analytical category in which Socrates has pitched the prompting question, and so also serves as the analytical category for Glaucon to answer Socrates's questions. Insofar as it is retained as their analytical category, there are grounds for its likewise being retained as that of the dialogue's interpreters. Second, and building on that point, what is envisaged in (c′) is that the *archontes* of a *kallipolis* refer to one another in terms of the shared and common function that they are collegially aiming to carry out—namely, that of using the *taxis* of ruling in order to achieve the *telos* of rule: as argued in previous chapters, that *telos* being for Plato as for a long tradition in Greek thought, the good of the ruled.

In this light, the choice in (c′) by the *archontes* of a *kallipolis* of another term to refer to one another (distinct from the generic "*archontes*" itself) bears comparison with the workings of constitutional officeholding in various Greek cities of the time, in which some cities chose to use the generic term *hoi archontes* also as a specific name for particular offices, while adopting other names for other offices. Use of a more specific functional term or title by the *archontes* in referring to one another as co-guardians (*sumphulakas*) does not vitiate the analytical and conceptual point being made by both Glaucon and Socrates about *archontes* being the overall analytical category pertaining to those in positions of political power, both in existing cities and in a *kallipolis*. The question of how exactly to understand the *archein* carried out by such *archontes*—the *taxis* of it as rule, and its relationship to office as one kind of rule—is the burden of the next chapter.

For present purposes, it may be concluded that there is indeed to be, not only in Glaucon's perception but in the actual features of a *kallipolis* to which he is responding, a dependence of the *archontes* upon the people in the *kallipolis*. Describing this in the language of a wage would seem to bear the implication of circumstances in which the people could cease paying the wages should they so choose—parallel to Xenophon on the Persian soldiers remarking that Cyrus's cessation of his paymaster role has terminated their obligation to serve him. However, that implication is not drawn out by either Socrates or Glaucon. Instead, in presenting a success conception of the terms of address in a well-functioning *kallipolis*, Glaucon envisages that the rulers will have their dependence on wages paid by the ruled in the forefront of their dispositional attitudes and addresses to the ruled—but that the ruled will have their own dependence on the guarding and safeguarding to be performed by the rulers in

---

58. This potential objection was advanced by Jonny Thakkar on reading an earlier draft of the present chapter.

the forefront of their dispositional attitudes and addresses to the rulers. It would seem that in a well-functioning city, it is important that the rulers should actually be dependent upon wages, which are paid to make up for their deprivation of private property and wealth; important that the rulers should have this dependence, and the concomitant aim of serving the good of those who pay these wages, at the forefront of their minds; but equally important that the ruled should not think of themselves as epitactic superiors to the rulers in virtue of paying the latter's wages but, rather, should have at the forefront of their minds their own dependence on the rulers as epitactic and epistemic superiors who use their powers to care for and benefit the ruled.

How should this nonreciprocity of terms of address on each side be interpreted? One might think that a reciprocal and mutual understanding of one another's roles would be a condition for a good constitution, and that its absence means not only that the ruled in this scenario lack any ability to control the power of their rulers, and so to coconstitute their own good, but also that they live as if in two different realities, separated by an unbridgeable chasm.[59] My interpretation is different. There is no chasm between their realities: the ruled know that they pay the wages to the rulers, even if they do not address them as their waged hired hands; the rulers definitely know that they are reliant on the ruled for their wages, in addressing them as their paymasters. The point of the nonreciprocity is a subtler one. It is that sometimes it is appropriate in politics (and in other interpersonal relationships) not to seek to exploit all the control over someone else's actions that one could potentially exert. Glaucon does not deny that the people are in fact the paymasters of their rulers, and he does not deny them the knowledge that they are so. He only envisages that they should address the rulers in terms of the function that they serve rather than the dependence that they indisputably (and known to all parties) possess. As analyses of "knights versus knaves" in designing institutional incentives have emphasized, invoking the *telos* of the rulers' actions may in fact be a better way of encouraging them to act well than micromanaging them would be.[60]

Thus, wages—as well as the nonreciprocal terms of address envisaged about them—can be understood as fitting within an overall success portrait of rule as a service conception. It is only within a constitution and a city in which the rulers actually do see the ruled as their paymasters and provisioners (and do so in part because they as rulers lack the private wealth that would make them independent of such wages and provisions, as well as in virtue of other features of the constitution and city, such as the education it provides), that the rulers will be sufficiently and reliably oriented toward the proper *telos* of

59. This objection is a composite of challenges put to me on an earlier version of this chapter by Lisa Disch and Jill Frank in their respective "Comments on 'Rule.'"

60. See the brief overview in Brennan and Pettit's "Feasibility Issue" (271–73).

rule—namely, the good of the ruled. Conversely, however, for this constitution and city to function well according to the same argument, it must be the case that the ruled actually do see the rulers as their safeguarders, without being disposed to view them as agents whose wages can be started and stopped at will in order to control them. That is not to say that there are no limits to safeguard the safeguarders themselves. On the contrary: the very dependence on wages is one of those limits, along with the legal deprivations, the age-related educational testing, and so on. But it is to say that exercising control of office-holders from below by instrumentalizing the payment of wages, as it were, is not on the agenda of the dialogue.

How to bring about such a successful realization of a service conception of rule is a topic about which the dialogue says relatively little; this is less surprising in view of the fact that, in the work of Joseph Raz from which I drew the lineaments of a service conception in part I (for Raz, of authority; for Plato, of rule), this question is equally downplayed. Indeed, Plato arguably offers somewhat more reflection on this than does Raz. While this is not the main topic of the present chapter or study, relevant here are the well-known remarks in the *Republic* about the "smallest change" that could bring about such a constitution, as well as the notorious passage proposing the exile of everyone over the age of ten from an existing city. Less noted as relevant are remarks by Socrates in book 6 about people who are imagined as having initially responded with anger to the interlocutors' claim that philosophers must rule.[61] These book 6 remarks are set within the continuing ambit of the book 5 framing with regard to all three "waves" of potential ridicule, as to whether the changes proposed for each wave are both "beneficial" and "possible."[62] Socrates confirms the conclusion of that overall framing at 6.502c5–7, in the course of which speech he affirms that while it is hard for this code of laws [*hē nomothesia*] to come into being, it is nevertheless not impossible.

To bring him to this conclusion, part of what transpires is an interchange with Adeimantus (beginning from 6.499d8), as to whether it is reasonable to expect that those who respond with anger to the claim that philosophers must rule can be expected to be gentled by the explanation of the true nature and way of life of philosophers, which is different from that of those who appear to be philosophers in existing cities but who lack that true nature and practice. Socrates asks Adeimantus to agree that such people will indeed be gentled by

61. This claim was announced in book 5 in the "third wave," and was subsequently supported with the book 6 analysis of the philosophical nature, culminating in portraying the philosopher as a "painter of constitutions" to whom the city is to be handed over (6.501c5–9).

62. Book 6 is where the argument is found that the book 5 third wave is "possible," an argument that is notoriously missing, or at best provided only indirectly, in book 5 itself. The relationship to that book 5 problematic is made clear by Socrates at 6.499b1–d6, initiating the train of thought that culminates at 6.502c8.

this explanation, and while Adeimantus is somewhat circumspect (first conditioning his agreement on such people being "disciplined" [6.501c10], then granting only that they will "perhaps be less [sc. angry]" [6.501e5]), Socrates asks him if he is willing to say that such people will have become fully gentled and persuaded, at least by shame, into accepting the claim (6.501e6–502a2), with which Adeimantus then concurs.

While Adeimantus's initial demurrals are worth noting, this little passage does show that part of the case that a *kallipolis* is possible depends on whether people in general can be expected to be persuaded that it is beneficial. The reason this is relevant then appears when Socrates asks: "If a ruler (*archontos*) somewhere laid down the laws and the practices which we have described, is it then impossible that the citizens (*tous politas*) will be willing (*ethelein*) so to act?" (6.502b6–8). In other words, part of the case that a *kallipolis* is possible depends on there being citizens who are willing to live according to its laws. The willingness of citizens to obey the laws established by a ruler is part of the success condition for the Platonic service conception of rule.

Finally, notice that while the discussion of wages is not taken up again beyond book 5, there is no indication that those guardians who attain the full philosophical education and serve in the maximally senior role of ruling from age fifty (as discussed in the next chapter) will cease to receive such wages. On the contrary, since there is no indication that they would be entitled to accumulate wealth or own land, they must receive wages, since there is no other way for them to receive such provisions. One may wonder, however, whether the safeguarding function of such wages falls away for the senior philosophers, once they are revealed as knowers of the Form of the Good in book 6 and placed at the summit of the educational program of book 7. It may seem that, in knowing the Form of the Good—a knowledge made possible only because of their original nature of loving learning more than bodily appetitive satisfactions,[63] as is made clear at the beginning of book 6—they can be expected to have no motive for the corruption or exploitation against which wages serve as a safeguard.[64] Perhaps wages are not actually needed as a safeguard for the senior philosophers, even though they will within the legal arrangements of the city still receive them. Against this, however, recall that the senior philosophers will in some generation be vulnerable to making mistakes in the tasks of ruling that involve calculation mixed with sense perception (tasks that include identifying which children have the right natures to be educated as and placed in the role of rulers). The senior philosophers, that is, are not epistemically infallible. And lacking epistemic infallibility, it seems possible that they could also succumb to moral failings, since virtue

63. Lane, "Virtue."
64. This objection was raised to me by Josiah Ober in discussing another part of this study.

requires and involves full knowledge. This suggests that wages for even the senior philosophers would continue to serve as a necessary legal safeguard in a *kallipolis*.

A final objection: are Plato's references to laws and legal safeguards in these contexts disingenuous or misleading?[65] While Plato uses legal vocabulary repeatedly to describe the wages and similar measures, as I have shown, to use that vocabulary today would typically suggest a measure of popular control over the laws that is absent in a *kallipolis* (and even from the constitutional project for Magnesia, though there the elected *nomophulakes* will have some powers to modify the laws that the pan-Cretan founding group will establish). The question is who within a *kallipolis* would have control over the laws, and how they would exercise that control: whether with any safeguarding limits or not.

Jill Frank reads the discursive founder-legislators of the *Republic* as the city's "extra-extra-constitutional rulers."[66] But a gap remains between the discursive legislation and any legal framework, and roles as rulers, that would be set up in a city founded in actuality and not simply in speech. Even if the set of discursively framed laws is to be entirely incorporated into that of the laws of the city in which actual guardian-rulers will appear, as Socrates expresses the hope that they will be (4.425e1–3), and even though such a city may be founded by philosophers who become kings or by kings who come to philosophize, the founding act of any actual civic legislation will not be identical to the discursive one. Likewise, it is not the discursive founder-legislators who would have the plenary power to override or violate the laws.

It is true that the laws are ultimately to be placed in the safeguarding hands of the eldest philosopher-guardians, over whom there are no further superordinate rulers. Indeed, the laws and the constitution as a whole will have been set up by a first generation of actual rulers (again, whether kings who philosophize or philosophers who become kings). And while Adeimantus and Socrates as the discursive founder-legislators envisage that these actual rulers and their successors would not find it difficult to make additions to the laws as needed (4.425d7–e3, implying that they will have the power to do so), there are no externally enforceable legal constraints on their power to make those legal changes.

---

65. I framed this objection following a helpful exchange with John Dunn on an earlier version of this chapter.

66. Frank, "Constitution," 48, applying the same description to the founder-legislators of the *Laws*. It is inapposite to the latter, however, given the gulf that Plato carefully constructs between their discursive legislation and the pan-Cretan commission who will be advised by it but whose task it will be to actually set up the legislation for Magnesia. It is thus even more clear for the *Laws* that the founder-legislators do not (pace Frank) wield force.

Yet is this so different from the situation in modern legal orders? There, too, there are no externally enforceable legal constraints on the decisions of, say, Supreme Court justices in the United States Constitution; they cannot be compelled to recuse themselves even for reasons that would require lower-court judges to do so, and there are no externally enforceable legal constraints on the merits of the verdicts that any majority among the justices may agree to reach. It is true, of course, that the selection process for Supreme Court justices does involve popularly elected senators, in a step of popular election that is absent from the constitution of a *kallipolis*. But the existence of a body that cannot be wholly legally constrained is not by itself an indication that the role of laws more broadly in a society is merely a smokescreen.

Theorizing Wages within a Service Conception of Rule

In the constitution of a *kallipolis*, I have argued, the dependence of the rulers and other guardians on wages paid by the ruled works both to indicate and to institute a service conception of rule, on which the *telos* of rule is the good of the ruled, ultimately understood in light of the Form of the Good simpliciter, which is tested by its encompassing the good of the ruled and not their exploitation for the good only of the rulers. Wages further play a role in impressing that self-understanding upon the rulers through the terms of address with which they are expected to address the ruled. However, as I have argued, the ruled are not expected to (and it is not part of the framing of a *kallipolis* that they should) adopt terms of address that reciprocally address the rulers as their hired servants; they are rather to address them as their "safeguard-ers" (*hoi sōtēres*, being so addressed in conjunction with the "auxiliaries" who support the safeguarders), focusing on their function in ruling rather than on their dependence on being paid wages in order to do so. Indeed, Plato nowhere suggests that the ruled are to impress or enforce a service conception of rule through any exploitation of the discretionary power that paying wages might seem, at least to modern readers, to provide.

In the constitutional project of the *Republic*, then, wages are not intended to evoke what modern scholars of contract and administrative law, and of sociology and politics more broadly, would call a principal-agent model of the relationship between the ruled and their rulers. On such a model, the ruled are construed as the principals, who appoint and control their agents, with wages (ex hypothesi in this case) as a means of exercising such control and enforcing the accountability of the agent to the principal. Jeremy Waldron, for example, interprets accountability as the relationship borne by an agent toward a principal in virtue of the fact that powers that originally belonged to the principal have been delegated or entrusted to the agent, who is reined in by the principal's ability to hold the agent to account (that is, to require them to give an account of their decisions.[67] In this perspective, officeholders are taken to be hired hands, or servants, as it were, who are necessarily entrusted with certain powers to act on behalf of the agent, but whose potential abuse or misuse of those powers the agent must seek to control.

Some theorists further treat such agents as "representatives" of their principals.[68] Representation, of course, brings its own minefield of interpretative debates, but one can broadly generalize that the relationship of representation is expected to carry with it some kind of relatively rich normative ties, however those are understood in detail. One complication is that most who focus on representatives focus on elected officials only, while in ancient Greek constitutions many officeholders were chosen by lot, or by procedures in which lot played some role.[69] Another complication in taking up a representative-focused approach to broadly "executive" officeholders is that most theorists have concentrated their attention solely on representatives in the role of legislators,[70] whereas the powers of Greek *archai* were on the whole more comparable to executive powers, some of them presiding over judicial and legislative processes but not primarily serving as legislators.

While framing a principal-agent model in the terms of representation is likely to be an especially poor fit for illuminating Athenian and Greek constitutional offices,[71] in fact, any application of the principal-agent model to political rule and office, to ancient Greek constitutional politics, or to the

---

67. Waldron ("Accountability and Insolence," 167–68, cf. 192) distinguishes this particular (he calls it "political") model of "agent accountability" as being one in which the standards of performance are set by the principal, in contrast to a "forensic" paradigm in which those standards are independently prescribed by law. In his view, forensic accountability characterized some republics, such as that of early modern Venice (176–77), whereas he classes ancient Athenian democracy under the heading of agent accountability (and thus of "democratic accountability"). Waldron describes Athenian audit procedures (*euthunai*) as applying only to officeholders chosen by lot, without referring to the fact that some Athenian officeholders were in fact chosen by election.

68. While Waldron (184–88) connects agent accountability to electoral representation, he does not rely on representation as an independent normative premise for his original model of agent accountability.

69. Ferejohn, in "Accountability and Authority," adopts a principal-agent model within the context of modern elected officials only.

70. I return to this point in chapter 11, in criticizing aspects of Kolodny's "Rule over None I" and "Rule over None II."

71. Cammack, "Representation." Focusing on certain linguistic expressions (such as *huper*, in the sense of "on behalf of" [which the article transliterates as "hyper"]), Cammack in this article neglects wider patterns of imagery and expressions with regard to rulers who serve, as discussed in this chapter and throughout this study. Moreover, she groups together some roles that technically counted as *archai* (offices), such as generals, with others, such as ambassadors (*presbeis*), that did not (577–79; as per Hansen, "Seven Hundred *Archai*," 152, 170–71), without either acknowledging or grappling with the significance of this distinction.

Platonic service conception of rule is likely to mislead. I take each of these points in turn. As to political officeholding in general: applying a principal-agent model (including both ancient Greek and modern cases) risks obscuring the epitactic powers of command and ordering that such officeholders (who are, after all, a species of rulers) enjoy. It is rare that agents are taken to have the power not only to act on behalf of their principals (for example, to bind them contractually) but also to give orders and commands directly to those principals. Yet this is the basic relationship between rulers and ruled. While the rulers may be accountable to the ruled in having their powers of ordering defined and limited by law, and controlled by (say) audit procedures that the ruled themselves democratically enforce, they remain empowered to give orders to the ruled that the ruled are generally bound to obey.

Thus, the tendency among certain political theorists to dismiss officeholders as being mere agents should be resisted. So should a similar tendency among certain scholars of ancient Greek officeholders. Indeed, the assumption of the principal-agent model that the principal originally possessed the powers that they delegate on terms to the agent fits ill with the ancient Greek figurations and descriptions of how political offices emerged and how their powers and roles might be interpreted, including those within and reflecting on democratic Athens. One part of those figurations was, as described in part I, the folk histories of Athenian political evolution told by contemporary and later Greek thinkers themselves, accounts in which the evolution of the powers of the *archai* and the *dēmos* in Athens were two intertwined but not identical stories. The account given in these potted histories (among them, one told by Plato himself in the *Menexenus*; another offered some centuries later by Pausanias) is one of the *dēmos* gaining powers—indeed, originally being granted them by Solon—not of their having had any role in granting those powers to the *archai*.[72] On the contrary, the earliest officeholders, such as, in Athens, the original three "archons," inherited the powers of the previous kings rather than being granted powers belonging to the people. Those powers are curbed by the imposition of various kinds of limits: initially, by the limitation of the previous life terms, and by the move to selection by election rather than inheritance. As democratic powers developed, the *dēmos* in its various institutional incarnations asserted new ways to control the officeholders. But it was the powers of control, not the original powers of executive action, that belonged to the people. The *dēmos* had never been able, even notionally, to issue directive orders or use coercive force. Rather, the original

---

72. Solon was credited with having given the *dēmos* the power to decide in the popular courts and the power to serve in the Assembly, but the fourth and lowest property class was excluded from holding any of the offices that the Assembly and courts were able to control—and I have suggested in "Claims to Rule" (271–72, nn7–8) that there is no very good reason to think that this restriction was ever formally lifted.

powers of executive action were not powers *of* the people but powers of the rulers, which the people in various ways, and to varying degrees of success, sought to bridle and control.[73]

This brings me to a survey of the language and imagery used for Greek rulers and (among them) officeholders prior to and contemporary with Plato, insofar as these figurations modeled service conceptions of rule that are not well captured by the strictures of a principal-agent model. This study has in earlier chapters dwelt on the image of the king as shepherd, which is clearly not well captured by a principal-agent analysis. Another significant image that emerged in the archaic period was that of the "steward" (*tamias*), a dispenser and distributor, someone who administered and regulated (*tamieuein*), linked terms that could be used in both household and nonhousehold contexts. Homer described Zeus himself as a *tamias*; Pindar described foreign kings as such; both uses showing that a steward was not necessarily the agent of another but could be a self-directing actor in possession of a plenitude of power and not merely delegated powers, albeit responsible for an appropriate dispensing of what is within their power.[74]

What about words and figures that more explicitly bespeak serving and servants? These words are definitely found in the context of democratic Athenian texts. The orators make much use of officeholders as public servants, especially using verbs such as *diakonein*, *therapeuein*, and *hupēretein*, the latter two (along with *epimeleisthai*) also featuring significantly in Plato, especially in the conjunction of all three in the *Statesman*.[75] And I noted earlier that Isocrates (7.26) depicts the officeholders (*tas archas*) whom the *dēmos* of a past idealized Athens chose, held accountable, and judged in disputes, as ideally acting "like servants," being ideally elite, wealthy men who use their leisure to care for the city's good—though here the analogizing move precisely puts such men outside the status of actual servants.

More explicit in exploring the status of officeholders as "slaves" (*oiketai*, which could mean slave or servant in context) is Aristophanes's *Knights* (l.5

---

73. This evolution of public powers bears comparison to one approach to constitutionalism in early modern and modern politics, identified by Möllers ("Pouvoir constituant," 190) as a "shaping of political power through juridification"; he discerns this approach especially in England and Germany, noting in both contexts that "the historic fear of unrestrained tyranny is closely connected to this idea of limitation of power" (also 190), an observation that fits the evolution of classical Greek polities as well.

74. Homer, *Il.* 4.84; Pindar, *Pythian Odes* 1.88, 5.62, and see also the related formulation at *Olympian Odes* 8.30, and the poet's portrayal of himself as steward at *Isthmian Odes* 6.57–58. Also notable are descriptions of persons stewarding their own mind and emotions (Theognis, 504–5) and their own appetites (Thuc., 6.78.2). Herodotus (2.121α2) uses the noun non-normatively in describing a builder exhorting his sons to make use of hidden access to make themselves stewards of a king's treasure.

75. Brock (*Greek Political Imagery*, 26) notes the use of these verbs as having become "a familiar trope in the orators," offering a range of relevant citations in note 8.

and passim), which depicts the household of a character named Dēmos (a personification of the *dēmos*), whose slaves (whom an Athenian theatergoer would have expected should be controlled by their master) show an unexpected ability to control him instead. Here, the master-slave relationship exceeds the bounds of the principal-agent model for the opposite reason: not because the purported agent is originally independent of any purported principal (as with the steward) but because an enslaved person does not hold discrete designated powers of delegated agency. The very lack of accountable control of slaves more broadly makes their powers of action appear, in the conservative comic world of the play, as a domestic and political threat.

By the end of the play, however, Aristophanes rows back from slavery as a way of figuring political office. Strikingly, as Roger Brock has observed, he has the character Dēmos resort to the language of stewarding (*tamieuein*), which he uses now as a transitive verb, describing the transfer of powers symbolized by his ring (ll. 947–48: "Return now the ring, for you are no longer to act as my steward").[76] As Brock further observes, when Dēmos decides to "entrust (*epitrepō*)" himself to the sausage seller, he is invoking not a principal-agent model, in which the principal can control the agent, but the kind of guardianship that is held by the tutor of a child (here adapted to the guidance of an old man). In this context, as in many of the archaic and fifth-century prose uses of the image of the steward, the guardian is not subject to comprehensive control by the principal. On the contrary: the guardian figure is in many contexts superior to their charge and must act outside and without the latter's full control.

Figures like guardians of young children—guardians who must be oriented to the good of those in their charge but who are not subject to their charges' explicit external control—are exactly the kind of guardians who are called for by Plato in the *Republic*. The analysis that I have offered of wages in a *kallipolis* comports with a similar model, not of principal-agent control but rather of guardianship (noting that I have allowed the slide from "guard" to "guardian" in translating *phulax* in the *Republic*, while avoiding merely assuming rather than arguing for that interpretation). For Plato in the *Republic*, as ultimately for Aristophanes in the *Knights*, the role of rulers and other guardians in serving the good of the ruled did not mean that they should be equated to servants in a subordinate sense. They remain epitactic issuers of orders, superior to those whom they rule in issuing those orders, even while they serve. In the *Republic*, the dependence of the rulers and other guardians on wages dramatizes not their subjection to the active control of the ruled who

76. I paraphrase Brock (*Greek Political Imagery*, 27), who writes: "When in *Knights* [lines] 947–8 Demos uses the verb *tamieuein* in demanding the return of his ring and handing it over to the sausage-seller, the term implies that the Paphlagonian has betrayed his trust." See also line 959.

pay those wages but the safeguarding (both materially and attitudinally) of their own orientation to the proper *telos* of rule as (tested by) the good of the ruled. Plato does not in the *Republic* rely only on the knowledge or virtue of the rulers to orient them toward the good of the ruled; as I noted in chapter 1, pace the influential critique by Karl Popper, Plato does not limit himself to the sole question of "who should rule?" Rather, he designs a *taxis* of roles that are to be limited and configured so as to safeguard the orientation of the guardians toward the good of the ruled. It is this overarching orientation of the role of the guardians (including a group of officeholders, as the next chapter will show)—one that eschews the narrower principal-agent model, which would make rulers the mere agents of those whom they rule—that is fundamental to the Platonic service conception of rule as configured in the *Republic*. How the limits of office (even reconfigured offices) can fit within the broader service conception of rule in that dialogue is explored in the next chapter.

CHAPTER SEVEN

Philosophers Reigning

RULERS AND OFFICEHOLDERS IN A
KALLIPOLIS (*REPUBLIC*, BOOKS 5–7)

IN A PASSAGE that (as argued in part I of this study) deserves more attention than it typically receives, Socrates in book 5 of Plato's *Republic* refers to political "officeholders" and "offices" (5.460b6–8), as I (and others) translate his two uses in that passage of *archai*—a plural of the noun *archē*, which can be translated in the singular either as constitutionally limited "office" or as more general "rule."[1] Yet discussions of the *Republic* seldom address the political and theoretical significance of the inclusion of offices (here and in other passages discussed in this chapter) in the constitutional project of the dialogue. The present chapter explains the place of office within that project as being held by apprentice rulers, who are subordinate to the full-fledged rule of philosopher-kings and philosopher-queens. The overarching framework of the *Republic* includes both officeholding and what I call "reigning" (translating *basileuein* in various passages as explained below) as two distinct kinds of rule, both articulated in terms of laws. In this way, Plato situates the *politeia* of the eponymous dialogue (its Greek title is *Politeia*, "Constitution") within a well-established fourth-century discourse in which a constitution is articulated in terms of offices and laws[2]—while exploring the ways in which officeholding may require safeguarding by a further kind of rule. In other words, Plato in this dialogue does not abjure a constitutional framework for

1. All quotations in this chapter are from Plato, *Republic*, according to the Slings OCT, and in my own translation, unless otherwise indicated.

As explained in overview in chapter 1 and in detail in chapter 2, while the noun can also bear other senses (such as "beginning" or "empire"), its spanning of general or abstract "rule" together with constitutionally limited "office" as a kind of rule is central to the argument of the present study. See pp.65–71 in chapter 2 in particular.

2. On the question of Greek constitutionalism, see note 53 in chapter 2.

the politics of a *kallipolis* but, rather, articulates one, a constitution that is simultaneously recognizable as such and distinctive in its contours.

Both the reigning rulers and the officeholders of a *kallipolis*, as kinds of rulers, together with younger trainees known as "auxiliaries," belong to an overall group of "guardians" (*phulakes*) (though sometimes Plato reserves the term "guardians" for only the subset of ruling nonauxiliaries). In the previous chapter of this study, I argued that in requiring and receiving wages, the role of the guardian group as a whole is framed in terms of a service conception: the guardians, including that subset of them who act as rulers, are to act in the service of the good of those whom they guard. Wages can thus be construed as central to the success of a service conception of rule in the dialogue, an idea I develop throughout this study, inspired broadly by Joseph Raz's service conception of authority. This chapter explores the further limits, in law and practice, that characterize the role of ruling as a service conception within the constitutional project of the *Republic* (as I sometimes refer to the articulation of a constitution "in speech" for a *kallipolis*). Its thesis is that the role of ruling is delineated in that dialogue far more precisely than has generally been recognized. Not only is the *telos* of rule, as serving the good of the ruled, clearly set out in *Republic* 1 (as I argued in chapter 5) but, moreover, the dialogue does not rest content with relying on the philosophical nature of the rulers, nor on their philosophical education or the content of the knowledge they so gain, in enabling this *telos* to be achieved. Rather, it also sets out a complex, age-differentiated *taxis* (order) of a range of roles defined by specific limits, which includes both some rulers who serve as officeholders and others who select those officeholders and play an important role in safeguarding their orientation to the good of the ruled. This complex *taxis* is necessary to enable the *telos* of rule to be realized, safeguarding the good of the ruled against exploitation by the rulers.

On my overall interpretation, Plato inquires into the implicit *telos* toward which existing forms of rule—especially constitutional offices—aimed, so as to reconfigure a *taxis* of rule, including office, capable of serving it (by his lights) more robustly. Within the limits of offices, typical Greek officeholders, including those in democratic Athens, were controlled by those whom they ruled, who were able to hold them accountable through audits (*euthunai*) and other limits and procedures. Beyond that, certain Greek constitutions, including that of Athens, set up institutions that were elevated above ordinary offices in order to play an overall safeguarding role for the constitution as a whole. For example, the Athenian Council of the Areopagus was composed of certain former officeholders who had successfully passed the *euthunai* at the end of their terms of offices (and were then subjected to a further kind of scrutiny),[3]

---

3. As I noted in chapter 2, membership of the Areopagus is once called an "office" in the [*Ath. Pol.*] (3.6), but as Hansen (*Athenian Democracy*, 294) points out in noting this, the fact that membership of the Areopagus did not preclude holding another office is decisive in showing that it cannot have technically counted as one: "as cumulation of magistracies

who then served in the Areopagus for the remainder of their lives without being subject to further accountability procedures.[4] What is of interest here is not just the fact of the Areopagus but the role it came to play in fourth-century ideological debates about the ancestral constitution, in which Plato can be understood to have participated in ways both resonant and rebarbative to his contemporaries. Here, my interest is primarily in emphasizing the resonance, for example, of Plato's language in the *Republic* with the language of Isocrates's idealization of the ancient Areopagus Council as having been made "sovereign (*kurian*) in taking caring charge (*epimeleisthai*) of good order [*eutaxia*]" (*Areopagiticus* 7.39).

The limits of offices manifest themselves in the *Republic* in terms of selection, age rotation, and distinct powers of office for the cohort of philosophers aged thirty-five to fifty. This cohort, like all the guardians in the city, is also dependent on wages paid by those whom it guards, as established in the previous chapter, though its members are not subjected to accountability procedures controlled by those ruled. Instead, they are further safeguarded by being subject to the control of their own epistemic and epitactic superiors, the eldest guardians, who are also fully educated philosophers (above the age of fifty). Those superiors oversee the education and selection of their juniors for progression into each political role, including ultimately selecting their own replacements. And there are hints that they may also play deliberative and judicial roles, which would also be analogous to the functions of the Athenian Areopagus. Yet their philosophical education equips them to safeguard the officeholders and the constitution and city as a whole more robustly, by Plato's lights, than the selection procedures for the Areopagus (composed of former officeholders, who were originally selected by lot, having been subjected to *dokimasia* and *euthunai* in conjunction with their former offices) would ensure. In lieu of imposing audit procedures to hold accountable these senior philosophers who are to reign as kings, Plato emphasizes that their education

---

[his word for what I call "offices"] was prohibited, the Areopagos [his preferred transliteration] cannot have been a magistracy."

4. While there seems to have been a requirement to submit collective financial accounts, this was arguably not an individual liability to further *euthunai* once having been appointed to the Areopagus Council. Aeschylus, 3.20, states that this council as a whole "is ordered by law to file its accounts with the *logistai* and to give an accounting [*euthunas didonai*]," which some have taken to imply individual liability to *euthunai*. But as Wallace (*Areopagos Council*, 95) argues in offering the translation I have reproduced in the previous sentence, "this phrase *euthunas didonai* probably refers only to the examination by *logistai* of the Areopagos' accounts," and refers to "the council as a whole, not individual members." (He cites on the same page the countervailing claim from Bekker's *Anecdota Graeca* [1.3.11.10–11] stating that those who had held office as *thesmothetai* [who were six of the nine archons] and who ascended to the Areopagus became *anupeuthunoi* [literally, not subject to *euthunai*]; while this seems prima facie to contradict Aeschin., 3.20, as just described, Wallace reads Bekker's claim as likely to mean only that the men in question had passed the *euthunai* at the end of their terms as *thesmothetai*.)

in philosophy has trained them in the reason giving that must more fundamentally underpin any kind of accountability at all, while simultaneously subjecting them to various other kinds of limits discussed in this chapter and the preceding one.

Whereas chapter 6 treated the guardians as a whole, in this chapter I focus on a distinction drawn by Plato among the "rulers" (so-called) between a group of officeholders, on the one hand, and a group of rulers senior to them who select and so safeguard the holders of those offices, on the other. The offices are confined to a group of middle-aged apprentice rulers aged thirty-five to fifty, who are tested and selected for holding the offices by the eldest rulers, who are aged fifty and above (and who were themselves tested and selected for each of the roles they have occupied by their own predecessors). This age hierarchy dramatizes the need for rulers who can safeguard the more procedurally limited and defined officeholders, so as to ensure that the powers of the latter are directed toward the good of the ruled and not instead toward their exploitation.

As was suggested in part I, the existence of "offices" and "officeholders" in a *kallipolis*—linguistically described with the same signals as conventional Greek offices, though the contours of their roles in the dialogue remain to be delineated—is a textual fact hiding in plain sight. Certain passages of the *Republic* make use of established conventional affordances of the verb *archein* and the noun *archē* so as to signal the holding of plural offices (the noun in the plural almost always means "offices" as opposed to "rule" in the singular, while the verb in the form of plural participles can mean either "officeholders" or "rulers" in context; both points depend on recognizing office to be a particular kind of rule). This was illustrated in chapter 2 with the book 5 passage describing those who will oversee the early childhood education in the city being founded "in speech," which I quote again in full:[5]

> the officers (*archai*) established for this purpose—men or women, or both, for presumably the offices (*archai*) are common to women and men. (5.460b6–8)[6]

---

5. One might also connect this to a passage in book 5, when, in the context of regulating anger-inciting disputes over injury and insult, Socrates specifies that someone older will be designated to "rule and discipline (*archein te kai kolazein*)" all those younger than him (5.465a5–6).

6. Translation quoted from Bloom, as in chapter 2, where that was done in order to make a point about standard translations of these terms. Nothing hangs on his use of the word "officials" as opposed to my preference for "officeholders." As I documented in chapter 2 (in which note 2 gives further information), influential translations in other languages track this point in practice by using similar language to "offices" and "officeholders" in translating this same passage (e.g., *Obrigkeiten, Behörde, magistrati, uffici, magistratos assignados*), in contrast to the language of "rulers" (e.g., *Regenten, Herrscher, governanti, gubernantes*), which they use in other passages in the same dialogue where the specific

By having Socrates use the plural noun *archai* here, which virtually always in a political context refers in the plural to offices, and exploiting it also to refer to the officeholders,[7] Plato clearly references the vocabulary for office, which was well established and sometimes unambiguous in Greek constitutions and texts of fifth- and fourth-century authors, especially in Attic. This is for reasons explained and documented in chapter 2: in brief, translating the plural *archai* as "rule" here would make no sense, whereas the plural noun was well established in Attic Greek usages as indicating "offices," as well as being available likewise to indicate their holders.

In what follows, I identify these "offices" as confined to a particular cohort of guardians: those at the penultimate stage of the educational progression, aged thirty-five to fifty, whose task is to go back into the Cave (an image that Socrates had introduced earlier for civic life). They are to gain experience there by engaging in "rule (*archein*) with respect to matters of war and with respect to those offices that befit young people (*hosai neōn archai*)" (7.539e5). It is these apprentice rulers, as I call them, who are to take on military commands (which were in many Greek cities themselves considered offices) and other offices (the content of which is further explored below). To be sure, the "offices" in question do not meet all the conventional parameters identifying such offices that in chapter 2 were drawn from Athenian fourth-century discourse (especially Aeschines's *Against Ctesiphon*) and from a wider family of officeholding constitutions in democratic and oligarchic regimes alike. To recall those parameters in an abbreviated version of the list assembled in chapter 2:

1. Performance audits: audits upon vacating an office (known as *euthunai*), with penalties if malfeasance of kinds specified in a given constitution was proven

2. Limited powers of office (specified powers, often as a collegial member of a board)

3. Limits on eligibility to serve: term limits; specified selection procedures usually by lottery, election, or a combination of both; scrutiny of civic standing as a test prior to installation in office (distinctive of classical Athens)

4. Other potential mechanisms of monitoring and sanctioning performance: (a) accusations brought against officeholders during a term of office (distinctive of classical Athens); (b) payment of wages (mainly in Athens and other democracies but only at certain periods)

---

linguistic signals of offices are absent. Yet the implications of this distinction for understanding the political theory of the dialogue have been scarcely explored.

7. As noted earlier in this study, this could standardly be done in Attic Greek: Hansen (*Athenian Democracy*, 226) notes that the noun *archē* (plural *archai*) was "used with just about equal frequency of the person holding the magistracy," a point made by him about Athens but which applies to other Greek constitutional polities as well.

The methods of selection of the officeholders in the *kallipolis* do not involve any combination of election and lot, though they do involve age eligibility. Moreover, and most strikingly, the methods of control of those officeholders do not involve any mention of procedural audits (*euthunai*) for holding them accountable, though they do involve wages. In terms of both selection and accountability, the officeholders are not subject to the control of the ruled (from below, as it were)—which is certainly different from officeholders in democratic constitutions such as Athens (and also different from what a principal-agent model of accountability would prescribe). Instead, they are subject to the control of a higher group of rulers, the fully fledged philosophers, who both select and safeguard the officeholders and thereby the constitution and city as a whole.

Within a *kallipolis*, its officeholders are among the "guardians" whose role is to safeguard (and so save and preserve) the city. Ensuring that they do so properly is to be achieved in part through the deprivation of wealth, which makes them dependent on wages—to be achieved through legally established safeguards. But it is also to be achieved by a superordinate group of guardians, the eldest cohort, who are tasked with safeguarding all of the guardians junior to them.[8] At this level, it is the bifurcation in the group of those called "rulers" in the *Republic*, between officeholders on the one hand and rulers whose role is to safeguard the officeholders and the constitution and city as a whole on the other, that answers the question I have treated in earlier chapters in regard to the *Statesman* and the *Laws*: the Juvenal conundrum of who shall guard the guardians, which I argue is answered in the *Republic* by identification of a group of "safeguarding rulers."

The officeholding guardians (who are rulers of a kind, since office is a kind of rule) are safeguarded by the most senior group of guardians (who are rulers of another kind—namely, reigning rulers). The latter are charged with the education and testing of each junior cohort so as to ensure that only those who are both motivated and capable to serve the good of the ruled will hold those offices. Indeed, the role of the senior rulers is described primarily as supervising the higher stages of the education and selection of the junior guardians at each stage of age progression (of those with the relevant natural capacities to begin with). There is also reference to the senior rulers' ability to make laws, which I connect to their capacity of deliberation and more broadly to their activity of maintaining through philosophical argument a full understanding of the Good as such. A final element in the role of these reigning rulers is that

---

8. Reference to the age hierarchy among the guardians should always be taken to include the role of selection at each stage: it is not age alone that qualifies one for this role but, rather, a selection for suitability to be promoted to the next age-differentiated rank, made by a superordinate cohort. Even the eldest guardians are not self-certifying, but are promoted to that rank by those who precede them in it.

they may serve as judges as well (though the textual evidence on this is not conclusive, as I discuss below). These senior rulers are described not in the language of officeholders but in the language of kings who reign (*basileuein*) and who are sovereign (*kurios*) over the most important matters in the state.

Yet the Juvenal conundrum must then be faced again at this higher level. In other words, one must ask: How will those supreme rulers, above whom there is no one superior who could play the role of safeguarding them, themselves be safeguarded so that they do not exploit their power but instead use it to serve the good of the ruled? The answer lies in a combination of the shape of the role of senior ruler (meaning the specific limits and order that it exhibits), the nature of those who are selected (by operation of the prior holders of the role itself) to take it up, and the knowledge of philosophy that they will possess. In other words, what safeguards the reigning rulers of the *Republic* is a combination of *taxis* (order); *phusis* (nature), developed and tested through education and experience; and the education that those with a suitable *phusis* can acquire in *philosophia*. In other words, rule in the *kallipolis* is ultimately safeguarded by a combination of its structural *taxis* and the qualities of the natural persons (both their nature and their education) who play roles within it, where central to the *taxis* is the process for identifying suitable candidates and ensuring that they and only they do in fact play those roles.

Indeed, in book 8, in offering a narrative of how this kind of constitution might decline into factional division (*stasis*), Socrates will use vocabulary cognate with *dokimasia* (featuring in parameter 3 in the list above) to describe this process of selection through education. There, he will argue that a certain generation of ruling guardians will eventually carry out a flawed scrutiny (*to dokimazein*) of the natures of the citizens (metaphorically described as gold, silver, bronze, and iron) (8.546d7–547a2), meaning that they will misidentify who should be the members of the next generation of auxiliaries (junior guardians) and rulers (senior guardians). This scrutiny is described by the same word that democratic Athenians used to describe the required testing of each person chosen to hold an office by election or by lot, prior to their being allowed to assume that role. In a *kallipolis*, such scrutiny must be passed before anyone is allowed to take up any role of guarding, including but not limited to officeholding.

The *taxis* of rule in a *kallipolis* is organized in part through legal safeguards. Together with all the other guardians, the supreme rulers too are to be dependent on wages as a provision enforced by law (as described in the previous chapter). For the full-fledged philosophers who have ascended to the role of reigning as kings through their nature, education, and experience, the role of these wages in constraining their behavior may seem otiose, given that they would not seek to enrich themselves as they have no appetite to do so. Yet given that they are human, and that the seeds of error and then corruption will necessarily eventually germinate as described in *Republic* 8, the legal limits imposed by wages on these rulers (as well as on the subordinate cohort of officeholders, and the auxiliaries below them) remain significant.

The *taxis* of rule is also organized in part through education and selection of those who will enter into that role (these processes being legally prescribed, while dependent upon the wisdom and virtue with which they are carried out). For while the eldest guardians are the supreme rulers in the city once they have reached the age (of fifty) required to play that role, their selection into it is carried out by the people who have held that role before them: the prior cohort of supreme philosopher-rulers, who select their own replacements and promote them to the highest ranks. This builds safeguarding of the guardians into the dynamic process of education and selection for the role of ruling, while conserving the supreme rule of a given cohort at any one time. While this still leaves the door open in theory to collusion and corruption of those in the highest rank over time, at least it closes the door to wholly uncontrolled self-selection. Not even those who fill the highest rank are self-certifying. They must be tested and selected by those who precede them in that rank.[9]

There is a further safeguard for the senior guardians provided in the dialogue, which lies in the content of their knowledge of the Good. As described, this is not merely contemplative knowledge but is gained and realized through the practice of philosophical dialectic, the exchanging of reasons. This is described in two important passages in book 7 in the language of *logon didonai*, giving and exchanging accounts, which was the same idiom used in Greek constitutional practices for the giving of accounts demanded by the accountability procedures for officeholders widely known as *euthunai*—and likewise used by Plato in other dialogues to describe Socratic inquiry and questioning (for example, *Theaetetus* 169a6, *Laches* 187e10). While scholars such as J. Peter Euben and Ryan Balot have noted the connections of Socratic inquiry to democratic accountability, against a wider backdrop by a range of scholars of assessments of resonances between Socratic and democratic practice and values, these scholars have not brought these points to bear specifically on the constitution of the city in speech in the *Republic* or connected them to the reconfiguration of office or rule therein.[10]

9. In this respect, such a mode of selection is comparable to the self-reproducing ranks of certain modern corporate boards (including certain nonprofit corporations), such as the Harvard Corporation that governs Harvard University.

10. Euben, *Corrupting Youth*, 91; Balot, "Democracy and Political Philosophy," esp. 188–93. See also Schlosser, *What Would Socrates Do?*, 29–54, 84–89, and passim. This point, and much of the literature relevant to it, was brought to my attention in work by Ian Walling ("Power and Vulnerability"). Markovits (*Politics of Sincerity*), Monoson (*Plato's Democratic Entanglements*), Saxonhouse (*Free Speech and Democracy*), and Schlosser (*What Would Socrates Do?*), are among other scholars who have highlighted resonances between Socratic practices and Athenian democratic ones more broadly, especially the value and practice of *parrhēsia*, or frank speech.

In *Republic* 7, Socrates emphasizes that the person who should be called "dialectician" is someone "who is able to lay hold of an account (*ton logon . . . lambanonta*) of the being of each thing" (7.534b3). In his complementary denial (also couched as what we would call a rhetorical question) he uses the precise phrase *logon didonai*, suggesting that the dialectician will be able not only to lay hold of such an account but also to give that account to others: "insofar as he's unable to give an account (*logon . . . didonai*) of something, either to himself or to anyone, do you deny that he has any understanding of it?" (7.534b4–6, trans. Grube/Reeve). He then drives the point home by applying it to knowledge of the Good (the Form of which had been alluded to in book 6):

> Then the same applies to the good. Unless someone can distinguish in an account (*diorisasthai tōi logōi*) the form of the good from everything else, can survive all refutations (*elenchōn*), as if in a battle, striving to test (*elenchein*) things not in accordance with opinion but in accordance with being, and can come through all this with his account (*tōi logōi*) still intact, you'll say that he doesn't know the good itself or any other good. (7.534b8–c5, trans. Grube/Reeve, modified)[11]

The maintaining of one's account against all possible refutations, in particular those rooted in being rather than mere opinion, is the highest achievement of the dialectician and a sign of their possession of knowledge. By invoking this high dialectical competence that the senior philosophers must achieve, Plato emphasizes that the logic of reason giving and account rendering is fundamentally a discursive logic.[12] Moreover, he implies that the epistemic test of such a discursive logic is in principle more comprehensive than any particular procedural version of accountability "to below" could adequately capture.

While the constitutional project of the *Republic* implies that procedural accountability controlled by those below (as it were) is neither necessary nor sufficient to achieve the function of safeguarding the good of those persons who are ruled, that project does incorporate education in the comprehensive logic of reason giving on which the very notion of accountability must rest. This relocates the underlying value of reason giving into a practice that is both mutual and potentially universal (though open in practice only to those who have reached the requisite level of dialectic), opening it to any challenge, in a way that Athenian and more broadly Greek institutions of accountability did not.[13] In

---

11. Grube/Reeve translate "striving to judge" where I translate "striving to test." The speech continues with the complementary denial of the same feat being possible for someone who has mere "opinion" (7.534c5–d1).

12. McCabe ("Philosopher Queens?" remarks that "central to dialectic is the idea of giving *and taking* an account; central to conversation is the speaking and listening relation between the two sides" (118, emphasis original).

13. Those procedures in Athens privileged the unaccountable *idiotai* in holding to account via defined procedures those who had exercised forms of institutional authority

this sense, rather than simply changing the subject in transposing the idea of accountability from political mechanisms to philosophical dialectic, Plato is zeroing in on the essence of both: the ability to offer reasons and to assess what counts as a valid reason. Politics depends on argument that is oriented to truth.

In this chapter, I begin by retracing the introduction of a group of guardians in *Republic* 2 and the subsequent distinction in book 3 between the junior guardians ("auxiliaries"), who are to be "ruled" by the senior guardians ("complete guardians"), who are to be the "rulers." While I follow Plato in sometimes emphasizing this divide between those whom I will call broadly "junior" and "senior," I also follow him in sometimes emphasizing a further subdivision, which is made in book 7. There, each of these two broad groups is further subdivided into two (either explicitly or implicitly), following the further educational stages, so as to highlight four distinct cohorts from the age of twenty upward. I focus especially on the cohort aged thirty-five to fifty (calling them "middle-aged"), who are to "rule . . . and hold such offices suitable to young people" as quoted below, and go on to assemble additional evidence for offices in this constitution and to argue that it is most likely (where not certain) this cohort who are intended to hold them. Finally I turn to the "reigning" role of the eldest rulers, assembling again the evidence for the limits on and powers of their role, weighing the extent to which these rulers—while not officeholders— are nevertheless distinguished by limits that serve some of the same functions as those typically found in Greek offices and serve to order their rule more broadly. Rulers who are not officeholders are not subject to externally enforced limits or controls. Yet, in a broader sense, their rule must exhibit order, for rulers cannot order their domain if they are not properly ordered in the constitution of their own activity.

The moral of considering the closeness, as well as the distinctness, of rule and office within the constitutional project of the *Republic* is that rule as such, including but not limited to rule exercised through constitutional offices, must be characterized by a *taxis* involving limits and boundaries of some kind. Rule must be bounded and limited—it must exhibit order—if it is to be able successfully to establish order for those within its domain. This is shown in the affirmative case of a *kallipolis* as depicted in *Republic* 5–7 in this chapter, and in the negative case of the flawed constitutions of *Republic* 8 in the next. The result is that, as already argued in this study in regard to the *Laws* and the *Statesman*, so too in the *Republic*, Plato's idea of rule is not exhausted by the identification of the *telos* of rule as the good—indeed, in the *Republic*, the Form of the Good—which in the framework of politics must be operationalized as the good of the ruled. On the contrary. Plato is as much concerned with

---

(such as officeholders) or institutionally channeled influence (such as orators). See Hoekstra, "Athenian Democracy," and Landauer, *Dangerous Counsel*.

the *taxis* of rule (including the place, role, and safeguarding of office), and what it must be like if that *telos* is to be realized, as any constitutional theorist of his or our day.

Age Cohorts: The Varied Roles of the Guardians in Relation to Ruling

I begin by supplying textual evidence for the overall age cohorts and their differentiated roles in relation to ruling. This requires evidence from several different points in the dialogue, especially books 3 (in which the overall distinction between auxiliaries and their seniors is first drawn) and 7 (in which the age progression in the education of the guardians is laid out). I take the overall evidence to suggest that all below age thirty-five are "auxiliaries" in that they are assisting the more senior rulers. The term "auxiliaries" sometimes functions in this broad sense, especially when the original bipartite distinction is in view. In a narrow sense, however, the "auxiliaries" are only those aged twenty to thirty, who play the roles of soldiers and procreators, overseen by their seniors. Likewise, in a broad sense, both the "officeholders" and those who "reign" as kings are "rulers" (comporting with the insistence throughout this study that officeholding was always viewed as a kind of ruling, as their linguistic overlap in Greek suggests). In a narrow sense, however, only the group of guardians who "reign" are the supreme and so true or complete rulers, in that they are not simultaneously ruled over by any further set of people who are senior and superior to them.

As noted above, within the group of guardians who had been introduced in book 2, a bipartite division is made by Socrates in book 3, as follows:

—"Auxiliaries": the junior guardians, here renamed "auxiliaries," who are to be "ruled" by more senior guardians
—"Complete guardians": the "rulers" over those junior guardians, who are to be the best of those who are more senior, here renamed the "complete guardians" (both points, 3.412c1–414b6).

He elaborates in this passage on the need to "choose those men from among the other guardians" who are "the superlative guardians of the city" (3.412d9, b10–11), success in this role requiring that they "take the initiative with respect to being knowledgeable, being capable, and also being caretakers (*kēdemonas*) of the city" (3.412c13–14). The noun *ho kēdemōn* typically referred not just to anyone engaged in an act of caregiving, but specifically to the role of someone whom one might call a caretaker: someone who had a charge to serve in that role, such as legally appointed guardians.[14]

---

14. While venturing "caretaker" as my own translation, I build on the remarks of Giulia Sissa ("Caregivers," 187–90 and passim) noting the connection between guarding and what

This reference to caretakers—applied specifically to that subset of guardians who are to be the "rulers" over the others—links the roles of guarding and ruling to an orientation of caring for the good of another, which a guardian is expected to exhibit. It operates in the same ambit as the language of legal guardianship, which was sometimes invoked in Athenian political discourse—for example, as noted previously in this study, by Aristophanes at one stage in the *Knights* (a role that would also be drawn upon as a model and metaphor in Roman political thought).[15] Continuous with the idea of rule as defended by Socrates against Thrasymachus in *Republic* 1 (discussed above in chapter 5), the dialogue again here commits itself to a service conception of rule.

What exactly is the nature of the rule to be exercised by the senior guardians over the junior ones? The question must be asked in the context of a further subdivision of each group that is drawn in book 7, in tracing the educational progress of the guardians and their roles at each stage.[16] There, each of the two overall groups of guardians—the auxiliaries and the rulers—is further divided into two, as follows:

Auxiliaries

Age twenty to thirty:[17] soldiers and procreators—"auxiliaries" in the
   narrow sense
Age thirty to thirty-five:[18] philosophy students who spend five years
   "participating in arguments" (7.539d5)

---

she translates as "caregiving (*kēdesthai*)" (188): "To defend, to protect, to rule, are ultimately modifications of one crucial task," with the mission of guarding being "minding to, tending to, heeding to, securing, safeguarding, and caring for," such that "government can only be the sublimation of that same endeavour." Discussing this paper with her at a conference in Zurich in 2016 opened my eyes to the importance of caring in Platonic political thought generally, which previously I had noticed primarily in the *Statesman*.

15. On Roman legal guardianship and its political appropriations in antiquity and beyond, see Atkins (*Roman Political Thought*, 32) and Lee (*Popular Sovereignty*, 121–57 and passim).

16. My reading emphasizes the continuous development of the portrait of these guardians from book 2 through book 7 (and the allusions at the beginning of book 8), in contrast to Vegetti (*Repubblica*, 4:364), who contrasts the "*archontes*-filosofi" (philosopher-rulers) of books 2–4 (though they are not yet philosophers in any full sense) and the "filosofi-re" (philosopher-kings) of books 5–6 with the fully developed philosophers of book 7 who know dialectic. An even stronger division among the philosophers in different parts of the dialogue, contrasting those who are philosophers by nature with those educated to serve that purpose in a *kallipolis*, is posited by Weiss in *Philosophers*.

17. See 3.414b4–6 for term "auxiliaries"; 7.537b7–d2 for the period from twenty to thirty, which includes the testing of their ability to remain "steadfast" both in their studies and "in war and in other pursuits according to the laws" (7.537d1–2). I leave aside the early childhood education, before age twenty, though this is clearly also important for the overall education program.

18. Advancement into this cohort is "tested by the power of dialectic" (7.537d2–8). Insofar as those in this age cohort are insulated from participating in war during their

Rulers

Age thirty-five to fifty (apprentice rulers who are middle-aged): "ruling" (*archein*) as military commanders and "officeholders" (*archai*), gaining political experience "in the Cave" (see below for treatment of the key passage identifying this group, 7.539e2–540a2)

Age fifty and above: the eldest and maximally senior "complete guardians," who have succeeded through philosophical dialectic in comprehending the Form of the Good—"reigning" as kings, "ruling" over all of their juniors in supervising their education and testing their eligibility for promotion to the next age cohort set to an assigned role (see below for the key passages in both book 5 and book 7)

For membership of each cohort, the age criterion for eligibility is necessary but not sufficient. Each cohort is composed only of those who are "selected" on the basis of having passed the test of performance in the previous cohort, described as a previously "selected" group whose members are tested for promotion to the next rank. The selection is done by means of "testing," with the verb *basanizein* repeatedly used to denote the testing of each age cohort, a verb drawn from the testing of the nature and purity of metals by rubbing them against a proving stone.

Having introduced the process of such selection in book 3, Socrates in book 7 explicitly refers back to this earlier selection of rulers in developing its stages further (7.535a6–7). Whereas the book 3 selection had focused on picking out the older people who had successfully passed tests of their stability and courage, and had highlighted the need for them to be knowledgeable, capable, and motivated to serve as protectors of the city, the corresponding book 7 selection (identified as such at 7.536c7–9) is focused on the more demanding challenge of identifying those youths who are by nature intellectually and temperamentally capable of the learning that must culminate in the study of dialectic.

Earlier in this educational journey, the children are to be given compulsory physical training. The earliest childhood education was described in book 5, in a passage I cited earlier, as being assigned to the *archai* who may be women or men or both (5.460b6–8); since the only group later described as holding *archai* is the age cohort thirty-five to fifty, it would seem that these are the ones charged with educating, testing, and selecting potential guardians from the cohort of youngest children. However, once book 7 takes up the education of those from the age of twenty onward, it seems likely that those charged with educating, testing, and selecting each subsequent cohort are the eldest guardians. Such education, testing, and selecting of the natural persons fit to serve as guardians in each rank is central to the task of ruling, conceived as safeguarding those who serve in the offices (the penultimate cohort of guardians),

---

studies, they seem temporarily exempted from the ranks of the auxiliaries in the narrow sense, though they belong broadly to the auxiliaries group.

as well as safeguarding the whole group of junior guardians more broadly, in order to ensure that they in turn will (safe)guard the city well.

I discuss below further evidence that this role in education and selection is central to the role of the eldest guardians, who are the supreme rulers. For now, I return to the educational progression of the guardians from the age of twenty, when (as noted above) they enter into the group of auxiliaries, who are the most junior of the guardians. As Socrates states in book 7, at the age of twenty, some of those who had been educated to that point are selected and given more *timas* ("honors") than others (7.537b7–8), as well as a continued education, designed to test their dialectical natures as well as their abilities in war and in the other activities "prescribed by law" (*nomimois*) (7.537c9–d2). It is presumably those in this group, aged between twenty and thirty, who are entered into the rank of "auxiliary" guardians, since they are of the age to pursue war as well as to procreate.

Socrates indicates that a further selection from this group will be made at the age of thirty, with those successful being granted further honors and recognitions. (Thirty was also the age at which male citizens became eligible to hold political offices (*archai*) in democratic Athens.) At this stage (e.g., 7.537b–d), Plato repeatedly uses language that unmistakably alludes to established terminology—*ek prokritōn*—for preliminary selection as a stage in an overall selection of candidates for offices in Athens, which might include nomination or election at the first stage and then election or lottery at a second stage. For example, a two-stage procedure known as *klērōsis ek prokritōn* began with a preliminary selection made by election, followed by a subsequent selection from that preselected group made by means of lottery.[19] Here, by contrast, the same vocabulary is appropriated for a two-stage procedure differing from that in Athens in at least two respects: the same procedure of preselection is used at both stages, and each stage is carried out by the same body of selectors (those already established as the eldest guardians).[20] Note also the pointed absence of election and lottery at either stage, the two available methods that could be used, mixed or matched, in such Athenian procedures for selecting officeholders. Instead, in the *Republic*, selection through education and testing serves the function that in Athens (and indeed in other Greek constitutions, with patterns varying especially between democracies and oligarchies) would be achieved by lottery, election, or both.

---

19. Hansen ("ΚΛΗΡΩΣΙΣ ΕΚ ΠΡΟΚΡΙΤΩΝ," 229) reviews the various sources of evidence, which are prima facie in tension on various points, including which offices were so selected and for what period; his overall conclusion is that this was "a fifth-century [Athenian] procedure, introduced in 487/86 (Ath. Pol. 22. 5) and attested no later than 458/57 (Ath. Pol. 26. 2)."

20. Gomme, Andrewes, and Dover (*Historical Commentary*, 5:221), note (in discussing historical material regarding the late fifth century, in book 8 of Thucydides) that "*prokrisis* is not normally performed by the same body that makes the final choice."

Those guardians so selected at age thirty are to be assigned "still greater honors," and then again to be "tested [*basanizein*] by the power of dialectic" (7.537d3–5). Such testing is applied further (using the same verb and its cognates) to the next stage of their education and role in the city from age thirty-five to fifty, and to the selection that is to be made at the end of that stage (*basanisteoi*, 7.540a1), so as to choose those who can be brought to see the Good itself. These guardians, who have "come safely through [the process of testing] and excelled in every way in the deeds as well as the epistemic studies" of the stage from thirty-five to fifty (7.540a4–6), are chosen to be compelled to see the Form of the Good and to embark on the ruling-as-reigning role of the most senior of the guardians. Before turning to that role of ruling as reigning, however, in the next section I return to the cohort aged thirty-five to fifty, in order to flesh out the evidence that this cohort is to hold "offices," and to explore what kind of offices those might be, and what the significance is of their being described (in some passages unambiguously) as such.

Apprentice Rulers: Offices and Officeholding for the Middle-Aged Cohort of Rulers

The description of the role of the cohort of guardians aged thirty-five to fifty makes clear (when a range of passages are properly contextually interpreted) that the constitution of a *kallipolis* is to include political offices. Consider how the role of this cohort in the city is described, in a passage found near the pinnacle of book 7, after the educational requirement of the study of dialectic has been explained and defended (the passage was mentioned above but is discussed now in further depth). At this juncture of the dialogue, Socrates addresses himself to what is to happen after the philosophers in training have completed five years of education in dialectic,[21] at which point they would have reached the age of thirty-five. At that point, still counting as among the relatively "young," they are to embark on fifteen years of "ruling" (*archein*):

> And after that [the five years of study of dialectic, from ages thirty to thirty-five], they will be made by you [Glaucon][22] to descend again into the Cave, and be compelled to rule (*archein*) in affairs of war and in such offices as belong to youth (*hosai neōi archai*), in order that they not lag behind the others in experience. And after this they must be tested (*basanisteoi*) as to whether they remain stable when pulled in every direction or whether they move about. (7.539e3–540a2)

21. This is a number about which he seems relatively relaxed, proposing five years in response to Glaucon's query as to whether he intends six or four (7.539d8–e3).

22. Glaucon, in his role of one of the three joint legislators for the city "in speech," is apostrophized by Socrates as playing the role of compelling these philosophers to return to the Cave.

The reference to "youth" here is clearly relative: these women and men will be aged thirty-five to fifty, better described as middle-aged, although still youthful as compared with the senior guardians whose role is to rule over and test them. They are, however, no longer auxiliaries. Rather, they are candidate senior guardians, who are still in the position of being ruled themselves by those eldest guardians who are in the process of testing them. They are to gain experience as apprentice rulers while being safeguarded by being tested both to enter into this role and ultimately to be promoted to the highest rank. And what at the latter stage is to be tested? Their ability, during fifteen years of gaining experience within the city, to engage in "rule" (*archein*) over other people in the city, in commanding troops in war, and in engaging in the appropriate offices for people at their (relatively late) stage of youth to occupy.

How does *archein* function in the above quotation describing the roles of this middle-aged cohort of rulers?[23] *Archein* in regard to "matters of war" may reasonably be translated as having the specific sense of military command. *Archein* with regard to matters that are such as pertain to "offices (*archai*) which befit young people" clearly signals (if in a more complex way than was typical) the *archein . . . archas* construction signifying "rule" in a more limited sense—that is, rule in the sense of "hold offices."[24]

To be sure, military commands were themselves paradigmatic examples of offices in many Greek constitutions, including that of democratic Athens (in both the fifth and fourth centuries). Because *te . . . kai* always conjoins two distinct entities rather than redescribing the same one in epexegetic terms (which a *kai* alone can do), one could read the second clause as adding additional kinds of offices to the military ones in identifying all of those that are suitable for young people; that would help make sense of what is otherwise a rather awkward conjunction of military affairs and political offices. Even if one does not read the first clause in the sense of making reference to "offices," however, their presence in the second is unambiguous: the plural of the noun

23. *Archein* here takes a demonstrative pronoun in the accusative (*ta*, accented) as its direct object. Levin ("APXΩ and APXH," 75) notes that "ἄρχω does not normally take an object in the accusative," but points out several exceptions; e.g., in Herodotus (1.120.5, 6.67.1–2; cf. 3.80.6). In the present *Republic* passage, the direct object is cashed out through a *te . . . kai* construction in which each clause has a different grammatical structure: the first (*te*) clause describes matters in regard to which the ruling is done, using the preposition *peri*; the second (*kai*) clause fills out the previous demonstrative pronoun with mention of *archai*.

24. As Levin ("APXΩ and APXH") notes: "ἀρχὴν (or ἀρχὰς) ἄρχω [*archēn* (or *archas*) *archō*] means 'to hold office(s)' and is not applied to monarchs or commanders but only to civil magistrates. Accordingly we often meet it in Attic . . ." (76); "When ἄρχω [*archō*] does not govern the genitive, it may signify 'rule' in a more limited sense—that is, 'hold office.' It can take various complements" (100).

archē almost always signifies "offices," and the context supports its doing so here. Moreover, the context of gaining political and military experience naturally supports the same translation: in a Greek city, one would typically have gained such experience precisely through the holding of offices. Thus, this cohort of philosophers comprises guardians engaged in "rule" over others in the city and its military affairs, and engaged in holding "offices," even while (and although) they themselves are still subject to rule by their seniors.

So far in this chapter I have identified two passages making clear that there are to be "offices" in the constitution of a *kallipolis*, when interpreted in the context of the existing affordances of the *archein* and *archē* vocabulary: the brief book 5 passage referring to the *archai* supervising early childhood education, and the book 7 passage about the role of the cohort of guardians aged thirty-five to fifty just discussed. Book 7 also features a third passage that I believe should be read as making reference to the "offices" to be held by some of the rulers in a *kallipolis* (as distinct from a final book 7 passage that uses a similar expression (*tōn megistōn*, "the greatest") but which, as I argue in the next section, is best construed as not making any reference to offices). The third passage that does (in my view) make reference to "offices" comes at a peak moment in book 7, where Socrates refers back to an earlier stage of the philosophical education of the progressive cohorts of guardians.

In this passage, Socrates highlights the need for calculation (*logistikē*) and arithmetic to be made compulsory for a "guard" (*phulax*) who must be "both a warrior and a philosopher" (7.525b6–7).[25] He then specifies those for whom "it would be appropriate . . . to legislate this subject [sc. calculation and arithmetic]" thus: "For those who are going to share in the highest [object unspecified; I suggest supplying 'offices'] in the city" (*tous mellontas en tē polei tōn megistōn methexeien*) (7.525b9–c1). This sentence does not feature any variant of the vocabulary of *archein* or *archē*. However, it does make use of the verb *metechein*, which was part of established Attic idioms for "sharing in" various civic matters, including the constitution and the offices.[26] And so, through a metonymic chain, this reference to "share in" *tōn megistōn* is most naturally

---

25. This was a point made in book 2, at 375e8–10 and following, on the philosophical dogs, as well as more famously in book 5.

26. Blok, *Citizenship*; the idiom is discussed briefly in my "Popular Sovereignty." By itself, apart from verbs for "sharing" or "participating in," the phrase *tōn megistōn* could refer not to the highest offices but more generally to "the most important matters," as I argue below is the case in another book 7 passage. Plato in the *Republic* and elsewhere makes ample use of both affordances: the political sense is unambiguously used, with the verb *metechein*, of offices in the city at *Leg.* 9.856b6–7, for example; however, the alternative sense of "the most important matters," is used by Plato in loci including *Plt.* 305d3, *Grg.* 487b5, and, specifically with reference to justice and other goods, at *Resp.* 1.367c6 and *Leg.* 10.890b8.

read as "share in the greatest offices in the city," with "offices" being supplied from that metonymic reference.

What offices would these be? The context in which this claim is situated suggests that these are the *archai* suitable to those aged thirty-five to fifty, in which case those would be the highest offices qua offices (above which the roles of the eldest guardians, above the age of fifty, would be those of rulers who are not themselves officeholders). After all, the context of this passage conjoins the role of a guard who is both "a warrior and a philosopher," and it is only the cohort aged thirty-five to fifty who can be properly said to be both: these guardians have been trained in philosophy from the ages of thirty to thirty-five, and then from ages thirty-five to fifty are directed to return to the Cave (metaphorically) to rule in matters of war, and to hold the other offices such as are suitable to their (relative) youth. Conversely, as the next section of the chapter will show, descriptions of the ruling role of the eldest guardians make no clear linguistic reference to the holding of any offices.

At this point, two questions about this ascription of "offices" to the constitution of a *kallipolis* must be confronted. The first is the extent to which the parameters that mark them as offices reconfigure the family resemblances typical of such parameters in Greek constitutions at the time, and whether this reconfiguration allows them still to be justifiably counted "offices" in more than name alone. The second: how to assess the theoretical significance of their being described, precisely, as "offices." That is, granted that the vocabulary and syntax here must in the affordances of Attic Greek be translated as "offices," to what extent are these offices recognizable according to the family of parameters by which political offices were conventionally framed as such? And to the extent that these offices evince a significant reconfiguring of those parameters, what is the point that the dialogue should be taken to be making in so doing? Is Plato's point that this is what genuine offices must be, once their role in a constitutional *taxis* enabling the realization of a service conception of rule is properly understood?

To address the first question, recall again the list of the parameters of offices in Athens and (in some cases) other Greek constitutions of Plato's day, which was surveyed earlier in this study, as consisting (in brief) of performance audits (*euthunai*); limited powers of office; limits on eligibility to serve; and other potential mechanisms of monitoring and sanctioning performance. The *euthunai* as audit procedures, most strikingly, are missing from the account given of a *kallipolis*. However, I argued in the previous chapter that the guardians' dependence on wages functions (alongside certain legal prohibitions) to achieve a similar function to that of *euthunai* and other accountability procedures, of safeguarding the orienting of these rulers toward the good of the ruled. Other parameters are arguably met although also reconfigured to varying degrees. The very language of plural "offices," as used in

Resp. 7.539e and in several other passages discussed below, implies that each office will be accorded a set of discrete, and thereby limited, powers. Limits on eligibility to serve are imposed by age, including the fifteen-year period from ages thirty-five to fifty during which these apprentice rulers will be engaged in holding military commands and political offices, and more broadly by the extensive educational testing that serves in lieu of election and lottery as a method of selection.

Thus, even though little is said about the nature of the "offices" held by the thirty-five- to fifty-year-olds beyond the fact that they exist as a plural set of roles that this cohort must fill, the family of parameters that conventionally defined Greek offices do for the most part apply to them, though with more or less reconfiguration in each case of how the functions served by those parameters are to be met—and with the glaring absence of procedural *euthunai* carried out by the people whom the officeholders rule. Rolling up the various parameters into a central point: what distinguished Greek "offices" as a kind of rule was that the limits applied to them are enforceable by someone else. In democracies, this enforcement or control came from below, as it were, enforced by the people or some subset thereof. In a *kallipolis*, as outlined in the *Republic*, it will be enforced by control from above, by a senior group that is charged with carrying out the education, selection, testing, and supervision of its juniors. The senior guardians, who are the supreme rulers, have the role of educating and testing each cohort of younger guardians for promotion to the next rank.

The offices of a *kallipolis* have (being described as plural) discrete powers and are to be oriented to the good of the ruled, in accordance with the overall service conception of rule. They are safeguarded by legal provisions and also by the control over their holders (the role identification) exercised by their seniors and superiors. True, little is said to flesh out exactly how these offices are to work in practice or to name each of them in detail. But this in a way proves a larger point: that a Greek constitution would normally, indeed almost necessarily, be articulated at least in terms of its offices and its laws. That Plato indicates unambiguously, but without much detail, the existence of offices within the constitution of a *kallipolis* is a sign of the inescapability of offices as a political idea that he takes from the contemporary context. Yet he does not incorporate the same content of the parameters that conventionally shaped those offices. Nor does he limit his account of a constitution to offices and laws. Rather, in a *kallipolis*, the officeholders are to be inherently controlled, answerable not to those below, nor to their own peers, but to their seniors, who were themselves answerable to those who preceded them in the same role. No group is self-certifying or free from an ordering and limiting selection process. I turn now to flesh out the ruling (and safeguarding) role of those eldest guardians further.

Ruling as Reigning: The Role of
the Most Senior Guardians

A good place to begin is with the other book 7 passage featuring the phrase *tōn megistōn* (consideration of which was postponed earlier), in which the phrase appears again with an unspecified referent, but this time without the verb *metechein*. Here, my interpretation of the passage is that offices are not in question (contra those translators, including Grube/Reeve, who have jumped to the conclusion, based on *tōn megistōn* as a phrase, that they must be):

> Then, as for those children of yours whom you're rearing and educating in speech, if you ever reared them in actuality, I don't think that you'd allow them to be sovereign *archontas* of the most important [things, the content of which must be determined] in the city (*archontas en tē polei kurious tōn megistōn einai*) while they are as irrational as incommensurate lines. (7.534d3–6).[27]

As per the general rule of thumb introduced in part I, *archontas* as a participle of *archein* can be translated in different contexts either with the sense of "rulers" or with the sense of "officeholders." While *tōn megistōn* could sometimes be shorthand for an implied object so as to mean "the greatest offices" (as I argued was the case in the other book 7 passage referring to offices for some of the rulers), in the present context, neither the context (lacking any verb such as *metechein*, which features in that other passage) nor the grammar gives support for doing so.[28] I would argue therefore that in the present passage, *tōn megistōn* is more plausibly be taken to refer, not to the offices in particular, but to the most important matters in the city generally, which could in this context mean the education (in philosophy and in experience) and selection of those who are ultimately to rule.

On this reading, as the passage gives no signal that the sense of "officeholders" is intended, *archontas* is best translated here more generally as "rulers." And a further clue to the referent being not all the rulers (both apprentice and senior) but the eldest guardians alone, is found in their characterization here as *kurious* (plural of *kurios*). While there is debate about whether *kurios* should generally be translated as "sovereign" or as "authoritative" within a given

---

27. Grube/Reeve: "I don't think that you'd allow them to rule in your city or be responsible for the most important things." Their translation suggests an epexegetic *kai*, whereas in fact the participle *archontes* is in the accusative case, as is the adjective *kurious*, and both are dependent on the overall syntax "you wouldn't allow [*easais*, the finite verb] . . . to be (*einai*)."

28. The verb *archein* could be used with the plural of *archē* in the accusative (*archas*), but not typically with the genitive of that noun (though it was used with the genitive of other nouns, implying "absolute, unrestricted power"): Levin, "ΑΡΧΩ and ΑΡΧΗ," 98.

domain,[29] here it points to the eldest guardians, whom, as I have argued, are the "rulers" in the fullest sense of ruling over their juniors, while not being subject to rule by anyone else. Whereas the Athenian *dēmos* was, in later fourth-century accounts, *kurios* over its officeholders as well as serving as their paymasters (at least for those few offices that definitely received wages in the fourth century), the role of being *kurios* here is assigned to the philosophers, whereas the role of paymaster remains with the people (as argued in the previous chapter).[30]

In describing the rulers as being "sovereign" over *tōn megistōn* (which I have argued is in context to be interpreted as "the most important matters," book 7 adds a new dimension to the overall characterization of the task of ruling in a *kallipolis*, which in book 5 was described in the language of kingship—as were many of the earlier figurations of rule in Greek thought with which this study opened. Famously, in inviting a so-called "third wave" of criticism in elaborating such a constitution, Socrates identifies the following as the single smallest change that could allow a city as close to this one as "possible" to be founded "in deeds" (*toi ergōi*), meaning in actuality, as opposed to merely "in speech" (*logōi*) (5.473a5–6):

Unless philosophers (*hoi philosophoi*) come to reign (*basileusōsin*) in cities or those who are now called kings (*hoi basilées*) and political power-holders (*dunastai*)[31] come genuinely and adequately to philosophize, that is, until this falls together (*sumpesēi*)[32] into the same

29. In defense of translating *kurios* as "sovereign" in certain contexts, see my "Popular Sovereignty." Caveats are offered by Hoekstra in "Athenian Democracy" and a critique propounded by Cammack in "*Kratos*." While I agree that *kurios* does not always mean "sovereign," it is consistent with the arguments of Hoekstra and Cammack that it sometimes can, and I maintain that here it does. However, it does not necessarily signify sovereignty in the sense of kingly powers (one can be *kurios* within the *oikos*, for example).

30. This connection was pointed out to me by Jacob Abolafia in a virtual Stanford seminar on a precursor of chapter 6.

31. As explained by Jordović ("Did the Ancient Greeks Know"), *dunasteia* was a general way to describe certain kinds of conventional political power, including those of figures who had not come to power through hereditary channels. This language will recur in book 8 when Socrates points out that the four kinds of constitution that he is proposing to trace are not exhaustive of all political forms. So the figures who might come to engage in philosophical activity or form the kind of passion for philosophy that would presumably lead them to do the same need not be kings in the sense of holding a particular political status.

32. The infinitive of this verb is *sumpitnein*, a poetic form of *sumpiptein*; given the sense in LSJ (for *sumpitnō*) of "fall or dash together, of waves." While the verb can be used in the plural of multiple entities that fall in line together (as by Aeschylus, *Pers.* 432, of multiple waves, and in *Ch.* 299), it can also be used in the singular, as by Euripides, for everything (itself cast in the singular) falling in line (*Hec.* 846), or for a particular person falling in line with another (*Hec.* 966), or, in a dubious line of text, for one entity that fails to fall in line with another (*Hec.* 1029, with the latter entity in the dative). It is also used in an infinitive form in Pindar to describe falling in with another person in wrestling (*Isthmian*

identity (*eis tauton*)—namely,[33] political *dunamis* and philosophy—
while the many, who belong to those who by nature now go along without one or the other, are kept out by force of necessity, there will be no
end to evils in cities, Glaucon, nor it seems to me for the human race.
And, until this, the constitution (*politeia*) which we have been recounting "in speech" (*logōi*) will never first grow up to the extent possible or
see the light of the sun. (5.473c11–e2)

What precisely is being said here about the envisioned conjoining of politics
and philosophy? Political *dunamis* is often read as referring solely to a position of political power (*dunamis* meaning a power or capacity). But *dunamis* can also denote any kind of power or capacity to act, including the
power associated with a particular kind of expertise; the latter a point that
Socrates will make within *Republic* 5 a few Stephanus pages later. Concern
with the *dunamis* of various kinds of expertise, including, centrally, political
expertise, is likewise an organizing feature of the *Statesman* (as discussed in
chapter 4).[34]

Recognition of the relevance of epistemic as well as political power to the
role of ruling is essential to making sense of what Socrates calls in book 5
the "third wave" (the greatest of three waves of expected ridicule for claims put
forward in that book), which refers to the claim that either kings must philosophize or philosophers must reign. In the formulation of that claim, political
dunamis refers in the first instance to the actual holding of political power—
such that by either means, political power and philosophy come to coincide
in a single person. Yet, the power that a person in such a role would have to
exercise must include connecting *philosophia* to the role of ruling or, in other
words, developing an epistemic outlook that is oriented toward and applicable
to political ruling. So while the *Republic* does not name a political art or expertise as a distinct domain of knowledge, the argument here does require that

---

Odes 4.51), a sport used as a metaphor at other important points in Plato's *Republic* (e.g.,
when Glaucon asks Socrates to, "like a wrestler, give me the same hold again" (8.544b4),
meaning the same hold as at the turning point between books 4 and 5, when Socrates had
been about to explain the four flawed constitutions and individuals, a project not resumed
until this moment in book 8).

33. I insert "namely" (which does not correspond to a particular word in the Greek) to
explicate the logic of the clauses. Adam and Rees (*Republic of Plato*, ad loc.) suggest that
the phrase *dunamis . . . philosophia* should be taken to be "in explanatory apposition to the
whole phrase" preceding it (*touto . . . xumpesei*).

34. As noted in chapter 4 (in an excursus while discussing the *Statesman*), Socrates in
Republic 5 analyzes a "power (*dunamis*)" in terms of "that over which (*epi*) it is [set] and
what it effects (*apergazetai*)" (5.477d2). In fact, that explanation is launched in order to
identify the philosophers, a task that is essential to defending the "third wave" claim itself.
It does so by characterizing them as holding fast to the project of knowing (illustrated by
knowing the beautiful itself), as opposed to the project of opining, which is unable to grasp
the beautiful itself and which characterizes the lovers of sights and sounds (5.476a10–d6).

philosophia be deployed by the person who is engaged in the task of political ruling. Or, to put it another way: like any power, political power (*dunamis*) will succeed only where it is knowledgeably directed to attain its end.

Thus, political power, which must be guided appropriately epistemically, and philosophy must be conjoined together. Conjoined not abstractly, but *eis tauton*. Within its immediate context and the following clause, *eis tauton* refers to a coincidence (Adam uses the words "coalition" and "coalescence" to gloss this) of political power and philosophy. But this conjunction belongs to an overall "until" construction (launched at the beginning of Socrates's speech) setting a condition about persons: either persons who are already philosophers must enter into positions of political power, or persons who are already in positions of political power must embark upon philosophizing. Given that the "until" sentence opens by discussing persons—their roles and activities—it makes sense to take the next part of the sentence (linked by a *kai*), which describes the coincidence of political power and philosophy, as being brought about by and through one of those two routes regarding the roles and activities of persons.

On this interpretation, then, while *eis tauton* immediately refers to the coincidence of political power and philosophy, the way in which this coincidence will be brought about is through a coincidence of a person, an activity, and a role: a person who is a philosopher (an identity that requires the doing of philosophy) who is also in a role of political power. And as books 5–7 unfold, it is almost exclusively one of the two possible routes to this coincidence that is emphasized: namely, that a person who is a philosopher, engaged in doing philosophy, should come into a role of political power.

Not just any role of political power will do, however. Rather, this role is described in the "third wave" passage as the role of "reigning" (using the verb *basileuein*). This is the first use of this verb within the dialogue, and it is a new way of describing the role of those in the constitutional project who had so far, in books 3–5, been described as engaged in "ruling" (*archein*), a role assigned to the most senior of the guardians, who are collectively also engaged in "guarding" (*phulattein/phulassein*). The verb *basileuein* will be used five more times in the course of the dialogue, three of these instances being especially significant.[35] Its centrality to the dialogue has been little discussed, despite its thematically significant invocation of kingship, and the fact that it contrasts with a way of considering kingly reign within a democracy that would be described by the orator Aeschines some years after Plato's death as follows: that "in a city living democratically, the private citizen reigns as a king (*basileuein*) by

---

35. The other two uses of the verb within the *Republic* are at 7.509d2, in describing the intelligible realm in the context of the analogy of the Line; and 10.607a6, describing the danger to the city of admitting the Muses and so allowing pleasure and pain to reign in the city in place of law or reason. Both of these contexts would repay further study.

means of the law and his vote."³⁶ The Platonic appropriation of the language of reigning within the *Republic* remains to be explored.

Twice in book 9, Socrates uses the verb *basileuein* in summing up a contrast between the characteristic quality, and the resulting happiness, of a city in which (implicitly, from the word "reign") kings reign, on the one hand, and one in which a tyrant is in power, on the other (9.576d3, 576e4).³⁷ The use of "reign" (*basileuein*) in the conclusion of the overall arc of argument from book 2 onward, about the happiness of these respective cities, and then about the happiness of the corresponding individuals—described a little later in book 9 as the individual who is "most kingly (*basilikōtaton*) and reigns (*basileuonta*) over himself," as opposed to the person who is "most tyrannical over himself and over the city" (9.580b9-c5)—highlights its significance in capturing the distinctive nature of rule in the best (and most just) city and analogously within the soul and life of the best (and most just) person.

Despite highlighting the significance of "reigning" by using the verb in these pivotal passages—in the "third wave" of book 5 to introduce the special character of the rule of philosophers, and in the culmination of the judgment in book 9 about the relative happiness of a *kallipolis* and a tyranny and of the corresponding types of individuals—Plato does little explicitly to define it or to relate it to the role of ruling (*archein*) or of officeholding as a kind of rule. In this section, I seek to flesh out the role of "reigning" by taking it to be reserved for the role of the most senior guardians, above whom there is no further group charged with selecting, testing, or supervising them apart from their predecessors in the same role. These eldest guardians who reign are those who can most precisely be described as kings. While they can also be described as rulers, they share the latter role with the immediately junior cohort, whom I called above the apprentice rulers: those who rule over others in the city through command of military affairs and through holding distinct offices (as shown above, described precisely as such).

Thus reigning turns out to be a subset of a broader category of ruling. Reigning is a kind of ruling, just as officeholding is another kind of ruling. The apprentice rulers rule over others in the city as officeholders and are also philosophers still in training (they have not yet come to know the Good). By contrast, the kings and queens, who are philosophers in the fullest sense of knowing the Good, reign over the whole city and, in particular, reign (their distinctive kind of ruling) over all the cohorts of guardians who are junior to

---

36. Aeschin., 3.233, my translation; a remark called to my attention by Landauer ("*Idiōtēs* and the Tyrant," 156).

37. I translate *aretē* at 9.576d3 as "quality" rather than (as elsewhere) "virtue," as it applies in the former context both to a tyranny and to a city in which kings (previously described as philosophers) reign.

themselves. This role of reigning revolves centrally around the supervision of education of the junior cohorts, as has been described already above.

The next passage that bears out the role of the eldest guardians in ruling as reigning is a reprise in book 6 of the "third wave" passage in book 5 that was considered above. In the reprise, the conjoined epistemic orientation of philosophy and politics is highlighted as involving an orientation to caring for a city, just as it involves an orientation to the erotic pursuit of philosophy. The passage emphasizes not simply the possession of power but that such power be oriented to its proper *telos*:

> We were compelled by the truth to say that neither a city nor a constitution nor an individual man, similarly, will ever become perfect, until:
>
> [1] some necessity comes about due to chance to those few and not vicious philosophers (the ones who are now called useless) such that they (whether willingly or not) take caring charge (*epimelēthēnai*) of a city, and to the city such that it comes to obey them, or
>
> [2] until, from inspiration from some god, a genuine passion (*erōs*) for genuine philosophy [*philosophia*] falls upon (*empesēi*)[38] those who now are power-holders (*tōn nun en dunasteiais*) or kings (*basileiais*) or their sons. (6.499b2–c1)

No verb for "reigning" or "ruling" features in this reprise passage, unlike in the original statement of the "third wave." Instead, the description of the philosophers taking up political power (1) is cast in the language of caring (*epimeleisthai*), the same verb that furnishes one of the three strands of the *dunamis* of statecraft in the *Statesman*.[39] Here, I have translated the verb not just as "caring" but as "taking caring charge of," in order to capture the explicit reciprocal requirement that the city must obey them in this role.

The other route (2), that those now in power in some kind of role should come to philosophize, also calls out "kings" as at least one kind of existing role to which this could apply. As argued in part I, reference to "kings" in Plato can be reasonably expected to bring with it their function as orderers (notice,

38. Notice again the striking choice of a poetic verb: here it is *empitnein*, the poetic form of *empiptein*, which is closely semantically related to *sumpitnein* and plays the precise parallel role in the reprise as did the latter verb in the original third-wave passage. The primary sense in LSJ for *empitnō* is "fall upon," though without the poetic image of the waves captured by *sumpitnein*; rather, the poetic contexts in this case involve more literal and prosaic kinds of falling upon (a wrestler falling on his opponents in Pindar, *Pythian Odes* 8.81; a daimon falling upon a household in Aeschylus, *Agamemnon* 1468; Ajax falling murderously and simultaneously upon two sheep whom he mistakenly thinks to be two of the Greek commanders in Sophocles, *Ajax* 58).

39. Lane, "Statecraft," as well as chapter 4 of this study.

for example, the role of the rulers as involved in the issuing of orders [*epitattein* or *epitassein*] and the auxiliaries in obeying them, at 5.458b9–c4), as well as their function as oriented to caring for the good of the ruled (building on, while refining, the Homeric trope of the king as shepherd of the people). Both of those functions are here condensed into the description of the philosophers in route 1 as "taking caring charge" of a city. Those philosophers who do so are the best candidates for counting as "kings": namely, those whom I have called the eldest guardians, whom Socrates calls in book 3 the "complete guardians" and the "rulers" in the narrow sense of the term—that is, those who have passed every educational, philosophical, and practical test imposed by their seniors and finally succeeded in grasping the Form of the Good. They take charge as natural persons who are fit for a role that is at once epitactic, epistemic, and oriented to caring for the good of those whom they are charged with ordering.

I have retraced (in reverse order) the significance of the philosophers "reigning" in book 5 and being "sovereign" over the most important matters in book 7. It is a few pages later in book 7 that the description of the education of the philosophers reaches the height that comes after they have seen "the Good itself," meaning, after the age of fifty, at which point those capable from the earlier cohort (of the apprentice rulers) are enabled to ascend to this final dialectical peak. Those who ascend to this point constitute the final and highest age cohort described. In the language of book 3 noted earlier, they are the "best" of the senior guardians, those who will "rule" (*archein*) over the junior guardians, who are in turn to be ruled by them.

Indeed, at this moment in book 7, Socrates adopts the language of taking "a turn" (*to meros*) in describing the role that these eldest guardians will fulfill within the city, within the overall context of the life they will lead. That life is a life of philosophizing: they are not only to be philosophers in a perfective state (that they have become philosophers) but in an active and ongoing state—they are "to spend most of their time with philosophy," pursuing it actively in the sense of busying themselves with it. Within that life, and so within the cohort of those pursuing that life along with them, their "turn" (*en merei . . . to meros*) will come for playing a role in the city's political life.[40] That role is as follows (numbering introduced to divide up Socrates's speech, in Greek part of a single long sentence, the beginning of which, from 7.540a4, is not quoted below):

> [1] Once they've seen the good itself, they must, using it as their model, set in order (*kosmein*) the city, its individual members, and themselves, for the remainder of their lives, doing so each in turn:

40. Hatzistavrou ("Happiness") emphasizes this turn taking as a solution to how it is that the philosophers will be happy (insofar as they spend enough time philosophizing) even while being necessitated to spend some of their time in ruling.

[2] for the most part, each will spend their time with philosophy, but, when their turn (*to meros*) comes, they must each labor and rule with regard to political affairs (*pros politikois epitalaipōrountas kai archontas*) for the sake of the city, not as if this were a fine thing to do, but rather doing it as something necessary.

[3] Then, having educated others like themselves to take their place as guardians of the city, they will depart for the isles of the blessed and dwell there. And, if the Pythia agrees, the people will make memorials and sacrifices in the city to them, as divine beings, but if not, then as happy and godlike ones. (7.540a4–c2)

The initial part quoted from the overall long Greek sentence, in point 1 above, is a description of the whole period of life remaining to those who have, after the age of fifty, ascended to this final educational and civic height. Notice that the overall task assigned to these people—who belong to the group of "rulers," and who have also been described as "reigning" (either being philosophers who will reign or kings who will philosophize)—is that of "setting in order" (*kosmein*). This resonates with the account of ruling as ordering that I have been developing as a Platonic one throughout this work, building as it did on previous Greek ideas of ruling as ordering (especially, of ordering as being part of the role of kings), as argued in part I.[41] In this light, again, it is only this supreme cohort that has the full role of "ruling": its members alone are able to set themselves in order, as well as to order others in the city and the city in general, the latter having been what the apprentice rulers were tasked with during their fifteen years of military command and political officeholding.

While the task of setting themselves in order is one that they could presumably do continuously for the remainder of their lives, the task of setting in order the city and its individual members is one that (as I construe the sentence) they take "each in turn" in the course of the remainder of their lives (since this is a cohort out of which they do not age but pass out of only by death, as point 3 in the sentence quoted makes clear). Rotation according to one's turn (*to meros*) was a standard feature of Greek officeholding, as Aristotle would make proverbial. The purpose of rotation in existing Greek constitutions was to control and limit any appetite to abuse or exploit power. Indeed, the oldest epigraphical evidence of Greek law is a law from Dreros prescribing punishment for any *kosmos* (an officeholder) who should seek to serve beyond their allotted term, as noted in chapter 2. In the case of the eldest philosophers who play the role of maximally senior rulers, by contrast, rotation by *meros* is to serve an inverse function: to necessitate their exercising political power for a prescribed rotation, rather than to prevent them from exceeding that

---

41. For an overview, see Atack's *Discourse of Kingship*.

rotation.[42] Nevertheless, the result is the same insofar as the role of actually exercising rule will be a time-limited one, rotated among those eligible to hold it. This imposes a limit on the *taxis* of rule, even if its motivation is to enforce a turn in ruling rather than to restrict incumbents to just their allotted turn.

What is it precisely that they take "each in turn"? It is specified in point 2 within the Greek sentence as a whole:

> For the most part, each will spend their time with philosophy, but, when their turn (*to meros*) comes, they must each labor and rule with regard to political affairs (*pros politikois epitalaipōrountas kai archontas*) for the sake of the city, not as if this were a fine thing to do, but rather doing it as something necessary.

I translate the *kai* conjoining reference to "labor" and "rule" as epexegetic, meaning that "rule" is explicative of what it is to "labor" with regard to political affairs. It is "labor" not only in the sense that it is objectively hard and time-consuming work but also because it is to be regarded as "necessary," rather than as something one pursues in order to achieve some prized excellence ("as if this were a fine thing to do"). The verb for "labor" resonates with the book 1 insistence on a wage that is a penalty, and also with the insistence of books 3–5 that the rulers should not only receive a wage (and need to do so in order to subsist) but think of themselves more broadly as dependent on those whom they rule for so receiving it, as argued in the preceding chapters 5 and 6 of this study.

While all these associations of "labor" are relevant, the most informative and important word in the sentence, for present purposes, is "rule" (the verb *archein*, conjugated as the participle *archontas*). These are, after all, the rulers par excellence in the city: they are the only group that will rule without being ruled by anyone else. Their rule is a form of labor, and it is to be done with regard to political affairs. It is not described in the idiom of office, yet it incorporates limits, some of which (such as turn taking or rotation; age minimum; testing and selection, though not by election or lot; wages) are straightforward versions of the parameters that typically or sometimes structured offices; others of which (such as the lifetime tenure once selected) bespeak institutions that were not technically offices but which played a safeguarding role above them, as did the Athenian Areopagus. The rule of the philosophers reigning as kings (or kings reigning who are also philosophers) is not an untrammeled or undefined role. It is limited and constitutional, even though not accountable through the same procedures that officeholding rule in Greek constitutions would conventionally involve.

Besides safeguarding the officeholders and so the constitution, through education, selection, and supervision of their juniors, Plato offers indications of three additional functions that the eldest rulers may play. In order of

---

42. Josiah Ober helped me in discussion of a previous draft of part of this study to see this contrast, though we may not fully agree on its significance.

explicit clarity in the text, these are lawgiving, deliberation, and judging. For lawgiving: there is one clear reference in regard to the philosophers' imagined willingness to take over a city, in regard to their putative refusal to take on tasks that include (inter alia) "to write laws" (6.501a6) except on certain conditions. For deliberation: a deliberative function is mentioned in book 4, at a point at which Socrates is concerned to prohibit exchanges of "tools and honors (*ta . . . organa . . . kai tas timas*)" (4.434b3–4) among the different occupational groups of the city. He is particularly concerned about one kind of exchange, which would "bring the city to ruin," in a case in which:

> someone who is by nature a craftsman or some other kind of money-maker . . . attempts to enter the class of soldiers, or one of the unworthy soldiers tries to enter the deliberative and guarding class (*to tou boul-eutikou kai phulakos*), and these exchange their tools and honors (*tas timas*), or when the same person tries to do all these things at once. (4.434a9–b6, trans. Grube/Reeve, modified)[43]

Especially interesting here is the contrast between the "deliberative and guarding class" and the class of the soldiers, meaning that the former must be the "complete guardians," who serve as rulers over the soldiers, who are auxiliaries. While much has been said to this point in the dialogue about the function of guarding, nothing has been said about the "deliberative" function—a term closely associated with the institution of a *boulē*—which is here conjoined with it. This function is not further allocated in books 5–7 between the most senior rulers and the middle-aged apprentice rulers who hold the offices under them. But if the eldest rulers are to exercise safeguarding functions that parallel in certain respects (as already shown) the Athenian Areopagus, this would be grounds for allocating the deliberative function of a council to them as well. (Doing so would have the interesting implication that the plurality of the senior rulers would matter, insofar as conciliar deliberation was standardly conducted among a plurality, if one can take that feature to carry over.)

Finally, for judging: book 4 also makes mention of a role of judging, one that Socrates links to the role of those engaged in ruling (at that point in the text, the only distinction having been drawn within the group of rulers being between rulers proper, or "complete guardians," and auxiliaries). He does so by posing a rhetorical question to Glaucon as to whether, as a cofounding legislator for the city "in speech," he will "order" (*prostaxeis*) the rulers (*tois archousin*) to "judge the legal cases" (*tas dikas . . . dikazein*) (4.433e1–2). Glaucon's assent assigns the role of judging to at least some group of the "rulers" as part of their role of ruling. But what exactly does this mean?

---

43. Grube/Reeve translate "judges and guardians," despite the fact that the term used is clearly relevant in institutional terms to a council (that said, one of the key functions of the Areopagus Council was to serve as a homicide court).

The role of judging was well established in Greek constitutions in various ways. In democratic Athens, for example, every officeholder was assigned the role of presiding over certain kinds of cases in court, though in most cases the actual verdict would be reached by a popular jury. To be sure, the jurors in those popular law courts were not holders of offices in the technical sense defined in part I. But Aristotle would in *Politics* 3 treat them as quasi-officeholders, since they exercise significant civic powers. And in Plato's *Republic*, the role of a juror is elsewhere said to require not only virtue but also an epistemic expertise.[44] For the noun for juror in Athens (which could also in other contexts mean any kind of judge), *dikastēs*, had been used by Socrates in book 3, in advancing the claim that the city they are founding would need both doctors and *dikastai* (plural), along with the corresponding forms of professional expertise.[45]

The identification of an epistemic expertise corresponding to the role of a judge suggests that those playing this role would need to have pursued fairly advanced studies. Moreover, Socrates had earlier, in book 3, discussed the qualities of good doctors and good judges, arguing there that "a good judge must be not young but old" (3.409b4–5). The age associated with someone who is a *gerōn* ("old person") would most likely be fifty and above—that is, the age of the eldest rulers in the context of books 5–7 rather than the thirty-five to fifty years of the cohort of officeholders described there. If so, the senior philosophers would also play the role of judging what lawsuits did arise, most likely to be among the ordinary citizens.[46]

Insofar as the "kings" of a *kallipolis* do not hold specific offices while in the ranks of the eldest guardians, their reigning clearly involves them in the supervision of education and selection of their juniors to play other roles within the

44. The virtue of a juror is also identified by the Platonic Socrates in Plato's *Apology* as one to which the jurors trying him should aspire, and as one ideally cultivated and reinforced by the swearing of the juror's oath. In chapter 4, I noted the expertise characterizing the role of a judge or juror in Plato's *Statesman*.

45. Note the resonance with the *Statesman*, in which judging was presented as corresponding to a specific kind of expertise as well; here, likewise, Socrates uses a term for jurisprudence, or *dikastikē*, 3.409e4–5.

46. Book 5 specifies that, in virtue of the laws depriving them of "the possession of money, children, and families" (5.464e1–2), "lawsuits and mutual accusations" will "pretty well disappear from among them, because they have everything in common except their own bodies" (5.464d6–e2), adding there that the absence of such lawsuits and accusations will enable them to live *astasiastois* (free from *stasis*). Socrates further asserts that "lawsuits (*dikai*) for acts of violence (*biaiōn*) or assault (*aikias*)" (both of these being established kinds of *dikai* in Athenian law) will not "justly occur among them" (5.464e4–6), since they'll be subject to what is revealed to be not only moral suasion but in fact a law, *ho nomos* (5.465a1), requiring them to vent and so resolve their anger in physical altercations with others of the same age (5.465a1–3). Hence the guardians and auxiliaries themselves will be pretty well (though the qualification implies not entirely) free from lawsuits, presumably meaning among themselves.

city and ultimately to replace themselves. They may do so while functioning as a kind of deliberative (and perhaps also judicial) council, engaging in deliberation so as to keep the city as a whole properly oriented toward the true *telos* of the good of the ruled, as part of their role of guarding as safeguarding. Even if this is too speculative a conclusion, the age progression of roles for the guardians—moving from auxiliary status to officeholding as a form of ruling for the apprentice rulers (aged thirty-five to fifty), to ruling as reigning among the over-fifty cohort who take turns in reigning—demonstrates a much more differentiated, nuanced, and even limited *taxis* of rule within the *Republic* than has normally been recognized. In particular, the senior guardians' role as safeguarding rulers has been imbued with versions of some of the limits characteristic of office, as a way of bringing out the fact that rule itself must be limited in some sense (must have a recognizable *taxis*) if it is to count as rule at all.

The role of the senior rulers, in the education, selection, and supervision of their juniors, is to safeguard those juniors with regard to their own orientation to the *telos* of rule—namely, the good of the ruled. Supervising the procreation and education of the young safeguards the roles of future rulers and officeholders, by ensuring that these roles will be filled only by natural persons who have the nature and education and disposition fitting them for those roles.[47] These senior guardians play the role of safeguarding rulers, safeguarding those occupying other roles in the city, including the penultimate age cohort, who occupy the political offices properly so called.

Conversely, roles cannot achieve their purpose if they are filled by candidates who are as natural persons unable or unwilling to carry out the *taxis* requisite to achieve their assigned *telos*. And in the case of the political roles of ruling and officeholding, these roles cannot achieve their purpose if they are held by persons who are incapable of steadily knowing and pursuing the good of the ruled, or who simply fail to care about doing so. The rulers must act as safeguarders to ensure that their own roles, and all the other roles within the city, are properly filled and exercised.

Yet the dialogue also emphasizes the role of philosophizing, among those natural persons with the nature, disposition, and upbringing to be capable of this epistemic pursuit, in providing another kind of safeguard. True philosophers will have no motivation to abuse their rule to enrich themselves rather than benefit the ruled, even while, in the roles of the rulers and officeholders of the dialogue, they will also be carefully deprived of ways and means to do so. Rather than rely on nature, education, or proceduralism alone, Plato knits them together in order to provide what the dialogue presents as the only adequate *taxis* for safeguarding the *telos* of rule.

47. Lane, "Virtue."

Conclusion

Can there be offices without the audit procedure of *euthunai* that most Greek constitutional regimes considered a distinctive parameter thereof? I have argued that in light of the full family of parameters that variously picked out Greek offices, Plato was able in the *Republic* to put forward a configuration of "offices," which are linguistically so termed, even without including the audit procedures of *euthunai*, which were often understood to be central to those parameters and to be key to making offices accountable and so (on the conventional understanding) as counting as offices at all. Instead, he develops a panoply of other limits on the powers of officeholders in the constitutional project of the dialogue, which contribute to the same function of orienting the officeholders toward the *telos* of the good of the ruled as did the conventional procedures of audit. The legal deprivation of property and kinship, along with the legal institution of wages for officeholders; the conservation of age-related eligibility and rotation; the limited, age-related powers; and the alternative educational method of selection and testing, supervised by senior rulers, all play a part as limits on these reconfigured offices. The result is a *politeia* featuring a *taxis* of offices that look in important respects very different from most Greek offices (even though the offices are described as such with conventionally recognizable syntax and vocabulary), but still identifiably share the functions that the standard limits on such offices served.

Moreover, for the senior rulers, the accountability for reason giving that is essential to their philosophizing (a pursuit in which they continue to engage for most of their time after age fifty, apart from when taking their turn in ruling) joins with the age-related selection and testing to which they themselves have been subjected by their predecessors to safeguard their orientation to the good of the ruled. The full *taxis* of rule in a *kallipolis* includes rulers who reign in order to safeguard their fellow "kings" and "queens," as well as to safeguard the apprentice rulers who hold offices under them. The whole group of rulers is subject to certain kinds of legal limits (including deprivation of wealth and payment of wages), as well as other kinds of supervision and control. The officeholders are controlled not by those over whom they rule but rather by those who test and select for fitness for office from above. The kingly rulers who reign are themselves controlled by the members of the earlier cohort in the same role, who test and select their successors' fitness for office from above.

Thus the *Republic*, no less than the *Laws*, shows Plato to be cognizant of the need for offices in a constitution; of the need to safeguard the orientation of officeholders toward the good of the ruled; and of the ways in which both rule and office need to be subject to limits (which in the case of the latter are externally controlled), including through the nature, disposition, and education of their holders, if the ultimate *telos* of the good of the ruled is to be politically ensured. That *telos* is one that the conventional *taxis* of Greek offices sought to achieve through accountability procedures and other limits making the officeholders subject to control by others (in democracies, by those whom they ruled).

Some individual or aspiring officeholders in those constitutions misunderstood the content of the *telos* of the good of the ruled (from Plato's perspective), taking it to be gratification of the citizens' appetites rather than cultivation of their virtue.[48] Other such aspirants to power, alongside some of those who offered to teach them the rhetorical tools to gain office (such as Callicles and Polus, respectively, in Plato's *Gorgias*), rejected the overall evaluative claim that rule should seek the good of the ruled, instead positing that it should be used to benefit the ruler. Against both directions of criticism, the *Republic*, from book 1 onward, recommits itself to the service conception of rule and the traditional (though not unchallenged) evaluative view of the *telos* of rule as the good of the ruled—even while offering a radically demanding account of what Goodness fundamentally is.

Plato's critique in the dialogue begins as an immanent one of the *telos* of office and rule, even though it leads to a kind of radical rejectionism of all but the truly understood *telos* (to use Michael Walzer's categories of social criticism, discussed in chapter 2). And that rival account of the true *telos* in turn generates an extensive reconfiguration of the *taxis* of both office and rule in order to realize that *telos* more robustly. Plato in the *Republic* is not oblivious to the harm that procedures and institutions can do if filled by the wrong people. By his lights, he is more attentive to that harm than were existing procedures and institutions of constitutional office, seeking to control it not only through education and selection but also through a complex distribution of roles in which each is subject to some kind of external control (albeit not that of the ruled themselves) in seeking to serve the good of the ruled.

One may close by asking: What kind of a *politeia* is the constitution of a *kallipolis* so described? At the end of book 4, Socrates says that the constitution described up to that point would be the same kind of constitution whether one or several figures should distinguish themselves among the rulers: it would have two different names, kingship in the former case and aristocracy in the latter (4.445d4–7). The point would have been provocative to Plato's contemporary readers, in challenging the way that existing discourses of constitutional classification treated names of constitutions as designating mutually exclusive kinds. Considered as kingship, the *Republic*'s constitution straddles the boundary between office and other kinds of rule, since kingship was typically hereditary and lifelong in ways that diverged from the usual parameters of office, yet was widely understood to be shaped by some kind of order that allowed it to create order in its turn. Considered as *aristokratia*, the

---

48. On the *Gorgias* as a form of "social criticism," I have learned much from Walling's "Power and Vulnerability."

constitution would have appeared distinctive, in that this was not an attested name of any actual Greek constitution (though it featured as a word in various debates), perhaps in part because it inverts the association of *kratos* otherwise mainly with democracy.

The two possible names indicated for the same constitution of a *kallipolis* indicate that this constitution is neither a typical -*archia* nor a democratic -*kratia*. It is not limited to offices, as was the identification of constitutions as -*archia* (who holds the offices: one, few, or many); nor is what makes it distinct the collective people's power to do things, but rather the hierarchical safeguarding. The mosaic of *archein* and *archē* here is too complex to fit into the existing constitutional classifications.[49] Conversely, Socrates's remark about constitutional names at the end of book 4 would in principle make the *Republic* and *Statesman* complementary on this point: in asserting that the plurality of rulers actually described in *Republic* 5–7 should not be taken to be essential to the nature of the constitution as such. Yet the plurality that I take to be necessary in the *Republic* for the military function that the guardians originally serve, as well as their procreative function, may also support an implicit collegiality that would allow both deliberation and mutual checking through judging. The plurality of rulers plays a function in the *taxis* of the constitution of a *kallipolis*, even though it is said to be officially a matter of indifference.

Whatever name is applied to the constitutional project of the dialogue, Plato in the *Republic* in no way seeks to abolish all limits on its rulers or to advance a project of untrammeled rule. Instead, he has Socrates work assiduously to institute limits of various kinds (including deprivation of any accumulation of wealth and dependence on wages, both limits that are said to be imposed by law) on the powers of its rulers. This includes those apprentice rulers who are to hold various offices: while those offices are not subject to the audit procedures (*euthunai*) that conventionally characterized Greek constitutional offices, other mechanisms within the dialogue can be understood as seeking to achieve the same function—namely, ensuring that the officeholders and other rulers aim at the *telos* of the good of the ruled. Even the reigning of philosopher-kings and philosopher-queens as rulers is shown to be subject to certain limits so as to be safeguarded in serving the ordering function of rule at all. What happens when all such constitutional safeguards are breached is the subject of part III.

---

49. I am grateful to Avshalom Schwartz for urging me to consider this issue, which builds on an important article by Josiah Ober ("Original Meaning of Democracy"). I have argued elsewhere ("Political Expertise," 78–79) that Plato makes a similarly iconoclastic gesture (with respect to Greek constitutional categorization) in the *Statesman*, by having the Eleatic Visitor claim that what is usually called "democracy (*dēmokratia*)" is actually and simply "the rule of the multitude (*hē tou plēthous archē*)" (*Plt.* 291d7–8), overriding the distinction between *kratos* and *archē* of the kind that Ober in "Original Meaning" argues underpinned Greek understandings of democracy.

PART III

Degenerations of Rule and Office

CHAPTER EIGHT

The Macro Narrative

FLAWED CONSTITUTIONS WITHIN
CITIES (*REPUBLIC*, BOOK 8)

The Macro and Micro Narratives of
Flawed Constitutional Orders

Before having fully outlined the constitution of a *kallipolis*, but having already hinted at the political and economic arrangements that would be laid out more fully in books 5–7, Socrates had in book 4 of Plato's *Republic* described the constitution of such a city as relatively sustainable: "if one time the constitution is set in motion well, it will go on as if growing in a circle" (4.424a5–6).[1] It is a *kallipolis* alone that harbors the potential for such relatively long-lasting sustainability, one that may be undone by material flaws but in which the educational, social, and political arrangements, as well as the values pursued and dispositions exhibited by the older generation at any given time, are suited to cultivate the same values and dispositions among the younger generation.[2]

Socrates had in book 4 glossed his circle-growing remark in precisely these terms:

> For appropriate nurture and education, being safeguarded, produce good natures, and again, appropriate natures, being in turn well educated,

---

1. See page 169, note 70, on my debts in regard to this passage. One might translate *hapax* here more colloquially as "as a one-off," rather than "one time." All quotations in this chapter are from Plato, *Republic*, according to the Slings OCT, and in my own translation, unless otherwise indicated; that said, in this chapter I make more use of published translations than in other chapters of this study, in part to maintain continuity with many of the translations used in my "How to Turn History."

2. This is an insight grasped by Lear ("Inside and Outside," 239)—namely, that all cities except the best one (a *kallipolis*) are unstable: "The point of Plato's argument is to show that there is only one relatively stable equilibrium point between inside and outside."

grow up even better than their predecessors, both in their offspring and in other respects, just like other animals. (4.424a6–10)

By contrast, any constitution in which the values and dispositions of (at least a key portion of) the older generation fail in practice to cultivate their reproduction among (at least a key portion of) those younger will be inherently liable to degeneration. Such a failure is likely to arise owing to contradictions in the social and political arrangements (the "constitution" in both the narrower political and broader way-of-life senses), which may both elicit and offer opportunities for actions and dispositions to act that are unsustainable in terms of the original aims of that constitution.[3]

Book 8 of the *Republic* embarks on a narrative of a sequence of constitutions that are flawed and unsustainable for precisely this reason. That is what I call the "macro narrative" of *Republic* 8: this book details a sequence of potential constitutional changes at the level of a city, starting with the constitution of a *kallipolis* (should one ever exist or have existed),[4] which changes

3. Frank ("Constitution," 55) points out that the "virtuous circle" point is made by Socrates also by comparison to animals, but that later in book 4 (at 430b) he distinguishes between the way in which animals form correct beliefs and the workings of both education and law. However, I take him in the "virtuous circle" passage to be referring only to the abstract possibility of self-sustaining development over time, rather than to its specific mechanisms. (Frank and I often disagree insofar as I take a given Platonic point to be making a pointed and limited abstraction from some case, whereas she takes all details of the same case to be apposite to the point being made. It is not clear how one should resolve such disagreements.) Similarly, she points out on the same page that the constitution of a *kallipolis* will eventually decline, but, as with a similar point in the *Laws* (see note 26 in chapter 10), I take the point to be that a *kallipolis* is relatively more stable because it ex hypothesi harbors no internal *stasis* but is eventually undone by the flaws in materiality and perception that in Plato's ontology are to be expected of embodied persons. Frank would likely reply that a *kallipolis* is in fact replete with internal *stasis*, as she argues earlier in the same paper, in that she sees uses of force as a sign of failure of persuasion, whereas I do not believe that Plato draws a sharp binary between them.

4. Here I correct one contention of my "How to Turn History" (82n5), from which the discussion of the constitutional macro narrative here is adapted with significant modifications (including translating some key passages afresh rather than, as there, relying on Grube/Reeve). The contention being corrected is the following:

> nowhere in that discussion of how and whether Callipolis could "come to be" is there any suggestion that it has ever historically existed in the past (consider for example [5.]473d6–e1, [7.]541a8–b1, and [8.]548c9–d4). Since Callipolis has never existed in the past or present, the implication is that its decline and the subsequent sequence of constitutional degeneration must be conceived as lying in the future.

In fact, the possibility that a *kallipolis* (as I transliterate in this book) had existed in the past, or is even now existing in the present, is left open at 6.499c7–d4, a point that I owe to Rachel Barney. Nevertheless, since Socrates's point in this passage is that if a *kallipolis* did or does exist, it is unknown to him, it follows that he cannot tell the narrative of decline as a historical narrative of some known past event (as is misleadingly suggested

successively into a timocracy, oligarchy, democracy, and tyranny.[5] That sequence is paired with what I call the "micro narrative," beginning in book 8 and concluding in book 9: this details a sequence of intergenerational changes of character between successive fathers and sons at the level of an individual person, starting with a father who is living roughly according to the political norms of a *kallipolis* but doing so amid a degenerating civic institutional culture, who begets a timocratic son; and continuing as this son becomes the father of an oligarchic son, who in turn becomes the father of a democratic son, who in turn eventually begets a tyrannical son.[6]

The ultimate purpose of both narratives is to enable Socrates to obtain Glaucon's and Adeimantus's agreement that a just life (which depends on a just soul) is valuable independently of the rewards that one living justly may or may not receive from gods or other humans.[7] Their agreement depends on their willingness to judge the maximally unjust life—which both they in book 2 and Thrasymachus in book 1 had identified as the life of the political tyrant—as maximally miserable as opposed to maximally happy and blessed.

---

by Adam's comments (*"Republic" of Plato*) on 8.545c5ff., that "Plato invites us to conceive of his perfect city as having already existed long ago," and that "Plato's Utopia appears as prehistoric Athens"); the use of aorists in narrating the degeneration sequence does not necessarily imply that it is set in the past. Thus Socrates in book 8 must still, for analytical purposes, "turn history into scenario," as I more broadly argued in my book chapter of that title. In fact, Socrates makes clear that there are other kinds of regimes and individuals as well, which are "somewhere intermediate between these four" (8.544c8–d3 more broadly).

5. These constitutional types are defined by reference to past and present existing exemplars and are identified as those for which names already exist (8.544c1–2). In some cases, established descriptive names of constitutional types are used ("oligarchy," "democracy," "tyranny," 8.544c3–6). The recognizably Cretan or Laconian constitution (so identified at 8.544c2–3), however, is given two possible generic names as a constitutional type, both of which may be Platonic coinages: "timocracy [*timokratia*]" or "timarchy [*timarchia*]" (8.545b7–8). The former is striking as it is modeled on *dēmokratia* (the only parallel formulation of a constitutional name in actual Attic Greek), which has been interpreted by Josiah Ober ("Original Meaning of Democracy") as having embodied a new kind of power (*kratos*), the power of the people to act collectively. On Ober's view, this contrasted with the traditional embodiment of political power through officeholding, expressed in the *archē* root (as in *oligarchia*) interpreted as "rule," which is constitutive of the other proposed name here, *timarchia*. As I argued at the end of chapter 7 (pp. 245–46) that he does in another context of the *Republic*, when proposing two alternative and very different names for the constitution being summed up at the end of book 4, and also in the *Statesman*, Plato is arguably (at *Resp.* 8.547b7–8) rejecting the whole tradition of constitutional differentiation that would put weight on these different roots, instead insisting that the Spartan constitution and regimes like it are not different in fundamental kind from the Athenian constitution and regimes like it, and vice versa.

6. Because each of these persons is explicitly gendered as male, I refer to them in gendered terms in what follows.

7. On the details of the book 2 "division of goods" on which Glaucon's original challenge to this point hinges, see Anderson's "Wages of Justice."

Thus, both narratives are needed to explain the condition and fate not only of a person with a tyrannical soul but also of a person with such a soul who lives out the life of a political tyrant. To do so, each narrative also generates explanatory accounts of what may be thought of as political science and political psychology, both of which are of interest for political theory in their own right.

The identification of five distinct kinds of both city and individual man was first adumbrated at the end of book 4 and the beginning of book 5, when Socrates had ventured the claim that "there are as many types of soul (*psuchēs tropoi*) as there are specific types of political constitution (*politeiōn tropoi*)"— namely, five in each case, of which four are distinctly flawed.[8] Following a "turning" in the argument[9]—in the course of which Socrates explains the "three waves" consisting respectively in the equality of female guardians, the communally organized procreation and absence of private property among the guardians, and the necessity for philosophers to reign as kings or kings to become philosophers (this last point in turn requiring an account of the nature of philosophers, what they must know and be able to do to be qualified to rule, and how they can be so educated)—Glaucon ultimately recapitulates that whole phase of the dialogue (books 5–7) as having offered a description of "a still finer city and man" than those that had been described by the end of book 4 (8.543d1–544a1, trans. Grube/Reeve).[10]

8. In fact, Socrates makes clear that there are other kinds of regimes and individuals as well, which are "somewhere betwixt and between these," the latter being those already identified (8.544d2). Of the five distinct kinds identified, he had already observed in book 5 that four are "bad and mistaken, their badness being of four kinds" (5.449a3–5, building on 4.445d2). The fifth and contrasting case in book 5 is the correct constitution, and the corresponding man, as adumbrated in books 2–4; later, a *kallipolis* and a philosopher will be introduced as still better kinds of city and individual respectively. Glaucon recalls this promised but interrupted book 4–book 5 discussion in book 8, saying, "I'd at least like to hear what four constitutions you meant" (8.544b8–9, trans. Grube/Reeve).

9. The purported source of the "Digression" label is a remark at the beginning of book 8 when Socrates asks Glaucon to recall "the point at which we took the turning (*exetrapometha*) that brought us here, so that we can go again on the same [sc. road, path, or similar, implied]" (8.543c4–6), using the verb *ektrepein* in its sense of "*to turn out of the course, turn aside*" (LSJ, *ektrepō*). However, this turning is better considered not as a digression but, rather, as a necessary part of the argument as a whole: one might imagine it as a longer route that covers the same distance from point A to point B as a shorter route, but which includes importantly different scenery along the way. I am indebted to discussion with André Laks in Princeton in 2019, who urged that one should not call books 5–7 the "Digression" on the ground that the detour is not a detour but is essential to deepen and so to be able to complete the original inquiry.

10. Also relevant to the evaluation of the relationship of the project of book 8 to the project of book 4, and to the overall arc of the inquiry, are the lines at 4.444e6–445c7, in which Socrates turns from summing up the virtues (and especially the justice) of the individual and the city to recall the original question posed by Glaucon's and Adeimantus's book 2 challenges as to whether it is "more profitable . . . to act justly . . . and be just . . . or to act unjustly and be unjust," setting aside effects of reputation and excluding ex hypothesi

In so doing, he integrates the whole of the argument so far, and anticipates similar integration of the micro narrative to come, into the overall inquiry that he and his brother had demanded of Socrates in book 2—namely, to determine "which man is best and which worst, and . . . whether the best is happiest and the worst most wretched or whether it's otherwise" (8.544a5–8, trans. Grube/Reeve). For the micro narrative will culminate in just such an explicit determination in book 9, in this way providing an answer to the interrelated challenges posed by Glaucon and Adeimantus in book 2. For its part, the macro narrative, standing apart from (though in parallel to) that overarching framework of the dialogue, serves to confirm that it is only the constitution of a *kallipolis* that counts sensu stricto as a genuine constitution at all. In this way, the macro narrative provides an answer to the challenge posed by Thrasymachus in book 1 (the sophist having taken all political constitutions to be exploitative of those ruled, as part of a claim that the most unjust life, the life of a tyrant, is also the happiest).[11]

The twinned narratives play three significant roles from the point of view of the present study, which I articulate in the terms of the *telos* (purpose) and *taxis* (order) of a given form of rule (this being the schema of rule introduced in chapter 2 and deployed throughout this study). First, the macro narrative demonstrates the ways in which constitutional orders of officeholding that lack safeguarding rulers can malfunction. Such malfunctioning is variously shown at work in the timocracy, oligarchy, and democracy depicted in book 8. For its part, the tyranny depicted there turns out not to be a proper officehold-ing order at all; it is, rather, a form of *anarchia*, an absence of any kind of rule (including office as a species or kind of rule). This term is initially introduced in the context of a democratic constitution, which turns out to harbor the potential for transformation into a tyranny within itself.

---

the prospect of punishment (4.444e6–445a4, trans. Grube/Reeve). Glaucon responds that "this inquiry looks ridiculous to me given the way the topic under discussion has already unfolded" (4.445a5–6), to which Socrates replies in a speech the translation of which has been disputed (4.445b5–7), regarding whether his response (which begins by affirming Glaucon's view that it is ridiculous) is meant to confirm that they have already proven this to be ridiculous or, alternatively, that they are now in a position to go on to do so. As Nicholas White ("Rulers' Choice," 35–39, a reference that I owe to Merrick Anderson) has argued, given the adversative phrase that Socrates uses (*all' homōs*), it is better to follow Burnet's punctuation in the original OCT and to construe the Greek (with Shorey) so as to yield something like this translation (my own): "but nevertheless, seeing that we have come here [to this point], we must not grow weary before we have seen with full clarity that these things are the case."

11. The overarching motivation for the accounts of the four flawed cities (*hēmartēmenas*, 8.544a1; *ta hamartēmata*, 8.544a4), and the four flawed individuals "who are similar to them" (8.544a4–5), is explicitly signaled as stretching back to Thrasymachus's challenge in book 1 as to whether the most unjust life or the most just life is the best life, and pre-paring the way for the final judgment (*krisis*) of this issue that will come in book 9 (here, 8.544a5–8, with mention of Thrasymachus at 8.545a4–b2, 9.590c7–d6).

Second, the micro narrative unpacks the ways in which rule in the soul of a given individual must exhibit a kind of order, and the various ways in which that order can be undermined. Such malfunctioning of rule is variously shown at work in the souls, or, more precisely, the embodied souls and the lives led, of the timocratic, oligarchic, and democratic men (all described in book 8). For his part, the tyrannical man described in book 9 turns out not to harbor any kind of ordered or (therefore) properly ruled soul at all: his soul is, rather, a manifestation of *anarchia*, an absence of rule. Third and finally, both narratives exhibit the ways in which the malfunctioning of rule results from distortions of both its *telos* and its *taxis*, and how they interact. I speak here of constitutions as the structures of cities and souls alike (though in the main part of this chapter, I shall generally reserve the term "constitution" for political formations).

However, while constitution can be deployed as a concept common to both city and soul, there are two significant discrepancies between the two. The first discrepancy is that there is within the soul no equivalent to the distinction that loomed large in my discussion of the constitution of a *kallipolis*: namely, the distinction between accountable officeholders as one kind of rulers and the role of rulers who carry out a safeguarding function for those officeholders. This is clearly a significant divergence, and because that distinction has been central to my overall argument, the reader may wonder what to make of it.[12]

The answer is that a higher-level parallel still obtains. *Taxis* within the soul is constituted by the relationship of rule between one part and other parts, and that relationship is characterized not only by which part rules but also by how it rules, which bears concomitantly on the interlocking phenomena of whether, why, and to what extent the other parts obey. In other words, while rule in a city can (but need not) be expressed through the procedures of accountable officeholding, rule in a soul exhibits order in a more generic sense, without precise parallels to the accountability mechanisms that are typical of political offices. The ordering required to bring about a given *telos* is at the psychological level achieved by the means that a soul part employs (and the kind of relationship that such means can constitute among the various parts) in maintaining its rule over the other parts, as will be illustrated in chapter 9.

The second discrepancy arises in regard to how the *telos* at each level— namely, the good pursued—is operationalized. The proper *telos* of rule of a city is the good of the whole city; to exclude exploitation, this is operationally cashed out in terms of the good of "the ruled" as opposed to the good of "the rulers."[13] The proper *telos* of the rule of a soul is the good of the whole soul; to

12. I am grateful to Alan Patten for pressing this objection to a presentation of part of an earlier draft of this work.

13. The overall good would involve a definite description covering the persons of the rulers, but not qua their role as such.

exclude misdirection, this is operationally cashed out in terms of the good of the properly ruling part—that is, the rational part. The discrepancy between the two levels is an index of the difference in Platonic thought between the political predicament and the personal one. While the challenge for most people's souls is to succeed in being ruled for the good of the rational part (which is able to grasp what is good for the soul as a whole), the challenge for most cities is to succeed in being ruled for the good of the ruled (as opposed to the temptation of the rulers to exploit their power for their own benefit).

Rule over others is the fundamental political predicament, one that Plato refuses to cloak in the language of self-rule when discussing interpersonal rule: in political rule, some persons are always ruling other persons, even if rotation means that their roles may sometimes be reversed. Yet if every individual could achieve proper self-rule, then the need for politics would disappear.[14] In contrast, there is no substitute, even theoretically, for self-rule within the embodied soul, except for the possibility that the very partitioning of the soul consequent upon embodiment could pass away. Politics can at best disappear in favor of personal self-rule; personal self-rule can at best disappear to the extent that the soul recovers its pure incomposite nature.

For all kinds of rule, because an appropriate *telos* can be fully achieved only through the appropriate *taxis*, then if the *telos* of a given form of rule is distorted, it follows that its *taxis* will have to be distorted to accomplish that flawed end. Conversely, if the *taxis* structuring either a *kallipolis* or the psyche of a just person unravels, in the sense that the ruling elements are no longer able or willing to use their roles effectively to aim at the appropriate *telos*, then it follows that the *telos* being pursued will have already become a distorted one. While the *telos* has analytical pride of place in these explanations, as befits a theory premised fundamentally on the nature of the Good, the two are likely in any given case to be degenerating in tandem and through interaction.

What underpins a valuable *taxis-telos* interaction is the presence of wisdom: the knowledge able to identify the proper (best) *telos* and so both to establish a proper (best) *taxis* and to operate through it in order to achieve that *telos*. It is wisdom, which grasps the true Good, that animates the safeguarding function of the reigning rulers (the philosopher-queens and philosopher-kings) within the constitution of a *kallipolis*. Likewise, it is wisdom, grasping the true Good, that animates the power of the properly ruling rational part within the constitution of a well-ordered soul.[15] Without wisdom, no *taxis* can achieve its true purpose. To be sure, the order expressed

14. See Lane, *"Antianarchia,"* 62–64, and chapter 11 below.

15. Mara (*Civic Conversations*, 63) observes that in Plato's *Protagoras* and *Charmides*, "rationality is eventually represented as a perfecting rather than strategic activity," and I think that the same is true of the *Republic* and the other two dialogues that are the focus of this study.

in any given *taxis* has itself some prima facie value, since without it no good purpose of any kind could be achieved. However, when such a *taxis* is misdirected to a flawed or false object instead of a genuinely good one, its prima facie value is undermined.

The points above will be deepened gradually over the course of this chapter and the next. One might think that books 8 and 9 of the *Republic* (and so chapters 8 and 9 of this study, which discuss those books) are redundant in terms of the explication of office and rule: that it should have sufficed for Socrates to point out at the end of book 7 of the *Republic* (and for me to have done so at the end of chapter 7 of this study), that both the *taxis* and the *telos* must in all constitutions other than a *kallipolis* be essentially flawed.[16] However, it is only by charting the interlocking permutations of flawed *taxis* and *telos* at both the macro (civic) and micro (individual) levels that one can ultimately appreciate the significance of a *taxis* that comes completely undone. This is the dissolution into anarchy (*anarchia*) that is exhibited by both the political tyranny and the tyrannical man, both lacking entirely in any meaningful order, and so unable to achieve the genuine Good for anyone, even, in the case of the tyrannical man, for himself.

Doing such charting means, at the macro level, showing how officeholders distort the proper purpose of rule when there are no safeguarding rulers to educate, orient, and test them. And at the micro level, it means showing how individuals distort the proper purpose of rule when they lack a proper education. Education on the basis of wisdom that understands what is truly good is the sine qua non without which the holders of accountable offices will undermine the values those procedures are intended to serve, and likewise without which individuals more generally will aim their lives at inherently flawed and self-undermining purposes. No form of constitutional ordering at either the civic or the individual level can be as stable as one aimed at the true Good.

I use the terminology of "macro" and "micro" narratives because it is misleading to refer to the two narratives as those of "city" on the one hand and "soul," or even "individual," on the other, as does most of the scholarly literature.[17] For the macro narrative, which focuses on the character of cities as given by their constitutions, cannot do without reference to some individual persons and the characters that they possess in virtue of their kinds of souls. Conversely, the micro narrative, which focuses on the character of individual persons as given by the order and motivations (the interlocking *taxis* and *telos*) of their souls, expressed in their embodied ways of life, cannot do without

16. I am grateful to Jill Frank for pressing me in discussion of an earlier version of this study to respond to this potential objection.

17. As do the titles of two influential works on this part of the *Republic*, Williams's "Analogy of City and Soul" and Ferrari's *City and Soul*.

reference to some particular civic order (or relative disorder) in which they find themselves situated. The "analogy" between city and soul, as the project set out by Socrates in book 2 (2.368d1–369a5) has conventionally come to be called, is involved in both the macro and micro narratives, but it is only one element of those narratives, both of which must feature complete individuals and their characteristic ways of life.

An alternative reading of books 8 and 9 as presenting what is merely an analogy between city and soul (exactly akin to the analogy of books 2–4) has been insisted upon by G.R.F. Ferrari, who has criticized those who have "refus[ed] to accept that the analogy is just an analogy"; for him, this means rejecting Jonathan Lear's alternative contention "that it [sc. the analogy] also links city and soul by causal relations."[18] Ferrari illustrates his view with the claims that "timocracy is like a timocratic man; it does not contain timocratic men, nor was it made by timocratic men," and, conversely, that "timocratic man is like a timocracy; he is not part of one, nor has he made one."[19] Ferrari

18. Ferrari, *City and Soul*, 55. This sequence of scholarly interventions began with Williams, in "Analogy of City and Soul" (201), asserting that Plato posited a relationship between a democratic city and a democratic man, in particular, which was logically flawed: "Plato seems disposed to confound two very different things: a state in which there are various characters among the people, and a state in which most of the people have a various character, that is to say, a very shifting and unsteady character." Rejecting Williams's charge of a misleading conflation between the (democratic) city and (democratic) man, Lear ("Inside and Outside," 230, 234–35, and passim) proposed a different way of understanding the city-soul analogy both in earlier books (2–4) and in books 8 and 9 as involving two reciprocal dynamics. On the one hand, "internalization," whereby the people, and especially the youth, of a city are shaped psychologically by the dominant culture and values in the city in which they grow up; on the other, "externalization," whereby the dominant group, especially of adults, in a given constitution shape the culture of that regime in their own psychological and normative image. While I accept some of Ferrari's specific criticisms of Lear (though not others, as noted in the main text above), Lear's mechanisms of externalization and internalization can be rehabilitated. Externalization works when one identifies offices and officeholders, and the attitudes of and toward them, as its defining moments, such that new values are externalized into a constitutional regime of office and attitudes of and toward the officeholders, which then itself has further causal efficacy. Internalization works when one recognizes (in the spirit of Lear's overall account) that the new values internalized through a process of (mis)education are median points forged by triangulation between old inherited familial values and new forms of social and ideological pressure. Thus, Lear remains correct that instabilities in each city, in particular in regard to its attitudes to and practices of officeholding, generate the unstable social psychology that gives rise to the next city. (A different rebuttal of Williams, targeted to his analysis of the democratic constitution and democratic souls or characters, is offered by Schofield [*Plato*, 114–17]).

19. Ferrari, *City and Soul*, 65–66. He adds that the timocratic man has the "character of that regime," not "the character of the rulers of that regime" (70, citing [8.]549a). He notes further (86) that the analogy generates linguistic metaphors in one direction only: political

is correct that, at each stage, a given political constitution need not, and in each stage of the macro narrative is not, wholly populated by individuals of the corresponding type. Indeed, even in its genesis, a constitution need not be brought about by individuals of the fully fledged corresponding type: such individuals may come into being (at least in more than a handful of cases) only within the corresponding constitution. Nevertheless, there will be some characteristic typology among at least some of the group of individuals who contribute to bringing a given constitution into being (yet who may, at the outset of the transition to that constitution, be a numerical minority in the population of citizens). Moreover, while Ferrari is right to point out that the timocratic man in the micro narrative (as I call it) is not shown to arise in or necessarily to inhabit a timocratic city, at other stages the two narratives do intersect in ways that challenge the force of his overall argument.

Most important in this regard is that the maximally unjust person turns out, on Socrates's account, to be not merely the representative tyrannical man (the man with a tyrannical nature) but such a man when living the life of a political tyrant, dominating a city, which is thereby ipso facto made into a tyranny. In the case of the political tyrant, the macro narrative must rely upon the micro one, as the latter furnishes the individual who is necessary to (though not exhaustive of) the causality of the former. For while Socrates stresses that it is a contingent matter whether any individual tyrannical man actually becomes a tyrant in a city, there can be no tyranny in a city without such an individual tyrannical man. A tyrannical man's characteristic way of life simply is the life of a political tyrant, and when such a person lives out such a life, he thereby makes his city into a tyranny (though this is to simplify the more complex causal story told in the text, in which the incipient tyrant's henchmen and bodyguards, as well as the early reactions of members of the populace, are also crucial). A tyrannical man (a person with a tyrannical nature) is depicted in Socrates's micro narrative (as I describe more fully in chapter 9) as born, not only to a democratic father, but also in a city in which the people with whom he associates cultivate both lawlessness and a frenzied erotic love in him. This creates a kind of anti-order within his soul, rooting out any beliefs or desires that contradict it, which is ultimately expressed in his way of life.

It is the whole way of life pursued by the maximally unjust person—whom Thrasymachus had from the outset identified with the tyrannical man, an identification that Socrates accepts and deploys for his own purposes—that causes his maximal unhappiness. In the macro narrative of the emergence of a tyranny (located in book 8), Socrates completes his account of the political tyrant as standing "in the city's chariot, having been perfectly realized as a tyrant rather

---

and constitutional language is used metaphorically to describe psychological formations (citadels, bodyguards, and so on), but psychological language is not used metaphorically to describe any particular political formation (no part of a city is ever described as "the rational part" (*to logistikon*), for example).

than a popular leader (*prostatou*)" (8.566d2–3), only to turn to a topic that he has not explicitly treated in any of the preceding stages of constitutional change: "the happiness of this man and of the city in which a mortal like him comes to be" (8.566d5–6, trans. Grube/Reeve), an (un)happiness that in the case of the political tyrant consists in killing the best of the citizens until "he is left with neither friend nor enemy of any worth" (8.567b6–8, trans. Grube/Reeve).

The same thematizing of the lack of friendship returns in the explicit consideration of the happiness of the tyrannical man, together with that of the tyrannical (or, rather, tyrannized) city, in the micro narrative of that individual's emergence, characteristic nature, and way of life (located in book 9): he is "most wretched" for a set of interlocking reasons, including the fact that such persons "live their whole life without any friends, always being a master to someone or a slave to someone else (*aei de tou despozontes ē douleuontes alloi*), a tyrannical nature always [being] without the taste of freedom or true friendship" (9.576a4–6, a passage that will be central to my thematic analysis of Platonic political thought in chapter 10). This unhappiness, consisting in significant part in an inability to enjoy friendship, is common to both the macro and micro narratives; it will flower in book 9 into the repeated overall judgment (presented in terms of three proofs) that the tyrant is the unhappiest of men, answering the challenges originally posed by Thrasymachus in book 1 and by Glaucon and Adeimantus in book 2.[20]

Thus, any analysis of the relationship between macro and micro narratives that claims them to be confined to "separate tracks," as does that offered by G.R.F. Ferrari, should be suspect—notwithstanding the parallel narratological strands in the text to which Ferrari has rightly drawn attention.[21] In fact, Ferrari in his original argument conceded that the tyrannical man plays a causal role in changing the constitution of the city so as to bring into being a constitution that is similar in type to himself.[22] This concession, however, was already sufficient to overturn his "separate tracks" metaphor. Were railroad tracks ever to cross, it would result in catastrophe, yet on Ferrari's own

20. Already in book 8, in taking up the macro-narrative case of democracy, Socrates connects consideration of that case to the ultimate aim of the whole project of discussing the flawed kinds of constitutions and individuals; namely, "in order, furthermore, that knowing the character of such a man [sc. one similar to the democratic constitution], we can set him forth for judgment" (8.555b4–7)—that is, judgment as to his happiness and its ranking in relation to the happiness of the tyrant and the other individuals being considered.

21. Ferrari, *City and Soul*, 60.

22. He makes this concession in discussing Lear, whose analysis had described interlocking dynamics of what Lear called "internalization" (of civic forces into individuals' psyches) and "externalization" (of psychic forces out to the civic sphere). While rejecting Lear's proffered evidence for these phenomena as counting generally, and illicitly, as cases of what Ferrari rejects as track-crossing, Ferrari concedes that in one case—the case of the tyrant—a dynamic of externalization is indeed in play, as he observes in *City and Soul* (95): "both tyranny and the tyrannical man have a special bond of the phenomenon of externalization."

account, it is essential for the macro and micro narratives of the tyrant to intersect, such that the tyrannical man who will be the subject of the micro narrative is already a key causal agent in the macro narrative.

Moreover, I shall show (pace Ferrari) that it is not solely in the case of tyranny and the tyrant that substantive intersections between the two narratives are to be found. On the contrary: the two narratives had much earlier come to share a common and repeated term of analysis, when the imagery of drones was introduced in the macro narrative in describing the oligarchic constitution and then used in the micro narrative of the oligarchical representative man to describe his "dronish" appetites (8.552c2–4, 554b7). The same imagery returns again in both macro and micro narratives in describing the democratic city and the democratic man, and, again, the tyranny and the tyrannical man. In what may be called a realist key, Plato shows the cases of oligarchy, democracy, and tyranny—and the corresponding characters (all gendered male)—to be closely interwoven; by contrast, the timocracy and timocratic man stand somewhat apart, as did Sparta and Crete (the overt cases from which the timocratic constitution is drawn) from political developments in other parts of Greece.

What function is served, then, by the narratological doubling, given the not insignificant interplay between the two strands, and the fact that souls (of embodied individuals) and cities must necessarily affect one another? I suggest that the doubled literary narratives serve an epistemological function. Their pairing demonstrates that the relationship between individuals and the city in which they live can be analyzed at either of two levels. At one level is a political-theoretic analysis in which the principles of constitutional change hinge on the nature and quality of rule in the city, which in the case of the flawed regimes analyzed in book 8 is (at best) officeholding deprived of any safeguarding by rulers who are not officeholders. At the other level is an individual-theoretic analysis in which the principles of psychological development hinge on the nature and quality of rule in the soul.[23]

These two levels of analysis correspond to different epistemological disciplines, what one would today call political science (developed in the form of political theory) and social psychology (which is lived out in the interpersonal interactions that form part of an overall way of life). Just as both political science and social psychology can, indeed must, take account of both individual and social factors, yet operate at different levels of analysis and take different phenomena as their primary objects accordingly, so too do Socrates's twin narratives. Combined, the two narratives together would warrant description as a unified humanistic social science or social theory, bearing comparison to

---

23. Ferrari (*City and Soul*, 79) does acknowledge the moral and epistemological value of the doubled narratives (without conceding their intersection beyond the one case of the tyranny), writing that "the symmetrical correspondence of city and soul, soul and city, contains instruction on how to live in society."

the theories of social and political and intellectual change variously offered by Marx, Weber, and Nietzsche.[24] As would studies articulated in terms of political science and political psychology today, the macro and micro narratives are shaped by different sets of principles and exhibit different degrees of freedom. And as one would expect today of the different kinds of narratives offered by sociologists and by psychologists, both social and political conditions and individual characteristics play a role in both narratives, without the two kinds of narratives thereby being collapsible into one, but, conversely, without its being illicit to learn from one narrative in telling the other. Both narratives engage with the dynamics of office and rule—recalling that on the argument of the present work, office is a kind of rule but may coexist with another kind of rule that is not cabined by the procedures and institutions typical of officeholding.

The macro narrative is at each stage, from timocracy through democracy, a narrative of political office without any further kind of rule, in which officeholders who lack the supervision and education (that safeguarding rulers could, as in a *kallipolis*, have provided) to direct their *taxis*-constituted powers at the proper *telos*—the good (the true Good) of the ruled—instead use those powers to pursue flawed ends. When uninformed by wisdom as to the true nature of the Good, the institutional *taxis* of office in the *polis* fails to achieve a proper *telos*, and may ultimately become so wholly undone so as not to be able to achieve any kind of *telos* at all.

The micro narrative is a narrative of psychological rule without the rule of reason, in which whatever part comes to rule instead lacks the education to direct the *taxis* of the soul at the *telos* of what is truly good, and instead uses its powers to pursue flawed ends. When uninformed by wisdom as to the true nature of the Good, the ordered *taxis* of rule in the soul fails to achieve a

24. I was helped to see this by the generous response given to a precursor of this chapter by a great student of Thucydides, the late Geoffrey Hawthorn. Raymond Geuss ("Thucydides," 226–27) has suggested that the ancient historian was "specifically interested not in the *past*, but in understanding those forms of collective human behavior that are recurrent and thus comprehensible"—a form of inquiry perhaps better called in modern terms, Geuss suggests, not "history" but rather "social and political theory" or even, with caveats, "behavioral science" (227). But if so, Plato's project in *Republic* 8 is closer to this dimension of Thucydides than many have been willing to admit (including Geuss himself, at least insofar as he implies his agreement with what he reports of Nietzsche: "Thucydides," 223). In "How to Turn History" (83), I discussed this point by drawing a contrast between Thucydides's project, which confined its material to the study of happenings in the actual past, and what I called "Plato's willingness to consider instead a future (or at least a scenario whose temporal location is unknown) as the material for his political theorizing remains instructive." So put, the point holds, though see note 4 in this chapter, above, for acknowledgement that the Platonic text also canvasses the possibility that a *kallipolis* had existed in the past or was existing in an unknown foreign land in the "present" time in which Socrates is depicted as conversing with his interlocutors (itself narratively framed by Socrates in the first person as taking place in a past the date of which is not made precise in the dialogue [Nails, "*Republic* in Its Athenian Context"]).

proper *telos*, and may ultimately become so wholly undone so as not to be able to achieve any kind of *telos* at all. Both narratives detail the effects of lack of ruling knowledge of the true *telos* of the Good. In the case of the macro narrative, this takes the form of officeholders without any additional safeguarding rulers or other form of safeguarding; in the case of the micro narrative, it takes the form of a ruling part that lacks the safeguarding capacity of reason.

However, while the narratives are twinned and parallel, their analytical frames are distinct, and for complementary reasons. Books 2–4 had already begun to elaborate a theory of social psychology, developing technical distinctions between the *logistikon* (rational part), *thumoeidēs* (spirited part), and *epithumetikon* (appetitive part). So the micro narrative that begins in book 8 can proceed by further elaborating what is already a more developed account of psychological theory, rather than needing to introduce new general principles thereof. Socrates accordingly embarks on the micro narrative without setting out any overarching principles, instead appealing to and elaborating upon the tripartite theory of the soul as he goes along.

By contrast, the political science of books 2–4 had been drawn with a very light touch, identifying three groups and functions in relation to rule, and sketching a very general principle of constitutional composition (the case of what I call the Thracians principle, considered below), but no account of the dynamics of constitutional change. (The original introduction of the city-soul analogy had depicted the origin of a simple city and then simply stipulated its transformation into a luxurious city.) For this reason, the macro narrative of book 8 requires the introduction of principles to govern its comparative political science, or, one may say, political theory. This may be because organic constitutional change has not been a feature of Socrates's analysis at the civic level before book 8; while he had recounted an origin story of the emergence of the city of pigs, which lacked any form of rule, that city was simply stipulated to have become luxurious and the constitution of a *kallipolis* was built up in response to those conditions. Its form of rule was depicted as having no predecessor, no preexisting form of political rule from which it had emerged. By contrast, in embarking upon the political-theoretic macro narrative, Socrates begins by explicitly proposing two principles to govern its analysis, which are presented further below.

Introducing the Macro Narrative: Constitutional Orders at the Level of a City

The book 8 macro narrative at the level of the city follows on directly from book 7, and, likewise, from the topic of the previous chapter of this study (focused on a *kallipolis* as described in books 5–7, and, more broadly, rooted in the city founded "in speech" initially in books 2–4). In chapter 7, I argued that, in the constitution of a *kallipolis*, the middle-aged cohort of apprentice rulers will hold positions described as "offices" (despite the fact that the parameters of these offices are not all the same as most conventional ones), while the senior philosophers will "reign" as kings and queens. As rulers who are superordinate to the officeholders, the philosopher-kings and philosopher-queens exercise wisdom by playing their part in the overall order (*taxis*) of the constitution:[25] supervising the education and selection of those occupying the offices (and in prior and subsequent age ranks of the guardians); more generally, safeguarding the purpose (*telos*) that those officeholders and the constitution overall pursue. The *taxis* of offices and rule that is outlined in the text (though most often overlooked), delineated through the issuing of laws "in speech," is constitutive in enabling the *politeia* of a *kallipolis* to achieve its *telos*. This interlocking of office, rule, and law is characteristic of Greek approaches to constitutions generally, as has been shown in this work so far.

Thus, a reader of the *Republic* should by the end of book 7 be able to infer that office, as a (political) kind of rule, and rule more broadly must be exercised by means of the appropriate *taxis* in order to achieve their appropriate *telos*—namely, the good of the ruled. In the case of a constitutional *kallipolis*, both *taxis* and *telos* are overseen by rulers who are capable of safeguarding the officeholders, who are subordinate to them, and the constitution as a whole. However, as this chapter will show, the role of such complete rulers (as Socrates calls them at one point, as noted in chapter 6) disappears with the disintegration of a *kallipolis*. Without safeguarding rulers, the *taxis* of offices in other constitutions will be unable to achieve any proper *telos* even should its officeholders wish to do so—albeit that, deprived of the education that only such rulers could provide and ensure, they are doomed to lack any such wish.

Any reader of book 8 is liable to recognize two contradictory tendencies within it. On the one hand is the sense that there is something worse about each successive constitutional stage from the timocracy to the tyranny, or, at the very least, that tyranny is clearly depicted as the worst of all the flawed constitutions. On the other is treatment of no constitution other than that of a *kallipolis* as being a constitution at all—implying that all others are equally valueless, in being equally nonexistent as genuine constitutions. And this latter claim, made in earlier books of the dialogue and noted in earlier chapters of the present work, comports with the fact that the timocracy already abjures the fundamental *telos* of aiming at the good of the ruled. Its officeholders aim to exploit the ruled for their own benefit (as I document below), and so from this perspective are already devoid of the true *telos* of rule.[26]

These two aspects of the macro narrative of book 8 can best be reconciled by treating *taxis* itself as having two faces, one purely descriptive and one

25. On the role of wisdom in the *Republic*, I have learned much from Yau's "Wisdom."

26. After writing an initial version of this material, I was pleased to learn of (and be allowed to read) Piñeros Glasscock's "What Makes Degenerate Regimes," in which the kinds of flawed rule that Plato condemns are illuminatingly termed "selfish ruling"; that paper draws contrasts with a *kallipolis* and with the corresponding soul, but draws no connection between rule and office.

inherently evaluative. Considering the descriptive face of *taxis*, one finds it existent to some extent even in an order of officeholders lacking knowledge of the true *telos*. (Indeed, it appears that a *taxis* of office itself, insofar as it involves officeholders whose orders are generally or at least purportedly obeyed by those ruled, has some minimal evaluative worth, insofar as it embodies some degree of order, which is a structural feature of goodness.) Considering the evaluative face of *taxis*, however, a *taxis* not directed toward a proper *telos* (and thereby necessarily misdirected toward a *telos* that is bad) can be held to have forfeited its overall value. At different moments in book 8, Plato will emphasize one or the other of these dual perspectives on the character of each constitution (until reaching the tyranny, which lacks any *taxis* at all).

The Two Principles of the Macro Narrative: Predominance and Disunity

In embarking on the macro narrative, Socrates introduces two principles to govern its composition. The first principle is one that I construe as explaining the emergence of constitutions and call here the Predominance principle (or simply Predominance).[27] The second principle posits disunity among officeholders as a general principle about the degeneration of constitutions; I call it here the Disunity principle (or simply Disunity).[28] On my account herein, both are principles of dynamics.[29] Predominance explains the transformative

27. Williams, in "Analogy of City and Soul," had called this the "Preponderance Principle," and I followed him in my "How to Turn History." However, on reflection, I think that Ferrari's terminology better corresponds to the political framework of officeholding and the eligibility for office through which, as I argue (going well beyond his own account), the principle is in practice shown to operate. Ferrari himself is oddly resistant to what he calls the "predominance principle," despite its clearly showcased explanatory role in the text. This is largely due to his failure to recognize the crucial role of what I shall call "political predominance" (borrowing his word) in explaining the workings of Predominance. For example, one piece of evidence that he marshals against the principle is that back in book 4, when Socrates describes what makes a city disciplined or moderate (having the virtue of *sōphrosunē*), the account is a matter of relationships between groups in the city rather than a feature of individuals within it. As Ferrari writes, "There is no suggestion here [at 4.431e] that a city is self-disciplined only if its citizens are" (*City and Soul*, 48). But, in fact, the self-discipline of such a city does depend on its ruling officeholders being self-disciplined and being able to impart that virtue through their rule. Similarly, it is the character of constitutions that is the specifically political context to which the Predominance principle is confined and directed.

28. Again, I have changed my terminology here from previous work. In "How to Turn History," I called this the "Simple Principle of the Unity of Officeholders." I thank Rachel Barney for suggesting "Disunity" instead.

29. In earlier drafts of this chapter, presented in various fora in 2021, I termed Predominance a principle of "statics" and Disunity a principle of "dynamics." Because Predominance characterizes the developed state as it has come into existence, it can appear from a certain perspective to be a principle of statics, but this is an illusion: the developed

coming into being of a given constitution, while Disunity explains its transformative passing away. More succinctly: Predominance explains coming into
being, while Disunity explains passing away. Predominance appeals to the
characters of certain individuals in giving a causal explanation of the emergence and distinctive character of the constitution under which they live, while
Disunity appeals to the characters of those occupying the roles of officeholders (or in its first application, more broadly, rulers of another kind) in giving
a causal explanation of the breakdown of one constitution which prepares the
way for the emergence of another.

Predominance posits that the characters of certain individuals, who act in
a way that tips the scales (but may do so by acting each individually, with a composite effect), explain the character of their city. Disunity posits that the cause
of constitutional change is factionalized division arising among what should
be a structured and ordered group of officeholders, dividing them as to their
purposes and actions qua officeholders, as I shall show below. While only Disunity makes explicit reference to political office (referring to those who hold the
offices in a given constitution), my interpretation of Predominance as applied
within the macro narrative emphasizes that those who in practice tip the scales
in shaping the character of their city are those in office (or more broadly eligible
for office). Thus both principles as applied in the macro narrative center on the
role of political office. Disunity implies a prior unity among the officeholders of
a given constitution (itself shaped by Predominance), which at some point is
sundered, becoming the proximate cause of a constitutional change.

Before presenting these principles in detail, it is useful to recall an earlier
claim made by Socrates in book 4, which is a kind of precursor of Predominance
and often used to interpret the latter. The book 4 claim—call it the Thracians
claim—was in fact very weak (much weaker than it is often taken to be). It was
not a principle of dynamics but, rather, an explanatory though very general statement about the character of any constitution that has (somehow) been established: to wit, that the characters of (some unspecified number of) individuals
have something to do with explaining the character of a constitution.[30] Socrates
stated the Thracians claim with what has become a famous illustration:

> It would be ridiculous for anyone to think that the spirited part does
> not come to be in cities out of individuals (that is, those having this

---

state is explicable only as the product of a prior transformation, and it is this transformative process that Predominance explains.

30. In fact, the Thracians claim is made in the service of a converse and more significant theoretical move: in order to establish that individual souls must have "in each
of them the same kinds and characteristics as are in cities" (namely, the famous three so-
called parts of the tripartite psychology), since, he says, "there isn't any place else from which
they have come" (4.435e1–2). This makes it less surprising that the claim is so relatively unin-
formative in the explanation that it offers, since the ultimate explanation being generated
overall (for which it furnishes a single step) resides at the micro rather than the macro level.

same quality), such as the Thracians and the Scythians and pretty much all those who live to the north, or the love of learning, which anyone would most ascribe to our locale, or the love of money, which someone might say is found not least among the Phoenicians and those in Egypt. (4.435e2–436a3)[31]

Socrates had previously asserted that the souls of all embodied individuals must have all three parts, as do all cities (beyond the city of pigs); these tri-partition claims are staples of the psychological and political theories of the dialogue. So the Thracians claim cannot be asserting the existence of a spirited part in some cities but not others. Rather, it is asserting the characteristic strength and notability of a quality associated with a given part: spiritedness (if not necessarily the full-fledged virtue of courage), associated with the spir-ited part; love of learning (if not necessarily the full-fledged virtue of wisdom), associated with the rational part; and love of money, which is of course only one of the possible drives associated with the appetitive part (and an unusual, if important, one at that).[32] The point is that the characteristic strength and notability of such qualities among individuals, which contribute to the role of a given soul part in shaping that individual's life and actions, must in some sense feature in explaining the characteristics of a city.

The Thracians claim is actually extremely weak. For despite what the illustrations may seem to suggest, it need not imply that all individuals of a population must share in a given characteristic in order for that characteristic to be present in the city. Rather, the claim requires only that there is some causal relationship between the characteristic's existence among (some unspeci-fied number of) individuals and its presence in the city. (In other words, all that is ruled out is that the kinds of characteristics in question—and notice that they are limited to those typically associated with given soul parts—should be entirely emergent at the level of the city.)

Moreover, the Thracians claim offers a unidirectional explanation. Its explanation goes only from individual soul parts among individuals to cities, not the reverse; indeed, this order of explanation is actually invoked in order to establish a more significant theoretical claim about individual psychology. So, despite the self-reinforcing circularity between the good constitution and the individuals nurtured within it that he had stated shortly before in book 4, in the Thracians claim Socrates is merely asserting that the characteristics of (at least some) individuals, which might feature in a micro narrative, should feature in explaining the existence of corresponding characteristics in a given *polis*. While the Thracians claim is causally explanatory in this broad way and

31. Reading *to peri* at 4.436a1 with the main manuscripts.
32. The importance of love of money in the psychic and civic economies of the *Republic* has been stressed by Schofield in *Plato* (250–81) and Thakkar in *Plato as Critical Theorist* (274–327); see, more broadly, Seaford, *Money*.

to this limited extent, it is far from complete. It sets one parameter of any explanation of the character of a constitution at any given moment, but offers no further dynamics to explain how such a constitution came into being. For the dynamics of such a causal explanation, the reader must wait until book 8, in which Socrates puts forward the principles of Predominance and Disunity.

Near the start of book 8, in replying to Glaucon's question of which four political constitutions were the flawed (vicious) ones that Socrates had had in mind to explain at the end of book 4, Socrates recurs to something like the Thracians claim. He asks Glaucon:

> Do you realize that of necessity there are as many kinds (*eidē*) of men (*anthropōn*) as there are of constitutions (*politeiōn*)? (8.544d5-6)

In the Predominance principle, once again, as in the Thracian claim, what appears to be an inference from constitutional types to individual types turns out to be founded on the inverse relationship:

> Don't you know that the kinds of human beings must be of the same types as those of constitutions? Or do you think that constitutions come to be "out of oak or rock"[33] and not from the characters (*ēthōn*) of those who, in cities, are the ones who tip the scales and drag the others along with them? (8.544d5-e2)[34]

Unlike the Thracians claim (to which it is often wrongly assimilated), the Predominance principle proposes a mechanism driving the dynamics of causality of the character of a constitution: namely, the claim that it is the character of (certain) people in a city that tips the scales in determining the character of a given constitution and drags the other people in that city along in so doing. This tipping of the scales is often interpreted purely in psychological, and sometimes in strictly mathematical, terms.[35] In contrast, I argue that

---

33. Saxonhouse ("Democracy, Equality," 277) identifies a source of this quotation and its relevance: "Socrates draws us to the scene where Penelope questions Odysseus, disguised as a stranger and stripped of any identity. She asks: 'From where are you? For you are not sprung from an oak of ancient story nor from stone' ([Homer, *Od.*] 19.162-3)." In fact, the "[not] from oak or rock" trope is also used by Homer in the *Iliad* (of Achilles, *Il.* 22.125) and once by Hesiod (*Th.* 35). In all three of these poetic figures, the emphasis is on a contrast with generation and human birth, and so especially relevant to the Platonic passage in question—a point that I owe to Malina Butorovic.

34. My translation of *oisthe oun* as "don't you know" may be a slight overtranslation, but I think it captures the interrogative conversational force of the sentence overall. Note that my translation of this important passage here differs from that which I accepted from published translations in "How to Turn History."

35. A notable exception (despite its slightly misleading title) is Sikkenga's "Plato's Examination"; among other points, the article glosses this principle in these terms—"the regime acquires its own character from the *psyche* of those who establish and hold the ruling offices" (378)—and offers translations involving "offices" or "ruling offices" of relevant

Predominance is to be understood as coming about through the framework of offices and officeholding in each flawed constitution. It will be at play either through the setting of the terms of eligibility for office or through the tendencies operating in the actual selection from among those eligible, or both. In other words, Predominance is on my reading not to be interpreted merely as an aggregation of individual psychologies, nor as a sheerly numerical balance. It is rather (albeit only implicitly) a principle of *political* predominance, one obtaining with regard to the self-appointed composition of the political class (whether the actual officeholders, or the eligibility of the group from which they are drawn) of the city.[36]

Predominance expresses the character given to a constitution by means of the definition of eligibility and entitlements, selection, attitudes, and actions of its officeholders qua officeholders, and the attitudes and actions of others in the city toward them qua officeholders. That constellation comes about as a constitution is established in virtue of the new values and broader social forces, which lead to a new definition of offices and practice of selection of officeholders being followed. Once the constitution is established, the actions and attitudes of its officeholders lead to further changes in both the institutions and attitudes (including normative values) within the city more broadly. So the Predominance principle, understood in terms of political predominance, is at once an expression of how a temporary (if in the long run unstable) equilibrium comes into being, and the catalyst for that equilibrium starting to unravel.

On my reading, the Predominance principle does not require that all individuals in a city, or even any individuals, possess the mature character corresponding to a constitution of a city in order for that constitution to come into being. Instead, a certain group of politically predominant individuals need only harbor characteristics that play into a process of change, the latter unfolding so as to bring a new constitution about, while at the same time developing their own characters more fully to be of the same type and inspiring the emulation of others to do the same. In other words, all that Predominance requires is that there be some group of people, who may well be a numerical minority at the beginning, with characters that impel political change in a certain direction while also pushing both their own characters and the characters of others

passages. Hitz ("Degenerate Regimes," 110) also briefly remarks on the centrality of political office to the constitutional macro narrative.

36. Whereas the book 4 Thracians claim made use of what psychologists and linguists call "generics"—by saying that Athenians love learning, what is meant is that most, though not all, Athenians love learning, or perhaps even that typical Athenians, whether or not they are the numerical majority, love learning—the book 8 Predominance principle makes clear that not all, or even most, of the citizens of a city must share the psychological characteristic in order for it to become predominant. Rather, the character of some tips the scales and drags along the others.

in a parallel direction too. The precise dynamics of such impulsion in each case will be explained further in what follows.

Whereas Predominance explains the character of constitutions in terms of the character of those individuals predominant as officeholders (as well as, more broadly, eligible to become officeholders) within them, Socrates's second principle focuses on whether the state of mind of that dominant group is united or subject to factional division. He describes this as a "simple principle" explaining "the cause of change in any constitution," and it is this that I have called the Disunity principle:

> Is it not a simple principle that constitutions in general[37] change from out of[38] that [unspecified: body or group] holding the offices (*echontos tas archas*), when factional division (*stasis*) arises within that [body or group] itself? But on the other hand, if this group remains of one mind—however small it may be—is it not the case that the constitution will be incapable of changing? (8.545c8–d3).[39]

37. While Grube/Reeve's translation of *pasa politeia* as "any constitution" works well in English and captures the overall sense of the phrase (one could relatedly express this as "every constitution," as I did in "How to Turn History" [87]), André Laks has helped me to see that this distributive sense is better understood as being rooted in the phrase having a general meaning of "constitution(s) in general." Such a reading makes the best sense of *pasēi politeia* later in book 8, at 8.564b9, where the parallel offered, *peri sōma*, is best taken to mean "body in general"—from which sense it applies to every individual body; likewise of *psuchē pasa* at *Phaedrus* 245c5 (albeit that this is a philosophically loaded context), where "soul in general" can be taken to apply to every individual soul, without having that as its actual grammatical meaning (as the *gar* clause that follows makes clear). It also compares well to the related syntactic formulation at *Laws* 3.683e1–3, *basilea . . . ē kai tis arkhē pōpote kateluthē*, in the context of a question from the Athenian Visitor that is also thematically relevant to the *Republic's* Disunity principle: "Now when a kingdom is destroyed, and indeed when any kind of rule (*tis archē*) has ever hitherto been destroyed, surely no one but they themselves are to blame," with "kingdom" and "rule" both being taken implicitly to furnish the agents (the king, the rulers) who are to blame for destroying their own regime. Other related references are noted by Poddighe ("Aristotle on Legal Change," 192), discussing Arist., *Pol.* [2.]1269a25–26, which she translates with the distributive sense ("in every constitution"), with note 70 citing another alternative possibility of translating the phrase as "in every part of the *politeia*," and claiming that "this is the meaning it appears to have in Plato (*Ep.* [*Letters*] VII 325) and Antiphon (*Tetr.* III.1.1)." However, in both *Letters* 7 and Antiphon, the phrase includes a definite article, so her parallels are of limited relevance to the present passage in Plato, which does not.

38. Again, in contrast to Grube/Reeve's translation here, which I previously followed, I choose "from out of" in accordance with the leading sense of *ek* (as per LSJ). One could even make a case for construing that as "in consequence of," in line with an additional sense of *ek* given by LSJ of "cause, instrument, or means" in explaining something's origin.

39. Compare the most divergent aspect of Grube/Reeve's translation from the one I have offered: "the cause of change in any constitution is civil war breaking out within the ruling group."

The core of the above speech, in which the Disunity principle can be isolated, is this: "that constitutions in general change out of that [unspecified: body or group] holding the offices (*echontos tas archas*)." Notice the centrality of office and offices to this principle. As established in the opening chapters of this study, this syntactical combination of verb and noun, treating the noun for office as an office held by a person or persons, makes clear that the referent is not ruling in a general sense but, rather, officeholding, which is procedurally limited and controlled. The phrase "holding" (or, more literally, "having") an office was an established part of the institutional vocabulary for Greek offices, and could be construed in one of two senses: either more broadly as the entire group who are eligible to hold the offices (thus meaning the group holding the offices in the sense of monopolizing them), or more narrowly as the subset of that group who are actually holding the offices at a given time. This is shown both in the *Republic* and in contemporary historical reflection to be an extraordinarily fruitful framework, as a recent scholar of Greek oligarchy has observed: stasis or faction among the ruling elites of such regimes can be shown to have been key to their fragility, and a likely (though not singular) path to the destruction of such constitutions.[40]

So specified, the Disunity principle provides an explanatory template for each case to come of how the constitutional regimes change into one another, or, to put it another way, emerge out of one another.[41] That template is one in which there are only officeholders (without any additional kind of rulers who could safeguard the officeholders), and this is indeed the case for every constitution that is not a *kallipolis*, including the four types on which the macro narrative of book 8 will focus. It is the doings of officeholders that constitute the proximate explanation for the change of character from one (type of) constitution to another.[42]

---

40. Simonton (*Classical Greek Oligarchy*, 248 with n94) cites this as the "Simple Principle" enunciated at *Resp.* 8.545d; he also claims that same principle is quoted repeatedly by Hawke in *Writing Authority*, but, in fact, Hawke refers three times to *Leg.* 711c (on 9, 189, 194) but never to *Resp.* 8.545d. Simonton also adduces a relevant comparison passage in Aristotle, *Pol.* 5.1306a9–10: "An oligarchy which is of one mind [*homonoousa*] is not easily overthrown from within" (260); on the related idea of *homonoia* in Plato, see Kamtekar's "What's the Good."

41. The centrality of *stasis* to each stage of the macro narrative has been remarked by Hitz ("Degenerate Regimes," 107 with n31), who also remarks on the description of the sailors as *stasiazontas* with one another in the Ship of State (6.488b3–4). I would add that this is the converse of its absence from the *kallipolis* in book 5, which was explained as deriving from the shared belief in and language for common kinship among the guardians (due to the community of procreation and rearing among the military auxiliaries), so producing "common pleasures and pains" among the guardians (5.463b9–464b7).

42. Thus I must disagree with the assertion by Arruzza (*Wolf in the City*, 60) that "books VIII and IX do not articulate a constitutional theory proper. . . . These pages include no details about citizenship rules, deliberative institutions and mechanisms, or

Accordingly, it is the unity of the group of officeholders in each constitution, and how that unity is ultimately breached, that explains the sequence of constitutional changes from a *kallipolis* to a timocracy, oligarchy, democracy, and tyranny. Without safeguarding rulers to supervise and educate these officeholders, the constitutions they govern are necessarily flawed and unstable. Their *taxis* is disordered, at the very least by the absence of safeguarding rulers, and in several cases by the undermining of an ethos of order(ing) and obedience. And those imperfect constitutions will dramatize, by inversion, both the requirements of a good *taxis* and the value of the normative *telos* of the good of the ruled that good officeholders (and good rulers more generically) should pursue.

Now the syntactical emphasis on those "holding the offices" in the Disunity principle might seem to be unduly restrictive in regard to its intended initial application to the transformation of a *kallipolis* into a timocracy, given my argument in chapter 7 that it is the middle-aged apprentice rulers who hold the offices in a *kallipolis*, whereas the most senior guardians are better characterized as having a safeguarding role as rulers. However, this restriction precisely tracks a discussion of the unity of the city in an important passage of book 5. There, Socrates had explained that the kinship names to be used in a *kallipolis* (discussed in another context in chapter 6) fundamentally indicate "the having and expressing" of a conviction of common identification with others faring well or badly, which in turn will be "accompanied by the having of pleasures and pains in common." He further explained there that "in addition to the other institutions, the cause of this is the having of women and children in common by the guardians"—that is, specifically by the auxiliaries, as he specifies a few lines later (5.463e4–464b6, referring to *tois epikourois* at b6).[43]

All of this is what lies at the root of Socrates's ultimate claim in this stretch of book 5, that "if there is no factionalizing (*stasiazontōn*) among the guardians, then there is no danger that the rest of the city will engage in a stand-off (*dixostatēsēi*) either against them or among themselves" (5.465b9–11).[44] To be sure, as sometimes throughout book 5, especially when speaking of the group of guardians as a whole, Plato reverts here to a broader categorization

---

the distribution of offices"; on the contrary, each of the first three flawed constitutions is defined by some combination of its citizenship rules and distribution of offices. Nevertheless, I have benefited from Arruzza's discussion in that work of Plato on tyranny, as will be evident below.

43. I adopt Grube/Reeve's translations of the quotations in this paragraph.

44. The identity of the subjects of this sentence ("the guardians") has to be supplied not from the general *hoi andres* at 5.465b6–7 but from the larger preceding context in the course of which it is several times clearly spelled out—e.g., at 5.464c6. My translation of *dixostatēsēi* as "engage in a stand-off" seeks to capture the implication that what is being ruled out is not any ordinary disagreement but rather the kind that would risk engendering factionalization of the *polis*.

than the detailed one that I excavated in chapter 7. Whereas I argued there that the officeholding cohort was not the auxiliaries aged twenty- to thirty-five whom one might think of as the primary reproductive group, nevertheless the thirty-five- to fifty-year-olds whom I identified as the officeholding cohort are still of potential childbearing age, and their unity has to be maintained among persons who are not yet knowers of the Form of the Good (so it is unsecured by full wisdom). Thus this group of officeholders, like and together with the younger auxiliaries, is more broadly subject to a need for unity that is both imperative and insecure.

The principles of Predominance and Disunity alike are focused on the character of a constitution. The Predominance principle offers an explanation of the emergence of a constitution (recall its formulation in terms of how a constitution "comes to be") focused on explaining the character of a constitution that has come into being and achieved a brief though temporary and relative stability. In contrast, the Disunity principle focuses on explaining how a given kind of constitution degenerates before it mutates into another kind. In both cases, the explanation offered is what I shall call proximate. By this I mean that both principles identify the cause that explains the proximate effecting of the change of constitutional kind, either into one (Predominance) or out of one (Disunity). It follows that they may interact more closely than I have so far suggested, and, indeed, I shall identify at least one moment in the macro narrative when an implicit appeal to Predominance is made in the course of explaining the changes consequent upon the triggering of the Disunity principle (this is the moment of the transformation of timocracy into oligarchy).

Neither principle entails the claim that such a proximate cause need be the only cause involved in any overall time slice of the macro narrative. There may well—indeed, one would imagine that there must—have been broader social and economic or psychological and normative changes that preceded and prepared, or even in some sense necessitated, this change in the unity of officeholders. That is, the explanatory schema of the two principles invokes the actions (and inactions) of officeholders as the proximate cause of constitutional character and change, without necessarily claiming to be an explanation at the only or most fundamental level. The two principles are compatible with a much richer and more complex causal framework, which Plato indeed sketches, as I shall show.

Transition to Timocracy: Kallipolis *as the Paradoxical Source of the Constitutional Decline*

While presented as a general claim (referring to "constitutions in general"), the Disunity principle is introduced in the context of the first change of constitution that needs to be explained: namely, the change from the constitution of a *kallipolis* to another kind of constitution, which Socrates has baptized with two names ("either timocracy or timarchy") and characterized as "the honor-loving constitution" (8.545b7–8, b6, trans. Grube/Reeve). And while Disunity will continue to be demonstrated in each subsequent change of constitution in the macro narrative, the epistemology of this initial phase shift (to adopt a modern locution) is presented as unusually challenging. For the protasis of the conditional stated as the opposite of a case explained by Disunity (namely, that "if this group [of those 'holding the offices,' from d1–2] remains of one mind—however small it may be—is it not the case that the constitution will be incapable of changing") is precisely the characterization explained earlier in this study of what makes a constitution a *kallipolis*: that those "holding the offices" are characterized by a profound unity, and that this unity, which is achieved in part through the safeguarding role of rulers who are not office-holders, in turn makes possible the broader unity of the city.

In applying Disunity to introduce the narrative of the first constitutional change to be described, Socrates broadens its scope beyond that stated in the principle, which had focused on those "holding the offices." For he asks:

How then, Glaucon, will our city be changed, and how will the auxil-iaries (*hoi epikouroi*) and the rulers (*hoi archontes*)[45] become faction-ally divided either in regard to each other or each among themselves? (8.545d5–7)

In having Socrates pose this question, Plato seems willing to countenance a less than strict application of Disunity to this first case, allowing *stasis* to arise not solely among the "officeholders" in a restricted sense (whom I argued in the previous chapter are in a *kallipolis* the apprentice rulers aged thirty-five to fifty), but rather among the whole group of guardians, including both aux-iliaries and rulers. This may serve to dramatize the fact that a *kallipolis* is the only constitution of the five considered in book 8 to feature at least some rulers who are not officeholders. Thus a principle designed to explain consti-tutional change in constitutions featuring officeholders alone will necessarily sit awkwardly in one in which the officeholders are only part of a broader ecology of guardians, sandwiched between younger auxiliaries in training to become officeholders themselves, and older rulers who are capable of safe-guarding the officeholders and auxiliaries under them.

On my analysis, then, this opening question that inaugurates the macro narrative of constitutional change does not precisely instantiate the Disunity principle. Rather, it initiates a process through which the very role of any kind of ruler other than officeholders will disappear, so that further constitutional changes will emanate from the group of officeholders alone. This will hap-pen in the transition to a timocracy, as the "rulers" first lose insight into the

---

45. As I argued in chapter 7, the reference to *hoi archontes* in contexts such as this one is best construed as referring to the eldest guardians.

judgments needed to realize the proper *telos* of such a constitution, and then, over several generations, lose commitment to pursuing that *telos*. Indeed, this change is concomitant with the eventual disappearance (as the timocratic constitution is instituted) of the distinction between officeholders and safeguarding rulers altogether. (I detail this process further below.)

Socrates asks Glaucon whether he wishes that they should, like Homer, pray to the Muses to tell them (speaking in the first person plural) "how *stasis* first fell upon (*empese*)" an unspecified object that is here presumably the *polis* (8.545d7–e1).[46] In envisaging how the Muses will speak, Socrates asks Glaucon whether he expects that they would do so "tragically, playing and jesting with us as if we were children" (8.545e1–3, trans. Grube/Reeve). The combination of adverb and verbs here is somewhat jarring, since speaking "tragically" was in the classical period typically associated with a serious and formal style, as opposed to a comic one, so contrasting with the idea of a playfulness appropriate to children. The idea may be that the Muses (or rather, and significantly for this point, Socrates imagining and speaking on their behalf) will be speaking in a mock-tragic style, not actually offering a full-blown or serious account but rather playing at doing so.[47] Indeed, when Socrates actually introduces what he imagines to be the Muses' story, he frames it with a disclaimer ("somehow like this (*hōde pōs*)," 8.546a1), so injecting an element of provisionality and uncertainty into his recounting of their tale.

Why Muses?[48] The epistemology of any change away from the constitution of a *kallipolis* is not something that can be easily accommodated within the terms of its discursive legislation before this point. As noted above, a *kallipolis* has been deemed the only kind of constitution capable of stably reproducing itself (4.424a5–6). How then should it ever swerve out of that circular reproduction and into a linear sequence of degeneration? Invocation of the Muses serves to address this seemingly insoluble conundrum. They

---

46. The *polis* was named in the nominative in his previous question at 8.545d5, though here a dative must be implied. *Empese* is a defective imperative form of *empitnein*, the poetic form of *empiptein*, the same verb that Socrates had used at 6.499b7–c1, discussed in chapter 7. The reference to Homer (*Il.* 16.112) invokes a passage in which Homer asks the Muses to tell him how "*proton . . . empese*": how first something fell upon something else—namely, how fire first fell upon the ships of the Achaeans. Plato here substitutes *stasis* generated from within for the Homeric recounting of fire seemingly generated from without. In Burnyeat and Frede (*Pseudo-Platonic Seventh Letter*, 168), Myles Burnyeat suggests, however, that this silent substitution invokes the Homeric narrative logic showing that the Trojan firing of the ships occurred as "the ultimate nightmare consequence of the dissension between Achilles and Agamemnon," and so was in reality an internally caused *stasis* among the Greeks themselves.

47. I thank Joshua Billings for suggesting this way of interpreting the line (as I interpreted his comments in a passing conversation).

48. For a review of the Muses' significance, see Hellwig (*Adikia in Platons "Politeia,"* 78–92).

are imagined to speak from the standpoint of a general account of biological nature and change—"everything that comes into being must pass out of existence" (8.546a2), a claim that is applied to humans alongside all plants and animals—as well as a mastery of mathematics, in giving their account of how a city with a constitution making it a *kallipolis* ("so composed") could come to change at all.[49] And what they are explaining, as Socrates eventually makes clear, is linked to the Disunity principle, by explaining the origin of the *stasis* to which it appeals: "*Stasis* must be said to be 'of this lineage,' always and wherever it should come about" (8.547a5–6).

The story that Socrates vocalizes on behalf of the Muses, rests, as I have argued elsewhere, on the "Achilles' heel" of "applying knowledge in time."[50] At some point, Socrates imagines the Muses telling Glaucon, a generation educated to be "leaders (*hēgemonas*) in your city," although they are "wise," nevertheless suffer an affliction in "calculation together with sense perception" (8.546b2–3, trans. Grube/Reeve)—that is, in their ability to perceive the manifestation of their calculations in the phenomenal world and in relation to its temporal changeability.[51] This leads to mistakes in the timing of the mating prescribed for the candidate auxiliaries, who are meant to reproduce their own good natures, and so to a much wider variation in the kinds of children who are born. The result is that the older guardians will prescribe sexual intercourse leading to procreation at the wrong times, generating a cohort of children who are "unworthy" in their natures to serve as guardians, even though the best of that unworthy second generation are chosen to do so.

This fatally flawed second generation of guardians will, when they replace their fathers' generation, "begin, being guardians (*phulakes*) who are ruling (*arxontai*), to neglect us [the Muses]" (8.546d5).[52] And the result, in the third generation of rulers so produced (*archontes*, 8.546e1), also constitutes evidence for the interwoven structure of ruling and officeholding in a *kallipolis*. For, as noted briefly in the previous chapter, the failure of this third generation of ruling guardians lies in their flawed carrying out of a scrutiny (*to dokimazein*) of the natures of the citizens (metaphorically described as gold, silver, bronze, and iron) (8.546d7–547a2), meaning that they misidentify the proper members of the next generation of auxiliaries (junior guardians) and

49. While the nature of the constitution of a *kallipolis* makes any change "difficult," any such city is, like every city, the kind of thing that comes into being and can pass away. This intriguingly brings a city into the scope of the biological generalization, either in its own right as a generated entity, or in virtue of its constituent human members (8.546a1–3).

50. Lane, *Method and Politics*, 146.

51. What they miscalculate bears on their grasp of the *kairos*, the opportune moment for action; on the *kairos* here, elsewhere in Plato, and in other authors, see my *Method and Politics* (139–46, 171–202).

52. Cf. Grube/Reeve: "they will begin, as guardians, to neglect us Muses," failing to translate the verb *arxontai*.

rulers (senior guardians). This scrutiny is described in a phrase using the same verb that democratic Athenians used to describe the required testing of each person chosen to hold an office by election or by lot, prior to their being allowed to assume that role.[53] Scrutiny both in Athens and in a *kallipolis* tests the quality and suitability of natural persons to embark on roles of rule.

This failure of properly conducted scrutiny would result in "intermixing" of the various types among an emergent fourth generation, resulting in "lack of likeness and unharmonious inequality," which "always breed war and hostility," summed up as the origin of *stasis*, or civil war (8.547a2–6, trans. Grube/ Reeve). The members of the next generation of auxiliaries and rulers must include people of both gold and silver types of soul (since it is only in the final sorting that the gold-natured alone will be allowed to become senior guardians). If there is intermixing of the gold and silver types with the bronze and iron types, this would affect the pool of auxiliaries as well as rulers. While the origin of *stasis* here is actually more encompassing than the narrow language of the Disunity principle would suggest, that is because only a *kallipolis* features rulers who are not officeholders (and indeed auxiliaries as well), offering a more variegated cast of ruling characters than will be found in any other constitution to which the principle will be applied.

Note that the final phase of this initial decline is not about procreation per se. It is, rather, about the failure of the full-blown rulers (the senior guardians) to properly scrutinize those to be permitted to serve as guardians in the age ladder of that role, and so to become candidates to replace the senior guardians in the next generation themselves. In recapitulating the three stages of the narrative of decline, the role of rulers in overseeing the selection of officeholders figures crucially at each step (I paraphrase the text in order to condense the account).

In the first generation in which the rot begins to set in, the original source of decline is the failure of calculation and sense perception—arguably, a random failure, rooted in the imperfection of the material world and the unstable nature of becoming. This leads a first generation of rulers to fail to properly direct marriage and procreation, which in turn undermines the education of a second generation, who are born with natures making them unsuitable candidates to serve as auxiliaries and so as candidates to become ruling guardians in their turn. Nevertheless, since no suitable candidates exist, some of these are indeed promoted to the role of rulers, and in that role fail in their turn to properly direct the education of the third generation. That third generation, when they in turn become ruling guardians, fail to properly conduct the scrutiny (*to dokimazein*) of the members of the fourth generation to become auxiliaries and rulers in their turn.

---

53. While Plato does not here use the noun (*dokimasia*) that was the name for such a process of scrutiny in Athens, the use of the definite article with the infinitive functions as an equivalent.

In other words, from the first generation described onward, some of those who become rulers are unsuitable for that task, meaning that they will be unable to maintain the unity of rational understanding required by that role. Moreover, this includes those who are to supervise education: a role that is explicitly identified as the task of those serving as "officeholders," as I have argued in this study, drawing on an unambiguous statement to that effect by Socrates at 5.460b6–8. Hence, *stasis* among the officeholders—and, more broadly, among the rulers who include the officeholders—is central to this process of degeneration, just as the Predominance principle would imply.

Which exact stage in this sequence counts as a change in the constitution per se? It is reasonable to think that it is not the stage of the first generation: their failing involves a failure of judgment that does not formally alter the existing constitutional institutions. Nor is it the stage of the second generation: for that, again, involves a failure of judgment that does not formally alter the existing constitutional institutions. It is only at the stage of the third generation that an institutional breakdown is manifest, one that bears directly on the composition of the fourth-generation group of auxiliaries and rulers (including officeholders as well as senior rulers), owing to the failure to properly conduct the scrutiny of those who are allowed to enter into it—that is, a failure by the rulers to safeguard a constitutional institution as it is meant to be operated.

And, indeed, we see in the relationship of the third and fourth generations a breakdown of unity that corresponds precisely to an application of the Disunity principle. For the fourth generation features a group of potential rulers who have received a flawed education from the flawed generation of their parents (the third generation). While there may also be conflict within the ranks of senior guardians at this stage and between the senior and junior guardians, the focus of the Muses' story is on the disunity that such a flawed education produces within the group "holding the offices," with *stasis* arising within that group itself such that it no longer "remains of one mind." What such a failure creates is a group of senior guardians (here using the term broadly, to cover both the middle-aged officeholders and the eldest safeguarding rulers) who are precisely not united in their natures and so in their values, but are rather unlike one another. And it is this that leads directly to *stasis*, just as the Disunity principle postulates: "that every constitution changes out of that [unspecified: body or group] holding the offices (*echontos tas archas*), when factional division (*stasis*) arises within that [body or group] itself" [phrased as a rhetorical question], while conversely "if this group remains of one mind—however small it may be—is it not the case that the constitution will be incapable of changing" [phrased as a rhetorical question] (8.545c8–d3).

Accordingly, it is at this stage of the emergence of the fourth generation as officeholders that the constitution of a *kallipolis* begins to change into one of a timocracy or timarchy (even though, as noted above, important changes for the worse have already happened at intellectual, psychological, and educational levels). In place of the previous stable group of auxiliaries composed entirely of the so-called gold (potential senior guardian) and silver (auxiliary alone) natures, the new group is composed of some who have natures of pure gold or silver, alongside others who have natures of iron or bronze (the metaphor for candidates to be farmers or artisans). These comprise two factions "striving and struggling with one another" (8.547b7–8), the one faction (of gold and silver) to maintain "virtue and the old [constitutional] order," the other (of iron and bronze) to pursue the goal of "money-making and the acquisition of land, houses, gold, and silver" (8.547b2–7) (all quotations in this sentence trans. Grube/Reeve).

In this scenario, neither group at the onset of this factional division has the precise character of the timocratic officeholders (figured by silver alone) whose establishment in office will be confirmatory and characteristic of the new timocratic constitution, though there may well be silver-natured people who are initially to be found among the faction in favor of the old order. This supports my earlier claim that the Predominance principle does not require the numerical preponderance of a majority, or even the existence of a full-fledged minority group, in order to explain how a change in constitutional character comes about. Instead, the principle articulates the proximate cause of a change in constitutional character as happening when a group of a corresponding character "tips the balance" in favor of constitutional change.

Before that tipping of the balance, and setting the stage for it, Socrates describes an "agreement on a middle way (*eis meson hōmologēsan*)" (8.547b8)[54] between the two factions, which serves to institute a set of social and economic changes in the society:

> They distribute the land and houses as private property, enslave and hold as serfs and servants (*perioikous te kai oiketas*)[55] those whom they previously guarded as free friends and provisioners (*hōs eleutherous philous te kai tropheas*), and occupy themselves with war and with guarding against those whom they've enslaved. (8.547b7–c4, trans. Grube/Reeve, modified)

Note that the abandoned role of guarding the producers and artisans as "free friends and provisioners" involves an abandonment of the relationship of the rulers of the *kallipolis* to those whom they had served in ruling, and who

---

54. On the phrase *eis to meson*, see Simonton (*Classical Greek Oligarchy*, 85n46).

55. As Adam notes (*"Republic" of Plato*, 211), the references to the *perioikoi* clearly evoke Sparta, "but also . . . Crete, Thessaly and Argos." Adam reads *oiketas* as a reference to the lowest order in each city of this kind; for example, the Spartan helots, who acted as, inter alia, "domestic servants."

in turn had served as their "paymasters and provisioners" (*misthodotas te kai tropheas*), as discussed above in chapter 6.[56] This is a clear sign that the original constitution has already begun to change, as Glaucon confirms in his response ("I think that is the way this transformation begins," 8.547c5, trans. Grube/Reeve). The very nature of guarding, originally directed solely against external enemies, is now directed internally against the artisan and producer group, whom the timocrats have newly enslaved. These arrangements consolidate a wealthy elite who use their political (and not merely economic) power for purposes of domination and exploitation.

The Timocratic Constitution

The new constitution constitutes "a sort of midpoint (*tis en mesō*)" (8.547c6, trans. Grube/Reeve) between the aristocratic constitution (the term used in book 8 to refer to the constitution of a *kallipolis*) and the oligarchic constitution. Socrates explains that by so situating it, he means that the new timocratic constitution maintains some of the institutions, practices, and attitudes of the aristocratic constitution, while introducing some characteristic of oligarchy, but also manifesting certain features of its own, given its unique placement between them. It is worth considering each of these sets of features in turn.

The aristocratic features that are maintained include honoring the rulers (albeit that they cease to be philosophers), alongside maintaining the "fighting class" (the auxiliaries) in their practices of common meals and education for war, and, conversely, in their being prohibited from making money (8.547d5–9). As in a *kallipolis*, in the timocratic constitution it will remain the case that:

> The rulers (*tous archontas*) will be respected; the fighting class will be prevented from taking part in farming, manual labor, or other ways of making money; it will eat communally and devote itself to physical training and training for war. (8.547d5–8, trans. Grube/Reeve)

But while the rulers will continue to be respected as such, their composition will change crucially from a *kallipolis* to a timocratic constitution, in that if the auxiliary pool is now wholly silver, there will be no gold natures available to be promoted to the ranks of senior guardians. Instead, the silver natures alone will (it is implied) fill those ranks, and then oversee the education of the next generation in their own (flawed) image.

In keeping with Predominance, the unique features (*idia*) of the new constitution revolve around the specific role played by those who hold the offices

---

56. Notably, the adjective "free (*eleutherous*)" was not used in passages of earlier books in which the service conception of rulers whose role is to guard the producers and artisans was outlined.

within it. To appreciate this point requires careful attention to the Greek text and its translation:

> Therefore [it] [referring back to "the constitution" at 8.547c7] will be afraid to vest (*agein*) wise people (*sophous*) in the offices (*epi tas archas*), inasmuch as [it] has acquired for itself people such as this (*tous toioutous andras*) who are no longer simple and earnest (*haplous te kai ateneis*) but rather mixed, and [it] will instead incline towards spirited and simpler people (*epi de thumoeideis te kai haplousterous*), who are more naturally suited for war than peace. (8.547e1–548a1, drawing in part on Grube/Reeve)[57]

It is undeniable that this passage uses recognizable Greek vocabulary for identifying political offices as such—namely, the prepositional phrase *epi tas archas*, used with the verb *agein*, one of the family of such phrases and verbs discussed in this context in chapters 1 and 2. More debatable is how to interpret the referent of the phrase *tous toioutous andras* ("people such as this"). On my view, this does not refer back as "they" to "wise people" (*sophous*) at the beginning of the sentence, as many translators (including Grube/Reeve) have taken it to do.[58] Rather, this phrase—*tous toioutous andras*, which I translated above as "people such as this"—refers to the pool of potential officeholders. And it is this pool that is now, as was argued above, precisely a group that is mixed: mixed not in the sense of being composed of individuals who are

---

57. The feminine subject of all of Socrates's interventions at 8.547c6–548a3 is *hē politeia* enunciated at 8.547c7. I am grateful to Jonathan Beere, Verity Harte, Emily Hulme, and Anders Dahl Sørensen for discussing the Greek of this passage with me, and especially to Emily for adducing relevant comparisons, though the final resolution is my own responsibility. Note that some details of the translation and reading of the passage given here differ from those in my "How to Turn History," albeit the overall argument as to the import of the passage is the same. "Vest" is not a literal sense of *agein* but reflects my effort to capture the figure of speech being used.

58. "They" is in any case too weak a translation of the phrase, which explicitly involves reference to a previous kind of characterization and so is rendered here by "such as this." Plato uses *toioutos* several times in book 8 and elsewhere in the *Republic* to refer generally to a relevant class of people, rather than to pick up a specific previous referent. Consider, for example, 8.545b8–9, where the timocratic man is introduced as *ton toiouton andron* as a general parallel to the timocratic constitution, and 10.619d2, where Socrates generalizes from a single example to a much more general description of a class as *toioutois*. And, indeed, immediately following the passage that we are concerned with, quoted at length above, Socrates uses *hoi toioutoi* (8.548a5) once again, clearly to discuss the whole group of timocrats—the description there is manifestly not limited to the wise alone. Therefore I take *tous toioutous andras* in the passage under consideration, at 8.547e2–3, to be invoking the whole group of people who are full citizens in the timocracy and (by its constitutional definition) among those entitled to serve as its officeholders, as opposed to those who have been excluded from constitutional membership by being subordinated through enslavement as "serfs and servants."

mixtures but in the sense of being a group of different kinds of individuals, as argued above, in terms of the metaphorical metal of their character types. This key move in establishing the political structure of the timocratic constitution exploits the distinction in Greek practice noted earlier, between the ruling group construed broadly as those eligible to hold the offices and those who are actually chosen to hold office at a given time. For what distinguishes the timocratic regime is that those who, out of the ruling group as a whole, will be vested in the offices (*epi tas archas agein*) no longer include the combined pool of gold and silver natures who would have served as auxiliaries in a *kallipolis*, and from whom the ultimate selection of gold natures only to serve as ruling guardians (both officeholding and later safeguarding) could be made. (The safeguarding rulers, indeed, are now vanishing, or vanished.) Instead, those who will be selected as officeholders in the timocratic constitution are solely the "spirited and simpler" people, the silver natures who direct the constitution toward the goal of making war. They are "simpler (*haplousterous*)" in the sense of being always inclined to war rather than peace,[59] and perhaps also in the sense of *haplous* as being truth telling or frank, in that in this new constitution, it is only these silver-natured people who can frankly aver their motivations of loving war and honor, such as are supported by the constitution (though even they will harbor secret motivations as well, as money lovers and money hoarders, that do not match the constitution's formal structure).[60]

As the Predominance principle would predict, it is in and through this new set of constitutional practices in regard to officeholding that the new constitution is formally enshrined. The political predominance of the silver natures in holding the offices is what confirms the new constitution in its timocratic character. Indeed, by eliminating any other kind of ruling role for those with gold natures, the new constitution makes redundant the distinction that had been central to the constitution of a *kallipolis*: that between the senior guardians who serve as safeguarding rulers, overseeing education and the overall constitution, and those junior to them who serve as officeholders and (junior to the officeholders in turn) auxiliaries. That distinction may, as I argued in chapter 7, be interpreted as resonating with acts of the Athenian Areopagus in overseeing the constitutional arrangements in spirit as well as in certain specific roles (roles that, in Athens, varied over time). By contrast, Plato implies here that the Spartan and Cretan constitutions, with which Socrates identifies the timocratic one (8.544c2–3), lacked such a meaningful institutional

---

59. Indeed, the alternative name for timocracy, "timarchy" (*timarchia*), that Socrates had proposed at 8.545b7–8—in his own right (saying "I"), so underlining that the purported speech of the Muses has merged into his own voice—captures this point already.

60. In the *Hippias minor*, Hippias describes Homer's Achilles as the "most simple (*haploustatos*)" (paired with "most truthful") (364e7), and as "simple (*haplous*)" (365b4), both points contrasting with his reading of Homer's Odyssey. I owe this point to Johannes Haubold in comments on a precursor of this chapter.

distinction;[61] the same will be seen to be the case also with the oligarchy and democracy (and a fortiori the tyranny) that follow.

The absence of such a distinction—which can be fully spelled out as a distinction between certain people ruling outside the constraints of office and others ruling wholly within the institutional constraints of officeholding— means that there is no body charged with the spirit of constitutional oversight of the kind that Plato builds into the constitution of the *kallipolis* in the *Republic* and (differently) into the constitution designed with Magnesia in view in the *Laws*. Nor is there anybody with the knowledge of the proper *telos*—that is, the good of the ruled—in a position of office or of any other kind of rule (a fortiori, since there is no other kind of rule than office in this new constitution). Instead, the timocratic officeholders pursue their own good and the good of the group to which they belong, to the exclusion and at the expense of those over whom they rule. The constitution is already bankrupt in terms of its *telos*, but its *taxis*, while fatally hollowed out, still has some semblance of order, with officeholders being obeyed.

Among those officeholders, however, is a new and endemic source of instability. This is expressed in a gulf between the public professions and laws established by the timocratic officeholders and their private economic aspirations. Having newly established private houses makes it possible for the timocrats to acquire and hoard money, since they now have a place to hide it, which was lacking in the common barracks of the *kallipolis*. Now, they make use of their private houses to build "private treasuries and storehouses" for the precious metals that they "value" but "are not allowed to acquire . . . openly" (8.548b4–5, trans. Grube/Reeve). These, indeed, are features shared by the timocratic and oligarchic constitutions. Such features are both psychological (the timocratic people "desire money just as those in oligarchies do, passionately adoring gold and silver in secret") and socioeconomic (they possess "private treasuries and storehouses, where they can keep [sc. their money] hidden, and have houses to enclose them, like private nests") (8.548a5–b2, trans. Grube/Reeve).

Yet the timocrats seem to be distinctive in their Janus-faced attitude to obedience. For while "the rulers are respected" in the timocratic constitution (as noted above), nevertheless, Socrates remarks, the timocratic rulers go "running away from the law like boys from their father" (8.548b6–7, trans. Grube/Reeve). If he has a specific law in mind here, it seems likely to be the

61. In *Laws* 3, the Athenian Visitor's discussion of the history of the Spartan constitution assimilates the council of elders, or *gerousia*, to the role of the kings, treating both more like proto-executive officeholders; neither the *gerousia* nor the ephors there are accorded the kind of constitutional oversight role of the Athenian Areopagus, or the broadly comparable roles that I have outlined as those of the Daily Meeting (as I argued in chapter 3 the oft-so-called "Nocturnal Council" can better be termed) of the constitutional project of the *Laws*, and of the senior guardians of the constitutional project of the *Republic*.

law that would officially ban the possession of such precious metals as they nevertheless secretly amass and hoard.[62] More generally, this lawlessness on the part of the timocrats, expressed in a tendency to evade the law secretly rather than to defy it openly, is an indication that those in office would be inclined to violating the normative purpose of the law (and so of their roles as officeholders established to uphold the law) in secret, even as they pretend to uphold it in public. Yet the fact that they are compelled by shame (as is implied) to do so only in secret, at least has the merit of leaving public respect for the order of offices and law intact, for the time being. The *taxis* involving command and obedience to rule embodied in offices retains at least an intact façade, even as the *telos* of rule in and through office has already flipped from service to exploitation.

Transition to Oligarchy

None of the further stages of the macro narrative, beyond the emergence of the timocracy, is explicitly ascribed to the Muses.[63] While some have thought that their story encompasses all of the subsequent stages, I disagree. As argued above, Socrates introduces the Muses to overcome one specific problem: how it is that the self-reproducing and therefore stable (for a time) constitution characterizing a *kallipolis* could ever come to change. Since the explanation of that problem requires a general knowledge both of past, present, and future times and places and of the general characteristics of things that come to be and so must pass away, it is this that the Muses are needed to explain. Beyond that first change, however, the change of a timocracy into an oligarchy, and subsequent phase changes in the macro narrative, do not pose the same difficulty.

I have argued that the monopoly on office held in the timocracy by the silver natures (who were previously, in the *kallipolis*, confined to auxiliary status) is central to timocracy as the means by which the dominance of silver natures is enshrined and sustained. Nevertheless, the most self-evident case of the significance of office among the flawed constitutions is that of oligarchy: the very

---

62. Insofar as the timocracy is explicitly said to be modeled on the Cretan and Laconian constitutions, it is relevant here to consider Aristotle's comment (*Pol.* 2.1270a16–19) on how Spartan laws allowed some Spartans to become poor and others rich: "For because some of the Spartans came to own too much wealth and others very little, the land passed into the hands of a few. This is poorly organized by the laws as well [meaning, in addition to the laws' poor organization of matters relating to women]" (trans. Reeve).

63. Zhang ("Muses") argues that the macro or constitutional narrative is the only part of the overall narrative of these books assigned by Socrates to the Muses, and that, in contrast, the micro narrative (as I call it) is narrated by Socrates himself, making use (and offering further elaboration) as it does of the tripartite psychology that Socrates had developed in books 2–4. I have come to appreciate the value of this insight, although I would still wish to highlight the significant parallels (and intersections) between the comparative political science of the macro narrative and the comparative social psychology of the micro narrative.

name of which denotes the number of those ruling in the sense of being eligible for, and of holding, office in what is in this constitution, as in all of the flawed nontyrannical constitutions, the only form of ruling. As a form of Greek constitution, *oligarchia* specifies the number (*oligo-*, "few") of those ruling in the sense of being eligible for and holding offices (*-archia*, from *archē*), since in such existing constitutions, as argued in part I, rule could be understood to be entirely subsumed in officeholding. Accordingly, *oligarchia* is presented in *Republic* 8 as "the constitution according to a property valuation . . . in which the rich hold office (*archousin*), while the poor do not share in office (*ou metestin archēs*)" (8.550c11–12).[64] Socrates reiterates this description in his later summing up of "the constitution called oligarchy" as "the one which brings into being its officeholders (*echousan tous archontas*) in accordance with a property valuation" (8.553a1–2).[65]

These linked definitions by which oligarchy is introduced and then summed up are elaborated in Socrates's account of how this constitution comes into being ("how timarchy is transformed into oligarchy" (8.550d2–3)). Once again, a transvaluation of values comes first, involving and generating social and economic changes as well as changed attitudes to the laws and the officeholders. All this fractures the unity of the previous group of officeholders, as per the Disunity principle, and so leads to a transformation of the constitution defined by a change in regard to office. In the case of this constitutional transition, the change involves not only informal practices of election to offices from among a fixed officeholding class but also a formal redefinition of the criterion defining the membership of that class itself.

To fill in the detail: The timocratic constitution is eventually "destroyed" by the proliferation of individual treasure houses filled with gold (8.550d8). Having already each acquired a private storehouse (so far kept hidden), these men now begin to enjoy not merely the secret accumulation of money but actually spending the money. This leads them to "divert (*paragousin*)" the laws (8.550d10)[66]—a remark that may mean that they misapply the laws, or block their application, to exempt themselves and their friends, a failing that already

---

64. Note that this definition of oligarchy is clearly meant to be familiar to Adeimantus, who has taken over as interlocutor as of 8.549b5.

65. A property valuation (*timēma*, used here in the plural) is characterized by LSJ in the relevant sense as "the value at which a citizen's property was rated for taxation, his rateable property," and as being a synecdoche for the idea of "a government where the magistrates were chosen according to property, a timocracy" (though this is not a timocracy in the sense of *Republic* 8). The verb *echein* arguably here has the sense of being brought into some condition (here that of office), as opposed to that of merely having or possessing (contrast *Resp.* 8.545d1–2, used of offices but in the latter sense).

66. My translation draws on various senses of the verb *paragō* in LSJ. Socrates presumably means in particular that they divert the law against possessing money, which, as I inferred above, must have characterized the timocratic constitution from which the oligarchic one emerges.

tacitly invokes their role as officeholders. Eventually, together with their wives, they "disobey" the laws altogether (8.550d10).[67]

Whereas the erstwhile timocrats' increasing boldness in diverting and ultimately disobeying the law is presented as a widespread phenomenon, it is not described as an automatic or lockstep process. Rather, Socrates explains its spread (to the "majority") by invoking a psychological mechanism that he describes in terms of certain people's acting *eis zēlon*, a term for emulation that is imbued with a competitive or rivalrous air—one dimension of which could be translated as "aping," another as "outdoing," both of which I seek to capture and combine in the admittedly clumsy phrase of "competitively emulating." The key sentence is this: "As one person sees another doing this and goes about competitively emulating (*eis zēlon*) that person, they make the majority like themselves" (550e1–2).[68] This is a pivotal sentence, but also an enigmatic one. Its subject is an unidentified "they" (implicit in the plural verb, picking up on those in Socrates's preceding speech). The logic of the sentence dictates that this "they" cannot yet be a majority of the timocrats—since it purports to describe precisely the process by which "they" become a "majority." And the mechanism by which this transpires is, on the one hand, a set of actions taken by individuals: each acting *eis zēlon* in response to seeing what another does, whether indulging in spending, diverting the laws, disobeying the laws, or any combination thereof. But, on the other hand, it is an overall action that some individuals are said to *do to others* ("they make the majority like themselves")—in other words, to "make others like themselves," precisely as the Predominance principle postulates.

The best way to make sense of this is to take the original "they"—the group of timocrats and their wives who are newly emboldened in their avarice— as being in fact a minority. They are a minority who are referred to without numerical specification, however, as they will prove to be the key actors in the transformation of the timocratic constitution as well as the politically predominant figures in the oligarchic one to follow (these two roles go together here, but we should monitor whether they come apart in subsequent stages). This original minority "they" does not, then, pick up the reference to "one person" at the start of the sentence above. Rather, this "they" is simultaneously those described as "another" in the key sentence—in other words, the objects of emulation, not the ones doing the emulating. And we should imagine this taking place among the women as well as among the men who are in the politically predominant group of timocrats. Because of the snowballing emulative actions of other individuals, the cumulative effect is that the original "they"

---

67. The purported role of women in this decline will be echoed in Aristotle's criticisms of Spartan women in *Politics* 2.

68. I am grateful to the participants in my 2019 graduate seminar on *Republic* 8 and 9 for illuminating discussion of this sentence.

(the newly emboldened) are the ones who succeed in "mak[ing] the majority like themselves." The paradox is that they themselves do not do this making directly. Rather, by existing as charismatic objects of rivalrous emulation, they attract others to seek to outdo them by, and in, becoming like them.

To put all this in metaphorical terms, this role of an original minority in the process of social norm transformation and psycho-socio-political change is not that of causal locomotives but, rather, of magnetic attractors that can also play a causal role. It is perhaps best captured by modern accounts of snow-balling changes in norms, especially positional norms ("keeping up with the Joneses")—or, in another idiom, by René Girard's studies of mimicry, except that this is for Plato not *mimeisthai* but rather a rivalrous and competitive drive, emulation as a form of aping that inherently seeks to outdo that which it copies. And, strikingly, it places an individual psychological dynamic at the heart of this stage of the macro narrative.

Notwithstanding the formal distinction between the sequences of macro and micro narratives, then, and in contrast to the influential interpretation of G.R.F. Ferrari, the dynamic relationship between individual and constitution is relevant here within the macro narrative (and will also be seen to be relevant within the micro narrative at a corresponding point). The specific individual dynamic here in question is one applying to individuals who are members of a ruling elite, and who operate as (corrupt) officeholders in their power to divert the laws in order to reflect their changing aspirations. While the role of psychology in the macro narrative is crucial, it is embedded in the affordances of the political order of offices and laws. The *taxis* of office goes wrong both because it lacks institutional safeguarding and, concomitantly, because the wrong people are put into the offices.

As moneymaking, and wealth generally, become the ever more explicit and dominant goal, so virtue—on the opposite side of the axiological scales—declines in being valued and so in being practiced. The result is a transformation in the character of, and the typical *telos* pursued by, the previously politically predominant group of men in the regime:

> Victory-loving and honor-loving (*philonikōn kai philotimōn*) men become lovers of making money and money-lovers (*philochrēmatistai kai philochrēmatoi*). (8.551a7–8, trans. Grube/Reeve, modified)

And this in turn leads to a transformation as to whom among themselves the members of the ruling group most admire, and accordingly in whom they choose, from among themselves, either to "bring into office" or conversely to "dishonor" in the sense of excluding from office:

> And they praise the wealthy man and admire him and vest him in the offices (*eis tas archas agousi*), but dishonor (*atimazousi*) the poor man. (8.551a8–10)

At this point in the macro narrative, a new set of norms for choosing office-holders has emerged from within the existing timocratic constitution. For while "praise" has an old-fashioned ring to it, it was for the Greeks expressed in concrete social practices (such as epideictic rhetoric), and it equates to what we today might call an expression of what a society values. And whereas previously that (personified) constitution was said to incline toward appointing to the offices "spirited and simpler people . . . more naturally suited for war than peace" (8.547e1–548a2, trans. Grube/Reeve), now the unspecified "they" here, who have become the majority (as we saw in the sentence above), apply a new standard to their election of officeholders (election being clearly implied insofar as the mechanism of selection must allow them to apply a standard to their choice, which lottery would not). In short, the majority of timocrats now elect to the offices not the warlike but the wealthy. This changes the character of the constitution from within, as it were. Its institutions are still the same at this stage, but the people who are chosen to hold the offices within them—and so to shape the overall regime in line with their political predominance—are of a fatally different breed.

How do the explanatory principles enunciated by Socrates at the start of the narrative apply here, at this crucial juncture of constitutional change or transition? Once again, the Predominance principle explains the character of the constitution when understood in the terms of political predominance. But, this time, we see that it allows for a subtle change within the politically predominant group itself. This begins when one part of the group succumbs to material and psychological temptations, setting in motion a magnetic process of competitive emulation by which the majority convert themselves to this new tendency or direction and then express these new values by remaking the specific composition of the officeholders from within the broader politically eligible class. All this transpires within the existing unchanged institutional framework of the timocratic constitution. Yet it also creates a new reality within those institutions, as the people now typically elevated to the offices that they specify pursue a very different set of values from those who had been typically elevated to them before.

When it comes to the change from one constitution to the next, however, it is not Predominance but Disunity that is supposed to operate. And here, the fact that the new values are said to be embodied by a "majority"—but never said to apply unanimously—is crucial. For while Socrates does not dwell on the cleavage within the timocratic political class that this whole set of changes has produced, the term "majority" at 8.550e1–2 implies that there is a remaining minority who hold to the old values (a rump of Ciceros, as it were, still fighting a rearguard action against the Caesars and Pompeys). And so, less clearly, perhaps, than in the previous case, but once again, we see the Disunity principle at work, understanding officeholders now in the broader sense of those eligible for office rather than only those holding it. For it is the disunity within this broader political class that brings about the transition from the timocratic constitution to an oligarchical one.

The Oligarchic Constitution

That moment of transition is highlighted by Socrates as inhering in the passage of a new law,[69] serving to settle the "defining mark [*horos*]" of an oligarchic constitution:

> So then isn't a law made, settling a defining mark of the oligarchical constitution—a majority who are monied (more so where it is more an oligarchy, less so where it is less so), and declaring that the offices (*archōn*) must not be shared in (*metechein*) by anyone who should lack the wealth[70] specified by the property requirement? (8.551a12–b3)[71]

As a recent scholar of actual Greek oligarchies has observed, Plato's hypothetical account here rests on firm empirical ground: "*oligarchia* was a *politeia* in which access to the authoritative magistracies (*archai*) was restricted to those in possession of a certain (usually quite exclusionary) property requirement (*timēma*), who constituted the sovereign ruling element (*kurion politeuma*)."[72] Note that this requirement was a restriction not on the franchise but rather on who was eligible to hold the offices (*archai*), including service on the council (*boulē*).[73] In other words, what made a constitution an oligarchy was not the extent of its popular franchise, which might be narrower or wider, but rather the setting of a relatively high property assessment as the requirement for holding the offices—exactly as Socrates puts it here. Once again, Plato provides a detailed, and realistic, political science of Greek constitutions.

With this *horos* as the defining mark of the kind or type (*poia estin*) of the oligarchic constitution, Socrates goes on to discuss "what are its faults

---

69. Socrates's next speech after the introduction of the law clearly signals an end to the "coming to be" phase of the narrative for this constitution (8.551b7) and a shift to discussion of its nature, though that issue is immediately turned into an enumeration of its previously mentioned multiple faults (8.551b8–9, referring back to 8.544c4–5). Plato appears alert to the fact that actually existing past and present oligarchies (as of the time that he was writing) varied significantly in the level of the property qualifications that they established.

70. That is, excluding the poorer timocrats, as observed by Sikkenga ("Plato's Examination," 382–84).

71. I have modified the translation that I offered in "How to Turn History" (98), in part owing to discussion with André Laks (though the responsibility for the translation here is my own). Unlike Grube/Reeve, I construe *horon* with *taxamenoi*.

72. Simonton, *Classical Greek Oligarchy*, 40.

73. Simonton, 37 with n154; see also 95n95 on oligarchic offices.

(*hamartēmata*)" (8.551b8–9).[74] In fact, he identifies as the first fault "the very mark (*horos*) that defines it," and does so by asking about the nature of rule (*archē*, 8.551c6) that it exhibits. Here I think that the translation of the noun *hē archē* as "rule" is warranted, for reasons to do with Plato's consideration of rule in the *Republic* as a whole. That rethinking of rule begins already in book 1 of the dialogue, as argued in chapter 5, and the relevance of that context is underscored here by Socrates's invocation (to make the present point) of a central comparison used in that same project of book 1. Socrates asks: "What would happen if someone were to choose the steersmen of ships by a property valuation, refusing to entrust (*epitrepoi*) the ship to a poor person even if he were a better steersman?" (8.551c2–4)—to which Adeimantus responds emphatically, "They would make a poor journey of it" (8.551c5).

While briefly stated, this condemnation of the oligarchic constitution is as trenchant as the better known condemnatory use by means of the same comparison in the "Ship of State" image (*eikos*) in *Republic* 6 (6.488a1–489c5). That passage is generally read as a coded condemnation of Athenian-style democracy. But, in fact, Socrates introduces it by describing it as "what the most decent people suffer in relation to their cities" (6.488a2–3). In light of the use of the same image to condemn the oligarchic constitution specifically in book 8, I suggest that we should take Socrates at his word in book 6: the "Ship of State" is not meant to be a coded reference (only) to Athens or to democracy, despite certain features of the image (such as the use of persuasion or execution, and the semantic echoes of Socrates's fate) that do pick up on features of that regime. Rather, it is a condemnation of any and all cities in which the "true philosophers" do not rule: any city that is not a *kallipolis*.

Returning to the juncture of book 8 reached above: Socrates's next move is to generalize the case of the steersman to the case of "the rule [*archē*] of anything else whatsoever" (8.551c6, trans. Grube/Reeve).[75] He then drives home the point that this applies (a fortiori) to the case of rule "of a city," a point that Adeimantus again emphatically endorses, characterizing this case of *archē* as "the [kind of] rule that is most difficult and most important" (8.551c8–10). The second fault that Socrates identifies, however, takes issue with the strict application of the term "city" here, for it inheres in the fact that the city governed by an oligarchical constitution "of necessity . . . isn't one city but two—one of the poor and one of the rich" (8.551d5–7, trans. Grube/Reeve).[76] Yet, while this

74. Socrates here picks up his earlier observation that the oligarchic constitution would be attended by a "host of evils (*kakōn*)" (8.544c4–5, trans. Grube/Reeve).

75. Reading *ē tinos* in this line with the manuscripts despite Slings's seclusion of it from his OCT: the line in full being *oukoun kai peri allou houtōs hotououn ē tinos archēs*. As Adam (*"Republic" of Plato*) notes on this line of text, *peri* governs *archēs*, so as to draw a contrast between the rule of a city and the rule of anything else.

76. Rejecting Adam's proposed transposition of *anankē* from d5 to c5.

is a memorable indictment of oligarchy, it is merely an application of a general point made earlier in the dialogue: that no city except "the kind of city we are founding [i.e., a *kallipolis*] is worthy of being called a city [*polis*]," since any other apparent city will in reality consist of "two cities at war with one another, one of the poor, the other of the rich" (4.422e1–2, 422e6–423a1).

By contrast, the third fault of oligarchy enumerated is explained in terms specific to that particular constitution: it is the fact that "oligarchs probably aren't able to fight a war." This is said to be because doing so would require them either to arm the poor majority, thus endangering their own rule, or show up on the battlefield, revealing themselves in doing so as being few in number (punning on the semantic root *oligo-* ["few"] in their name; 8.551d9–e3). Conversely, the fourth is a fault that, while new in the sequence of degenerating constitutions, will turn out not to be unique to oligarchy, as it will be shared also by democracy. This is "the meddling in other people's affairs (*to polupragmonein*) that we [says Socrates] condemned before" (8.551e4)[77]—namely, that in this constitution "the same people [will] be farmers, money-makers, and soldiers simultaneously" (8.551e4–552a3) (translations in this sentence, Grube/Reeve).[78] The fifth and final fault will likewise be characterized as one that the oligarchic constitution is "the first to admit" (8.552a5, trans. Grube/Reeve), implying that it will be the first but not the last to do so, or, in other words, that on this score also democracy may be expected to follow in its footsteps.[79]

In fact, in turning to what should in sequence count as the fifth fault, Socrates reverts to his earlier and more intense word choice: he calls this fifth one not merely a "fault" but rather "the greatest of all evils (*tōn kakōn*)" (8.552a4–5, trans. Grube/Reeve). This is a striking superlative, given that it is presented as different from and greater than the first fault—the factionalizing of a single city into two cities, which itself would seem to have been fatally bad. In what does "the greatest of all evils" consist? It consists in:

> allowing someone to sell all his possessions and someone else to
> buy them and then allowing the one who has sold them to go on living in the city, while belonging to none of its parts, for he's neither a

77. The back reference may be meant to pick up any one of a number of passages in book 4 defining justice, and then specifically justice in the city (as well as in the individual)—for example, the account of justice as "doing one's own work and not meddling with what isn't one's own (*to ta hautou prattein kai mē polupragmonein*)" (4.433a8–9, trans. Grube/Reeve, recalling and stating a general definition of justice), applied specifically to the case of a city at 433d1–4 (*ouk epolupragmonei*); cf. 434b8–c10, 4.441d7–9, and passim, for the positive definition in the case of the city.

78. Here, as sometimes silently elsewhere, for the sake of smoothness of presentation, I convert what are in Greek posed as rhetorical or leading questions into English statements.

79. This is a point that Adeimantus already seems to grasp in replying "[the] first," meaning, as Grube and Reeve gloss his lapidary reply, that "it is the first to allow that" (8.552b3).

money-maker, a craftsman, a member of the cavalry, or a hoplite, but a poor person without means. (8.552a7–b2, trans. Grube/Reeve)

This breaching of the whole-part relationship of the city, in which an individual is allowed to live in a city without being a proper part of it, is counted as a bad in itself. In my terms, it counts as a distortion of the proper *taxis* of the constitution. And Socrates again spells out that this lack of proper membership in the city characterizes the profligate spendthrift oligarch even before he has taken the final step of selling all his possessions:

> When the person who sells all his possessions was rich and spending his money, was he of any greater use to the city in the ways we've just mentioned than when he'd spent it all? Or did he merely seem to be one of the officeholders (*tōn archontōn*) of the city, while in truth he was neither officeholder nor subject (*oute archōn oute hupēretēs*) there, but only a squanderer of his property? (8.552b8–11, put in the form of a rhetorical question; trans. Grube/Reeve, modified)[80]

Here Plato treats office in a strict evaluative sense, to return once again to an idea introduced in chapter 1. Like the wealthy oligarch here, someone can be nominally "employed," as it were, as an officeholder (so characterized according to the descriptive face of the idea), yet (according to its evaluative face) not be a real or true officeholder at all.

Remarkable here is that it is not solely the bankrupted poor person who no longer counts as a part of the city (8.552a8–9). No more a part of the city is someone who is actually ensconced in office, but who squanders his substance and so fails to conserve the basis on which he was eligible for office in the first place. While the aim of accumulating wealth and the use of that as a threshold for office is an imperfect and flawed way to define a constitution, it is nevertheless the criterion by which this regime is established and governed. To flout it by trying to remain in office while impoverished is to flout the constitutional order that the erstwhile oligarch is supposed to be upholding. Here it is an officeholder who is first disobedient to the skeletal order (*taxis*) of rule, not any one of those over whom he rules.[81] If the exploiter of office for private gain violates the *telos* of office as a species of rule, which was first analytically advanced in book 1, the spendthrift oligarchical officeholder violates the *taxis* of office in failing to obey the legal requirements for holding the office that he

---

80. One could alternatively preserve "ruler" in the translation of *oute archōn oute hupēretēs* because of the neat contrast with "subject," as I did in "How to Turn History" (99), but construe "ruler" in the specific sense of "officeholder."

81. This reinforces the point that Plato is entirely willing to entertain the disobedience of officeholders as the first step in the degeneration of a constitution, consistent indeed with the Disunity principle (which disobedience by officeholders is one way of manifesting)— pace Sørensen, "Political Office," as discussed earlier, 138n54.

does. Both, in different ways, distort the idea of office understood in evaluative terms.

At this point, Socrates introduces the image of the drone, or, more specifically, various kinds of drones. This image will become central to all that follows in both the macro and micro narratives, as each moves from the case of oligarchy (oligarchic individual) to democracy (democratic individual) to tyranny (tyrannical individual and his role as a political tyrant). As such a shared trope, it gives structure to the unified comparative political science of oligarchy, democracy, and tyranny that Socrates highlights as emerging within the broader explanatory schemata already in play. In particular, the two constitutions that were actual contenders for power in Greek cities in the mid-fifth to mid-fourth centuries (spanning the dramatic setting of the dialogue as well as the likely time of Plato's having composed it) are presented by Plato here as sharing key analytical characteristics. These characteristics not only link them in a likely sequence of degeneration but also shed light on their respective workings—points that are underlined by Socrates's presentation, as we shall see.

The image of the drone builds on a Greek view evident in Hesiod and Aristophanes:[82] that drones were different in kind from bees, the former being treated in these texts as invasive parasites that would infect a beehive, such that a good beekeeper would try to keep them out of the hive or cut out the infected part of a hive if necessary (see the later recapitulation of this point in the transition from democracy to tyranny, 8.564b–c). Here in the *Republic*, they are used metaphorically for people who were once (or at least could potentially have counted as) internal parts of the city, but who become an alien element, one that poses a criminal threat and no longer counts as a proper part of the city—in contrast to Aristophanes's portrayal, for example, in which jurors are wasps (bees) with stings who get angry, while demagogues are drones who live off the substance of the people. However, as Danielle Allen has observed, Plato diverges from Hesiod and Aristophanes in a key respect: "Socrates redefines the category of drone to include not only stingless types but also drones with stings, a category that did not exist in Hesiod or Aristophanes and that does not exist in nature"; a move that he makes, in her view, in order to vilify and transform democratic Athenian attitudes toward anger.[83] The very depiction of the dynamics of democratic politics in the dialogue incorporates that transformation.

As the image is initially developed at this point in the dialogue: the spendthrift oligarch is presented as a drone, but a winged one, implying (as the

82. Hesiod (*Theogony* 504, *Works and Days* 304), and for Athenian democratic culture, Aristophanes (*Wasps* 1114–16).

83. D. Allen, "Angry Bees," 97. Brock (*Greek Political Imagery*, 187n134) credits this insight already to Pelletier in a 1948 article in *Revue de philologie, de littérature et d'histoire anciennes*.

image unfolds) that he (at least initially) possesses property. And all winged drones are held to be stingless, a quality that is not defined here, but that later will be said to indicate the more cowardly of the drones who are followers of the bravest, stinged drones who emerge as leaders (8.564b4–7). Here, it is rather the wealth of the winged drones that seems to explain why they will not become common criminals, those who carry out any one of a number of crimes— "thieves, pickpockets, temple-robbers, and all such evil-doers" (8.552d4–5, trans. Grube/Reeve)—referring here to those that the just person was said not to be likely to commit in book 4 (4.442e4–443b3, where temple robberies, thefts, and embezzlement were among the specific crimes excluded).

By contrast, wingless (poor) drones are divided into two groups. Some are stingless: they are beggars (who presumably are followers in the sense of making no trouble for the constitutional order as such). Others, those who are wingless but have stings, become common criminals (who presumably are leaders in the sense that they challenge the laws of the constitutional order), albeit that they are controlled by the oligarchic officeholders by means of legal force (8.552c4–e4).[84]

Socrates sums up this part of the discussion by explaining that such people (the various kinds of drones enumerated above) arise in the city owing to "lack of education, bad rearing, and a bad constitutional arrangement" (8.552e5–7, trans. Grube/Reeve). Education and its failings in rearing or upbringing more broadly—a fundamental failure due to the lack of rulers capable of safeguarding the educative and selective process—lies at the heart of the transvaluation of values that will soon unfold within this unstable oligarchic constitution, just as it does in the transvaluation of values at each state of the macro narrative (and, indeed, of the micro narrative as well).

Transition to Democracy

Having seen how the oligarchy is born, its character, and its faults, how then does its demise take place?[85] Socrates begins with a sketch of the transition, asking: "Isn't the city changed from an oligarchy to a democracy in some such way as this, because of its insatiate desire [*aplēstia*] to attain what it has set before itself as the good (*tou prokeimenou agathou*); namely, the need to

84. Simonton (*Classical Greek Oligarchy*, 71 with n304) notes this passage and comments more broadly on the use of *epimeleia* characteristic of oligarchs; cf. 108 and passim.

85. For the timocracy, the transition is traced before the nature of the new constitution is stated; for the oligarchy, the nature of the new constitution is stated briefly before the transition is outlined and then the nature is restated. For the democracy, Socrates makes a methodological remark recalling the need to discuss first *genesis* ("how it comes into being (*genomenon*)") and then what I generally refer to as *poios tis*, here in the grammatical form *poion tina* ("what it is," in the sense of what character it has when it does).

become as rich as possible?" (8.555b9–11, trans. Grube/Reeve, modified).[86] Notice here the emphasis on the flawed conception of the good (flawed in regard to the true Good) as the *telos* adopted by the oligarchy in decline. And once again, this psychological motivation (stated here as belonging to the city generally, but implied by the Predominance principle to be the psychological motivation of the politically predominant group) is mediated through the constitutional institution of officeholding in order to bring about the transition to a different kind of constitution. Indeed, Socrates specifies that the entrenched position of ruling or holding office on the basis of wealth creates an ideological blind spot in the officeholders. Their short-sighted motivation to gain more and more wealth, and as a result more and more honor (which may signify also continuing to be elected to offices), leads them to be unwilling to pass laws that could check the spendthrift tendencies of the young. This unwillingness is what will ultimately undermine their rule and the oligarchical constitution itself.

To put this point in model-theoretic terms,[87] the oligarchical officeholders cannot collectively protect their own constitutional game because they are individually too invested in the project of private moneymaking to be willing to rein in the dangerous consequences that their private projects threaten:

> Since the officeholders (*archontes*) in the city are the officeholders (*hoi archontes*) because they own a lot, I suppose they're unwilling to enact laws to prevent young people who've had no discipline from spending and wasting their wealth, so that by making loans to them, secured by the young people's property, and then calling those loans in, they themselves become even richer and more honored. (8.555c1–5, trans. Grube/Reeve)

Here, the proper *telos* of office is articulated by way of its absence. It is the lack of public purpose, of a willingness to use office for the benefit of the ruled rather than resort to exploiting it for one's own private gain, that eventually brings down the oligarchy. Even while the oligarchic officeholders retain a sufficiently ordered constitution (in the shape of a *taxis* of officeholding with broadly adequate powers of command and concomitant expectations of obedience) to potentially use their powers for the right purposes, they refuse to do so. It is their own misuse of (including the failure to properly use) the powers of their office that brings about their constitution's demise.

Once again, as in the earlier presentation of the character of the oligarchic constitution, this initial statement uses an unspecified "they," which

---

86. In the extended context of this passage, Socrates also characterizes the oligarchy as having an "insatiate desire for wealth" as its key destructive flaw (8.562b4–5). No analogous point is made about the *kallipolis*'s desire for virtue, or the timocracy's desire for honor.

87. Here I am thinking of a comparison to Ober and Weingast's "Sparta Game."

might seem to imply that the oligarchs are at least remaining united in their self-destructive purposes. Against such a reading, however, is the fact that its positing of the group of officeholders causing the demise of its own constitution as a united group would violate the Disunity principle. Therefore, following a principle of interpretative charity, a better reading of the unspecified "they" would take it to play a similar role to the unspecified "they" in the timocratic case: namely, as appearing in the service of tracing a schism that opens up within the officeholding group. For the neglect of moderation that the officeholding oligarchs encourage leads to some among the broader group bankrupting not only others (as above) but also themselves. And since the oligarchic constitution by definition disenfranchises anyone who falls below the property requirement, these people "sit idle in the city . . . with their stings and weapons—some in debt, some disenfranchised (*atimoi*), some both—hating those who've acquired their property, plotting against them and others, and longing for a revolution" (8.555d7–e2, trans. Grube/Reeve).

The still-monied make matters worse through continued moneylending, and once again refuse—as officeholders—to pass either the law mentioned above or a "second-best one which compels the citizens to care about virtue by prescribing that the majority of voluntary contracts be entered into at the lender's own risk" (8.556a9–b2, trans. Grube/Reeve). Instead, they double down on their own neglect of virtue and on their neglect of it in the education of their children. Whereas an institutional solution could in theory stabilize the regime (though a legal change without a better educational system to engender virtue would probably be of only temporary use), these officeholders put their private interests above securing the stability of the constitution in which they serve (or, one might say in ironic tones, "serve"). Once again, while the *taxis*, which relies upon sufficient normative acceptance of the roles of command and obedience by the citizens and the officeholders generally, is still intact, the *telos* which that officeholding order serves as an instantiation of rule is further and characteristically corrupted.

The Disunity principle is honored in this account of the dynamics of the breakdown of oligarchy and its transformation into democracy: it is the breach in the unity of the oligarchic class by the indebtedness, impoverishment, and in some cases disenfranchisement of some of them by others that explains how it is possible for the constitution to change. For the breach of this unity, due to *stasis*, which factionalizes the politically predominant few, results in some of the erstwhile oligarchs becoming bankrupted agitators among the greater body of the poor. And that in turn will result in a revolution from below (a possibility also noted by Aristotle).[88] Here, the dynamics of the Disunity principle are embedded in a larger class divide—itself also a matter of *stasis*—between

---

88. *Pol.* 5.1306a9, a connection noted by Newman in his commentary on the *Politics*, as cited by Simonton (*Classical Greek Oligarchy*, 248n94).

the rich and the poor characterizing the oligarchic city, which explains the further dynamics of the revolution to follow. Nevertheless, this more complex explanation does not breach the Disunity principle, since the group acting from "below" includes disenfranchised and otherwise disenchanted erstwhile oligarchic officeholders among them.

The analysis of those further dynamics will take on the character of a diagnosis, underscored by the comparison to the medical diagnosis of a sick human body. Before that medical comparison is invoked, Socrates describes the social encounters between the complacent and indolent rich (who have abandoned the timocratic virtue that had enabled their forebears to suppress and exploit the poor) and the poor who are members of the city. In an oligarchy, as Plato observes (once again realistically), the poor are participants in the city's festivals, embassies, and wars, even though they are by its very constitutional definition excluded from its offices:

> But when officeholders and those ruled (*hoi te archontes kai hoi archomenoi*) in this condition meet on a journey or some other common undertaking—it might be a festival, an embassy, or a campaign, or they might be shipmates or fellow soldiers—and see one another in danger, in these circumstances are the poor in any way despised by the rich? Or rather isn't it often the case that a poor man, lean and suntanned, stands in battle next to a rich man, reared in the shade and carrying a lot of excess flesh, and sees him panting and at a loss? And don't you think that he'd consider that it's through the cowardice of the poor that such people are rich and that one poor man would say to another when they met in private: "These people are ours; they're nothing"? (8.556c6–e2, trans. Grube/Reeve, modified).[89]

Matthew Simonton draws on this passage, along with other parts of Plato and Aristotle, in his game-theoretic account of *stasis* in the context of transitions away from oligarchic regimes in ancient Greek history. As "setting[s] where rulers and ruled in an oligarchy are likely to encounter one another," he highlights precisely the festivals (*theoriai*) and military campaigns (*strateiai*) mentioned in this passage.[90] He also highlights Socrates's subsequent observation that such a city is like a sick body, which "needs only a tiny imbalancing-weight (*mikras ropēs*)[91] from outside to become ill"—an outside weight that in the

---

89. Grube/Reeve translate *hoi te archontes kai hoi archomenoi* as "rulers and subjects," and embroider (albeit persuasively) the bit of imagined closing dialogue (which reads in Greek, *Andres hēmeteroi. Eisi gar ouden*) as "'These people are at our mercy; they're good for nothing.'"

90. Simonton, *Classical Greek Oligarchy*, 237, and 224–73 more generally.

91. Simonton (246) helpfully translates *mikras ropēs* as a "tiny imbalance," which I have adapted; contrast Grube/Reeve's translation as "slight shock," which obscures the metaphorical framework of a balancing scale.

case of a city might be constituted by "one side bringing in allies from an oligarchy or the other from a democracy." Indeed, as Simonton notes, Socrates remarks that a city may sometimes find itself "in a state of civil war (*stasiazei*)" even without any such external imbalancing (8.556e4–10). Once again, Plato is remarkably realist in his political science here, to the extent that his account can serve modern scholars as evidence of the actual dynamics of Greek oligarchies, even as their studies help to illuminate Plato's text in turn.

The Democratic Constitution

As per his procedure with regard to the timocracy and the oligarchy, having recounted the process by which a constitution has been brought about, Socrates offers a formal definition of the nature of that constitution. In the case of the democracy, it goes as follows, beginning with a summation of the process of constitutional change that has just been described:

> And I suppose that democracy comes about when the poor are victorious [in the revolution against the rich described above], killing some of their opponents and expelling others, and giving those who remain (*tois . . . loipois*) an equal share in the constitution and in the offices (*ex isou metadōsi politeias te kai archōn*), and for the most part assigning people to the offices (*hai archai*) in the constitution by means of lot. (8.557a2–5, trans. Grube/Reeve, modified)[92]

The verb translated here as "giving . . . an equal share" (*metadidōmi*), is used of offices already in Herodotus (7.150), and in a number of fourth-century texts as well.[93] Sharing in "offices," as Plato astutely uses it here, is the maximal form of political participation and status; a related verb was used in exactly

92. For the reasons developed in this chapter and throughout this study, I translate *archōn* and *hai archai* here both in terms of offices: while the former is a judgment call, the plural-noun form of the latter makes the sense of "office" unambiguous, given the technical vocabulary for office established in Greek politics at the time. Contrast Grube/Reeve's translation of these terms as "ruling" and "positions of rule" respectively, both of which are less precise in specifying the intended sense; they also translate *tois . . . loipois* as "the rest," implying that this is a reference only to the "rest" of the rich, whereas I translate "those who remain" to capture the reference as being to all those remaining in the city after some of the rich have been killed and others exiled. André Laks suggested to me that the final clause of the sentence could mean that democracies generally assign people to the offices by means of lot, rather than that they use lot for the most part but also at other times election; both readings are possible, but given that even Athens at its most democratic did not use lot exclusively, I find the reading that I have given in the main text more plausible.

93. See Aristotle (*Pol.* 4.1306a25), Isocrates (13.10), and others. A phrase that is very similar to Plato's description of democracy at 8.557a2–5 is used by the orator Lysias (25.3): *tois mēden adikousin ex isou tēs politeias metadidonai* (to give an equal share in the constitution to those who have committed no injustice).

this sense back in the initial identification of the oligarchic constitution, when Socrates declared that in such a constitution the poor "have no share in office (*ou metestin archēs*)" (8.550d12). But sharing in the "constitution," which also features in the present passage as an object of *metadidōmi*, could have a broader meaning, whereby one might be either ineligible, or in practice unlikely, to hold office, yet be able to engage in other forms of political participation, such as controlling the officeholders by holding them to account, as argued in earlier chapters.[94] In an extended and loose sense, every citizen in a democracy might be considered eligible for office (and so within the scope of Predominance), though various Greek democracies did set low property thresholds for citizenship, office, or both.

To be sure, the idea of "sharing in the constitution" was more commonly associated with the verb *metechein*. As one scholar has helpfully explained of Athenian usage:

> In democratic Athens, the verb commonly used for participation was *metechein*, "to have a share," with the connotation "a share to use actively with others." Its usage in combination with "the *polis*"—that is, "to have a share in the *polis*" meaning "to be a participating citizen"— emerged in the early fourth century . . . to become a popular expression in Athenian political discourse. *Metechein* in the *polis* meant belonging to the group and participating in all it did, while *metechein* in the *politeia* usually meant participating in the political decision making of the *polis*.[95]

This formulation features both in Athenian democratic contexts and also in Aristotelian or Aristotelian-connected texts.[96] The Aristotelian circle's (if it

94. Indeed, the original meaning of *politeia* was "citizenship," and understanding it here to signal an equal share in citizenship would be in line with these practices, though in the next line the back reference by means of *en autēi* is better construed as "constitution."

95. Blok, "Citizenship," 168, citing (inter alia) Lys., 2.77, 16.3; Isoc., 21.2, 18.49; Pseudo-Aristotle, *Rhetorica ad Alexandrum* 1424a39–b14.

96. Notably, however, the same verb can be used outside democratic contexts as well, and there the line between "sharing in the constitution" and "sharing in the offices" can be blurred. For example, the fourth-century *Rhetorica ad Alexandrum* (2.18–19) advises that "in the case of oligarchies, the laws should assign the offices on an equal footing to all those sharing in the constitution (*tois tēs politeias metechousi*)." This could in principle mean a restricted citizen roll. But in the next sentence, which begins in the next section (2.19), the sequel suggests that the poor (described as the *plēthos*) in such oligarchies are also citizens, who are liable to resent the insolent treatment that should be prohibited by law—even though they do not "share in the constitution" in the sense of being eligible to hold office. I translate "all those sharing in the constitution" as opposed to the translation by Rackham in Benson and Prosser's *Readings in Classical Rhetoric*, as "all those sharing in citizenship": their translation of this phrase cannot be correct, since the conclusion of the discussion is that the multitude in an oligarchy will be citizens but will be excluded from office. I adapt part of this note from my "Popular Sovereignty" (57).

is not Aristotle's own) historical recounting, in the *Constitution of the Athenians*, declares that under the "primitive constitution" and the constitution introduced by Draco, the people "had virtually no share (*metechontes*)" in the "constitution" (2.3),[97] whereas in contrast Solon enabled the poor multitude to share (*metechein*) (implicitly, in the constitution), by making them assemblymen and jurors. And in the *Politics* (3.11), Aristotle himself develops an argument in which the poor multitude can count as *kurios* without sharing (*metechein*) in the offices, by electing the officeholders and holding them to account by means of *euthunai* or formal accountability procedures.[98] So within the ambit of Greek constitutional practice and thinking, one might live in a regime without counting as a citizen, or count as a citizen without being eligible to hold office, or be eligible to hold office without actually holding it. Plato's text can again be called realist in its sensitivity to all of these permutations that were so important to the Greek understanding of political organization in different constitutional orders.

Interestingly, whereas in the case of oligarchy Socrates organized his subsequent discussion of what this kind of constitution is (like), its kind or (in a loose sense) nature (*poia estin*, in a question by Adeimantus, 8.551b8–9) in terms of faults in the constitution itself, in the case of democracy he yokes the question of its kind to a question about "how . . . these people live" (8.557a9–b1).[99] This introduces a discussion of the way of life of the people in a democratic city, a theme that is explicitly highlighted only in the cases of democracy and tyranny, though a similar account was provided unheralded as such in the cases of oligarchy and timocracy—each containing a distinct commentary on the characteristic people who are elected to the offices and (in the case of the oligarchy and democracy) how they characteristically misuse those offices in each constitution and harbor people who distort the obedience that offices should require.

In the case of the timocracy, following the account of which people will in the timocratic constitution be elected to offices (8.547e1–548a4), Socrates canvassed the following dimensions of such a city: psychological (love of honor, but also secret love of money), domestic and economic (private houses with secret treasuries and storehouses), and educational (neglect of the Muse of discussion and philosophy, and neglect of music and poetry) condition of the

---

97. "Constitution" must be supplied as the object of *metechontes*, having been mentioned two lines earlier.

98. "To give them no share and not to allow them to share (*metechein*) at all would be cause for alarm (for a state in which a large number of people are excluded from office and are poor must of necessity be full of enemies)" (3.1281b28–30, trans. Reeve, modifying his punctuation). See also 4.1290a7–13. For the general expression and idea in Aristotle, see Schofield (*Saving the City*, 141–59), and my "Popular Sovereignty."

99. The Greek is *tina dē oun . . . houtoi tropon oikousi; kai poia tis hē toiautē au politeia.*

timocrats (8.548a5–d5). The same themes were covered in the case of the oligarchic city: psychological (love of money, now publicly manifest [8.551e2]), domestic and economic (*to polupragmein*, or playing multiple roles in the constitution and city simultaneously), and educational (allowing beggars and criminals to develop, though keeping them in check through force). In the case of the democracy, however, while expounding the psychological desires of the politically predominant group within the democratic constitution (thus demonstrating the Predominance principle), and then explaining the distinctive characteristics of the officeholding group, Socrates only briefly comments on its domestic, economic, and educational arrangements. In doing so, he focuses primarily on its failure to insist on carrying out legal sentences of death or exile;[100] its educational failure in despising the kind of care that a *kallipolis* would by definition take in educating the potential guardians; and its related political failure in choosing people for office while "giving no thought to what someone was doing before he entered public life and . . . honoring him if only he tells them that he wishes the majority well" (8.558b5–7, put as a rhetorical question, trans. Grube/Reeve).[101] Once again, education is crucial in generating the transvaluation of values that expresses itself in transformed attitudes to law and office, among the officeholders and those who are meant to be ruled by them alike.

Socrates opens his account of the character of the democratic constitution by invoking one feature of the democratic city: freedom. This might tempt the reader to believe that it is the "love of freedom" that characterizes and motivates those who are politically predominant in that city, parallel to the "love of honor" and "love of money" in the preceding two constitutions.[102] But, in

---

100. Nails ("*Republic* in Its Athenian Context," 13) comments on this line, beginning by translating it in full as follows: "'people condemned to death and exile under such a constitution stay on at the center of things, strolling around like ghosts of dead heroes, without anyone staring at them or giving them a thought' (8.558a4–8)." She explains that "the incident that provokes the remark is the sacrilege scandal of 415," which (as she details: I paraphrase her) had involved the mutilation of the city's herms (boundary markers engraved with images of the god Hermes), and the accusation of a number of prominent men of having profaned a celebration of the Eleusinian mysteries, and notes that several of these men were subsequently recalled to active military and political service, and that others then returned to Athens despite having been sentenced to death or exile: "Plato was then [in 415] about nine, and about seventeen when the condemned and exiled men began returning to Athens and strolling around."

101. "Honoring (*timai*)" is a broader notion here, which includes without being limited to the choosing of someone to hold an office. Recall that in the democratic constitution as presented earlier, lottery is said to be used to choose officeholders only "for the most part," implying that election is used for the rest (as was the case in democratic Athens in both the fifth and fourth centuries).

102. The "love of honor" and "love of money" are mentioned as two motives for ruling, as opposed to the penalty that motivates the best people to rule (1.347b1–4), as discussed above in chapters 5 and 6.

fact, he does not use the phrase "desire for freedom" until the later description of the degeneration of the democratic constitution into a tyranny, when he characterizes the "insatiate desire for freedom and the neglect of other things" as what will "change this constitution and put it in need of a dictatorship."[103] Rather, in the democratic constitution in its normal (nondegenerating) condition, as it were, freedom is the condition that allows individuals in the city (in particular, those who are politically predominant—namely, the democratic majority) to pursue whatever it is that they individually desire ("Doesn't everyone in it have the license to do what he wants [?] . . . And where people have this license, it's clear that each of them will arrange his own life in whatever manner pleases him" [8.557b5–c3, trans. Grube/Reeve]). It is this variety in the individual desires of the democratic majority—unlike the relative uniformity in the individual desires of the politically predominant timocrats and oligarchs—that explains Socrates's claim that the democratic city, like a multicolored (poikilon) cloak, "contains all kinds of constitutions on account of the license it gives its citizens."[104]

The same phenomenon of license explains the distinctively problematic relationship of the democratic majority to officeholding: a majority who now count as numerically preponderant as well as politically predominant. This is because, while in the other flawed cities of book 8 (barring the tyranny) each constitution is formally defined in terms of the eligibility for officeholding—in this case, giving those remaining in the city "an equal share in the constitution and in the offices (ex isou metadōsi politeias te kai archōn)," 8.557a4—the relationship of the officeholders to their offices is in the democratic city doubly complex. On the one hand, any democratic citizen is eligible to hold office (in the simplified portrait of book 8, which does away with the property qualifications for office that all actual Greek democracies had, even Athens at least in the fifth century and arguably in the fourth). On the other hand, some of them

---

103. 8.562c4–6, trans. Grube/Reeve. My observation on this point dovetails with Nicolay's "Plato on the Origins" and also Origins of License, in both of which he more broadly traces a shift in the attitudes of the democratic majority as the narrative of the democracy progresses (or degenerates), from valuing freedom as instrumental to satisfying their nonnecessary desires to a second-order valuing of freedom for its own sake, work from which I have learned a great deal.

104. 8.557c5, 8. 557d2, respectively, trans. Grube/Reeve. On the cloak image: Villacéque ("De la bigarrure") situates the writing of the Republic in the 380s in Athens, at which time a himation poikilon, a multicolored coat or cloak (a garment with resonances of Odysseus and Medea), carried connotations of poikilia being transposed from a previously aristocratic value to one that Plato associates with elite competition within the democracy and with democratic spectacles (she points out Plato's avoidance of the term dēmos here in favor of the plural hoi polloi). As for Plato: Euthphr. 6c2–4 explicitly refers to the cloak woven by the women of Athens and brought in procession to the Parthenon every four years in celebration of the Panathenaia festival; Blondell ("Fleece to Fabric") argues that the closing image of the cloak in Plt. 311b7–c7 likewise does so implicitly.

may have an aversion to doing so, and more of them will manifest an aversion to being ruled by those who happen to occupy the offices at a given time.[105] Socrates describes the democratic constitution as imposing "no requirement to rule (*archein*), even if you're capable of it, or again to be ruled (*archesthai*) if you don't want to be" (8.557e1–3, trans. Grube/Reeve), a sentence in which the reference to rule is clearly cashed out in the surrounding context as ruling in the form of officeholding. Moreover, the same constitution is said to fail to prevent anyone who wishes to "serve in public office or as a juror (*kai archēis kai dikazēis*)" from doing so, "even if there is a law forbidding you to do so" (8.557e5–558a1, trans. Grube/Reeve, modified).[106]

In other words, it appears that the slack enforcement associated with the democratic constitution's *taxis* of office opens the door to whomever among its citizens seeks to avoid holding office, on the one hand, or being bound by the orders of the officeholders, on the other. Conversely, the same slack enforcement also opens the door to whomever among its citizens seeks to hold office or serve as a juror even when the *taxis* of officeholding as defined would prevent them from doing so. In other words, while Socrates does not quantify the proportion of people falling into one or the other of these groups, it seems safe to infer that members of the politically predominant group in the democratic constitution manifest both an aversion to obeying officeholders and also a potential aversion (at least for some of them) to holding office when they should (presumably in virtue of their superior knowledge and expertise) be expected to do so.

Here, in the breach, not only the *telos* of office is being violated but so too the basic expectation of command and obedience that is central to the *taxis* of constitutionally defined offices, and to any kind of rule more broadly. Not being ruled if you do not wish to be is a violation of the role relationship of order and obedience between ruler and ruled, whereas choosing not to rule even when you could rule well is a violation of the *telos* of office. Thus the democrats have no stable ideological investment in officeholding. As with everything else they do, their attitude to it is a matter of whim. If the timocrats and the oligarchs misuse (and so distort) office, the democrats cannot be said to use it at all—or, perhaps, to hold it in anything more than mere name. When the requirements of rule as a fundamental *taxis* are breached, in

---

105. For an attribution of similar aversion to being ruled to democrats (implicitly including Athenians) by Xenophon, see my "Xenophon (and Thucydides)."

106. Grube/Reeve translate *kai archēis kai dikazēis* as "serve in public office as a juror." But *kai* can also be translated as "or," and given the fact that jurors did not technically count as holding offices in the Athenian democracy, it makes at least as much sense so to translate it here, taking serving in public office as one of the cases to which Socrates's stricture applies, jury service as another. In the latter part of the passage quoted, the sudden shift to the second person singular may be a pointed suggestion that Adeimantus is one of those who might be tempted to violate the legal limits on officeholding.

other words, the basis for any kind of constitutional order at all is beginning to disintegrate.

This is the key to the meaning of *anarchos* at 558c2, the adjective corresponding to the word *anarchia* that appears again in the context of the tyrannical man becoming a political tyrant in book 9 (9.575a1). Here in *Republic* 8, it is used in summing up the democratic constitution:

> It would seem to be a pleasant constitution, one in which there is no one in office (*anarchos*) [an adjective unpacked in the translation by the prepositional phrase "one in which"] but there is great variety, and which distributes a kind of equality to both equals and unequals alike. (8.558c2–4)

Anarchos, as an adjective, must be understood—in light of the intertwined Greek vocabulary for office and rule that this study has explained (beginning in part I)—specifically as the privation or absence of rule, either understood broadly, or understood specifically in the sense of office.[107] In this context, given that this is a democratic constitution in which the rulers are all office-holders, it should be taken to indicate an absence of an officeholder that is not absence in any accidental or contingent sense. It is not here a simple vacancy of office or rule, nor (yet, as it will be in the tyranny) the effective abolition of the roles of office and rule altogether. Rather, it refers here to an office not being properly constituted by the appropriate dispositions of both its holders and their subjects, such that there can be no meaningful exercise of or obedience to office.[108]

(There is an ironic moment in Sophocles's *Antigone* in which Creon asserts "that there is no evil worse than *anarchia*" [line 672]. The newly established Theban ruler begins his reflections by stating the crucial importance of obedience [*kluein*, literally "to hear" in the sense of "comply with, obey"] to anyone whom the city should "set up" as ruler [line 666]. This is echoed at the end of his speech in "obedience" in the specific sense of "obedience to command" (*peitharchia*) [line 676].[109] Even a tyrant can demand obedience, but as the

---

107. Having in 2017 presented as the Else Lecture at the University of Michigan–Ann Arbor the initial fruits of my research on *anarchia* in Greek usage, I then learned of (and from) the work of Laffon ("ἀναρχία (anarchia)") on the senses of the word and its use in various contexts.

108. Cf. Johnstone, in "Anarchic Souls," who reads *anarchos* as meaning "not ruled in a stable and enduring way" (140; see also passim), failing to recognize the technical vocabulary of office here, and, similarly, Saxonhouse ("Democracy, Equality," 280), who reads *anarchos* as "being without rule." Of course, office is a kind of rule, as this study contends, but the context of the democratic constitution makes a reference to office the better (because more informative) translation.

109. Creon also invokes both ruling and being ruled as capacities appropriate to a good ruler (*archein . . . archesthai*, lines 668–69).

play unfolds we find that Creon rejects the voices of the people of the city and the customary unwritten religious laws alike, which would and should moderate rule at least to approximate an evaluative purpose (*telos*) of benefiting the ruled. On a Platonic account, Creon's sway itself would turn out to be a form of the very *anarchia* that he decries.)[110]

As I have argued elsewhere, *anarchos* here signifies a "disobedience [which might be by officeholder or by subjects of the office] which is so great as to be tantamount to a destruction of the proper constitution of office"[111]—albeit that, in the whimsical reference to the degenerating democratic constitution as breeding "anarchy even among the animals" (8.562e3–4, trans. Grube/ Reeve), the meaning can be only metaphorically related to officeholding. But back in the description of the nature of the democratic constitution as such, Socrates had envisaged that no one eligible to hold office in this constitution (including, but not limited to, the politically predominant democratic majority) has any stable, as opposed to occasional or whimsical, ambition to serve in office. And, conversely, those who have been barred from office or jury service may nevertheless serve if they so choose.

Both of these features of the democratic constitution suggest that the legal entitlements and duties of office are being hollowed out in spirit even if purportedly followed. The very idea of rule, as expressed in the specific form of a *taxis* or order of constitutional office, is here disintegrating, and taking the *telos* of office and rule with it. One finds here a kind of shadow play in which people are purportedly chosen for office and nominally claim to hold it, but in so doing violate the most basic expectations of command and obedience without which it becomes meaningless, such that there is really no one in office at all, insofar as no one is disposed either to command or to obey.[112] In the

110. As would Trump's: Lane, "Why Donald Trump."

111. Lane, *"Antianarchia,"* 68.

112. Bloom ("Interpretive Essay," in *"Republic" of Plato*, 418) observes that "democracy is essentially a transitional regime because its principle, freedom, does not encourage the respect for law requisite to the maintenance of a regime." I add to this, more specifically, respect for office and obedience to officeholders. In "Placing Plato," with regard to Plato, and in "Xenophon (and Thucydides)," with regard to Xenophon, I have argued that both of these two Socratics emphasized that Sparta was more characteristically suited than Athens to the kind of freedom that is compatible with obedience to officeholders as well as to laws. As I put this point in "Xenophon (and Thucydides)" (130–31):

> The laconizing tradition, expressed more straightforwardly (though not without caveat and limit) in Xenophon than in Plato, is of course *parti pris*. Yet the psychological insight that it offers here in both authors—that there is a risk to political obedience stemming from an unwillingness to be thought slavish in obeying one's fellows—is nevertheless an insight worth taking seriously. It reminds us that the so-called rule of law can never be wholly bloodless. The rule of law must also always involve the rule of some humans over others, and those others being willing to obey the officeholders as their rulers as well as (and not only) the laws alone.

degenerating democratic constitution's misunderstanding of political freedom as incompatible with willing obedience to rule, Plato offers an implicit
indication (to be explored further in chapter 10) of the way in which political
freedom should be conceived in order to preserve that compatibility. *Anarchia*
marks a case where the compossibility of rule and freedom has broken down.

Before turning to the narrative of the transition to tyranny, it is worth
reflecting further on the relationship between anarchy and tyranny in Greek
texts prior to or contemporaneous to Plato, in order to delve into the meaning of their close juxtaposition in these passages of the *Republic*.[113] Before
Plato, the relationship between anarchy and tyranny was most commonly,
and significantly, taken to be one of opposition: anarchy being an absence of
(properly constituted, whether in the sense of legitimate or effective or both)
leaders or officeholders, whereas tyranny was a condition characterized by an
all-too-present and powerful leader. This is manifest in Aeschylus's *Eumenides* at line 696, in the course of Athena's establishment of the Athenian tri-
bunal to try Orestes: "Neither anarchy nor tyranny (*to mēt' anarkhon mēte
despotoumenon*)—this I counsel my citizens to support and respect, and not to
drive fear wholly out of the city" (696–97, trans. Smyth).[114] Aeschylus's Athena
positions anarchy and tyranny as two extremes, both of which the Athenians
should seek to avoid in their city, a positioning prefigured in very similar language by the chorus of Erinyes (Furies) earlier in the same play (527–28).[115]
A similar contrast between anarchy and tyranny is drawn in Isocrates's *Panegyricus*: "finding the Hellenes living without laws and in scattered abodes,
some oppressed by tyrannies [*dunasteiai*], others perishing through anarchy
[*anarchia*] . . ."[116]

113. The remainder of this section is adapted from my "*Antianarchia*" (66–69) and
"How to Turn History" (105–6). I developed an account of the occasional history of *anarchia* in classical and postclassical Athens (as refracted in later or contemporary texts and
inscriptions) in "Office and Anarchy."

114. As LSJ comments, here *to . . . anarchon* functions grammatically as the equivalent
of the noun *anarchia*.

115. The Furies use very closely related phrasing: *mēt' anarcheton bion mēte despotoumenon ainesēs* ("Do not approve of a lawless life or one subject to a tyrant") (525–26,
trans. Smyth).

116. *Panegyricus* 4.39, trans. Norlin. Ebrey, in "Value of Rule" (a reply to my "*Antianarchia*"), criticizes my interpretation of this passage, and in so doing takes himself to rebut
my more general argument, writing as follows:

> Note that both those that are oppressed by tyrannies and those perishing
> through anarchy are living without laws (ἀνόμως ζῶντας), and so tyranny and
> anarchy are aligned here. In fact, Lane's philological examination of *anarchia*
> helps us appreciate what Isocrates is saying. *Anarchia* is not simple lawless-
> ness; it is the lack of a ruler or officeholder. Isocrates is here relying on the
> idea that there are two different ways people can live without laws: they can
> do so because they lack a leader, or they can have a leader but one with no
> regard for law—a tyrant. Thus, it is not a Platonic innovation to align anarchy

Indeed, the idea of anarchy as an absence of obedience to ruling office-holders, while tyranny is a kind of excrescence of ruling authority (or at least power), makes intuitive sense. Nevertheless, at a deeper level, Plato's intervention in the *Republic* reveals an alignment between anarchy and tyranny rather than an opposition between them. This occurs insofar as Socrates posits an extended description of avoidance, rejection, and resistance in the degenerating democratic city to any kind of rule or leadership, including that of officeholders. (In the course of that description, the *anarchia* of that city is said to extend to its animals, a reductio of its view of extreme freedom.) It is the unwillingness to submit to rule, leading to and constituting complete *anarchia*, that is the "origin" (*archē*, in its other, though related, sense) from which tyranny in the city seems to Socrates to "evolve" (8.563e3–4).

To identify a case of *anarchia* even where there is the shadow play of office (as in a democratic constitution that has not broken down completely) is a realist judgment as much as an ethical one (it can be realist only because it takes account of the ethical question). Indeed, the macro narrative through the case of the democratic constitution reveals that the very meaning of political office as the means of structuring the landscape of political power must have an evaluative core. For it is not possible to articulate its purposes, even the most minimal, and even when most distorted or undermined, without it. Plato in *Republic* 8 and 9 gives reason to think that the basic categories of constitutional order must involve the epitactic rule of officeholders or other rulers. To put the point epigrammatically: Plato is a realist precisely because he is also a moralist;[117] or, in other words, he recognizes the evaluative dimension of ethics and politics as ineliminable.

How does the democratic constitution begin to degenerate? Is the Disunity principle at work in that narrative, as its postulation as the principle governing the dynamics of constitutional change would suggest that it should be? Here is Socrates on the origin of the degeneration of the democratic constitution:

> When a democratic city, athirst for freedom [*eleutheria*], happens to
> get bad cupbearers for its leaders, so that it gets drunk by drinking more

---

and tyranny; Isocrates, and quite possibly others, sees them as both involving lawlessness. (79)

While Ebrey's invocation of the overall context of the contrast is helpful (though requiring further discussion, as the relationship between laws and leadership in Greek thought is not necessarily that the former is dependent on the latter), it does not invalidate the *men/de* contrast in the Isocrates passage in question on which my original point relied. It remains the case that Isocrates is contrasting two different forms of living without laws and a proper constitution (*politeia*, same section, as he goes on to say), the one constituting *anarchia*, the other tyranny.

117. Here I dissent from Gerson (*Plato's Moral Realism*), as well as from the claim made by Geuss in "Thucydides, Nietzsche, and Williams" that Thucydides is the "better guide to human life" (219) because Plato resorts to "the moralization of the basic categories in [his] theory of human psychology" (223).

than it should of the unmixed wine of freedom,[118] then, unless the officeholders (*tous archontas*) are very pliable and provide plenty of that freedom [*eleutheria*], they are punished by the city and accused of being accursed oligarchs. (8.562c8–d4, trans. Grube/Reeve, modified)

Analysis of this passage must begin with its metaphor of the symposium.[119] A cultural institution found in archaic, aristocratic, and oligarchic contexts as well as in Athenian democracy, a well-ordered symposium was always governed by a *symposiarchos*.[120] This was a leader or, literally, a ruler of the symposium, the name of whose role is formulated on a related principle to that of a general political officeholder or magistrate, an *archōn* holding an *archē*. One of the key roles of the *symposiarchos* was to prescribe the proportions on any given occasion in which wine and water would be combined, a ritual to be performed in one of the *kratēr* mixing vessels provided for the ritual, as diluting wine with water was central to Greek cultural identity. For anyone to serve unmixed wine in violation of this ritual role would have been immediately recognizable to a reader of Plato's at the time as a sign of cultural and political danger, of a world beginning to be turned upside down.[121] More broadly, the requirement of rule, that some are empowered to command while others are required to obey, emerges here in the criticism of the degenerating democracy in which it comes to be lacking.

The movement of the metaphor from the undermining of the role of the official governing the symposium to that of officeholders more generally is spelled out in Socrates's claim that as drunkenness on unmixed freedom sets in, the actual rulers in the city—who are those holding the offices—will be "accused of being accursed oligarchs." For an oligarch is precisely understood in such a democracy as someone who has usurped power, someone who does not deserve to rule. To call the holders of properly installed offices "oligarchs" is to undermine the very basis of democratic rule, and in such a regime, therefore, of constitutional rule as such.

118. While the Greek text lacks the noun "wine" (a more literal translation of the relevant part of the passage would be "drinking more than it should of unmixed freedom itself"), the imagery of cupbearers and drunkenness supports a looser but felicitous Grube/Reeve translation as the "unmixed wine of freedom."

119. For a brief overview of many of the details of the Greek symposium, see Dalby's "Symposium."

120. One anonymous elegist wrote, "let us obey the symposiarch: this is what good men do, and it produces the best deliberation": Adesp. Eleg. fr. 27.7–10 West, as quoted in Simonton (*Ancient Greek Oligarchy*, 85), who explains that "the symposiarch . . . mirrors the presiding officials and eponymous magistrates familiar from Archaic Greek deliberative bodies."

121. Pace Tecuşan ("*Logos Sympotikos*," 244–45), who in an otherwise helpful article claims that *Laws* 6.773c8–d4 is Plato's only reference to mixing wine. *Laws* 1, of course, is a locus classicus for discussion of ideal sympotic practice.

The same motif is expressed in a further speech by Socrates describing the degenerating democratic constitution. Such a city, he says, "insults those who obey the officeholders (*tōn archontōn*) as willing slaves (*ethelodoulous*) and good-for-nothings and praises and honors, both in public and in private, rulers who behave like subjects and subjects who behave like rulers" (8.562d6–9).[122] As throughout book 8, shifts in predominant dispositions to praise and other evaluative attitudes drive concomitant changes in constitutions and individual characters.

What this sentence says is that, as democracy devolves into tyranny, praise attaches to those who negate the duties of commanding (ordering) and obeying associated with the *taxis* of officeholding, and in so doing abdicate the very idea of constitutional order and rule itself. For if we consider the meaning of "rulers who behave like subjects" and vice versa—or, as this line could equally well be translated, "officeholders who behave like subjects" and vice versa—this is a recipe for the nullification of the very possibility of office and indeed of any other kind of rule. And this is fatal. If a subject behaves like a ruler or officeholder, or a ruler or officeholder like a subject, that means that there can be no maintenance of a principle of obeying rulers in virtue of their office, or, indeed, of obeying them at all.

As in the accounts of degeneration of the preceding constitutions, Socrates uses a generalized plural in the first part of this account, which can be confusing. For if it is taken to apply to *everyone* within the politically predominant group (or the city as a whole), then it would seem to rule out the applicability of the Disunity principle—by implying that all officeholders are in fact behaving in the same (unified) way. But, as in the previous cases, though with less explicit indication in the text, the account should be taken rather to be highlighting a tendency within the politically predominant group of officeholders, but not one within the unified group as a whole—hence as allowing for the Disunity principle to be at work.

In this case, one might appeal to the gap between the broader notion of political predominance—that is, the group eligible to hold the offices (in the democratic constitution, everyone, and in particular, the poor majority)—and the narrower notion of those actually holding them. For if the officeholders behave like subjects, while those over whom they rule, who are themselves eligible to be officeholders, behave as if they were actually officeholders when they are not, this constitutes a breach of the unity of the politically predominant class construed in the broader sense—just as the Disunity principle

---

122. I translate *tōn archontōn* as "officeholders" but *archontas* / *archomenois* and *archomenous* / *archousin* as rulers / subjects // subjects / rulers—since, as office is on my analysis a kind of rule, both officeholding and ruling as translations of these participles are possible. Again, where the correlative relationship of obedience is invoked, "rulers" makes a neater juxtaposition in English with "subjects" than would "officeholders."

would require. The danger identified is the unwillingness to obey rulers, or specifically (in a constitution with no safeguarding rulers) those ruling in the form of institutional officeholding. And that unwillingness stems specifically from freedom (*eleutheria*) being allowed to go its fullest length (8.562d9–10). It is the unmixed, and so unlimited, engagement in political freedom that destroys the principle of ruling and being ruled, and so its instantiation in the constitutionally limited forms of office.

By erasing any meaningful distinction between subjects and rulers, as part of the disintegration of the very meaning of officeholding, the democracy of book 8 prepares to snuff itself out in an act of suicidal self-abolition. It does so because it has already undermined the *taxis* defining a constitution predicated on office, as were most Greek constitutions of Plato's day. Socrates links the erasure of the meaningfulness of this political relationship of command and obedience to the erasure of other relationships of command and obedience that were established in Greek societies at the time, including the abomination of slavery: fathers-sons, humans-animals, citizens-foreigners, masters-slaves, men-women. The result is a heightened psychological sensitivity in the souls of the citizens to any attempted application[123] of mastery—accompanied by a heightened social sensitivity to the mastery of the law: "In the end . . . they take no notice of the laws, whether written or unwritten, in order to avoid having any master at all" (8.563d6–e1, trans. Grube/Reeve).[124]

Socrates marks this as the precise "origin from which tyranny seems to me to evolve" (8.564e3–4), placing a dividing marker in the narrative: prior to this point, he had described the origin of tyranny in the democratic constitution, whereas subsequent to this origin, he will chart the development of a common disease that develops in democracy as in oligarchy: namely, the group of stinged and stingless drones. I noted earlier that the decline of the timocracy was marked by the timocrats and their wives diverting and then disobeying the laws (regarding private wealth), and that of the oligarchy by a failure to pass bankruptcy laws necessary to stabilize the regime, reflecting a refusal on the part of the officeholders to put their interests as constitutional officers above their private moneylending concerns. So, too, the decline of the democracy is marked by a change in attitude to the laws by the democrats as a whole,

123. Against Grube/Reeve's translation of *prospheretai* as reflexive ("if anyone even puts upon *himself* the least degree of slavery"), I accept a point made to me by René de Nicolay, that the middle-passive verb here is better construed as constraint applied by someone else—such as an officeholder.

124. On the term "unwritten law": Thomas ("Written in Stone?," 16) argues that the real novelty at this historical Greek moment was *written* law (taking the moment in a broad sense as beginning from the earliest epigraphic evidence of Greek laws in the second half of the seventh century, and continuing through the late fourth), since "you do not distinguish unwritten laws from written until you are beginning to see written law as a definite category."

who of course likewise constitute the officeholding group in the broad sense of those eligible to hold office.

Transition to Tyranny

In embarking on the narrative of the transition from democracy to tyranny in the sense of the destruction of democracy and the evolution of tyranny, Socrates offers two generally neglected comments. The first yokes the destruction of the oligarchy to the destruction of the democracy as both being generated by "the same disease," albeit when it arises in the democracy it is "more widespread and virulent [lit. stronger, *ischuroteron*] because of the general permissiveness" of that constitution, and will ultimately serve to "enslave" it (8.563e6–9, trans. Grube/Reeve). Before spelling out the nature of this common disease, however, he refers back to even broader principles of change affecting seasons, plants, and bodies, as well as constitutions (8.563e9–564a1), which he had originally introduced in the context of imagining how the Muses would narrate the degeneration—mentioning plants, animals, and timing—of a *kallipolis*. There, he had united these in announcing the general principle that "everything that comes into being must decay" (8.546a2, trans. Grube/Reeve); here, he announces a different general principle, that "extreme action in one direction usually produces in return a great change in the opposite direction" (8.563e9–10).[125] The specific change that he has in mind is that from "extreme freedom"—which characterized the already-degenerating democracy—to the "extreme slavery" that characterizes the tyranny (8.564a3–8, trans. Grube/ Reeve).This overarching principle of action and reaction explains the swing from one extreme to another, offering a more analytically polarized depiction of the relationship between democracy and tyranny than the sequencing of the macro narrative here would otherwise suggest.

That narrative itself picks up with the account of the disease common to oligarchy and democracy, which is the role of "that group of idle and extravagant men, whose bravest members are leaders and the more cowardly ones followers," metaphorically described as stinged and stingless drones respectively (8.564b4–7, trans. Grube/Reeve). Comparing their agitating effects within "constitutions in general"[126] to the effects of phlegm and bile within a body (so

---

125. Grube/Reeve translate: "excessive action in one direction usually sets up a reaction in the opposite direction," which is not wrong, but obscures the reference to "great change," as well as the fact that *to agan ti poiein* here will be picked up by *hē . . . agan eleutheuria* and *eis agan douleian*, both in 8.564a3–4.

126. So construing *pasē politeia*, in contrast to the distributive sense of Grube/Reeve's "every constitution" (see 269n37 in this chapter, above). In this context, the comparison to phlegm and bile in regard to "body"—as well as the fact that the disease has been identified specifically in oligarchy and democracy, implying that it is not universal—supports the construction that I offer.

picking up on the body-constitution comparison that he had just adumbrated more broadly), Socrates pronounces that:

> It's against them that the good doctor and lawgiver of a city, no less than a wise beekeeper, must take advance precautions, first, to prevent their presence, and, second, to cut them out of the hive as quickly as possible, cells and all, if they should happen to be present. (8.564c2–5, trans. Grube/Reeve, modified)[127]

The widespread Greek understanding of drones being an alien, invasive, and parasitic species in a beehive is picked up again in this image, and further elaborates the unified comparative political science that emerged first in the case of oligarchy and continued in the case of democracy. In the latter case, the analysis focuses on the people as dominated by the numerically preponderant, as well as politically predominant, many (described as the *plēthos* at 8.564e4)—it is the many and the poor who (in this particular version of democracy) are eligible to hold the offices and so to whom the Disunity principle will apply.

Indeed, Socrates underscores the unified political science encompassing democracy and oligarchy (and ultimately generating tyranny) by dividing the democratic city into three kinds "in reasoning (*tōi logōi*)" to match the three kinds that it has in fact (8.564c10–d1), and comparing the role of each kind systematically to its role in an oligarchy (8.564d1–565a3, translating *to genos* throughout as "class" in the generic sense of a distinctively featured group). Both constitutions feature a group of "idle and extravagant men,"[128] who in an oligarchy arise because of the bankruptcies of young or unlucky oligarchs, but who as a group are by definition in such a constitution "prevented from sharing in the offices (*tōn archōn*)" (8.564d6–7), and so prevented from fomenting the kind of *stasis* that (according to the Predominance principle) would undermine the constitution. In a democracy, however, this same class arises "because of the general permissiveness" and is enabled to become "far fiercer," precisely because, there, those who waste their financial wealth are nevertheless able to take part in politics, a phenomenon that Socrates illustrates by using the word for the speaker's platform in the Athenian Assembly (*ta bēma*), and by asserting that they will therefore be able to steer all political affairs in the constitution (8.564d2–e2).

This suggests an implicit modification of the Predominance principle, as in the oligarchy, to consider as the relevant group of officeholders the whole group eligible for office, and position this as the group within which *stasis* will emerge. At the same time, it highlights a peculiarity in democracy, compared

---

127. I translate the clause about the wise beekeeper that Grube/Reeve unaccountably omit.

128. This class is identified as such by a back reference to 8.564b4–5.

to the preceding constitutions: that the officeholders are not the only people with meaningful power within the workings of the constitution at any given time.[129] To be sure, in every constitution there is a kind of latent power of the excluded, should they group together, commit sabotage, or rise up more publicly. This is the kind of power that the poor were shown to exercise within the oligarchic constitution, resulting in a military uprising and revolution, and thereby bringing about the establishment of the democratic constitution. But in a democracy, there is also a special kind of power of those who are not officeholders within the workings of the constitution itself: they are able to speak up in the assembly and thereby exercise power directly, even without holding office themselves. In democratic Athens, the Assembly had power to elect those officeholders who were chosen by election rather than by lottery; to bring charges against any officeholder for misusing the powers of their office; and to vote on certain fundamental policy questions, such as making war or peace, directly.

Plato here acknowledges a similar distinction, and uses a superlative form of the same word *kurios*—namely, *kuriōtaton*—to do so. The "fiercest" members of the kind of idle and extravagant men arrogate power to themselves within the workings of the Assembly (clearly indicated by the reference to the speaker's platform, or *bēma*), and they use the powers of "talking and acting" in that context as a group that "manages everything." Such general control of affairs is independent of the officeholder, though it makes use of other formal features of a democratic constitution, such as the existence of an assembly. And, ultimately, as already noted in the workings of the democratic constitution itself, the people who are eligible to hold office hold excessive sway over the officeholders at any given moment, hollowing out the latter positions to a kind of shadow play.

Of this group of extravagant wasters, as one might think of them, the "fiercest" are positioned as the drones. A second group in both constitutions (the democratic and the oligarchic) is positioned as the "drone fodder," being the relatively wealthy who possess the metaphorical honey that the drones seek to extract (8.564e4–15). And the third group in both constitutions is those whom one might consider the silent majority: those who farm their own land but are relatively poor. Socrates comments that while they are not generally active in democratic politics (in contrast to the drones), "when this group is convened, it is the largest and most decisive (*kuriōtaton*) group in a democracy" (8.565a1–2).[130]

---

129. I am grateful to Matthew Landauer for emphasizing this emergence of a new kind of power in the democracy in discussions at Princeton in 2019, drawing on my own previous work as he did so.

130. I translate the verb *athroizein* as "convened" (in contrast to Grube/Reeve's "assembled"), so as to make clear that in this context it implies a formal political convocation. The

Socrates proceeds to elaborate these dynamics of democratic politics. On the one hand, the *dēmos* are reluctant to convene politically unless by doing so they "get some share in the honey," something that they do "always" succeed in getting, though their leaders keep the lion's share for themselves by manipulating political processes so as to expropriate wealth from the rich and distribute it to the poor (8.565a6–8). This in turn compels "those whose wealth is subject to such expropriation to ward it off by speaking in front of the people and acting in whatever way they can" (8.565b2–3), or, in other words, by defending themselves in lawsuits, or perhaps resisting expropriating moves in the assembly or council. But, finding themselves, "even when they have no appetite for revolution at all, charged by the drones with plotting against the people and of being oligarchs" (8.565b5–7, trans. Grube/Reeve, modified), the oligarchs in the original social sense of the wealthy few end up becoming oligarchs in the political sense of holding a polarized partisan position (while still operating within a democratic constitution).

In summing up these dynamics, Socrates invokes principles of the explanation of action in terms of knowledge and ignorance, which are familiar to readers of Plato from arguments in the *Gorgias* and other dialogues but are here integrated into a comparative political science specifically of oligarchy and democracy, which will stretch forward into an account of tyranny as well, these three constitutions being linked also by the social psychology of the so-called drones (even though other aspects of the political science, including the transvaluation of values and the roles of education, law, and office, apply to the timocracy as well). Doing so makes good on the philosophical claim that the teleologically structured action of ordinary human beings, aiming at what they believe to be the good, is best explained by their ignorance or knowledge of what the good actually is. Specifically, Socrates suggests, the *dēmos* "do not act willingly (*ouk hekonta*)," but rather do as they do "because they are ignorant and deceived by the drones," while the newly minted oligarchs likewise "do not act willingly (*ouk hekontes*)" but rather (it is implied) are forced into action or reaction owing to the stinging of the drones (8.565b9–c4, trans. Grube/Reeve, modified). Ignorance and force explain the lack of pursuit on each side of the true Good. That said, it would be better for them at least to stabilize the democratic constitution rather than letting it degenerate into tyranny, even if the true Good would involve a better constitution (a *kallipolis*) still.

The developments that follow once again manifest Plato's close attention to the distinctive institutions and practices of Greek political life, and especially those of a democracy such as Athens. The democratic constitution is beset by "impeachments, judgments [in lawsuits], and trials on both sides," in the course of which the *dēmos* will always eventually have recourse

---

superlative adjective is hard to translate in terms of "sovereignty" in English, though the decisiveness of this body does give it a power of that kind within the constitution.

to "setting up one man as their special champion, nurturing him and making him great" (8.565c6–12, trans. Grube/Reeve). Maintaining the horticultural metaphor, Socrates remarks that "whenever a tyrant grows up, this special championing is the sole root from which he sprouts" (8.565c12–d2, trans. Grube/Reeve, modified).

Notice that within the story of the destruction of the democratic constitution (termed "enslavement"), and the origin of the tyranny (which is a kind of anticonstitution, hence I devote no section to it), Socrates has introduced a mini-narrative of the origin and growth of the tyrant himself. This mini-narrative simultaneously illustrates again how the story of the individual man and the story of the constitution interact within each technically distinct narrative, and counts as a case of track crossing in Ferrari's terms (the one such case conceded by Ferrari himself, as noted earlier). Socrates highlights this mini-narrative by referring to the "origin"[131] of the change from the "champion of the people" into a tyrant (8.565d4), only to give a startling metaphorical account of this origin: comparing it to a story about the temple of the Lycaean Zeus in Arcadia (Zeus the wolf-god)—namely, that anyone who tastes the piece of human innards mixed up with those of sacrificial animals will himself become a wolf. Similarly, and in another account of detailed institutional procedure, Socrates suggests that the same happens when one of these "champions of the people" (using sometimes the word *prostatēs*, sometimes the word *proestōs*, in 8.565c9–568a6), having gotten "control of a docile mob" (following Shorey's translation here), "brings someone to trial on false charges, and murders him," this amounting to tasting the blood of one's fellow citizens in another vulpine metaphor. In what seems to be a gloss on these processes, not all involving murder strictly but also giving a taste of wealth that can be purloined, as well as blood, Socrates asserts: "He banishes some, kills others, and drops hints to the people about the cancellation of debts and the redistribution of land" (8.565e7–568a2, trans. Grube/Reeve).

Such a man is "inevitably fated either to be killed by his enemies" (who might thereby short-circuit the degeneration at least for a time, as the passing of better bankruptcy laws in the oligarchy might also have done) "or to be transformed from a man into a wolf by becoming a tyrant" (8.566a2–4, trans. Grube/Reeve; another rhetorical question by Socrates). It is this man who "stirs up civil wars against the rich"—a clear application of the Disunity principle in the context of the eligible officeholders being constituted by the democratic majority together with the rich—and, "if he's exiled but manages, despite his enemies, to return" (another contingency that could short-circuit the degeneration for a time), will "come back as a full-fledged tyrant" (8.566a6–10, the latter a rhetorical question, trans. Grube/Reeve). To be sure, he has enemies who try to

131. The word for origin is *archē*, used in a sense distinct from (though connected to) the sense of office and rule.

expel him or put him to death through a judicial process or plot secretly to kill him, but because the people give him a bodyguard, he can escape this, and stand "in the city's chariot" now as a complete tyrant rather than as a champion of the people.

At this point, Socrates embarks on the assessment of the happiness of this man, the tyrant, and of "the city in which a man like him comes to be" (8.566d5–6), highlighting that, in this case, the city in which the tyrant comes to be (that is, in which a young man comes to be a tyrant) is the same city that is becoming (or has become) a tyranny, such that the macro and micro narratives intersect in the account of their genesis, or coming into being. When the character and way of life of the tyrannical man are detailed in book 9, we will learn that such a man need not in fact become a political tyrant: it is a misfortune should that fate befall him.[132] But in the book 8 macro narrative, the same dynamics that transform the democratic constitution into the tyranny are those that produce the tyrant; necessarily so, as a tyranny cannot exist without a tyrant at its helm. And so the very purpose of the whole exercise stretching from book 2 to book 9—to decide whether the tyrant is the happiest of men— is launched within the macro narrative, even though it will be resumed and concluded within the micro narrative considering the evolution and character of the tyrannical individual (and his happiness, a desideratum not added to any of the preceding stages of the micro narrative) that opens book 9.

It remains to be observed that in the political dynamics bringing tyranny to its final nadir (that is, to its full realization and establishment), the new tyrant's erstwhile companions, "who helped to establish his tyranny and who hold positions of power within it" (8.567b1–2, trans. Grube/Reeve)—before they were swiftly liquidated—are not characterized by any of the terms for "office" or "officeholder" that I have been tracing throughout book 8. The tyrant is described as suspecting people of "not favoring his rule (*archein*)" (according himself that honorific description), while according only "positions of power" to his henchmen—who are soon to be purged.[133] Those on the tyrant's side are consistently described only as those serving as his "bodyguard"—for example, at 8.567d6—rather than in the terms for "office" used in describing the three previous flawed constitutions in book 8.[134] The conditional demands on a tyrant "if he intends to rule (*archein*)" once again refer to his self-conceived project (8.567b6–7, trans. Grube/Reeve); the reality of his power, however, is now command without any stable relationship to the *taxis* that either office

---

132. A nice illustration of the idea here is the case of Oedipus, who would indeed have been better off had he never come to rule, a point I owe to Wintor Scott and René de Nicolay in discussion at Princeton.

133. The references are respectively 8.567a6, 8.567b1 (*tōn sugkatastēsantōn*), trans. Grube/Reeve.

134. I borrow this sentence from my "*Antianarchia*" (68).

or any kind of proper rule would require.[135] As one of Aristotle's distinctions between kingship and tyranny would suggest, tyranny's power is not "according to order" (*kata taxin*), the kind of order (*taxis*) that Aristotle would in the *Politics* invoke in conjunction with a constitutional order of offices. Rather, it manifests an absence of order and limit: it is "unbounded" (*aoristos*) (Arist., *Rhetoric* 1.1366a2).[136]

The assessment of the tyrant's happiness, which begins as the macro narrative of the emergence of tyranny is concluded, involves Socrates in elucidating further political dynamics of the tyranny. Most important is that it is "necessary for a tyrant to be always stirring up war" and to do away with the bravest of his original allies and of anyone who has any virtues or wealth who would come to oppose him, instead hiring foreign mercenaries and freeing slaves to be his bodyguard. Socrates eventually returns to the fact that "the people, who fathered the tyrant, will have to feed him and his companions" (8.568e3–4, trans. Grube/Reeve), claiming that if they resist and seek to drive him out, the tyrant will become a parricide (of the people who metaphorically fathered him—to be matched by the individual tyrannical man's crimes against his actual father and mother in the micro narrative). It is at this point that the language of enslavement that was mooted for this particular degenerative constitutional change is made fully good (or, rather, bad), since "in seeking to escape from the 'frying pan' of enslavement to free men, the *dēmos* would find themselves having fallen into the 'fire' of being mastered by slaves" (8.569b9–c2).

Conclusion

Tyranny turns out to be both slavery and anarchy, for the tyrant as well as for their subjects: it is tantamount neither to freedom nor to genuine power. In their very willingness to instrumentalize everything to their own benefit, negating the very idea of any boundedness or constraint (legal or otherwise) on their own power, the tyrant negates not only the normative purpose of rule (its *telos*) on Plato's conception but also its very structure or order (its *taxis*). In other words, tyranny collapses into anarchy. Bad rule, rule for a malign purpose (which negates and inverts the actual normative purpose of rule), collapses into being no rule at all, as Plato understands it.

How exactly does this come about? Consider this first from the standpoint of the tyrant, and then from the standpoint of their subjects. On the one hand, without any concern to maintain an order (*taxis*) of hierarchy between ruler

---

135. Note references to the tyrant's "rule" by Socrates (*archein*, 8.567a6; *arxein*, 8.567b7), by Adeimantus (*arxei*, 8.567c8), and again by Socrates in the micro narrative (9.575e4). I read these as descriptive uses, devoid of evaluative content.

136. I owe this reference to Hoekstra ("Athenian Democracy," 48).

and ruled as such, the tyrant ends up fawning on their subjects rather than being able to rely on commanding them, while also being willing to treat their own whims as entirely malleable and thus erasing any boundaries on the purpose that they might choose to try (however self-defeatingly) to pursue. (This will be demonstrated further in passages in book 9, considered in the next chapter.) On the other hand, without any reason to respect such an order of hierarchy, the subjects are likely to evade the tyrant's commands and seek to overthrow them if they can. The tyrant recognizes no limitations on their own power or its uses, including the moral and epistemic constraints that a concern for the good of the ruled would import, but which evaporate when the tyrant is concerned only with whatever they take their own personal good, the good of the ruler, to be.

Indeed, if the tyrant were to recognize the distinction between their seeming good and their actual good, as Socrates urges in the *Gorgias*, this would in fact impose a limitation on their use of power (and Socrates in that dialogue would say even their possession of it). Indeed, this resonates with and helps us to make sense of the broader dimension of that notorious Socratic argument in the *Gorgias*: that properly understood, tyrants lack any actual power at all. This is precisely because they are incapable of acting for their own true benefit (incapable both epistemically and dispositionally, though, again, properly understood in Socratic terms, those two causes are really one).[137]

For Plato, then, rule is evaluative all the way down. And this is a point that he makes not only as an idealist, as it were, but also as a certain kind of realist. Tyrannies are in reality unstable, and his analysis in terms of normative values shows why this should be so. The evaluative status of rule derives from both its *telos* and its *taxis*, and from the relationship between them; conversely, a complete negation of the value of either will end in undoing of the other. Thus, tyranny and anarchy respectively illustrate key axes of Plato's understanding of rule, as well as demonstrating the inevitable intersection of those axes. Tyranny calls attention to the axis of purpose (*telos*); anarchy to the axis of order (*taxis*). In principle, *taxis*—which for Plato must always incorporate a hierarchy of ruler and ruled in terms of the epitactic relationship between them in principle—has prima facie value in its own right. But, if the *telos* of a *taxis* is negated and inverted, that *taxis* loses its value. Indeed, as we have just argued, in so doing it is ultimately undone as a genuine *taxis* altogether. Absolute power without any limits inevitably turns into its opposite: no actual power at all.[138]

---

137. Thanks to Alex Lee for asking about the relationship to this argument in the *Gorgias* in discussion of an earlier version of this chapter as the 2021 Langford Lecture at Florida State University.

138. Thanks to Rachel Barney for helping with this formulation in discussing an earlier version of this monograph.

CHAPTER NINE

The Micro Narrative

FLAWED CONSTITUTIONS WITHIN SOULS
(*REPUBLIC*, BOOKS 8–9)

AT THE END of what I call the micro narrative, in which each of the flawed individuals corresponding to the flawed constitutions has been described, Socrates invites Glaucon to issue a rank-ordered verdict of the happiness of five types of individual: "the kingly one, the timocratic one, the oligarchic one, the democratic one, the tyrannical one" (9.580b1–5).[1] Glaucon's verdict is that they should be ranked from happiest to least happy in the order of their appearance in the dialogue (the order just mentioned), implying that the kingly person was introduced prior to the timocratic one and the others of books 8 and 9. Socrates glosses part of the verdict thus: "the happiest one is the best and most just person, this person being the kingly one who reigns over [*basileuein*] themselves" (9.580c1–3). While Socrates does not specify that this kingly person is necessarily a philosopher, he has previously argued that only such a person would therefore be capable of reigning over a city. He completes his gloss on the verdict as follows: "the most miserable one is the most evil and the most unjust person, this person being the one who should happen to be most tyrannical over themselves and to the greatest extent tyrannize the city" (9.580c3–5).

This maximally miserable person is not simply anyone with a tyrannical nature but anyone with such a nature who actually wields the power of tyrannizing a city. The destination of the micro narrative is the tyrannical man. But the destination of the dialogue's arc of argument—from book 1 (Thrasymachus's challenge that it is tyranny that is the maximally unjust and happiest life: 1.344a4–6) and book 2 (Glaucon's and Adeimantus's linked challenges as

---

1. Grube/Reeve translate "the king, the timocrat, the oligarch, the democrat, and the tyrant," but the Greek uses adjectives as substantives, referring to character types, rather than the noun denoting each role. All quotations in this chapter are from Plato's *Republic*, according to the Slings OCT, and in my own translation, unless otherwise indicated.

to whether it is most profitable to become a tyrant and act unjustly, so long as one can escape human or divine punishment for it, 2.357a1–367e4)—is the demonstration that the political tyrant is that person whose life is not maximally happy (as one might think) but, rather, maximally miserable.

Given the importance of the micro narrative to the argumentative arc of the dialogue, it is surprising that, in contrast to his explicit introduction of two principles early in book 8 to explain the macro narrative of constitutional change in cities that then unfolds, Socrates announces no new principles to govern the parallel micro narrative of constitutional change in the souls, and hence the lives, of individuals. The subjects of the micro narrative are those whom, following Ralph Waldo Emerson, I call in this chapter "representative men": explicitly gendered male in each case in being described as fathers and sons, these are the individuals animated by distinctively ordered (or, rather, relatively or wholly disordered) souls and, as a result, living characteristic ways of life. They are the timocratic man, the oligarchic man, the democratic man, and the tyrannical man.[2] From a formal literary perspective, the overall structure of the micro narrative is given by the similarity of each representative man to the constitution to which he corresponds (which also yields the narrative order, transposed from the macro to the micro case).

Each man (apart from the first) is the son of the preceding stage's father, and (apart from the last) father of the subsequent stage's son. Thus each type featured in the micro narrative arises from intergenerational (mis)education.[3] As a father, each of the main characters in turn proves to be unable in the course of raising his son to pass on an intact set of his own values: values that are articulated in terms of the rule within his soul, expressed in each case in the language of the psychology of tripartition, and also his concomitant way of life, including especially his participation or nonparticipation in officeholding and the political life of his city. It is this failure that gives rise to a transvaluation of values in the character of the son and the life he will lead, meaning that, in the micro narrative, the familial dynamic involves a degeneration across generations from one representative case to the next.

2. Note that, as introduced, the analogy is between the justice of a "single man" and a "whole city" (2.368e2–3; cf. 2.368e5, noting that "a city is larger than a single man," trans. Grube/Reeve): it is a city-man, or city-individual, analogy, rather than (as usually labeled) a city-soul analogy.

Correspondingly, the argument in book 4 culminates in identifying the various virtues within "the individual" as compared with the city (4.441c8–443c3), albeit that they reside in the individual case "within the soul" of each individual (4.441c5–6). Thus it should not be a surprise when the spotlight of book 8 is trained (in both the macro and micro narratives) on the city-man comparison rather than on a city-soul comparison specifically, albeit that the soul of an individual is crucially relevant to explaining their attitudes and actions.

3. On the importance of education in what I call the micro narrative, see Hitz's "Degenerate Regimes," as well as Helmer's "Histoire, politique et pratique."

There is a sense in which the micro narrative can be taken to have begun back in books 5–7, or even in book 4. Glaucon can be seen to be acknowledging this at the beginning of book 8, when he remarks that Socrates had earlier said (then addressing Glaucon in the second person) that "you would class both the city you described and the man who is like it as good," pegging this to the end of book 4, even though "as it seems, you had a still finer city and man to tell us about" (8.543c9–544a1, trans. Grube/Reeve), implying that the latter are respectively the *kallipolis* and the philosopher of books 5–7. It would seem, then, that Glaucon takes Socrates to have identified the philosopher as the implicit first stage, or prelude, to the micro narrative of intergenerational degenerating characters that will unfold in books 8 and 9. True, no stage in the micro narrative identifies such a figure as clearly as the constitution of the *kallipolis* is positioned as the first stage (or one might say in some way the prelude) of the macro narrative. Still, Socrates had himself asked, at the very end of book 7, "then isn't that enough about this city and the man who is like it?" (7.541b1–2, trans. Grube/Reeve), retrospectively casting (as I take it) "the man who is like" the *kallipolis* to be the person with a philosophical nature who is not corrupted through their education. While the portrait is only glancingly cast in this role of prelude to the micro narrative, I think this remark shows that it is meant to play that role.

In any case, certainly by the end of book 4, the essential role of rule in the psychology of the embodied tripartite soul—consisting of the rational part (*to logistikon*), thumotic part (*to thumoeidēs*), and appetitive part (*to epithumetikon*)—was made clear. Tripartition itself calls for an account of order (*taxis*) among the parts, and Socrates had adverted to the language of rule in order to define that *taxis*, which was well-ordered only when directed at the proper *telos*—namely, the Good itself. Indeed, not only does the micro narrative make repeated and precise use of the technical language of the tripartition of the soul introduced in book 4, in so doing, it also offers a further analytical elaboration of this schema, especially from the case of the oligarchic man onward. For whereas what is dominant in the timocratic man is an already-identified soul part (the *thumoeidēs*), all three of the representative men who follow—oligarchic man, democratic man, and tyrannical man—are dominated by their appetitive parts, albeit with different content for the dominant *telos* of each such part and with different ways in which each exerts its dominance.

These latter three representative men can be distinguished from one another only insofar as the specific kinds of appetites and desires that are dominant in each one's *epithumetikon* (appetitive part), as well as the precise manner in which the soul is ruled and ordered in each representative man, are distinguished. In other words, rule in the soul is shown to involve not only the fact of a hierarchical order (or, rather, relative order) but also the particular kind of order (whether brought about by force or by persuasion) involved in each case. That order is in each case given a different character by the identity of its dominant soul part and, in the case of the appetitive part, the identity of a given dominant set of appetites (rule by the moneymaking appetites being different in quality from rule, or rather sheer domination, by untrammeled erotic love).[4]

Digging into the literary structure at a finer level of detail: each case of the micro narrative exhibits a clearly marked sectioning in the treatment of each case, between two distinct topics (with the order in which they are treated varying from case to case). On the one hand, the topic of how the representative youth comes to be, or his genesis; on the other, his character type, or, in Greek, literally, "what he is like" or "what [quality] he is" (*poios tis*) (other related expressions are used as well).[5] As noted above, in the case of the democratic man Socrates adds a third topic, of the way of life of this man, which was anticipated implicitly in the accounts of his forebears and is repeated in the case of his progeny (the tyrannical man); and for the tyrannical man a further fourth section is added, discussing whether he is the happiest or most wretched of men.

In presenting the micro narrative, I begin with the final individual in the sequence, who is the tyrannical man, and work in reverse order from there (inverting the order of individuals presented in the micro narrative). This is because the tyrannical man is the counterpart to the political tyranny in the macro narrative with which the previous chapter of this study concluded (and in the course of discussing which, aspects of the tyrannical individual, both as a private person and in the role of tyrant in a city, were already broached). Thus I shall work backward from the tyrannical man as presented in book 9 to his father (the democratic man), paternal grandfather (the oligarchical man), and paternal great-grandfather (the timocratic man), each of whom was presented in the reverse order in book 8. I do so partly in order to keep the tyranny and tyrannical man in proximity in my discussion, and partly because the method of reading Plato backward can be a fruitful one.[6] While doing so presents narrative challenges, given that the elaboration of the tripartite

4. On the overall account of tripartition in the soul in the *Republic*, see Lorenz (*Brute Within*, pts. 1–2).

5. In Burnyeat and Frede's *Pseudo-Platonic Seventh Letter*, Burnyeat translates the related phrase *to poion ti* as "what it is like" (131), while observing that this expression, used in the dubious (and in Burnyeat and Frede's view, definitely spurious) *Seventh Letter*, is found only three times in late Plato and "always as a long-winded interrogative . . . never as the nominalization of the answer to that question, which is the usage found in [the *Seventh Letter*]" (128). He does not discuss the repeated ways in which the phrase *poios tis* is used both as an interrogative and as a nominalization of the answer to that question in *Republic* 8 and 9.

6. Following a fruitful conversation with M. M. McCabe, I chose to follow this method on a larger scale in devoting the final three (of six) Carlyle Lectures in sequence to aspects of *Republic* 9, 8, and 1, and in discussing the *Laws*, *Statesman*, and *Republic* in that order in the chapters of this study.

psychology builds forward in the Platonic text of books 8 and 9, it thereby shakes up the reader's expectations and highlights unexpected junctures of the argument—at least that is my hope.

The Tyrannical Representative Man

Consider, then, the tyrannical representative man in the micro narrative. To be sure, the depiction of the rise of the tyrant in the macro narrative has already anticipated this, since there cannot be a tyrant without a tyrannical man who rises to political power; conversely, however, as the micro narrative will show, not all tyrannical men become political tyrants. The case in the micro narrative is taken up at the outset of book 9, with a programmatic outline that includes four parts—the most extensive program for any case of the micro narrative:[7] first, "how (*pōs*)" he comes to be, in this case out of a democratic father (*ek dēmokratikou*); second and third, his kind of character and how he lives (*genomenos te poios tis estin kai tina tropon zē*); and a final fourth point, which picks up the original purpose of the inquiry from book 2, and indeed from book 1, onward:[8] to decide whether this tyrannical man's

7. The original program for the first two cases had been bipartite: how the man in question comes to be (his genesis, which I like to gloss, following Gigon ["Timokratie und Oligarchie"] as his *Werden*) and what his character type is (like) (or, again following Gigon, his *Wesen*, though this is not the person's essence as a human being but rather his type as a flawed embodied character). In the presentation of the timocratic man, *Wesen* precedes *Werden*; in that of the oligarchic man, it is the other way round, as it is for the democratic man, in the case of whom Socrates tacitly expands the program to add a description of how "he lives" (8.561a6 (*zēi*), c6 ["lives on (*diazēi*)"], d8 (*ton bion*), the latter echoed by Adeimantus at e1, glossing it as "the life of a legally equal man (*bion isonomikou tinos andros*)" [8.561e1–2]). The fourth part of the program is introduced only in the case of the tyrannical man, for whom the *poios tis* (call it the second element) is expanded by the third "in what way he lives (*tina tropon zē*)" (9.571a3). In other words, the interlocutors must look into three questions in two steps, with a resumptive *genomenos te* introducing the two last questions (the second of which is really a prolongation of the first, which I indicate by adding punctuation): ". . . to examine, both (*te*) how he grows out of the democratic type and (*te*), once he has come into existence (*genomenos*), of what kind he is (*poios tis estin*) and (*kai*) in what way he lives (*tina tropon zē*)" (9.571a1–3). Grube/Reeve's translation of *poios tis . . . zē* as "what he is like when he has come into being" obscures the way in which the grammar of this third section functions on a par with—and not as a subsection of either of—the other two; in my view, the *genomenos* applies both to the *poios tis estin* and to the *kai tina tropon zē*. I am grateful to André Laks for discussion of how to construe and translate the Greek here, though I have further modified the translation he had suggested in conversation.

8. Socrates first refers to blessed happiness when classing justice "among the finest goods, as something that should be desired by anyone who would be blessed by it (*makariō*) both through itself and through what comes about as a result of it" (2.358a1–3), putting this question on the agenda of the inquiry, though Glaucon uses a different term, *eudaimonesteros* (2.361d3) in setting the terms of his challenge (and Adeimantus uses different

life is "wretched or blessedly happy (*athlion hē makarion*)" (9.571a1–3, trans. Grube/Reeve).

This is because assessment of the tyrant's way of life is the case that bears directly on the original book 1 and 2 inquiries (connected by Glaucon and Adeimantus when they raise and revise Thrasymachus's original challenge) to which an answer is being sought. In the macro narrative, Socrates had already described just such a man who had become an actual political tyrant, asking there about "the happiness of this man and of the city in which a mortal like him comes to be" (8.566d5–6, trans. Grube/Reeve). However, in the micro narrative of the tyrannical man that this programmatic set of questions launches, his private and public lives will be distinguished—indeed, this may be the reason that the question of how he "lives" is called out separately in this case alone. The supreme misery will be reserved for the man who "is tyrannical but doesn't live a private life, because some misfortune provides him with the opportunity to become an actual tyrant" (9.578c1–3, trans. Grube/Reeve).

In embarking on this case, Socrates offers a final extension of the explanatory theory of human psychology, which had begun with the tripartition of the soul in book 4 and is now to be completed by distinguishing "the kinds and numbers of our appetites" (9.571a7–9). The new distinction needed is within the class of "unnecessary pleasures and appetites"—note the two being yoked together here as in the previous elaboration of the psychology in the service of delineating the democratic man—by distinguishing one subset of them as those that are "transgressive (*paranomoi*)" (9.571b3–4).[9] These appetites are the ones that are "awakened in sleep, when the rest of the soul— the rational, gentle, and ruling part (*logistikon kai hēmeron kai archon*)— slumbers" (9.571c3–5, trans. Grube/Reeve). Indeed, Socrates asserts, "there is a dangerous, wild, and unlawful (*anomon*) kind of appetite in everyone, even in those of us who seem to be entirely moderate or measured—this is evident in our dreams" (9.572b1–6, trans. Grube/Reeve, modified), even though he had earlier observed that in most people such appetites are "held in check by the laws and by the better appetites in alliance with reason" (9.571b5–6, trans.

---

terms as well). However, Thrasymachus had previously claimed that "the most fully realized injustice"—which he specifies to be "tyranny"—makes the doer of injustice the "happiest (*eudaimonestaton*)," and leads to his being "called happy and blessed (*eudaimones kai makarioi keklēntai*)" (1.344a4–7, b7–c1). The special relevance of the tyrant to the original question is already highlighted by Socrates in his programmatic statement near the beginning of book 8 (8.545b4–c4), in which he also segues from the "man" corresponding to the tyrannical constitution (supplied from *andra* in the oligarchic and democratic cases at 8.545b9 and c1 respectively) to the "tyrannical soul" (8.545c4).

9. I venture "transgressive" as a translation of *paranomos* in the spirit of Adam's note (*"Republic" of Plato*, to 9.571b9) that "παράνομοι [*paranomoi*] is more like our 'unnatural' than 'lawless'" and that "the phrase οὐ κατὰ νόμον [*ou kata nomon*] in Hdt 1.1.61 has the same connotation." I reserve "lawless" for translating the word *anomos*. There is further discussion of the nature of these appetites in Johnstone's "Tyrannized Souls."

Grube/Reeve, modified). It would seem that, while each type of representative man is a product of a discrete psychosocial formation, with his familial upbringing and civic context combining to yield a variously flawed education, the appetite for becoming a tyrant is at least latent within the dreams of anyone.

In order to narrate the genesis of the tyrannical man, Socrates reaches back to summarize the genesis and character of his father—the democratic man (the intertwining between father and son at each stage of the micro narrative being one reason that my reverse-order presentation can work). Having been "pulled in both directions" between his oligarchic father and household, and the civic pressures from outside influences, which we have argued are already those of a democratic city, the proto-democratic youth matures so as to live in the following way. As described, this youth:

> settles down in the middle of both ways of living . . . And enjoying each in moderation, as he supposes, he lives a life (*bion zēi*) that is neither slavish nor transgressive (*oute aneleutheron oute paranomon*) and from having been oligarchic he becomes democratic. (9.572d1–4, trans. Grube/Reeve, modified)

Paranomos signifies a broadly political attitude and qualifies a way of life; it will be further elaborated in the psychological theory of appetites that is completed as apparatus for describing the rise of the tyrannical man, where the political sense here will be brought to bear as well.

It is this democratic man who, when older, becomes a father, with a "young son who is brought up in his father's ethos" (9.572d6–7, trans. Grube/Reeve, modified). As this son grows up, people outside the home pressure him to engage in "all the kinds of transgressiveness [*paranomia*]" that they "call freedom" (9.572d10–e2), a similar set of pressures to those that had been brought to bear on his father during his own youth.[10] In the case of the proto-tyrannical youth, while his democratic-man father and parental household seek to nourish his more moderate appetites, those driving the vanguard of ideological transvaluation in the wider city ("those clever enchanters and tyrant-makers") implant in the young man "a powerful erotic love, like a great winged drone, to be the leader [*prostatēs*] of those unproductive desires ready to spend whatever is at hand" (9.572e3–573a1, trans. Grube/Reeve, modified). Within the youth's soul, the other appetites then "implant the sting of craving" in the drone, which as the "leader of the soul (*ho prostatēs tēs psuchēs*)" then "adopts madness as its bodyguard" (9.573a8–b1, trans. Grube/Reeve) and purges the soul of any remaining more moderate and shame-sensitive appetites.

Adeimantus responds to this description that "you've perfectly described the evolution [*genesis*] of a tyrannical man" (9.573b5, trans. Grube/Reeve).

---

10. Arruzza (*Wolf in the City*, 44–46, 153–83), discusses the tyrant's *paranomia* and its relation to his *erōs* as a broader trope of Greek literature.

Socrates concludes this account of the tyrannical man's genesis with a short précis, which posits the ambition to rule over others as central to the tyrannical man's psychology (notwithstanding that the burden of the macro narrative, as I argued in the previous chapter, implied that the actions of a political tyrant cannot count as proper rule). Recalling that "erotic love (*ho erōs*) has long been called a tyrant,"[11] and that a madman (like such a lover) "attempts to rule (*archein*) not just human beings, but gods as well," he concludes that "a man becomes tyrannical in the precise sense (*akribōs*)[12] when either his nature (*phusei*) or his way of life (*epitēdeumasin*) or both of them together make him drunk, filled with erotic desire, and mad" (9.573b6–c9, trans. Grube/Reeve). The distinction between "nature" and "way of life" points up the fact that, since all of us have a nature that harbors at least some *paranomos* appetites, those whose nature is filled with more powerful ones may be especially liable to becoming tyrannical. Yet so too are those whose nature may not be exceptional in this regard but whose "way of life" happens to foster the uncontrolled and extreme growth of those appetites in the direction of mania. Indeed, it is striking that the noun *epitēdeuma* is used here (in a dative plural), since this often has the connotations of a *collective* way of life, suggesting again the impact of the broader psychosocial-ideological formation of the city in which this individual genesis is taking place.

This is the juncture to what I called the fourth and final part of the program for this phase of the micro narrative—namely, the question of how the tyrannical man lives, or his way of life (9.573c11–12). Dominated by his internal drive of erotic love to satisfy his resultant costly appetites, the tyrannical man soon "expends (*analiskontai*)" all of his income (9.573d10), and begins to borrow and eat into his capital. (The technical financial terms used in this stretch of dialogue highlight Plato's alertness to socioeconomic, as well as sociopolitical and socio-psychological, dynamics and institutions in the micro as well as the macro narrative.) Having exhausted his resources (like a junkie, though driven by erotic love leading his other appetites rather than drugs), the tyrannical man is driven to use deceit or force to acquire further

11. Here and elsewhere, many editors and translators capitalize the first letter of *erōs* to indicate that they believe Plato is here referring to the Greek god of that name; in contrast, I have decided to keep all occurrences of *erōs* in Greek in lowercase (contra some choices made by the OCT editions used and quoted). As Richard Hunter (*Plato's "Symposium,"* 15) points out in discussing this very term, notably, "Greeks did not have our conventions of distinguishing capital and lowercase letters." I commented on the ambiguity of the Greek *erōs* in the "blurring of lines between external and internal subjection, to the god and to one's own desires," in my "Placing Plato" (705).

12. This is an interesting reprise by Socrates of an adverb first employed by Thrasymachus (and then echoed by Socrates) in book 1 in a similar sense, as I noted in chapter 5: to express a precise and technical meaning of a term. I argued that for Socrates, in contrast to the sophist, the "precise sense" of any term to which he applies that characterization has an irreducibly evaluative dimension.

wealth, having concluded that "he deserves to outdo (*pleon echein*)" even his own parents (9.574a7-9, trans. Grube/Reeve)—using a phrase that was deeply if controversially rooted in Athenian democratic ideology, a variant of the combined verb *pleonektein* and also linked to the noun *pleonexia*, the appetite or drive to have more than others.[13] The fact that it is his own parents against whom he first turns also deepens the inversion of familial authority relationships that had begun in the life of his democratic-man father.

Following these domestic crimes, the tyrannical man then turns to appropriate wealth from others in the city, by means of burglaries and robberies, in particular temple robberies (9.573e3-574d5), which picks up on Socrates's confirmatory point in book 4, as agreed by Glaucon, that a just person would have nothing to do with such crimes (he also mentions thefts, but using a different word) (4.443a3-5).[14] Socrates then moves to comment not only on the appetites and actions of the tyrannical man but on his "opinions" (*doxas*, 9.574d5). In fact, he suggests that it was not only appetites but opinions that had undergone a dramatic change, in that "the old traditional opinions that he had held from childhood about what is fine or shameful—opinions that he had accounted just—are overcome by the opinions, newly released from slavery, that are now the bodyguard of erotic love and hold sway along with it" (9.574d5-8, trans. Grube/Reeve).[15]

Note that the "slavery" that these opinions had undergone seems to have been their forcible suppression into sleep, which had been the case "when he himself was under the laws and his father and had a democratic constitution inside him (*dēmokratoumenos en heautōi*)" (574e1-2).[16] Instead of a democratic

13. The translation "outdo" is not quite literal (the sense would be "out-possess," if that were a word, akin to "out-compete"). A note in the Grube/Reeve translation ad loc. helpfully refers back to their note on [1.]343e (actually on 1.344a1-2), pointing out that "*pleonexia* is, or is the cause of, injustice ([2.]359c) . . . [and] is contrasted with *doing or having one's own*, which is, or is the cause of, justice ([4.]434a, [4.]441e)." It is significant that the tyrannical man is described here as believing that he deserves to *pleon echein* (roughly, "have more than") his own parents, since such an appetite has been identified as paradigmatically unjust, thus continuing to set up the judgment of the paradigmatically unjust and just persons in terms of their happiness or wretchedness that will culminate later in book 9. On *pleonexia* in Plato (and Aristotle) here and more generally, I have learned from Zimecki's "(Ambiguous) Moral Status."

14. The reading of this part of book 4 as offering "confirmatory argument" is defended by Burnyeat in "Justice" (216 and passim).

15. A progressive freeing from shame had already unfolded in the democratic phases of both the macro and micro narratives. In the former, the democratic constitution, in the course of its degeneration, is said to foster the disappearance of any "shame" or "fear" felt by sons toward their parents (8.562e7-563a1). The role of shame in the latter is detailed below.

16. A note in the Grube/Reeve translation in Cooper's *Plato* (ad loc.) helpfully refers to 7.538c, a mini-portrait of a person in whom exposure to dialectic leads them to reject the childhood convictions "about just and fine things" (7.538c6-8), so that "from being law-abiding he seems to become transgressive of law (*paranomos . . . doxei gegonenai ek*

way of life and the force of the democratic laws and patriarchal customs, the
tyrannical man now has a mini-tyrant within him:

> Erotic love (*erōs*) lives (*zōn*) within him tyrannically, in complete *anar-*
> *chia* and lawlessness (*en pasē anarchiai kai anomiai*), seeing that it is
> his sole ruler (*monarchos*), and drives him, as if he were a city, to dare
> anything that will provide sustenance for itself and the unruly mob
> around it (some of whose members have come in from the outside as a
> result of his keeping bad company, while others have come from within,
> freed (*eleutherōthenta*) and let loose by his own habits). Isn't this the
> life (*ho bios*) of such a man (*toioutou*) [a tyrannical man]? (9.575a1–8,
> trans. Grube/Reeve, modified).[17]

There is a tension here: Socrates personifies *erōs* as living "tyrannically" within
the tyrannical man, in a state of complete *anarchia* and *anomia*—and yet
also as doing so seeing that (or because) it is *monarchos*, using a term for a
single ruler that could indicate a king, which presents a direct semantic conflict with *anarchia* in the sense of the absence of any officeholder or ruler for
which I argued in the macro narrative of book 8. This semantic conflict is best
resolved by leaning on the difference between a properly ordered *taxis* of rule
and something else that is a shadow-twin of proper rule, what one might today
call power without constitutional authority. There is no proper ruling within
the (metaphorical) city of the tyrannical man's soul. Rather, *erōs* rules that soul
autocratically, as its sole ruler (*monarchos*), but without a genuine *taxis* of rule
in place (thus, leaving the soul in a condition of *anarchia*) and without any
proper obedience to laws, not even of the shadow-play kind that the democratic man exhibited (thus, leaving the soul in a condition of *anomia*).

At this point, I must anticipate the next section of this chapter in order to
briefly recall what in the narrative sequence precedes the case of the tyrannical man: namely, the life of the democratic man who will eventually father

---

nomimou)" (7.539a3), strikingly using the same *ek* formulation for genesis as throughout
book 8, as well as the term *paranomos*, which names the transgressive appetites that arise
in sleep in the psychological theory elaboration prefatory to the narrative of the genesis of
the tyrannical man in book 9.

17. I have left *anarchia* untranslated for discussion in the main text below. Note that
en pasē here must have the sense of "complete," as opposed to the distributive sense that
I noted in some earlier passages. Notable in this passage is the parenthetical remark (as
interpreted and printed in the English) highlighting that some of the appetites have been
fostered by interaction with others in the city outside the household, while others were
born internally and "freed" (note the sinister appropriation of a democratic ideological
term) by his own *tropoi*, a term that picks up the programmatic *tina tropon zē* (roughly,
"what kind of way of life") (9.571a3) with which this section of the micro narrative had been
heralded. Furthermore, the shift from describing this representative man's way of living (*zē*)
to that of his life conceived as a whole (*ho bios*) prepares the way once again for the summing up of his happiness or misery to come.

him. In the early life of the eventual democratic representative man, Socrates notes a possible turn of events that could temporarily keep such a youth from going down that developmental path. That would depend upon the some-time victory (in cases of internal conflict) of the metaphorical oligarchic party within him, which would induce "shame (*aidōs*)" in him (8.560a4–7). But this fragile equilibrium is eventually overturned by "his father's ignorance about his nurture [*trophē*]" (8.560a10)—highlighting the role of education and its failures at every stage in the micro narrative—which allows the further appe-tites that spring up in the youth to flourish without constraint. These dan-gerous appetites are further fostered by his internalization of new forms of civic rhetoric, which involve a transvaluation of values. This is illustrated by the rhetorical redescription (using the technique known as *paradiastolē*) of a number of evaluative terms that are central to political life.[18] Among them, Socrates highlights the redescription of shame (*aidōs*) as "folly" and, likewise significant for the present argument, of *anarchia* as "freedom (*eleutheria*)" (8.560d3, e5). The disorder inherent in *anarchia* is viewed in such character-istically democratic rhetoric not as dangerous but as the valorized democratic attachment to freedom.[19]

What, then, does *anarchia* mean when applied to the tyrannical man at 9.575a1–2 (the beginning of the last inset quotation above)? Recall that Socrates had used the adjective *anarchos* in book 8, in the description of the democratic constitution in the macro narrative, which I translated as describ-ing a constitution "in which there is no one in office" (8.558c2). The word *anar-chia* also featured in the degenerative phase of that same democratic city, in the whimsical reference to the degenerating democratic constitution as breed-ing "anarchy even among the animals" (8.562e3–4, trans. Grube/Reeve), where the meaning can be only metaphorically related to officeholding but describes a general breakdown of the norm of obedience to rule. In the previous chapter, I interpreted both references to *anarchia* in the macro narrative of book 8 as indicating that the legal entitlements and duties of office and rule are being hollowed out by a kind of shadow play in which people are purportedly chosen for office and nominally claim to hold it, but in so doing violate the most basic normative expectations associated with office as a kind of rule.

While the democratic constitution lacked (in Socrates's presentation) rul-ers who are not officeholders, the underlying idea of *archē* is that of rule, since, on my overall analysis in this work, office is a kind of rule. In the case of the soul, as there is no exact analogue for constitutional office, the idea of rule is

---

18. *Paradiastolē* was called to my attention in work by Quentin Skinner to which I am much indebted, beginning with his "Thomas Hobbes."

19. Note that this must be democratic rhetoric, even though it is arising in a city in which a democratic youth is only beginning to emerge. This is another counterexample to Ferrari's strict separation between the two narratives (apart from the single exception he acknowledges), discussed in chapter 8 of the present study.

what should instead be emphasized. Within the soul, the vacancy indicated by *anarchia* is not a simple vacancy of a position of rule. Rather, it indicates the absence of a ruler in virtue of a flawed *taxis*, such that there can be no meaningful exercise of or obedience to the putative ruler even if one is notionally installed. In other words, in living this kind of life, as Socrates observes, the representative tyrannical man is not merely under the passing sway of his psychological whims, as was his democratic father. Rather, he is under the tyrannical power of a stinging drone-like *erōs*, one that drives him to commit crimes of all kinds in order to satisfy his erotic and other appetites. That tyrannical power is no form of constitutional rule; the soul of such a person is in its grip, which may be described as rule but is in fact devoid of proper constitutional ordering, hence it is a condition of *anarchia* and *anomia*.

Having summed up "the life that such a [tyrannical] man leads," it would seem that the programmatic outline of the beginning of book 9 has been fulfilled. Yet Socrates continues the narrative, doing so—it turns out—in order to draw a distinction between the life that such a tyrannical man leads in private life and the life of such a man should he actually rise to the power of a political tyrant. This phase of the micro narrative begins, interestingly, by multiplying the number of such men as a hypothetical case: "if there are only a few such men in a city, and the rest of the people are moderate" (9.575b1–2), the former group will leave the city to serve as bodyguards of a tyrant elsewhere or as mercenaries, but if there are no foreign wars for them to fight, they instead stay in the city and commit a number of "evils" there (9.575b5)—the enumeration of which is telling:

> They steal, break into houses, snatch purses, steal clothes, rob temples, and sell people into slavery. Sometimes, if they are good speakers, they become sycophants and bear false witness and accept bribes (9.575b7–10) (trans. Grube/Reeve throughout this sentence).

The initial list of crimes generalizes over those that Socrates has already mentioned of burglary and robbery of clothes, as well as robbing temples, with two of the verbs used here (for stealing and temple robbing) also having been used in confirming the actions expected of the just man in book 4 (4.443a3–5).[20] But in addition to adding the selling of people into slavery, Socrates adds several more "evils" that pertain especially to a democratic political system, and were notably found in democratic Athens: the role of people acting as "sycophants," false witnesses, and bribers, all in virtue of an ability to speak well— meaning, by implication, in the courts.

While Socrates and Adeimantus banter about how bad such evils are if the people committing them remain few in number, Socrates insists that it

---

20. On the confirmatory nature of this argument, see Burnyeat, "Justice" (216 and passim).

is "when such people become numerous and conscious of their numbers, it is they—aided by the foolishness of the people—who beget a tyrant," the man who emerges in that role being the one who "has in his soul the greatest and strongest tyrant of all" (9.575c3–8, trans. Grube/Reeve). That most tyrannical man either finds himself willingly received by a city or else brings in outsiders in order to enslave his homeland. Indeed, enslaving others is "the purpose (*telos*) toward which such a man's appetites are directed" (9.575d2–e1). Notice Socrates's use of the vocabulary of *telos* here, which informs the terminology of *telos* and *taxis* deployed throughout the present study.

What is the explanatory status of this mini-narrative? It does not correspond to any of the standard phases of the micro narrative, those dedicated to the emergence, nature, or way of life of a particular representative man. It is rather about what happens when a good number of such tyrannical men emerge and make common cause. In fact, it is close to being governed by the Disunity principle that was enunciated as governing the macro narrative: now that there has been a breach within the democratic majority who constitute the officeholding group within this democratically governed city (a fact about the city argued for above), a group with a new set of transformed values is able to remake the constitution—not this time in a compromise with the values and remaining defenders and embodiments of the previous regime, but in what will be a wholesale transformation of a democracy into a tyranny.

Should one be surprised to find something like the Disunity principle at work here? Its appearance supports my rejection in chapter 8 of the construal (championed by G.R.F. Ferrari) of the macro and micro narratives as separate tracks that should not be allowed to cross (even though Ferrari himself had conceded some track crossing in the case of tyranny). What is happening at this point is that the micro narrative about the emergence of a tyrant as an individual representative man is turning into a macro narrative of the emergence of a tyranny as a political regime out of a city that has been a democracy. The two accounts enrich each other precisely as I have argued in chapter 8 that the reader should both allow and expect.

Having offered this mini-narrative, however, Socrates returns—in the plural—to the case of the multiple tyrannical men whom he had been describing previously (as it were, contrasted with the singular tyrant who rises out of that group to political tyranny), to consider "what these men have become like (*gignontai*) in private life and before ruling (*archein*)" (9.575e3–4), with *archein* in my view being used descriptively, shorn of its usual evaluative burden. Describing the dynamics of such people's association with flatterers who obey them, or, conversely, their willingness to flatter those from whom they need anything, Socrates sums up their condition thus—still in the grammatical plural for the first part of the sentence, before their "tyrannical nature" becomes the singular subject for the second part:

So they live their whole life without any friends, always being a master to someone or a slave to someone else (*aei de tou despozontes ē doul- euontes allōi*), a tyrannical nature always [being] without the taste of freedom or true friendship. (9.576a4–6)[21]

In a parallel to the end of book 4, where he had confirmed that the just person was of a certain character and would characteristically undertake certain actions and not others, Socrates continues here in book 9 to confirm that such people should be called "untrustworthy" (*apistous*) (9.576a8), and then that they are (again in the plural) "truly just about as unjust as anyone can be, if what we earlier agreed about justice [the virtue of justice: *dikaiosunē*] was right" (9.576a10–b1)—a reference that must likewise be back to the end of book 4, where the nature of justice as a virtue had been agreed. Thus Socrates has here confirmed that these men with tyrannical natures and private tyrannical lives embody the unjust man whose happiness or unhappiness has been the overall subject of the whole inquiry from book 2 onward.

Socrates then sums up the description that has been offered of this man, whose "waking life is like the nightmare we described earlier" (9.576b3–4). He emphasizes that this worst kind of life characterizes not just anyone with a tyrannical nature but only such a person who has become a political tyrant:

> . . . he [sc. *ton kakiston*, supplied from 9.576b3, "the most evil person"] comes to be (*gignetai*) from someone by nature most tyrannical who acts as sole ruler (*monarchēsēi*), and the longer that he is in this tyrannical way of life, the more he becomes such a person [sc. *ton kakiston*]. (9.576b6–8)

It is Glaucon who agrees to this as "necessary" (9.576b9), and he to whom Socrates reinforces the point, that "the man who comes to light as most vicious [will] also come to light as most wretched," and that "the one who for the longest time acts most of all as a tyrant, will in truth become such [sc. most wretched] to the greatest extent and for the longest time" (9.576b10–c4, converting rhetorical questions into statements for ease of presentation).

What follows between Socrates and Glaucon will return to occupy part of chapter 10. Here, I note the verb *monarchein*, which picks up the previous mention of the tyrannical man's soul, in which *erōs* is the *monarchos*. There, the role of *erōs* as *monarchos* did not prevent the actual condition of the soul from being one of *anarchia*. So here, one should not be misled by the use of this verb into taking the tyranny, either inside the tyrant's soul or in the city over which he holds sway, to be any kind of stable and appropriate ordering that would correspond to properly constitutional rule. On the contrary, the

---

21. This passage will be central to chapter 10.

lack of proper *taxis* in a tyrannical soul is a lack of stable and appropriate order, just as is the lack of proper *taxis* in the so-called rule of a political tyranny. A strictly evaluative interpretation of what a constitution requires (of an individual or a city) disallows the tyrannical man and tyranny in the micro and macro narratives alike to count as such. Both individual and political constitutions must be appropriately responsive to reasons, and to reason, if they are to count as constitutions at all.

The Democratic Representative Man

I turn now backward in the micro narrative, to the coming to be, and then the characteristic type, of the democratic man, one of whom will become the father of the tyrannical youth just described.[22] The democratic man is born to a father described as "that miser and oligarch"[23]—in other words, to an oligarchical representative man. As a boy, the child is initially raised in his oligarchical father's ways, ruling by force over a certain set of his pleasures, described as the "spendthrift" ones (I return to the significance of ruling "by force" below).

In order to understand the psyche of this oligarchical father and the related and developing psyche of his son, Socrates draws a distinction within the overall class of appetites, between necessary and unnecessary ones (*tas te anankaious epithumias kai tas mē*), a proposal that Adeimantus endorses. Necessary appetites are defined conjunctively. They include "those that we can't desist from and those whose satisfaction benefits us," which are jointly ("both") described as "those which it is necessary by nature for us to satisfy," in contrast to "those that someone could get rid of if he practiced from youth on, those whose presence leads to no good or even to the opposite," which are again taken as a conjunction and jointly called "unnecessary" (8.558d11–559a6, trans. Grube/Reeve).

Illustrating with the case of food, Socrates describes necessary appetites as including the appetite for bread as well as that for beneficial (say, nutritious) delicacies, whereas desires that go beyond these would count as unnecessary. Applying a different set of terms to the same distinction, he dubs the latter "spendthrift" and the former "moneymaking" (8.559c3–4, trans. Grube/ Reeve). This gloss is interesting both because of the resonances of "spendthrift" that have already appeared in the macro narrative at the oligarchical stage, and because of the wider extension that it gives to the notion of "moneymaking" appetites than one might have expected. In giving free rein to his

22. Socrates first asks who the "private individual" is who resembles the democratic constitution, but then proposes that they should first, parallel to the sequence adopted for the democratic constitution, investigate in what manner such a person comes to be (*tina tropon gignetai*, 8.558c6–8).

23. 8.558c10–d2.

"moneymaking," in other words, the oligarchic representative man is not to be thought of as seeking money alone; he is also seeking to satisfy appetites including bread and certain delicacies, the same being true of sex (8.559c6) and other desires. Moneymaking as an appetite is not only treated as both instrumentally and intrinsically valuable as a putative good but also encompasses objects that are more extensive than money alone.

At this stage Socrates applies this new distinction to a contrast that he had drawn one stage before in both the macro and micro narratives (the latter of which I am deliberately recounting backward): a contrast between a person called a "drone," who is "ruled (*archomenon*) by the unnecessary" appetites and pleasures, and a "miserly and oligarchic man [sc. who is ruled by] his necessary [sc. pleasures and appetites]" (8.559c8–11). The figure of the drone was first introduced by Socrates in the macro narrative at the stage of the oligarchical constitution, as noted in chapter 8. It was then analogized in a description of the oligarchical man as possessing "dronish appetites" (8.554b7; cf. d6–7), but, again, ones that he is able to forcibly control, by subjecting them not to reason but to the moneymaking appetites themselves.

Now returning to the familial narrative of the birth of the democratic man: here, of course, the oligarchical man is the father, whose son is reared "in the miserly and uneducated manner we described" (8.559d5–6, trans. Grube/ Reeve, referring to the way of life of the oligarchical man, as the rearing of his offspring has not yet been described). The fateful moment of constitutional transformation begins when the son "tastes the honey of the drones" (8.559d6, trans. Grube/Reeve). The language of political rule applied to the soul is developed into a language of civil war, revolution, and counterrevolution, displaying similar political dynamics to those at work in the transformation of the oligarchic constitution into a democratic one in the macro narrative. In the emergent democratic youth's soul, there is an *acropolis* or citadel, with its best "guardians" being "knowledge, fine ways of living, and words of truth" (8.560b7–9, trans. Grube/Reeve); there are figurative royal gates, ambassadors, and expulsions; and, finally, new evaluative language arising to capture the transvaluation of values that has taken place.[24]

The democratic youth who emerges "spends as much money, effort, and time on unnecessary pleasures as on necessary ones" (8.561a6–8, trans. Grube/ Reeve), continuing to treat them equally even once he has welcomed back some of the exiled unnecessary ones in his mature life. He insists that "all pleasures are equal and must be valued equally" (8.561c3–4, trans. Grube/Reeve), and

---

24. There is a play here on the question of guardians, with the language of a "guardhouse (*to phrourion*)," which at 8.561b8–9 still seems to exist in a kind of shadow-play role (a point I owe to Amanda Greene). I transliterate *acropolis* as this spelling is more recognizable in English.

already from youth "lives always surrendering rule over himself (*tēn heautou archēn*) to whichever pleasure comes along, as if it were chosen by lot, until it is satisfied, and then again to another, not devaluing any of them but rather fulfilling them all equally" (8.561b4–5, trans. Grube/Reeve, modified).[25] The analogy of the nature of rule in the democratic man's soul, and life, to democratic sortition, indicates an order (*taxis*) that is at the same time a disorder. For a purported order of rule that lacks any principle of prioritization but instead is hostage to whatever pleasure pops up ("as if . . . by lot") is no genuine order at all.

The lack of order in the soul leads to a lack of order in his life, as Socrates spells out in an important sentence: "There is neither order nor necessity in his life (*kai oute tis taxis oute anankē epestin autou tōi biōi*)" (8.561d6–7, trans. Grube/Reeve, modified).[26] Lacking proper *taxis* in his soul and in his life, the democratic man takes politics no more seriously than any other activity. His engagement in politics is frequent (*pollakis de politeuetai*), involving his "leaping up from his seat and saying and doing whatever comes into his mind" (8.561d3–5, trans. Grube/Reeve)—implying that the context is an assembly or council meeting, since jurors would not (at least in Athens) be allowed to speak.[27] But his political engagement is as sporadic as his engagement in other activities, whether drinking, music, physical training, or philosophy. His pursuits are a kind of shadow play, parallel to the shadow play of rule and office in the democracy. The problem here is not just ignorance of the good, but a lack of meaningful order and ordering in the democratic man's way of life.

The result is that the democratic man is in himself a kind of compendium of (ill-formed and evanescent) characters, "a complex man, full of all sorts of

25. Adeimantus's responses throughout the democratic phases of both the macro and micro narratives are notably enthusiastic and definite, perhaps reflecting his own intimate experience of living in a democratic constitution. However, when at 8.559e3 he remarks *pollē anankē*, translated by Grube/Reeve as "It's inevitable that this is how it starts" (picking up on the "beginning of his transformation" remark at 8.559e1), this should be construed not as necessarily meaning that the change from the oligarchic young man to the democratic one is inevitable but that once a change has begun (in the way that Socrates describes in the remarks eliciting the response *pollē anankē*), such a process of change so initiated will necessarily lead in a democratic-man direction. The question of how deterministic the overall account of either narrative is intended to be is too large to resolve here.

26. Johnstone ("Tyrannized Souls," 435) notes this passage but also argues that while the life of the democratic man lacks order, "his soul is relatively calm." He takes this (unpersuasively, in my view) to refute the claim made by Annas in *Introduction to Plato's "Republic"* that the democratic man is already disunified (reported by Johnstone on 432–33).

27. To be sure, such political activity is but one of the activities that the democratic man may take into his head to pursue. What occasions his choice between such activities as drinking heavily or dieting, training or being idle, and even pursuing philosophy, is whether he happens to desire to "competitively emulate (*zēlōsēi*)" those who practice them (8.561d5), echoing the crucial role of *eis zēlon* at 8.550e1, in the transformation of the timocracy into an oligarchy in the macro narrative, as noted in chapter 8.

characters, fine and multicolored" (8.561e3–4, trans. Grube/Reeve). In this he is "just like the democratic city" (8.561e4–5, trans. Grube/Reeve), a city that harbors all kinds of ways of life: in such a city there may well be oligarchic types, as well as dedicated artists or culture vultures, dedicatedly pursuing a particular set of passions, alongside the democratic representative men themselves who are surely also present.[28]

The Oligarchic Representative Man

Continuing to move backward, I turn now to the origin story (genesis) of the oligarchic man.[29] The narrative of this intergenerational transforming begins with the case of the "child (*pais*)" (8.553a9) of the timocratic father, the word *pais* underscoring the fact that in question is the emergence of a new kind of character from childhood and adolescent experience, rather than the change of an already developed character from one kind to another. In describing the growth of this child, Socrates uses a verb related to a key prepositional phrase that featured in the macro narrative precisely in the parallel transformation of timocracy into oligarchy (*eis zēlon*, 8.550e1). The timocrat's child begins his growth by "competitively emulating (*zēloi*)" his father, in a pattern that would if unhindered result in his coming to resemble his father with a similar character. Instead, the nascent oligarchic youth suffers a sudden reversal of attitude when he sees his timocratic father punished for holding office, a key moment in which the role of office is both unmistakable and central:

> . . . he suddenly sees him [the father] crashing against the city like a ship against a reef, spilling out all his possessions, even his life. He had held a generalship or some other high office (*ē stratēgēsanta ē tin' allēn megalēn archēn arxanta*), was brought to court (*dikastērion*) by false witnesses, and was either put to death or exiled or was dishonored (*atimōthenta*) and had all his property confiscated. (8.553a10–b5, trans. Grube/Reeve)

The mention of a generalship as an illustration of what counts as a case of "high office [*megalē archē*]" makes the translation of *archē* as "office" inescapable, as does the pairing of the verb *arxanta* with the noun *archē*, which would be redundant if one were alternatively to translate *archē* as "rule." The vocabulary of *hai megalai archai* was well established both in Athenian and in broader constitutional language in Greek writings. Other aspects of the

---

28. See the discussion of Williams's problem, and ways of replying to it, in chapter 8, above.

29. In the case of the oligarchic man, the order of discussion of "how he comes to be (*hōs te gignetai*) and what sort of man he comes to be (*hoios te genomenos estin*)" (8.553a3–4) follows the sequence of that original programmatic announcement.

vocabulary here are technical terms, specifically, of the Athenian democracy in Plato's day: the term *dikastērion* used of a popular jury court; the role of false witnesses (*sukophantes*) for hire, a label bandied about by their opponents but also used descriptively and analytically;[30] and the punishments of death, exile, dishonor—losing one's entitlement to pursue *timē* in the sense of office—and property confiscation, were all actual punishments attaching to the Athenian trials that followed upon either accusations brought in the course of *euthunai* (audit procedures) or the other procedures for holding officeholders to account that were introduced above in part I.

Thus the micro narrative drama here depends on the timocratic man's son—the budding oligarchic youth—being witness to his father's holding office and being subjected to accountability procedures, which are institutionally recognizable from a range of Greek cities and especially akin in several respects to those of democratic Athens, complete with jury courts, "sycophants," and typical sanctions. Unlike the case of the budding timocratic youth, in which the role of his mother and the family's servants, together with a wider public opinion, are highlighted as fanning the flames of his rebellion against his father's values, here it is the sheer spectacle of his father's fall as witnessed by the youth himself that brings about the transvaluation of his values.

Having suffered the loss of the family's property and fearing for his own life as a result of his father's actions, the son undergoes this transvaluation as follows: he "immediately drives from the throne in his own soul the honor-loving and spirited part that ruled there" and instead establishes "his appetitive and money-making part on the throne, setting it up as a great king within himself, adorning it with golden tiaras and collars and girding it with Persian swords" (8.553b8–c7, another of Socrates's many rhetorical questions, trans. Grube/Reeve). Key here is the specification of the nature of the appetitive part (*to epithumetikon*) of the oligarchical man: it is referred to as specifically being a moneymaking part (*philochrēmaton*). This begins the elaboration of the appetitive part, which, as shown above, Socrates continues to unfold further in the course of characterizing the democratic and tyrannical men as well.

Notice too that the politicization of the psychology here turns not just to the language of rule but to the language and trappings specifically of the Persian monarchy. This is a kind of political rule that was widely perceived as in tension with the rule embodied in Greek constitutional officeholding, in that (as imagined by many Greeks) the Persian king dominated his subjects and aggrandized himself with the wealth and power of his position, rather than being accountable to them for ruling for their good. That portrait of domination is fleshed out further as Socrates continues that such a man "makes the rational and spirited parts (*to . . . logistikon te kai thumoeides*) sit on the ground beneath [the appetitive and moneymaking part—supplied

30. See Osborne's "Vexatious Litigation" on sycophancy in democratic Athens.

from 8.553c5], one on either side, reducing them to slaves" (8.553d1–2, trans. Grube/Reeve). He thereby subjugates his rational part to merely instrumental reasoning about wealth acquisition, and his spirited part to valuing and honoring wealth and its getting alone.

That completes the development of the oligarchic "youth"; or, at least, as Adeimantus comments, "there is no other transformation of a young man (*neou*) who is an honor-lover into one who is a money-lover that's as swift and sure as this" (8.553d8–e1, trans. Grube/Reeve), suggesting that there could be a family of such psychological and familial dramas having the same result. Socrates then turns to the next programmatic question, which is whether he is "similar" [*homoios*, 8.553e3] to the oligarchic *politeia*, this being the way in which he frames the transition to *poios tis* (in this case, the term used was *hoios*; both meaning, roughly, "what he is like" or "what type he is"). This generates a series of comparisons, specific ways in which the oligarchic youth is "like" (or resembles) the oligarchic constitution, which I reorganize in what follows to bring out the underlying analytical structure.

One pole around which these characteristics revolve is (his appetite for) money, his defining appetite as noted above, informing his character in the following respects (all quotations in this sentence trans. Grube/Reeve):

- His "attaching the greatest importance to money" (8.554a2–3)
- His "being a thrifty worker, who satisfies only his necessary appetites, makes no other expenditures, and enslaves his other desires as vain" (8.554a5–8)
- His being "a somewhat squalid fellow, who makes a profit from everything and hoards it—the sort the majority (*to plēthos*) admires" (8.554a10–b1)

The second pole around which these characteristics revolve is his (lack of) education, an education that could in theory provide a better conception of the good as a *telos* in place of money. This pole is introduced when Socrates responds to Adeimantus's summary of the above ("money is valued above everything by the city and the man," 8.554b2–3, trans. Grube/Reeve) with the inference that "I don't suppose that such a man pays any attention to education," to which Adeimantus responds that "if he did, he wouldn't have chosen a blind leader for his chorus and honored him most" (8.554b4–6, trans. Grube/Reeve).[31]

The result of this lack of education is narrated by Socrates as follows: "because of his lack of education, the dronish appetites—some beggarly and some evil—exist in him, but . . . they're forcibly held in check by his carefulness

---

31. This is a reference to the blind god of wealth, Plutus, as various editions of the dialogue point out. There is a textual issue at 8.554b6–7, which does not affect the present argument.

[*epimeleia*]" (8.554b7–c2, trans. Grube/Reeve).[32] Socrates will add (with an oath), relative to the above, that "most of them have appetites akin to those of the drone, once they have other people's money to spend" (8.554d5–6, trans. Grube/Reeve)—a point that recalls the oligarchical constitution of the macro narrative, in which the politically predominant oligarchs in the offices were able to appropriate money from others, whom they drove to bankruptcy.

Putting these poles into interplay within the overall psychology of this emerging oligarchic youth: the love of money is a flawed *telos*, setting the "good" of satisfying his necessary appetites at odds with the characteristic goods of the rational and spirited parts. And because this *telos* is inherently divisive, it elicits and reinforces a concomitantly flawed *taxis*: one that must use repressive force rather than persuasion to control his other appetites and dominate his rational and spirited parts, as well as his unnecessary appetites.

The education that he lacks is what would in theory give him a better *telos* and a concomitantly more robust *taxis* (since his *telos* would in that case no longer be inherently divisive). Without it, the result is a set of "evildoings," or opportunistically unjust actions in particular settings, that characterize the oligarchical man's way of life whenever he can get away with them: "the guardianship of orphans or something like that, where they [the oligarchical man, described in the plural] have ample opportunity to do injustice with impunity" (8.554c7–9, trans. Grube/Reeve). This stands in contrast to the just actions that he forces himself to perform whenever he has a sufficient fear of being caught: "In those other contractual obligations, where he has a good reputation and is thought to be just, he's forcibly holding his other evil appetites in check by means of some decent part of himself," using "compulsion and fear" rather than "taming them with arguments" (8.554c10–d3, trans. Grube/Reeve).

Socrates draws three conclusions from all of the above about the characteristic nature of the oligarchical representative man (all quotations in this list trans. Grube/Reeve):

- "Someone like that wouldn't be entirely free from internal civil war and wouldn't be one but in some way two" (8.554d9–e1)—compare to the oligarchy, which was said to be not one city but two (see p. 290).
- "For this reason, he'd be more respectable than many, but the true virtue of a single-minded and harmonious soul far escapes him" (8.554e4–6).
- "This thrifty man is a poor individual contestant for victory in a city or for any other fine and much-honored thing. . . . [H]e fights like an oligarch, with only a few of his resources. Hence he's mostly defeated but remains rich" (8.555a1–6).

32. I noted the oligarchic associations that *epimeleia* could bear also in the context of the macro narrative of the *Republic* in book 8 (and in chapter 8 above). As this study argues, Plato in other contexts renovates *epimeleia* into a positive value, especially in the *Statesman*, and in other parts of the *Republic*.

Before leaving the oligarchic man, consider two final points. The first is his characterization as a "miser," precisely mirroring the description of the oligarchic officeholding class in the macro narrative.[33] In fact, there is a striking out-of-sequence parallel between this description of the oligarchic man and the description of the timocratic officeholding class in the macro narrative. In the micro narrative, Socrates generalizes about the oligarchic man that most such people "have appetites akin to those of the drone, once they have other people's money to spend" (8.554d5–7, trans. Grube/Reeve). In the macro narrative, Socrates remarks of the timocratic officeholders that "such people will desire money just as those in oligarchies do" (8.548a5–6, trans. Grube/Reeve), and then offers this striking parallel to the oligarchic man: "They'll be misers with their own money (*pheidōloi chrēmatōn*), since they value it and are not allowed to acquire it openly, but they'll love to spend other people's because of their appetites" (8.548b4–5, trans. Grube/Reeve, modified).

This close parallel suggests that those who are the (politically) predominant men within the timocratic constitution—those who are, by the Predominance principle, themselves timocrats—already share a key feature of the oligarchic man's psychology. This explicit comparison across the two narratives invites us to consider the parallels between those who are predominant in a constitution, who are indeed the dominant men within it, and those who are like that constitution, whom one can expect will be similar to those dominant men (albeit not to all of the people within that constitutionally governed city). However, in this particular case, there is the extra complication that the wires seem to have been crossed: that the (timocratic) men of the timocratic constitution in the macro narrative are being compared to the oligarchic man of the micro narrative.

How to explain this? The fact that the timocrats of the macro narrative already harbor the appetite for wealth is crucial to explaining the passing away of the timocratic constitution and its transformation (this time using the verb *metabainein*, 8.550d2, d5) into the oligarchic constitution. As I noted in chapter 8, the key analysis of its origin is this:

> The treasure house filled with gold, which each possesses, destroys the constitution. First, they find ways of spending money for themselves, then they divert the laws relating to this, then they and their wives disobey the laws altogether. (8.550d7–10, trans. Grube/Reeve, modified)

So while the original character of the timocrats in the macro narrative is to be misers with their own money, it seems that the secret store of gold that they each possess leads them to desire to find ways of spending it—contrary to the laws, which would presumably continue, as in the *kallipolis*, to ban their

---

33. For the individual: *ho pheidōlos* (8.555a1); *ton pheidōlon*, (8.555b1) (cf. Grube/Reeve, "thrifty"); for the oligarchic officeholding class in the macro narrative, *pheidōloi chrēmatōn* (8.548b4).

handling of gold and silver (even though the laws of the timocratic constitution now allow them to hold private land and houses, unlike in the *kallipolis*: 8.547b8–c1).

Indeed, the timocrats' original appetite to acquire money had been immediately linked by Socrates to a desire to spend it: the original mention of their "private treasuries and storehouses" goes on to a remark that within the "houses to enclose them, like private nests," they "are able to spend (*dapanōnto*) [sc. of their money, *chrēmatōn*, supplied from 8.548a5], using it up either on women or on anyone else they wish" (8.548a8–b2, trans. Grube/Reeve, modified). The optative mood of the verb conjugated here, *dapanōnto*, is significant: it indicates that it is possible for the timocrats to spend their hoarded money (so long as they do so within the privacy of their own homes, at least in the mature constitution, as it were), but not that they actually engage in doing so to the full extent possible. It is immediately after indicating that capacity for private spending that Socrates adds the remark about their being "misers with their own money" but loving to spend that of others because of their "appetite [*epithumia*]" (8.548b4–5, trans. Grube/Reeve).

When one puts all this together with the passage about the origin of the degeneration of the timocratic constitution, it suggests that the timocrats' appetites for pleasure and luxury—originally held in at least some check owing to the combined force of the law and the specific love of hoarding money—eventually break out into a desire for spending that leads them to divert the laws and eventually to disobey them. Perhaps this further suggests that the "diverting" of the laws includes their distortion to allow the spending of public funds.

How and why is this paralleled in the oligarchic man of the micro narrative? Before tackling this question directly, it helps to look again at the oligarchs, who are the (politically) predominant group in the oligarchic constitution in the macro narrative, in the full flowering of the mature constitution. There were hints there that, on the one hand, these oligarchs are misers just as their timocratic forebears were (indeed, some of them may be the same people, who have undergone the psychosocial transformation—the transvaluation of values—described earlier): for example, in the remark that "they'd be unwilling to pay mercenaries, because of their love of money" (8.551e2, trans. Grube/Reeve), notable because the hiring of mercenaries by a Greek city would be a civic expenditure. In other words, whereas the timocrats seem to be able to sever their private money from their view of public monies, the oligarchs do not. On the contrary, the latter seem to consider even public expenditure (from taxation primarily of themselves, as the predominant and perhaps the only group of full citizens in an oligarchic constitution) as coming directly out of their own purse, as it were (akin to more recent taxpayer revolts). However, as described in the macro narrative, at least some of them nevertheless become spendthrifts of their private wealth, these being the ones who become bankrupted (Socrates explicitly refers to such a person at the time when he "was rich and spending his money" as "a squanderer of his property" [8.552b8-11, trans. Grube/Reeve]).

Thus, among the oligarchic men of the oligarchic constitution, the politically predominant attitude seems to be miserliness in respect of expenditure on public military needs, at least on mercenaries. But at least some of them— even before the constitution's decline—give in to the appetites that must by implication be possessed by them, appetites perhaps inherited from their timocratic forebears or indeed still possessed by them from the timocratic constitution's time, which lead them to spend money rather than only to hoard it. And there is a similar complex psychology at work in the oligarchical man of the micro narrative, to whom I now return.

"Humbled by poverty," the nascently oligarchic youth "turns greedily to making money, and, little by little, saving and working, he amasses property" (8.553c2-4, trans. Grube/Reeve); the implication seems to be that he gives up on the life of political (including military) honor (including office), having been humiliated by his father's failure to securely enjoy it, and so instead starts to care about making money. As noted earlier, the description of his newly enthroned dominant soul part is complex: "the appetitive part and money-making part (*to epithumetikon te kai philochrēmaton*)," with the *te kai* indicating here conjoined but not identical elements. This description suggests that, indeed like his timocratical and oligarchical forefathers, the nascent oligarchic youth possesses bodily appetites that require spending to satisfy them (with their origins in the body, but extending to complex appetites such as spending on mistresses, as mentioned in the earlier macro narrative cases), as well as the specific appetite for money or wealth, which serves both an instrumental and an intrinsic purpose in his psychological economy. Again, this double role was presaged earlier in the micro narrative, with the reference to the timocratic man, who "as he grows older . . . shares in the money-loving nature" (8.549a9-b2, trans. Grube/Reeve) that he had as a young man despised.

Thus, one direction of development of the oligarchical man is the life of someone who spends and squanders his wealth to the point of bankruptcy—to use a modern term for what Socrates describes as him "sell[ing] up everything (*panta*, in the sense of all his possessions)" (8.552a7) and, in a striking phrase, "the person who has used up (*anēlisken*) [sc. everything, *panta*, supplied from 8.552a7]" (8.552b8). (This is also a verbal echo of the macro narrative's description of the timocratic men's appetites, which they "could" [but seemingly did not] fully act upon privately.) Now, in the micro narrative, at least the less self-controlled among the oligarchical men fail to control their appetites and so "use up" their whole wealth.

At this point, Socrates makes the narratives intersect. He invokes the social psychology of the drones whom he had identified within the oligarchy in the macro narrative (8.552c6-e8), identifying (as outlined above) a set of "dronish appetites" within the oligarchic man, some of them "beggarly" and others "evil" (again, closely paralleling the oligarchs of the macro narrative), but which his "carefulness [*epimeleia*] holds in check by force" (8.554b7–c2). Here, in the absence of education oriented to the true Good, the orientation of care (*epimeleia*) for the good required of a true ruler has been negatively transmuted into a distorted, blinkered, and aggressive grasping for a good construed merely as economic gain.

In the macro narrative, the oligarchic city was said to harbor drones, some of them winged (propertied), others wingless (poor), and of the latter, some of them (the stingless ones) beggars, others (with stings) criminals. Here in the micro narrative, the oligarchical man is described as resembling the oligarchic city in harboring drones (dronish appetites), some of them beggarly, others evil. The social psychology of the drones in the macro narrative is adapted as individual psychology in the micro narrative. And while the oligarchical man uses "compulsion and fear" to hold his evil appetites in check, those appetites are there, as I noted earlier in comparing this individual to the timocratic officeholders and office-eligible class in the timocratic constitution. Moreover, as I noted above, a pun on the word "oligarchs" (the few being officeholders) in both narratives highlights likely military failure, which in the micro narrative is converted into a failure in individual competitions for victories and honors (8.555a2–5): civic competitions, which would naturally include competitions for office. The individual oligarchical representative man is someone who is likely to fail in competitions for office among his peers; the oligarchs of the oligarchic city are likely to fail in military competitions with other cities. While the oligarchic constitution is defined in terms of eligibility for office, it is still open to individual oligarchs to choose how to compete for that office. By contrast, the oligarchical man is defined as having been transformed from "a young man who is honor-loving (*philotimou*)" into one who is "money-loving (*philochrēmaton*)" (8.553d8–e1, trans. Grube/Reeve), someone who ceases to love (and so seek) the honors that in Greek cities always included the holding of office (and, in democracies, especially of the high elected offices).

The Timocratic Representative Man

This brings me back, finally, to the timocratic man, who will become the oligarchic youth's father, and who emerges at the first stage of the sequence of the flawed representative men in the micro narrative. Taking over from his brother Glaucon at just this moment of book 8, Adeimantus begins with the question of what he is like (*poios tis*), by comparing such a man to Glaucon himself in respect of the timocratic man's *philonikia* (8.548d8–9), and Socrates responds by offering a general description of the timocratic man's qualities and behaviors, which (he says—perhaps protesting too much?) are unlike those of Glaucon.[34] With the comparator being Glaucon's own character, his characteristics are as follows, organized in terms of his education; his *telos* of chosen aims, including his attitude to money (which begins to anticipate that of his oligarchical offspring to come); and his attitude to the *taxis* of order and obedience required by political office:

- Being less well educated in music and poetry than Glaucon
- Loving poetry and rhetoric, without being a rhetorical expert
- Loving office/rule and honor (being a lover of office/rule, and lover of honor (*philarchos*[35] *te kai philotimos*): being very obedient to office-holders (*archontōn de sphodra hupēkoos*) but also exerting his own claim to "rule (*archein*)" (understood in the sense of holding office) not on "his ability as a speaker" but on "his abilities and exploits in warfare and warlike activities"
- Despising money when young but loving it more as he gets older, because "he shares in the money-loving nature and isn't pure in his attitude to virtue" (quoting, glossing, or closely paraphrasing the text at 8.548e4–549b7, drawing at points on the Grube/Reeve translation)

The key to his overall character type is his (lack of) proper education. The result: "he lacks the best of guardians (*phulakos*)" within his soul—namely, "reason (*logos*), mixed with music and poetry," which "alone dwells within the person who possesses it as the lifelong safeguarder (*sōtēr*) of his virtue" (8.549b3–4, 6–7, trans. Grube/Reeve, modified). Lacking reason as a guardian within his soul, he is unable to play the part of a guardian capable of being a safeguarder of the city.

Socrates's emphasis on the youthfulness of the timocratic representative man, whose character as such he analyzes, highlights the broader importance of (inadequate) education in giving him, and each of his offspring to follow,

34. That is to say, he begins, as it were, with the *poios* . . . *tis*, and only then turns to the question of genesis. This by itself is not a drastic departure from the proceedings in the macro narrative, where at least a brief statement of the character of oligarchy (at 8.550c8–d1) and tyranny (8.564a6–8) precedes in each case the account of the genesis of the regime.

35. *Philarchos* is a rare word in Attic Greek (an observation that I owe to Anders Dahl Sørensen). Plato uses it only one other time (*Phaedo* 82c7, in the plural), and it serves to underscore that the timocratic man does not just love honor earned in any possible way, but especially loves honor earned through serving in political office. This is reinforced by Theophrastus's discussion of the oligarchic character type, which opens with the definition of *hē oligarchia* as seeming to be "a certain kind of *philarchia*" (*philarchia tis*) that "covets power and profit (*ischuos kai kerdous*)" (Theophrastus, *Characteres* 26.1, Loeb trans., modified). Unlike Plato's oligarchic representative man, however, Theophrastus's is oriented to seeking office, or, ambiguously, to seeking a political arrangement that will give him and his fellows secure power in the city: see Theophrastus, *Characteres* 26.3, called to my attention by René de Nicolay.

his representative character. As each gets older, interaction with his flawed environment brings out latent dimensions of his soul. In the timocratic youth's case, this is exemplified by his developing his latent love of money, owing to his lack of virtue, due in turn to his flawed education.

This theme of an inadequate education precisely mirrors the inadequate education that characterized the second stage of the decline of the constitution of a *kallipolis*, as recounted in chapter 8. There, a new generation of "unworthy" guardians began to "neglect us Muses" and to "have less consideration for music and poetry than they ought," so that "young people [the third generation] will become less well educated in music and poetry" (8.546d3–7, trans. Grube/Reeve), a degeneration of education that implicitly carries on into the fourth generation and the men who set up the formal timocratic constitution. How does this precise mirroring between macro and micro narratives, in regard to a flawed education, specifically one neglecting music and poetry, bear on the question of their relationship (and the scholarly debates about it) discussed in the preceding chapter?

It is true, as Bernard Williams maintained, that not everyone in (say) a timocratic city need be (or probably will be) a timocratic man.[36] It is also true, as G.R.F. Ferrari has emphasized, that a timocratic man need not in principle be born in a timocratic city. Yet the marked parallel between the kind of flawed education that brings about and (presumably) persists in a city with a timocratic constitution and that which brings about the emergence of a timocratic representative youth suggests a further way of understanding the relationship between the macro and micro narratives.

The key point is that the kind of education that tends to produce a certain kind of character can be provided either in the city or in the household. The macro narrative focuses on the effects of such an education when provided by the city, in the shape of its characteristic, and predominant (though not univocal or monolithic), social relations, ideologies, and values. The micro narrative focuses on its effects when provided (in the characteristic patriarchal vein of this narrative in particular) by a father within the household, in the shape of the characteristic social relations, ideologies, and values of that father, which are meant to be predominant in that household, though those cultivated by the broader household will again not be univocal or monolithic.

Thus, the fact that the kinds of education cultivated in the two domains can have parallel tendencies and aims, and indeed can reinforce each other, is what explains a closer relationship and interconnection between each kind of city and the corresponding kind of man than Williams (or Ferrari) would allow, although not one that goes as far as claiming that it is only one kind of city that can produce the corresponding kind of man, or vice versa. To be sure, the direction of that tendency will only be partially or fully realized depending

36. See the discussion in chapter 8 above.

on the social context, as well as other factors of the nature of the person being educated. Plato's sensitivity to this caveat should be taken to be a strength, not a weakness. It is comparable to the way in which the unfolding of genes depends on the signals of other genes as well as the pressures and affordances of the environment in which the organism lives. Such a story can be told at both micro and macro levels, with a lack of determinism at both levels, and no prohibition on their multiple points of intersection.

As for the timocratic man's genesis: that part of the story begins at 8.549c1 (Socrates: *Gignetai de g'* . . .), with a setting of the scene. Socrates offers an explicit, and striking, description of the city in which the timocratic youth grows up:

> He's the son of a good father who lives in a city that isn't well governed (*ouk eu politeuomenēi*), who avoids honors, offices, lawsuits (*tas te timas kai archas kai dikas*), and all such meddling in other people's affairs (*tēn toiautēn pasan philopragmosunēn*), and who is even willing to be put at a disadvantage in order to avoid trouble. (8.549c1–5, trans. Grube/Reeve)

As envisioned by Socrates, the city in which the proto-timocratic youth is born is governed by an officeholding constitution (the plural noun *archas* makes clear that these are offices, not any other form of rule) that is characterized by lawsuits in which those eligible to hold the offices are described as potentially taking part. In contrast, in a *kallipolis*, as I argued in chapter 7, those eligible for office—who are a subclass of the ruling guardians—are not subject to lawsuits, having no eligibility to hold the money or property around which Greek lawsuits would typically revolve. (For its part, *timas*, the plural of *timē*, could name offices as well as other kinds of civic honors, as noted earlier in this study.) So the timocratic man is one who is motivated to seek the competitive approbation embodied in holding office, in contrast to his father's aversion to office and to other forms of public life.[37]

Second, note that this city is also characterized by the description of honors, offices, and lawsuits as among the kinds of "meddling [*philopragmosunē*] in other people's affairs"—using a noun that may be coined by Plato but that Aristotle considered synonymous with the well-established and characteristically democratic-Athenian term *polupragmosunē*.[38] While the timocratic youth's "good father" (549c1–2) is said himself to stay aloof from such public

---

37. As my reverse-order recounting of the micro narrative allows me now to recall, once the timocratic youth grows up and himself becomes a father, he will come to grief on the shoals of accountability, by being severely sanctioned in the course of holding public office—and it is this failure that his own son, the proto-oligarchic youth, will witness.

38. *Topics* 111a8–11. On the significance of *polupragmosunē* in Athenian democratic practices and ideology, as well as its salience for critics of such practices and ideology, see Carter's *Quiet Athenian*.

affairs, he is clearly being positioned as living within a context in which the possibility of such meddling is rampant.

So is this city of the timocratic youth's birth a degenerate *kallipolis*, or a city like democratic Athens, or what? Surprisingly, the question of just what kinds of cities this youth and the other representative men are born in has been scarcely addressed in the literature. The negative strictures offered by Williams and Ferrari—namely, that each such city need not be the one corresponding to the character of the similar youth—do not ask, let alone answer, the question. I would venture that Plato may be meaning to characterize each of these cities not so much by a single kind of constitution (instead leaving that open) but by the kind of flawed education it provides. This makes the different cities that are home to each of the representative men more similar to one another than one would otherwise expect.[39]

At the level of the particular household being described, that education is an intersection of the negligence and quietism exhibited by the father (a man who does not care about money or fight his own battles in the courts), compounded with the reactive social aspirations of the mother and servants. At the level of the city, the values championed by the mother and servants are instilled and reinforced by prevalent ideologies: "Those in the city who do their own work (*ta autōn prattontas*) are called fools and held to be of little account, while those who do the opposite are honored and praised" (8.550a2–5, trans. Grube/Reeve).[40] Once again, the micro narrative cannot do without appeal to the dynamics of a city at the macro level, even though these do not always correspond point by point to the macro narrative itself.

A triangulation among these different directions of education is performed, Socrates emphasizes, by the budding timocratic youth himself, who "hears and sees all this [in the city], but he also listens to what his father says, observes what he does from close hand, and compares his ways of living with those of the others" (8.550a5–7, trans. Grube/Reeve). And it is the resultant vector that shapes the development of the budding timocratic youth's soul, using the technical psychological vocabulary of tripartition that Socrates had developed in book 4 (435b9–441c7 and passim), charting the trajectory of that psychic development (back in book 8) as follows: "His father nourishes the rational part (*to logistikon*) of his soul and makes it grow; the others nourish the spirited and appetitive parts (*to te epithumetikon kai to thumoeides*)" (8.550b1–3, trans. Grube/Reeve).

39. In "Plato's Neglected Critiques" (still work in progress at the time of writing), I discuss the question of just what kind of city is indeed presupposed as the city in which each of the successive representative men is born—a question that Ferrari (*City and Soul*), for example, entirely fails to address, though his overall thesis (laid out above in chapter 8) puts it very much on the table.

40. Grube/Reeve translate "those who meddle in other people's affairs," but this is not spelled out in the Greek, which merely negates the "do their own work" for the contrast.

The resolution of these social and psychological pressures within the formation of the timocratic youth's soul is as follows, in a description using the same kind of highly politicized vocabulary that features at each stage of the micro narrative:

> Because he isn't a bad man by nature but keeps bad company, when he's pulled in these two ways, he settles in the middle and surrenders the rule [*archē*] over himself to the middle part—the victory-loving and spirited part (*te kai philonikōi kai thumoeidei*)—and becomes a proud and honor-loving (*philotimos*) man. (8.550b4–6, trans. Grube/Reeve)

Once again, this is a notable parallel to the timocratic constitution in the macro narrative, which also involves agreement on "a middle way" in setting up a constitution that is "a sort of midpoint between aristocracy [the constitution of a *kallipolis*, as Socrates terms it here] and oligarchy" (8.547b8, c6–7, trans. Grube/Reeve). It is obvious that the "middle" nature of the timocracy and the timocratic soul is unique among the types of constitutions and men: in the timocracy, the group of silver-natured soldiers are predominant, who had been the middle group of the *kallipolis*; in the timocratic soul (and, hence, the man with that soul), the *thumoeides*, which is the middle of the three parts of the soul, is predominant. By contrast, none of the other constitutions or representative men is described with the language of the "middle." All are rooted in the appetitive class or part (in the soul, *to epithumetikon*), which is, as it were, an extreme, rather than a middle.

In both the timocracy and the timocratic man, the predominance takes a specifically political shape, as one part (the middle part) that comes to "rule": in the timocracy, ruling in the guise of officeholding; in the timocratic man, the "surrendering" of "rule over himself" by the whole person to the middle part, or *to thumoeides*, of his soul. And in this case, the language of "surrender" (*paradidōmi*) of "rule over himself"—a highly politicized word, as it was commonly used, inter alia, for the military surrender of a city—is common also to the democratic man (8.561b5). The timocratic man abdicates rule by the educated reason that he still, to some (imperfect) extent, possesses; the democratic man abdicates stable rule by either reason or appetite, handing it over instead to the temporary sway of passing pleasures. In contrast, figuration of the oligarchical man is not in terms of surrender but of coercion, this man being a person who sets up a certain kind of appetitive part as ruler (on the model of a Persian king) and reduces the other parts to its slaves (as shown above).[41]

---

41. See Lorenz (*Brute Within*) for a general argument that it is the dominant soul part rather than the whole soul that determines action in each case. This is compatible with the argument I have developed about the way a given soul part shapes an overall way of life for each representative man in the micro narrative.

In the case of the tyrannical man, his internal *erōs* serves as "leader of the soul." The comparison of the tyrannical man to a drunkard who has abdicated not only stable self-rule but any sort of agency is telling. Whereas the timocratic, oligarchical, and democratic men all play an active part as whole human agents in settling their characters, the tyrannical man does not. For his soul, and hence his life, is so disordered that he is not truly capable of being an agent at all. This psychology is considered further in chapter 10.

Conclusion to Part III as a Whole

The macro narrative featured constitutions that are all profoundly flawed, each of them having abandoned the true *telos* of rule, and the first three (timocracy through democracy) having gradually undone its *taxis* as well. Indeed, the timocratic constitution had already emerged as a scene of domination, in which the unphilosophical officeholding (and office-eligible) group subjugates and exploits a group of producers. While this constitution is not explicitly termed by Socrates a *stasiōteia* as opposed to a *politeia*, nor is it explicitly said (as is the city featuring an oligarchic constitution) to be two cities rather than one, it has already abandoned and turned against the fundamental civic goals of unity stated in *Republic* 6. It likewise violates the aims of ruling, caring, and weaving together opposed groups in the civic body, as stated in the *Statesman*, and the legislative aims of freedom, friendship, and wisdom stated in the *Laws*.

No such disunified constitution will be able to reproduce itself in the stable way that belongs to a *kallipolis* alone. Only a *kallipolis* is stable for a time not because of repression but because people's motivations and values stably interact to produce and reproduce a valuable form of social relationship. Similarly, only a person whose reason rules their own soul will be immune (or as immune as human nature and mortal chance allows) to temptation and corruption over time, not because of repression but because their motivations and values are stably organized to produce and reproduce a valuable way of life. The rule of reason is what enables virtue (and constitutes the virtue of wisdom, which is one part of a united whole). Being capable of ruling oneself is what makes a person "kingly," as noted at the outset of this chapter; otherwise, one needs ideally to live in a constitution ruled over by those described as kings (whether in the *Republic* or the *Statesman*), or, as a second-best, in a constitution that embodies the values of rational order and law and so can promote these in and through its officeholders, safeguarded by an understanding of the rationality of the laws that they uphold.

Short of these kingly standards, there are constitutions of city and of soul that may be relatively rankable, but that all fall absolutely short of the true constitution in each case. Each of these flawed constitutions, political and psychic, is inherently unstable. At one point of the macro narrative, Socrates suggests that the officeholders of the oligarchic constitution may use their official powers more or less well or badly. By doing so, they may stabilize their regime to a greater or lesser extent, and for a longer or shorter period. Yet the innate flaw in the oligarchic constitution is the same as that in the timocratic one: its officeholders are oriented to exploit for their own advantage those whom they rule, rather than to serve them. In other words, no modification of their *taxis* can ultimately or fully compensate for the distorting effect of a flawed *telos*. This is the fundamental flaw making these two constitutions not only vicious (as opposed to virtuous) but also (and therefore) ultimately unstable. Indeed, while the powers accorded by each constitution to its officeholders might be used in somewhat better or somewhat worse ways, the inherent instability of both of them makes the trajectory of degeneration ultimately inescapable. The path of the macro narrative appears to be broadly, if in detail somewhat variably, deterministic, and it is governed by explicit principles (Predominance and Disunity), as shown in chapter 8. Indeed, a path of degeneration is inevitable, given Disunity, which means that there has been a privatization of ideas of the good, such that a common and genuinely valuable *telos* is no longer shared among all those who are politically predominant in relation to the offices that give each constitution (apart from tyranny and *kallipolis*) its political *taxis*.

Not so the micro narrative. If a timocratic constitution seems fated to evolve (or, rather, degenerate) into an oligarchic one, and so on, the men who are born under any given constitution may evolve (or degenerate) in many different directions, depending on how the characters of their parents and household interact with the ideological pressures endemic to that constitution and the city that it orders (or disorders). Those ways are multifarious, arising from nuanced interactions between each individual father's values and those of the city in which they live. Some individuals within the same city may be sports of nature, others not; they may also be lucky or unlucky in their particular parentage and the character of others in their household.

Or, to put it in other words: the entire micro narrative of *Republic* books 8 and 9 is couched in terms mounting a critique of the various ways in which political education—in cities presented as sharing many of the hallmarks of democratic Athens—could go wrong. This comports with indications elsewhere in the dialogue of the ways in which a philosophical education in a democracy might on some rare and blessed occasions go right.[42] The micro narrative that harbors these possibilities is the one that at once speaks directly to the readers of the dialogue (especially those implied to be living in a democracy such as Athens) and simultaneously undoes the seeming determinism of the macro narrative about the life choices of individuals, and, perhaps, the political possibilities that those individuals may choose to foster. Plato does

---

42. This case is argued in detail in my "Plato's Neglected Critiques."

not appeal solely or even primarily in this part of the dialogue to the good life that a philosopher qua philosopher will live. Rather, his emphasis is on the value of psychic self-rule and the just life that it makes possible. And even if this is a value that only philosophers may be fully able to achieve, it has an everyday relative dimension in experience to which the argument of the dialogue is fully alive.

As to rule: like the macro narrative at the constitutional level, the micro narrative at the individual level exhibits the unstable pathologies arising from the interaction of a flawed *telos* and a *taxis* attempting to achieve such a flawed *telos*. Each of these flaws is a source of instability that undermines the ordering role of rule. While within the life of an individual, and within their psyche, there is no exact analogue to the procedural mechanisms of accountable office, a broader analogue lies in the fact that rule must be inherently ordered itself if it is to be able to perform its ordering role. It is ultimately the tyrannical man whose erotic drive toward lawless pleasures is so inherently unbounded that it fails to count as an orienting *telos* in any sense of rule, and simultaneously undermines any *taxis* of individual conduct at all. But from the timocratic youth onward, the flaw in the *telos* pursued from the standpoint of what reason would prescribe also results in a flawed *taxis* of individual conduct (shaped by a flawed *taxis* within the soul). *Telos* and *taxis* must go hand in hand in specifying any kind of rule. The concluding chapters of this work reflect on this point more broadly across Plato's work.

PART IV

Thematizations of Rule and Office

CHAPTER TEN

Against Tyranny

PLATO ON FREEDOM, FRIENDSHIP, AND THE PLACE OF LAW

THE CHAPTERS OF PART III of this study both revolved around a diagnosis of the tyrannical man who might come to power within a city. Even before coming to power, such a man was diagnosed by Socrates as inherently lacking the ability to enjoy freedom or friendship. In a passage of *Republic* 9 noted in chapter 9 above, discussing such tyrannical men:

> So they live their whole life without any friends, always being a master to someone or a slave to someone else (*aei de tou despozontes ē doul-euontes allōi*), a tyrannical nature always [being] without the taste of freedom or true friendship. (9.576a4–6)[1]

The incapacity to enjoy freedom or friendship is due to a lack of order in their lives, which makes it impossible for them to trust others or to be trusted by them, or, to spell that out, to cooperate in an appropriately reliable way with others and to be treated by them as such a cooperative partner. While that lack of order in their lives is generated by the lack of order in their souls (the utter domination of erotic love as a tyrannical appetite being incompatible with any actual order), it is manifest in their relations with other persons. The lack of freedom and friendship is attributed to the quality of those interpersonal relations rather than being solely attributable to the internal order (or, rather, lack of order) within their souls.

The same holds true of the life of such a man should he rise (or, rather, sink) to the condition of political tyrant within a city. In a passage of the

---

1. This chapter focuses on passages from both the *Republic* (according to the Slings OCT) and *Laws* (the only OCT of which is edited by Burnet); I indicate which dialogue is being quoted with its abbreviated title only when the context does not make this clear. Translations are my own unless otherwise indicated.

same dialogue, which I shall place in context and analyze later in this chapter, Socrates reaches the following conclusion about the political tyrant: "In truth, then, and whatever some people may think, the real tyrant is really a slave (*doulos*), compelled to engage in the worst kind of fawning, slavery, and pandering to the worst kind of people" (9.579d10–11, trans. Grube/Reeve, modified).[2] It is not the tyrant's soul but his social relations that are at stake in this statement of the proposition that he is really a slave.[3] His counting as a slave is meant to explain both that he is unfree, despite being legally a free person in a city with chattels and other relationships of legal slavery, and also that he is friendless, since the fawning and pandering in which he is compelled to engage are antithetical to true friendship. The tyrant who seems all-powerful in having abolished all constitutional limitations on his power in fact ends up having to fawn, out of fear, on the very subjects whom he would dominate— for lack of any protection from a commonly accepted rule of law and *taxis* of ruling in which they share. If Hegel's stylized master in the *Phenomenology of Spirit* is dependent on his slave for the services that minister to his power, Plato's tyrant is dependent even more radically for his own power on that of his subjects, a dependence that ends up negating the value of that very power and the freedom that it would normally be expected by Greek citizen men to provide.[4]

As both passages above suggest, freedom and friendship are at a pivotal moment in the *Republic* presented as self-evident values, the lack of which are key to explaining why the tyrant's life is to be judged maximally miserable rather than (as Thrasymachus, and after him Glaucon and Adeimantus, had earlier in the dialogue asserted) maximally happy and blessed. In fact, the contrast with tyranny, as I shall develop the way in which it is presented, demonstrates how civic freedom and friendship can be fostered for free citizens (but not for their slaves) by a constitutional order of office and law, the very order that a tyrant undermines and destroys. The first part of this chapter is devoted to demonstrating the relationship among these ideas, and in particular the place of freedom and friendship, in the *Republic*: these being values that are rarely taken to animate that work. In the second part of the chapter,

---

2. Socrates uses a participle of the verb "to be" in order to signal that he is making this claim about the tyrant considered in terms of the strict evaluative sense of that idea (only the true tyrant counts as a tyrant at all in this sense, as opposed to a looser descriptive sense): see chapter 1 for these two senses.

3. I make this point about this particular crux in the argument only. Of course, part of the broader thesis of book 9 is that the tyrant is also psychologically enslaved to his own *erōs*, as Arruzza (*Wolf in the City*, 183) puts it: "Plato's response to the fantasy that only the tyrant, like Zeus, is free, is that under the tyranny of eros conjoined with appetites, nobody is free."

4. Thanks to Lindsay Van Horn for pointing out the significance of this dependence in discussion at Princeton in 2021.

consideration is given to a later moment in book 9 of the *Republic* in which a speech by Socrates seems prima facie to challenge its valorization of freedom, by making use of the language of "slavery" to describe the relationship of ruler and ruled. How and why Plato uses the language of slavery to describe a relationship of rule that he has in the same stretch of the dialogue presented as fostering freedom (and friendship) is a seeming paradox that I attempt to resolve by taking the "slavery" in question to extend only to the abstracted epitactic dimension of rule, but not to the exploitative *telos* that actually existing legal slavery in Greece at the time supported (as *Republic* 9 itself implies). This is still to abstract from slave relations and their full materiality, which continue to cast a shadow over the discussion of values from any part of Platonic or other ancient Greek texts.

Thus the plot thickens as to the relationship among rule, freedom (and slavery), and friendship, in ways that I undertake to clarify both in these sections on the *Republic* and in the next part of the chapter, which treats the same themes in the *Laws*. There, too, rule is described as a relationship involving a kind of "slavery," set against the backdrop of ways in which rule is aligned with freedom and friendship in the *Laws*. In regard to both dialogues, in order to make sense of their various valorizations of freedom alongside their uses of the vocabulary of slavery to capture the epitactic dimension of rule, I argue that the key is making freedom appropriately compossible with rule (drawing on the notion of compossibility originally developed by Leibniz) in terms of its *taxis*, while at the same time insisting that any rule that can be willingly obeyed must be for the good of its subjects. Both the *taxis* and the *telos* of rule have to be made compossible with willing obedience.

The language of slavery is used to indicate that rule must involve epitactic ordering. This was a dimension of the actually existing legal slavery in Plato's day. However, such legal slavery involved the *telos* of exploitation of the ruled, rather than the *telos* of serving their good as Platonic rule posits. Hence Plato's invocations of rule as a form of willing slavery rest on the condition (counterfactual for actually existing legal slavery) that the purpose of any such relationship must be the good of the ruled. This does not remove the stench of the metaphor. But it at least makes it possible to challenge further appropriations of it as justifying rank exploitation and coercion.

From a standpoint that empathizes with slaveholders, as I show, Plato in *Republic* 9 develops an account of freedom and friendship for legally free men (whose masculine gender is emphasized in the text), which is presented as being easily recognizable to Socrates's interlocutors in that part of the dialogue (who are themselves legally free Athenian citizens). This pivotal book of the dialogue, which brings to a peak the demonstration that the life of a tyrant, who is the maximally unjust person, is maximally miserable as opposed to maximally happy, rests not so much on the special features of a *kallipolis* or the life of a philosopher but rather on the enjoyment by free citizens of the everyday constitutional practices of offices and laws that tyranny would overturn. That enjoyment includes the values of civic freedom and civic friendship, which are shown in the dialogue to be fostered in practice by office and law, which both reflect and shape the cooperative disposition among citizens on which both freedom and friendship are built.

In other words, the values of freedom and friendship themselves turn out to be interlocking for those with the status of free citizens: both rely, as I explain with help from Plato's *Gorgias*, on an underlying cooperative disposition among the citizens to engage in partnership or association (*koinōnia*). These values are needed to underpin the *taxis* of a constitution organized through office and law, so as to orient these at least partially and roughly toward the proper *telos* of rule (the good of the ruled). Conversely, that very *taxis* of office and law operates to reinforce and support such a cooperative disposition among the citizens, even as they express that disposition in enabling such a constitution to function. By and through this entire interlocking process, civic freedom and friendship are supported. This is a kind of garden-variety constitutionalism, which does not invoke the higher-order safeguarding function that a constitution would ideally possess. Rather, the fundamental diagnosis of what is wrong with tyranny, as summed up in *Republic* 9, rests only on appeal to a constitutional experience in which offices and laws are relatively well respected and so can serve to underpin the cooperative disposition among the citizens on which both freedom and friendship depend. Again, this is presented as being an everyday, garden-variety experience for those who enjoy the privileged status accorded fully to male citizens, not for those whom Plato in this same part of the dialogue takes for granted that the legal order will enable them to enslave.

Preliminaries: Compossibility

Before turning to the details of that *Republic* 9 account, I offer a word about the notion of compossibility (*compossibilitas logica*, in the neo-scholastic Latin of Leibniz, who coined the term), which I adapt in a less rigorous form for purposes of this chapter.[5] For Leibniz, the concept serves to distinguish multiple possible worlds from the actual world, the latter being a world in which only those concepts that are compossible can be jointly realized. For present purposes, the key underlying idea, which can survive abstraction from Leibniz's distinctive ontology and cosmology, is, as Benson Mates explains,

---

5. While it is surprising that relatively few modern political philosophers have taken up the notion of compossibility, its fruitfulness in the hands of Hillel Steiner suggests its utility for explicative purposes in political theorizing more generally: see, for example, Steiner's *Essay on Rights*.

that "some things that in themselves are possible are not compossible."[6] Mates states a technical definition of compossibility as follows: "A pair of individual concepts, A and B, are compossible if no contradiction follows from the supposition that there are corresponding individuals for both of them—that is, if the statements 'A exists' and 'B exists' are consistent with one another."[7] As he illustrates with a choice of Leibnizian examples:

> There could be a world in which there was no sin, and there can be (indeed, is) a world in which there is forgiveness of sin, but there cannot be a world with both of these features; likewise, there could be a world in which there was no poverty, but such a world would exclude the exercise of charity, which in itself is possible (and also desirable).[8]

Like Plato in the *Timaeus*, Leibniz depended on further evaluative and ontological commitments to underwrite the thought that the present world is the best of all possible worlds.

Here, my concern is with the compossibility of freedom and friendship on the one hand and of rule, office, and law on the other, in Plato's analysis of political constitutions. I use the vocabulary of compossibility more loosely than Leibniz (or Mates), to refer to the substantive corealization of certain values—in particular, freedom and rule—rather than solely to their logical noncontradictoriness.[9] Both *Republic* 9 and *Laws* 3 sketch portraits of constitutions (in a parable of *Republic* 9, and in the quasi-history of ancient Athens in *Laws* 3) in which officeholders and laws make freedom possible by securing mutual forbearance and trust. Freedom, in particular, is valuable only when configured so as to be compossible with rule—that is, insofar as obedience to rule becomes willing or voluntary, expressing freedom as an adverbial modification of rule.

A constitutional *taxis* of office and law enables this in a distinctive way, with willing obedience being fostered by the limitations and protections built into the powers of officeholders and the demands of law. This in turn supports a certain kind of freedom, which Susan Sauvé Meyer has called (in discussion of Plato's *Laws*) "civic freedom," and which in turn underwrites a certain kind of friendship.[10] To be sure, this can go wrong, if citizens cease to be willing to

---

6. Mates, *Philosophy of Leibniz*, 43.

7. Mates, 75, citing (n36) Leibniz, *Textes inédits*, 325: "The compossible is that which, with another, does not imply a contradiction."

8. Mates, 43–44.

9. While I argue that they must be configured in certain ways so as to be corealizable, so making a kind of necessity claim, I speak of "compossibility" to indicate the need to modify each in order to make it compatible with the other.

10. Meyer, "Civic Freedom." El Murr ("*Philia* in Plato," 26) refers to "civic friendship," arguing that in the *Republic* Plato considers it as "a consequence, rather than a cause, of civic unity," in contrast to the *Laws*. However, his discussion of the *Republic* is only of

obey officeholders and laws and come to do so only grudgingly or not at all. Nevertheless, it is a common and distinctive path to the realization of these values as compossible.

Yet while this garden-variety constitutionalism involving office and law is acknowledged at key moments in both dialogues (of course, taking a more elevated Platonic form in the divinely inspired laws and carefully reconfigured offices of the constitution depicted in the *Laws*), it is not necessarily the only path to freedom and friendship that Plato contemplates. Both freedom and friendship can be understood as flowering out of a common root, which is a cooperative disposition, expressed in a willing obedience to rule. Such rule need not necessarily take the form of office and law, though Plato recognizes that it is less likely that citizens will manifest willing obedience to rule when it does not. The fundamental issue of obedience to rule and of the definition of rule will be treated further in the next chapter. Here, the focus is on office as a kind of rule, one that goes hand in hand with law and provides a distinctive path to freedom and friendship that is seldom appreciated as a Platonic one outside the *Laws*.

Preliminaries: Friendship and Freedom

A helpful perspective on the interrelationship between friendship and freedom can be developed from Plato's *Gorgias*, which in its final stretch (before the closing myth) features Socrates speaking in his own person, summing up and extending the claims that have emerged from his examination of Callicles. The themes and claims that emerge there are highly resonant with those in my chosen trio of dialogues (*Republic, Statesman, Laws*), as Socrates contends that "a person who wants to be happy (*eudaimona*) must evidently practice discipline [*sōphrosunē*]" and, if in need of discipline and restraint, "must pay his due [in a legal context] and must be chastised (*kolasteon*), if he's to be happy (*eudaimōn*)."[11] Indeed, he applies this to how he should act in "direct[ing] all of his own affairs and those of his city." In contrast, Socrates contends that a person who lives as Callicles had been advocating, cultivating the incessant effort to satisfy appetites that are wholly undisciplined, is someone who "could not be dear (*prosphilēs*) to another man or to a god, for he is incapable of partnering (*koinōnein . . . adunatos*), and where there's

---

friendship within a *kallipolis*, rather than attending to its arising within the garden-variety constitutionalism that in this chapter I identify in a stretch of *Republic* 9. I was prompted by Panos Dimas, commenting on a draft of part of this study, to recognize the centrality of friendship to its themes.

11. *Grg.* 507c9–d6, trans. Zeyl, modified; I have adopted Moore and Raymond's proposal made in another Platonic context (introduction to Plato's *Charmides*, xxxvi–xxxvii) to translate *sōphrosunē* here as "discipline."

no partnership (*koinōnia*) there can be no friendship (*philia*)."[12] What does Socrates mean in suggesting that the state of *koinōnia*, itself underpinned by a person's ability to "be a partner," both with other persons and with gods, is necessary for *philia*? Such partnership is the opposite of a state of enmity or *stasis*. *Stasis* is what tears human communities apart, destroying their ability to realize any interpersonal goods. The chapters in part III traced this destructiveness in the flawed constitutions of the cities of *Republic* 8 (and of the souls in 8 and 9), while the need to avoid *stasis* also featured in the various cities discussed in the constructive constitutional projects of the *Republic*, *Statesman*, and *Laws* alike, as discussed in part II.

Drawing on Plato's *Laws* advances the analysis a step further. There, the Athenian Visitor speaks as generally of *koinōnia* as does Socrates in the *Gorgias*. He goes further in asserting that every *koinōnia* requires a ruler.[13] In turn, a willingness to rule and a willingness to obey are required on the part of the ruler and the ruled, a willingness that is made possible by making freedom compossible with rule.[14] This willingness itself requires *koinōnia*, in a mutually constitutive relationship in which the disposition to cooperate underpins rule, and rule underpins stable cooperation. In other words, *koinōnia*—the basic disposition to cooperate with one's fellows rather than to confront them with hostility—is what makes freedom possible (as I shall argue in analyzing moments in both the *Republic* and the *Laws*) and likewise makes *philia* possible (as the *Gorgias* explicitly avows).

Of course, bringing the *Gorgias* to bear on the *Republic* and *Laws* is a speculative move. My argument, however, does not hinge on the *Gorgias*. I invoke that dialogue simply as a convenient way of beginning to explicate what will become legible in the text of the *Republic* in its treatment of freedom and friendship in book 9, and what is explicitly articulated in the text of the *Laws*: namely, taking civic freedom and friendship to be interpersonal valuable relationships that must be corealized simultaneously in both the *taxis* and the *telos* of rule if they are to be realizable in either. It is only if rule is configured so as to be compatible with freedom, through the willingness of obedience by the ruled, and if it is configured so as to be compatible with friendship—so jointly serving to exclude the limiting case of tyranny—that both freedom and friendship can be secured for and as part of the good of those ruled. This is most readily and recognizably achieved in a constitution manifesting the *taxis* of office and law.

How precisely are freedom and friendship in this chapter, and in the portions of Plato on which it primarily draws, to be understood? As I have argued

---

12. *Grg.* 507e3–6, trans. Zeyl, modified.

13. *Leg.* 1.639c1–5, a passage discussed further in chapter 11.

14. The willingness to rule, while it cannot be taken for granted, is more readily found than is the willingness to obey.

elsewhere, freedom in Plato—in the significant invocations of it in *Republic* 9 and *Laws* 3 (as well as 4 and 9) discussed below—is to be understood in an interpersonal sense.[15] Employing the triadic formula introduced by Gerald C. MacCallum Jr, analyzing the freedom of an agent x as a relation in which "'x is (is not) free from y to do (not do, become, not become) z,'"[16] freedom in these passages is treated as the freedom of one person, x, from actual or potential interference by others to do the everyday actions that are commonly assumed by x and their peers to befit the social and political status enjoyed by x.

The focus in these particular Platonic contexts is especially on the case of free male citizens, who would expect to be able to move around their city freely, to travel to other cities at their own choice, and to be able to build bonds of friendship with their peers: all these actions are taken for granted as the kinds of actions that such citizens would generally take to befit their free status. Tyranny—meaning the nullification or abolition of office and law—deprives these citizens of this freedom, both because it removes the stable framework of trust underpinning the expectation that they should be able to enjoy it and because it threatens potential interference according to the whims of the tyrant. Plato extends that analysis to the political tyrant himself. While such a tyrant will presumably suffer little to no actual interference with his actions so long as he succeeds in holding sway, *Republic* 9, as I argue below, emphasizes the inhibiting fears of potential interference from subjects (including close associates and bodyguards) who have been given good reason by the tyrant's own actions to rebel.

Thus *Republic* 9 shows this everyday sense of interpersonal freedom to be under threat of potential or actual interference in a tyranny, for everyone, including the tyrant himself. The arguments of that book do not rely upon any conception of freedom more ersatz than that. Proceeding from the negative case of the abolition of meaningful office and law in a tyranny, *Republic* 9 suggests that interpersonal freedom in a *polis* for those enjoying free-citizen status is dependent upon that very constitutional framework. That, however, raises a new problem: How can freedom be delimited in order to remain compatible with rule, including constitutional rule through office and law? For while office and law in fact foster freedom on the showing of *Republic* 8 and 9, they may nevertheless be believed by many people to inhibit or threaten it.[17]

That problem is addressed by Plato in *Laws* 3, which provides an analysis of how such interpersonal freedom can be made compossible with rule, including its species of office. That compossibility depends on citizens exhibiting a

15. Lane, "Placing Plato"; I emphasize here the republican dimension of such freedom more than I did there. See, for example, the emphasis on "potential interference" in Pettit (*Just Freedom*, 35).

16. MacCallum, "Negative and Positive Freedom," 314.

17. This is persuasively shown to be a diagnosis offered by Plato in Nicolay's "Origins of Licence."

willing obedience (sometimes termed "voluntary slavery") to laws as well as to rulers, who in certain contexts of that part of the dialogue are specifically shown to be officeholders. The disposition of "willingness" that informs the actions and attitudes constituting "obedience" is the same disposition that earlier I glossed as "cooperative." Both the enjoyment of freedom and its security over time rely on this disposition.[18]

A final preliminary caution: while garden-variety constitutionalism presents office and law as necessary to enable freedom and friendship (at least in complex societies, barring the primitivist societies sketched at the beginning of *Laws* 3), they are not sufficient. This is for twin reasons. Considered, as it were, from above, office and law require safeguarding of some kind to secure the correct epistemic and caring orientation to the *telos* of the good of the ruled, lest their proceduralism become perverted or empty. Considered, as it were, from below, office and rule require a cooperative disposition among the citizens, lest their procedures become a matter for factional dispute (*stasis*) rather than a framework for cooperation. Office and law risk becoming shadow play, or, even worse, mere shills in the struggle for power, in the absence of the kind of education that their procedural forms alone cannot provide, and in the absence of the kind of disposition to cooperate that such an education would inform and sustain.

Recall the telling moment limned briefly in *Laws* 4 (and discussed near the end of chapter 1), one that strikingly makes use of Thrasymachean language from the *Republic* in outlining a dystopian possibility (and claiming it to be, in many if not all *poleis* of the day, reality), of claims to officeholding that have been shaped entirely by and to the advantage of those in power. Plato in this passage shows himself to be well aware of the destructive possibility of a kind of zero-sum political battle, which the Athenian Visitor describes as follows:

> When officeholders are so made by fighting over their positions (*archōn perimachētōn genomenōn*), the winners take over the affairs of state so completely that they totally deny the losers and the losers' descendants any share in office (*archēs . . . metadidonai*). Instead they live in close watch (*paraphulattontes*) on each other to prevent anyone who comes into office (*eis archēn*) who would, remembering the past wrongs, overturn the present arrangements.[19] (*Leg.* 4.715a8–b2)

In contrast to such *stasioteiai*, a true *politeia* will involve freedom that is mixed with rule, limited so as to be compossible with it, in order to be valuable, and

---

18. The role of security in relation to other values (including freedom) is something I have learned from Emma Rothschild and Amartya Sen over many years, in part through participating with them in activities of the Common Security Forum and the Joint Centre/ Center for History and Economics.

19. See chapter 1 page 33, above, for a note on this translation.

it is only in this sense that one may value "freedom" as such as a proper aim of good legislators.[20] But likewise, as the Athenian goes on to insist here, in a sentiment that Cicero and Augustine would later echo: "laws which are not established for the good of the whole state are not correct laws" (*Leg.* 4.715b3–4). The legal form without the animating spirit of a cooperative disposition is a hollow shell.

Rule and Freedom: *Office and Law, Freedom and Friendship, in* Republic 9

I turn now to Plato's account in *Republic* 9 of how a constitution of rule involving law can play a role in underpinning freedom and friendship, as elements in the good of the ruled that are unavailable in a tyranny even to the tyrant himself. In a relatively neglected stretch of dialogue after having completed the presentation of the tyrannical man, Socrates argues that it is when living the life of a political tyrant—a life that throughout the work he has agreed with his various interlocutors in classing as the maximally unjust one—that this man will be most thoroughly unhappy and wretched. This passage, discussed in depth below insofar as it centers on what I call the parable of a transported slaveholder, is retrospectively classed by Socrates as the first of three proofs that the tyrant is the most unhappy person (answering the challenges set by Thrasymachus in book 1 and by Glaucon and Adeimantus in book 2).

Nothing in these culminating indictments of the life of a tyrant in book 9 hinges on the distinctive nature of a *kallipolis*. Rather, they invoke lower-key, everyday, experiential contrasts with tyranny, in the shape of constitutions of office and law, with which Glaucon is assumed to be familiar. These parts of the dialogue show the *Republic* to be concerned not only to vindicate the *kallipolis* as the ideal constitutional *taxis* combining a role for safeguarding rulers with rule by officeholders, not only to indict the flawed constitutions of book 8 for their respective failures to constitute a *kallipolis*, but also to be engaged in explaining just how ordinary constitutions of office and law (however flawed with respect to the ideal fulfillment of the schema) can work to secure the goods of freedom and friendship, in contrast to a tyranny. Flawed as these everyday constitutions will be when considered from a strict evaluative perspective, they nevertheless exhibit how freedom and friendship can be made compossible with and by office and law, and so why in practice a schema in rule might be valuably fleshed out in this way.

The passage to which I now turn, a parable of a transported slaveholder as an analogy for a political tyrant, rests on a repugnant presumption: that of the purported benefit to masters of enslaving other human beings. This must

---

20. Contra Laks ("Freedom, Liberality, and Liberty"), whose focus on the mean between freedom and obedience I otherwise accept.

be presumed insofar as Plato in this passage enlists the sympathy of the dialogue's interlocutors—and, it is most reasonable to assume, also his imagined
readers—with an imagined slaveholder transported outside the constitutional
legal protections (including, at the time, the legal protection of his slavehold-
ing) that free men could normally take for granted in a *polis* at the time. This
parable hinges on recognizing the actual bad of slavery for the enslaved, whom
the parable recognizes would naturally seek in such a situation to rebel. Its
paradoxical upshot is that a constitutional order of office and law serves to
foster freedom and friendship for those whom it protects, even as it strips
away, from those whom it exploits, the opportunity to enjoy those goods
securely or at all.

It must be acknowledged that the transported slaveholder parable does
nothing for the benefit of the legally enslaved apart from acknowledging
their actual exploitation. Its aim is to rein in their masters with regard to
one another: to persuade them that the mutual opportunity for freedom and
friendship rests, in the case of everyday experience for Plato and his fellow
legally free Greeks, upon the compossibility of both with office (a species of
rule) and with law. Plato's defense of office and law here is a contribution to
the conditions of freedom and friendship among equals, but one that presupposes that those equals are simultaneously dominating and exploiting others
in the extreme terms of enslavement. Reading it today might be an invitation
to consideration of the conditions of creating freedom and friendship among
equals while simultaneously recognizing the ways in which various kinds of
domination invade those relations of putative equality (or simply exclude
many people from their reach).

The transported slaveholder passage is located at a pivotal moment in the
Republic's quest to prove that it is advantageous (in its relation to one's happiness) to be just. Building on the analysis of the tyrannical man discussed above
in chapters 8 and 9 (as it happens, discussing *Republic* 8 and 9), Socrates sums
up the predicament of such tyrannical men in the passage with which this
chapter opened:

> [T]hey live their whole life without any friends, always being a master
> to someone or a slave to someone else (*aei de tou despozontes ē doul-
> euontes allōi*), a tyrannical nature always [being] without the taste of
> freedom or true friendship. (9.576a4–6)[21]

What does he mean by this? The broader context of the overall argument of
the dialogue is relevant. From *Republic* 1 onward, Socrates has accepted Thrasymachus's positioning of the tyrant as paradigmatic of maximal injustice.
What he will eventually refute is Thrasymachus's contention (at 1.344c5–7)

---

21. I have slightly modified the translation of this sentence from that which I offered
in "Placing Plato."

that the injustice of the tyrant is comparatively "freer" than is justice, a refutation that he undertakes by proving its opposite. As quoted earlier, contrary to the freedom that Thrasymachus had associated with injustice and its paradigm exemplar of tyranny, "the real tyrant is really a slave" (9.579d10–11), a sentence that applies to the case of a tyrannical man who has actually gained political power as a tyrant in the city.

It is often assumed that this proposition invokes the ideal of virtuous psychological self-mastery that has been developed in the course of the dialogue. However, as I have argued elsewhere, while that ideal of self-mastery is certainly central to the dialogue, it is not labeled or celebrated as "liberty" or "freedom," and no new idea of freedom is needed in order to articulate that ideal, which relies instead on existing ideas of the badness of slavery in particular.[22] Similarly, one might expect the conclusion that "the real tyrant is really a slave" to be drawn by Socrates as an implication of the account of the tyranny of *erōs* within the soul of the tyrant, with the proto-tyrannical youth as "someone in whom erotic love (a tyrant) (*erōs turannōs*) dwells" (9.573d4). But, in fact, that description, relying on a deeply ingrained sense in Greek poetry of the badness of being tyrannized over by *erōs* (whether interpreted as an internal drive or as the Greek god of the same name, a distinction not marked in Greek texts) was nothing new. Its badness is deeply rooted in the language of Greek poetry. The work of the dialogue is not needed to make *that* point persuasive; it already would be to anyone like Glaucon and Adeimantus, and to Plato's readers.[23]

Rather, the innovative point being driven home at this juncture of *Republic* 9 is that while such people—should they gain the power of political tyranny—will (relative to their unfortunate subjects) be "masters and free" (9.577c7, trans. Grube/Reeve), the free status that they nominally possess will not bring in its train the normal concomitants of free actions and a free disposition. In actions and dispositions, the nominally free and masterful tyrant will be

---

22. Lane, "Placing Plato." This is an article in which I primarily used the English term "liberty" in keeping with its role in structuring the special issue of the journal in which that paper appeared. Here, I have changed my terminology to a more consistent use of "freedom." I also am delighted here to take note of Carl Young's "Plato's Concept of Liberty in the *Laws*," which appeared simultaneously with my paper in 2018, though it treats only the *Laws*, not (as mine did) also the *Republic*. Young's paper, like mine, vindicates the idea that Plato is not unconcerned with what Berlin called "negative" liberty, but devotes itself primarily to the argument that the virtue of self-control (as he translates *sōphrosunē*) is central to Plato's political ideal of liberty in the *Laws* and is connected to the ideal of the mixed constitution.

23. No new conception of "positive liberty" is advanced or required to make sense of it, any more than of Socrates's subsequent description of a tyrannical man as someone who cannot even control himself and so cannot be expected to rule others (9.579c6–d1). On the association of tyranny with anarchy (*anarchia*) that Socrates makes at 9.575a1, see chapter 11, as well as the chapters in part III.

condemned to slavishness, in the sense of relating to others as if imprisoned or enslaved. It is not only the psychic life of tyrants that is slavish. Rather, and central to my argument, is the fact that their interpersonal and political life is slavish as well.

Indeed, this claim is encapsulated in the way that the conclusion that "the real tyrant is really a slave" is in fact supported in the sentence in which it appears:

> In truth, then, and whatever some people may think, the real tyrant is really a slave (*doulos*), compelled to engage in the worst kind of fawning, slavery, and pandering to the worst kind of people. (9.579d10–11, Grube/Reeve, trans. modified)

As I noted above, it is not the tyrant's soul, but his social relations, that are at stake here. To understand this proposition more fully, I return to the neglected Platonic thought experiment upon which it rests, designed to show that even more wretched than the tyrannical person living a private life is the tyrannical man who becomes an actual tyrant in a city.[24] The issue here is whether the political tyrant can, or will, be happy, and the answer will be that they cannot: precisely because they lack freedom in the interpersonal sense, and also interpersonal friendship. It is the absence of freedom and friendship, an absence deriving from the tyrant's own abolition of any constitutional order of rule, that plays a key role in dooming the tyrant to unhappiness. To be sure, that abolition itself stems from the woeful condition of the tyrant's soul or psyche, their utter inability to rule themselves in the sense of imposing any order on their whims, lusts, and urges. But Plato's focus here is on the interpersonal relations that the tyrant's psychological condition brings about.

In the thought experiment, a wealthy slaveholder is to be imagined as suddenly transported with his slaves to an uninhabited place where he cannot rely on the law or the officeholders to protect him anymore (9.578e1–579b1). Socrates argues that the transported slaveholder would become unable to act in the ways generally open to free persons, because he would not be able to trust the laws and officeholders to protect him from his own slaves. He would be unprotected by the compact of mutual defense of free men against slave revolts that the laws of every Greek *polis* effectively established and assumed; as Socrates remarks, outside the thought experiment, a "whole city is ready to defend each of its individual citizens" (9.578d13), including and especially focusing here on those of the citizens who own fellow humans as slaves.

Absent that defense by the law and the officeholders who uphold it, Glaucon avers that such a slaveholder would be greatly in fear lest (as Socrates puts the question to him) "he and his children and his wife should be killed by the

---

24. While this episode in the dialogue has been relatively neglected in Platonic scholarship, it is notable that duBois (*Slavery*, 60) uses an extract from it (9.578e–579a) as an epigraph for her chapter "Ancient Slavery."

[i.e., their] slaves" (9.578e5–7). The assumption made here is important: it is that slaves who would be able to attack their masters with the expectation of impunity would do so. So unwilling is their obedience (rightly) understood by Plato to be. Slavery as an instance of sheer hierarchical command and obedience, with a *telos* aimed at benefiting the ruler rather than the ruled, would indeed be incompatible with willing obedience.

Again, it is a morally repugnant fact that the thought experiment, and the dialogue more generally, devised in a slave society, assumes that a key benefit of constitutional rule among free citizens is that they can use the power they so gain to dominate their slaves. Likewise repugnant is the fact that Socrates's thought experiment rests on an assumed sympathy of the interlocutor, and reader, for a (transported) slaveholder. As in the founding documents of the American Republic in the United States, the ideal of constitutional rule and of mutually secure free citizens is here articulated, in a society in which its applicability to enslaved persons was brutally curtailed so as to allow them to be dominated and exploited. The effort to wrest ideals of constitutional rule for a society of equals from such documents must be acknowledged to be, certainly in the case of Plato here, going against the evident expectation of the text (which in this passage relies on a reader's presumed sympathy for the transported slaveholder). Likewise, in writing about the history of political thought in order to better understand ideals of constitutional rule for contemporary purposes, one must acknowledge that making any such ideals a reality for all requires a political struggle against those forces imposing inequality and allowing continued domination and exploitation. The project of this chapter is one of intellectual reconstitution of the mutual interlocking of the values of freedom, friendship, and constitutional rule in the belief that these today can, and must, be made relevant to all, as opposed to being reserved for the exploitative elite (in this case, slaveholders) with whom Plato is manifestly in this passage concerned.

The moral of the parable, as Plato has Socrates articulate it, is that it is because of this lack of trust and so unwillingness to cooperate as equals, due to a lack of effective legal assurance, that the slaveholder would be "compelled to fawn on some of his own slaves . . . and . . . become a panderer to slaves" (9.579a1–3, trans. Grube/Reeve). Indeed, it is this compulsion to fawn on others that explains the claim that the tyrant is sometimes a slave (as well as sometimes a master). Without the ability to trust in others to uphold and enforce the expected norms and entitlements of free status, his ability to engage in the actions befitting of a free person (as he and his peers in free legal status in a given society would view them) is effectively curtailed—actions that in the context assumed in Plato's presentation here were expected to include the domination of slaves. The freedom being limned here is unmistakably freedom for some, to use Hegel's terms, but not for others, but it still can reveal the contours of equality among that group in ways that help shape the compossibility of freedom and equality more broadly.

Socrates draws an analogy between the transported slaveholder and the political tyrant: the person who is not only a tyrannical man but also holds tyrannical power in a city. In what sense is a political tyrant unfree? In the sense that he finds himself living in a "prison" (the noun is *desmōterion*), "like a woman, mostly confined to his own house," unable to travel abroad, and so on, using gendered assumptions that again rely on Greek (and in this case especially Athenian) practices that would be broadly rejected today. In Socrates's analysis, this set of confining conditions makes the political tyrant unlike "other free men" (*hoi alloi eleutheroi*) (9.579b4–c1, trans. Grube/Reeve, modified). Notice that while the tyrant is still nominally a free man in status, he is deprived—just as the transported slaveholder would be—of the usual capacity for free actions that would be assumed by such a free male citizen to befit his status as such.

In the thought experiment, the lack of solidarity with others results from the actions of a deus ex machina who is able to whisk away the law and the political community of free men who would normally be able to rely upon one another to enforce it. The added twist in the case of any actual political tyrant is that (as the analogy implies) it will be his very own actions that rebound upon him, making him unable to rely on the very conditions of free action that he as a nominally masterful, free person would normally in such societies expect to enjoy, in the way that free men who live in well-ordered and constitutionally ruled cities can routinely do. Having made the previously free persons of his city into, effectively, his slaves, he must now live among them as if isolated in a sea of untrustworthy, because untrusted, enemies—just as would a transported slaveholder.

While the tyrant is not literally or physically enslaved in relation to everyday expectations of freedom of action, he has condemned himself to living as if he were so. And he has done so by undermining the conditions of garden-variety constitutional rule. Thus the proposition that "the real tyrant is really a slave" is not asserted, in its immediate argumentative context, in virtue of the tyrant's internal psychic structure. It is asserted, rather, in virtue of his self-constructed inability to rely on cooperation with other persons as guarantors of a space for his free action in the way that would generally be understood by him and his peers to befit someone typically enjoying the free legal status that he does. To be sure, that self-constructed inability stems ultimately from his psychic order, or, rather, lack of order: it is the tyrant's inability to command his own actions that gives rise to his inability to interact with others on terms of friendship or freedom. But it is the latter consequence, thematized as a violation of constitutionalism, that has been largely overlooked in readings of the dialogue.

The *Republic* glosses the consequences of this lack of solidarity and trust as a deprivation not only of freedom but simultaneously of friendship. Tyrants are unable to enjoy friendship. This fact is one of the worst, and most miserable, aspects of their status—a key member of the class of attributes that Glaucon readily agrees makes the status of tyrant (who counts as the maximally unjust person, as agreed by Socrates already in book 1) the most unhappy and least desirable, rather than the happiest and most desirable as Thrasymachus had initially argued it to be. And far from being associated with greater freedom as Thrasymachus had claimed, it is precisely the injustice of the tyrant toward those around him that will deprive him of the capacity to engage in the characteristic (free) actions associated with the status of being a free man.

Hence the image of a masterful, free tyrant is not challenged here by direct appeal to his miserable psychic condition. Instead, it is undermined by showing that his tyrannizing, unjust disposition and actions undermine the very possibility of his performing the actions that conventionally (in that society) befit someone free, and so being able to enjoy the free actions that a free person would normally have expected to be able to enjoy. What explains that incapacity is the destruction of garden-variety constitutional rule, involving offices and laws capable of underpinning the trust that freedom requires. That whole framework depends on the cooperative disposition that fosters friendship but that has been undermined by the actions of the tyrant himself.

In other words, Plato argues in *Republic* 9 that the problem with tyranny is not only that it is unaccountable, though it is that. He also offers a further and deeper diagnosis of tyranny: that the tyrant is the epitome of someone who is untrustworthy and so unsociable, or, in a word, uncooperative. Or to borrow a term from Facebook, the tyrant is both unfriendable and unfree, and unfree not only in his soul but resultantly also in his social relations. It is because he is uncooperative that he proves unable to enjoy either freedom or friendship for himself, let alone to secure either for his subjects—freedom requiring a cooperative disposition expressed in willing obedience of the rulers by the ruled (here, illustrated by the converse case of tyranny), and friendship requiring a cooperative disposition that can be realized in appropriate relations of trust among citizens sufficient to secure their mutual continuation.

In this moment of *Republic* 9, law itself and constitutional arrangements of officeholding more broadly are presented as counting among the expressions of this cooperative disposition, and serve to express and support it. There can be no basis for the trust and the security of expectations that provide the basis for freedom and friendship alike, and hence no genuine or effective constitutional order of law, under a tyrant aiming solely to satisfy his own most bestial desires and driven to negate any constraint—including the constraints of law and office—that would prevent him from doing so. Or, to put it another way, focusing on freedom alone: the legal status of being a free person (as opposed to being legally enslaved) is insufficient to enable one to securely enjoy the value of freedom. Freedom as part of the good of a citizen, which is the *telos* of rule, can be realized only when it is incorporated into the *taxis* of rule, potentially of office and law, and these in turn must be made compossible with freedom through the willing obedience of those who are subject to their powers.

Yet it is not only the tyrant who is deprived of the very possibility of freedom and friendship in virtue of the trust in the law and in one's fellow free citizens that his own mode of ruling undermines. The same is true of his subjects, and in virtue of the same absence—that is, an efficacious political constitution. For it was the absence of such an efficacious political constitution in the imagined slaveholder case and, by analogy, in the political tyrant case that made their subordinated populations into societies of (literal or metaphorical) slaves chafing to revolt, rather than free persons mutually upholding political rule. It follows that a necessary condition for making a "whole city . . . ready to defend each of its individual citizens" (9.578d13, trans. Grube/Reeve) is the obedience of those citizens not only to the laws but also to those ruling who exercise power in accordance with those laws. Slavery (figured as the status of those deprived of the protection that a free constitution affords to free persons) is an assumed bad not only for the tyrant but also for the citizens who are made into his subjects.

Rule as Slavery? The Paradox of Willing Obedience in the Republic

The transported slaveholder parable and the lessons drawn from it figure as the first of three proofs that the tyrant is the most unhappy of the five representative men considered in books 8 and 9. Once those proofs have been completed, Socrates proposes a new "image of the soul in words, so that the person who says this sort of thing [namely, that 'injustice profits a completely unjust person who is believed to be just'—which had been said by Glaucon himself in book 2] will know what he is saying" (9.588b10-11, with the interjection quoting 9.588b2-4, trans. Grube/Reeve). Socrates continues to urge that such a person (his address to Glaucon being tactfully disguised through anonymization) consider what they may be assuming and be offered gentle persuasion to change their mind. Throughout this stretch of the dialogue, it is everyday experience, as well as poetic example and metaphor, that is used to "persuade . . . gently" (9.589c6). That is, as in many of the passages of book 9 responding to the original challenges made by Thrasymachus (in book 1) and by Glaucon and Adeimantus (in book 2), it is lived experience of the value of constitutional order in general, in what I have called garden-variety constitutionalism, rather than the theoretically distinctive excellence of a *kallipolis*, that is being invoked.

Socrates sums up the lesson of the soul image by returning to his appeal to the relationship between freedom and constitutional rule—this time transposed to the psychic domain. This appeal is prefaced by a startling invocation of slavery as a way of describing good (or at least necessary) political rule, to which I turn shortly—startling given that it appears shortly after the transported slaveholder passage in which slavery itself is an assumed bad. But before I turn to that invocation, let me introduce the appeal to freedom and constitutional rule within the soul, as this sums up a number of themes of this chapter so far and the study as a whole (the *telos* and *taxis* of rule, and their relationship to constitutions, guardianship, and law).

> SOCRATES: "It is better for everyone to be ruled (*archesthai*) by divine and wise reason, it being best that [sc. this is] his own within himself, but if not, being imposed from without, so that as far as possible all will be alike and friends (*philoi*), steered (*kubernōmenoi*) by the same thing."
>
> GLAUCON: "Yes, that's correct."
>
> SOCRATES: "Clearly, then, this is also what the law aims at, being the ally of everyone in the city. And it is also what rule (*archē*) over children aims at, in not allowing them to be free (*eleutherous*) before a constitution [*politeia*] is established in them as in a city, and by caring for their best part with our own, we set up a substitute guardian [*phulax*] and ruler [*archōn*] similar to our own within it. Then, and only then, we set them free (*eleutheron aphiemen*)" (*Resp.* 9.590d3–591a3).

The *telos* of rule is set out clearly in the first statement by Socrates quoted above: friendship is made possible by common subjection to rule by divine and wise reason. This rule may be instantiated intrapsychically, for those who are capable of cultivating such divine and wise reason within the best part of themselves—their *logistikon* (this ranking of the parts of the embodied has just been reiterated in the metaphor of the human being as containing a miniature human being, a lion, and a multicolored beast). For those for whom that is not possible, however, it should be imposed from without, meaning in the form of interpersonal rule of one person over another.

It is the establishment of a constitution within the soul, including this safeguarding function of ruling, that makes freedom possible. Notice the vocabulary of "guardian [*phulax*]" and "ruler [*archōn*]." This is exactly the same vocabulary that was earlier used to designate the political constitution of a *kallipolis*. Rule over children aims to set up a guardian and ruler within each child's own soul, capable of establishing and safeguarding its order (*taxis*) and keeping it oriented to the proper *telos*. As Dimitri El Murr has emphasized, it is such internal psychological rule, achieved by some citizens for themselves and by others through the rule of external guardians, that forges the "alikeness" among citizens on which their mutual standing as "friends" depends.[25]

---

25. El Murr, "*Philia* in Plato," 24–25.

Likewise, the law that will regulate rulers even within a *kallipolis* (as shown in earlier chapters of this study) serves to foster psychic rule as well. The inter-personal *taxis* of rule involves the law, which is the ally of everyone in the city in the sense that it is directed to helping them realize their good.

Is this passage invoking a new ersatz sense of psychic freedom as opposed to interpersonal freedom? No: I would contend that this is freedom in the same interpersonal sense invoked earlier in the analysis of the tyrant. It is the freedom of one person from actual or potential interference by others, to do the everyday actions that would be assumed by that person and their peers to befit the social and political status that they enjoy. Both references to free-dom (*eleutherous einai*, as the object of what the adults in question will allow for the children being reared, and *eleutheron aphiemen*, in which the adults set free the children) are to future states in which the children are to be left to their own devices. Freedom is not being used to describe the condition of their souls directly; there is no mention of *erōs* as a dominating drive depriv-ing them of freedom, for example. On the contrary. Constitutional rule is cul-tivated within their souls so that they may be set free to enjoy the ordinary opportunities to do the everyday actions that they take to befit their social and political status (with Socrates's use of the first-person plural in the latter part of the second statement, invoking kinship with Glaucon, building in the presumption that such status is the same status as free male citizens, which he and Glaucon share).

This passage does not, however, simply connect rule, friendship, freedom, law, and guardianship. It is prefaced by a positive invocation of slavery to describe the kind of obedience that such rule requires.[26] While slavery is an

---

26. Frank (*Poetic Justice*, 116–18) challenges my reading of the choice of means between force and persuasion in Plato in this passage of *Republic* 9 (about to be discussed in the main text), as in the means described for the education of books 2 and 3, and argues more generally that "there appears to be nothing 'voluntary' about the submission of the ruled" in a *kallipolis* as described in the *Republic* (though the laws and rule of books 5–7, discussed above in chapter 7, receive less attention from her). In "Constitution" (51–54), she endorses "willing obedience" as an ideal, but finds the purported "willing acquiescence" of citizens envisaged in Plato's dialogues to be undercut and absent in practice in the depiction of the *Laws'* constitutional project (51–53), and likewise undermined in that of the *Republic* (54). While it can be difficult to adjudicate between readings that operate from such different premises as hers and mine, the tensions that she highlights—between the way in which the double theory of law is presented in the latter dialogue and the actual deployment of the laws and preludes that follows—are to my mind a sign of the lack of a sharp binary between persuasion and force in Platonic thought, rather than of the tacit undercutting of that binary. Nevertheless, owing in large part to conversation and engagement with Frank and her work, I would now wish to withdraw my own contention in "Persuasion et force" (195) that (to translate my own words there) good rule "does not involve any constituting role for those ruled." The emphasis of the present study is on the way in which a *taxis* of rule can indeed involve a constituting role for the ruled, so long as that is consonant with what must (at least in principle) be the epitactic role of the ruler. I return to this question in the next chapter.

assumed bad as a legal status putting one outside the benefits of constitutional rule, it can be employed as a good when used as a way to describe the necessity of rule and of obedience to that rule. This is in contrast to the assumed badness of enslavement to *erōs*, and to the assumed badness of a putatively free person's being unable to rely on the civic friendship, as it were, needed to support acting in the ways that such free status would normally facilitate—actions including at the time, as for Plato in the transported slaveholder parable above, being able to securely and legally exploit one's slaves.

The key to resolving this paradox is that Plato does not invoke slavery in these descriptions of political rule in merely descriptive terms. Rather, he conserves its epitactic dimension only, while replacing the *telos* of exploitation of the slave with a postulated *telos* (within the description of political rule) of what is genuinely good for the person ruled. That is morally odious insofar as it purports that such slavery for the benefit of the slave could actually exist. But it puts a condition on Plato's invocation of slavery, and reveals its connection to the logical structure of his thought, while entertaining the counterfactual possibility of a relationship of slavery that is purportedly beneficial to the slave. (That this would have been considered counterfactual follows from the widespread fear and bemoaning in Greek texts of the fate of falling victim to enslavement, showing that the exploitative nature of that domination was widely recognized.)

To fill in the context for this move, which immediately prefaces the passages considered in the inset section above: this is a point in *Republic* 9 when Socrates has just taken up the case of a "manual worker" who is "despised" in virtue of his "best part" being "naturally weak" (9.590c1–5, trans. Grube/Reeve)—working out the moral of the "image of the soul in words," or metaphor, as containing homunculus, lion, and beast. Here is how he discusses the case of the manual worker, in a statement that leads directly into (and overlaps below) with those I was considering immediately above:

> Therefore, to ensure that someone like that is ruled (*archētai*) by something similar to what rules the best person, we say that he ought to be the slave [*doulos*] of that best person who has a divine ruler (*to theion archon*) within himself. It isn't to harm the slave that we say he must be ruled (*archomenos*), which is what Thrasymachus thought, but because it is better for everyone to be ruled (*archesthai*) by divine and wise reason. (*Resp.* 9.590c7–d4, trans. Grube/Reeve, modified)

This text has sometimes been read as suggesting that Plato intended his ideal city to enslave the lower classes; indeed, such a reading of this passage as "advocat[ing] that members of the lower classes be 'slaves' to the philosophers" is central to the adverse evaluation offered by Christopher Bobonich of the political program of the *Republic* as compared to the *Laws*.[27] This putative

27. Bobonich, *Plato's Utopia Recast*, 203.

contrast between slavery as characterizing the position of ordinary citizens in the *Republic* and freedom as characterizing that of the ordinary citizens of the *Laws* must first of all be challenged. For, as Malcolm Schofield has argued, it is a gross misreading of this passage to take it to be advocating that the lower classes of a *kallipolis* are literally to be slaves to the philosophers,[28] not least because Socrates will go on to propose terms on which the members of these groups will indeed (according to his analogy to parents rearing children) be "set . . . free" (9.590e3–591a3). Bobonich's reading is more broadly antithetical to the whole construction of the *kallipolis*, in which members of the lower class (the manual workers) are clearly presented as free citizens, being contrasted with occasional mention of slaves.[29]

The key to a better understanding of the passage begins with Socrates's reference to Thrasymachus. As argued above in chapter 5, Thrasymachus's focus in *Republic* 1 was not on legal chattel slavery but, rather, on the nature of political rule and obedience. He argued "that the virtue of justice and what is just is really the good of another, the advantage of the stronger and the ruler, and harmful to the one who obeys (*peithomenou*) and serves (*hupēretountos*)" (1.343c3–5, trans. Grube/Reeve, modified). That is, obedience to a ruler is inherently exploitative of the subject. He went on to argue that the epitome of a ruler so aiming to exploit his subjects for his own benefit is the tyrant (1.344a7), who "kidnaps and enslaves (*doulōsētai*) the citizens" (1.344b5–7, trans. Grube/Reeve).

That is the sole time that Thrasymachus mentions enslavement. Hence it must be the argument to which Socrates is reverting in book 9 when he mentions the Chalcedonian by name. If so, then in asserting that those whose best (rational) parts are naturally weak should be "slaves of the best person," whose best (rational) parts are sufficiently strong so as to rule in themselves and be able to foster that rule in others, Socrates is discussing not the literal status of slavery but rather the question of subjection to rule in general. He is using slavery as a synecdoche for the epitactic dimension of rule—but only for that dimension.[30] The *telos* of the "enslavement" relationship in this case of good

28. Schofield, *Plato*, 273–74, with n57.

29. Vlastos, "Slavery in Plato's Thought,"151–52, and passim.

30. I described slavery as a synecdoche for rule in "Persuasion et force" (195 and passim). The understanding of synecdoche on which I rely is given by Seto ("Distinguishing Metonymy from Synecdoche," 92): "Synecdoche is a conceptual transfer phenomenon of semantic inclusion between a more comprehensive and a less comprehensive category." In this case, slavery would be the less comprehensive category from which semantic inclusion is extended to the more comprehensive category of rule. However, as I indicate in the main text, I would argue now that it is only the epitactic dimension of slavery (as it were, its *taxis* rather than its *telos*) to which this analysis applies—since slavery does not belong to the evaluative category of Platonic rule in virtue of not sharing the *telos* of the good of the ruled. Laks (*Plato's Second Republic*) calls the use of slavery in these passages a metaphor by analogy, with which I now also agree: the lack of complete subsuming of legal

rule is the good of the ruled, whereas the *telos* of legal enslavement in Greek cities was (as implied by the transported slaveholder parable) their exploitation. Slavery itself, like other legal relations, is being shown by Plato to depend evaluatively primarily on its *telos*, with its *taxis* being potentially put to both good (in his eyes) and bad ends.

Thus, in his deployment of slavery as a synecdoche for one dimension of rule here (the epitactic dimension of its *taxis*), Socrates insists that its purpose must be "not to harm the slave." In this he inverts the *telos* of actually existing legal relationships of slavery. The Socratic antithesis of harm is, of course, benefit. So slavery could count as a case of rule only if, and when, its *telos* is to benefit the ruled—fitting with the idea of rule as normative all the way down. This is how Plato can imply that actually existing Greek slavery was an exploitative relationship (given that, in the transported slaveholder parable, Socrates assumes that slaves would kill their masters if they could), while here treating its epitactic dimension of command and obedience as potentially serving a different value—namely, the good of those ruled politically. This reading is supported by Socrates's linked appeal, in the inset quotation above, to the way in which parents rule over their children, in "not allowing them to be free before a constitution is established in them as in a city." The comparison is clearly meant to invoke the establishment not of intrapsychic coercion but rather of a regular order of rule, with one part of the soul ordering for the good of the actions of the others. Political freedom depends on the parallel *taxis*: it must reject *anarchia* at any and every level. It also depends on benefit to the ruled.

Indeed, this defuses one potential objection to my account of Plato's deployment of slavery as a synecdoche for the epitactic dimension of rule—namely, that such a deployment must contradict the willing nature of the obedience that Plato elsewhere (including in the *Republic*'s discussion of the value of temperance or discipline [*sōphrosunē*] in book 4) connects with the ideal of rule. The incompatibility of actual chattel slavery with willing obedience was something of which Plato was clearly aware: the very moral of the transported slaveholder story in *Republic* 9, as argued above, hinges upon the assumption that slaves who were able to attack their master with the expectation of impunity would do so, so unwilling is their obedience (rightly) understood to be. Slavery as an instance of sheer hierarchical command and obedience, with a *telos* aimed at benefiting the ruler rather than the ruled, would indeed be incompatible with willing obedience. So the key to the *Republic* 9 assertion that "it is not to harm the slave that we say he must be ruled" is that here legal slavery is being used as a synecdoche for one dimension of rule (its epitactic one), while not being used to model the actual purpose of the rule in

---

slavery within the more comprehensive category of rule means that the relationship has to be metaphorical for the whole of each category even though synecdochic with regard to one shared dimension.

question, which is instead posited as being to the postulated genuine benefit of the ruled. Again, to be clear, that *telos* does not hold of any actual slave relationship. But it does make sense of the intentionally paradoxical aspects of this text, as of the discussion of "willing slavery" in the *Laws* with which this chapter will eventually conclude.

Rule and Freedom, Rule as Slavery? The Paradox of Willing Obedience in the Laws

In Plato's *Laws*, the Athenian Visitor recounts purported histories of Persia and Athens, in the service of demonstrating how each embodied in ancient times at least a rough balance between the principles of monarchy (*to monarchikon*) and liberty (*to eleutheron*), which had been upset in the course of their more recent political development (or, rather, decline) (3.693e5–694a1).[31] In the case of Persia, the balance was literally between monarchy and liberty, since the empire was always subject to a single ruler, though the Visitor also describes the Persians collectively as rulers over their imperial subjects. The "measured combination of slavery and freedom" that was achieved under Cyrus bespeaks the making compossible of obedience to rule—the epitactic relationship that "slavery"[32] is used here to denote—with a kind of freedom that consists in free speech and an openness to the subjects' military and political participation (3.694a3–4 and, more generally, through 694b6). That freedom, however, comported with military relationships of command and obedience, and with the king as ruler of the empire as a whole.

Whether ancient Persia is being viewed as an officeholding constitution is unclear; kingship had a liminal status as an office in Greek constitutional thought at the time, as was explored above in part I, and the description of ancient Persia does not feature any unambiguous signals of office of the kind considered throughout this study. All things considered, it seems better to read

31. I describe this as a "rough balance" since the Visitor says that they had achieved this in ancient times in some way (*pōs*), but "less so" in the present day (the imprecisely chronologically located late fifth-century dramatic context of the dialogue: see note 11 in chapter 3 above).

32. Meyer ("Civic Freedom," 518) argues for translating *douleia* as "subjection" in certain political contexts insofar as subjection, as opposed to slavery, "comes in degrees." While this is a good point, she herself translates it as "slavery" in certain passages of *Laws* 3, including a number in the very stretch concerned with ancient Persia and ancient Athens that I am discussing here. Because I am interested in the contrast between freedom and slavery more generally, I highlight that through my translations. I am more broadly indebted to Meyer's reading of political freedom in *Laws* 3 overall (which also builds in part on my own previous work), which she defines as follows (514): "a polity is free to the extent that its structure of governance or 'rule' (*archē*) mitigates the inequality that is inherent in the relation between those who wield political power (*archontes*) and those who are subject to that rule (*archomenoi*)."

this account as one in which freedom arises from willing obedience to rule, in which that rule is not narrowly cabined by the typical limits of office, but in which features of the relationship between ruler and ruled make it compossible with freedom and so friendship alike. The Visitor highlights that this combination of rule and freedom made possible both "friendship" and "commonality of reasoning," with friendship capturing the relative equality of dispositional interactions that Cyrus fostered, even within the constraints of hierarchical military command and imperial rule (3.694b5–6 and, more generally, 694a3–b6).

Here he builds on an overall valorization of compossible freedom, friendship, and wisdom (values named differently in different passages within book 3) as values characterizing a city as a whole (3.693d8–e1),[33] which he contends can be achieved only through a combination of monarchy and democracy, as the cases of ancient Persia and Athens are deployed to illustrate. In a postmortem on the subsequent corruption of the Persian constitution, the Visitor implies that such friendship and commonality are the fruits of freedom, explaining that it was when the people were deprived of freedom, and the despotic principle (*to despotikon*) was exaggerated, that both friendship and commonality were killed off (3.697c7–d1). (The closeness of freedom and friendship, however, is such that other passages in Plato treat them as coeval, both being fruits of a cooperative disposition.) Ancient Persia shows that freedom and friendship can be made compossible with rule, even when that is not necessarily shaped by the order of constitutional officeholding according to the full range of its conventional parameters.

The paradoxical need for an appropriate balance of both freedom and slavery, where the latter is deployed to denote the epitactic dimension of rule (rather than literal legal slavery), is further emphasized in the Athenian Visitor's description of the constitution of ancient Athens. The moral of the story is announced in advance as reiterating that of the narrative of ancient Persia— namely, as showing "that freedom which is total and from all rule, is to no small degree worse than is rule by others according to measure" (3.698a10–b2). Note that, in this case, the monarchic principle has to be interpreted metaphorically as meaning rule in terms of office, as at the start of the Visitor's narrative, Athens had already passed from its legendary kings to "a constitution . . . in which offices (*archai*) were assigned according to a property valuation establishing four classes" (3.698b4–5). The *taxis* of the ancient Athenian constitution was one of officeholding and, as the Visitor soon makes clear, also law.

---

33. For the variations on these values and the relationship among these various passages, see Meyer's "Civic Freedom." I have learned a great deal from discussing these passages with her and with others, including Amanda Greene, André Laks, Matthew Landauer, René de Nicolay, Jeremy Reid, and Jiseob Yoon.

It is in that context of rule carried out through offices, and governed by law, that the Visitor explains how freedom and slavery were balanced in the ancient Athenian constitution. At that time, when the Persians had attacked the Greeks, the Athenian constitution was such that "shame (*aidōs*) was . . . a despot (*despotis*) who made us live in willing enslavement to the laws then in force (*douleuontes tois tote nomois zēn ēthelomen*)" (3.698b5–6). And he adds a similar gloss in summing up the overall nature of that ancient constitution: "When the old laws applied, my friends, the people were not sovereign (*kurios*): on the contrary, they lived in a kind of willing enslavement (*tropon tina hekōn edouleue*) to the laws" (3.700a3–5).[34] In these two passages, the Visitor develops a conception of "willing enslavement" that is deliberately paradoxical.[35] Indeed, for the reader whom I earlier followed Malcolm Schofield in terming the practiced Platonic reader,[36] Plato here inverts the related expression of "willing slaves (*etholodoulous*)" used as an insult by the democrats of the deteriorating democratic constitution in *Republic* 8 (8.562d7), as noted above in chapter 8.

To interpret this paradox, I again read "slavery" here as a synecdoche for the epitactic dimension of rule, as argued above, and couple this with the idea of a "willing" relationship of obedience to that rule. One can act freely in obeying the epitactic orders of a ruler, even though in submitting to those epitactic orders, one is in that respect acting in a way that is common to democratic (and other) citizens and legal slaves alike. Voluntariness, or willingness, both translations that can be used to describe action that is performed *hekōn*, modifies obedience to rule. It does not replace or cancel such obedience. And it is precisely not to be conceived as authoritativeness, still less via the modern metaphors of authorization or authorship that have played so crucial a role for modern thinkers from Hobbes onward, but rather as a willingness to engage in subjection, an obedience to the orders of officeholders that applied even in the context of democratic rule.[37]

That does not mean that there was no difference in Plato's thinking between democratic rule (or other political rule) and legal slavery. Indeed,

---

34. I have offered a more literal translation of these two passages than I did in "Persuasion et force" and "Placing Plato," aiming to better capture the participial form of *douleuontes*, and to highlight the invocation of the vocabulary of legal slavery. Other aspects of this chapter further modify the claims which I made in those two earlier articles.

35. Similarly, the "rulers" (*archontas*) are to be redescribed as the "servants of the laws" (*hupēretas tois nomois*) at 4.715c6–7.

36. Schofield, "Religion and Philosophy," 3.

37. Klosko (*Development*, 245) is to this extent right when he says that Plato's *Laws* does not offer "a theory of popular consent," using "consent" in the juridical and legitimating sense of the social contract tradition (245). Klosko does, however, countenance speaking of "consent," whereas I would use instead the Athenian's language of being willing and well-disposed, a dispositional rather than juridical point.

I argued above that in *Republic* 9 Plato implies that legal slavery does not aim at the good of the slaves, whereas political rule to count as such must at least take itself to be aiming at the good of the ruled (depending on how strictly one applies an evaluative approach to the idea of rule). Yet all such relationships share an epitactic dimension of someone giving orders to someone else, and are to that extent hierarchical. This is true of democratic officeholders too, office being a kind of rule. To the extent that democratic officeholders and citizens—that is, rulers and subjects—are unwilling to acknowledge this, but instead come to take freedom to reside in the absence of rule rather than to be compossible with it, to that extent democracy itself will be in jeopardy. This is a fate that Plato narrates for the democratic constitution of ancient Athens in its more contemporary days in *Laws* 3, as well as for the democratic constitution of *Republic* 8.

To demonstrate the significance of willing obedience to rulers (in ancient Athens, being officeholders), one must attend to another passage in the Visitor's account of ancient Athens, which intervenes between those two quoted immediately above.[38] Speaking in the first person plural as a fellow Athenian to the ancestors whose constitution he is describing, he remarks that at the time of the Persian threats to the Greeks in the early fifth century, fear of the Persian army: "enslaved (*douleusai*) us in even greater slavery [*douleia*] to the officeholders (*tois te archousin*) and the laws (*nomois*)" (3.698b8–c2).[39] To be sure, the comparative formulation here sits somewhat awkwardly with the translation of "slavery" and "enslavement" (as opposed to "subjection"). But my choice of translation serves to highlight the way in which the military threat at the time intensified the willingness (out of fear) to obey not only the laws but also the officeholders. This mention of officeholders, who are a species of rulers, so harking back to the emphasis on "freedom . . . from all rule" in the original overview of what the ancient Athens story will eventually reveal in its decline, is significant. For in *Laws* 3's concluding narrative of the degeneration of ancient Athens as a constitution, the initial role will be played precisely by a breakdown in the people's willingness to subject themselves to *rulers* in the shape of officeholders—just as in the degeneration of the democratic constitution of *Republic* 8. Here, the Visitor traces out the gradual disintegration of the realized compossibility of freedom and slavery, understood as signifying obedience to the epitactic dimension of rule (which in an officeholding

---

38. I have modified my translation of the two quotations that follow to bring out the significance of these rulers being, specifically, officeholders, which was a point I had not yet noticed when writing "Placing Plato."

39. This passage, with the verb for enslavement reinforcing the noun to express a reflexive activity and its result, is a good example of when "enslavement" can be construed as a synecdoche for a more general idea of "obedience" to epitactic orders, with all the shock value involved in such a move, but without importing the exploitative aim of existing relations of legal slavery, as argued above.

constitution is limited and shaped by law), and so of friendship as a consequence of the loss of that compossibility.[40]

He begins, notoriously, by remarking on the corruption of music in ancient Athens (speaking in the collective first person of these ancestors as his fellow Athenians): "From music began for us the belief of every person that they were wise about everything, as well as transgressiveness (*paranomia*), and freedom followed too" (3.701a5–7).[41] The danger lies in each person deciding that he is wise about every subject, beginning with music. It is not just that people start to disregard the laws. It is that they start to do so because of believing themselves to be "wise"; indeed, by implication, wiser than the rulers.[42]

It is this unwillingness to submit to the rulers—who in this democratic constitution are specifically officeholders, as I pointed out above—that eventually spurs a fatal disregard for the laws and thence for the gods. This is spelled out in the Visitor's next speech:

> Next from such freedom [*eleutheria*] would arise unwillingness in regard to enslavement (*douleuein*) to the officeholders (*archousi*), then from this, they would flee from the slavery [*douleia*] and admonitions of their fathers and mothers and elders, and near the end, they seek to avoid hearkening to the laws; and they are already at the end when they stop paying heed to oaths and promises and divine matters altogether. (3.701b5–c2)[43]

Here, enslavement and slavery are again being used as figures for the epitactic dimension of rule, but with the *telos* of the good of the ruled, which, however, these errant ancestors are failing to recognize or heed for themselves. Without

40. Schöpsdau (*"Nomoi" (Gesetz) Buch I–III*, 487) comments on the relationship between slavery, law, and friendship in the history of ancient Athens, specifically on 3.698a9–c3, that "insofern ist die 'Unterwerfung unter die Gesetze' (*douleuein tois nomois* [in Greek font in original]) eine Voraussetzung für Freundschaft" (in this respect, "subjugation to the laws" [*douleuein tois nomois*] is a presupposition for friendship).

41. I have made a more literal translation here than the one in "Placing Plato." Saunders translates *eleutheria* here as "complete license," but Greek does not have this kind of pejorative word for excessive freedom; Plato instead makes pejorative use of *eleutheria* in some contexts, or describes it as "extreme" using varying formulations, though no adjective is used here. Cicero, however, in his influential gloss in *De re publica* (1.66–68) on this passage of Plato's *Republic*, introduces the notion of *licentia* in Latin into his account of Plato's Greek. I owe this observation to Nicolay, "Licentia."

42. A rich discussion of the nuances of this passage is offered by Nicolay in "Origins of Licence."

43. Again, I have offered a more literal translation than that of Saunders (which I quoted for this passage in "Placing Plato"), aiming thereby to take heed of the significance of the vocabulary of officeholding, which I had not fully recognized when writing that paper. On the significance of oaths in Athens and other Greek societies as a method for (in my terms) seeking to align the actions of officeholders and others with the *telos* of rule, see the work by Alan Sommerstein and various collaborators, including Sommerstein and Bayliss's *Oath and State*.

a willingness to obey rule, which must involve obedience to rulers—who in a democratic constitution, as in this narrative, will be officeholders—no kind of order (*taxis*) can be sustained. Incorporating willing obedience to rule into one's schema of political values requires a reshaping of freedom to accommodate it compossibly, making freedom a limited, measured value, a mean rather than an unbounded absolute.

In a constitution of office and law, free actions as citizens must be limited by willing obedience not only to laws but also to the rulers, if a constitutional order is to be sustained. That necessity to subject oneself to rulers, specifically in the form of officeholders, is likely to be a vexed psychological and sociological difficulty especially for democratic constitutions and citizens, or so Plato suspected it would ultimately prove.[44] On the view developed here, understood as broadly common to the *Republic* and the *Laws*, Plato is not the ancestor of Rousseau in the way that Isaiah Berlin and others have believed, as the forefather of the ideal of "positive liberty." On the contrary, if we want to think about the relationship between Plato and Rousseau, it is more interesting to see the former as a critic of the latter avant la lettre, as to whether it is possible at bottom for humans collectively to be free because and insofar as they rule themselves. I have argued that for Plato, in both the *Republic* and the *Laws*, the deeper truth is that rule, even in the form of office and law, must always involve the rule of some human beings over others. In other words, on Plato's account, one cannot hide behind a Rousseauean formula in which obedience to laws means that one obeys only oneself. Rather, any such move is unmasked as a sleight of hand that can only obscure the painful and difficult fact that constitutional order—including officeholding—requires some human beings willingly to obey others.

Unwillingness to be ruled, while likely to prove an Achilles' heel of democracy, is not unique to democracies. At another moment in the *Laws* (in book 8), the Athenian Visitor observes that no constitution in which the citizens are unwillingly ruled—naming democracy, oligarchy, and tyranny—is a proper *politeia* at all. These regimes should rather most correctly be called *stasiōteiai* (factionalisms), "because under none of them do willing rulers rule willing subjects, but, rather, rulers willingly rule over unwilling subjects always by employing some kind of force" (8.832b10–c5). Whether the hierarchy involved in such rule on Plato's view must offend against relations of democratic equality, whether political rule must make use of coercion, and whether political rule is always and for everyone necessary at all are topics to be considered in the next and final chapter.

---

44. On this point in Plato, see also Nicolay's "Origins of Licence." A similar suspicion is expressed by Xenophon, as I argued in "Xenophon (and Thucydides)."

CHAPTER ELEVEN

Against Anarchy

THE HORIZON OF PLATONIC RULE

RULE AND FREEDOM can be made compossible through willing obedience, a relationship that can be helpfully mediated by law. This, I argued in the last chapter, is Plato's view as developed in part of the *Republic* (in particular, part of book 9) as well as more explicitly in the *Laws*. In his double theory of law in the latter dialogue, law itself necessarily makes use of the threat of coercion, potentially (and ideally) supplementing this with persuasion aimed at reducing the exercise of that threat, and so the need for it, without ever being able to abolish that altogether.[1] Law, as I shall shortly explain further, is for Plato inherently coercive. Platonic rule is almost certain in practice to have to make use of law. But this does not mean that such rule is defined by the use of coercion. Once again, Plato is no Weberian. Political rule like other kinds of rule is in principle epitactic and teleological, as per the Platonic schema of rule laid out above in chapter 2: a ruler must act in and through a *taxis* of some kind of order, which is oriented to some kind of *telos*. That *taxis* must at least in principle be epitactic—capable of issuing orders—as is the case for officeholders in law-governed constitutions, as for any other kind of rulers on Plato's account. But political rulers need not qua rulers attach coercive measures to their orders. As in the philosopher Joseph Raz's theory of authority, it is the directiveness toward a good that is fundamental to Platonic rule, not the particular means by which such directiveness is enforced.

While not inherently coercive, the epitactic nature of rule (a ruler being capable of issuing orders to the ruled) is for Plato necessarily hierarchical, as well as axiomatically opposed to anarchy. This means that the way in which it comports with values such as social equality will on Plato's view challenge the ideal of "rule over none" that has been advanced by one prominent democratic

---

1. This sentence invokes claims made by Laks' "Legislation and Demiurgy."

political theorist, and a more straightforward endorsement of democracy as a kind of "anarchy" by others. Nevertheless, while staunchly rejecting political anarchism, Plato at moments entertains an idyll of philosophical anarchism: not the standard account thereof (which is actually a philosophical attitude toward political anarchism) but rather an aspiration to self-rule that could obviate the need for political rule.

Individuals who can rationally rule and order themselves do not need to be ruled by others in order to live virtuous and so happy lives. It is less clear whether they could realize the relational goods of civic freedom and friendship in their spontaneous relationships with others. But for a whole body of citizens to realize those latter goods, it would seem that political rule would be necessary in order to encompass them all in those relationships, and thus that political rule would have value in coordinating the realization of that good even for those who are capable of ruling themselves. For Raz, political authorities will generally be able to secure coordinated relationships (which better enable individuals to act in accordance with reasons that apply to them) better than can any individuals themselves (albeit that the reach of authoritative directives, in the sense of the justification for their applicability, may vary according to the epistemic and other capacities of a given individual). Similarly for Plato, the need for political rule is variegated according to individual epistemic capacities, even while political rulers will generally be able to secure coordinated relationships (which are among genuine goods for individuals) better than can any individuals themselves.[2]

In its next section, this chapter addresses the relationship between law and coercion, and more generally between law and rule, in Plato, arguing that while Plato makes use of law in the principal constitutional projects of each of the three dialogues studied herein (*Republic, Statesman, Laws*) and defines written law as inherently coercive, he never identifies rule by its use of any particular means, whether coercion or persuasion. Rather, in the *Statesman*, where his most explicit and developed account of rule is found, rule is identified in terms of the role of a ruler who possesses and deploys political expertise. As set out in that dialogue, such expertise defines the *telos* of rule as the good of the ruled, toward which the ruler must be oriented (described as their "caring" for the good of the ruled). In addition to caring for the *telos* of the good of the ruled, the ruler must make use of epitactic orders (at least, they must have the capacity to do so in principle, though their speech acts may be more complex and variegated in practice): this epitactic capacity must be part of the *taxis* of

2. This chapter discusses passages from the *Republic* (according to the Slings OCT), *Statesman* (according to the Robinson edition of the dialogue in the Duke et al. OCT), and *Laws* (the only OCT of which is edited by Burnet); I indicate which dialogue is being quoted with its abbreviated title only when the context does not make this clear. Translations are my own unless otherwise indicated.

any kind of rule. It is part of the definition of the role of ruler that they have that capacity.

However, as was anticipated in my opening chapter, no more than Joseph Raz does Plato normatively justify rule in terms independent of the condition of the ruled. Instead, similar to the way that Raz locates the normative justification for expecting obedience (where it is expected) to authoritative directives in reasons that independently apply to their subjects, so Plato implies that it is the fact that the *telos* of rule is for the good of the ruled that should, in a well-ordered polity, lead the ruled to willingly obey. Where the ruled do not recognize that fact, fail to grasp what is truly good, or resist obedience for any other reason, the polity is not well ordered. Like Raz, Plato offers a success theory of rule rather than a universally obligating one. What defines rule as such is neither its use of coercion nor its imposition of universal obligation. This way of thinking about the nature of rule carves up the boundaries of political theorizing very differently from those traditions of analysis that focus on the monopoly of violence as definitional of the political or of the state.

That said, however, in every constitutional project that Plato outlines at any length, both office and law are in fact included as part of the *taxis* of rule. The chapters in part II showed this, arguing that both offices and laws feature in the constitution of a *kallipolis* as outlined in the *Republic*, in the city ruled by a true statesman at the end of the *Statesman*, and, of course, in the constitution delineated with Magnesia in view in the *Laws*. In each of these constitutional projects, political rule is necessary, and will in practice involve both office and law, even though neither features in the definition of what makes it count as rule.

In being epitactic, the political rule featuring in each of these constitutional projects is also and necessarily hierarchical. The next two parts of the chapter consider this account of Platonic rule in relationship to two contemporary lines of thought that argue from different premises that hierarchical rule is neither necessary nor desirable. On the one hand, I consider the relational egalitarian democratic theory of Niko Kolodny (taking this as illustrative of a broader line of thinking about democracy as "no rule" in relational egalitarian democratic theories); on the other hand, I consider a range of postmodern theories that also idealize "no rule." In contrast to both of these lines of thought, Plato defends the necessity and value (in most circumstances) of political rule, on condition that it be genuine or true rule that is oriented toward the good of those ruled. It is in this sense that Plato is committed to what I have called elsewhere *antianarchia*.[3]

Yet this commitment to *antianarchia*—in terms of the need for rule—is paradoxically compatible with a kind of philosophical anarchism. As the final part of the chapter will show, Plato occasionally toys with an idyll in which

---

3. Lane, "*Antianarchia.*"

everyone is able to rule themselves so completely that the need for political rule, as it were, withers away.[4] Nevertheless, in practice, such psychological self-rule requires for most people being fostered through law, political rule, or both.

Plato on Law and Rule: The Place of Coercion

In the *Laws'* account of the need to foster willing obedience in order to make rule and freedom compossible, as discussed in the preceding chapter, a mediating role is placed by the distinctive theoretical shape that Plato there gives to law itself. This is the double theory of law introduced in book 4 of that dialogue, according to which law proper in the narrow sense is a command backed by the threat of force, which should be coupled with a persuasive prelude (sometimes translated "preamble") to reduce the need to realize that threat. This theory of law treats it as incorporating conditional commands that are fashioned by lawgivers (in the dialogue the *Laws*, only "in speech"), but are then to be carried out by the orders of the rulers who, in the constitutional project being delineated at this point in the dialogue, will specifically be officeholders (as argued above in chapter 3).

The role of the preludes has been celebrated by scholars such as Christopher Bobonich as making it possible for the citizens of Magnesia to enjoy moral and so political freedom, and by Malcolm Schofield as thereby placing the dialogue's political ideal in relationship to a hypothetical version of the social contract tradition.[5] I argue that while the preludes are indeed one means of making rule and freedom compossible, one must remember that they are simply one such means. They neither alter the nature of rule itself nor change the basis on which it is exercised. The preludes are a means of encouraging willing obedience to the rulers (in Magnesia, the officeholders) and the laws themselves. By so doing, they do make civic freedom possible, but not because they respect a prior moral status on the part of the ruled, nor because they secure their authorization of rule in a way that would make it legitimate. Rather, they contribute to the compossibility of rule and freedom expressed in the willing obedience that they foster.

In book 4, with a reprise in book 9 mentioned briefly earlier in this study, the Athenian Visitor deploys an account of a relationship between the free doctor and the free patient outlined in the dialogue, as a metaphor for the relationship between the epitactic ruler, who must enforce the conditional commands issued by the lawgiver, and the person(s) being ruled. According

---

4. This widely quoted phrase is found in Engels (*Dühring's Revolution in Science*, 355), and became widespread in subsequent socialist literature, including being used by Lenin, as I cite below.

5. Bobonich, *Plato's Utopia Recast*; Schofield, *Plato*, 84–88. Schofield, however, does observe (*Plato*, 85) that "the legislation of the *Laws*, including its preludes, is . . . *actually* an instrument of social control" (emphasis original).

to this medical analogy, the coercive threat intrinsic to any law corresponds to the activity of an assistant doctor when ministering to slaves, whereas the addition of a persuasive prelude characterizes a free doctor ministering to free patients.[6] Illustrating the theory with the (philosophical) issuance of a law about marriage containing both elements, the Visitor identifies the purpose of the prelude as being "to make the person to whom he promulgated his law accept his orders—the law—in a more well-disposed frame of mind (*eumenōs*) [and] because of this (*dia tēn eumeneian*), more tractable and willing to learn (*eumathesteron*)" (4.723a4–6).[7] The final expression of this aspiration in the comparative (*eumathesteron*) is significant. The preludes help to foster an aim of rule; their success in doing so will fall along a spectrum, rather than marking a bright line of any kind between legitimacy and illegitimacy.

Likewise, notice that it is *willingness* that the prelude, as part of the double formation of a law, seeks to foster. By contrast to the "doctor of slaves" acting "stubbornly like a tyrant," the free doctor treating the free patient "does not give orders (*epetaxen*) prior to having somehow persuaded, and then having made the patient gentle (*hēmeroumenon*) and always preparing him by means of persuasion, leading him to health, and trying to complete this [his return to health]" (4.720d7–e2).

Now there is no doubt, given that the doctor of slaves has been compared to a tyrant, that the appearance of persuasion in the context of the free doctor of free men implicitly invokes a rhetorically common contrast in Greek between force and persuasion, embedded in a context between tyranny and freedom. However, two aspects of the last quotation condition just what this does and does not mean. First, the "somehow (*pēi*)": this suggests that persuasion can happen in a number of different ways, not all of them necessarily as a result of a fully voluntary action by the patient. Second, the mention of "gentling (*hēmeroumenon*)" the patient. This resonates (albeit by using a different Greek word) with an opening analogy made by the Visitor to the way in which children might seek medical treatment. Just as the children were seeking gentle treatment from their doctors, so the doctor treating a free patient

6. As I argued in "Persuasion et force," the contrast is actually between two different professional statuses, characterizing a doctor and the doctor's assistant, on occasions when they treat patients of different legal statuses (free and enslaved, respectively). While the doctor's assistants are said to be either free or enslaved, it is not their own legal status that defines their role in the analogy but, rather, that of the patients they treat.

7. Debate about the interpretation of this passage has rightly concluded that one must not suppress the cognitive dimension of *eumathesteron*; but nor must one exaggerate it: to make someone more willing to learn is not to establish their learning as a criterion for how to treat them. The German and Latin translations offered by Görgemanns (*Beiträge*, 40) are helpful: for *eumenēs*, he offers *wohlwollend* and *benevolus* (both in the broad sense of "benevolent"); for *eumathēs*, *leicht belehrbar* and *docilis* (both of which can have the sense of "teachable").

should treat him gently and so make him gentle (whereas a doctor treating harried slaves has no leisure for such niceties). The purpose of law is to foster a willingness in its subject to obey the orders given by an imagined lawgiver (invoked in various roles throughout the dialogue), who corresponds to the doctor in the analogy, and so by extension the orders of a ruler, who in this context will be an officeholder, who is tasked with enforcing the laws.

Law is a modality of rule, one that in certain configurations can work better than others to foster willing obedience to rule (note the comparatives in the quotations in the previous paragraph).[8] I call it a modality to recognize the fact that, when employed as a means, it will shape the ways in which the overall relationship between rulers and ruled is experienced and expressed, and so shape the way in which its *telos* may be interpreted and realized. Nevertheless, the use of law is not presented by Plato as a criterion, or even an indispensable instrument, of rule. As I have argued in a more extensive treatment of the preludes elsewhere, the ruler is no more or less a ruler in virtue of making use of law or of the double theory of law, any more than the doctor is more or less a doctor in virtue of using persuasion in the way described (which I glossed there as having a good bedside manner).[9] Persuasion and coercion, the latter a necessary feature of law and the former a desirable one, are possible means of rule.[10] Yet rule might operate without making use of either of these means, neither of which serves to constitute a ruler as a ruler.

8. The Athenian concludes his account of the two methods of doctoring by asking for an evaluation, which is again framed in the comparative, as to whether the double method of pairing persuasion and order will make a doctor "better" at doctoring or a gymnastics trainer similarly better at training (4.720e2–5). The choice between these methods does not define what it is to be a doctor, or what it is to be a doctor of a certain kind (a doctor, or a doctor's assistant). The definition of being a doctor, as opposed to the better or worse ways of doctoring, depends solely on the nature of one's knowledge, so long as that knowledge incorporates (as on Platonic terms it must) the goodness of the *telos* at which the profession aims.

9. Lane, "Persuasion et force," which engages with much of the literature on the preludes as it stood at that time; see the updated discussion and references in Laks's *Plato's Second Republic* (a work that was in process of production as this study was being finalized, but that I had been privileged to read in earlier versions).

10. Arendt noticed this Platonic (and more broadly, she thought, ancient) treatment of violence as a means relative to some end, and so as not fundamental even to the misinterpretation of political action as a kind of making or work that she took Plato to have engendered:

> Up to the modern age, this element of violence [as necessary for making] remained strictly instrumental, a means that needed an end to justify and limit it, so that glorifications of violence as such are entirely absent from the tradition of political thought prior to the modern age ... because ... all articulations of the *vita activa* [as opposed to the exercise of contemplative reason], fabrication no less than action and let alone labor, remained themselves secondary and instrumental. (*Human Condition*, 228)

Where does this leave the question of whether Plato is a rule of law theorist? Of course, in the *Laws*, the role of laws that specify and enforce procedural accountability for all officeholders is central to the (second-best) political ideal. Yet not even in the *Laws* is Plato committed to a purely proceduralist view of the value of law. This is for two reasons. On the one hand, the laws must have the proper *telos* in order to be part of a valuable normative ideal of rule. Plato shows himself to have been well aware, as expressed not only in the challenge that he puts in the mouth of Thrasymachus but also in the Athenian Visitor's observations in *Laws* 4 (714b3–715b2), of the dystopian possibility (and, indeed, in many if not all existing *poleis* in his day, reality) of a rule of law in which the laws have been shaped entirely by and to the advantage of those in power. On the other hand, even laws with a reasonably good *telos* (or, at least, avoiding the most exploitative kind of bad one) must be underpinned by a mutually cooperative disposition and relationship among the citizens, if the rule they support is to be both actual and valuable.

Plato's respect for the role that law can play in certain kinds of constitutions in no way equates to legal fetishism. It is to law, not to rule, that Plato attaches coercion as the use (or threat) of force. Moreover, it is specifically to written laws. While the writtenness of the laws is not central to the double theory of law as threat and preamble, it does play a central role in the envisaging of how the constitution for Magnesia will be able to foster virtue. As noted in chapter 3, the Athenian Visitor goes so far as to discursively prescribe that the eventual citizens of Magnesia should study and memorize the written law code as a central part of their education.[11] Written laws characterized what one may think of as the "modern state" of Plato's time, this being a time in which the codification of laws as written was very recent (in the wake of 403/402 in Athens, with attendant debates about the role of writing and its value in the late fifth century, in which Plato himself participated in the mid-fourth).

That said, in an anthropological excursus in book 3 of the *Laws*, the Athenian Visitor describes the "origin" of a "*politeia*."[12] According to the Athenian's speculative prehistory, a series of floods has periodically destroyed all the tools and discoveries developed by each wave of *poleis*, leaving only the current period's advances extant. As humanity regrouped gradually after the last cataclysm without knowledge of mining and lived with minimal arts such as pottery and weaving, herding and hunting, but without gold and silver and so without *stasis* or lawsuits, people initially "felt no need for lawgivers

11. *Leg.* 7.811b6–e1, discussed in Nightingale, "Writing/Reading," 289. See also more generally on the writtenness of law in the *Laws*, Nightingale's "Plato's Lawcode in Context."

12. *Leg.* 3.676a1–2; or rather, of an indefinite number of *politeiai*, since the Athenian posits the coming to be and passing away of multiple *poleis* in the "indefinitely long period of time" in which people have "lived under some sort of political organization (*politeuomenoi*)" (3.676a8, b3–4, trans. Saunders).

(*nomothetōn*)" and did without "written laws (*grammata*)," living together on the basis of "accepted usage and 'ancestral' law, as we call it (*ethesi kai tois legomenois patriois nomois*)" (3.680a3–7, trans. Saunders, modified). Such a constitution involved ruling (*archei*) by the eldest member of the family over a single "flock" (though the comparison animals are birds, not sheep as in the *Statesman*). The Athenian calls this a "patriarchal" system, glossing the role of the ruler as "kingly" (3.680e1–4), so emphasizing its commonality in this respect with the roles of kingly rule articulated in the *Statesman* and *Republic*.

Here, then, is a portrait of a primitivist polity with laws of a kind, rulers, and a constitution—all this without written laws. It is a portrait of rule and even law but without the coerciveness attached to written laws that character-ized the modern state, as it were, of Plato's day—as of our own. In other words, Plato here makes clear that rule does not require the form of coercive threat embedded in (written) law. The context of primitive social evolution, and the language of "custom" and ancestral laws, suggests that the enforcement in mind at this stage is rather that of informal social norms. Of course, tribal leaders (as I have glossed them) may well have disposed of force, but they are clearly not being conceived here as operating a proto-state mechanism of formal legal threats of force.

Thus, Plato is willing to entertain the idea of rule without specifying the idea of coercive force, or its embedding in any kind of proto-state machin-ery. In this respect, despite his hostility to *anarchia*, he shares something in common with later anarchists (as well as Marxists envisioning the eventual condition of communism), who are willing to entertain informal mechanisms of enforcing social cooperation, which may (even necessarily) involve certain kinds of hierarchy, but who eschew the full panoply of formal, legal, written threats of state force. His point is that people must not be disposed to flout the epitactic commands necessary for the maintenance of political order, rather than that such commands must inherently be backed by (a monopoly of) coer-cive force.

Fundamentally, once again, it is a question of cooperative dispositions, not of procedures or institutions—dispositions that must underpin orientation to the role of ruler as well as the role of ruled. This means that Plato is free from legal fetishism. To be sure, whenever designing a city "in speech" (in both *Republic* and *Laws*), he does so in and by using laws and offices. And in so doing, as in his reflections on the garden-variety constitutionalism familiar in his own day (discussed in the preceding chapter), he respects and highlights the role that law can play in structuring social cooperation and so fostering distinctive forms of both freedom and friendship.

Nevertheless, law and office will become hollow shells unless underpinned by the cooperative disposition that must animate freedom and friendship even as law and office can then support and bolster them. Law, with its coercive force, is but one means that a ruler may choose to use, and it is entirely possible for law and legal procedures and institutions to be turned to a nefarious *telos*, in which case it would count as part of a regime of bad rule rather than good rule. In this sense Plato is, once again, as contended in the conclusion to part III (on the basis of other parts of his writings), revealed as a realist of a distinctive kind: one who recognizes that no realistic assessment of interpersonal relationships and political institutions can entirely eschew an evaluative standpoint.

Rule as a Role: The Defining Mark of Rule in the Statesman

I have been arguing that, from Plato's perspective, a state with written coercive law was the modern state of his day. Yet he resists its self-proclamation of a unique legitimacy. In the *Statesman*, the Eleatic Visitor rejects Young Socrates's questioning of the claim that (as the youth puts it) "rule may exist even without laws (*aneu nomōn*)" (293e8), a claim that the Eleatic had actually cast in terms of whether rule is "according to written laws or without them (*kata grammata . . . aneu grammatōn*)" (293a7) (trans. Rowe). In defending the irrelevance of laws (as well as other potential means or specifications of rule) to what makes rule count as such, the *Statesman* is not mainly to be taken to be theoretically opening the door to tyranny, which is the usual idiom in which commentators have assessed these passages. It is rather to be read as insisting that rule need not make use of law in order to count as rule. The subtle way in which this does and does not comport with anarchistic aspirations in later political theorizing will be considered below. In this section, I focus on the argument of the *Statesman* on this point, as it lays out an account of the nature of rule.

To be a ruler is to occupy a role.[13] It can be identified as a role only in terms of some kind of boundedness or limitation: not necessarily the institutional and procedural limits of office, and not necessarily the legal limits imposed by law, but conceptually some kind of boundedness, such that not everything will count as acting in this role. Or, to put it another way: the minimal *taxis* of rule inheres not solely in the epitactic role of command but also in the value

---

13. A useful definition of a role is offered by Emmet, in *Rules, Roles and Relations* (13–14): "A role is a capacity in which someone acts in relation to others," adding that it "suggest[s] a way of acting in a social situation which takes account of the specific character of the relation, and which is considered appropriate in a relation of that kind, either for functional reasons or from custom and tradition." Emmet elsewhere, like many others, invokes the notion of a *persona*, from the masks in Greek and Roman drama, which were turned into a more general figure by Cicero in *De officiis*.

of the *telos* that gives that epitactic role an inherent boundedness, directing it to give such and only such commands in circumstances that conduce to the realization of the *telos*. In the language of the *Statesman*, the ruler must care for the good of the ruled, and this caring will necessarily orient and so bound their actions, making them recognizable as part of a role.

Another way to think of this is that the ruler must conceive of themselves as occupying a role and orient their own action accordingly. While their potential scope of action may be in principle open-ended, it must be oriented so as to count as action *as a ruler* rather than simply action according to their whims as a natural person. While this may seem a difficult constraint to operationalize in the absence of the enforceable institutional or legal limitations of office, Plato dramatizes the point in the tyrant of *Republic* 9, who is presented as a natural person and whose impulsive behavior stems entirely from his psychological makeup, without any boundedness at all. What the tyrant does is whatever it occurs to the tyrannical man to do and that he finds himself able to do. The tyrant does not (genuinely) rule, if one takes rule in its strict evaluative sense (though he may be loosely described as a ruler); he does not genuinely rule because there is no bound on what he does, and so no order discernible in his behavior. He does not occupy the role of ruler because he does not (cannot) occupy any role at all. It is thus that tyranny and anarchy converge.[14]

Nevertheless, while the ruler must occupy a role, this role need be shaped only by an epitactic *taxis* and a *telos* of the good of the ruled for which the ruler cares (the caring can be taken to describe the *taxis* as it is oriented to the *telos*, hence as connecting them). No particular means is either required of the ruler or prohibited to them, so long as they are characterized by the basic lineaments of the role just described. This is emphasized at a crucial juncture in Plato's *Statesman*, when the Eleatic Visitor takes an uncompromising stance on the question of what makes a political constitution "correct in comparison with the rest, and alone a constitution" (293c5–6, trans. Rowe)—invoking this again in the strict evaluative sense in which only a genuine constitution counts as a constitution at all. Indeed, he derives the answer to this question about constitutions from an underlying question about the nature of *tous archontas* (the rulers of such a constitution), showing that the constitution in question is shaped essentially by the nature of its ruler(s).

The answer given by the Visitor is focused on the epistemic capacity of those rulers. But it is not merely a theoretical capacity. Rather, it is a capacity that is expressed in an orientation to caring for the good of that over which they rule. Here is the account of "the only correct defining mark" of "any . . . sort of rule [*archē*] whatsoever" (293c2–3), which the Eleatic illustrates with

---

14. In practice, it was often the flouting of the laws that signaled tyranny, whereas it was more obviously the vacancy (descriptively or normatively judged) of office that signaled anarchy (as argued by Bordes in *Politeia*).

medicine, resonating with the account of *technai* as forms of *archai* in *Republic* 1 (discussed in chapter 5 of this study):

> We say no less that they are doctors, so long as they preside over us according to expertise, whether purging or otherwise reducing [sc. our bodies] or else building them up, so long as each of these carers safeguard [*sōizein*] what is in their care, [sc. presiding] solely with the aim of the good of these bodies, making better what was worse. (*Plt.* 293b5–c1)

Notice the emphasis on the expertise in virtue of which these experts rule, described in the same speech as their "being in charge [*epistatein*] on the basis of *technē*" (293b5–6):[15] their ruling is ascribed a caring orientation and a safeguarding function, aiming at the good of the ruled (in the case of doctors, the body of the patient being what is ruled).

Just before the above conclusion, the Visitor had laid out a set of three bifurcated conditions, insisting that for any ruler (illustrated by the case of a doctor) the correct defining mark of rule is, as above: "whether they rule over the willing or the unwilling, whether according to written laws or without written laws, and whether they themselves are rich or poor" (293a6–8).[16] He then transposes this defining mark, and the three contrasting conditions, to the case of a political constitution. In assessing which kind of constitution is "correct . . . and alone a constitution" (293c5–6), he pins the analysis on the question of whether in it "the rulers (*tous archontas*) would be found truly possessing expert knowledge, and not merely seeming to do so" (293c6–8). But one should not be misled by this condensed transposition to take the expertise in question to be purely technical and potentially non-normative. Rather, the clearly marked parallels with the preceding passage about the doctor show that political expertise here must be taken to be a kind of expertise that aims at the good of the ruled, with a caring orientation toward safeguarding that good so far as possible (since contingencies may permit only partial improvement ["bettering"] rather than realization of the full good).

Socrates drives home that very point in explicit terms. After introducing the three political analogues to the postulated range of medical actions (purging as analogous to killing or exiling; reducing, to colony formation; building up, to making immigrants citizens), he concludes that the only constitution "which alone we must say is correct" is one in which the rulers "safeguard

---

15. The verb *epistatein* has the sense of "presiding over," "being in charge of," or "having the care of"; like *archein* and *ho archōn*, this verb had a corresponding noun (*ho epistatēs*) used to designate certain officeholders, including the presiding officers in certain constitutional bodies in democratic Athens.

16. I follow Rowe in taking [*ta*] *grammata* in context to signify "written laws," as it often does, though the word technically means just "the writings." On doctors and other therapeutic experts counting as "rulers," see chapter 5 above, on *Republic* 1.

[*sōzein*] [sc. the city] on the basis of expert knowledge and what is just, making it better (*beltiō*) than it was so far as they can" (293d8–e1, trans. Rowe, modified). Again, the language of "safeguarding" (and the same Greek verb) resonates with the role of the safeguarding rulers in the *Republic* (as per chapters 6 and 7 above especially). Both of these passages in the *Statesman* treat the *telos* of rule, and of any constitution distinguished by the existence of a genuine ruler or rulers, from what might be called a black-box standpoint. Whatever the ruler should do, so long as it genuinely counts as bettering the ruled and so acting for their good, this is sufficient to make the ruler count as a true ruler, the rule count as genuine rule, the constitution count as a correct constitution.

The emphasis in these passages is on the *telos* of rule, though the *taxis* is drawn in terms of a caring orientation in ruling that is oriented toward and by that very *telos*. This does give some minimal content to the *taxis* as well. A tyrant who was oriented only to their own pleasure, for example, would violate the teleological orientation of the order (*taxis*) here. Nevertheless, in this significant stretch of the *Statesman*, no more content is offered about the *telos* or *taxis* of genuine rule than what has been adumbrated above. Instead, the Eleatic will later go on to apply this argument to the question of the "name" to be given to someone who meets the criteria above, first considering the case of a medical practitioner, then of a political one (the word "name" and the idea of naming will recur in what follows). That application, picking up on where I here left off, will come after a famous turn in the conversation, in which the Eleatic responds to Young Socrates's expressed discomfort with regard to what the older figure glosses as "the correctness of those who rule without laws" (294a3–4, picking up on one of the three bifurcated conditions set aside above).

In returning to the medical case, Socrates reverts initially to the first of the bifurcated conditions that had been raised and set aside: not the question of (written) laws but the question of ruling over willing or unwilling subjects (back at 293a–6). Here, he glosses that question by asking what should be said of someone who "forces the better without using persuasion" (296b1; notice how "better" clearly picks up the earlier discussion). Illustrating that question by returning to the medical example, he entertains the following possibility:[17]

> If, then, someone engaged in doctoring does not persuade, but has expertise in the correct way, and, against what has been written down, necessitates some child or man or woman to do what is better

---

17. As noted above, he had previously invoked the example of the doctor at 295c1 as analogous to the statesman, there having added the doctor to the gymnastic trainer already canvassed from 294d8–9. These are of course favorite Socratic examples, providing some ammunition to an interpretation of the Eleatic Visitor and Socrates as developing complementary rather than opposed views.

(*to beltion*),[18] what is to be the name (*tounoma*) for this use of force? Would not any name be better than that [sc. given to] what we previously called an unhealthy and inexpert mistake? And is it not wholly correct to say what [sc. was said] previously with regard to someone being forced in regard to such a situation, that is, anything except that he had unhealthy and inexpert things (*nosōdē kai atechna*) done to him by the force-wielding doctors? (296b5–c3)

The back reference, with a very close verbal echo, invoked in the phrase "an unhealthy and inexpert mistake" is to the Visitor's initial invocation of the doctor, pairing him with the gymnastic trainer, in a more elaborated thought experiment in which such a figure leaves written instructions for his patients while he is out of the country but then comes back unexpectedly.[19] The Visitor had there posed the rhetorical question (expecting, and receiving, an emphatic negative reply from Young Socrates) of whether such a doctor:

must[20] staunchly[21] think that neither he nor the patient should step out of line with those ancient laws that had once been laid down (*nomothetēthenta*), neither he himself by ordering other actions, nor the patient by daring to do different things contrary to what was written down—the alternative actions being medically indicated and healthy ones; must he think [supplied] that things that happened differently were unhealthy and not part of his expertise (*nosōdē kai ouk entechna*)? (295d2–7)[22]

Putting these closely linked passages together shows that the question of how to name the actions of an expert therapeutic practitioner (for both the doctor and the statesman are positioned earlier, as I showed, as cases of

18. I construe *to beltion* as referring to what is better from the standpoint of the *telos* of the patient's good, in line with its use in the earlier passages to which reference is clearly indicated, pace Rowe and others, who translate so as at least to imply that what it is "better" than is "what has been written down."

19. While both the itinerant doctor and gymnastic trainer are invoked in the initial framing of the point, in what follows I focus on the doctor only, for simplification.

20. Rowe translates the *dein* as "would," but, as I argued in chapter 4 with regard to another part of the *Statesman*, this is often better translated with the force of "must," as opposed to "should" or "would."

21. Rowe translates the participle *karterēn* as "obstinately," but the verb *kartereō* generally has a more positive valence according to LSJ.

22. In addition to the choice of translation for individual words noted in the footnotes immediately above, I construe the phrase *hōs tauta onta iatrika kai hugiena* at 295d5–6 as depending on *an hēgoito* at 295d3, and as further characterizing the positive alternative courses of action in the phrases immediately preceding it. This is pace Rowe, who takes it as an independent clause that begins to characterize the contrasting negative course of action; in my view, that negative course of action begins to be indicated only with the next phrase, *ta de* ... (295d6).

experts oriented to the good of that which they rule) is invoked by the Eleatic at three levels:[23]

—First, in the passage immediately above, at the level of the doctor reflecting on his own reasoning and that of his patient, so as to exclude any prohibition for the actions he must take that would invoke the (specious) grounds that acting as his expertise dictates would be "unhealthy and not part of his expertise (*nosōdē kai ouk entechna*)"

—Second, in the passage that follows it (cited higher above), at the level of the interlocutors of the dialogue making their theoretical assessment of the situation

—Third, at the level of the patient within the analogy

It is striking that the Eleatic posits that the same reasoning is appropriate at each of these levels. Patient, doctor, and philosophical interlocutors must all exclude any name for the acts of a genuine doctor (or statesman) that would imply that they were unhealthy and inexpert—that is, contrary to the *telos* of medicine and to the knowledge that characterizes it as a genuine form of expertise. At the same time, the Eleatic does not insist that such a genuine doctor or statesman would necessarily in fact succeed in attaining the full good of those he rules in so acting. Indeed, he clings to the comparative language (what is "better (*beltionōn*)"), which also figures in an earlier part of this extended passage at 295c9). This comparative but not absolute formulation may be due to the black-box standpoint from which Plato focuses this extended stretch of dialogue, to the imperfect results such a figure might attain (due to material limitations and contingencies), or to both.

The Eleatic then turns to a full application of the point to the case of the statesman, building on his prior prefiguring of it (as in the use of the language of legislation (*nomothetēthenta*) while describing the acts of a true doctor). To do so, he first defines the criteria for "what we have been calling the mistake in contravention of the [implied: true] political expertise," as involving (the pursuit of) "the shameful, bad, and unjust" (296c5–7). These three words, linked with *kai* into a single group object (pace Rowe's translation), jointly characterize a *telos* that is the opposite of the good, or bettering, of the city that was the object posited at the outset of this passage.[24] In applying the point, the Eleatic chooses to address it again to the level of the subjects of the statesman, rather

---

23. On the significance of names and naming in the dialogue more broadly, see my *Method and Politics* (31–33 and passim).

24. The Eleatic is about to specify the *telos* as bettering the people within a city who are acted upon by the statesman; he does not limit these to the citizens, or even to the free persons, and at the end of the dialogue will indeed specify that "both slave and free" are to be covered by the cloth fabric, perhaps a *peplos*, woven by the true statesman as the *ergon* of his expertise.

than to the statesman's own reasoning or that of the interlocutors (albeit that all three levels are expected, as already indicated, to align):

> Then those who have been forced, contrary to what has been written down and to ancestral custom, to do different things that are more just, better, and finer (*dikaiotera kai ameinō kai kalliō*) than what they did before—tell me, if people in this kind of situation for their part should censure this kind of use of force, or rather, if their censure isn't to be the most laughable of all, mustn't they rather say anything on each occasion other than [sc. saying] that those who have been forced have been affected [sc. to do] shameful, unjust, and bad things, by those who did the forcing? (296c9–d5, trans. Rowe, modified)

Once again, the question is what can rightly be said of rulers (here presented in the plural, as those doing the forcing) who use some modality of rule—in this case force rather than persuasion—to bring it about that those whom they rule act more justly, better, and more finely than they did previously or would otherwise do. And once again, the case is phrased (at least in this positive part of the claim) in comparative terms. These rulers using force to make their subjects act in more just, better, and finer ways—and remember that the criteria just announced for inexpert mistakes were (jointly) the shameful, bad, and unjust, which perfectly match up (more just/unjust, better/bad, finer/ shameful)—are to be named as anything other than people who are making the kind of mistake that is characteristic of nonexperts. That is, putting all of these passages together, they are to be called anything other than true statesmen or true rulers.

All of this yields what the Eleatic calls a *horos*: literally a boundary mark, counting here as the "defining mark" of a properly governed city, one that rests on an underlying relationship of genuine political rule.[25] This defining mark is "that the wise and good man will govern [*dioikein*] for the good of the ruled," as the Eleatic goes on to claim in his next speech (the lines cited being 296e3– 4). This states the *telos* of rule, as understood on the basis of the expertise that both grasps the good of the ruled and orients the ruler to care for it. Such a mark exhausts the identification of rule as such. Its expression underscores the emphasis throughout this passage on what one can rightly say (including what

---

25. Trivigno ("Above the Law," 157) proposes "criterion" to translate *horos*, while reserving "mark" for a less rigorous role: he distinguishes "between the *criterion* of right rule and the *marks* of right rule: A mark of right rule is a typical, but not inevitable, feature of right rule, whereas the criterion is that which makes right rule right." According to Trivigno, still on the same page, the use of "laws" and the "consent of the citizens" are both marks of right rule, which facilitate its realization of its *telos*, but are neither necessary nor sufficient to its counting as a case of rule. While he and I use different English terminology, in that I use "defining mark" for what he calls "criterion," our understandings of the substance of the relevant passages are otherwise closely aligned.

name can be correctly applied) with regard to any of the cases of putative rule that are under consideration.

Rather than offering the kind of justification of the rule of a true ruler in terms of an explanation of why those they claim to rule are obligated to obey, which modern political theorists would tend to seek, Plato instead stays within the ambit of the very nature of rule itself. The justificatory force comes indirectly, in two ways. First is the appeal to the good of the ruled, which is treated as an objective truth, in the same way that Razian authority appeals to reasons that apply to its subjects as objectively holding. Second is the repeated contrast drawn between the true ruler and those who only claim or believe to count as such rulers, failing to meet the criterion for reasons that may include lack of true expertise or sheer lack of caring for the good of the ruled (all required in the schema, as emphasized above). This rhetorical unmasking of purported expert after purported expert (as by Socrates), in the *Statesman* manifesting as rivals to the true statesman, exerts a kind of illocutionary force that is supporting the contrasting account of the nature of true rule.

In spelling out the *horos* of rule, the Eleatic links the role of another kind of therapeutic practitioner—here a steersman—to the case of a ruler, and then by extension from a ruler directly to the correct kind of constitution. And in contrast to Thrasymachus in *Republic* 1, in excluding the possibility of "mistake" from such a case, the Eleatic Visitor does not consider normatively perverse cases (as did Thrasymachus in characterizing all rulers as ruling for their own good or advantage), nor even normatively neutral ones. Instead, he rules out the attribution of any "mistake" to "wise rulers, whatever they do, so long as they guard (*phulattōsi*) one great thing, that by always distributing what is most just to those in the city, according to wisdom and expertise, they safeguard (*sōzein*) them and so far as they can bring it about that they are better than they were" (297a5–b3).[26] Notice the guarding and safeguarding language, in vocabulary identical to that used in delineating a *kallipolis* in the *Republic*. Here, as there, rule must be properly therapeutic for the ruled to be proper rule. That therapeutic aim will be in accordance with justice, but nothing more about its specific content is said here.

From what I have called the black-box standpoint on the *telos* of rule adopted in this part of the dialogue,[27] whatever the benefit (including the

---

26. There is a potential tension between the emphasis on the good of the ruled as individuals, which was identified in *Republic* 1 as the *telos* of rule (as per chapter 5, above), and the *Statesman*'s primary emphasis on the good of the city. One may hypothesize the following relationship: the good of the city must ultimately serve to benefit the individual good of each of the ruled; however, in some cases, that good can consist only in putting an end to their morally vicious actions by whatever means possible. See similarly Trivigno, "Above the Law," 162.

27. And also, I would argue, in the stretch of *Republic* 1 that was the main focus of chapter 5. The partial parallels of the *Statesman* to *Republic* 1 tell against efforts to drive

relative betterment, if that is all that is on offer) to the ruled, so long as it is indeed benefit, that fulfills the *telos* criterion for rule to count as correct. Moreover, exactly what sort of *taxis* is involved here to flesh out the role of ruling or "presiding over" also remains opaque. It may be inferred that there will be circumstances in which wise rulers cannot achieve the betterment of the ruled, or cannot achieve it to the full extent that the normative ideal of the interlocking *telos* and *taxis* of rule would require. Nevertheless, once again, this black-box standpoint shows that by simply inspecting a *taxis* oriented to a correct *telos*, rule can be judged to be expert and not inexpert—that is, to be genuine. The means that it may or may not employ are irrelevant to that determination.

It remains open, from the black-box standpoint, as to whether all goods for the ruled—and, in particular, the relational goods of civic freedom and friendship—can be achieved by any and every kind of rule. The garden-variety constitutionalism considered in the course of a parable in *Republic* 9 (as discussed in the previous chapter) and the second-best constitution outlined "in speech" in the *Laws* both show ways in which freedom and friendship can in practice arise within and be supported by a constitutional *taxis* of office and law. Both are rooted in a cooperative disposition, which is in turn recursively supported by the trust and willingness fostered by that very *taxis*. The *Statesman* passages considered in this section, by contrast, do not make clear whether freedom and friendship can be attained by just any or every kind of rule that is properly named "rule," nor by just any or every means that such rule might employ. The emphasis in these passages is on the *telos* that an expert ruler is knowledgeably (and, it must be said, caringly) able to pursue alone. However, once one begins to consider how such a ruler will interact with their subjects, and how their role would in practice manifest the bounds and limits necessary to mark it out *as* rule (as opposed to anarchy), then one finds oneself in the territory of office and law as the almost inevitable practical means of rule. (*Almost* inevitable, on grounds described below.)

The Idea of Platonic Rule versus the Ideal of "Rule over None"

While Platonic rule need not be coercive, I have argued that in the political domain it must be (at least in principle) epitactic and in that respect hierarchical: a ruler must in principle be empowered to issue orders to those they rule. That implies an ineliminable relational hierarchy, or hierarchical relationship, between the person(s) in the role of ruler and the person(s) in the

---

a wedge between the *Statesman* and the Socratic dialogues by Straussian scholars who take the Eleatic Visitor to be inherently anti-Socratic (in contrast to my emphasis on the complementarity in regard to office and rule of the *Republic*, *Statesman*, and *Laws*). See, for example, Zuckert, *Coherence*, 680–735; S. Rosen, *Plato's "Statesman,"* 6–7.

role of being ruled. And that is on Plato's view true of all kinds of political rule, including officeholding which is limited by law and held accountable to those who are ruled. Even in a democracy, as *Republic* 8 and *Laws* 3 demonstrate in the negative, political rule must involve such hierarchy, which cannot be erased by features peculiar to democratic society.

Plato's stance can be clarified by considering the contrary view common to (or at least overlapping among) a certain range of democratic theorists:[28] by considering both the cogency of their alternative to the Platonic contention (as I have reconstructed it) and the cogency of what a Platonic critique of that alternative would be. In this section, I treat that view as articulated by a theorist of a relational egalitarian view of democracy; in the next, by more radical theorists, for whom the democratic ideal actually amounts to what they call "anarchy."

Here, I consider the view defended by Niko Kolodny that democracy properly understood amounts to an ideal of no rule at all, or, as he describes it, "rule over none," by which he means that the social relations of equality can nullify the relations of hierarchy that political rule would otherwise involve. I argue that Plato would say that this is impossible. Neither in a democracy nor in any other constitution can the relations of hierarchy involved in political rule be obviated by social relations of equality.

While Kolodny never actually defines what he means by "rule," he implies that it is to do with the making of "social decisions" or, later, "political decisions" in a context involving institutions, authority, and legitimacy.[29] Characterizing democracy as "a constituent . . . of a society in which people are related to one another as social equals, as opposed to social inferiors or superiors,"[30] his basic move (and one that is characteristic of relational egalitarian democratic theories more broadly) is to argue that political rulers and ruled remain social equals in the relevant sense because the rulers are merely the agents of the ruled, who are the principals (acting collectively).[31] The thought is

---

28. While I focus on relational egalitarianism in the analytical democratic theory tradition, a similar idealization of democracy—as if it need not and should not be valorized as a kind of rule—is advanced in Bonnie Honig's agonistic democratic theory. Similar to Kolodny and the relational egalitarians in this respect, Honig (*Antigone, Interrupted*, 9) defines democratic theory as "the branch of political theory devoted to enhancing and rethinking equality" (taken to exclude the hierarchy that rule requires), although it should be noted that she positions Antigone as an example of a political actor who exemplifies "counter-sovereignty and solidarity" as opposed to standard political rule.

29. Kolodny, "Rule over None I," 195, 197, and passim. Eventually explaining the nature of "political decisions" more fully, Kolodny writes: "Because political decisions are inescapable for all of us, are taken to have final authority over all of us, and use force against all of us, to deprive any of us of equal opportunity to influence them would amount to a kind of subordination" (228).

30. Kolodny, 196.

31. Introducing the idea of representation, Kolodny ("Rule over None II," 317) argues that it is true in both nonpolitical and political contexts that "if a person, or group, as

that political officeholders are akin to other professional fiduciaries, and that the kind of relationship between any individual citizen and their collectively employed rulers is no different from the kind of relationship that ordinary citizens might have with their "lawyers, doctors, accountants, and financial planners," to quote Kolodny once again.[32] On this view, political officeholders are positioned within a broader principal-agent model—a model that I argued in chapter 6 does not capture either officeholders and rulers in general (given their epitactic powers over their subjects) or the ancient Greek or specific Platonic ideas of officeholders and rulers in particular.

In fact, Kolodny takes a curious intermediate step. In arguing that such a principal-agent relationship does not (or, at least, need not, and typically does not) offend against social equality, he moves from the "ordinary, nonpolitical contexts" of citizens delegating to doctors and other professionals to "political contexts"—but not immediately to the political context of most interest, which is of citizens delegating to executive officeholders. Instead, he makes an intermediate appeal to the political context of legislatures, "[which] regularly delegate decisions to subsidiary officers or bodies," in which cases, he claims, "no question of the social inferiority of the legislature, or its members, to the delegate arises."[33] His thought seems to be that when the legislature delegates to (say) an executive body, this creates a principal-agent relationship but one that does not offend against social equality.

But this thought is inapt, or at least problematic, to support the extension to the case of political officeholders who have epitactic powers over citizens (today typically called executive officeholders, though their ancient Greek counterparts also enjoyed certain powers today considered judicial), on at least three grounds. First, in constitutional systems, the legislature does not necessarily create the executive body to which it may choose to delegate (in some cases it may do so, but in others it does not). Second, the legislature is itself a collective artificial body, so that it is not clear what it would mean for it (as a collective entity) to be engaged in social relations at all, or how or whether anything it might do could offend the principle of social equality applying to individual natural persons. Third, the relationship between legislatures (as artificial bodies) and subsidiary officers or bodies does not normally

---

'principal,' delegates to another person, as 'agent,' certain powers . . . this need not imply the social inferiority of the individual principal (or the members of the group principal) to the agent." He argues further that, in the political context, each of the ruled must enjoy the "equal opportunity to influence political decisions" ("Rule over None I," 227; repeated on 229). It is in this context that he introduces the idea of delegation of "the citizenry" to an "official—say, representative in the legislature," considered further in the main text above (Kolodny, "Rule over None II," 317).

32. Kolodny, "Rule over None II," 317.

33. Kolodny, 317.

involve everyday "ongoing social relations" of the kind that are in question between citizens and political officeholders.

Kolodny's actual concern—the case that he is seeking to illuminate by invoking the purported evidence from the "ordinary, nonpolitical contexts" as well as from the (problematic) case of "political contexts" involving the legislature as the delegator—is described as "the relationship between the citizenry and official," the "official" being immediately glossed with an em-dash clause as "say, representative in the legislature."[34] It is typical of democratic theorists operating in this space to take the case of a legislator (a representative, or member, in a legislative body) as paradigmatic of a political "official" or officeholder. Yet this choice is awkward for the project of the present study, given that a modern legislative representative would not in fact count as a paradigmatic officeholder in the typical Greek sense set out in part I of this study. Unlike a paradigmatic Greek officeholder, an individual legislator (call them a legislative representative) has typically few or no powers of command, though a collective body of legislative representatives does typically have certain powers of command, such as the subpoena power enjoyed by each committee and subcommittee of the United States Congress. Choosing a legislative representative as the paradigm for discussing the nature of political rule obfuscates the question of the epitactic power of ordering (or command), which today attaches primarily to individual executive branch officeholders, as it did for the Greeks to the holders of individual *archai* as they understood that term (and even though many of the *archai* were organized into collective boards).

It makes more sense, therefore, to take instead an elected executive branch officeholder—say, a state governor, in the United States federal system—as the paradigm case for assessing Kolodny's argument, and more broadly relational egalitarian democratic theory. Is it then correct to conclude that a state governor embodies a form of "rule over none"—in virtue of being understood as an agent for the people as principal, in a principal-agent relationship that does not impair the social equality that would otherwise exist among them as natural persons? The impediment to drawing such a conclusion lies in the very nature of the "*ongoing relations* with others" with which Kolodny and his fellow relational-egalitarian democratic theorists are concerned.[35] It is the very fabric of everyday ongoing relationships to which they wish to direct analytical attention. But in the case of executive officeholders, such as a state governor in the US federal system, the fabric of their "*ongoing relations* with others" necessarily involves the power of command: either its actual exercise or, at least, its possible exercise (as public health crises tend to make abundantly clear).

The fact that such officeholders are elected by the public (and so in some sense are their agents, as principal-agent models of accountability would

34. Kolodny, 317.

35. Kolodny, "Rule over None I," 228, emphasis original.

claim) does not negate the power of command that the governor possesses, or the corresponding requirement of obedience that falls upon the ruled. And that relationship of rule—in the terminology of this study—is precisely a feature of the *"ongoing relations* with others" that obtain between rulers and ruled in any kind of relationship of political rule. Those ongoing relations must involve—indeed, they are defined by—the power of the rulers to command and the obligation of the ruled to obey. A relationship in which one has the power to command while the other must obey is inevitably experienced as a hierarchical relationship. A state governor is clearly not a political equal of those whom they govern in and during the time in which they play the role (and in this case occupy the office) of governing, and this is true even if they are subjected to periodic election (or selection by lottery) and other mechanisms of accountability and control by the governed.

The fact that an agent is authorized by a principal to occupy a certain role does not nullify the features of that role as facts about the social relations in which its occupant, qua occupant, engages. Recall the cases of "ordinary nonpolitical contexts" to which Kolodny appeals to begin building his principal-agent argument: "lawyers, doctors, accountants, and financial planners." These are (or ideally should be) all fiduciary relationships, ones that Plato would class as "caring" or "therapeutic," in the terms used in chapter 5. Indeed, as observed there, doctors and accountants are the two examples of roles chosen by Thrasymachus in *Republic* 1 to exemplify rule. Even one of Plato's most cynical characters has no trouble in thinking of doctors and accountants as rulers insofar as they exercise therapeutic *technai* that give orders to others.[36]

Crucially, for Plato as opposed to Kolodny, these practitioners of the therapeutic *technai* are indeed to be conceived as rulers. They are positioned in the *Republic*, as in the *Statesman*, as epitactic rulers, even though they do not necessarily dispose of coercive means of enforcement. Their epitactic nature resides in their ability to issue orders or directives that are oriented to the good of the ruled. It is that *telos* which makes this an appropriate form of *taxis*. To be sure, the *Statesman* distinguishes between the advisor, who knows the content of the appropriate command (in a command-apt form, as I have argued elsewhere),[37] and the king or statesman, whose role is (unlike that of the advisor) epitactic. But this means that it is their role to promulgate or issue the order, not (necessarily) to back it up with force. The form that their expertise takes is that of what Joseph Raz would call the issuing of authoritative

---

36. In part, this is because various Greek polities (including democratic Athens) had public doctors and public accountants, and Thrasymachus is arguably thinking of just such civic roles, not of ordinary private ones (there being a kind of public-private distinction in ancient Greek practice, albeit one that does not align neatly with our own).

37. Lane, "Value of Knowledge."

directives. As is the case for Raz, whether or not these directives are binding depends on independent facts about the world and the person to whom those directives are addressed. The important issue for Plato is that the nature of ruling involves the capacity to issue such orders, toward a *telos* of the good of the ruled. His account of the idea of rule does not hinge on whether a subject (or patient, in the case of a doctor) is obligated to obey but rather on whether the ruler is acting qua ruler when they issue their orders.

It is for this reason that Plato has his protagonists dwell on the case of the doctor when defining the role of the political ruler. Recall again the point made by the Eleatic Visitor in the *Statesman*, as discussed above:

> If, then, someone engaged in doctoring does not persuade, but has expertise in the correct way, and, against what has been written down, necessitates some child or man or woman to do what is better (*to beltion*),[38] what is to be the name (*tounoma*) for this use of force? Would not any name be better than that [sc. given to] what we previously called an unhealthy and inexpert mistake? And is it not wholly correct to say what [sc. was said] previously with regard to someone being forced in regard to such a situation, that is, anything except that he had unhealthy and inexpert things (*nosōdē kai atechna*) done to him by the force-wielding doctors? (296b5–c3)

A doctor who uses force to impose treatment on a patient, treatment that is (stipulatively) better for them, is not making "an unhealthy and inexpert mistake." In other words, such a doctor is acting appropriately *as* a doctor: they are acting within the boundaries of their (expert) social role. Given this view, Plato would reject Kolodny's assumption that medical doctors do not count as giving orders, and that (by analogy) statesmen—political rulers— likewise do not, an assumption predicated on viewing such doctors and statesmen as agents of their respective principals (patients and citizens). On the contrary, Plato underscores the epitactic nature of political rule, and of therapeutic relationships likewise.

Kolodny might reply that in a republican political constitution, and in the case of political agents, someone occupying the role of (say) a state governor cannot lord it over their fellow citizens. Rather, there is an underlying equality of status that is rooted in the rotational, limited nature of political office as well as in the broader legal and social features of such a regime, which mitigates against any offensive social inequality attaching to political hierarchy.[39]

---

38. I construe *to beltion* as referring to what is better from the standpoint of the *telos* of the patient's good, in line with its use in the earlier passages to which reference is clearly indicated, pace Rowe and others, who translate so as at least to imply that what it is "better" than is "what has been written down."

39. Indeed, he indicated the direction of such a response in a gracious discussion of a precursor of this chapter in a virtual Berkeley seminar in April 2021; I am indebted to all

Nevertheless, I would contend that to hold that a single moment of principal-agent authorization, such as a periodic subjection to election, nullifies the significance of the ongoing relationship of command and obedience is to give up on the fundamental insight of relational political theorizing in the first place. To claim that such election (and additional features) could make democracy not a form of rule of some over others but rather a form of "rule over none" is akin to the claim, ridiculed by Rousseau, that the election by the English of their members of the House of Commons (then once every seven years) makes them free other than for the precise moment of the voting.[40]

If one is truly concerned with *"ongoing relations* with others," then one must recognize that any form of political rule—including democracy—must precisely involve ongoing relations of command and obedience between rulers and ruled. The fundamental insight of relational egalitarians—namely, that the ongoing fabric of social relationships matters—is what makes this true, once it is consistently applied to political relationships of rule as it should be. Why have so many relational egalitarians blinded themselves, for the case of political hierarchy, to this implication of their own fundamental insight?

Consider, first, the "paradigms" that Kolodny offers, on the one hand, for the kind of social relations ("relations of social superiority and inferiority") that he hopes to avoid: "We know the paradigms. The servant is 'subordinate' to the lord of the manor, the slave 'subordinate' to the master, and so on."[41] The servant-lord and slave-master paradigms have been made famous by republican theorists and adopted by relational egalitarians, who are more interested in the general relationship of being able to look someone in the eye without having to truckle or bow and scrape than in the specific cases of political domination for which these paradigms were long invoked.[42] It is true that democratic citizens should not have to truckle or bow and scrape before their political officeholders, insofar as a democratic polity is unlikely to adopt such norms. Republican theorists, however, have been concerned not *only* with the truckling aspect of social relations but also with the specific problem of political domination (even if that is but one example of a broader phenomenon of relationships of social domination): servants and slaves have been paradigmatic not just of the

---

the participants in that conversation and to Jonny Thakkar for further comments along similar lines.

40. Rousseau, *Social Contract*, bk. 3, ch. 15: "The English nation thinks that it is free, but is greatly mistaken, for it is so only during the election of members of Parliament; as soon as they are elected, it is enslaved and counts for nothing."

41. Kolodny, "Rule over None II," 292, for both quotations in this sentence to this point.

42. See especially the oeuvre of Philip Pettit—for example, *Just Freedom*—in which he popularized the "eyeball test" as to whether someone is so situated as to be able to "look others in the eye without reasons for fear or deference" of certain kinds, and therefore to be able to "walk tall and assume the status of an equal with the most powerful in the land" (xxvi).

need to truckle but of the vulnerability to arbitrary decisions and treatment by their respective lords and masters. Yet taming that arbitrariness does not take away the hierarchical nature of the relationship of rule that remains: a hierarchy necessarily experienced as such in "ongoing social relations" (even election-punctuated ones).

What republican theorists have tended to get right, and democratic relational egalitarians have tended to forget, is that the political relationship is one in which political rulers (including officeholders) will inevitably enjoy powers of command: the power to make decisions and impose certain treatment on their subjects. Plato would counsel that politics requires us to consider how such relationships of rule can be made ethically valuable, rather than to evade the question by seeking to stipulate or define them away by an evasion maneuver. It is simply evasive to claim that so long as rulers are bound by the rule of law, the problem of rule "by men" (in the traditional formula) disappears. Plato's concern with rule highlights that rule by persons remains a feature of any rule of law, and that obedience to persons as rulers remains necessary. Democratic social norms and expectations may tend to erode such obedience; they cannot make the need for it disappear. The burden of the Platonic dialogues considered in the present study is that an ongoing hierarchical social relationship is inescapable in practice, given the role of rule, which is defined by having powers of command that make a claim on others to obey. (The theoretical exception of a condition in which each person is fully able to rule themselves is considered further below.) Such an ongoing social relationship of rule means that political hierarchy is practically inevitable.

Whether such political hierarchy offends against relational egalitarian sensibilities—whether it makes impossible a society that is genuinely free from social inequality—is for relational egalitarians themselves to reconsider. In other words, Plato would challenge Kolodny to the effect that political hierarchy is a relationship that cannot be reduced by democratic sleight of hand to political equality. Neither periodic elections nor selection by lottery, nor other forms of accountability and control, can exempt political officeholders from this fundamental fact about rule. Rule can never be "rule over none." To this extent, Lenin, with his famous question "who whom?" was right (albeit that in *State and Revolution* he toyed with an idyll in which a certain kind of rule, associated with the modern state, would disappear). But against Lenin in turn, Plato would contend that the question of rule is a question of evaluatively oriented order, which may be either good or bad, rather than necessarily reducible to sheer domination.

Against Rule: Democratic Appeals to Anarchy

A similar conclusion applies if one sets Plato in dialogue with nominally similar claims to Kolodny's "rule over none" that have been made from very different political idiom and theoretical traditions, often under the sign of "anarchy," with which I have shown that Plato explicitly engaged. Consider in particular Claude Lefort's assertion that "power becomes and remains democratic when it proves to belong to no one."[43] Jacques Rancière draws on Lefort in denouncing Plato's *Republic* in particular as the original antithesis of such aspirations: he takes Plato to have advanced there an "archipolitics" (playing on the twin senses of *archē* as rule and as origin) that replaces freedom and indeed politics itself with a disciplining ideal of "moderation." For Rancière, Plato in one sentence in the *Laws* (book 3) points to "democracy" as involving (through lottery) "the complete absence of qualifications for governing," an absence that undoes the "particular quality of *arche*" and instead makes possible what Rancière understands to be "politics."[44] (This overlooks the fact that Plato in the course of the *Laws* does not identify democracy with the absence of elections or the sole use of lottery, any more than the Athenians did.) Invoking Lefort, Rancière argues that, in one respect, Lefort's idea of democracy as involving a "structural void," "refers to *an-archy*, to the absence of an entitlement to rule that constitutes the very nature of the political space."[45]

To be sure, Rancière does not expel the ruling-ruled relationship from democracy per se; what he expels, and counts as *an-archy*, is "the absence of an *entitlement* to rule" (emphasis added). But Lefort's original definition of democratic power cited above was stronger: that democratic power is power that "proves to belong to no one." Other broadly postmodern authors, including interpreters of classical texts in that spirit, make play with an ideal of anarchy as precisely an absence of a relationship of rule. In reading Euripides's *Iphigeneia at Aulis*, for example, Nicolas Lema Habash draws on Judith Butler's idea of an "anarchistic moment" to impose an idea of *anarchia* (using the Greek word but without locating it in the play) on the text, understood in part as "acting . . . against social hierarchies."[46] Habash is actually making an anachronistic use of anarchy in the Greek context by explaining it as "lawlessness" (which the Greeks, including Plato, called rather *anomia* or, in a related sense, *paranomia*), rather than an absence of office or rule. Setting that aside, how should one understand the range of modern ideals of anarchism, and what Plato might say in response to them?

A word of definition as to modern ideas of anarchism first, meaning those formulated as normative ideals. They have been focused on opposition to state power and to the very existence of the state: whether "political anarchism,"

43. Lefort, *Democracy and Political Theory*, 27, quoted in Wohl, *Love among the Ruins*, 218n8.

44. "Thesis 3" in Rancière, Bowlby, and Panagia, "Ten Theses."

45. "Thesis 5" in Rancière, Bowlby, and Panagia, referring to Lefort, *Democracy and Political Theory*.

46. Habash, "Lawlessness Controls the Laws," 180, 182. For the term "anarchistic moment," Habash (179) cites Butler's "Critique, Coercion" (214), which further defines the "anarchistic" (glossing Benjamin) as "that which is beyond or outside of principle."

which directly rejects state legitimacy, or "philosophical anarchism," which rejects arguments for the legitimacy of the state though remains open to other considerations before drawing political conclusions (in fact, philosophical anarchism is better termed philosophical-political anarchism, given that its focus remains on the state). Consider as illustrative of both political and philosophical anarchism so understood, the words of Bakunin: "If there is a state, then necessarily there is domination and consequently slavery. A state without slavery, open or camouflaged, is inconceivable—that is why we are enemies of the state."[47]

For Bakunin, what allows the state to serve as an instrument of class oppression is its monopoly (or, at least, its claimed monopoly) on the use of force, invoked so as to impose obedience on the ruled, who (if clear-eyed about their situation) would not obey willingly. However, as I argued above, for Plato rule is not necessarily or inherently a relationship making use of coercion. The modern state of written law and its coercive application, as it were, might wither away, without the need or possibility of political rule disappearing.

Indeed, an appeal to functional, temporary, noncoercive relationships of rule has often been made as a way of thinking about how to replace the state, whether in the context of an ideal of mutual aid or in the context of an ideal of communism, as expressed by Lenin in a moment of reflection in *State and Revolution* (far from the practices that he would go on to enforce).[48] If only rule could be voluntarily obeyed without the need for a state apparatus, a certain form of anarchism, it has long been imagined, could be realized.

The paradox is that Plato—for all his hostility to *anarchia*—can be construed in one respect as having entertained a similar ideal. His exploration of the idea of rule as such is of course (having taken place in antiquity) independent of the modern state. But, more to the point, as argued above, it is independent of the idea of force or violence as the instrument through which rule must operate. When Plato thinks about force, he thinks about it as a feature of *law* (and, in particular, written law): force is the defining feature of law in what the Athenian Visitor calls the "single" sense of a coercively backed command

47. Bakunin, *Statism and Anarchy*, 178. I was directed to this quotation by its citation (in another translation) in Fiala's "Anarchism," which provided useful guidance for this section more broadly.

48. Lenin, in *State and Revolution*, describes the power of the state as consisting (following Engels) mainly in "special bodies of armed men having prisons, etc., at their command" (316), which must be "broken, smashed" (329), being replaced (as the state "withers away") with "democratic measures" on which "all officials, without exception, [sc. will be] elected and subject to recall *at any time*, their salaries reduced to the level of ordinary 'workmen's wages'" (341, emphasis original to the translation). Notice that there will still on this view be a hierarchical relationship of rule in the shape of officeholders empowered to give orders to others, though Lenin anticipates the relational egalitarian aspiration to make such hierarchy conform to relations of social equality.

(or, to simplify, threat), even though this is not a fully adequate ideal of law, which should rather be construed in the "double" sense of having a persuasive preamble attached to the coercive threat. Yet he never defines *rule* by its use of any particular means; indeed, as argued above in regard to the *Statesman*, the Eleatic Visitor is at pains to resist any such definition.

When Plato in the *Laws* embarks on a consideration of rule, he defines it as a feature of human interaction and community rather than in terms of force.[49] As noted earlier, his Athenian Visitor asks the Cretan Cleinias: "You understand that each and every assembly (*sunoidois*) and gathering (*koinōnias*) to do with any kind of activity (*praxeōn*) whatever should invariably have a ruler (*archonta*)?" (1.640a4–6). The context is entirely general—any gathering for any kind of activity—and as the Athenian goes on to illustrate his point, he invokes not only the general of an army (1.640b3) but also the symposiarch of a symposium (1.640b6–d8; the case has already been introduced at 1.639d2). Indeed he had already discussed the cases of goatherds and captains as well as army commanders, in making the point generally earlier:

> Take any social gathering [*koinōnia*] you like, which functions naturally under a ruler (*pephuken te archon einai*) and serves a helpful purpose under his guidance: what are we to think of the observer who praises or censures it although he has never seen it gathered with its ruler (*koinōnousan met' archontos*), but always with no ruler (*anarchon*) or with bad ones (*meta kakōn archontōn*)? (1.639c1–5).

The context of the symposium suggests that no monopoly of violent force, much less that backed by any kind of proto-state apparatus, need be involved in the idea of rule or the corresponding idea of a ruler. While the Visitor does presume that symposia will suffer "a certain amount of disturbance" due to drunkenness (1.640c1–2), and invokes this as a premise for the proposition that such a body will need a leader (*archontos*) (1.640c4), he makes no reference to the use of force by such a symposiarch—though he does later compare them to military commanders (*stratēgous* at 1.671d7, picked up for the comparison at d9). The symposiarch will exercise their rule through influence and social norms, rather than through coercively backed threats, but they count as a ruler issuing commands, and one who will be more or less willingly obeyed (they must, to be sure, maneuver deftly with the drunken ruled).[50]

---

49. Compare Aquinas in *De regimine principum* (a treatise some other sections of which are ascribed to another author), arguing that "one man is the master of another as a free subject when he directs him either towards his own good, or towards the common good," and holding that such a relationship would have obtained even in the "state of innocence" before the Fall (4).

50. On the symposiarch and the symposium generally in this passage, see Tecuşan's "*Logos Sympotikos*."

More generally, in defining the nature of rule (as in *Republic* 1, as well as here in *Laws* 1), and even the nature specifically of political rule (as in the *Statesman*), Plato never invokes coercion or the monopoly of use of force. The *Statesman*, as noted in chapter 4, ultimately defines the nature of political expertise as involving ruling, caring, and weaving. Ruling is the epitactic relationship of order and obedience, but it is modeled on the *architektōn*, who is akin to a foreman of works, responsible on site for keeping the workers on task until the overall work is completed.[51] There is an epitactic relationship here but not a relationship of force: the image could be at home in Engels's or Lenin's idylls of communism (understood, as argued above, as a form of anarchism in the sense of having dispensed with a state that would have withered away). While the post-state epitactic relationship would for Engels in *Anti-Dühring* be directed at "the administration of things and the direction of processes of production,"[52] both of these tasks will still require direction in the sense of a hierarchical command of some persons over others. Even the idyll of short-term, revocable, and severely constrained powers in such post-state roles cannot ultimately abolish rule altogether.

Pure Philosophical Anarchism

Indeed, it may be no accident that Plato flirts with the possibility of political anarchism at certain moments and in certain moods, even while consistently rejecting psychological or cosmic anarchism as an ideal. Call this pure philosophical anarchism: not the "philosophical anarchism" that challenges the normative legitimacy of the state while perhaps allowing for its utility (and so is arguably still a form of political anarchism) but, rather, the philosophical anarchism that holds political rule to be unnecessary for certain individuals to achieve psychic rule. *Taxis*, or order, is essential to rule, and psychic rule is essential for virtue and so happiness. But the means by which it might be achieved vary from intra-psychic moderation to interpersonal command and obedience, to *polis*-backed use of force embodied in written law. For those who can rationally rule themselves, political rule may not be necessary, though in order that others should be ruled who need to be, they may have to be incorporated into a constitution of political rule as well.

An idyll akin to philosophical-political anarchism, in which legislation vanishes into self-rule, governed by self-persuasion, is briefly entertained by Adeimantus in *Republic* 2, in his wistful vision of the way the world would be had his elders "persuaded" his own generation from their youth that justice is really the greatest good of the soul:

---

51. Lane, "Politics as Architectonic Expertise?"
52. Engels, *Dühring's Revolution in Science*, 355.

For if all of you had spoken in this way from the beginning and persuaded us, from youth onwards, we would not keep guard [*phulattein/
phulassein*] over each other for fear injustice be done, but each would be
his own best guard (*phulax*), afraid that in doing injustice he would
dwell with the greatest evil. (2.367a1–5)

The term *phulax*, of course (related to the verb *phulattein/phulassein* translated above as "keep guard") is the same that will be used for the guardians
and eventually the philosopher-rulers later on in the text. So sufficient persuasion inducing self-rule would have done away with rule by guardians—that is,
in the terms of the *Republic*, it would have done away with political rule at
all.[53] Both of these moments could be described as idealizing Socratic conversation to the extent that politics entirely disappears.

It is this kind of moment in Plato of which Allan Silverman was presumably thinking when he claimed that "Plato . . . is committed to philosophical
anarchy, the condition in which each soul rules itself. Philosophical anarchy
is the ideal *nonpolitical* condition sought by reason."[54] But notice that this is
not an ideal of universal anarchism or *anarchia*; on the contrary, as Silverman
himself observes, it is a "condition in which each soul *rules* itself" (emphasis
added). Insofar as such psychological self-rule is impossible for most embodied
human beings, however, the rejection of political *anarchia* remains essential: this is what I have meant by attributing to Plato the pattern of thinking,
characterized in the negative, that I call *antianarchia*.[55]

From a Platonic point of view, philosophical anarchism is confused insofar
as it takes itself to authorize political anarchism. The order that rule provides
is essential in souls, and thus, in all of Plato's constructive political dialogues,
necessary in cities. In providing such order, meanwhile, rule must itself be
bounded, in ways that at least parallel and may include the formal procedural
limits of office and law.

Platonic political thought opposes anarchy as much as tyranny, but also
tyranny as much as anarchy. Both sides of that equation are revelatory. Plato's
idea of rule recognizes the value of office as part of its potential *taxis*, while
insisting that any procedural and legal limits—albeit needed for office and
rule to be capable of being recognized as such—will be hollow without orientation toward the *telos* of the good of the ruled. Tyranny violates both the
taxis and the *telos* of rule; anarchy fails to achieve the *telos* because it fails to
count as a *taxis* at all. The idea of rule captures the indispensability of order
(including potentially an order of offices) if any individual or political good is
to be realized.

53. Lane, introduction to Plato's *Republic*, xxvi.
54. Silverman, "Ascent and Descent," 63, emphasis added.
55. Lane, "*Antianarchia*," from which I have adapted these paragraphs.

ACKNOWLEDGMENTS

THIS STUDY EXPANDS and selectively develops the written text of the 2018 Carlyle Lectures, which I was honored to deliver at the University of Oxford, entitled "Constitutions before Constitutionalism: Ancient Greek Ideas of Office and Rule." I am grateful to the Electors for the invitation to serve as Carlyle Lecturer; George Garnett for his care in overseeing the lectures, as well as the help of the staff of the Faculty of History; and the Warden and Fellows of All Souls for their hospitality, and the staff of the college for their assistance, including the staff of the Codrington Library. More details on the lectures and their relationship to the present book, as well as to past publications, are provided below, as are further thanks connected with that stay at Oxford. I thank the team at Princeton University Press, in particular Rob Tempio, Matt Rohal, and Chloe Coy on the editorial side, and Jenny Wolkowicki and Maia Vaswani on the production side, for their patience and support during my revision and expansion of the Carlyle Lectures for print, and the two anonymous referees for the Press for their helpful comments.

The study is also the belated metamorphosis of a previously planned book, which had the working title "The Rule of Knowledge: Platonic Psychology and Politics." While working on that project in 2012–13 at the Center for Advanced Study in the Behavioral Sciences at Stanford University, with the additional support of the John Simon Guggenheim Memorial Foundation (in the form of a fellowship) and Princeton University, I came to realize that in order to think about the rule of knowledge in Plato, I had first to clarify his idea of rule. That realization was roughly coeval with the germination of my interest in Greek and specifically Platonic ideas of office, developed through (inter alia) papers on office in the *Statesman* (for the VIII International Plato Symposium Pragense in Prague in 2011), in Aristotle (for the AHRC Popular Sovereignty Network in 2012), in the oligarchical constitution of *Republic* 8 (for the Yale–King's College London Seminar, and then a conference in honor of Paul Cartledge, in 2014), and in relation to rule and anarchy (in Toronto for the Workshop in Ancient Philosophy in 2016). Add to that papers on law in the *Republic* in 2010 (for the IX International Plato Society Symposium in Tokyo) and liberty in the *Republic* and *Laws* in 2015 (for the AHRC Research Network on Liberty), and the shape of the argument of the present work can already be dimly seen (though roughly three-quarters of it is previously unpublished).

Teaching courses at Princeton on political theory from Athens to Augustine, the *Laws* and specifically *Laws* 3, *Republic* 8 and 9, and the *Statesman* (twice, including in the Zoom-inflected spring of 2020), and a Politics junior workshop on political office, as well as sitting in on courses on the *Laws* taught by André Laks and the *Oresteia* by Josh Billings, was also formative for these ideas, and I thank all of the students and other participants in these courses. So too was a summer as scholar-in-residence in ancient studies at the American Academy in Rome, thanks to its then director John Ochsendorf, where I began to think about how to transform the Carlyles into a monograph and to draft a new introduction.

Preparation of the Carlyle Lectures was supported by research leave from Princeton University in fall 2017, and their delivery by permission from Deborah A. Prentice (then dean of the faculty) to spend seven weeks at Oxford in January and February 2018, further facilitated by knowing that I could rely on Maureen Killeen to keep the University Center for Human Values operating smoothly. Princeton University supported another sabbatical in fall 2020, supplemented by a spring 2021 leave thanks to the award of an Old Dominion Research Professorship for 2020–21 by the Princeton Humanities Council; I am grateful to the council for that honor, to Michael Smith for relieving me of the directorship of the University Center that year and serving as acting director with panache even in pandemic circumstances; and to Regin Davis and Janine Calogero for their indispensable contributions as assistant director and acting assistant director during that period. I would also like to thank Sue Winters and Dawn Disette for their work as my administrative assistants within the center, and all the staff members of the center as well.

In addition to (and in between) those two periods of research leave, I was also fortunate to receive unstinting understanding and practical support from Princeton University while I coped with major medical challenges in 2019–20. The generous arrangements made by Sanjeev Kulkarni (then dean of the faculty), Alan Patten (chair) and Amanda Kastern (senior manager, Finance and Administration) in Politics, and Jed Atkins (who selflessly undertook to teach my undergraduate course while visiting Princeton on sabbatical), enabled me to continue to direct the University Center, with the thoughtful help of all of its staff, led by Regin Davis (assistant director), and to advise graduate students during that year, though the writing of this book had to be put on hold. Among so many family members, friends, and colleagues to whom I am more grateful than I can say for their practical and emotional support, I can mention only a foremost few: the unstinting guidance of longtime friends Doctor Anne Hallward and Doctor Saul Weiner; the stalwart familial support of Sheila and Norman Lane, Diana Lane and Yonatan Malin, the extended Lane family on all sides, and the extended Lovett and Ditchfield families; and the special support offered by Pam Edelman, Barbara Graziosi, Johannes Haubold, Diana Lipton, Jacob Lipton, Jonah Lipton, and Rabbi Julie Roth—and Andrew Lovett, above all.

Princeton University also provided funds for a Carlyle manuscript conference to be held in December 2017; a workshop on the revised manuscript was convened by the Princeton Program in Classical Philosophy on Zoom in February 2021; and another Zoom workshop on a further revision informally by me in May 2021. I also presented parts of the original lectures and of their revision and expansion for this study in multiple formal and informal contexts during 2017–22, as well as benefiting immensely from conversations about Plato and Greek ideas in classrooms, workshops, meals, Zoom chats, walks, and so on, with dozens of colleagues, students, and friends. I am indebted to far more of the participants in such events and conversations than I can name (though the Plato Club of 2018–19 deserves a special mention: at its core were Amanda Greene, Matthew Landauer, and André Laks). While it is invidi-ous to have to draw lines in being unable to name everyone at large events, I wanted to mention at least the formal occasions for presentation of material in this study, and those who gave extensive, written, or especially germina-tive comments, from the time that the Carlyle Lectures crystallized in draft in fall 2017 through the composition of this note in spring 2022. Conversely, I have mentioned some people only once, even where they have played mul-tiple roles and been longtime conversation partners on Plato; and I have not repeated the acknowledgements found in published papers in full. To all those not named: please forgive the oversight, which is unintentional, and know that I am indeed grateful.

2018 Carlyle Lectures at Oxford University

CONSTITUTIONS BEFORE CONSTITUTIONALISM: ANCIENT GREEK IDEAS OF OFFICE AND RULE

I. Office and Anarchy
II. Office and Accountability
III. Ruling and Being Ruled
IV. Rule, Law, and Liberty
V. Office and Rule in Constitutional Change
VI. The Purposes of Office and Rule

Active Oxford participants in Carlyle Lectures and associated events in Hil-ary Term 2018: Teresa Bejan, Daniel Butt, Ursula Coope, Jás Elsner, Silvia Elsner, Cécile Fabre, Gail Fine, Elizabeth Frazer, Michael Freeden, George Garnett, Terence Irwin, Ben Jackson, Jonathan Katz, Neil Kenny, Tae-Yeoun Keum, Cécile Laborde, David Leopold, Avi Lifschitz, Noel Malcolm, David Miller, Alan Ryan, Kate Ryan, Sophie Smith, Amia Srinivasan, Rosa-lind Thomas, Leslie Topp, Peter Wilson, Annette Zimmermann.

Visiting participants in Carlyle Lectures: Fiona Campbell, Greg Conti, Jane Ditchfield, Christina Hemsley, Dictynna Hood, Susan James, Norman Lane, Sheila Lane, Hansong Li, Diana Lipton, Jonah Lipton, Andrew Lovett,

Eileen Lovett, Leon Lovett, M. M. McCabe, Chaim Milikowsky, Quentin Skinner, Richard Tuck.

Other important presences in Oxford that term: Margaret Bent, Myles Burnyeat (the last times that I was able to see him, to whom I owe so much, before his death), and Rhianon Trowell.

And a final note in regard to the Carlyle Lectures: the first lecturer invited to speak on aspects of antiquity, in an extension of the original remit, was Peter Garnsey in 2005 (the lectures that became his brilliant book on the history of ideas of property). I am honored to have followed in his footsteps as Carlyle Lecturer and those of so many other friends and mentors, above all those of Quentin Skinner (1980), whom I understand to have inaugurated the series and who has been a longtime mentor and friend, and the late Judith Shklar (1986), from whom, immediately upon her return from Oxford to Harvard (while I was an undergraduate at Radcliffe College), I would begin to learn to read, write, and think as a political theorist.

Other Lectures, Workshops, and Seminars

Other named lectures, plenary lectures, and plenary panels in which I presented material related to the Carlyle Lectures or this study (2017 onward only, listed roughly in chronological order of delivery):

Philip Hallie Lecture, Wesleyan University
Gerald F. Else Lecture in the Humanities, University of Michigan (Ann Arbor)
Charles McCracken Distinguished Guest Lecture, Michigan State University
Sir Malcolm Knox Lecture at the University of St Andrews
Royal Society of Edinburgh/Royal Institute of Philosophy Annual Lecture
Britain and Ireland Association for Political Thought Annual Lecture
EUREX Workshop Keynote Lecture, held at the University of Oslo
Bergen Ancient Philosophy Symposium Keynote Lecture
Plenary Symposiast, Joint Session of the Aristotelian Society & the Mind Association
UK Civil Service Leadership Academy Seminar
Hebrew University Public Lecture
Langford Family Lecture, Florida State University

Conferences or seminars at the following organizations or locations (some multiple times in different contexts) in addition to the lectures listed above:

Associations: American Philosophical Association, American Political Science Association, Institute for Historical Research, International Conference for the Study of Political Thought

Universities: Arizona, Bamberg, Bergen, Berkeley, Cambridge (special thanks to John Robertson and to the B Club), Columbia, Duke, École Normale Supérieure, Georgetown, Georgia, Humboldt-University, Northwestern, Oslo, Oxford (including also the Corpus Classics Centre), Stanford, Toronto, Zhuhai

Graduate students and former graduate students who served as my research assistants, each of whom also participated in various activities listed below, and who shaped this work through their own research and our conversations—I owe each of them for expert contributions at crucial stages, with Ian Walling shouldering the final round of delegated tasks with good humor and capacious insight:

Emily Hulme, René de Nicolay, Ian Walling, Jiseob Yoon

Other graduate students whom I advised (and learned from) on related topics in this period:

Olaowulatoni (Toni) Alimi, Merrick Anderson, Wenjin Liu, Jeremy Reid (Arizona), Gabriel Shapiro, Darius Weil, Claudia Yau, Christen Zimecki

Other graduate students who participated in various specific discussion fora regarding this work or related courses (without being able to list all who participated in the latter):

Classical Philosophy: Bridget Brasher, Malina Butorovic, Joseph Moore, Wintor Scott, Adele Watkins, Giulia Weißmann, Megan Wicks, Norah Woodcock
Political Theory: Elly Brown, Utku Cansu, Max Ridge, Emily Salamanca, Lindsay Van Horn

Commentators, conveners, special guests, and others at Princeton-convened discussions of this work in draft for the Carlyle Lectures or this study (which also included many of the graduate students listed above as well as others):

Jed Atkins, Rachel Barney, Charles Beitz, Josh Billings, David Cannadine, Linda Colley, Greg Conti, Kathleen Crown, Jill Frank, Giovanni Giorgini, Michael Gordin, Barbara Graziosi, Amanda Greene, Emily Greenwood, Verity Harte, Antony Hatzistavrou, Johannes Haubold, Kinch Hoekstra, Desmond Jagmohan, Nannerl Keohane, Mirjam Kotwick, André Laks, Hendrik Lorenz, Steve Macedo, Sara Magrin, M. M. McCabe, Benjamin Morison, Jan-Werner Müller, Dimitri El Murr, Debra Nails, Josiah Ober, Dan-el Padilla Peralta, Alan Patten, Philip Pettit, Kim Lane Scheppele, Starry Schor, Anna Stilz, Jeff Stout, Benjamin Straumann, Jonny Thakkar, Voula Tsouna, Katja Maria Vogt, Susan Wolfson

Chairs, commentators, and others who particularly engaged in discussions convened elsewhere (apart from Oxford or Princeton) of this work in draft for the Carlyle Lectures or this study (not repeating those named above; not including all those who participated in discussions of such material prior to 2017; and surely though inadvertently neglecting many others whom I would wish to thank):

> Danielle Allen, Julia Annas, Valentina Arena, Cinzia Arruzza, Carol Atack, Ryan Balot, Rachel Barney, Jonathan Beere, Gábor Betegh, Joseph Bjelde, Richard Bourke, Annabel Brett, the late Sarah Broadie, Lesley Brown, Ian Campbell, Amber Carpenter, Paul Cartledge, Emmanuela Ceva, Josh Cohen, Robert Connor, Chiara Cordelli, Giuseppe Cumella, Nick Denyer, Avner De-Shalit, Panos Dimas, Lisa Disch, John Dunn, David Ebrey, Mark Fisher, Sara Forsdyke, Hallvard Fossheim, Peter Garnsey, Lloyd Gerson, Alex Gottesman, Jon Gould, Alex Gourevitch, John Haldane, Stephen Halliwell, Bonnie Honig, Christian Illies, Susan James, Demetra Kasimis, Niko Kolodny, Richard Kraut, Jun-Hyeok Kwak, Matthew Landauer, Jeffrey Lenowitz, Hansong Li, Jacob Lipton, Alex Long, Tony Long, Minh Ly, Karuna Mantena, Patchen Markell, Jeff Masse, Alison McQueen, Christopher Meckstroth, Susan Sauvé Meyer, Christopher Moore, Charles Nathan, Josiah Ober, Olof Pettersson, Christopher Raymond, Jeremy Reid, Christoph Riedweg, John Robertson, Emma Rothschild, Arlene Saxonhouse, Malcolm Schofield, Avshalom Schwartz, David Sedley, Rachel Singpurwalla, Quentin Skinner, Svetla Slaveva-Griffin, Michael Sonenscher, Anders Dahl Sørensen, Brian Spisiak, John Wallach, James Warren, Leif Wenar

Advice and consultation on issues regarding this work (persons not otherwise listed above):

> J. G. Allen, Victor Caston, Michael Flower, Emily Foster-Hanson, Jane Gerhard, Ivan Jordović, Filip Karfik, Janet McLean, Jonathan Price, Emilio Rosamilia, Matthew Simonton

—————

Finally, it is impossible to imagine the last five, ten, indeed nearly thirty years, without the constant companionship and care of composer Andrew Lovett, without whom I would not have been able to write or complete this work or to do (and enjoy) so much else. This book's dedication is the barest expression of my love and gratitude.

GLOSSARY OF SELECTED GREEK TERMS

THIS LIST IS INTENDED as a rough-and-ready aid for readers of the present study, giving a brief account of relevant senses of words used often in this study and (in some cases) some of the ways in which they appear morphologically in Greek quotations herein (but omitting articles, and giving only certain instances of cases and conjugations). I have sometimes grouped together terms with cognate formations or functions. This glossary is in no way intended to replace or correct the entries in any published lexicon or other authoritative reference source.

ABBREVIATIONS USED IN THIS GLOSSARY

acc.	accusative
adj.	adjective
inf.	infinitive (in an active voice unless designated "m-p" for middle-passive)
n.	noun
nom.	nominative
part.	participle of a verb
pl.	plural
sg.	singular
v.	verb
—	represents alternative or distinguishable senses
–	represents varying ways to translate the same sense

GLOSSARY TERMS

agathos (nom.)/*agathon* (acc.)	good (adj., can be used as a n.)
aneuthunos (adj.)	unaccountable (see by contrast *hupeuthunos*)
anupeuthunos (adj.)	unaccountable (see by contrast *hupeuthunos*)
archē (n. sg.)	rule—office (n.) (other senses: beginning; empire)
archai (pl. nom.)	
archas (pl. acc.)	
archōn (pl. gen.)	
archein (v. inf.)	to rule—to hold office (rule as an officeholder)
archōn (n./part. sg. nom.)	part. (can function as n.): ruler–officeholder
archontas (n./part. pl. acc.)	
archontes (n./part. pl. nom.)	
archōn basileus	king archon (a particular one of the three so-titled *archons* in Athens; by another count, including six additional officeholders, there were nine so-titled archons)
basileia (n.)	kingship
basileuein (v.)	to reign (as a king)
basileus (n.)	king

basilikē (adj.)	kingly; kingly expertise (used as name of expertise)
dēmos (n.)	people (often as contrasted with the elite few)
douleia (n.)	slavery–subjection
douleuein (v. inf.)	to serve as a slave
doulos (n.)	slave
eleutheria (n.)	freedom
eleutheros (adj., can be used as n.)	free—free person
epikouros (n. sg.)	servant
epikouroi (n. pl.)	
epimeleia (n.)	care
epimeleisthai (v. inf. m-p)	to care for, take caring charge of
epistēmē (n. sg.)	(kind of) knowledge or expertise
epitaxis (n. sg.)	order–command (see also *taxis*)
ergon (n. sg.)	task–product–function
erōs (n. sg.)	erotic love (also used as name of a Greek god)
euthunai (n. pl.)	audits–accountability procedures
hupēretein (v. inf.)	to serve
hupēretēs (n. sg.)	servant
hupēretai (n. pl.)	
hupeuthunos (adj.)	accountable
kallipolis (n. sg.)	beautiful city (used as an identifier for the constitution developed in Plato's *Republic*)
kēdemōn (n./part. sg.)	caretaker
kosmos (n. sg.)	order
misthodotēs (n. sg.)	wage earner–mercenary
misthos (n. sg.)	wage
misthoi (n. pl.)	
nomothetein (v. inf.)	to legislate
nomothetēs (n. sg.)	lawgiver–legislator
nomothetai (n. pl.)	
nomos (n. sg.)	law
phulax (n. sg.)	guard–guardian
phulakes (n. pl.)	
phulattein/phulassein (v. inf.)	to guard (two variant spellings)
politeia (n. sg.)	constitution
politeiai (n. pl.)	
politēs (n. sg.)	citizen
politai (n. pl.)	
politikē (adj., can be used as n.)	political (adj.), statecraft (as name of expertise)
politikos (n. sg.)	statesman
sōtēria (n.)	safeguarding–preservation
sōzein (v.inf.)	to safeguard–preserve
stasis (n.)	faction–civil war
taxis (n.)	order
technē (n. sg.)	expertise–craft–profession
technai (n. pl.)	
telos (n.sg.)	purpose
therapeia (n. sg.)	care
therapeuein (v. inf.)	to care for
trophē (n. sg.)	nurture–provisions–food

Adam, James. *The "Republic" of Plato*. With an introduction by D. A. Rees. Cambridge: Cambridge University Press, 1963. https://doi.org/10.1017/CBO9780511897856.

Aeschines. *Aeschines*. Translated by Christopher Carey. Austin: University of Texas Press, 2000.

———. *The Speeches of Aeschines*. Translated by Charles Darwin Adams. Cambridge, MA: Harvard University Press, 1948.

Aeschylus. *Aeschyli "Eumenides."* Edited by Martin West. Boston: DeGruyter, 2012.

———. *"Agamemnon"; "Libation-Bearers"; "Eumenides"; Fragments*. Translated by H. W. Smyth. Cambridge, MA: Harvard University Press, 1960.

———. *Aischylou "Hepta epi Thēbas."* Edited and translated by T. G. Tucker. Cambridge: Cambridge University Press, 1908.

———. *Eumenides*. Edited by Alan H. Sommerstein. Cambridge: Cambridge University Press, 1989.

———. *The Oresteia*. Translated by David Grene and Wendy Doniger O'Flaherty. Chicago: University of Chicago Press, 1989.

———. *Septem contra Thebas*. Edited by G. O. Hutchinson. Oxford: Clarendon, 1985.

———. *The Seven against Thebes*. Translated by C. M. Dawson. Englewood Cliffs, NJ: Prentice-Hall, 1970.

Allen, Danielle S. "Angry Bees, Wasps, and Jurors: The Symbolic Politics of ὀργή in Athens." In *Ancient Anger: Perspectives from Homer to Galen*, edited by Susanna Braund and Glenn W. Most, 76–98. Cambridge: Cambridge University Press, 2004.

Allen, Jason G. "The Office of the Crown." *Cambridge Law Journal* 77 (2018): 298–320.

Anderson, Merrick. "Thrasymachus' Sophistic Account of Justice in *Republic." Ancient Philosophy* 36 (2016): 151–72.

———. "What Are the Wages of Justice? Rethinking the *Republic*'s Division of Goods." *Phronesis* 65 (2020): 1–26.

Annas, Julia. *An Introduction to Plato's "Republic."* Reprint with corrections. Oxford: Clarendon, 1982.

———. *Virtue and Law in Plato and Beyond*. Oxford: Oxford University Press, 2017.

Antiphon and Andocides. *Antiphon; Andocides*. Translated by K. J. Maidment. Vol. 1 of *Minor Attic Orators*. Cambridge, MA: Harvard University Press, 1941.

Applbaum, Arthur I. *Ethics for Adversaries: The Morality of Roles in Public and Professional Life*. Princeton, NJ: Princeton University Press, 2000.

Aquinas, Thomas. *De regimine principum*. In *Aquinas: Political Writings*, edited by R. W. Dyson, 5–51. Cambridge: Cambridge University Press, 2002.

Arendt, Hannah. *The Human Condition*. Chicago: University of Chicago Press, 1958.

———. *On Revolution*. New York: Viking, 1965.

———. "What Is Authority?" In *Between Past and Future: Six Exercises in Political Thought*, 91–141. New York: Viking, 1961.

Aristophanes. *Aristophanes comoediae*. Edited by F. W. Hall and W.M. Geldart. Vol. 1. Oxford: Clarendon, 1907.

———. *Wasps*. In *"Clouds," "Wasps," "Peace,"* edited and translated by Jeffrey Henderson. Cambridge, MA: Harvard University Press, 1998.

Aristotle. *The Athenian Constitution*. Translated by P. J. Rhodes. Harmondsworth, UK: Penguin, 1984.

——. *Politics*. Translated by C.D.C. Reeve. Indianapolis: Hackett, 1998.

——. *"The Politics" and "The Constitution of Athens."* Edited and translated by Stephen Everson. Cambridge: Cambridge University Press, 1996.

—— [Pseudo-Aristotle?]. *Atheniensium respublica*. Edited by F. G. Kenyon. Oxford: Clarendon, 1951.

Pseudo-Aristotle. *Rhetorica ad Alexandrum*. Translated by H. Rackham. In *Readings in Classical Rhetoric*, edited by Thomas W. Benson and Michael H. Prosser. Bloomington: Indiana University Press, 1972.

Arruzza, Cinzia. *A Wolf in the City: Tyranny and the Tyrant in Plato's "Republic."* Oxford: Oxford University Press, 2019.

Atack, Carol. *The Discourse of Kingship in Classical Greece*. New York: Routledge, 2020.

——. "The Shepherd King and His Flock: Paradoxes of Leadership and Care in Classical Greek Philosophy." In *Paradox and Power in Caring Leadership: Critical and Philosophical Reflections*, edited by Leah Tomkins, 75–85. Northampton, MA: Edward Elgar, 2020.

Athenaeus. *The Learned Banqueters*. Vol. 5, *Books 10.420e–11*. Translated by Douglas S. Olson. Cambridge, MA: Harvard University Press, 2009.

Atkins, Jed W. *Roman Political Thought*. Cambridge: Cambridge University Press, 2018.

Bakunin, Michael. *Bakunin: Statism and Anarchy*. Edited by Marshall Shatz. Cambridge: Cambridge University Press, 1990.

Balot, Ryan. "Democracy and Political Philosophy: Influences, Tensions, Rapprochement." In *The Greek Polis and the Invention of Democracy: A Politico-cultural Transformation and Its Interpretations*, edited by Jóhann Páll Árnason, Kurt A. Raaflaub, and Peter Wagner, 181–204. Chichester, UK: Wiley Blackwell, 2013.

Bambrough, Renford. "Plato's Political Analogies." In *Philosophy, Politics & Society: A Collection*, 1st Series, edited by Peter Laslett, 98–115. Oxford: Blackwell, 1956.

Barker, Ernest. *Greek Political Theory: Plato and His Predecessors*. London: Methuen, 1918.

Barney, Rachel. "Last Night in Suburbia." Nellie Wallace Lecture (number 1) delivered as part of the Nellie Wallace Lectures, "The Just Society and Its Enemies, Rereading Plato's *Republic* in 2022," Oxford University, 2022.

Bartels, Myrthe L. *Plato's Pragmatic Project: A Reading of Plato's "Laws."* Stuttgart: Franz Steiner Verlag, 2017.

Beck, Hans, ed. *A Companion to Ancient Greek Government*. Chichester, UK: Wiley-Blackwell, 2013.

——. "Introduction: A Prolegomenon to Ancient Greek Government." In *Ancient Greek Government*, 1–6.

Beere, Jonathan. "Philosopher-Kings and the Possibility of the Ideal City in Plato's *Republic*." Unpublished manuscript. Microsoft Word document, version of 2022, on file with author.

Billings, Joshua. *The Philosophical Stage: Drama and Dialectic in Classical Athens*. Princeton, NJ: Princeton University Press, 2021.

Bleicken, Jochen. *Die athenische Demokratie*. Zurich: Ferdinand Schöningh, 1985.

Blok, Josine. *Citizenship in Classical Athens*. Cambridge: Cambridge University Press, 2017.

——. "Citizenship, the Citizen Body, and Its Assemblies." In Beck, *Ancient Greek Government*, 161–75.

Blondell, Ruby. "From Fleece to Fabric: Weaving Culture in Plato's *Statesman*." *Oxford Studies in Ancient Philosophy* 28 (2005): 23–75.

——. *The Play of Character in Plato's Dialogues*. Cambridge: Cambridge University Press, 2002.

Bloom, Allan. *The "Republic" of Plato*. Translated with notes and an interpretive essay. New York: Basic Books, 1968.

Bobonich, Christopher. "Persuasion, Compulsion, and Freedom in Plato's *Laws*." *Classical Quarterly* 41 (1991): 365–87.

———. *Plato's Utopia Recast: His Later Ethics and Politics*. Oxford: Clarendon, 2002.

Bordes, Jacqueline. *Politeia dans la pensée grecque jusqu'à Aristote*. Paris: Les Belles Lettres, 1982.

Braund, Susanna Morton, ed. and trans. *Juvenal and Persius*. Cambridge, MA: Harvard University Press, 2004.

Brennan, Geoffrey, and Philip Pettit. "The Feasibility Issue." In *The Oxford Handbook of Contemporary Philosophy*, edited by Frank Jackson and Michael Smith, 258–79. Oxford: Oxford University Press, 2005.

Brisson, Luc, and Jean-François Pradeau, eds. and trans. *Platon: "Le politique."* Paris: Garnier Flammarion, 2003.

Brock, Roger. *Greek Political Imagery from Homer to Aristotle*. New York: Bloomsbury, 2013.

Bronstein, David. "Learning from Models: 277c7–283a9." In *Plato's "Statesman": A Philosophical Discussion*, edited by Panos Dimas, Melissa Lane, and Susan Sauvé Meyer, 94–114. Oxford: Oxford University Press, 2021.

Brown, Eric. "Justice and Compulsion for Plato's Philosopher-Rulers." *Ancient Philosophy* 20 (2000): 1–17.

Brunschwig, Jacques. "Rule and Exception: On the Aristotelian Theory of Equity." In *Rationality in Greek Thought*, edited by Michael Frede and Gisela Striker, 115–55. Oxford: Clarendon, 1999.

Burnet, John, ed. *Platonis opera*. Vol. 1. Oxford Classical Texts. Tetralogiae 1–2. Reprint. Oxford: Clarendon, 1961. First published 1901. (Includes *Statesman*)

———, ed. *Platonis opera*. Vol. 2. Oxford Classical Texts. Tetralogiae 3–4. Oxford: Clarendon, 1901.

———, ed. *Platonis opera*. Vol. 3. Oxford Classical Texts. Tetralogiae 5–7. Oxford: Clarendon, 1903.

———, ed. *Platonis opera*. Vol. 4. Oxford Classical Texts. Tetralogia 8. Reprint. Oxford: Clarendon, 1978. First published 1902. (Includes *Clitophon, Republic, Timaeus, Critias*)

———, ed. *Platonis opera*. Vol. 5. Oxford Classical Texts. Tetralogia 9, Definitiones, Spuria. Reprint. Oxford: Clarendon, 2011. First published 1907. (Includes *Laws*)

Burnyeat, Myles. "Justice Writ Large and Small in *Republic* 4." In *Politeia in Greek and Roman Philosophy*, edited by Verity Harte and Melissa Lane, 212–30. New York: Cambridge University Press, 2013.

———. "Utopia and Fantasy: The Practicability of Plato's Ideally Just City." In *Plato 2: Ethics, Politics, Religion, and the Soul*, edited by Gail Fine, 297–308. Oxford: Oxford University Press, 1999.

Burnyeat, Myles, and Michael Frede. *The Pseudo-Platonic Seventh Letter*. Edited by Dominic Scott. Oxford: Oxford University Press, 2015.

Burtt, J. O., trans. *Minor Attic Orators*. Vol. 2. Cambridge, MA: Harvard University Press, 1962.

Butler, Judith. "Critique, Coercion, and Sacred Life in Benjamin's 'Critique of Violence.'" In *Political Theologies: Public Religions in a Post-Secular World*, edited by Hent de Vries and Lawrence E. Sullivan, 201–19. New York: Fordham University Press, 2006.

Caillemer, E. "ARCHONTES (Ἄρχοντες)." In *Dictionnaire des antiquités grecques et romaines*, edited by Ch. Daremberg and Edm. Saglio, 382–88. Graz, Austria: Akademische Druck-u. Verlaganstalt, 1969.

Cammack, Daniela. "The *Kratos* in *Dēmokratia*." Unpublished manuscript. Accessed May 2, 2022. www.danielacammack.com.

———. "Representation in Ancient Greek Democracy." *History of Political Thought* 42 (2021): 567–601.

Camp, John McK., II, and John H. Kroll. "The Agora Mint and Athenian Bronze Coinage." *Hesperia: Journal of the American School of Classical Studies at Athens* 70 (2001): 127–62.

Campbell, Blair. "Poliatrics: Physicians and the Physician Analogy within Fourth-Century Athens." *American Political Science Review* 76 (1982): 810–24.

Carpenter, Amber D. "Civic Function and the Taxonomy of Skills: 287b4–290e9." In *Plato's "Statesman": A Philosophical Discussion*, edited by Panos Dimas, Melissa Lane, and Susan Sauvé Meyer, 136–55. Oxford: Oxford University Press, 2021.

Carter, L. B. *The Quiet Athenian*. Oxford: Clarendon, 1986.

Carugati, Federica. *Creating a Constitution: Law, Democracy, and Growth in Ancient Athens*. Princeton, NJ: Princeton University Press, 2019.

Chambry, Émile, ed. and trans. *Platon: Œuvres complètes*. Vols. 6–7, *"La république."* Paris: Collection des Universités de France, 1933.

Cicero. *Cicero's Orations*. Translated by Charles Duke Yonge. Mineola, NY: Dover, 2018.

Condren, Conal. *Argument and Authority in Early Modern England: The Presupposition of Oaths and Offices*. Cambridge: Cambridge University Press, 2006.

Cooper, John, ed. *Plato: Complete Works*. Associate editor D. S. Hutchinson. Indianapolis: Hackett, 1997.

Cordelli, Chiara. *The Privatized State: Why Government Outsourcing of Public Powers Is Making Us Less Free*. Princeton, NJ: Princeton University Press, 2020.

Dalby, Andrew. "Symposium." In *Encyclopedia of Greece and the Hellenic Tradition*, edited by Graham Speake, 1594–95. London: Fitzroy Dearborn, 2000.

Danzig, Gabriel. *Apologizing for Socrates: How Plato and Xenophon Created Our Socrates*. Lanham, MD: Lexington Books, 2010.

Dauber, Noah. *State and Commonwealth: The Theory of the State in Early Modern England, 1549–1640*. Princeton, NJ: Princeton University Press, 2016.

Demosthenes. *Demosthenis orationes: Tomus I*. Edited by M. R. Dilts. Oxford: Oxford University Press, 2002.

———. *Speeches 18 and 19*. Translated by Harvey Yunis. Austin: University of Texas Press, 2005.

———. *Speeches 20–22*. Edited and translated by Edward M. Harris. Austin: University of Texas Press, 2008.

De Vaan, Michiel. *Etymological Dictionary of Latin and the Other Italic Languages*. Leiden: Brill, 2008.

Dio Chrysostom. *Dio Chrysostom*. Vol. 2. Translated by J. W. Cohoon. Cambridge, MA: Harvard University Press, 1950.

Disch, Lisa. "Comments on 'Rule.'" Presented at International Conference for the Study of Political Thought conference on Anatomies of Power: Praxis, Violence, Rule, May 14, 2022. Unpublished Microsoft Word document, 2022, on file with author.

Dixsaut, Monique, Dimitri El Murr, Marc-Antoine Gavray, Alexandre Hasnaoui, Étienne Helmer, Annie Larivée, Antoine de la Taille, and Fulcran Teisserenc, eds. and trans. *Platon: "Le politique."* Paris: Vrin, 2018.

Dolgert, Stefan. "Dungeon Master Socrates: A Role-Playing Game Meta-theory of Plato's *Republic*." Paper delivered at the Annual Meeting of the American Political Science Association, San Francisco, 2017.

duBois, Page. *Slavery: Antiquity and Its Legacy*. Oxford: Oxford University Press, 2009.

Duke, E. A., W. F. Hicken, W.S.M. Nicoll, D. B. Robinson, and J.C.G. Strachan, eds. *Platonis opera*. Vol. 1. Oxford Classical Texts. Tetralogiae 1–2. Oxford: Clarendon, 1995. (Includes *Politicus (Statesman)*, translated by Robinson, cited as Duke/Robinson translation)

Duncan, Christopher M., and Peter J. Steinberger. "Plato's Paradox? Guardians and Philosopher-Kings." *American Political Science Review* 84, no. 4 (1990): 1317–22.

Ebrey, David. "The Value of Rule in Plato's Dialogues: A Response to Melissa Lane." *Plato Journal: Journal of the International Plato Society* 16 (2016): 75–80.

Egan, Timothy. "Kamala Harris, the Prosecutor Trump Fears Most." *New York Times*, August 14, 2020. https://www.nytimes.com/2020/08/14/opinion/kamala-harris-trump.html.

Eggers Lan, Conrado, ed. and trans. *Platón: Diálogos IV; "República."* Madrid: Gredos, 1986.

Ehrenberg, Victor. *The Greek State.* 2nd ed. London: Methuen, 1969.

Ellis, Samuel. "Sole Rule and the Greek Polis: Legitimising Monocratic Power from the Archaic Period to the Early Hellenistic Period." PhD thesis, University of Edinburgh, 2021.

El Murr, Dimitri. "Kingly Intertwinement: 308b10–311c10." In *Plato's "Statesman": A Philosophical Discussion*, edited by Panos Dimas, Melissa Lane, and Susan Sauvé Meyer, 239–59. Oxford: Oxford University Press, 2021.

———. "*Philia* in Plato." In *Ancient and Medieval Concepts of Friendship*, edited by Suzanne Stern-Gillet and Gary M. Gurtler, 3–34. Albany: State University of New York Press, 2014.

———. "Platon contre (et avec) Thrasymaque." In *L'esprit critique dans l'antiquité*, vol. 1, *Critique et licence dans la Grèce antique*, edited by Bernard Collette-Dučić, Marc-Antoine Gavray, and Jean-Marc Narbonne, 343–64. Paris: Les Belles Lettres, 2019.

———. *Savoir et gouverner: Essai sur la science politique platonicienne.* Paris: Vrin, 2014.

Emerson, Ralph Waldo. *Representative Men: Seven Lectures.* Cambridge, MA: Belknap Press of Harvard University Press, 1996. First published 1850.

Emmet, Dorothy. *Rules, Roles and Relations.* London: Macmillan, 1966.

Engels, Frederick [Friedrich]. *Herr Eugen Dühring's Revolution in Science (Anti-Dühring).* Translated by Emile Burns. Edited by C. P. Dutt. London: Electric Book Co., 2001.

Euben, J. Peter. *Corrupting Youth: Political Education, Democratic Culture, and Political Theory.* Princeton, NJ: Princeton University Press, 1997.

Euripides. *Fragments: Aegeus-Meleager.* Translated and edited by Christopher Collard and Martin Cropp. Cambridge, MA: Harvard University Press, 2008.

———. "*Hecuba*"; "*The Trojan Women*"; "*Andromache.*" Translated by J. Morwood. Oxford: Oxford University Press, 2001.

———. "*Iphigenia among the Taurians*"; "*Bacchae*"; "*Iphigenia at Aulis*"; "*Rhesus.*" Translated by J. Morwood. Oxford: Oxford University Press, 1999.

———. *The Plays of Euripides.* Translated by E. P. Coleridge. London: George Bell and Sons, 1891.

Farrar, Cynthia. "Taking Our Chances with the Ancient Athenians." In *Démocratie athénienne, démocratie moderne: Tradition et influences; neuf exposés suivis de discussions*, edited by Alain-Christian Hernández, with contributions from P. Ducrey and M. H. Hansen, 168–217, with discussion 218–34. Geneva: Vandœuvres, 2009.

Ferejohn, John. "Accountability and Authority: Toward a Theory of Political Accountability." In *Democracy, Accountability, and Representation*, edited by Adam Przeworski, Susan Carol Stokes, and Bernard Manin, 131–53. Cambridge: Cambridge University Press, 1999.

Ferrari, G.R.F. *City and Soul in Plato's "Republic."* Sankt Augustin, Germany: Academia Verlag, 2003.

Feyel, Christophe. *Dokimasia: La place et le rôle de l'examen préliminaire dans les institutions des cités grecques.* Nancy, France: Association pour la diffusion de la recherche sur l'antiquité, 2009.

Fiala, Andrew. "Anarchism." In *The Stanford Encyclopedia of Philosophy Archive*, Spring 2018 edition, edited by Edward N. Zalta. https://plato.stanford.edu/archives/spr2018/entries/anarchism/.

Foucault, Michel. "Omnes et Singulatim: Towards a Criticism of Political Reason." In *The Tanner Lectures on Human Values*, vol. 2, edited by Sterling McMurrin, 298–325. Salt Lake City: University of Utah Press, 1981.

Frank, Jill. "Comments on 'Rule.'" Paper presented at the International Conference for the Study of Political Thought, Anatomies of Power: Praxis, Violence, Rule, May 14, 2022. Unpublished manuscript. Microsoft Word document, 2022, on file with author.

———. "Constitution." In *A Cultural History of Law in Antiquity*, edited by Julen Etxabe, 41–58. London: Bloomsbury, 2021.

———. *Poetic Justice: Rereading Plato's "Republic."* Chicago: University of Chicago Press, 2018.

Frank, Jill, and Sarah Greenberg. "Weaving Politics." In *The Routledge Handbook on Women in Ancient Greek Philosophy*, edited by Sara Brill and Catherine McKeen. New York: Routledge, forthcoming.

Freytas-Tamura, Kimiko de. "A British Town Weighs Its Officials' Merits, with Scales." *New York Times*, May 18, 2016. http://www.nytimes.com/2016/05/19/world/what-in-the -world/high-wycombe-england-annual-weigh-in.html.

Fröhlich, Pierre. *Les cités grecques et le contrôle des magistrats (IVe-Ier siècle avant J.-C)*. Geneva: Droz, 2004.

———. "Governmental Checks and Balances." In Beck, *Ancient Greek Government*, 252–66.

Gabrielsen, Vincent. *Remuneration of State Officials in Fourth Century B.C. Athens*. Odense, Denmark: Odense University Press, 1981.

Gagarin, Michael. *Early Greek Law*. Berkeley: University of California Press, 1987.

Gagarin, Michael, and Paula Perlman, eds. *The Laws of Ancient Crete, c.650-400 BCE*. Oxford: Oxford University Press, 2016.

Geiger, Rolf. "'Die jetzt so genannten Könige und Machthaber.' Zur Kritik politischer Begriffe in den Platonischen Dialogen." Paper presented at Philosophie für die Polis: Fünfter internationaler Kongress der Gesellschaft für antike Philosophie, Zurich, 2016.

Gerson, Lloyd. *Aristotle and Other Platonists*. Ithaca, NY: Cornell University Press, 2005.

———. *Plato's Moral Realism*. Cambridge: Cambridge University Press, forthcoming 2023.

Geuss, Raymond. *Philosophy and Real Politics*. Princeton, NJ: Princeton University Press, 2008.

———. "Thucydides, Nietzsche, and Williams." In *Outside Ethics*, 219–33. Princeton, NJ: Princeton University Press, 2005.

Gill, Mary Louise. "Models in Plato's *Sophist* and *Statesman*." *PLATO: Journal internet de la Société platonicienne internationale* 6 (2006): 1–16.

———. *Philosophos: Plato's Missing Dialogue*. Oxford: Oxford University Press, 2012.

Giorgini, Giovanni, ed. and trans. *Platone: "Politico."* With introduction and notes by Giorgini. Milan: BUR, 2005.

Glotz, Gustave. *The Greek City*. Translated by N. Mallinson. London: Routledge, 2011. First published 1929.

Goldie, Mark. "The Unacknowledged Republic: Officeholding in Early Modern England." In *The Politics of the Excluded, c. 1500-1850*, edited by Tim Harris, 153–94. New York: Palgrave, 2001.

Gomme, A. W., A. Andrewes, and K. J. Dover. *A Historical Commentary on Thucydides*. Vol. 5. Oxford: Oxford University Press, 1981.

Gordon, Jill. *Turning toward Philosophy: Literary Device and Dramatic Structure in Plato's Dialogues*. University Park: Pennsylvania State University Press, 1999.

Görgemanns, Herwig. *Beiträge zur Interpretation von Platons "Nomoi."* Munich: C. H. Beck, 1960.

Greene, Amanda R. "When Are Markets Illegitimate?" *Social Philosophy and Policy* 36 (2020): 212–41.

Griffith-Williams, Brenda. "The Succession to the Spartan Kingship, 520–400 BC." *Bulletin of the Institute of Classical Studies* 54, no. 2 (2011): 43–58.

Grube, G.M.A., trans. *Apology*. By Plato. In Cooper, *Plato*.

———, trans. *Euthyphro*. By Plato. In Cooper, *Plato*.

———, trans. *Phaedo*. By Plato. In Cooper, *Plato*.

Grube, G.M.A., trans., rev. C.D.C. Reeve. *Republic*. By Plato. In Cooper, *Plato*.

Guarducci, Margherita. *Inscriptiones creticae, opera et consilio Friderici Halbherr collectae*. Vol 4. Rome: Libreria dello Stato, 1950.

Habash, Nicolas Lema. "Lawlessness Controls the Laws: *Nomos*, 'The Ethical,' and the (Im)-possibilities of Anarchia in Euripides' *Iphigenia at Aulis*." *Arethusa* 50, no. 2 (2017): 169–92.

Hall, Jonathan. "Rise of State Action in the Archaic Age." In Beck, *Ancient Greek Government*, 7–21.

Hansen, Mogens Herman. *The Athenian Democracy in the Age of Demosthenes*. Translated by John A. Crook. Oxford: Blackwell, 1991.

———. "ΚΛΗΡΩΣΙΣ ΕΚ ΠΡΟΚΡΙΤΩΝ in Fourth-Century Athens." *Classical Philology* 81 (1986): 222–29.

———. "*Misthos* for Magistrates in Classical Athens." *Symbolae Osloenses*, 54 (1979): 5–22.

———. "*Misthos* for Magistrates in Fourth-Century Athens?" *Greek, Roman, and Byzantine Studies* 54 (2013): 404–19.

Harding, Phillip, ed. *From the End of the Peloponnesian War to the Battle of Ipsus*. Cambridge: Cambridge University Press, 1985.

Harel, Alon. *Why Law Matters*. Oxford: Oxford University Press, 2014.

Harris, Edward M. "Trials, Private Arbitration, and Public Arbitration in Classical Athens; or the Background to [Arist.] *Ath. Pol.* 53, 1–7." In *Athenaion Politeiai tra Storia, Politica e Sociologia: Aristotele e Pseudo-Senofonte*, edited by Cinzia Bearzot, Mirko Canevaro, Tristano Gargiulo, and Elisabetta Poddighe, 213–30. Milan: LED, Edizioni universitarie di lettere economia diritto, 2018.

Harte, Verity. "Knowing and Believing in *Republic* V." In *Rereading Ancient Philosophy: Old Chestnuts and Sacred Cows*, edited by Verity Harte and Raphael Woolf, 141–62. Cambridge: Cambridge University Press, 2017.

Hatzistavrou, Antony. "Happiness and the Nature of the Philosopher-Kings." In *New Essays on Plato: Language and Thought in Fourth-Century Greek Philosophy*, edited by Fritz-Gregor Herrmann, 95–124. Swansea: Classical Press of Wales, 2006.

Haubold, Johannes. *Homer's People: Epic Poetry and Social Formation*. New York: Cambridge University Press, 2000.

———. "'Shepherds of the People': Greek and Mesopotamian Perspectives." In *Mesopotamia in the Ancient World: Impact, Continuities, Parallels*, Proceedings of the Seventh Symposium of the Melammu Project held in Obergurgl, Austria, November 4–8, 2013, edited by Robert Rollinger and Erik van Dongen, 245–54. Münster, Germany: Ugarit-Verlag, 2015.

Hawke, Jason. *Writing Authority: Elite Competitions and Written Law in Early Greece*. DeKalb: Northern Illinois University Press, 2011.

Heath, Joseph. *The Machinery of Government: Public Administration and the Liberal State*. New York: Oxford University Press, 2020.

Hellwig, Dorothea. *Adikia in Platons "Politeia": Interpretationen zu den Büchern VIII und IX*. Amsterdam: B. R. Grüner, 1980.

Helmer, Étienne. "Histoire, politique et pratique aux livres VIII–IX de la *République*." In *Études sur la "République,"* vol. 1, edited by Monique Dixsaut, 149–68. Paris: Vrin, 2006.

———. *Oikonomia: Philosophie grecque de l'économie*. Paris: Classiques Garnier, 2021.

Herodotus. *The Persian Wars*. Vol. 1, *Books 1–2*. Translated by A. D. Godley. Cambridge, MA: Harvard University Press, 1920.

Hitz, Zena. "'Degenerate Regimes in Plato's *Republic*." In *Plato's "Republic": A Critical Guide*, edited by Mark L. McPherran, 103–31. Cambridge: Cambridge University Press, 2010.

Hobbes, Thomas. "Preface to the Readers." In *On the Citizen*, edited and translated by Richard Tuck and Michael Silverthorne, 7–15. Cambridge: Cambridge University Press, 1998. First published 1642 (in Latin).

Hoekstra, Kinch. "Athenian Democracy and Popular Tyranny." In *Popular Sovereignty in Historical Perspective*, edited by Richard Bourke and Quentin Skinner, 15–51. Cambridge: Cambridge University Press, 2016.

Homer. *The "Odyssey" of Homer*. Translated by Richmond Lattimore. New York: Harper Perennial Modern Classics, 2007.

———. *The "Iliad" of Homer*. Translated by Richmond Lattimore. Introduction and notes by Richard Martin. Chicago: University of Chicago Press, 2011.

Honig, Bonnie. *Antigone, Interrupted*. Cambridge: Cambridge University Press, 2013.

Hulme Kozey, Emily. "Another *Peri Technes* Literature: Inquiries about One's Craft at Dodona." *Greece and Rome* 65 (2018): 205–17.

———. "The Good-Directedness of Τέχνη and the Status of Rhetoric in the Platonic Dialogues." *Apeiron* 52 (2019): 223–44.

———. "Is Farming a *Technē*? Folk Concepts in Plato and Aristotle." *Ancient Philosophy* 42 (2022): 443–51.

———. "*Philosophia* and *Philotechnia*: The Techne Theme in the Platonic Dialogues." PhD dissertation, Princeton University, 2019.

Hunter, Richard. *Plato's "Symposium."* Oxford: Oxford University Press, 2004.

Irwin, Terence. *Plato's Moral Theory: The Early and Middle Dialogues*. Oxford: Clarendon, 1977.

Ismard, Paulin. *La démocratie contre les experts: Les esclaves publics en Grèce ancienne*. Paris: Éditions du Seuil, 2015. (Translated as *Democracy's Slaves: A Political History of Ancient Greece* by Janet Marie Todd. Cambridge, MA: Harvard University Press, 2017.)

Isocrates. *Isocrates*. Vols. 1 and 2. Translated by George Norlin. London: Heinemann, 1928.

———. *Isocrates*. Vol. 3. Translated by LaRue van Hook. London: Heinemann, 1928.

Johnstone, Mark A. "Anarchic Souls: Plato's Depiction of the 'Democratic Man.'" *Phronesis* 58 (2013):139–59.

———. "Tyrannized Souls: Plato's Description of the Tyrannical Man." *British Journal for the History of Philosophy* 23 (2015): 423–37.

Jordović, Ivan. "Did the Ancient Greeks Know of Collective Tyranny?" *Balcanica* 36 (2005): 17–33.

———. *Taming Politics: Plato and the Democratic Roots of Tyrannical Man*. Stuttgart: Franz Steiner Verlag, 2019.

Kamtekar, Rachana. "The Politics of Plato's Socrates." In *A Companion to Socrates*, edited by Sara Ahbel-Rappe and Rachana Kamtekar, 214–27. Oxford: Blackwell, 2006.

———. "What's the Good of Agreeing? Ὁμόνοια in Platonic Politics." *Oxford Studies in Ancient Philosophy* 26 (2004): 131–70.

Klosko, George. *The Development of Plato's Political Theory*. 2nd ed. Oxford: Oxford University Press, 2006.

———. "The Nocturnal Council in Plato." *Political Studies* 36 (1988): 74–88.

Knobe, Joshua, Sandeep Prasada, and George E. Newman. "Dual Character Concepts and the Normative Dimension of Conceptual Representation." *Cognition* 127, no. 2 (May 1, 2013): 242–57. https://doi.org/10.1016/j.cognition.2013.01.005.

Kolodny, Niko. "Rule over None I: What Justifies Democracy?" *Philosophy and Public Affairs* 42 (2014): 195–229.

Kolodny, Niko. "Rule over None II: Social Equality and the Justification of Democracy." *Philosophy and Public Affairs* 42 (2014): 287–336.

Krapinger, Gernot, ed. and trans. *Platon: "Der Staat."* Ditzingen, Germany: Reclam, 2017.

Kraut, Richard. "Return to the Cave: *Republic* 519–521." *Boston Area Colloquium in Ancient Philosophy* 7 (1991): 43–62.

Laffon, Amarande. "L'ἀναρχία (anarchia) en Grèce antique." PhD dissertation, Paris 4 Sorbonne, 2016.

Laks, André. "Freedom, Liberality, and Liberty in Plato's *Laws.*" *Social Philosophy and Policy* 24 (2007): 130–52.

———. "Legislation and Demiurgy: On the Relationship between Plato's *Republic* and *Laws.*" *Classical Antiquity* 9 (1990): 209–29.

———. *Plato's Second Republic: An Essay on the "Laws."* Princeton, NJ: Princeton University Press, 2022.

———. "L'utopie législative de Platon." *Revue philosophique* 116 (1991): 417–28.

Laks, André, and Glenn Most, trans. and eds. *Early Greek Philosophy.* 9 vols. Cambridge, MA: Harvard University Press, 2016.

Landauer, Matthew. *Dangerous Counsel: Accountability and Advice in Ancient Greece.* Chicago: University of Chicago Press, 2019.

———. "Drinking Parties Correctly Ordered: Plato on Mass Participation and the Necessity of Rule." *Journal of Politics* 84 (2022): 2011–2022.

———. "The *Idiōtēs* and the Tyrant: Two Faces of Unaccountability in Democratic Athens." *Political Theory* 42 (2014): 139–66.

Lane, Melissa. "*Antianarchia*: Interpreting Political Thought in Plato." *Plato Journal: Journal of the International Plato Society* 16 (2016): 59–74.

———. *The Birth of Politics: Eight Greek and Roman Political Ideas and Why They Matter.* Princeton, NJ: Princeton University Press, 2015.

———. "Constitutions before Constitutionalism: Classical Greek Ideas of Office and Rule." The 2018 Carlyle Lectures, delivered at Oxford University. Unpublished manuscript. Microsoft Word document, 2018, on file with author.

———. *Eco-Republic: What the Ancients Can Teach Us about Ethics, Virtue, and Sustainable Living.* Princeton, NJ: Princeton University Press, 2012.

———. "'Emplois pour philosophes': L'art politique et l'étranger dans le politique à la lumière de Socrate et du philosophe dans le *Théétète.*" Translated by Fulcran Teisserenc. *Les études philosophiques* 74 (2005): 325–45.

———. "Founding as Legislating: The Figure of the Lawgiver in Plato's *Republic.*" In *Dialogues on Plato's "Politeia" ("Republic"): Selected Papers from the Ninth Symposium Platonicum,* edited by Luc Brisson and Noburo Notomi, 104–14. Sankt Augustin, Germany: Academia Verlag, 2013.

———. "How to Turn History into Scenario: Plato's *Republic* Book 8 on the Role of Political Office in Constitutional Change." In *How to Do Things with History,* edited by Danielle Allen, Paul Christesen, and Paul Millett, 81–108. Oxford: Oxford University Press, 2018.

———. "The Idea of Accountable Office in Ancient Greece and Beyond." *Philosophy* 95 (2019): 1–22.

———. Introduction to *Plato: The Republic,* translated by Desmond Lee, xi–xl. London: Penguin, 2007.

———. "Lycurgus, Solon, Charondas . . . : Figuring the Legislator in Platonic Political Thought and Its Aftermath." Paper delivered as the Nicolai Rubinstein Lecture, Queen Mary, London, 2019. Microsoft Word document, 2019, on file with author.

———. *Method and Politics in Plato's "Statesman."* Cambridge: Cambridge University Press, 1998.

———. "Office and Anarchy." Carlyle Lecture (number 1) delivered as part of the Carlyle Lectures, "Constitutions before Constitutionalism: Classical Greek Ideas of Office and Rule," Oxford University, 2018.

———. "Persuasion et force dans la politique platonicienne." Translated by Fulcran Teisserenc. In *Aglaïa: Autour de Platon; Mélanges offerts à Monique Dixsaut*, edited by Aldo Brancacci, Dimitri El Murr, and Daniela P. Taormina, 165–98. Paris: Vrin, 2010.

———. "Placing Plato in the History of Liberty." *History of European Ideas* 44 (2018): 702–18.

———. "Platonizing the Spartan *Politeia* in Plutarch's *Lycurgus*." In *Politeia in Greek and Roman Philosophy*, edited by Verity Harte and Melissa Lane, 57–77. New York: Cambridge University Press, 2013.

———. "Plato on the Value of Knowledge in Ruling." *Aristotelian Society Supplementary Volume* 92 (2018): 49–67.

———. "Plato's Neglected Critiques of a City like Athens in *Republic* 8 and 9: The Democratic Cities Nurturing the Four 'Representative Men.'" Paper presented at the 2021 Annual Meeting of the Society for Classical Studies.

———. "Plato's Political Philosophy." In *The Blackwell Companion to Ancient Philosophy*, edited by Marie Louise Gill and Pierre Pellegrin, 170–91. Oxford: Blackwell, 2006.

———. *Plato's Progeny: How Plato and Socrates Still Captivate the Modern Mind*. London: Duckworth, 2001.

———. "Political Expertise and Political Office in Plato's *Statesman*: The Statesman's Rule (*Archein*) and the Subordinate Magistracies (*Archai*)." In *Plato's "Statesman": Proceedings of the Eighth Symposium Platonicum Pragense*, edited by Aleš Havlíček, Jakub Jirsa, and Karel Thein, 49–77. Prague: OIKOYMENH, 2013.

———. "Politics as Architectonic Expertise? Against Taking the So-Called 'Architect' (Ἀρχιτέκτων) in Plato's *Statesman* to Prefigure This Aristotelian View." *Polis* 37 (2020): 449–67.

———. "Popular Sovereignty as Control of Officeholders: Aristotle on Greek Democracy." In *Popular Sovereignty in Historical Perspective*, edited by Richard Bourke and Quentin Skinner, 52–72. Cambridge: Cambridge University Press, 2016.

———. "Self-Knowledge in Plato? Recognizing the Limits and Aspirations of a Self as Knower." In *Self-Knowledge in Ancient Philosophy*, edited by Fiona Leigh, 51–70. Oxford: Oxford University Press, 2020.

———. "Statecraft as a Ruling, Caring, and Weaving *Dunamis*: 303d4–305e7." In *Plato's "Statesman": A Philosophical Discussion*, edited by Panos Dimas, Lane, and Susan Sauvé Meyer, 195–216. Oxford: Oxford University Press, 2021.

———. "States of Nature, Epistemic and Political." *Proceedings of the Aristotelian Society* 99 (1999): 211–224.

———. "*Technē* and *Archē* in *Republic* I." *Oxford Studies in Ancient Philosophy* 57 (2019): 1–24.

———. "Virtue as the Love of Knowledge in Plato's *Symposium* and *Republic*." In *Maieusis: Essays in Ancient Philosophy in Honour of Myles Burnyeat*, edited by Dominic Scott, 44–67. Oxford: Oxford University Press, 2007.

———. "When the 'Thirty Tyrants' Got Their Name, and Why It Matters." Lecture delivered as the keynote for the Britain and Ireland Association for Political Thought Annual Conference, held at Oxford University, 2018.

———. "Why Donald Trump Was the Ultimate Anarchist." *New Statesman*, February 8, 2021. https://www.newstatesman.com/world/americas/north-america/us/2021/02/why-donald-trump-was-ultimate-anarchist.

———. "Xenophon (and Thucydides) on Sparta (and Athens): Debating Willing Obedience Not Only to Laws, but Also to Magistrates." In *Philosophie für die Polis: Akten des 5. Kongresses der Gesellschaft für antike Philosophie 2016*, edited by Christoph Riedweg, 121–32. Berlin: De Gruyter, 2019.

Nicolay, René de. "Licentia: Cicero on the Suicide of Political Communities." *Classical Philology* 116 (2021): 537–62.

———. "The Origins of Licence: Excessive Freedom in Ancient Political Philosophy." PhD dissertation, Princeton University and the École Normale Supérieure, 2022.

———. "Plato on the Origins of Freedom Fetishism in Athens." Paper delivered at the Meeting of the Society for Classical Studies, Chicago, 2021.

Nightingale, Andrea. "Plato's Lawcode in Context: Rule by Written Law in Athens and Magnesia." *Classical Quarterly* 49, no. 1 (1999): 100–122.

———. "Writing/Reading a Sacred Text: A Literary Interpretation of Plato's *Laws*." *Classical Philology* 88, no. 4 (1993): 279–300.

Ober, Josiah. *Democracy and Knowledge: Innovation and Learning in Classical Athens.* Princeton, NJ: Princeton University Press, 2008.

———. "The Original Meaning of Democracy: Capacity to Do Things, Not Majority Rule." *Constellations* 15 (2008): 3–9.

———. *Political Dissent in Democratic Athens: Intellectual Critics of Popular Rule.* Princeton, NJ: Princeton University Press, 1998.

Ober, Josiah, and Barry R. Weingast. "The Sparta Game: Violence, Proportionality, Austerity, Collapse." In *How to Do Things with History*, edited by Danielle Allen, Paul Christesen, and Paul Millett, 161–84. Oxford: Oxford University Press, 2020.

Olympiodorus. *Commentary on Plato's "Gorgias."* Translated and edited by Robin Jackson, Kimon Lycos, and Harold Tarrant. Leiden: Brill, 1998.

———. *Olympiodori "In Platonis Gorgiam commentaria."* Edited by Leendert Gerrit Westerink. Leipzig: Teubner, 1970.

Osborne, Robin. "Vexatious Litigation in Classical Athens: Sykophancy and the Sykophant." In *Athens and Athenian Democracy*, edited by Robin Osborne, 205–28. Cambridge: Cambridge University Press, 2010.

Pausanias. *Description of Greece.* Vol. 2, *Books 3–5 ("Laconia," "Messenia," "Elis 1").* Translated by W.H.S. Jones and H. A. Ormerod. Cambridge, MA: Harvard University Press, 1926.

Pettit, Philip. *Just Freedom: A Moral Compass for a Complex World.* New York: W.W. Norton, 2014.

Philip, J. A. "The Platonic Corpus." *Phoenix* 24 (1970): 296–308.

Philostratus. *Apollonius of Tyana.* Vol. 1, *"Life of Apollonius of Tyana," Books 1–4.* Edited and translated by Christopher P. Jones. Cambridge, MA: Harvard University Press, 2005.

Pindar. *Pindar.* Vol. 1, *"Olympian Odes"; "Pythian Odes."* Edited and translated by William H. Race. Cambridge, MA: Harvard University Press, 1997.

———. *Pindar.* Vol. 2, *"Nemean Odes"; "Isthmian Odes"; Fragments.* Edited and translated by William H. Race. Cambridge, MA: Harvard University Press, 1997.

Piñeros Glasscock, Allison. "What Makes Degenerate Regimes Unhappy?" Unpublished Yale University Qualifying Paper, 2014. Microsoft Word document, 2014, on file with author.

Plato. *Apology.* See under Grube.

———. *Charmides.* See under Moore and Raymond.

———. *Euthyphro.* See under Grube.

———. *Gorgias.* See under Zeyl.

———. *Hippias minor.* See under Smith.

———. *Ion.* See under Woodruff.

———. *Laches.* See under Sprague.

———. *Laws.* See Burnet OCT. See also under Schofield, Meyer, Morrow, Saunders, Schöpsdau.

———. *Letters*. See under Morrow.

———. *Menexenus*. See under Ryan.

———. *Phaedo*. See under Grube.

———. *Protagoras*. See under Lombardo and Bell.

———. *Republic*. See Slings OCT, Burnet OCT. See also under Adam, Bloom, Chambry, Eggers Lan, Grube and Reeve, Krapinger, Lee, Leroux, Radice, Rufener, Sartori, Schleiermaacher, Vegetti.

———. *Sophist*. See under White.

———. *Statesman*. See Duke/Robinson OCT, Burnet OCT. See also under Brisson and Pradeau, Dixsaut et al., Giorgini, Migliori, Rowe.

———. *Theaetetus*. See under Levett and Burnyeat.

———. *Timaeus*. See under Zeyl.

Plutarch. *Vitae decem oratorum*. Edited by Anton Westermann. Leipzig: Theod. Becker, 1833.

Pocock, J.G.A. 1987. "The Concept of a Language and the *Métier d'Historien*: Some Considerations on Practice." In *The Languages of Political Theory in Early-Modern Europe*, edited by A. Pagden, 19–38. Cambridge: Cambridge University Press, 1987.

Poddighe, Elisabetta. "Aristotle on Legal Change." *Araucaria: Revista Iberoamericana de filosofía, política, humanidades y relaciones internacionales* 21 (2019): 183–207.

Popper, Karl R. *The Open Society and Its Enemies*. 2 vols. Princeton, NJ: Princeton University Press, 1963. First published 1945.

Posidonius. *Posidonius*. Vol. 1, *The Fragments*. Edited by Ludwig Edelstein and I. G. Kidd. Cambridge: University Press, 1972.

Pritchard, David M. "The Public Payment of Magistrates in Fourth-Century Athens." *Greek, Roman, and Byzantine Studies* 54 (2013): 1–16.

———. *Public Spending and Democracy in Classical Athens*. Austin: University of Texas Press, 2015.

Pritchett, W. Kendrick. *The Greek State at War*. Pts. 1 and 2. Berkeley: University of California Press, 1974.

Quandt, Kenneth. "A Commentary on Plato's *Republic*." OnPlatosRepublic, version of October 20, 2020. http://www.onplatosrepublic.com/.

Raaflaub, Kurt A. "Archaic and Classical Greek Reflections on Politics and Government: From Description to Conceptualization, Analysis, and Theory." In Beck, *Ancient Greek Government*, 73–92.

———. "Homer to Solon: The Rise of the Polis, the Written Sources." In *The Ancient Greek City-State: Symposium on the Occasion of the 250th Anniversary of the Royal Danish Academy of Sciences and Letters, July 1–4 1992*, edited by Mogens Herman Hansen, 41–105. Copenhagen: Munksgaard, 1993.

Radice, Roberto, ed. and trans. *Platone: "La repubblica."* In *Tutti gli scritti*, edited by Giacomo Reale. Milan: Bompani, 2000.

Rancière, Jacques. "Does Democracy Mean Something?" In *Adieu Derrida*, edited by Costas Douzinas, 84–100. Basingstoke, UK: Palgrave Macmillan, 2007.

Rancière, Jacques, Rachel Bowlby, and Davide Panagia. "Ten Theses on Politics." *Theory and Event* 5, no. 3 (2001). https://doi.org/10.1353/tae.2001.0028.

Raz, Joseph. *The Morality of Freedom*. Oxford: Clarendon, 1986.

Rehfeld, Andrew. "On Representing." *Journal of Political Philosophy* 26, no. 2 (2018): 216–39.

Reid, Jeremy. "Changing the Laws of the *Laws*." *Ancient Philosophy* 41 (2021): 413–41.

———. "The Offices of Magnesia." *Polis* 37 (2020): 567–89.

———. "Voting for the Guardians: Election, Lottery, and Moderated Democracy in Plato's *Laws*." Paper presented at the Meeting of the Society for Classical Studies, Chicago, 2021.

Rhodes, Peter J. *A Commentary on the Aristotelian "Athenaion Politeia."* Reprint of 2nd ed. Oxford: Oxford University Press, 2006.

Rhodes, Peter J., and Robin Osborne, eds. *Greek Historical Inscriptions, 404–323 BC.* Oxford: Oxford University Press, 2003.

Roberts, Jennifer Tolbert. *Accountability in Athenian Government.* Madison: University of Wisconsin Press, 1982.

Robinson, Eric W. *The First Democracies: Early Popular Government outside Athens.* Stuttgart: F. Steiner Verlag, 1997.

———. *Democracy beyond Athens: Popular Government in the Greek Classical Age.* Cambridge: Cambridge University Press, 2011.

Rosen, Michael. "Liberalism, Republicanism and the Public Philosophy of American Democracy." In *Die Weltgeschichte—das Weltgericht? Stuttgarter Hegel-Kongress 1999*, edited by Rüdiger Bubner and Walter Mesch, 261–79. Stuttgart: Klett-Cotta, 2001.

Rosen, Stanley. *Plato's "Statesman": The Web of Politics.* New Haven, CT: Yale University Press, 1995.

Rousseau, Jean-Jacques. *"The Social Contract" and "The First and Second Discourses."* Edited by Susan Dunn. New Haven, CT: Yale University Press, 2002.

Rowe, Christopher J. Introduction to *Plato: "Statesman."* Edited and translated by Rowe, 1–20. Warminster, UK: Aris and Phillips, 1995.

———, trans. *Statesman.* By Plato. In Cooper, *Plato.*

Rufener, Rudolph, ed. and trans. *Platon: "Der Staat."* Düsseldorf: Artemis and Winkler, 2000.

Ryan, Paul, trans. *Menexenus.* By Plato. In Cooper, *Plato.*

Sandel, Michael J. *Democracy's Discontent: America in Search of a Public Philosophy.* Cambridge, MA: Harvard University Press, 1996.

Sartori, Franco, ed. and trans. *"Repubblica": Platone.* Bari, Italy: Laterza, 2005.

Saunders, Trevor J., trans. *Laws.* By Plato. In Cooper, *Plato.*

Saxonhouse, Arlene W. "Democracy, Equality, and *Eidē*: A Radical View from Book 8 of Plato's *Republic." American Political Science Review* 92 (1998): 273–83.

———. *Free Speech and Democracy in Ancient Athens.* Cambridge: Cambridge University Press, 2006.

Schleiermacher, Friedrich, ed. and trans. *Platons "Staat."* Berlin: G. Reimer, 1828.

Schlosser, Joel Alden. *What Would Socrates Do? Self-Examination, Civic Engagement, and the Politics of Philosophy.* Cambridge: Cambridge University Press, 2014.

Schofield, Malcolm. *Cicero: Political Philosophy.* Oxford: Oxford University Press, 2021.

———. "The Disappearing Philosopher King." In *Saving the City*, 37–54.

———. "Law and Absolutism in the *Republic." Polis: Journal for Ancient Greek and Roman Political Thought* 23 (2006): 319–27.

———. *Plato: Political Philosophy.* Oxford: Oxford University Press, 2006.

———, ed. *Plato: "The Laws."* Translated by Tom Griffith. New York: Cambridge University Press, 2016. Translation cited as Schofield/Griffith.

———. "Plato, Xenophon, and the Laws of Lycurgus." *Polis: Journal for Ancient Greek and Roman Political Thought* 38 (2021): 450–72.

———. "Religion and Philosophy in the *Laws.*" In *Plato's "Laws": From Theory into Practice, Proceedings of the VI Symposium Platonicum; Selected Papers*, edited by Samuel Scolnicov and Luc Brisson, 1–13. Sankt Augustin, Germany: Academia Verlag, 2003.

———, ed. *Saving the City: Philosopher-Kings and Other Classical Paradigms.* Florence, KY: Taylor and Francis, 1999.

Schöpsdau, Klaus, trans. *Platon, Werke*. Vol. 9.2. *"Nomoi" (Gesetze) Buch I–III*. With commentary by Schöpsdau. Göttingen, Germany: Vandenhoeck and Ruprecht, 1994.

——, trans. *Platon, Werke*. Vol. 9.2. *"Nomoi" (Gesetze) Buch IV–VII*. With commentary by Schöpsdau. Göttingen, Germany: Vandenhoeck and Ruprecht, 2003.

——, trans. *Platon, Werke*. Vol. 9.2. *"Nomoi" (Gesetze) Buch VIII–X*. With commentary by Schöpsdau. Göttingen, Germany: Vandenhoeck and Ruprecht, 2011.

Scott, Dominic. *Listening to Reason in Plato and Aristotle*. Oxford: Oxford University Press, 2020.

Seaford, Richard. *Money and the Early Greek Mind: Homer, Philosophy, Tragedy*. Cambridge: Cambridge University Press, 2004.

Sedley, David. "Philosophy, the Forms, and the Art of Ruling." In *The Cambridge Companion to Plato's "Republic,"* edited by G.R.F. Ferrari, 256–83. Cambridge: Cambridge University Press, 2007.

Seto, Ken-ichi. "Distinguishing Metonymy from Synecdoche." In *Metonymy in Language and Thought*, edited by Klaus-Uwe Panther and Günter Radden, 91–120. Philadelphia: John Benjamins, 1999.

Shapiro, Gabriel. "Essentialism in Late Plato and Aristotle's 'Categories.'" PhD dissertation, Princeton University, 2022.

Sikkenga, J. "Plato's Examination of the Oligarchic Soul in Book VIII of the *Republic*." *History of Political Thought* 23 (2002): 377–400.

Silverman, Allan. "Ascent and Descent: The Philosopher's Regret." *Social Philosophy and Policy* 24 (2007): 40–69.

Simonton, Matthew W. *Classical Greek Oligarchy: A Political History*. Princeton, NJ: Princeton University Press, 2017.

Sissa, Giulia. "Caregivers of the Polis, Partygoers and Lotus-Eaters: Politics of Pleasure and Care in Plato's *Republic*." In *Philosophie für die Polis: Akten des 5. Kongresses der Geschellschaft für antike Philosophie 2016*, edited by Christoph Riedweg, 173–99. Berlin: De Gruyter, 2019.

Skinner, Quentin. "Thomas Hobbes: Rhetoric and the Construction of Morality." *Proceedings of the British Academy* 76 (1991): 1–61.

Slings, S. R., ed. *Platonis "Rempublicam."* Oxford Classical Texts. Oxford: Clarendon, 2003.

Smith, Nicholas D., trans. *Lesser Hippias*. By Plato. In Cooper, *Plato*.

Sommerstein, Alan, and Andrew Bayliss. *Oath and State in Ancient Greece*. Berlin: De Gruyter, 2013.

Sørensen, Anders Dahl. "Political Office and the Rule of Law in Plato's *Statesman*." *Polis* 35 (2019): 401–17.

——. "The Second Best City and Its Laws in Plato's *Statesman*." *Archiv für Geschichte der Philosophie* 104 (2022): 1–25.

Sprague, Rosamond Kent, trans. *Laches*. By Plato. In Cooper, *Plato*.

Stalley, R. F. *An Introduction to Plato's "Laws."* Indianapolis: Hackett, 1983.

Steinberger, Peter. "Ruling: Guardians and Philosopher Kings." *American Political Science Review* 83 (1989): 1207–25.

Steiner, Hillel. *An Essay on Rights*. Oxford: Blackwell, 1994.

Stout, Jeffrey. "Religion since Cicero." Gifford Lecture (number 1) delivered as part of the Gifford Lectures, "Religion Unbound: Ideals and Powers from Cicero to King," University of Edinburgh, 2017.

Straumann, Benjamin. *Crisis and Constitutionalism: Roman Political Thought from the Fall of the Republic to the Age of Revolution*. New York: Oxford University Press, 2016.

——. "The Energy of Concepts: The Role of Concepts in Long-Term Intellectual History and Social Reality." *Journal of the Philosophy of History* 14 (2019): 147–82.

Tecuşan, Manuela. "*Logos Sympotikos*: Patterns of the Irrational in Philosophical Drinking; Plato outside the *Symposium*." In *Sympotica: A symposium on the Symposion*, edited by Oswyn Murray, 238–60. Oxford: Oxford University Press, 1990.

Thakkar, Jonny. *Plato as Critical Theorist*. Cambridge, MA: Harvard University Press, 2018.

Theophrastus. *Characters*. In *"Characters"; Herodas, "Mimes"; Sophron; and Other Mime Fragments*, edited and translated by Jeffrey Rusten and I. C. Cunningham, 3rd ed. Cambridge, MA: Harvard University Press, 2003.

Thomas, Rosalind. "Written in Stone? Liberty, Equality, Orality and the Codification of Law." In *Greek Law in Its Political Setting: Justifications Not Justice*, edited by Lin Foxhall and Andrew D. E. Lewis, 8–31. New York: Oxford University Press, 1996.

Thomson, Judith Jarvis. *Normativity*. Chicago: Open Court, 2008.

Thucydides. *History III*. Edited and translated by P. J. Rhodes. Warminster, UK: Aris and Phillips, 1994.

Todd, Stephen C. *The Shape of Athenian Law*. Oxford: Clarendon, 1993.

———. "Writing the Law in Early Greece?" *Polis* 11 (1992): 28–39.

Trivigno, Franco V. "Above the Law and Out for Justice." In *Plato's "Statesman": A Philosophical Discussion*, edited by Panos Dimas, Melissa Lane, and Susan Sauvé Meyer, 156–76. Oxford: Oxford University Press, 2021.

Tuck, Richard. *The Sleeping Sovereign: The Invention of Modern Democracy*. Cambridge: Cambridge University Press, 2016.

Vegetti, Mario, ed. and trans. *"La repubblica": Platone*. With commentary by Vegetti. 7 vols. Naples: Bibliopolis, 1998–2007.

Vermeule, Adrian. *Common Good Constitutionalism*. Cambridge: Polity, 2022.

Viehoff, Daniel. "Authority and Expertise." *Journal of Political Philosophy* 24 (2016): 406–26.

Villacéque, Noémie. "De la bigarrure en politique (Platon *République* 8.557c4–61e7)." *Journal of Hellenic Studies* 130 (2010): 137–52.

Vlastos, Gregory. "Slavery in Plato's Thought." In *Platonic Studies*, 2nd ed., 146–63. Princeton, NJ: Princeton University Press, 1981.

Vogt, Katja M. *Belief and Truth: A Skeptic Reading of Plato*. New York: Oxford University Press, 2012.

Waldron, Jeremy. "Accountability and Insolence." In *Political Political Theory: Essays on Institutions*, 167–94. Cambridge, MA: Harvard University Press, 2016.

Wallace, Robert W. *The Areopagus Council to 307 B.C.* Baltimore: Johns Hopkins University Press, 1989.

———. "Councils in Greek Oligarchies and Democracies." In Beck, *Ancient Greek Government*, 191–204.

Wallach, John R. *The Platonic Political Art: A Study of Critical Reason and Democracy*. University Park: Pennsylvania State University Press, 2001.

Walling, Ian. "Power and Vulnerability: Plato's *Gorgias* in Context." PhD dissertation, Princeton University, 2021.

Walzer, Michael. *The Company of Critics: Social Criticism and Political Commitment in the Twentieth Century*. New York: Basic Books, 1988.

Weiss, Roslyn. *Philosophers in Plato's "Republic": Plato's Two Paradigms*. Ithaca, NY: Cornell University Press, 2012.

White, Nicholas. "The Rulers' Choice." *Archiv für Geschichte der Philosophie* 68 (1986): 22–46.

———, trans. *Sophist*. By Plato. In Cooper, *Plato*.

White, Stephen A. "Thrasymachus the Diplomat." *Classical Philology* 90 (1995): 307–27.

Willetts, Ronald F. *The Law Code of Gortyn*. Berlin: De Gruyter, 1967.

Williams, Bernard. "The Analogy of City and Soul in Plato's *Republic*." In *Exegesis and Argument: Studies in Greek Philosophy Presented to Gregory Vlastos*, edited by

Edward N. Lee, Alexander P. D. Mourelatos, and Richard M. Rorty, 196–206. Assen, Netherlands: Van Gorcum, 1973.

Withington, Phil. *The Politics of Commonwealth: Citizens and Freemen in Early Modern England*. Cambridge: Cambridge University Press, 2005.

Wohl, Victoria. *Law's Cosmos: Juridical Discourse in Athenian Forensic Oratory*. Cambridge: Cambridge University Press, 2010.

———. *Love among the Ruins: The Erotics of Democracy in Classical Athens*. Princeton, NJ: Princeton University Press, 2009.

Wolfsdorf, David. *Trials of Reason: Plato and the Crafting of Philosophy*. Oxford: Oxford University Press, 2008.

Wolin, Sheldon S. *Fugitive Democracy and Other Essays*, edited by Nicholas Xenos. Princeton, NJ, and Oxford: Princeton University Press, 2016.

Woodruff, Paul. "Plato's Early Theory of Knowledge." In *Essays on the Philosophy of Socrates*, edited by Hugh H. Benson, 86–106. Oxford: Oxford University Press, 1992.

Worthington, Ian, Felix K. Maier, Stephan Schorn, and Hans-Joachim Gehrke, eds. "Jacoby Online." Leiden: Brill, August 17, 2007. https://brill.com/view/db/bnjo.

Xenophon. *Hellenica*. Edited by E. C. Marchant. Notes by G. E. Underhill. Salem, NH: Ayer, 1984.

———. *Hellenica: Books I–IV*. Translated by Carleton L. Brownson. Cambridge, MA: Harvard University Press, 2003. Translation first published 1918.

———. *The "Hellenica" ("Greek History") of Xenophon of Athens: A Facing-Page Critical Edition and Translation from Greek into English*. Edited by F. Donald and Ralph E. Doty. Lewiston, NY: Edwin Mellen, 2006.

———. *"Hellenika" I–II.3.10*. Edited and translated by Peter Krentz. Warminster, UK: Aris and Philips, 1989.

———. *"Hellenika" II.3.11–IV.2.8*. Edited and translated by Peter Krentz. Warminster, UK: Aris and Philips, 1995.

———. *Helléniques: Livres I–III*. Edited by J. Hatzfeld. Paris: Les Belles Lettres, 2003.

———. *The Landmark Xenophon's Hellenika: A New Translation*. Translated by John Marincola. Edited by Robert B. Strassler. Introduction by David Thomas. New York: Pantheon Books, 2009.

———. *"Memorabilia," "Oeconomicus," "Symposium," "Apology."* Translated by E. C. Marchant and O. J. Todd. Revised by Jeffrey Henderson. Cambridge, MA: Harvard University Press, 2013.

———. *Xenophon on Government*. Edited by Vivienne J. Gray. Cambridge: Cambridge University Press, 2007.

———. *Xenophon's "Spartan Constitution": Introduction, Text, Commentary*. Edited by Michael Lipka. Berlin: De Gruyter, 2002.

———. *Xenophontos: ELLHNIKA*. Edited by Carolus [Karl] Hude. Leipzig: B. G. Teubner, 1930.

Yau, Claudia. "Wisdom in Plato and Aristotle." PhD dissertation, Princeton University, 2021.

Yoon, Jiseob. "The Role of Law in Plato's Political Philosophy: A Prospectus." Dissertation prospectus, approved by the Department of Politics, Princeton University, 2020. Microsoft Word document, 2020, on file with author.

Young, Carl. "Plato's Concept of Liberty in the *Laws*." *History of Political Thought* 39 (2018): 379–98.

Zadorojnyi, Alexei V. "Transcribing Plato's Voice: The Platonic Intertext between Writtenness and Orality." In *Gods, Daimones, Rituals, Myths and History of Religions in Plutarch's Works: Studies Devoted to Professor Frederick E. Brenk by the International Plutarch Society*, edited by Luc Van der Stockt, Frances Titchener, Heinz G. Ingenkamp, and Aurelio Pérez Jiménez, 467–92. Logan: University of Utah, Department of History, 2010.

Zeyl, Donald J., trans. *Gorgias*. By Plato. In Cooper, *Plato*.

——, trans. *Timaeus*. By Plato. In Cooper, *Plato*.

Zhang, Alex. "The Muses and Political *Stasis* in *Republic* 8." Unpublished Yale University term paper. Microsoft Word document, 2014, on file with author.

Zimecki, Christian. "The (Ambiguous) Moral Status of Pleonectic Behavior." Unpublished Princeton University paper as part of doctoral dissertation research in progress. Microsoft Word document, version of 2022, on file with author.

Zuckert, Catherine H. *Plato's Philosophers: The Coherence of the Dialogues*. Chicago: University of Chicago Press, 2009.

abuse of power or office, 29–32, 29n65, 167–69, 171, 186–87, 205, 239, 243, 294. *See also* accountability; corruption; exploitation of the ruled; flawed constitutions in cities

accountability, 3–7, 3n1, 9, 15, 15n30, 19, 26, 31–32, 44, 53–54, 60, 60n47, 63–64, 97, 97nn29–30, 103–6, 109, 114, 188, 214–15n3, 214–15, 241, 336, 345n37; accountability to superordinate rulers, 15, 38–39, 53, 64, 218, 231, 244, 263, 273; accountability to the ruled, 54, 64, 69–70, 218; in Athens (*see under* Athens); of auditors (*euthunoi*), 97, 99–102, 102n38; in constitutional systems other than democracies, 59n42; in *Laws*, 36, 53, 97–98, 103–6 (see also *Laws*); and philosopher-kings/senior rulers, 27, 219–22, 244, 246; and practice of philosophical dialectic, 220–22; principal-agent model of, 207–9, 211, 398–401, 399n31, 403; in *Republic*, 9, 53, 218–22, 244, 246 (see also *Republic*); in *Statesman*, 9, 37 (see also *Statesman*); unaccountable rulers, 3, 4, 5, 8, 18n37, 95–96, 368; and wages (*see* wages). See also *euthunai*; Juvenal conundrum; office, parameters of/ limits on

Achilles, 49, 281n60

Adam, James, 235, 251n4, 278n55

Adeimantus, as interlocutor in *Republic*, 42, 75n87, 140, 161n54 (see also *Republic*; *specific topics*)

Aeschines, 57–58, 58nn39–41, 68n68, 69, 190, 200, 217, 235

Aeschylus, 49, 60, 60n46, 305

Agamemnon, 49, 274

age cohorts of guardians in *Republic*, 38–39, 178, 179n14, 201, 210, 214–16, 218–20, 222–44, 250, 263–64, 275–79; eldest cohort as rulers/reigning, 38–39, 176n8, 178, 183, 215, 218–19, 225, 232–44, 263 (see also philosopher-

kings/queens); middle-aged cohort as apprentice rulers (officeholders, military commanders), 38–39, 213, 216–18, 225, 227–31, 246, 262 (see also officeholders); youngest cohort as auxiliaries (soldiers, procreators, students), 39, 178, 223–27 (see also auxiliaries). *See also* guardians

Allen, Danielle, 107, 292

anarchos, 303–4, 303n108

anarchy/*anarchia*, 10, 26, 40–41, 72, 253, 305–6, 328, 382–84, 388, 405, 405n46, 409; and absence of rule in the soul, 254, 327, 329; *anarchia* defined, 305n116; and democracy, 303–6, 328, 404–8; and freedom, 305, 328, 374; and lawlessness, 305n116, 306; modern and post-modern ideas of democracy and anarchism, 404–8; philosophical anarchism, 382–84, 408–9; and the tyrannical man, 327–29, 327n17, 331; tyranny as form of anarchy, 39, 40, 47, 253, 306, 316–17

anax, 48n11

anomia, 327, 329, 405. *See also* lawlessness

antianarchia [English coinage by author], 40–41, 383–84, 409

anupeuthunos/aneuthunos, 14n28, 18n37, 60n47, 95–97, 97n29, 99, 215n4

appetitive part of the soul, 262, 266, 320, 321, 323–27, 323n9, 330, 332–34, 336–37, 339–42, 346, 353

Applbaum, Arthur, 25nn52–53

apprentice rulers. *See under* officeholders

Aquinas, Thomas, 407n49

archai (plural of *archē*), 43, 44, 65n56, 67, 124, 209, 216, 216n6; in *Republic*, 213, 216–17; in *Statesman*, 124, 136. *See also* officeholders

archē, 3n3, 4, 8, 10, 16, 33n73, 42–43, 45, 62, 62n49, 65–71, 65n57, 68n68, 142, 147, 193n48, 194, 213, 216–17, 229; as "empire," 52n26, 67n67; history of

archē (*continued*)
    term use, 65; in *Laws*, 9–10; as "office," 4, 10n16, 53, 68n68, 155, 162, 163, 172, 229, 335; in *Republic*, 9–10, 142, 147, 156, 158, 162, 163, 172, 179, 201, 213, 246; as "rule," 4, 65, 136, 142, 143, 147, 156, 158, 328; as "rule" or "office," 3, 42, 67, 179, 213; in *Statesman*, 9–10, 116, 136, 137, 138, 147n21

archein (to rule/hold office), 147n21, 193n48, 194; Arendt and, 13n26; and empire, 52n26; in *Laws*, 91n14, 97n29; in *Republic*, 148n23, 163–64, 179, 180n15, 201, 216, 235, 240, 246, 302; in *Statesman*, 10, 116, 117, 117n5, 121, 121n14, 124, 136, 137, 139, 147n21; and terms of address, 201, 202; translation issues, 3n3, 68, 68n68, 70, 117n5, 121n14, 164, 216, 228, 228n23; and vocabulary of rule and office, 8, 10, 42–43, 45, 65–71, 121, 121n14, 216–17, 229

archōn (participle of *archein*, also commonly transliterated as *archon*), *ho archon*, 62, 62n49, 67, 68, 113, 113n73, 117n5, 126, 126n29, 127; *archon basileus* (*see under* Athens: king-archon in). See also *archontes/archontos* (other frequently used participles of *archein*)

archontes/archontos (participles in nom. pl./gen. sg.), *hoi archontes*, 42, 42n1, 44, 62n49, 67, 68, 69, 69n72, 121, 121n14, 183n28, 201, 202, 232, 273, 273n45, 294, 297n92; board of *archontes* in Athens, 62, 68n68, 69, 127. *See also* terms of address

[*ho*] *archos* (military leader/naval commander), 65n57

Arendt, Hannah, 11–13, 11n17, 13n26, 148n25, 386n10

Areopagus Council, 15, 15n30, 19, 214–15n3, 214–15, 241

aristocracy, 143, 143n9, 245–46, 279

Aristophanes, 60n47, 160, 210–11, 224, 292

Aristotle, 15n30, 18, 28, 59n45, 68n68, 93n20, 134, 175, 283n62, 295, 298–99, 316

Arruzza, Cinzia, 270n42, 324n10, 354n3

Assembly, 60, 97nn29–30, 209n72, 299, 311, 312

Atack, Carol, 46n7, 48, 48n10

Athenian Visitor (protagonist in *Laws*), 30, 74–76, 80, 81, 88, 88n4 (see also *Laws*; *specific topics*)

Athens, 15, 51, 55, 59n45, 60–61, 100, 162–63, 191, 191n42, 191n44, 193–94, 228, 242, 298–99, 300n100, 312, 336, 375–77, 379; accountability of officeholders in, 5, 55, 60–61, 100, 100n34, 187n35, 214 (see also *euthunai*); Aeschines and, 57–58, 58nn39–41; ancestral constitution, 15, 62, 184, 215, 298–99, 376–78; and Areopagus Council, 15, 15n30, 214–15n3, 214–15, 241; Assembly (*see* Assembly); board of *archontes*, 62, 68n68, 69, 127; codification of laws, 387; degeneration of ancestral constitution, 378; as democracy, 5, 17, 55n33, 57, 58n39, 89, 100, 108n59, 121, 134, 172n1, 181, 189, 199, 209, 214, 226, 228, 242, 298–99, 301, 329, 336, 378; eligibility criteria for officeholders, 226, 301; *euthunai* (end-of-term audit procedures), 57–59, 100, 100n34, 208n67, 214 (see also *euthunai*); folk histories of Athenian political evolution, 3–5, 44, 209–10, 375–79; the Four Hundred, 61, 184n29, 189; king-archon (*archon basileus*) in, 3n1, 5, 102, 117; limits on offices and officeholders, 55–61, 55nn32–34, 230–31; *nomophulakes* (law guardians) in, 103; oligarchic regimes in, 61, 184n29 (*see also* the Four Hundred; the Thirty *under this heading*); Peisistratid dynasty, 46, 46n7; powers of offices, 16, 56, 56n35; scrutiny of chosen officeholders prior to taking office, 14, 55–57, 89; selection of officeholders, 57, 226, 297n92, 312; the Thirty, 15, 58n39, 161n53, 184n29, 189, 193–94, 193n48; transformation from kingship to accountable office, 3–5, 3n1, 44; unaccountable jurors and assemblymen, 60, 60n47, 97nn29–30; use of *archon* as title for officeholder(s), 3n1, 68–69nn68–69, 68–69; wages paid to officeholders, 55, 61, 89, 161n53, 175, 184n29, 189

auditors (*euthunoi*), 36, 88, 97, 99–103, 101n36, 102n38

audit procedures in Greek polities. See *euthunai*

auxiliaries (younger guardians in *Republic*), 178, 193–94, 214, 223–27, 270n41, 271, 275, 276, 278–83; and education, 39, 224, 227, 243 (*see also* education); and failures of scrutiny, 275–76; prohibited from having wealth, property, and kinship ties, 196–97 (*see also under* guardians); safeguarded by superordinate rulers, 38, 218, 243; as soldiers and procreators, 183n28, 223, 224, 226, 246; and terms of address, 199; wages for, 196–98. *See also* guardians

Bakunin, Michael, 406
Balot, Ryan, 220
Bambrough, Renford, 146
Barney, Rachel, 173n2
Bartels, Myrthe L., 77n91
basileuein, 38, 47, 178, 213, 219, 235–36. *See also* reigning
basileus, 46n7, 47–48, 48n11. *See also* kings
Beck, Hans, 17n35
Bekker, Immanuel, 215n4
Berlin, Isaiah, 380
Biden, Joseph R., 119n8
Billings, Joshua, 73n82
Blok, Josine, 65n56
Bloom, Allan, 42n1, 43n2, 216n6, 304n112
Bobonich, Christopher, 80, 372–73, 384
Bordes, Jacqueline, 36, 62, 62n49, 71
boulē, 108
Brock, Roger, 211, 211n76
Brown, Eric, 166n65
Brunschwig, Jacques, 96
Burnyeat, Myles, 274n46, 321n5
Butler, Judith, 405

Callicles (interlocutor in *Gorgias*), 19, 51, 173, 245
Cammack, Daniela, 68n68, 208n71, 233n29
Camp, J. M., 191n44
caring, 37, 58n41, 95, 106, 119, 119n9, 131, 382; caring for the good of the ruled, 19–20, 37, 49–51, 382 (*see also* good of the ruled); and defining mark of

correct rule, 390, 391; and guardians (*phulakes*), 181–82, 223–24 (*see also* guardians); intertwining of ruling, caring, and weaving in *Statesman*, 132–33; and kings as shepherds, 49–51, 119–20 (*see also* shepherds); in *Laws*, 106; and philosopher-kings/senior rulers, 15n32, 237, 238; in *Republic*, 37, 106, 149–52, 237; in *Statesman*, 37, 106, 117, 119–20, 123, 131, 382. *See also* good of the ruled; therapeutic *technai*

Carugati, Federica, 63n53
character of representative men in *Republic* books 8–9. *See* democratic man; flawed constitutions within souls; oligarchic man; timocratic man; tyrannical man

Cicero, 379n41, 389n13
cities: all cities except for a *kallipolis* as unstable, 249n2; city-man comparison, 319, 319n2, 320, 335, 337–38, 342, 347; city "of good men," 164–65; city-soul analogy, 257–58, 257nn18–19, 262; and civil war/revolution, 295–97, 312, 314; distinctions and parallels between rule in the soul and rule in a city, 254–55; divided into rich and poor, 288–89, 296–97; and drone imagery, 292–93; dystopian cities, 33–34, 34n74 (*see also* anarchy/*anarchia*; tyranny); and flawed constitutions (*see* democracy; flawed constitutions in cities; oligarchy; timocracy; tyranny); founding and establishment of constitutional order, 180–83, 206; happiness within, based on type of ruler, 236; and internalization of civic forces and externalization of psychic forces, 257n18, 259n22; lack of proper membership in, 290–92; and terms of address, 197–207; and Thracians principle, 265–67. *See also* Athens; Dreros; *kallipolis*; Magnesia

citizens of Greek polities, 70, 120, 123, 125, 132–35, 197–207, 246n49, 298–99, 366. *See also* *dēmos*; obedience of the ruled; officeholders; subjects of rule

Cleinias (interlocutor in *Laws*), 80, 81, 88, 88n4 (see also *Laws*)

coercion/force, 81, 332, 371n26, 384–89, 392–95; and double theory of law in *Laws*, 80, 89, 93, 93n19, 381, 384–86, 407; relationship between law and coercion, 381–82, 384–89, 406–7; rule as not necessarily coercive, 18, 388, 397, 401, 406–8; and rule in the soul, 320, 347; and unwilling subjects, 380
common good constitutionalism, 28–30
competitive emulation, 285–87, 335
compossibility, 355, 357–62, 375, 376, 378–80, 384; defined, 356–58
Condren, Conal, 66n60
constitutions (*politeiai*), 26, 34, 51, 61–63, 90, 122n18, 137, 188, 228; account-ability procedures in, 6, 55–56, 55n33, 137, 231 (*see also* accountability; *euthunai*; office, parameters of/limits on); articulated in terms of offices and laws, 71, 72, 213, 231, 244; Bordes and, 62, 62n49; classification of, 245; con-stitutional project for a *kallipolis* (see *kallipolis*; *Republic*); constitutional project for Magnesia (*see* Magnesia; *Laws*); constitutional project in *Statesman*, 72, 120–23, 133–39, 383, 390–92 (see also *Statesman*); and discursive legislation, 77–82 (*see also* discursive legislation); flawed consti-tutions and degeneration of rule and office, 39–40, 116n4, 136–39, 171, 219, 249–317 (*see also* flawed constitutions in cities); garden-variety constitution-alism, 10, 40, 356, 358, 361, 367–69, 388, 397; and Juvenal conundrum, 6–7, 15 (*see also* Juvenal conundrum); Lane and, 63n53; noocracy, 92; and parameters of office (*see* office, par-ameters of/limits on); Plato's *Politeia* translated as "*Republic*," 71; sequence of flawed constitutions in *Republic*, 39, 250–51, 271–317; and *Statesman*, 116n4, 136–39, 390–92; Straumann and, 63n53; translation issues, 6n8, 63n53; vulnerabilities of constitutional rule, 6–7, 32–34, 64, 114, 187 (*see also* Athens; Crete; democracy; flawed constitutions in cities; Juvenal conun-drum; *kallipolis*; oligarchy; Sparta; timocracy)

Cooper, John M., 166n65
cooperation, 40, 41, 356, 358, 361, 366, 368, 387–89. *See also* obedience of the ruled
Cordelli, Chiara, 16n34
corruption, 30, 32–34, 64, 90, 155, 169, 187, 286, 295, 376, 379; and *euthunai* procedures, 55n33, 99; and human nature, 95–96, 96n27; and philo-sophical nature of rulers, 187, 205; and prohibition of wealth, property, and kinship ties for guardians in *Repub-lic*, 177–78, 185–87; and psychology of the suitable candidate for role of ruler, 23, 168–69; rulers exploiting the ruled/pursuing their own good, 7, 18–19, 21–22, 40, 47, 145, 148, 153, 173, 192–93, 200, 245, 263, 279, 282–83, 317, 348, 349, 373, 396; safeguarded against by the rational part of the soul, 348; safeguarding against corruption of superordinate rulers, 187, 219–20; and under- and overidentification of a person with their professional role, 171; and wages, 219–20. *See also* abuse of power or office; accountability
Crete, 54, 61, 260, 281–82
Critias, 62
Ctesiphon, 58, 58n40, 68
Cyrus, 200, 202, 375–76

Daily Meeting, 94, 106–14, 107n54, 176n8
degeneration of rule and office, 39–40, 249–350; transition from democracy to tyranny, 301, 306, 309–16, 330; transition from *kallipolis* to timoc-racy, 272–79; transition from oligar-chy to democracy, 293–97; transition from timocracy to oligarchy, 283–88. *See also* democracy; Disunity princi-ple; education; flawed constitutions in cities; oligarchy; Predominance principle; timocracy; tyranny
Delian League, 51
democracy, 138n54, 301, 304–14, 377–80; and accountability to the people, 214, 218; and *anarchia*, 303–6, 328, 404–8; and aversion to obeying officehold-ers or holding office, 302, 304–6; and city-man comparison, 335; conflation

of democratic city and democratic man, 257n18; constitution described, 297–310; democratic Athens, 5, 17, 55n33, 57, 58n39, 89, 100, 108n59, 121, 134, 172n1, 181, 189, 199, 209, 214, 226, 228, 242, 298–99, 301, 329, 336, 378; and Disunity principle, 306, 308–9, 311–12, 314; and drone imagery, 260, 310–13; and education, 299; emergence from an oligarchy, 295–97; and epitactic dimension of rule, 378; faults of, 187, 290, 300–310, 313–14, 329; and freedom/permissiveness, 300–301, 301n103, 306, 309–11, 328; and hierarchical nature of rule, 398; kingly reign within, 235; Kolodny and, 383, 387–404, 398–99nn29, 31; and language of slavery, 378; and lawlessness, 138n54, 306, 309; Lefort and, 405; and modern and post-modern ideas of anarchism, 404–8; as "no rule," 383; and obedience to officeholders, 377–80; and oligarchs, 307, 313; and power gained by the *dēmos*, 209–10, 312–13; and Predominance principle, 298, 300, 311–12; problematic relation of democratic majority to officeholding, 301–4; proximate causes of constitutional change, 306–9; Rancière and, 405; and rule by the multitude, 70, 246n49; selection of officeholders, 297, 297n92, 300, 300n101; and sequence of flawed constitutions, 251, 259n20; and sharing in the constitution, 297–99, 298n96, 301–2; social classes in, 311, 312; and *telos* and *taxis* of rule, 302–4, 308–9; and terms of address, 198; and transition to tyranny, 301, 306, 309–16, 330; and wages paid to officeholders, 56, 89, 174–75, 178, 184; way of life in a democracy, 299, 301. *See also* Assembly; Athens; degeneration of rule and office

democratic man, 40, 251, 258, 260, 320, 322, 322n7, 324, 327–28, 332–35, 334n27; character of, 334–35; city-man comparison, 257n18, 335; genesis of, 324, 328, 332–34, 334n25; and rule in the soul, 334, 334n26, 347; way of life, 321, 324, 334, 334n26

democratic theory, 11n17, 31–32, 70n73; Honig and, 387n28; Kolodny's relational egalitarian theory, 383, 387–404, 398–99nn29, 31

dēmos, 33, 60, 62, 68n68, 97, 97n29, 147, 178, 198, 209–10, 209n72, 233, 313, 314. *See also* citizens of Greek polities; subjects of rule

Demosthenes, 58, 58nn40–41, 60, 182, 200

despotēs, 118n6

dialectic, 39, 220–22, 227

dialogues of Plato: author's approach to study of, 9n13, 30–31, 71–83; certain characters in dialogues as avatars of Plato, 9n13, 30, 74–76; cities in, 30–31 (see also *kallipolis*; Magnesia); commonalities, 72–73; as complementary to each other, 30, 73–74, 73n81; and constitutional project (*see* constitutions); developmentalist approach to, 73; and discursive legislation, 77–82 (*see also* discursive legislation); interpretive stances regarding, 71–83; political figures in, 44–64 (*see also* guardians; kings; officeholders; philosopher-kings/queens; statesman; tyrants); titles discussed, 71, 71n77; unitarian approach to, 73

Diogenes Laertius, 71n77, 74n85

discursive legislation (legislation "in speech"), 39, 77–82, 104, 182n26; in *Laws*, 77–82, 88, 88n5, 92, 96, 104, 107, 109, 111, 111n67; in relation to *Statesman*, 81–82, 123; in *Republic*, 39, 77–82, 140, 141, 176–77, 182, 182n26, 186, 206

Disunity principle, 264–65, 269–79, 284, 287–88, 291n81, 295–97, 306, 308–9, 311–12, 314, 330, 349, 361. *See also* degeneration of rule and office; *stasis*

doctors, 145n14, 150, 180, 242, 386n8, 401n36; and analogies/examples/metaphors of ruling, 131, 136–37, 144, 146, 146n18, 151, 170, 384–86, 385n6, 391–94, 401–2; and therapeutic *technai*, 149, 393–94, 401

dokimasia, 55, 56, 89, 89n8, 215, 219. *See also* scrutiny

Dreros, 54, 61

drone imagery, 260, 292–93, 309–13, 324–25, 333, 341–42

dual-character concepts, 24–25, 24nn49–50

dunamis (power, capacity), 123, 125, 125n25, 130, 136, 160, 234–35

dunasteia, 233, 233n31

Ebrey, David, 305n116, 306n116

education, 94, 101, 101n37, 104, 112, 122, 134, 169, 216, 225, 227–30, 249–50, 300; breakdown of, and flawed characters, 319, 324, 337, 338, 342–45, 349; breakdown of, and flawed constitutions in cities, 136, 171, 261, 276–77, 293, 299–300, 344; and decline of a *kallipolis*, 136, 276–77, 344; education and testing of potential officeholders and rulers, 38, 39, 61, 94, 104, 135–36, 159, 169, 215–16, 219–22, 224, 224n18, 225, 227, 237–38, 243, 244, 263; and *Laws*, 104, 136n49, 387; and *Republic* (*see specific topics under this heading*); and *Statesman*, 134–36

Eleatic Visitor (protagonist in *Statesman*), 30, 74–76, 75n86

election of officeholders. *See* officeholders, selection of

El Murr, Dimitri, 73n81, 370

Emerson, Ralph Waldo, 39, 319

Emmet, Dorothy, 389n13

Engels, Friedrich, 384n4, 406, 406n48

epikouroi, 173, 193–94, 196. *See also* auxiliaries

epimeleia/epimeleisthai, 106, 119, 119n9, 131, 181. *See also* caring

epitactic powers (power of issuing commands/orders), 18, 18n38, 109, 114, 127–28, 132, 309, 355, 371n26, 378–79, 400–402; as central to ruling, 124, 141, 381–83, 397–98, 404; double theory of laws as orders prefaced by persuasion, 80, 89, 93, 93n19, 381, 384–86, 407; and expert knowledge, 118–19, 123, 124, 126; and hierarchical nature of rule, 381, 383, 397–98, 401; and kings, 52–53, 118, 119, 124, 134; and master builder example, 127–28; political expertise as "command-apt," 119, 153, 401; slavery as synecdoche for

epitactic dimension of rule, 373–75, 377–79, 378n39; and statesmen, 117, 124, 130, 132, 401; and *taxis* of rule, 381–83; and tyranny, 317; and willing obedience, 377 (*see also* obedience of the ruled)

epitaktikē, 126, 153

epitaxis, 18, 18n38, 52–53. *See also* epitactic powers

epitrepein, 120, 120n12, 135

Eratosthenes, 193

ergon (task, product, result), 78, 79, 120, 130, 133, 135, 136, 180, 182

erōs/erotic love, 321, 324–25, 325n11, 327, 329, 331, 348, 353, 354n3, 364

Euben, J. Peter, 220

eunomia, 50

Euripides, 405

euthunai (end-of-term audit procedures), 5, 14, 55–60, 55nn32–33, 56, 58nn39–41, 69, 97, 99–100, 103, 186–88, 230, 299; absence of *euthunai* in *Republic* and *Statesman*, 8, 9, 186–87, 218, 230, 231, 244, 246; in Athens, 55nn32–34, 57–59, 100, 208n67, 214; expansion beyond financial oversight in Athens, 99–100, 103; in *Laws*, 59, 88, 97, 99–103; in many Greek constitutions, 88, 88n7, 217; as metaphor for accountable rule, 60

euthunoi (auditors), 6n9, 36, 88, 97, 99–102, 102n38

evaluative vs. descriptive sense of words and concepts, 23–25

exploitation of the ruled, 7, 18–19, 21–22, 40, 47, 153, 154, 173, 177, 187, 200, 263, 279, 283, 348, 349, 355, 373

factional division (*stasis*) among officeholders. *See* Disunity principle; *stasis*

factional regimes. See *stasiōteiai*

Ferrari, G. R. F., 257–60, 257n19, 259n22, 260n23, 264n27, 314, 328n19, 330, 344, 346

Feyel, Christophe, 57n38

flawed constitutions in cities, 39, 249–317; city-man comparison, 319, 319n2, 320, 335, 337–38, 342, 344; and city-soul analogy, 257–58, 257n18; and civic- and individual-level (macro and micro level) dysfunction, 256–57; constitutions other than a *kallipolis* as flawed, 256, 263; and distorted *taxis* and *telos* of rule (*see under taxis* of rule; *telos* of rule); and Disunity principle, 264–65, 269–72 (*see also* Disunity principle); and dynamic relationship between individual and constitution, 286; and flawed education, 136, 171, 261, 276–77, 293, 299–300, 344; instability of flawed constitutions, 348–49; and lack of safeguarding by rulers who are not officeholders, 261–62, 270–71, 281–82; and Predominance principle, 264–69, 272 (*see also* Predominance principle); proximate causes of constitutional change, 265, 270, 272, 277–79, 294–96, 306–9; sequence of flawed constitutions, 39, 250–51, 271–317; as *stasiōteiai* (factional regimes), 23n47, 361, 380; and transvaluation of values, 284, 293, 300, 313. *See also* degeneration of rule and office; democracy; Disunity principle; oligarchy; Predominance principle; timocracy; tyranny

flawed constitutions within souls, 318–50; and city-man comparison, 319, 319n2, 320, 335, 337–38, 342, 344; and city-soul analogy, 257n18; and dominant parts of the soul, 320–21 (*see also* appetitive part of the soul; rational part of the soul; rule in the soul; spirited/thumotic part of the soul); and flawed education, 319, 324, 337, 338, 342–45, 349; genesis of flawed characters, 321, 349 (*see also specific flawed character*); and rule in the soul (by force or persuasion), 320; and transvaluation of values, 319, 328, 333, 336, 340. *See also* democratic man; oligarchic man; timocratic man; tyrannical man

Form of the Good, 20–21, 67, 104n45, 159, 166n65, 205, 220–21, 225, 227, 238. *See also* Good, the

Frank, Jill, 72n80, 170, 206, 206n66, 249n3, 371n26

Frede, Michael, 274n46, 321n5

freedom, 12, 21, 28, 304n112, 356, 358, 360, 367, 370, 371, 374–77, 382; and *anarchia*, 305, 328, 374; as benefit of office and law, 40, 41, 356, 362–69, 388; compossibility of freedom and rule, 357–62, 375, 376, 380, 384; and democracy, 300–301, 301n103, 306–7, 309–11, 328; and disobedient citizens, 304n112, 309 (see also *anarchos*; anarchy/*anarchia*); and genesis of the tyrannical man, 324; and Magnesia, 384; nominal free status of the tyrant, 364–65, 367–69; political freedom, 374, 375; relationship among rule, freedom, and slavery, 355–80; and second-best constitution in *Laws*, 397; and the tyrannical man, 259, 353; and tyranny, 360; and tyrants, 354, 360, 364–69; and a tyrant's subjects, 369

friendship, 21, 28, 376, 382; as benefit of office and law, 40, 41, 356, 362–69, 388; and cooperative disposition among the citizens, 356, 358; lack of friendship for the tyrant/tyrannical man, 259, 331, 363, 365–69; and second-best constitution in *Laws*, 397

Fröhlich, Pierre, 55n34, 59

Gellius, Aulus, 74n85
Gerson, Lloyd, 72n80
Geuss, Raymond, 261n24
Gigon, Olof, 322n7
Girard, René, 286
Glaucon, as interlocutor in *Republic*, 42, 75n87, 140, 161n54. See also *Republic*; *specific topics*

Good, the, 20–22, 67; *dēmos* acting out of ignorance of the Good, 313; flawed conception of, 293–94; good of the soul, 254–55; known by philosopher-kings, 220–21, 236, 238, 255; operationalization in politics, 21; and philosophical study by potential rulers, 220–21; and the soul, 254–55, 320; and *telos* and *taxis* of rule, 255–56, 261; tyrants' inability to discern their actual good, 317; and understanding the actual good of the ruled, 52. *See also* Form of the Good

good of the ruled, 5–6, 18–23, 52, 63, 64, 98–99, 116, 129, 153, 188, 203–4, 355, 366, 378, 401–2; common goods, 28–30; and cultivating virtue in the citizens, 90, 100, 245; and debate in *Republic* over the meaning of rule, 144–58; and defining mark of correct rule, 390–91, 395–97; and fostering psychic self-rule, 371; and guardians in a *kallipolis*, 214, 231, 263; and Homeric king as "shepherd of the people," 9, 19 (*see also* shepherds); misunderstanding of, 245; and philosophers as rulers, 157; and political expertise, 123, 382, 391–92; and professions other than political rule, 149–53, 391; ruling for the good of the ruled as normative expectation in Plato's time, 19–20, 37, 52, 140, 153, 174; and service conception of rule, 123, 128, 142, 187–88, 211; and statesmen, 130; and *taxis* of rule, 41, 72–73, 212; as *telos* of rule, 18–23, 27, 41, 49, 52, 63, 72–73, 90, 140, 141, 170, 243, 244, 245, 372, 382, 383, 390, 395; a true ruler as caring for the good of the ruled, 37, 131, 140, 145, 153, 158, 164–65, 382, 390–92; Vermeule and, 28–30. *See also* caring; Good, the; therapeutic *technai*

Görgemanns, Herwig, 385n7

Gorgias (Plato), 51, 146n18, 173, 245, 313, 317, 356, 358, 359

Greene, Amanda, 25n52

Grube, G. M. A., 42n1, 43n2, 144n12, 151n35, 190n41, 193n46, 232, 232n27, 241n43, 269nn37–39, 296n89, 297n92, 310n125, 318n1, 322n7, 326n13, 334n25, 346n40

guardians (*phulakes*), 38–39, 174, 176n8, 177, 178, 183, 185–87, 192, 193, 199, 213–20, 218n8, 223–44, 242n46, 246, 252, 263, 270n41, 271–72, 275, 276, 278, 279, 281, 409; and age cohorts, 178, 222–27, 243 (*see also* age cohorts of guardians in *Republic*); and breakdown of hierarchical safeguarding system leading to timocracy, 275–79; and caring orientation/good of the ruled, 181–82, 214, 223–24, 231, 243, 244; "complete" guardians and rulers, 179n14, 193, 201, 222, 223, 225, 238, 241, 263

(*see also* philosopher-kings/queens; reigning); dependence on wages, 173–77, 183–85, 214, 218, 244, 246 (*see also* wages); divided into senior rulers and junior auxiliaries, 178, 201, 214, 223–25; divided further (among senior rulers) into eldest rulers and middle-aged officeholders, 218, 222; female guardians, 252; function of, 179–83, 218, 223–24; and hierarchical safeguarding, 38–39, 218, 244, 246; and Juvenal conundrum, 219; as mercenaries, 173, 175; military function, 182–83, 217, 225, 228, 230, 231, 246; philosophical education of, 215–16, 220–22, 224, 224n18, 227, 238; and prohibition of kinship ties, 177, 196, 242n46; and prohibition of wealth and property, 38, 174, 177, 185–87, 191, 196–97, 218, 242n46, 244, 246, 252; and rulers who are not officeholders, 230, 242, 273; scrutiny of potential guardians, 219, 275–77; and service conception of rule, 214, 224; in a timocracy, 279–83; and transition from *kallipolis* to timocracy, 273–79. *See also* age cohorts of guardians in *Republic*; *archontes/archontos*; auxiliaries; *epikouroi*; officeholders; philosopher-kings/queens

Habash, Nicolas Lema, 405

haireisthai, 121, 135

Hall, Jonathan, 3n1

Hansen, M. H., 10n16, 18n39, 184n29, 189–90, 189n37, 192, 195, 214–15n3, 217n7, 226n19

happiness: in cities, based on type of ruler, 236; of guardians, 174, 192; of kingly man, 318; and living a maximally unjust life, 251; and self-discipline, 358; and the tyrannical man, 259, 315, 323; and the tyrant, 251, 253, 258, 259, 316, 318–19, 323, 362, 365, 368, 369

Harel, Alon, 150n30

Harte, Verity, 150n33

Haubold, Johannes, 49n18, 51n23, 156n46, 281n60

Hawke, Jason, 270n40

Hawthorn, Geoffrey, 261n24

Heath, Joseph, 16, 17

Helmer, Étienne, 16n32

Herodotus, 46n7, 48–49, 65, 69–70, 69nn70–71, 143n10, 193, 210n74, 297

Hesiod, 48, 48n11, 49, 267n33, 292

Hippias, 281n60

history/folk history of rule and office in Greek thought and practice, 3–5, 9, 16, 44, 50–51, 53–54, 209–10

Hitz, Zena, 270n41

Hobbes, Thomas, 130, 140, 171

Hoekstra, Kinch, 233n29

hoi en telei (those in power), 66, 66n60

Homer, 210, 267n33, 274, 274n46; *Iliad*, 49, 50, 50n19, 267n33; *Odyssey*, 49, 50

Homeric kings, 48, 48n11, 49; as shepherds of the people, 19, 49–51, 49n18, 51, 120, 154, 210

Homeric society, 50–51

Honig, Bonnie, 398n28

honor, 161–63, 273, 294, 299, 336, 337, 342, 343

horos, 395–96, 395n25

Hulme Kozey, Emily, 83n112, 142n4, 149n28, 182n23

Hunter, Richard, 325n11

hupeuthunos, 14, 56

Ismard, Paulin, 16n33

Isocrates, 15, 15n32, 184, 210, 305n116, 306n116

Johnstone, Mark A., 303n108, 334n26

Jordović, Ivan, 73n82, 233n31

justice, 181, 181n18; and happiness, 322n8; and institutional corruption, 31–33; justice serving the stronger (Thrasymachus's account), 141, 143–44, 150, 165n62, 373; Socrates's response to Thrasymachus, 165n62

just life, 251, 252n10, 253n11, 258–59, 318, 331, 338, 362, 363, 368; disadvantages of being a just person (Thrasymachus's account), 154–55

Juvenal conundrum ("Who shall guard the guardians?"), 6–8, 6n9, 15, 22, 41, 99, 100, 111, 219; and *Laws*, 6n9, 7–8, 87–88, 93, 99–100; and *Republic*, 7–8, 176, 218–19; source of quotation, 87n2; and *Statesman*, 7–8

kairos, 116, 129, 275n51

kallipolis (beautiful city in *Republic*), 38, 43, 60, 80, 141, 159, 173n2, 175, 183–88, 219, 236, 252n8, 275–77, 275n49, 310, 320, 345, 371–73; absence of *euthunai* (audit procedures) in, 186–87, 218, 230, 231, 244, 246; age-differentiated *taxis* of roles in, 201, 214, 218, 223–43 (*see also* age cohorts of guardians in *Republic*; auxiliaries; guardians; officeholders; philosopher-kings/queens); constitution of, 140, 245–46, 249–50, 250n3, 263, 274, 279, 348; and corruption, 169, 185–87; education and selection of future rulers, 219, 220 (*see also* education); function of guardians, 179–83; and the good of the ruled, 214, 231, 263; guardians (*phulakes*) (*see* guardians); legal prohibitions on wealth and property (*see* wealth and property); and obedience of the ruled, 205, 371n26; political offices, 227–31, 244–46; rulers as senior cohort of guardians, 176n8, 178, 183, 232–43 (*see also* philosopher-kings/queens); and rulers who are not officeholders, 230, 242, 273; selection of officeholders, 218 (*see also* officeholders, selection of); and service conception of rule, 231; and *taxis* of rule, 219–20, 244, 263; and terms of address, 197–207; transition to timocracy, 271–79, 283; and wages, 172–212 (*see also* wages). See also *Republic*

kings, 44, 47–53, 118, 135, 175, 336; Atack and, 48, 48n10; contrast to officeholders, 56–57, 63; contrast to tyrants, 46n7, 47; distinction between kingship and tyranny, 316; eldest guardians reigning as kings, 225, 232–43 (*see also* philosopher-kings/queens; reigning); epitactic powers, 52–53, 118, 119, 124, 134; happiness of the kingly man, 318; Homeric kings, 19, 48–51, 48n11, 49n18, 51, 120, 154, 210; king as knowledgeable ruler, 47, 118, 129, 133, 135, 136, 140 (*see also* statecraft/political expertise); king as oriented to the good of the people, 48, 52; king as political weaver, 48, 120, 130, 132–33;

kings (*continued*)
  king as shepherd, 48–51, 49n18, 119–20, 210; king as steward, 210; king as unaccountable kind of ruler, 4; kingly man ruled by the rational part of the soul, 348; ordering role of, 46n7, 48, 49, 237–39; in *Republic*, 47, 232–43, 245 (*see also* philosopher-kings/ queens); rivals to title, 117, 119, 130; senior guardians (*see* philosopher-kings/queens); and service conception of rule, 130; in *Statesman*, 47–48, 115–20, 129, 130, 135, 136, 140; states-men identified with, 115–16, 130, 137, 139; transformation from kingship to accountable office in Athens, 3–5, 44. *See also* philosopher-kings/queens

Klosko, George, 377n37

knowledge, 72, 72n78, 91n14, 112, 116, 118, 129, 149–52, 242, 313; and epitactic powers, 123, 126; expertise in caring, 131; expertise needed by rulers, 391–92; kingly expertise, 118, 129, 133, 135; offices requiring specific expertise, 122; political expertise (*see* statecraft/ political expertise); rule of knowl-edge, 26, 52, 64, 115, 119, 138; types of expertise, 125n25, 126, 126n28, 134; and virtue, 74, 91, 167–68; wisdom, 91, 98–99, 255–56, 261, 379

to koinon, 125, 125n24

koinōnia, 356, 359

Kolodny, Niko, 383, 387–404, 398–99nn29, 31

kosmoi, 54, 59

kosmos, 9, 18n38, 54, 93n20

Kraut, Richard, 166n65

kritikē, 126n28

Kroll, J. H., 191n44

kurios, 219, 232–33, 233n29, 299, 312

Laks, André, 73n81, 76n89, 81, 92n17, 96, 96n27, 107n53, 184n31, 269n37, 297n92, 362n20, 373n30, 381n1

Landauer, Matthew, 18n38, 59n42, 101nn36–37, 187n35

Lane, Melissa [also M.S./Melissa S.], 63n53, 76n89, 119n9, 304n112, 305n116, 346n39, 360n15, 364n22,

371n26, 373n30, 377n34; approach to study of dialogues, 9n13, 30, 74–76

law guardians. See *nomophulakes*

lawlessness (*anomia*), 282–83, 305–6, 305n116, 309, 327, 329, 339–40, 405. *See also* anarchy/*anarchia*

laws, 54n30, 61–62, 90, 94–98, 138, 239, 294, 295, 309, 361–62, 386–88; codi-fication in Athens, 387; and coercion, 381, 382, 384–89, 406–7 (*see also* coercion/force); and cooperative dis-position among the citizens, 387–89; and discursive legislation, 206 (*see also* discursive legislation); divinely inspired law, 36, 50, 64, 91, 116n4, 358; double theory of laws as orders/ coercion prefaced by persuasion, 80, 89, 93, 93n19, 381, 384–87, 407; and founding a city, 206; freedom and friendship as benefit of office and law, 40, 41, 356, 362–69, 388; and Greek constitutions, 61–63 (*see also* constitutions); incorrect laws, 362; lack of institutional legal framework in Homeric society, 50; law guardians (*nomophulakes*), 91, 103–6; law as master of officeholders, 92; law not necessary as a criterion or instrument of rule, 386, 389; in *Laws* (see *Laws*); legislation "in deed," 92n17; legisla-tion "in speech," 39, 77–82, 92 (*see also* discursive legislation); loss of respect for laws, 300, 302–6, 304n112 (*see also* anarchy/*anarchia*); obedience to (*see* obedience of the ruled); in *Republic*, 39, 77–82, 140, 141, 186–87, 383; safe-guarding through the content of the laws, 176n8; senior guardians as law-makers, 218, 241; spirit of the laws, 94, 106–14, 176n8; unwritten laws, 309, 309n124, 388; written laws, 382, 388. *See also* accountability; constitutions; office, parameters of/limits on

Laws (Plato), 35–36, 40, 79, 87–114, 89n9, 90n11, 91n14, 136n49, 161, 183n28, 282n61, 283n63, 359, 378, 407; and accountability, 53, 97, 99–102; age requirements and term limits for officeholders, 88; Athenian Visitor as avatar of Plato in, 74–76 (*see also*

Athenian Visitor); and coercion, 384–89, 408; compared to other dialogues, 184–85; and compossibility of freedom, rule, and friendship, 357–61, 375, 376; constitutional laws (laws setting up offices), 54n30; constitutional project of, 53, 61–62, 72, 87–114, 183–84, 187, 282, 371n26, 383; and corruption, 32–34, 95–96; Daily Meeting, 36, 94, 106–14, 176n8; and discursive legislation (legislation "in speech"), 77–82, 88, 92, 96, 104, 107, 109, 111, 111n67; double theory of laws as orders/coercion prefaced by persuasion, 80, 89, 93, 93n19, 381, 384–87, 407; establishment of offices, 54n30, 93n20; and *euthunai* procedures, 59, 88, 97; and *euthunoi* (auditors), 36, 88, 97, 99–103; and freedom, 360, 397; and friendship, 376, 397; and garden-variety constitutionalism, 40, 358, 361; guarding the spirit of the laws, 36 (*see also* Daily Meeting *under this heading*); and initial establishment of new *polis*, 94; and interpretive stances, 72–83; and Juvenal conundrum, 6n9, 7–8, 87–88, 93, 99–100; lack of superordinate rulers overseeing officeholders in, 94; and language of caring, 106; and language of slavery, 40, 92; law guardians (*nomophulakes*), 91, 93–94, 101, 103–6; and limits of a *taxis* of offices, 27; and noocracy, 92; and obedience of the ruled, 359, 371n26, 375–80, 384; office and law in, 10, 35–36, 53, 88, 91–92, 94–98, 383 (*see also specific topics under this heading*); and penalties for rulers or officeholders, 184, 184n31; and political freedom, 375, 375n32; protagonist and interlocutors in (*see* Athenian Visitor; Cleinias; Megillus); and relationship among rule, freedom, and slavery, 355; and rulers and statesmen, 113–14; safeguarding through the content of the laws, 176n8; and second-best constitution/city, 18, 18n37, 31, 80, 96–97, 387, 397; selection of auditors, 100–101; selection of guardians of the laws (*nomophulakes*), 101; selection of

officeholders, 88, 89, 91, 170, 170n73; and service conception of rule, 175, 184–85; and *telos* and *taxis* of rule, 27, 90, 100, 105; title discussed, 72; use of *archē* and *archein*, 9–10, 91n14, 97n29; wages not paid to officeholders, 61, 89, 161n53, 183, 187; women as rulers, 115n1. *See also* Magnesia

Lear, Jonathan, 249n2, 257, 257n18, 259n21

Lefort, Claude, 405

Leibniz, G. W., 356–57

Lenin, V. I., 142, 142n6, 404, 406, 406n48, 408

leōs, 50, 105n49

Leslie, Sarah-Jane, 24n50

Leviathan (Hobbes), 171

Levin, Saul, 65n54, 148n23, 228nn23–24, 232n28

Lewis, V. Bradley, 107n54, 108, 108n58

logistai, 100n34

logos, 78–79, 79n97

Long, Alexander, 179, 182, 185

Lorenz, Hendrik, 347n41

lotteries. *See* officeholders, selection of

Luraghi, Nino, 3n1, 48n11

Lycurgus (Athenian orator), 62, 62n52

Lysias, 193–94, 193n48, 297n93

MacCallum, Gerald C., Jr., 360

macro narrative of flawed constitutions within cities, 249–317; connection between macro and micro narratives, 259–60, 286, 314–15, 328, 328n19, 330–31, 344–46; and Disunity principle, 264–65, 269–72, 270n41, 349 (*see also* Disunity principle); and political science, 260–62; and Predominance principle, 264–69, 272, 349 (*see also* Predominance principle); sequence of flawed constitutions, 39, 250–51, 271–317; and social psychology of drone imagery, 292–93, 313, 341, 342 (*see also* drone imagery). *See also* democracy; flawed constitutions in cities; oligarchy; timocracy; tyranny

Magnesia (colony envisaged in *Laws*), 53, 77n91, 80, 98–102, 112, 184n30, 383, 384; auditors (*euthunoi*), 99–103; and Cnossians, 105–6; Daily Meeting,

Magnesia (colony envisaged in *Laws*)
(*continued*)
106–14; and discursive legislation, 80,
81, 88, 88n5, 92, 96, 104, 107, 109, 111,
111n67; and double theory of law, 384–
86 (*see also under* laws); education of
the citizens, 91, 104, 387; founding and
establishment of constitutional order,
93n20, 105; and lack of wages, 161n53;
law guardians (*nomophulakes*), 103–6;
office and law in, 94–98, 383 (*see also
specific topics under this heading*);
and prelude to laws, 384; proposed
constitution (see *Laws*); selection of
officeholders, 170n73. See also *Laws*
March, James G., 54n29
Markell, Patchen, 11n17
Mates, Benson, 356–57
McCabe, M. M., 75, 75n88
Megillus (interlocutor in *Laws*), 80, 81,
88, 88n4, 105n51
Menexenus (Plato), 4–5, 209
Menn, Stephen, 62n50, 72n79
metechein, 298–99
Meyer, Susan Sauvé, 357, 357n10,
375n32
micro narrative of changing character
of individuals, 251, 256–57, 261–62,
283n63, 318–50; and city-man comparison, 319, 319n2, 320, 335, 337–38,
342, 344; and city-soul analogy,
257n18; connection between macro
and micro narratives, 259–60, 286,
314–15, 328, 328n19, 330–31, 340, 342,
344–46; representative man as son of
preceding stage's father, 319, 324; and
social psychology of drone imagery,
260–62, 292–93, 341, 342 (*see also*
drone imagery); and three parts of the
soul, 262, 283n63, 319. See also democratic man; oligarchic man; timocratic
man; tyrannical man
Minos (Cretan king), 90, 90n13
misthōtoi (mercenaries/hired hands), 173,
173n2, 180–81
misthos (wage), 172, 184n30, 188–92, 195,
197. See also wages
Möllers, Christoph, 210n73
money, 191, 191n44, 278; and guardians in
a *kallipolis* (prohibited to), 185–87,
191; monetary wages, 189, 191–92;

moneylending, 295, 309; moneymaking appetites, 266, 321, 332–33, 336–
37; and oligarchs, 294–96, 336–37,
342; and timocrats, 282–84, 299, 343,
344; and the tyrannical man, 325–26.
See also wealth and property
Moore, Christopher, 168n68
Morrow, Glenn, 88n7, 97n29, 103, 103n44,
110, 161n53, 184n31
Muses, 274–75, 274n46, 277, 283, 283n63,
310

Nails, Debra, 300n100
Nicolay, René de, 83n112, 301n103,
309n123
Nocturnal Council. *See* Daily Meeting
nomoi, 50, 62, 62n50, 71, 72, 78
nomophulakes (law guardians), 91, 93–94,
101, 103–6, 104n47, 112–13, 182n25
nomos, 18n37, 50, 72, 79, 82, 97, 186,
242n46
noocracy, 92

obedience of the ruled, 40, 343, 369–75,
371n26, 378, 383, 403, 404; breakdown in, 304n112, 309, 328, 378–80,
383 (*see also* anarchy/*anarchia*); and
compossibility of freedom and rule,
357, 359 (*see also* compossibility);
and cooperative disposition among
the citizens, 40, 358, 368; and doctor
analogy, 384–86; and friendship, 359,
368; and hierarchical nature of rule,
404; and language of slavery used to
describe rule, 355, 369–75; paradox
of willing obedience in *Laws*, 375–80,
384; and persuasive prelude to laws,
384–86; Raz and, 383; Rousseau and,
380; *taxis* and *telos* of rule compossible with willing obedience, 355;
unwilling obedience of slaves, 366,
374; willing obedience described
as voluntary slavery, 308, 361,
375, 377
Ober, Josiah, 17n35, 246n49, 251n5
Oedipus, 315n132
office, 7, 14, 17, 40, 41, 44, 54n30, 61–62,
106, 108–9, 122, 134, 228, 230, 242,
273, 356, 358, 361–69, 378, 400;
and accountability, 4–6, 53 (*see also*
accountability); and Aeschines's

dispute with Ctesiphon, 57–58, 58nn40–41; and age cohorts (*see* age cohorts of guardians in *Republic*); author's use of term, 4n4, 12–13, 217; and corruption, 32–34 (*see also* abuse of power or office; corruption); and democracy, 302, 304–6; and flawed constitutions, 136–39 (*see also* flawed constitutions in cities); history in Greek thought and practice before the time of Plato, 3–5, 9, 16, 44, 53–54, 209–10; lack of distinction between ancient Greek political and administrative offices, 16, 54, 103; in *Laws*, 88–99; material benefits of, 160–61, 361–62 (*see also* abuse of power or office; corruption); and oligarchy (*see* oligarchy); parameters of office (*see* office, parameters of/limits on); powers, in Athens, 16, 56, 56n35; powers, in *Laws*, 88; powers, limits on, 14, 55, 56, 215, 217, 230, 231; reconfiguration of offices in the constitution of a *kallipolis*, 230–31, 244–46; relationship between rule and office, 4, 11–12, 38, 42–43, 117, 120–23, 164; in *Republic* (see *kallipolis*; *Republic*; *specific topics under this heading*); in *Statesman*, 120–23, 133–39; and timocracy, 281–82, 286–87; and the timocratic man, 343; and tyranny, 253, 315; vulnerabilities of, 7, 114, 138 (*see also* Juvenal conundrum). See also *archai*; *archē*; vocabulary of rule and office

office, parameters of/limits on, 6, 14, 54–61, 55n34, 95n25, 217, 230–31, 244–46; and accountability, 5 (*see also* accountability); in *Laws* (see *Laws*); limits on eligibility to serve, 14, 54–57, 104n45, 215, 217, 230, 231, 284, 288, 301–2; limits on powers of each office, 14, 55, 56, 215, 217, 230, 231; performance audits (*euthunai*), 55, 55nn32–33, 57–60, 217 (see also *euthunai*); and prohibition of wealth and property, 38, 174, 177, 185–87, 191, 196–97, 218, 242n46, 244, 246, 252; and reconfiguration of offices in the constitution of a *kallipolis*, 230–31, 244–46; in *Republic*, 230–31, 244–46

(see also *kallipolis*; *Republic*); rotation of officeholders, 239; scrutiny of chosen officeholders prior to taking office, 14, 55–57, 89, 89n8, 217, 219, 275–77; and wages (*see* wages)

officeholders, 4, 44, 53–64, 117, 155, 160–63, 210–11, 263, 294, 301–4, 328, 335–36, 378, 382–83, 400; and accountability enforced by auditors (see *euthunai*; *euthunoi*); accountability to the ruled, 54, 64, 214; accountable to/safeguarded by superordinate rulers in a *kallipolis*, 15, 26, 27, 37, 38, 53, 57, 64, 136, 139, 213–15, 218–19, 244, 254, 263, 273; accusations against, 55, 55n34, 60–61, 217; apprentice rulers (middle-aged cohort) as, 213, 216, 217, 225, 227–31, 246; character thereof shaping constitutions (*see* Predominance principle); combined executive, legislative, and judicial functions, 16, 18n39, 56, 103; contrast to kings and tyrants, 56–57, 63; and corruption (*see* corruption); and democracy, 56, 89, 174–75, 178, 184, 297, 297n92, 300–306, 300n101; distinction between "reigning" and rule by officeholders, 213, 218, 236; distinction between statesman and officeholders, 124; and Disunity principle, 264–65, 269–72, 361 (*see also* Disunity principle); education of potential officeholders (*see* education); as epitactic rulers, 54, 400, 404 (*see also* epitactic powers); exploitation of the ruled, 294, 349, 361–62 (*see also* abuse of power or office; corruption; exploitation of the ruled; oligarchy; timocracy); inducements for good service, 161–64 (*see also* honor; penalties for officeholders and rulers; wages); lack of safeguarding in flawed constitutions, 261–62, 270–71, 281–82; in *Laws*, 53; obedience/disobedience to, 308–9, 378–80 (*see also* obedience of the ruled); and oligarchy, 89, 283–91, 294–96, 342, 349; as paradoxical kind of rulers, 63–64; and parameters of office (*see* office, parameters of/limits on); penalties for, 161–64, 166, 172, 184, 184n31; and Predominance principle, 264–69, 268n36, 272 (*see also* Predominance principle);

officeholders (*continued*)
and principal-agent model, 208–9, 398–401; and prohibition on wealth and property (*see* wealth and property); in *Republic*, 213–46 (*see also* guardians; *kallipolis*); and "rule over none," 400, 404 (*see also* democratic theory); selection of (*see* officeholders, selection of); in *Statesman*, 53; and terms of address, 197–207; and timocracy, 279–83, 349; and under- and overidentification of a person with their professional role, 171; unity among, 273; wages paid or not paid to, 56, 61, 89, 160–63, 161n53, 172–212, 218, 244 (*see also* wages); women as, 43, 216. *See also* accountability; *euthunai*; rulers

officeholders, selection of, 6, 57, 91, 98–100, 99n33, 104, 135, 136, 217; in Athens, 57, 226, 297n92, 312; and breakdown of selection system leading to timocracy, 276–77; and democracy, 297, 297n92, 300, 300n101; eligibility criteria, 14, 54–57, 104n45, 215, 217, 226, 230, 231, 284, 288, 301–2; in *Laws*, 88, 89, 91, 170, 170n73; officeholders chosen by combination of lottery and election, 14, 55, 57, 69, 101n36, 226, 300n101; officeholders chosen by election, 55, 57, 91, 135, 286–87, 297n92, 312; officeholders chosen by lottery, 14, 17, 55, 57, 69, 91, 297, 297n92; offices requiring specific expertise, 134; and oligarchy, 284, 286–88, 296; and Predominance principle, 268; preparation/education of potential officeholders, 64, 91, 104, 135–36 (*see also* education); in *Republic*, 38–39, 215, 218, 225–27, 243–44; scrutiny of chosen officeholders prior to taking office, 14, 55–57, 89, 89n8, 217, 219, 275–77; selection of auditors, 100–101, 101n36; selection of guardians through education and testing, 38–39, 215, 218, 225–27, 243–44; selection of law guardians (*nomophulakes*) in *Laws*, 101, 104–5, 104n47; selection of superintendent of education in *Laws*, 101n37; in *Statesman*, 121, 134–36; and

timocracy, 281, 286–87; and wealth, 99, 284, 286–87
officium, 12–13, 13n24
oikonomos, 118n6
oligarchic man, 40, 251, 320, 322n7, 332–33, 335–42; character of, 338–40; and city-man comparison, 337–38, 342; and drone imagery, 260, 333, 337–39, 341–42; genesis of, 335–37, 341, 342; and rule in the soul, 342, 347; way of life, 333, 338, 341
oligarchy, 39, 251, 287–97, 300, 307, 309, 311, 312, 332, 340–42, 349, 380; absence of wages for officeholders in, 89, 184n29; in Athens (*see under* Athens); and city-man comparison, 337–38, 342; constitution defined/ described, 284, 288–93; and Disunity principle, 295–96; and drone imagery, 260, 292–93, 310–12, 333, 342; emergence from timocracy, 283–88, 339–40; *euthunai* in, 59; and failure of lawmaking, 294, 295, 309; faults of, 288–93, 294–97, 311, 349 (*see also* specific faults under this heading); and Predominance principle, 294, 311; property valuation and officeholding, 284, 288; proximate causes of constitutional change, 294–95, 309; and revolution from below, 295–96; and selection of officeholders, 284, 286–88, 296; and *telos* and *taxis* of rule, 291, 294, 295; transition to democracy, 293–97; value placed on wealth and moneymaking, 286–87, 294–95, 300; way of life in an oligarchy, 300
Olsen, Johan P., 54n29
orders (commands). *See* epitactic powers
Otanes, 69–70, 69n72

Panathenaea, 51n23
paradeigma, 133, 133n44
parameters of office. *See* office, parameters of/limits on
paranomos, 323, 324, 325, 326–27n16
patrios politeia (ancestral constitution), 15. *See also under* Athens
Pausanias, 3–5, 8, 209
Peisistratid dynasty, 46, 46n7

penalties for officeholders and rulers, 161–64, 166, 172, 184, 184n31
permissiveness. *See* freedom
Persia, 40, 49, 336, 347, 375–76, 378
persuasion, 18n38, 80, 81, 320, 371n26, 384–86, 385n6; double theory of laws as orders/coercion prefaced by persuasion, 80, 89, 93, 93n19, 381, 384–86, 407
Pettit, Philip, 403n42
Philochorus, 15n31
philosopher-kings/queens (senior rulers in a *kallipolis*), 9, 47, 48n10, 213–46, 273; accountability of officeholders to, 38–39, 53, 218, 231, 244, 263, 273; accountability of/safeguards on, 27, 39, 219–22, 244, 246; and breakdown of selection system leading to timocracy, 275–79; and caring orientation, 237, 238; and corruption, 219–20; and deliberation, 241, 243; and discursive legislation vs. actual legal frameworks, 206; and failures of scrutiny, 276–77; and gold nature, 276, 279; as judges, 219, 241–42; and Juvenal conundrum, 219; and knowledge of the Good, 220–21, 236, 238, 255; as law-makers, 218, 241; not referred to as officeholders, 230, 242, 273; as not self-certifying, 39, 218n8, 220, 231; and objections to claim that philosophers must rule, 204–5; ordering role of, 237–39; philosopher-queens, 9, 15n32, 27, 29, 236, 246, 255; philosophers ruling as kings, or kings philosophizing, 181n22, 233–37, 240, 252; and practice of philosophical dialectic, 39, 220–22; as reigning/"complete" guardians/rulers, 179n14, 193, 201, 222, 223, 225, 232–43, 263; as rulers overseeing education and selection of their juniors, 39, 215, 218–20, 225–26, 237–38, 243, 244, 263, 276; selecting their own replacements, 39, 215, 220, 276; as supervisors safeguarding subordinates, 27, 38–39, 64, 213–15, 236–37, 243, 244, 254, 263, 273; as supervisors safeguarding the constitution, 15n32, 176, 215, 218, 263; and taking turns, 238–41; and wages, 219–20
philosophers, 38; and asceticism, 168, 176; and bodily desires, 168; and education, 169; as full knowers, 167; and happiness, 174, 318; inducements for ruling, 161–64; intrinsic motivations of persons with philosophical natures, 167–68; and lack of motive for corruption, 205, 219–20, 243; and love of learning, 167–68, 176, 205; moral and intellectual virtues of, 23, 167–68; and ordering for the good, 157; philosopher as a better kind of person, 252n8, 320; and psychic self-rule, 350; and psychology of the suitable candidate for role of ruler, 23, 159, 165–70; and temperamental fitness for rule, 165–70; and wages, 205–6
philosophical anarchism, 382–84, 408–9
phulakes, 111, 173, 182–83. *See also* guardians
Pindar, 50, 210, 233n32
Plato: characters in dialogues as avatars of, 9n13, 30, 74–76; dates of dialogues, 45n5; dates of lifespan, 45n5; development of ideas of rule and office, 4n6, 11–12; and discursive legislation, 77–82; and expectation that rulers care for the good of the ruled, 19–22, 26; influence of Greek poetry and prose on, 48–49; and interpretive stances on, 9n13, 30–31, 71–83; and Juvenal conundrum, 6n9, 7–8, 41; and language of kingship, 9, 47–48; as law theorist, 387; as opponent of *anarchia*, 10, 40–41, 72, 382–84, 388, 409; as opponent of tyranny, 10, 47, 72, 408; and philosophical anarchism, 382–84, 408–9; and preventing abuse of power/institutional corruption, 29–34; as realist, 41, 83, 171, 260, 288, 296, 297, 299, 306, 317, 389; and rule of knowledge, 26; schema of rule, 48, 52, 73, 78, 124–31, 153, 192, 222–23, 253, 362, 381; and strict evaluative sense vs. loose descriptive sense of words and concepts, 23–26; and terms of art in present study, 17–26, 35, 44, 193; terms possibly coined by, 155, 251n5, 345; theory of goodness, 20; virtue and Platonic ethics, 21; vocabulary of rule and office (*see* vocabulary of rule and office). *See also specific topics and works*

Platonic Forms, 52n27, 67. *See also* Form of the Good

Plutarch, 50, 51, 51n23

Pocock, J. G. A., 4n6

Poddighe, Elisabetta, 269n37

Polemarchus, 193

politeia. *See* constitutions

political expertise. *See* statecraft/political expertise

political figures, 44–64. *See also* auditors; guardians; kings; *nomophulakes*; officeholders; philosopher-kings/ queens; statesman; tyrants

political predominance, 264n27, 268, 281, 311. *See also* Predominance principle

politikē, 71, 125. *See also* statecraft/ political expertise

politikos. *See* statesman

Polus (interlocutor in *Gorgias*), 173, 245

Popper, Karl, 27, 29, 212

Predominance principle, 264–69, 264n27, 268n36, 272, 277–81, 285–87, 294, 298, 300, 311–12, 339, 349

principal-agent model of accountability, 207–9, 211, 398–401, 399n31, 403

Pritchett, W. Kendrick, 189, 191, 195

private property. *See* wealth and property

provisions, as a kind of wages, 188–92, 195

pseudo-Xenophon, 62

Raaflaub, Kurt A., 54n31

Rancière, Jacques, 11, 405

rational part of the soul, 255, 255n15, 262, 266, 323, 337, 343, 346, 348, 370

Raymond, Christopher, 168n68

Raz, Joseph, 20, 204, 214, 381, 382, 383, 396, 401–2

reason, 91, 92, 220–22, 262

Reeve, C. D. C., 42n1, 43n2, 144n12, 151n35, 190n41, 193n46, 232, 232n27, 241n43, 269nn37–39, 296n89, 297n92, 310n125, 318n1, 322n7, 326n13, 334n25, 346n40

Rehfeld, Andrew, 26n54

Reid, Jeremy, 97n29, 101n36, 102n38, 107, 108n56, 110, 110n63, 170n73

reigning, 38, 176n8, 178, 179n14, 183, 193, 201, 215, 219, 222, 223, 225, 232–43, 263, 318; distinguished from rule by

officeholders, 213, 218, 236. *See also* philosopher-kings/queens; rulers

"representative men" in *Republic*, 39–40, 319. *See also* democratic man; flawed constitutions within souls; micro narrative of changing character of individuals; oligarchic man; timocratic man; tyrannical man

Republic (Plato), 43, 43–44n4, 141, 184–85, 357, 396n27; absence of *euthunai* (audit procedures) in, 8, 9, 186–87, 218, 230, 231, 244, 246; and age cohorts (*see* age cohorts); and anarchy/*anarchia* (*see* anarchy/*anarchia*); and avoiding corruption, 185–87 (*see also* accountability; corruption); and caring orientation/good of the ruled, 9, 22, 37, 106, 140, 149–53 (see also *telos* of rule *under this heading*); constitutional project of, 37–39, 53, 72, 177n13, 178, 186–87, 207–9, 213–14, 222–23, 244–46, 383; and degeneration of rule and office (*see* degeneration of rule and office); and discursive legislation (legislation "in speech"), 39, 77–82, 140, 141, 186; and drone imagery (*see* drone imagery); and education (*see* education); and *epikouroi* (*see* auxiliaries); and flawed characters (*see* flawed constitutions within souls); and flawed constitutions (*see* flawed constitutions in cities); and founding a city, 180–83; and freedom and friendship, 353–56, 359–60, 362–69; and garden-variety constitutionalism, 358, 358n10, 397; and guardians (*see* guardians); interlocutors (*see* Adeimantus; Glaucon; Socrates; Thrasymachus); and interpretive stances, 72–83; and Juvenal conundrum, 7–8, 176, 218–19; and language of slavery, 40, 355, 369–75 (*see also* slavery); and the limits of office, 27, 215, 244 (*see also* office, parameters of/limits on); and macro narrative of flawed constitutions, 249–317 (*see also* flawed constitutions in cities); and the meaning of rule, 142–58; and micro narrative of changing character of individuals, 318–50 (*see also* flawed constitutions within souls); motivation of rulers/ officeholders, 38, 157–65; and natural person's temperamental fitness to rule, 165–70; and obedience of the ruled, 369–75, 371n26 (*see also* obedience of the ruled); parable of the transported slaveholder, 362–63, 365–67, 369; and philosopher-kings/senior rulers (*see* philosopher-kings/queens); and philosophical anarchism, 408–9; and reconfiguration of offices, 230–31, 244–46; and selection of officeholders, 38–39, 218, 225–27; and sequence of flawed political constitutions, 39, 250–51, 271–317; and service conception of rule, 142, 175–76, 185, 187–88, 204, 207–12, 214, 224, 231, 245; Socrates as avatar of Plato in, 30, 74–76, 140; superordinate rulers safeguarding officeholders, 15, 26, 27, 38–39, 64, 213–15, 236–37, 243, 244, 254, 263, 273; and *taxis* of rule, 170, 179, 202, 212, 214, 219–20, 222–23, 243, 244, 263; and *telos* of rule, 27, 140–71, 214, 243, 263, 396n26 (see also *telos* of rule); and tension between role of the ruler and the natural person who takes up role, 23, 166–67, 170–71; and terms of address, 197–207; title discussed, 71, 71n77; and tyranny (*see* tyranny; tyrants); use of *archē* in, 9–10, 142, 147, 156, 158, 162, 163, 172, 179, 201, 213, 246; use of *archein* in, 9–10, 163–64, 179, 180n15, 201, 228, 302; and wages paid to rulers and officeholders, 27, 38, 61, 160–63, 172–212, 214, 244 (*see also* wages); and women (*see* women). See also *kallipolis*

Rhodes, P. J., 55n32, 129n36
Roberts, Jennifer Tolbert, 55n33, 59n42
Robinson, D. B., 118n6
Rosen, Michael, 25n52
Rousseau, Jean-Jacques, 380, 403, 403n40
Rowe, Christopher J., 125n24, 155, 391n16, 393nn18, 20, and 21, 402n38
rule, 4n4, 7, 17–26, 18n38, 22n45, 29–30, 44, 51, 67, 118, 126, 225–26, 317, 350, 358, 370, 371, 374, 378, 382, 388; Arendt and, 11–12; bad rule, 19, 316–17,

389 (*see also* abuse of power or office; anarchy/*anarchia*; corruption; exploitation of the ruled; tyranny); benefit of rule, 10, 370–71, 373, 384; and coercion, 18, 384–89, 384n5 (*see also* coercion/force); compossibility of freedom and rule, 357–62, 375, 376, 380, 384; core elements, 122 (*see also* epitactic powers; *taxis* of rule; *telos* of rule); defining mark/*horos* of correct rule, 136–37, 389–97, 395n25; and definition of statecraft, 125–26; and democratic theory, 383; distinction between "reigning" by safeguarding rulers and rule by officeholders, 213, 218, 236, 254; distinctions and parallels between rule in the soul and rule in a city, 254–55; and doctor analogy, 136–37, 384–86, 391–93, 401–2; epitactic nature of rule, 18, 18n39, 124, 141, 381–83, 397–98, 404 (*see also* epitactic powers); and flawed constitutions, 136–39, 294 (*see also* flawed constitutions in cities); hierarchical nature of rule, 381, 383, 397–98, 401, 404; and Homeric society, 50–51; intertwining of ruling, caring, and weaving, 132–33; and kings (*see* kings; philosopher-kings/queens); language of slavery used to describe rule, 12, 40, 210–11, 355, 369–75; law not necessary as a criterion or instrument of rule, 386, 389; "no rule"/"rule over none" theories, 383, 397–404; obedience of the ruled (*see* obedience of the ruled); Plato's schema of, 48, 52, 73, 78, 124–31, 153, 192, 253, 362, 381; and political expertise, 119, 123, 153, 234–35 (*see also* statecraft/political expertise); political rule ideally obviated by self-rule (philosophical anarchism), 382, 384; political tyrant as not truly ruling, 317, 325, 354, 390; Popper and, 27; post-modern idealization of "no rule," 383; and principal-agent model, 207–9, 399–401; and professions other than political rule, 141, 146–49, 148n25, 401; and psychic self-rule, 10, 41; Rancière and, 11; Raz and, 381, 382, 383, 401–2; relationship

rule (*continued*)

between law and coercion, 382, 384–89; relationship between political rule and psychic self-rule, 10; relationship among rule, freedom, and slavery, 355–80; relationship between rule and office, 4, 11–12, 38, 42–43, 117, 120–23, 164; in *Republic*, 142–58; rule of knowledge, 26, 52, 64, 115, 119, 138 (*see also* statecraft/political expertise); rule as maintaining order, 46n7, 48, 49, 237–39; rule by the multitude, 69, 69n69, 70, 246n49; rule as not necessarily coercive, 388, 401, 406–8; rule within the soul as ultimate aim of any kind of rule, 21, 41, 370, 371; service conception of rule, 20, 20n41, 21, 38, 117, 123, 128, 130, 173–76, 184–85, 207–12, 214, 224; and serving the good of the ruled (*see* good of the ruled; *telos* of rule); in *Statesman*, 118–36, 389–97, 401–2; and strict evaluative sense vs. loose descriptive sense of words and concepts, 23, 25, 153–54; *technē* and, 142–58, 401; *telos* and *taxis* of (*see taxis* of rule; *telos* of rule); temperamental fitness to rule, 165–70; turn-taking or rotation by rulers, 238–41; and tyranny (*see* tyranny); willingness to rule, 157–65; Wolin and, 11n18. See also *archē*; vocabulary of rule and office

ruled, the. *See* subjects of rule

rule in the soul, 254, 320–21, 347, 350, 374; absence of, and anarchy, 254, 327, 329; absence of, and the tyrannical man, 254, 327–29, 332, 348, 353, 364, 365; benefit of, 10, 370–71, 373, 384; and the democratic man, 334, 334n26, 347; distinctions and parallels between rule in the soul and rule in a city, 254–55; guardian within the soul, 41, 370–71; and the kingly man, 318, 348; malfunction of rule in the soul, 254 (*see also* democratic man; oligarchic man; timocratic man; tyrannical man); and the oligarchic man, 342, 347; political rule obviated by sufficient self-rule, 41, 382, 384, 408–9; proper *telos* of, 254–55, 320; psychic

self-rule, 10, 21, 41, 327, 329, 350, 354; and rational part of the soul, 370; *taxis* of rule in the soul, 320, 329, 332, 334, 338, 350; and the timocratic man, 343, 347; as ultimate aim of any kind of rule, 21, 41, 370, 371

rulers, 21, 113–14, 124, 141, 142n7, 144–46, 173, 174, 183, 183n28, 193, 390–91, 394–95, 397, 407; and age cohorts (*see* age cohorts of guardians in *Republic*; guardians); apprentice rulers as officeholders, 213, 216–18, 225, 227–31, 246, 262; defined in precise sense introduced by Thrasymachus, 145, 153; distinction between "reigning" by safeguarding rulers and rule by officeholders, 213, 218, 236, 254; education of potential rulers, 141, 157, 159, 215–16, 219; eldest guardians as "reigning," 232–43, 263 (*see also* reigning); eldest guardians as rulers overseeing education and selection of their juniors, 39, 176n8, 178, 183, 215, 218–20, 223, 225–26, 232–44, 263; and issuing orders (*see* epitactic powers); lack of safeguarding by rulers who are not officeholders in flawed constitutions, 261–62, 270–71, 281–82; in *Laws*, 113–14, 407; master builder example, 126–28, 408; motivation of persons capable of ruling, 141, 157–65, 166; nature of persons capable of ruling, 23, 141, 159, 165–70, 219; obedience to (*see* obedience of the ruled); officeholders as rulers receiving a wage, 174–75; and principal-agent model, 207–9, 399–401; professionals (e.g., doctors) and examples of rule, 126–28, 144–48, 408; reluctant rulers as the best rulers, 159; role defined, 141; ruler as occupying a role, 389–97; rulers exploiting the ruled or pursuing their own good, 7, 18–19, 21–22, 40, 47, 145, 148, 153, 173, 177, 187, 192–93, 200, 245, 263, 279, 282–83, 317, 348, 349, 355, 373, 396; rulers as having professional expertise, 146 (*see also* statecraft/political expertise); rulers as safeguarders of a constitution, 15n32, 176, 215, 218, 263; rulers in the strict evaluative sense vs. the loose descriptive sense, 23–24, 153–54; rulers who are not officeholders, 230, 242, 273; safeguarding against corruption of highest/superordinate rulers, 187, 219–20; and service conception of rule (*see* service conception of rule); statesmen as rulers, 115, 124, 130, 132–33, 136; subordinates safeguarded by rulers, 15, 27, 37, 38, 136, 139, 244 (*see also under* philosopher-kings/queens); tension between role of the ruler and the natural person who takes up role, 23, 166–67, 170–71; and terms of address, 179, 197–207; in a timocracy, 279–81; a true ruler as caring for the good of the ruled, 37, 131, 140, 145, 153, 158, 164–65 (*see also* caring; good of the ruled); unaccountable rulers, 3, 4, 5, 8, 18n37, 95–96, 368; and wages (*see* wages); willingness to rule, 157, 158–65; women as rulers/philosopher-queens, 9, 15n32, 27, 29, 115n1, 228, 236, 246, 255. See also *archontes/archontos*; guardians; kings; philosopher-kings/queens; reigning; statesman

Saunders, Trevor J., 80, 111n65, 379n43
Saxonhouse, Arlene, 6n8, 267n33
Schofield, Malcolm, 13n24, 83n111, 87n1, 122n18, 373, 377, 384, 384n5
Schöpsdau, Klaus, 379
Scott, Dominic, 161n54
scrutiny (*dokimasia/dokimazein*), 14, 55–57, 89, 89n8, 217, 219, 275–77
Sedley, David, 76n89, 166n65
selection of officeholders. *See* officeholders, selection of
self-rule. *See* rule in the soul
service conception of authority (Raz's conception), 20, 20n41, 204, 214, 381, 396
service conception of rule, 20n41, 21, 38, 117, 123, 128, 130, 142, 173–76, 179, 184–85, 187–88, 194, 197, 205, 207–12, 224, 231, 245, 381–83, 401–2
Seto, Ken-ichi, 373n30
Shapiro, Gabriel, 24n50
shepherds, 19, 49–51, 49n18, 120, 149n28, 154, 156, 157, 160, 174, 180, 210

Shorey, Paul, 42n1, 43n2
Sikkenga, J., 267n35
Silverman, Allan, 409
Simonton, Matthew W., 270n40, 293n84, 296, 296n91, 307n120
Sissa, Giulia, 223n14
sitēsis, 189. *See also* provisions, as a kind of wages; *trophē*; wages
slavery, 12, 16n33, 29n65, 40, 117, 130, 198, 355, 362, 363, 365, 366, 372, 374, 377–78, 385, 406; language of slavery used in describing rule, 12, 40, 200, 210–11, 355, 369–75; parable of the transported slaveholder, 362–63, 365–67, 369, 374; as rejected by relational egalitarian democratic theory, 403–4; relationship among rule, freedom, and slavery, 355–80; as synecdoche for epitactic dimension of rule, 373–75, 373n30, 377–79, 378n39; *telos* of exploitation of the slave, 372, 374; and transition from *kallipolis* to timocracy, 278, 278n55; and the tyrannical man, 329–30, 353, 363; and tyranny, 310, 316; tyrant as a slave, 354, 364–67; willing obedience described as voluntary slavery, 308, 361, 375, 377
Socrates, as avatar of Plato in *Republic*, 30, 74–76, 140. See also *Republic*; *specific topics*
Socrates, Young. *See* Young Socrates
Socrates (Xenophon's version), 19, 19n40, 47, 51
Solon, 50, 55n32, 59n45, 70n73, 100, 209, 209n72, 299
Sophist (Plato), 123, 123n20
Sophocles, 66n59, 303–4
Sørensen, Anders Dahl, 137–38, 137n51, 138n56
sōtēria (safeguarding), 106, 109, 110, 110n64
soul: city-soul analogy, 257–58, 257n19, 262; flawed rule within the soul, 39–40 (*see also* flawed constitutions within souls; rule in the soul); psychic self-rule (*see* rule in the soul); and Thracians principle, 265–66, 265n30; three parts of, 262, 266, 283n63, 319, 320, 323 (*see also* appetitive part of the soul; rational part of the soul;

soul (*continued*)
    spirited/thumotic part of the soul);
    types of souls, 252, 276; types of souls
    and unsuitable candidates for rule and
    office, 276, 278, 279. *See also* flawed
    constitutions within souls; rule in the
    soul
sovereign rule. See *kurios*; reigning
Sparta, 90nn11–12, 97n29, 191n42, 260,
    278n55, 281–82, 282n61, 283n62,
    304n112
spirited/thumotic part of the soul, 262,
    265–66, 320, 336, 337, 346, 347
stasiōteiai (factional regimes), 23n47,
    361, 380
stasis, 219, 250n3, 265, 269–72, 270n41,
    359; Simonton's game-theoretic
    account, 296–97; and transitions
    between constitutions, 273, 275–77,
    295–96, 311–12. *See also* Disunity
    principle
statecraft/political expertise (*politikē*), 71,
    95, 118, 119, 122–26, 125n25, 128–33,
    135, 136, 153, 234, 382, 391–92; defined,
    125–26, 152–53
Statesman (Plato), 8, 9, 36–37, 52–53, 64,
    81–82, 115–39, 122n18, 123, 128–30,
    136, 138n56, 141, 155, 242n45, 382–83,
    389–93, 396, 396nn26–27, 408;
    Arendt and, 13n26; and caring orien-
    tation, 37, 106, 117, 119–20, 123, 131,
    382, 390–92; constitutional project
    of, 72, 120–23, 133–39, 383, 390–92;
    defining mark of correct rule, 136–37,
    389–97; definition of a statesman, 37,
    133; definition of statecraft, 125–26,
    152–53 (*see also* statecraft/political
    expertise); distinction between advi-
    sors and kings, 401; and distinction
    between kingship and tyranny, 47; and
    doctor analogy, 392–94; and flawed
    constitutions, 116n4, 136–39; and gen-
    uine constitutions, 390–92; and the
    good of the ruled (see *telos* and *taxis*
    of rule *under this heading*); Hobbes
    and, 130; identification of statesman
    and king, 47–48, 115–16, 130, 137, 139;
    and interpretive stances, 72–83; and
    Juvenal conundrum, 7–8; and office
    and officeholders, 53, 120–23, 133–39,

383; and political expertise, 20n41,
    72, 72n78, 118, 234, 382; and political
    weaving, 48, 120–21, 123, 130, 132–35;
    and relationship between rule and
    office, 117; rule connected to kingship,
    47–48, 51; and rule of knowledge, 115,
    119, 138 (*see also* statecraft/political
    expertise); and schema of rule, 124–31;
    Schofield and, 122n18; and service
    conception of rule, 117, 128, 130, 175;
    superordinate ruler(s) safeguarding
    officeholders, 15, 37, 136, 139; and *telos*
    and *taxis* of rule, 22, 27, 116–17, 119,
    123–24, 126, 131, 133, 382, 389–90,
    392, 395–97; title discussed, 71–72;
    use of *archē* and *archein* in, 10, 116,
    117, 121, 121n14, 124, 136, 137, 139,
    147n21. *See also* Eleatic Visitor
statesman (*politikos*), 37, 72, 115, 117, 119,
    122n18, 124, 125, 125n25, 128–31, 136;
    and caring orientation, 117, 131; as
    cipher in *Statesman*, 37, 38, 64, 124,
    141, 161, 166, 170; defined, 37, 72, 133;
    epitactic powers, 117, 124, 130, 132;
    and expert knowledge, 72, 133, 139
    (*see also* statecraft/political expertise);
    identification with a king, 115–16, 130;
    as nonsubordinate/superordinate, 117,
    136, 139; as political weaver, 120, 121,
    130, 132–33; *politikos* as term possibly
    coined by Plato, 155; rivals to title, 117,
    119, 130, 396; as ruler, 115, 124, 130,
    132–33, 136–37; and service concep-
    tion of rule, 117, 128, 130; and temper-
    amental fitness for rule, 165–70
Steiner, Hillel, 356n5
Stout, Jeffrey, 24n50
Straumann, Benjamin, 63n53
subjects of rule, 200, 201, 356, 360; coop-
    erative disposition among the ruled,
    40, 41, 356, 358, 361; and democratic
    theory, 387–404; exploitation of the
    ruled, 7, 18–19, 21–22, 40, 47, 153, 154,
    173, 177, 187, 200, 263, 279, 283, 348,
    349, 355, 373; and freedom and friend-
    ship (*see* freedom; friendship); good of
    the ruled (*see* good of the ruled; *telos*
    of rule); and interpersonal freedom,
    360, 370, 371 (*see also* freedom); lack
    of freedom and friendship for tyrant's

subjects, 369; language of slavery used in describing rule, 12, 40, 210–11, 355, 369–75; and obedience (*see* obedience of the ruled). *See also* citizens of Greek polities; *dēmos*

sullogos, 108, 111

sumpitnein, 233, 233n32

taxis, 18nn37–38

taxis (order) of rule, 6, 18, 28, 30, 37, 41, 49, 52, 116, 119, 123, 179, 240, 255–56, 263–64, 302–3, 308–9, 327, 376; age-differentiated *taxis* of roles in a *kallipolis*, 214, 244 (*see also* age cohorts of guardians in *Republic*); and caring orientation, 116, 157; compared to *taxis* of Vermeule's common good constitutionalism, 29; and compossibility of freedom and rule, 357; as compossible with willing obedience, 355; as core element of rule, 122, 141, 243; and defining mark of correct rule, 389–90; distortion of, 39, 40, 255–56, 261, 264, 286, 291, 302–3; and epitactic powers, 18, 52–53, 381–83; and flawed constitutions (*see* democracy; oligarchy; timocracy; tyranny); and *Laws*, 27, 90, 105; office and law as part of, 383; and realization (*ergon*), 116; reconfiguring institutions to keep *taxis* of rule oriented toward *telos* of the good of the ruled, 22–23, 30, 63, 72–73, 244; and *Republic*, 170, 179, 202, 212, 214, 219–20, 222–23, 243, 244, 263; and role of the ruled, 371n26 (*see also* obedience of the ruled; subjects of rule); and rule in the soul, 254, 320, 329, 332, 334, 338, 350; and *Statesman*, 27, 116–17, 119, 123–24, 126, 131, 133, 382, 389–90, 392, 397

technē (expert knowledge, profession), 37, 72n78, 118n6, 142n4, 155, 181, 182n23; and the meaning of rule, 142–58, 401; therapeutic *technai*, 141, 149–52, 391, 393–94, 396, 401, 402

Tecuşan, Manuela, 307n121, 407n50

telos, 18n37, 320, 338

telos of rule, 18–23, 31, 39, 51–52, 91, 186, 255–56, 263, 274, 355, 392, 394, 396, 397; achieved through a *taxis*, 18, 49,

63, 72–73, 105, 119, 157, 170; as core element of rule, 122; as cultivation of virtue in the citizens, 90, 100, 245, 387; and defining mark of correct rule, 390; and democracy, 302, 304; distortion of, 39, 40, 95–96, 98, 245, 253, 255–56, 261, 264, 271, 282–83, 286, 294, 295, 302, 317, 348–50; as flawed conception of exploitation of the ruled, 18–19, 40, 177, 200, 245, 263, 283, 349, 355, 372; as the good of the ruled, 18–23, 27, 41, 49, 52, 72–73, 90, 170, 243, 244, 245, 382, 383, 390, 395; and language of slavery, 372, 374; and *Laws*, 90, 100; and oligarchy, 294, 295; and *Republic*, 27, 140–71, 214, 243, 263, 396n26; and *Statesman*, 22, 116, 123–24, 126, 131, 133, 382, 389–90, 392, 395–97; and timocracy, 282–83, 286; and tyranny, 316–17; and tyrants, 46

telos of rule in the soul, 254–55, 320, 330, 337, 338, 343, 350

terms of address, 179, 197–207

terms of art, 17–26, 35, 44, 193

Thebes, 56–57n36

Theophrastus, 343n35

therapeia, 119n9, 131

therapeutic *technai*, 141, 149–52, 391, 393–94, 396, 401, 402

Theseus, 50, 51n23

thesmophulakes, 103

Thomas, Rosalind, 309n124

Thomson, Judith, 24n49

Thracians principle, 262, 265–67, 265n30, 268n36

Thrasyllus, 71n77

Thrasymachus (interlocutor in *Republic*), 19, 51, 140–45, 150, 153–56, 161, 165n62, 174, 251, 253, 253n11, 258, 259, 318, 363–64, 368, 373, 396, 401, 401n36

Thucydides, 51, 65, 68, 189, 194, 261n24, 306n117

timē, 65n56, 172n1; *timai* (plural), 122, 163

timocracy, 39, 79–80, 251, 260, 273, 278–83, 283n62, 284n66, 299, 309, 339–40, 347, 348; and absence of distinction between senior guardians and

timocracy (*continued*)
officeholders, 281–82; and city-man comparison, 344, 347; and city-soul analogy, 257–58, 257n19; and competitive emulation among timocrats, 285–87; constitution described, 273, 278–83; and Disunity principle, 284, 287–88; emergence from a *kallipolis*, 271–79, 281; faults of, 349 (*see also specific faults under this heading*); and Predominance principle, 279–81, 285–87, 339; proximate causes of constitutional change, 277–79, 309; and secret accumulation of wealth, 282–84, 299, 309; selection of officeholders, 281, 286–87; and *telos* and *taxis* of rule, 282–83, 286; as term possibly coined by Plato, 251n5; timarchy as alternative name, 251n5, 273, 281n59; transition to oligarchy, 283–88, 339–40; way of life in a timocracy, 299
timocratic man, 40, 251, 320, 322n7, 335–36, 339–40, 342–48, 345n37; characteristics of, 343, 347; and city-man comparison, 344, 347; genesis of, 336, 343–47; and rule in the soul, 343, 347
titai, 59
titles of rulers and officeholders. *See* terms of address
Todd, S. C., 68n69, 194, 194n49
Trivigno, Franco V., 395n25
trophē, 189, 196, 197, 197n53. *See also* provisions, as a kind of wages; wages
Trump, Donald, 304n110
Tuck, Richard, 16n34
turannos, 46, 46n7, 65n58. *See also* tyrants
tyrannical man, 40, 251, 258, 320, 322–32, 326n13, 326n16, 353; and absence of rule in the soul, 254, 327–29, 332, 348, 353, 364, 365; and anarchy/*anarchia*, 327–29, 327n17, 331; and *anomia*/lawlessness, 327, 329; and civic freedom and friendship, 259, 353–54; dangers of numerous tyrannical men in a city, 329–30; and Disunity principle, 330; and drone imagery, 260, 324–25; genesis of, 258–59, 322, 324–25; genesis of a political tyrant, 314–15; and lack of friendship, 259, 331, 353, 363; and lack of order in the soul, 353; as a

master or slave, 353, 363; and maximally unjust life, 251, 258–59, 331; as not necessarily becoming a political tyrant, 315, 322; political tyrant (*see* tyrants); as ruled by *erōs*, 327, 329, 331, 348, 354n3; and tyranny in a city, 258, 329; unhappiness of, 259, 315, 323, 331; way of life, 325–26, 329. *See also* tyrants
tyranny, 10, 39, 52n26, 72, 143, 143n9, 236, 251, 258–59, 315, 317, 380; absence of constitutional order in, 253, 329, 368; and anarchy/*anarchia*, 26, 39, 40, 47, 253, 306, 316–17, 329; and *anomia*/lawlessness, 305n116, 329; distinguished from kingship, 47, 316; and drone imagery, 260; emergence from democracy, 301, 306, 309–16, 330; faults of, 356, 368; oppositional relationship to anarchy prior to Plato, 305–6; Plato as opponent of, 10, 47, 72, 408; and *telos* and *taxis* of rule, 316–17, 408; and tyrannical man, 258, 259; as unstable form of rule, 317; Xenophon and, 47
tyrants (political tyrants), 44, 46–47, 46nn7–8, 47, 56–57, 175, 236, 251–52, 259n22, 260, 314–17, 323–25, 354, 360, 364–69; happiness or unhappiness of, 251, 253, 258, 259, 315, 316, 318–19, 323, 331, 362, 365, 368, 369; inability to rule themselves, 365 (*see also under* tyrannical man); as lacking actual power/not truly ruling, 317, 325, 354, 390; lack of freedom, 354, 360, 365–69; lack of friendship, 363, 365–69; lack of trust in others, 366–67; and maximally unjust life, 258–59, 331, 362, 363, 368; origin and growth of a political tyrant, 314–15; and parable of the transported slaveholder, 362–63, 365–67, 369; relationship to their subjects, 317, 354, 360, 365, 366; as ruled by *erōs*, 325, 354n3, 364 (*see also under* tyrannical man); tyrannical man not necessarily becoming a political tyrant, 315, 322; way of life, 323, 325

Vegetti, Mario, 224n16
Vermeule, Adrian, 28–30, 28n59

Villacéque, Noémie, 301n104

virtue, 21, 28n59, 64, 90, 91, 91n14, 98–101, 103, 167–68, 245, 249, 250n3, 266, 278, 286–87, 348, 384–87. *See also* wisdom

vocabulary of rule and office, 3–4, 4n6, 8, 10, 14, 18n37, 23–27, 35, 42–43, 45, 65–71, 68n68, 121, 121n14, 210–11, 216–17, 229

wages, 14, 55, 56, 61, 89, 156, 160–64, 172–212, 173n2, 184n29, 219–20; in Athens, 61, 175, 184n29, 189; content of wages for guarding (foodstuffs, housing, monetary wages, provisions, etc.), 188–98; conundrum of wages in a *kallipolis*, 172–212; and dependence on a paymaster, 197; justifications for, 61, 174–77, 183–88, 218, 230; and *Laws* (wages not necessary), 61, 89, 183–84; and reluctant rulers, 160; and *Republic*, 27, 38, 61, 160–63, 166n65, 172–212, 214, 244; and service conception of rule, 173–74, 184–85, 197, 204, 207–12, 214; and terms of address, 197–207; theoretical implications, 197–212. See also *misthos*; penalties for officeholders and rulers; *trophē*

Waldron, Jeremy, 207, 208nn67–68

Wallace, Robert, 15n31, 215n4

Walling, Ian, 24n50

Walzer, Michael, 82, 83n112, 245

wealth and property, 174, 278, 279, 282–87, 295–97, 326, 336; and eligibility for officeholding in Greek polities, 301; and the oligarchic man, 336–41; prohibition of wealth and property for guardians in a *kallipolis*, 38, 174, 177, 185–87, 191, 196–97, 218, 242n46, 244, 246, 252; property valuation and officeholding in an oligarchy, 284, 288; secret accumulation of, in a timocracy, 282–84, 299, 309; and selection of officeholders, 99, 286–87; and transition from oligarchy to democracy, 294–96; and value placed on wealth in an oligarchy, 286–87, 294–95, 300. *See also* money

weaving, 120–21, 123, 130, 132–35

Weber, Max, 18, 19

White, Nicholas, 253n10

White, S., 141n3

Williams, Bernard, 257n18, 264n27, 344, 346

wine, cultural ritual of diluting with water, 307, 307n118

wisdom, 91, 98–99, 255–56, 261, 379

Wolin, Sheldon, 11n18

women, 9, 15n32, 27, 29, 43, 115n1, 216, 225, 228, 236, 246, 252, 255, 271, 285, 285n67, 339–40, 367

Xenophon, 19, 47, 51, 67–68, 72n79, 194n50, 200, 202, 304n112

Xerxes, 49, 153

Yoon, Jiseob, 23n47, 79n96

Young, Carl, 364n22

Young Socrates (interlocutor in *Statesman*), 137, 137n50, 389, 392, 393

Yunis, Harvey, 58n40

Zeus, 48, 50n21, 90n13, 210, 314

Zhang, Alex, 283n63

A NOTE ON THE TYPE

THIS BOOK has been composed in Miller, a Scotch Roman typeface designed by Matthew Carter and first released by Font Bureau in 1997. It resembles Monticello, the typeface developed for The Papers of Thomas Jefferson in the 1940s by C. H. Griffith and P. J. Conkwright and reinterpreted in digital form by Carter in 2003.

Pleasant Jefferson ("P. J.") Conkwright (1905–1986) was Typographer at Princeton University Press from 1939 to 1970. He was an acclaimed book designer and AIGA Medalist.

The ornament used throughout this book was designed by Pierre Simon Fournier (1712–1768) and was a favorite of Conkwright's, used in his design of the *Princeton University Library Chronicle*.